Introduction to Management

Introduction to Management

Third edition

Richard Pettinger

palgrave

© Richard Pettinger 2002

First edition 1994
Reprinted twice
Second edition 1996
Reprinted five times
Third edition 2002

Published by
PALGRAVE
Houndmills, Basingstoke, Hampshire RG21 6XS and
175 Fifth Avenue, New York, N.Y. 10010
Companies and representatives throughout the world

PALGRAVE is the new global academic imprint of
St. Martin's Press LLC Scholarly and Reference Division and
Palgrave Publishers Ltd (formerly Macmillan Press Ltd).

ISBN 0–333–96807–7

This book is printed on paper suitable for recycling and made from fully managed and sustained forest sources.

A catalogue record for this book is available from the British Library.

Library of Congress Catalog Card Number. 2002025247

10 9 8 7 6 5 4 3 2
11 10 09 08 07 06 05 04 03

Editing and origination by Curran Publishing Services Ltd Norwich, Norfolk

Printed in China

Contents

List of figures

List of tables

List of example boxes

Acknowledgements

The genesis of this book lay in the undergraduate Management Principles course of the Bartlett School of Architecture, Building, Environmental Design and Planning, University College London. In the pursuit and completion of this project, therefore, special thanks and acknowledgement are due to Graham Winch, then of University College London, now of the University of Manchester Institute of Science and Technology. I also wish to thank others at University College London, including Andrew Scott, Linda Heeselman, Paul Griseri, and all of the staff at the UCL Management Studies Centre; and Bev Nutt, David Kincaid, David Woolven, and Stephen Gruneberg of the Bartlett School.

Many other people also contributed. Stephen Rutt, Sarah Brown and Jane Powell at the publishers were a constant and positive source of help and guidance throughout. I am indebted to Kelvin Cheatle of Broadmoor Hospital; Jim and Margaret Malpas and Sandra Madigan of Malpas Flexible Learning Ltd, a top-quality professional education and training company and consultancy; Ian Robinson of the University of Bath; David Scott of the Artisan Group; and to Rebecca Frith, who typed and edited the manuscript. I am also grateful to Keith Sanders, Ken Batchelor, Michael Hutton, James Pollock, and Roger and June Cartwright for their constant support and encouragement.

RICHARD PETTINGER

Preface

Everywhere in the world there is a revolution going on, a transformation of business and of the services needed and wanted by people. At the heart of this revolution is management. This is underlined by a realisation that, whatever the merits of how this was conducted in the past, new ways and new methods are essential for the future; above all, this means a better understanding of what management actually is.

The background against which this revolution is taking place is one of economic, social, technological and political turbulence and upheaval. The global environment is both unstable and volatile. The sophisticated post-industrial new economies of the West are undergoing radical transformation, driven by a combination of recession, technological advance and competition from emerging nations. This is exacerbated by the need for levels of investment and other resource commitments over periods of time that run contrary to prevailing political and economic pressures. The economies of the Far East have generated a business and commercial power bloc in the period since the Second World War which dominates the global electrical and consumer goods markets and makes them major operators in the car, white goods and finance sectors. This has been achieved through a combination of investment, technology and organisation founded in the reconstruction and regeneration of the world devastated by the Second World War. At the same time, the European Union is seeking to extend its influence by drawing in countries that were hitherto members of the communist bloc; this is driven by the desire partly to create the conditions in which economic stability and prosperity can be assured, and partly to create the political conditions in which peace, prosperity and stability can be maintained.

Ever-greater strains and demands are placed on the finite and diminishing resources of the world by an ever-increasing global population. These have therefore to be arranged, planned, ordered and organised to ensure that they are used to greatest possible advantage. In the particular context of pressure on the one hand and finity on the other, this constitutes a drive for constant improvement in efficiency, effectiveness, maximisation and optimisation.

This is the framework of the 'business sphere', the environment of business, and background against which business is conducted. It forms the backcloth to the 'management sphere', the actual and conceptual environment (global, organisational and departmental) in which the practice of management is conducted. The work is carried out in and by 'organisations', combinations of human and other resources drawn together for a distinctive business or social purpose.

The standpoint adopted in response to this is straightforward: management is a statement of excellence and quality and of expertise. There is a body of knowledge and skills that must be acquired by anyone who wishes to be a part of the managing – the direction and ordering – of the situation. There are capabilities and capacities required in people in the pursuit of this. High standards of behaviour, ethics and performance are called for. There is a personal commitment necessary in terms of energy, commitment, enthusiasm and ambition. There is increasingly a standard of education and training necessary, both as a prerequisite to entry to the field and in the maintenance of effective and current performance in it. Finally, in common with all true experts, managers must have personal pride and joy in the work itself, in the organisation in which it is carried out, and in the particular department in which the manager is working.

The nature of this expertise is complex and diverse. The practice of management requires both the recognition of this complexity and the capacity to reconcile the conflicting elements present in the pursuit of it. For the purposes of introducing the scale and scope of this expertise and in order to provide a framework for the recognition and understanding of it, the book is organised into four parts and 23 chapters, giving a comprehensive introduction and background to the environmental, economic, strategic, operational and behavioural aspects of management.

To bring the threads of these opening remarks together, the elements feed off each other. Good management engenders good business, good business creates good organisations, good organisations attract, retain and develop good managers, who in turn improve both the quality of organisations and of the business that they conduct. Organisations thus cannot afford bad managers or their bad practices.

The main conclusion drawn is in relation to the constant expansion of the subject, both as a field of study and as an area of practice, and of the consequent need for those who work in it to keep up to date with developments, to read, to acknowledge and to accept their responsibilities for their own continuous professional expansion and to act upon all of this. The commitment needed for this matches that of any classical profession such as medicine or the law.

This is an illustration and summary of the scope and coverage of the book. The overall purpose is to introduce concepts and features of the management sphere to the student coming to the subject for the first time; to those commencing professional studies and professional examinations who require an introduction to management or a general management reader; to those studying management as part of a technological, technical, engineering or computer course; and to make a contribution to the level and content of the debate in the field.

RICHARD PETTINGER

Part I
The foundations of management

1 Introduction

'Julius Caesar never asked anyone to do anything that he was not willing to do himself.' Gaius Suetonius, *The Twelve Caesars*.

'My staff – my people – were so fresh and full of enthusiasm. It would have been criminal to drill this out of them.' Shigeru Kobayashi, Sony, at the opening of the company's first factory, 1961.

'Everyone wants instant success. No one is prepared to put in the hard work.' David Cork, London Leisure Services Ltd, March 2000.

'If you don't like people, leave now.' Tom Peters, *The World Turned Upside Down*, Channel 4., 1986.

CHAPTER OUTLINE

Introduction

The professionalisation of management

Management as a field of study

Management research and literature

The foundations of modern management

Milestones in the development of modern management practice

The search for excellence

Conclusions

Summary.

CHAPTER OBJECTIVES

After studying this chapter, you should be able to:

begin to understand what management is, and what it is not

understand the key management tasks and concerns

understand the personal and professional qualities necessary to be a successful manager

understand the nature of the professionalisation of management

understand the piecemeal nature of the development of the body of knowledge of modern management, and the contribution of each

understand the foundations on which the expertise and practice of modern management are built.

Introduction

The purpose of this chapter is to identify the range of general and universal concepts and elements that ought to be present in any worthwhile study of the subject of management. These are highlighted in themselves and then drawn together in so far as this is possible. However, many of these elements are disparate or divergent and it is essential to recognise them as such.

There are many definitions of management; each tackles a part of the answer, and it is useful to see them as complementary rather than conflicting. Henri Fayol, in the early twentieth century, defined it as the process of 'forecasting, planning, organising, commanding, coordinating and controlling' (Fayol and Urwick, 1946). E.F.L. Brech (1984) called it 'the social process of planning, coordination, control and motivation'. Writing in the 1980s, Tom Peters defined it as 'organisational direction based on sound common sense, pride in the organisation and enthusiasm for its works' (1989). More recently still, Graham Winch of University College London described management as 'coping with change and uncertainty' (1996). It is clear that management is partly the process of getting things done through people; and partly the creative and energetic combination of scarce resources into effective and profitable activities, and the combination of the skill and talents of the individuals concerned with doing this.

Management is conducted in organisations; and organisations operate in their environment. Organisations are variously described as 'systems of inter-dependent human beings' (D.S. Pugh, 1986), or a 'joint function of human characteristics, the task to be accomplished and its environment' (Simon, 1967). They may be seen as combinations of resources brought together for stated purposes. They have their own life, direction, permanence and identity; and are energised by people.

The professionalisation of management

Management is variously defined as science, profession and art. The truth of its status lies somewhere between the three, and there are strong elements of each.

There are precise scientific aspects that have to be assimilated. Any manager must have a good grasp of certain quantitative methods and financial and statistical data, as well as certain, less scientific but well tried and tested, elements such as human motivations, and the effect of different payment systems on the performance of different occupations.

It is a profession in so far as there is a general recognition that there are certain knowledge, skills and aptitudes that must be assimilated and understood by anyone who aspires to be a truly effective manager. Management is not a formal or traditional profession in that it is not a fully self-regulating occupation, nor is there yet a named qualification that must be achieved before one is allowed to practise. However, pressure to be both educated and qualified is growing universally. There is a recognition also of the correlation between this and expert and effective practice.

Management is an art in the sense that within these confines and strictures there is great scope for the use of creativity, imagination, initiative and invention within the overall sphere of the occupation. The scientific methods and body of knowledge referred to must be applied in their own way to each and any given situation, issue or problem. This is the creative aspect of the manager's role and function, and anyone in a managerial position who seeks for prescriptive solutions to organisational problems is likely to fail.

The best managers are committed and dedicated operators; highly trained and educated, with excellent analytical and critical faculties. Beyond this, there is a body of skills and aptitudes, knowledge, attitudes and behaviour that the effective manager must have and be able to draw upon.

The personal qualities required include:

- ambition, energy, great commitment, self-motivation
- job, product and service knowledge
- drive and enthusiasm
- creativity and imagination
- a thirst for knowledge
- a commitment to improvement
- a commitment to continuous development, both personal and professional
- the ability to grow and broaden the outlook and vision of the organisation concerned
- a positive and dynamic attitude, self-discipline and empathy with the staff
- a love of the organisation, and pride and enthusiasm in the job, its people, its products, its services, its customers and clients (see Example Box 1.1).

These personal qualities provide the springboard for the successful and professional operator. The task also calls for a good general knowledge, understanding and grasp of basic economics, including the relationship between organisations and their environment, current issues and affairs, and constraints on the ability to conduct business. It is also necessary to understand:

- strategy and policy
- marketing
- behavioural sciences
- personnel and industrial relations
- the use and management of information
- the use and management of technology
- production, operations, systems, service, projects and facilities management
- and the management of initiative and innovation.

Currently, much of this is formalised and achieved through the study of business at school, college and university. This is by no means a universal requirement, however; there have been countless successful managers who never had this benefit, although their success was undoubtedly based on their own ability, however gained, in these areas.

Management is a global activity and lessons can be learned from everywhere in the world. This includes Western Europe, North America, Japan, Korea, the Philippines, Malaysia, Indonesia, the Middle East, Australia, New Zealand and South Africa, where managerial practices are well documented. This will inevitably be further developed as the economies of the former communist bloc and USSR, South and Central America, India and Pakistan, China and Africa, begin to grow and develop. All of these are industrialising and commercialising and having their own influence on business practices. In the future, such developments will undoubtedly embrace the rest

EXAMPLE BOX 1.1 Professions

The 'classical' professions are medicine, law, the priesthood and the army. The following properties were held to distinguish these from the rest of society.

- **Distinctive expertise:** not available elsewhere in society or in its individual members.
- **Distinctive body of knowledge:** required by all those who aspire to practise in the profession.
- **Entry barriers**: in the form of examinations, time serving, learning from experts.
- **Formal qualifications:** given as the result of acquiring the body of knowledge and clearing the entry barriers.
- **High status:** professions are at the top of the occupational tree.
- **Distinctive morality:** for medicine, the commitment to keep people alive as long as possible; for law, a commitment to represent the client's best interests; for the church, a commitment to godliness and to serve the congregation's best interest; for the army, to fight within stated rules of law.
- **High value:** professions make a distinctive and positive contribution to both the organisations and individual members of the society.
- **Self-regulating:** professions set their own rules, codes of conduct, standards of performance and qualifications.
- **Self-disciplining:** professions establish their own bodies for dealing with problems, complaints and allegations of malpractice.
- **Unlimited reward levels:** according to preferred levels of charges and the demands of society.
- **Life membership:** dismissal at the behest of the profession; ceasing to work for one employer does not constitute loss of profession.
- **Personal commitment:** to high standards of practice and morality; commitment to deliver the best possible service in all circumstances.
- **Self-discipline:** commitment to personal standards of behaviour in the pursuit of professional excellence.
- **Continuous development:** of knowledge and skills; a commitment to keep abreast of all developments and initiatives in the field.
- **Governance:** by institutions established by the profession itself.

Notes

1. In absolute terms 'management' falls short in most areas. Formal qualifications are not a prerequisite to practice (though they are highly desirable and ever more sought after). Discipline and regulation of managers is still overwhelmingly a matter for organisations and not management institutions. There is some influence over reward levels and training and development. Measures of status and value are uneven. Management institutions act as focal points for debate, and also have a lobbying function. They do not act as regulators.
2. There is a clear drive towards the professionalisation of management. This is based on

> **Example Box 1.1 (continued)**
>
> attention to expertise, knowledge and qualifications, and the relationship between these and the value added to organisations by expert managers.
>
> 3. In 1995, Charles Handy proposed that all business school graduates should be required to take the equivalent of the Hippocratic Oath, thus committing themselves to best practice and high standards and quality of performance.
>
> If management is viewed in this way, it is a highly professional activity and one that demands a set body of expertise and a large measure of commitment on the part of its practitioners. In traditional terms, management falls short of the full status of profession in that the elements outlined here do not constitute yet a formal entry barrier (in medicine, the law, the clergy and the military, it is essential to have the stated qualifications before being allowed to practise).

of Africa, and the more remote parts of Asia. It must be recognised, finally, that management is currently being conducted in a changing and turbulent environment. This has itself changed over the period since 1945 and the reconstruction of the world damaged by the Second World War. Then, everything was arranged to try to bring order, stability and performance steadiness to business, service and the markets and spheres in which they operated. Today all that has gone and the processes of technological advance, management education, automation, social change and political development, together with the globalisation of business and commerce, ensure that all concepts of management are subject to continuous change and revision. Truly expert and committed managers will always ensure that they keep themselves up-to-date with everything that impinges on both their job and their chosen profession. Many managerial institutions now insist that their members keep records of all continuous professional development activities that they undertake and, indeed, insist on this as a condition of continuing membership (see Example Box 1.1).

Management research and literature

There is a great range of management research and literature: textbooks, how-to books, personal and organisational histories, professional and commercial journals and periodicals, computer-based packages, databases, leaflets, checklists; and also university and commercial research programmes, monographs and learned papers. This can be broken down as follows.

- Some of it is intellectually extremely challenging. The ability, both to understand and to be an effective practitioner in certain aspects of the managerial sphere, requires a high degree of intellectual capacity, higher education and a basic grasp of some mathematical and economic theories as well as of behavioural and operational matters.
- Some of it addresses precise or defined issues that have a direct bearing on the business sphere. This is especially true of the areas of leadership, motivation,

perception, the formation of attitudes, standards and values which have their own body of knowledge in their own right, and which then require translation into particular managerial situations in different ways.

- Some of it dwells heavily on empirical research, case histories and anecdotal examples. This enables studies of the relationships between variables in given situations to be undertaken and assimilated, and 'what if' and other hypothetical discussions to take place in relation to real events of the past, but in overtly 'safe' situations at present. The body of the general knowledge and experience of the manager is thus developed and extended, as are his or her critical faculty, awareness and overall view of the sphere.

- Some of it illustrates particular successes and failures; this is especially true of the swelling array of books produced by successful business people. The lessons to be drawn here are often in the mind of the reader. Such books tend to reinforce only certain aspects of the whole managerial sphere. They provide a very useful library of what has worked in practice for comparison against a theoretical or academic base, although one by-product of this has been to create and develop a faddish approach (see Example Box 1.2).

Historical background

The subject of management has been studied over the centuries with the view of establishing what constitutes a successful manager or, in a closely related field, what makes a successful leader. The subject of leadership is dealt with fully later in the book. At this stage, suffice it to say that while the two concepts are closely related, they are not synonymous: a good leader is not necessarily a good manager, nor are good managers always brilliant leaders (though they should always be at least capable).

The subject of management has been developed from the earliest points of civilisation. Religious writings identify the fundamental elements of strength of character and purpose, positive morality and love of truth that anyone who aspires to a position of authority should have. Both archaeologists and those interested in organisational aspects have long concerned themselves with how the resources necessary to build the pyramids and temples of Egypt and South America were coordinated. They have speculated on the means by which these might have been achieved, without coming to definite conclusions overall.

Common threads running through the lives of the twelve Caesars, as told by Suetonius writing in the first century AD, related their overall success to their moral and ethical purposes, their ambitions, their policies for Rome and the Roman Empire and the standpoints for these. Also identified were elements that were necessary to survive in the situation and the extent to which they were successful in the pursuit of this. Julius Caesar, himself a writer of note, dealt extensively with the vision and the strategic and tactical awareness that he required to be successful in his twin careers of general and emperor. Later, histories of the Frankish Kingdom in the Middle Ages ascribe strong leadership, a clarity of purpose and the ability to persuade a range of disparate elements to a single point of view as characteristics of Charles Martel and Charlemagne in the establishment of the nation of France.

The nature and importance of power and influence were thus clearly established. Niccolo Machiavelli, the Florentine, writing in the fifteenth century, developed this much further. His book *The Prince*, recognised as an early authority on leadership,

EXAMPLE BOX 1.2 Fashions and Fads

The opposite to the rigour of developing expertise and a body of knowledge is a prescriptive approach. 'Fashions and fads' is a useful way of describing directive, prescriptive and simplistic approaches to management issues and problems. Some current issues are as follows.

- **Job evaluation:** the analysis of job and work activities according to present criteria in order to rank them in importance, status, values and place on the pay scale. In practice, job evaluation tends to be rigid, inconsistent and divisive.
- **Business process re-engineering (BPR):** attention to administration, supervision and procedures for the purposes of simplicity, clarification and speed of operation. The premise is that these improvements are always possible. In practice, BPR tends to be applied prescriptively to all functions without reference to organisational effectiveness or wider aspects of operations.
- **Total quality management (TQM):** attention to every aspect of organisational practice in pursuit of continuous improvement, the highest possible standards of practice, products, services and customer service. In practice, TQM tends to be prescriptive in approach and dominated by paperwork and administration systems rather than attention to products and customers.
- **Right first time, every time:** this rolls easily off the tongue/pen; it is a direct contradiction of the view that everything can be improved.
- **Benchmarking:** benchmarks set standards of activity against which other activities can be compared and rated; benchmarking also applies to placing people on salary scales, activity scales, job importance scales and other matters to do with status. In practice, it is usually rigid, inconsistent and divisive.
- **Virtual organisation:** organisation structures based on technology rather than physical presence. A useful concept that tends to get drowned, either by cost-cutting or technological processes; or conventional, adversarial supervision.

The major contribution of each (and all fashions and fads) is to broaden the debate on management issues, and to get people thinking about progress and improvement. Their weakness appears when they are taken as offering perfection, the absolute truth, and instant solutions to all-round management problems.

---

pushed back the ethical and moral boundaries and advocated the subordination of means to ends. He marks political awareness and astuteness, and the ability to translate innate abilities into particular situations, as further key characteristics; if one did not understand the environment and could not operate within it, one could not be truly effective.

The main common element of these historic studies was the separation of the role of the leader and the characteristics required of the leader from other business, political and military activities. A good soldier did not necessarily make a good leader; on the other hand, to be a good leader of soldiers it was necessary to have a good knowledge of what the components of soldiering were, and to be able to combine this with the other necessary characteristics of ordering, directing and planning.

Prior to the Western industrial revolution therefore, there was a large, if uncoordinated and undervalued, body of knowledge and experience available from which conclusions about the prevailing and ideal nature of leadership and management could be drawn.

The industrial revolution in Great Britain and Europe over the eighteenth and nineteenth centuries brought great social and political ferment and upheaval, as well as economic restructuring. Out of this ferment and transformation came particular initiatives, writings and scholarship, both in relation to work and also concerning society at large.

Marxism

The ferment of ideas that ran concurrently with the industrial and social upheaval brought with it the concept of communism. Written and developed by Karl Marx and Friedrich Engels, the *Communist Manifesto* propounded that industrial society as it stood was to be a place of permanent upheaval and revolution; that the workers, the wage slaves, would not tolerate the current state of industrial society, but would rather overthrow it and seize control of it for themselves. Egalitarian in concept, it rejected the then emerging concepts of capitalism, bourgeoisie (the middle and professional classes), and the fledgling wage–work bargain. Largely discredited as a philosophy (above all by the collapse of the communist bloc that *called itself* Marxist), Marxism never succeeded in translating into an effective code for the organisation of work. However, it does illustrate the extreme or radical perspective on working situations, the extent to which the workforce may become alienated either from the organisation for which they work or from its managers. It also voices genuine concerns for the standards, dignity and rights of those who work for others in the pursuit of supporting their own lives. It became the cornerstone of the trade union movement in the UK and elsewhere. Its attraction lay in the egalitarianism preached and the utopian vision of shared ownership of the means of production and economic activity (see Example Box 1.3).

Bureaucracy and the permanence of organisations

The work of Max Weber (1864–1920) developed the concept of the permanence and continuity of organisations, and was the basis of the theory of bureaucracy. Weber saw bureaucracy as an organisational form based on a hierarchy of offices and systems of rules with the purpose of ensuring the permanence of the organisation, even though jobholders within it might come and go. The knowledge, practice and experience of the organisation would be preserved in files, thus ensuring permanence and continuity. Authority in such circumstances is described as legal-rational, where the position of the office holder is enshrined in an organisation structure and fully understood and accepted by all jobholders. The organisation itself is continuous and permanent. Work is specialised and defined by job title and job description. The organisation is hierarchical, with one level subject to control by that (or those) above it. Everything done in the name of the organisation and its officials is recorded. Jobholders are appointed on the basis of technical competence; the jobs exist in their own right; jobholders have no other rights to the job. Ownership and control of the organisation are separated; effectively the

---

EXAMPLE BOX 1.3 Marxism and Egalitarianism

Paradoxically, at exactly the time when Marxism is discredited as a political and social philosophy, it is possible to identify more clearly a direct link between economic prosperity, organisational longevity, and high levels of organisational staff output and quality. For example:

- **Lincoln Electric:** which makes manufacturing, welding and electronic equipment for the American ship and automobile industries, has since 1932 paid out extensive bonuses to all staff, based on a combination of suggestions received and organisational profitability. The result has been that the company has not had a single lay-off since that date, and that the staff regularly earn, in productivity and performance-related bonuses, approximately double their income.
- **Semco:** the Brazilian manufacturing and internet corporation, always assigns 23 per cent of gross profits for distribution among the staff.
- **USAir:** in which the company trade union took a controlling interest, has been pulled back from bankruptcy through a narrowing of pay scales and differentials, and the introduction of profit-related salary payments and bonuses, at the instigation of the trade union.
- **Nissan UK:** based at Washington, Tyne and Wear, consistently achieves the highest levels of productivity of any car company anywhere in the world (with the exception of one factory in Japan and one in Korea); this is founded in the adoption of, and commitment to, single staff status for all those working for the company.

---

owners of an organisation appoint others to run it on their behalf. The work and the control of it are enshrined in rulebooks and procedures which must be obeyed and followed. Order and efficiency are thus brought to this state of permanence.

Thus, the overall purpose of bureaucratic structure was, and remains, to attain the maximum degree of efficiency possible and to ensure the permanence of the organisation. As organisations grow in size and complexity, the bureaucracy itself has to be managed. Failure to do this leads to red tape, excessive procedures, and obscure and conflicting rules and regulations. In the worst cases, the rules and procedures become themselves all-important, to the detriment of the product or service that is being offered.

The origins of welfarism

The Cadbury family, who pioneered and built up the chocolate and cocoa industries in Great Britain in the nineteenth century, came from a strong religious tradition (they were Quakers). Determined that their companies should be both profitable and ethical, they sought to ensure certain standards of living and quality of life for those who worked for them. They built both their factories and the housing for their staff at a model industrial village at Bourneville on what was then the edge of Birmingham. The village included basic housing and sanitation, green spaces, schools for the children and company shops that sold food of a good quality. The purpose was to ensure that the staff were kept fit, healthy and motivated to work in the factories, producing good quality products. Other Quaker foundations operated along similar lines, including the Fry and Terry companies (which also produced chocolate). Similar attitudes may also be found now at, for example:

- **The Body Shop:** where all staff are required to work one day per month on the social or environmental project or activity of their choice.
- **Sony UK:** where there is a commitment to lifetime employment, and a guarantee of no compulsory redundancies.
- More generally in organisations that have sought to balance the quality of working life and commitment of their staff, by introducing private healthcare, insurance and crèche and nursery facilities (examples include British Airways, British Telecom, Citibank).

This approach was by no means the rule, and many employers continued to treat their people very harshly, keeping them in bad conditions, under-paying them and using fear as the driving force. Graphic and apocryphal descriptions may be found in the poetry of William Blake, and *The Water Babies* by Charles Kingsley. However, the work of the Cadburys is important as one of the most enduring early industrial examples of the relationship between concern for the staff and commercial permanence, profitability and success.

Henri Fayol

The work of Henri Fayol (1841–1925) is important because he was the first to attempt a fully comprehensive definition of industrial management. It was published in 1916 under the title *General and Industrial Administration*. It identified the components of any industrial undertaking under the headings of technical, commercial, financial, security, accounting, and managerial. This last component comprised forecasting, planning, organisation, command, coordination and control of the others; the overall function is to unify and direct the organisation and its resources in productive activities. He also listed 14 'principles of management' on which he claimed to have based his own managerial practice and style and which he cited as the foundation of his own success:

1. **Division of work:** the ordering and specialisation of tasks and jobs necessary for greater efficiency and ease of control.
2. **Authority and responsibility:** the right to give commands and the acceptance of the consequences of giving those commands.
3. **Unity of command:** each employee has an identified and recognised superior or commander.
4. **Unity of direction:** one commander for each activity or objective.
5. The **subordination** of **individual** interests to the **organisational** interest.
6. **Remuneration** and **reward** in a **fair and equitable** manner to all.
7. **Centralisation** and **centrality** of control.
8. A discernible **top-to-bottom line of authority.**
9. **Order** as a principle of organisation, the arrangement and coordination of activities.

10. **Equity:** the principle of dealing fairly with everybody who works for the organisation.
11. **Employee discipline:** ensuring that everybody receives the same standard of treatment at the organisation.
12. **Stability of job tenure:** by which all employees should be given continuity of employment in the interests of building up expertise.
13. Encouragement of **initiative** on the part of everyone who works in the organisation.
14. *Esprit de corps:* the generation of organisation, team and group identity, willingness and motivation to work.

Fayol's work stands as the first attempt to produce a theory of management and set of management principles. Fayol also recognised that these principles did not constitute an end in themselves; that their emphasis would vary between situations; and that they would require interpretation and application on the part of those managing the situation.

Scientific management

The concept of scientific management, that is the taking of a precise approach to the problems of work and work organisation, was pioneered by Frederick Winslow Taylor (1856–1917). His hypothesis, based on his experience in the US steel industry, rested on the premise that the proper organisation of the workforce and work methods would improve efficiency. He propounded a mental and attitudinal revolution on the part of both managers and workers. Work should be a cooperative effort between the two. Work organisation should be such that it removed all responsibility from the workers, leaving them only with their particular task. By specialising and training in this task, the individual worker would become 'perfect' in his job; work could thus be organised into production lines so that items could be produced efficiently and to a constant standard. Precise performance standards would be predetermined by job observation and analysis and a best method arrived at; this would become the normal way of working. Everyone would benefit: the organisation because it cut out all wasteful and inefficient use of resources; managers because they had a known standard of work to set and observe; and workers because they would always do the job the same way. Everyone would benefit financially also from the increase in output, sales and profits, and the reflection of this in high wage and salary levels. In a famous innovation at the Bethlehem Steel Works, USA, where he also worked, Taylor optimised productive labour at the ore and coal stockpiles by providing various sizes of shovels from which the men could choose to ensure that they used that which was best suited to them. He reduced handling costs per tonne by a half over a three-year period. He also reduced the size of the workforce required from 400 to 140.

The great advances that Taylor and others who followed the scientific school made were in the standardisation of work, and the ability to put concepts of productivity and efficiency into practice. The work foreshadowed the production line and other standardised efforts and techniques that have been used for mass-produced goods and commodities ever since. In the pursuit of this, scientific management also helped create the boredom, disaffection and alienation of the workforces producing these goods that still remain as issues to be addressed and resolved into the twenty-first century (see Example Box 1.4).

The human relations school

The most famous and pioneering work carried out in this field of management was the Hawthorne Studies at the Western Electric Company in Chicago. These studies were carried out over the period 1924–36. Originally designed to draw conclusions between the working environment and work output, they finished as major studies of work groups, social factors and employee attitudes and values, and the effect of these at the place of work.

The Hawthorne Works employed over 30 000 people making telephone equipment. Elton Mayo, Professor of Industrial Research at Harvard University, was called in to advise the company because there was both poor productivity and a high level of employee dissatisfaction.

EXAMPLE BOX 1.4 Scientific Management Criticised

The great weakness of the scientific management approach is that it took no account of the human and social needs of those working in these conditions. Taylor reasoned that by guaranteeing high levels of pay, satisfaction would automatically follow.

This has consistently been shown not to be the case. For example:

- The Birds Eye frozen food factory at Skelmersdale in Lancashire was, until its closure, the only major employer in an unemployment black spot. Relatively high levels of prosperity and quality of life were enjoyed by those who worked at the company. Yet because it paid no attention to the human aspect of its activities, productivity declined and workforce strife increased. In vain did the company threaten the staff with factory closure and redundancy. In the end the staff accepted the closure, and the redundancy payments on offer, because they were collectively sick of the ways in which they were being treated from a human point of view.

- The UK coal mining industry lost 400 000 jobs between the years 1975 and 1995. The miners were among the best-paid workers in the UK. Despite exhortations from their trade union, when the miners were offered redundancy payments, the vast majority took them – again, because they were treated as a disposable commodity, rather than human beings.

- Those going to work in dot.com companies in the late twentieth century did so in the belief that they were part of a new industrial revolution. They quickly discovered that, apart from the chosen few who owned the companies, they were to be required to work in cubicles, in front of computer screens, for long periods of time. The directors of dot.com companies quickly discovered that, in contrast to their own zeal and enthusiasm, their staff were unwilling to be treated in this way.

The first of his experiments was based on the hypothesis that productivity would increase if working conditions were improved. The first stage was the improvement of the lighting for a group of female workers; to give a measure of validity to the results, a control group was established whose lighting was to remain unchanged. However, the output of both groups improved and continued to improve whether the lighting was increased or decreased. A second stage extended the experiments to include rest periods, variations in starting and finishing times, and variations in the timing and length of the lunch break. At each stage the output of both groups rose until the point at which the women in the experimental group complained that they had too many breaks and that their work rhythm was being disrupted. The third stage was a major attitude survey of over 20 000 of the company's employees. This was conducted over the period 1928–30. The fourth stage consisted of observation in depth of both the informal and formal working groups in 1932. The final stage (1936) drew all threads together and resulted in the commencement of personnel counselling schemes and other staff-related activities based on the overall conclusions drawn by Mayo and his team from Harvard and also the company's own researchers.

These may be summarised as follows.

- **Individuals** need to be given importance in their own right, and must also be seen as group or team members.
- **The need to belong** at the workplace is of fundamental importance, as critical in its own way as both pay and rewards and working conditions.
- There is both a **formal and informal** organisation, with formal and informal groups and structures; the informal exerts a strong influence over the formal.
- People respond positively to active involvement in work.

What started out as a survey of the working environment thus finished as the first major piece of research on the attitudes and values prevalent among those drawn together into working situations. The Hawthorne Studies gave rise to concepts of social man and human relations at the workplace. They were the first to place importance on them and to set concepts of groups, behaviour, personal value and identity in industrial and commercial situations.

Winning friends and influencing people

This work was carried out in the early part of the twentieth century by Dale Carnegie, a pioneer of concepts that have now become part of the mainstream of good business and management practices. Carnegie identified the barriers and blockages to profitable and effective activity. He summarised this as 'overcoming fears'. The starting point for nearly all transactions was having to deal with humans on a face-to-face basis as the prerequisite for commercial success.

To do this successfully he identified certain fundamental techniques for handling people. The main factor is empathy: the ability to put yourself in the other person's position, seeing things from their point of view, understanding their wants, needs, hopes and fears; and understanding what they want from the transaction (not your wonderful product *per se*, but rather the benefits that are expected to accrue). The customers are at the centre of the transaction and, therefore, are entitled to feel important and to have their wants and needs attended to and satisfied.

Carnegie identified other characteristics in support of this that would reinforce the effective capabilities of anyone who deals with customers. These are: learning to take a genuine interest in people; the development of a positive persona; listening attentively and responding to the needs of the customers, encouraging them to talk; speaking in terms of their interests; and being sincere. Language used should always be positive and couched in terms that encourage progress and positive responses. Staff should never argue with customers.

More generally, Carnegie preached the value of positive rather than negative criticism – above all, when it is necessary to tell someone that they are wrong, focusing on the wrong deed rather than criticising their personality. The person in question should also be allowed to save face. Criticism should always be followed by constructive help and by an item of praise. In general, all people should be praised and valued, and given a high reputation; the organisation is going to need their positive qualities, and not those engendered by any lasting resentment.

Carnegie also preached the more general virtues of honesty, openness, self-respect, commitment and clarity of purpose as being central to business and commercial success. The lessons taught by Carnegie run throughout the whole of the philosophy of human relations and are to be found in the practices of many successful companies and those regarded as 'excellent'. The importance of, and central position of, 'the customer' is a feature current in the offerings of business schools in the last decade of the twentieth century, as well as being a critical factor in the successes of Japanese industry and commerce.

The 'affluent worker' studies

The affluent worker studies were carried out at Luton, UK, in the early 1960s. There were three companies studied: Vauxhall Cars, La Porte Chemicals and Skefco Engineering. The stated purpose was to give an account of the attitudes and behaviour of a sample of affluent workers – male high wage earners at large and complex production companies – and to attempt to explain them. Both the firms and the area were considered highly profitable and prosperous.

The main findings were as follows. For the workforce, the job was overwhelmingly a means to an end: that of earning enough to support life away from the company. The affluent workers had little or no identity with the place of work or with their colleagues; this was especially true of those doing unskilled jobs.

Some skilled workers would discuss work issues and problems with colleagues. The unskilled would not. In general, the workforces felt no involvement with either the company, or their colleagues, or the work. Positive attitudes towards the company prevailed overall, but again these were related to the instrumental approaches to employment adopted: the companies were expected both to increase in prosperity, and to provide increased wages and standards of living. They were perceived to be 'good employers' for similar reasons.

The matters to which the affluent workers were found to be actively hostile were those concerning supervision. The preferred style of supervision was described as 'hands off'; any more active supervision was perceived to be intrusive. Work study and efficiency drives were also opposed.

There was a very high degree of trade union membership (87 per cent overall), though few of the affluent workers became actively involved in either national or branch union activities. Union membership was perceived as an insurance policy. The main point of contact between workers and union was the shop steward who was expected to take an active interest, where necessary, in their concerns.

No association was found between job satisfaction and current employment. It was purely a 'wage–work bargain', a means to an end. The most important relationship in the life of the worker was that with his family. The workers did not generally socialise with each other, either at work or in the community; thus membership of workplace social clubs was also low.

The view of the future adopted was also instrumental. There was no general aspiration to supervisory positions for their intrinsic benefits. The affluent workers would rather have their own high wages than the status and responsibility of being the foreman. More generally, the future was regarded in terms of increased profitability and prosperity, with an expectation that wages would grow and that standards of living and of life would, in consequence, grow with them.

The studies illustrated the sources and background of the attitudes and behaviour inherent in this instrumental view of employment. More generally, the studies concluded that levels of workplace satisfaction were conditional upon continued stability and prosperity; and that there were universal expectations of continuing growth in the situation.

The Peter Principle

Lawrence J. Peter worked as teacher, psychologist, counsellor and consultant in different parts of the American education sector during the post-war era. This included education in prisons and dealing with emotionally disadvantaged and disturbed children.

The Peter Principle, published in 1969, is based on the assumption and invariable actuality that people gain promotion to their level of incompetence. As long as they are successful in one job, people will be considered suitable candidates for promotion by the organisation in question; and only when they are unsuccessful at that level will they not be considered for the next promotion (see Example Box 1.5). The book is written in an essentially racy and light-hearted way; the lessons to be learned are nevertheless extremely important.

Promotions are clearly being made on a false premise, that of competence in the current job rather than the qualities required for the new one. It follows from this that assessments for promotion are fundamentally flawed, based on a misleading appraisal of the wrong set of characteristics. More generally, what is 'sound performance' in one job may simply be identified on the basis that the individual is not actually doing any harm.

Example Box 1.5 The Peter Principle

'The head's friends saw that the head was no use as a head, so they made her an inspector, to interfere with other heads. And when they found she wasn't much good at that, they got her into Parliament, where she lived happily ever after.'

Source: C.S. Lewis, *The Silver Chair*, 1953.

In the management sphere, the application of the 'Peter Principle' is only too universal. Time and again promotion to supervisory and management grades from within the ranks is based upon the operative's performance in those ranks rather than on any aptitude for supervision, management or direction. Organisations thus not only gain an incompetent or inadequate supervisor; they also lose a highly competent technician. This remains true for all walks of life – the best nurses do not *per se* make the best hospital directors; the best teachers do not make the best school heads; the best drivers do not make the best transport fleet managers.

The lessons to be drawn from this may be summarised as the ability to identify genuine levels and requirements of performance, and the attributes required to carry them out, and to set criteria against which they can be measured accurately. People may then be placed in jobs that they can do, and for which they are best suited. Aptitude for promotion, or any other preferred job for that matter, can then be assessed on the basis of matching personal qualities with desired performance, and organisational appointments made accordingly. Finally, the principle also has implications for growing and nurturing your own experts and managers and for succession and continuity planning.

Business policy and strategy

The importance of this as part of the field of the study of management was first fully developed by H.I. Ansoff, who postulated theories concerning both the totality of, and complexities of, organisational and operational strategy. This work was carried out in the 1950s and 1960s.

Ansoff's stance was based in the concern found among business managers of identifying rational and accurate ways in which organisations could both adjust to and exploit changes in their environment. Such ways he described as:

- **Traditional,** micro-economic theories of the firm which, while taking full account of 'the organisation in its environment', took no account of either its operational or behavioural procedures and practices.
- The need to reconcile **a range of decision classes** – strategic, administrative and operational – in both the allocation of, and competition for, the organisation's resources, priority, time and attention.
- **Transition** from one state to another due to changes in technology, markets, working practices, size or scale of the firm and its operations.
- The application of **science and technology** to the process of management which was ever-increasing at the time. This generated both interest and acceptance of more analytical approaches.

Ansoff was a pioneer in what was then recognised as a complex field of study, and one that offered great scope for research both from an academic point of view and also in the interest of the pursuit of profitable business. His work has been substantially developed by Michael E. Porter of the Harvard Business School, to include in-depth analyses of strategy processes, competitive positioning and competitive advantage, developing and refining the key concepts outlined above and also delving much deeper into the complexities that constitute effective corporate strategies.

This has included substantial analyses of the interrelationships between organisations and their environment, and between organisations in particular industrial and commercial sectors. In turn, he has related this to both the diversification and complexity of the organisations themselves as they operate in particular spheres. He has isolated the concepts of defensive and offensive strategies and when each should be used. His work has produced a comprehensive set of tools, techniques and methods for the analysis of companies, industries, sectors and markets.

Porter's concept of the analysis of the 'value chain' (see Figure 1.1) identifies the elements that are critical in devising and assessing profitable or effective strategy, where the particular links in the chain lie, and the effect of each upon the whole of the strategy adopted. These links include:

- costs and their behaviour
- the separation and combination of activities
- the technology that is available and the ability of the organisation to use it
- the identification of good and bad aspects of operations in the organisation and the market
- the identification of good and bad industrial and commercial sectors and competitors within them.

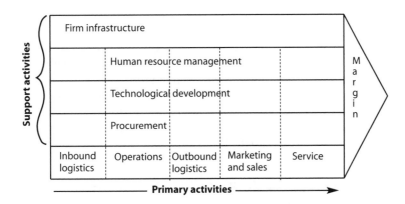

Notes:

The value chain breaks an organisation down into its component parts in order to understand the source of, and behaviour of, costs, and actual and potential sources of differentiation. It isolates and identifies the 'building blocks' by which an organisation creates an offering of value to its customers and clients.

- It is a tool for the general examination of an organisation's competitive position, and means of cost determination.
- It identifies the range and mix of characteristics necessary to design, produce, deliver and support its offerings.
- The value chain should be identified at 'business unit' level, for greatest possible clarity and accuracy.

The value chain

FIGURE 1.1

Source: M. E. Porter (ed.), *Competitive Strategy*, Free Press, 1981 and *Competitive Advantage*, Macmillan, 1985.

These are then related to both the segments in which the organisation is to operate and the structures and sub-structures that it adopts in order to do this effectively.

Business and public policy and strategy is currently a major field of enquiry. This derives from the change, turmoil and turbulence that are endemic throughout the business sphere at present. As organisations master the strategic approach, and understand the importance of conducting it and formulating it effectively, and in line with their own capabilities and capacities, they gain great advantages in their ability to compete in their chosen field.

Organisations, management and technology

The relationships between the technology required to conduct certain industrial and production activities and the nature and style of organisation required to energise this were studied by Joan Woodward, who conducted research among the manufacturing firms of South East Essex in the post-war conditions of the 1950s. The research looked at the organisational aspects of the levels and complexities of authority, hierarchy and spans of control in these organisations (see Figure 1.2). It also considered the nature and division of work: the clarity of the definition of jobs and duties, and the ways in which specialist and functional divisions were drawn. Finally, the nature of communications activities and systems in the organisations was analysed.

The conclusions drawn related the differences in these organisational aspects to the different technologies used in them. The technology was found to impinge on all factors: organisational objectives, lines of authority, roles and responsibilities, and the structure of management committees. The nature, complexity and personality of systems for control were also found to be related to the technological processes in place.

The work also defined the levels of production process and complexity in technological terms that are now universally understood and used: those of unit production, batch production, mass production and flow production. It further developed the relationship between these and the nature and complexity of organisation required in each case, and, above all, in regard to the highly capital-intensive mass and flow activities.

Socio-technical approaches: mechanistic and organic management systems

These model systems of management were proposed by T. Burns and G.M. Stalker in *The Management of Innovation* (1966). The mechanistic system of organisation was found to be appropriate to conditions of relative stability. Such conditions are highly structured, and those working in them have rigorous formal job descriptions, clearly defined roles and precise positions in the hierarchies (see Figure 1.3). Direction of the organisation is handed down via the hierarchy from the top, and communication is similarly 'vertical'. The organisation insists on loyalty and obedience from its members, both to superior officers and to itself. Finally, it is essential that the functionary is able to operate within the constraints of the organisation.

The organic model is suitable to unstable, turbulent and changing conditions where the organisation is constantly breaking new ground, addressing new problems, and meeting the unforeseen. A highly specialised structure cannot accommodate this. What is required is fluidity, continual adjustment, task redefinition and flexibility (see Figure 1.4).

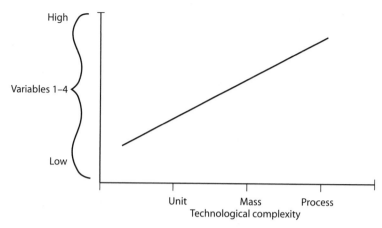

Variables:
1   Number of levels in management hierarchy
2   Ratio of managers and supervisors to total staff
3   Ratio of direct to indirect labour
4   Proportion of graduates among supervisory staff engaged in production

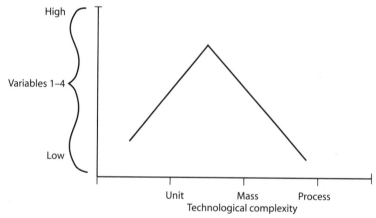

Variables:
1   Span of total of first time supervisors
2   Organisation flexibility/inflexibility
3   Amount of written communication
4   Specialisation between functions of management, technical expertise, time–staff structure

Organisations and technology

FIGURE 1.2

Source: P. A. Lawrence, *Management in Action*, Routledge and Kegan Paul, 1984. Used with permission.

Groups, departments and teams are constantly formed and reformed. Communication takes place at every level, and between every level. The means of control is regarded as a network rather than a personal commitment to it, and goes beyond the purely operational or functional.

Burns and Stalker developed their theme a stage further, to ascertain whether it was possible to move from the mechanistic to the organic. They concluded that this was

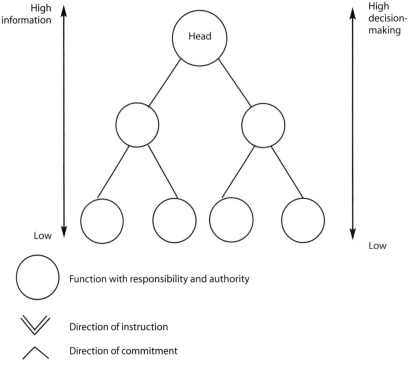

High
information

High
decision-
making

Head

Low

Low

Function with responsibility and authority

Direction of instruction

Direction of commitment

FIGURE 1.3 Organisation structures: mechanistic

Source: P. A. Lawrence, *Management in Action*, Routledge and Kegan Paul, 1984 (after Burns and Stalker).

unlikely. When mechanistic organisations seek change, committee and working party systems are created and liaison officer posts are established. Additional stresses are placed on the existing structure and channels of communication of the organisation, compounding the difficulties and clouding the issues that are to be faced. As a result, progress tends to be stifled rather than facilitated.

Excellence

The genesis of the work that subsequently grew into the management concept of 'excellence' was a review carried out in the latter part of the 1970s by McKinsey, the international management consulting firm, of its thinking and approach to business strategy and organisation effectiveness. This review was itself founded in a dissatisfaction with conventional approaches to these matters.

The approach adopted was to study both businesses and managers of high repute and/or high performance, and to try to isolate those qualities and characteristics that made them so. A model (the 7-S model; see Figure 1.5) for the design and description of organisations was also proposed. Those working on the study also identified those attributes that they felt ought to be present in such organisations and persons, and to test them against those studied.

In all, 62 organisations were studied. They were drawn from all sectors of US

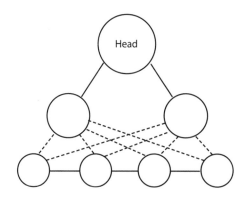

Notes:

External knowledge and experience important.
The synergy principle:
the whole is greater than the sum of its parts.

———— Predominant relationship

- - - - Secondary relationship

Organisation structures: organic   *FIGURE 1.4*

Source: P. A. Lawrence, *Management in Action*, Routledge and Kegan Paul, 1984 (after Burns and Stalker).

industry and commerce, and included many global firms (such as Boeing, McDonald's and Hewlett Packard).

'High performing' took on a variety of meanings:

- profitability
- a global organisation (such as IBM)
- a strong positive image (such as Marks & Spencer)
- a strong domestic organisation (Sainsbury's in the UK or 3M in the USA)
- a strong player in a slumped or declining market.

It was also related to aspects such as a strong general image; customer confidence; and staff and customer loyalty.

These characteristics may be summarised as follows.

- The leadership and management of business organisations requires **vision,** energy, dynamism and positivism; the placing of the customer and his needs and wants at the centre of the business; and the ability to change and improve as a permanent organisational feature.
- The closeness of the relationship between the **organisation** and its **customers** and **clients** must be maintained; if this is lost the customers will go elsewhere.
- The commitment, motivation, ability, training and development of all **staff** at all levels of the organisation are critical to the continuation of its success; closely related to this is a shared vision or shared values to which all members of the organisation must ascribe; staff must be held in high respect and well rewarded.
- **Supervision** levels, hierarchies, regional and head office establishments must be kept to a minimum; the purpose of these establishments is to service those who generate business of the organisation and not to impose a superstructure on them; such establishments should also be flexible and responsive and not hierarchical and inert.

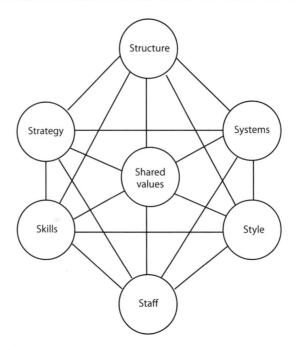

The 7-S framework
Purpose: a configuration of organisation, pattern and design that reflects the essential attributes that must be addressed in the establishment and development of an excellent organisation.

FIGURE 1.5   The concept of excellence applied to organisations

Source: T. Peters and R.H. Waterman, *In Search of Excellence*, Harper and Row, 1982.

- Organisations must stick to their **core business**; that which they are good at; and that which is profitable and effective.
- Organisations must constantly **innovate and improve**, update working practices, staff abilities, technology, customer response times and methods. They should constantly seek new applications and new markets for their existing products and services.
- Organisations must be **receptive** to ideas and influences from outside, and be able to evaluate them for use and value to them in their own circumstances.
- The bias of the organisation must be towards action not procedure.

The key findings were as follows.

The essential nature of organisation culture

In the organisations studied this was:

- a belief in being the best
- a belief in the importance of the staff and individuals as well as in their contribution to the organisation

- a belief in, and obsession with, quality and service
- a belief that organisation members should innovate and have their creative capacities harnessed
- a belief in the importance of excellent communication among all staff
- a belief in the concept of simultaneous loose–tight properties: measures of control that allow for operational flexibility
- a belief in the continuous cycle of development
- a recognition that there is always room for improvement
- attention to detail: the necessity to ensure that whatever the excellence of the strategic vision, it must always be carefully and accurately carried out
- a belief in the importance of economic growth and the profit motive.

The importance of macro-organisational analysis

This was the approach used to establish the concepts and elements that were present in the organisations described as 'excellent'.

Essentially, this is dependent upon the strength and style of leadership: the drive, determination, core values and strategic vision necessary to energise and make profitable the organisation's activities. In time, this becomes 'the way things are done here'. Managers underpin this through their day-to-day activities: the issues with which they concern themselves, the matters on which they spend resources, the people with whom they spend time. It is therefore a combination of both what they do and how they do it, and messages are given off by this to the rest of the organisation. Above all, leaders of organisations express the true organisational value through the means by which they conduct themselves in all activities.

These values become an integral part of the structures and systems of the organisation and affect all its activities. If the management style is energetic and positive, this is reflected in the ways in which senior managers wish to have things done.

The study also looked at the particular performance indicators of the organisation. These came from all areas of activity. They included asset growth and returns on capital invested; the organisations studied and from which the lessons were drawn had rates of return on these factors of between 10 and 60 times the sectoral average. Absenteeism was another factor studied. In a US steel works studied by Peters he found an uncertificated sickness rate of only two-fifths of 1 per cent, against a national average of 6 per cent and a sectoral average of 9 per cent. Organisation reputation was another factor assessed. This was conducted across all the organisation's activities (marketing, human resource policies, customer care and customer relations, equality of opportunity) and also across its wider general reputation in the environment and community, in which it invariably perceived itself to have a direct stake, interest and wider responsibility.

The other contribution of the 'excellence' studies was to identify the characteristics mentioned earlier as essential to both organisation and managerial success (see Example Box 1.6). The role of the senior manager is therefore the management of the organisation's culture, style and values; design and direction of strategy; and assessment of progress against precisely stated performance indicators.

EXAMPLE BOX 1.6 Criteria for Excellence

- High growth of assets, value, turnover and profits.
- Consistent reputation in sector as leader and pioneer.
- Solid and positive reputation with customers, community and general public.

Source: W. Goldsmith and D. Clutterbuck (1990).

- Professional organisations are lean and empowered.
- Professional staff require flat structures and autonomy for effective performance.
- Processes and procedures are speedy, simple and effective.

Source: C.B. Handy (1984).

- Excellence is performance thousands and thousands of percentage points over sectoral norms.

Source: T. Peters and R.H. Waterman (1982).

- Innovation and development leading to maximisation and optimisation of the human resource.
- Innovation in quality of working life.
- Promotion of full and genuine equality of opportunity.
- Models of good practice that offer their example to the world, and are pleased and proud to be studied.

Source: R.M. Kanter (1985).

Conclusions

The overall purpose here has been to illustrate the complexity, range and scale of the subject matter that is to be considered, the widely differing standpoints from which it has been tackled, and the progression of it as a field of study. The balance of the material quoted reflects the particular concern with it over the period since 1945 and its emergence as an area critical to both business and economic success, and also the wider prosperity of society at large.

This is not at all an exhaustive coverage. However, it does attempt to itemise major staging posts and fields of enquiry, and to illustrate the variety of studies that have been undertaken. Each study addresses different parts of the business and management sphere. Each makes its own particular contribution to the whole; none provides a comprehensive coverage of the field. What is clear, however, is that management is an ever-broadening sphere. The works illustrated here demonstrate just how far this has developed and the variety of approaches that have been taken in the pursuit of this.

There is no doubt that there has been a shift in approach to regard management as an occupation in its own right. What has been less certain the actual composition of this occupation and profession. This chapter has attempted to illustrate the basis of this and to introduce some of the major concepts, studies and ideas that have contributed to the state of its development.

Some more specific conclusions can also be drawn from this material. Management direction and leadership are separate from the functions, operations and activities of the organisation. Ability to generate the confidence, loyalty, trust and faith of all those in the organisation is essential. It is necessary to establish the identity of a common purpose to which everybody in the organisation can aspire and on which all the resources of the organisation are concentrated. People must be rewarded in response to the efforts that they put into the achievement of the organisation's purposes. Both the organisation and its managers must have both the knowledge and the ability to operate in the chosen environment and to influence it as far as they possibly can. Within particular constraints, organisations establish their own ways of working, cultural norms, procedures and practices as part of the process of making effective their daily operations. There is the recognition that business and managerial practice takes place in a turbulent global environment. The ability to operate within this is critical to continuity and success.

This, then, represents the backcloth against which the rest of the book is written. It enables a broad understanding of where the current state of the management art/science/profession is drawn, and where the current matters of importance and concern within it lie. It also indicates the range and complexity of the qualities and capacities required of the manager.

CHAPTER SUMMARY

This chapter highlights the major foundation stones on which the principles and practice of modern management are based. It is important that they are seen as complementary rather than conflicting. For example, it is essential that organisations address the key question of productivity – the maximisation and optimisation of resources over long periods of time – with exactly the same vigour and determination as Taylor. However, alongside this it is also essential that they address the human side of enterprise, and the need for permanence, order and stability. Indeed, you cannot have one without the rest. It should be apparent from the examples given in the chapter (see Example Box 1.5) that drives for productivity can only be sustained if the other aspects of order, permanence and humanity are also present.

It should also be increasingly apparent that management is indeed an occupation, trade or profession in its own right. There is no reason why managers should be paid more than the people that they manage. Indeed, in many successful organisations and industries this is not the case. For example:

- The managers of top UK and European football clubs, though paid extremely well, earn substantially less than their star players.
- Film directors earn substantially less than the star actors and actresses who work for them (though again, film directors are normally relatively well paid).
- Stockbrokers, financial and other commodity traders earn substantially more than those who run the organisations for which they work.

- Those who work at the frontline of oil and gas exploration earn substantially more than their managers in their company head offices.

- Those working in unskilled or semi-skilled occupations on building and civil engineering sites can earn a lot more than the site manager, provided that they are prepared to put in the hours.

This was one of the points that Peter (see page 17) was making when he ridiculed the notion of promoting people into managerial positions from those of technical excellence. In the UK this has been further underlined by the fact that, for the first time, the army training college at Sandhurst has introduced management training for its officer candidates. This flies in the face of the notion that was widely held until quite recently, that military training was the best possible management training of all!

It should also be apparent from the content of this chapter that there are no easy answers to the principles and practice of management. If the elements indicated are to be harmonised and made to work effectively alongside each other, then those charged with ensuring that this happens – the managers – have to understand the necessity for this, rather than picking on one to the exclusion of all others.

DISCUSSION QUESTIONS

1. Identify organisations where there is little evidence of humanity in managerial practice, yet (on the face of it at least) great evidence of economic success. What are the reasons for this? What effects do you think the addition of humanity to drives for productivity would have on these organisations?

2. What were the major influences of Tom Peters and the other writers on excellent organisations, on the development of principles of management?

3. Why do so many excellent professionals (e.g. doctors, lawyers, teachers, nurses, sales people) find it necessary to take promotion into managerial positions? What are the advantages and disadvantages of this?

4. Identify those principles of management that have endured through the ages; and contrast these with those that have only recently been identified. What are the main lessons for present day students of management to be drawn from Julius Caesar and Machiavelli?

CHAPTER CASE STUDY

POTTER'S GLASS LTD

Potter's Glass Ltd is a medium-sized manufacturer of industrial glassware. It is situated near the southern entrance to the Blackwall Tunnel in East London. Its core business is to produce sheet glass and finished window units for the construction industry.

The company employs a total of 190 staff, of whom 130 are engaged on glass manufacturing, 35 on sales, and 25 on management and administration.

The company has recently experienced a downturn in its order book, and at present has the capacity to produce 20 per cent more than it can sell. The company chief executive, Nicholas Potter, has run the company successfully for the past 25 years. He has managed to avoid any redundancies or lay-offs in spite of the recessions in the UK building industry in the 1980s and 1990s. This time however, matters are more serious, because he understands that he is being undercut on both price and productivity by alternative suppliers from mainland Europe.

He has accordingly held meetings with two firms of management consultants. The first, a major City of London institution, charged £8000 for a two-day fact-finding exercise. When the consultants presented their report, they recommended an immediate reduction in the workforce of 25 per cent, and a reduction of the number of sales staff to 20.

The second firm of management consultants, a small company owned by the friend of Nicholas' brother and operating out of Dartford in Kent, 20 miles away, spent a week analysing the factory. This company's recommendation was that Potter's should maximise productivity and sales efforts, and fight the continental opposition on price, value, and reliability.

Nicholas Potter has both reports in front of him. He is just wondering what to do, when his secretary walks into the room. She asks him what he is studying. When he tells her, she replies, 'Yes, I've been thinking about this too. Why don't we go into the production of glass ornaments?'

'What?'

'I said, "go into the production of glass ornaments". We could do it. I've done a little bit of research, and the people on the factory floor tell me that there is no reason why the machinery can't be re-jigged to produce excellent, durable glass ornaments for the gift shop sector.'

QUESTIONS

1. Briefly evaluate the information that you have been given. What further information do you require to arrive at an informed judgement?
2. On the basis of what you have been told, identify a much broader range of alternative courses of action open to Potter's Glass Ltd.

2 Managing in a Changing Environment

"We never had time to do anything properly. Consequently, we always had to find time to do it twice.' Marcus Aurelius, Roman Emperor, 120 AD.

'If instead of filming theBoat Race, the BBC entered it, the cox would be ordered to do all the rowing, while the eight crew shouted conflicting orders.' John Tusa, ex-BBC employee, 1999.

'Fewer than half the firms that have downsized since 1990 have seen long-term improvements in quality, profitability or productivity.' American Management Association Report, 25 January 1999.

'The key to success in the twenty-first century is the management of knowledge and expertise.' Peter F. Drucker, *Management Challenges for the Twenty-first Century,* 2000.

CHAPTER OUTLINE

Introduction

Barriers to effective change

Changing culture and structure

Change catalysts and agents

Other factors

Lessons from Japan

The present and future of management.

CHAPTER OBJECTIVES

After studying this chapter, you should be able to:

understand the main forces driving organisational and managerial change and development

understand and identify the operational and psychological barriers to change

understand the pressures on organisation structures, cultures and strategies

understand and recognise the effectiveness of particular approaches to the management of change

understand and identify the conflicting demands of particular stakeholders, lobbies and vested interests.

Introduction

The changes that have impinged on society over the period since 1945, and more particularly since the 1960s, have deeply affected the management of organisations. These changes may be summarised as:

- **Technological:** affecting all social, economic and business activities; rendering many occupations obsolete and creating new ones; and opening up new spheres of activity, bringing travel, transport, distribution, telecommunication, industry, goods and services on to a global scale; the development of fledgling virtual industries; the development by companies of virtual activities (see Example Box 2.1).
- **Social:** the changing of people's lives, from the fundamentals of life expectancy and lifestyle choice, to the ability to buy and possess items; to travel; to be educated; to receive ever-increasing standards of health-care, personal insurance and information; to be fed; to enjoy increased standards of social security and stability, increased leisure time and choice of leisure pursuits; and all commensurate with increases in disposable income and purchasing power, and choices of purchase.
- **Eco-political:** resulting in changes in all governmental forms; the state of flux and expansion of the EU, with the adoption of super-national laws and directives, and the single market; the collapse of the communist bloc and the former USSR; the fragmentation of the former Yugoslavia into its component states; the emergence of Taiwan, South Africa, Korea and Vietnam as spheres of political and economic

---

EXAMPLE BOX 2.1 LastMinute.com

LastMinute.com was founded in 1997 by Brent Hoberman and Martha Lane-Fox as a virtual/internet travel ticketing and gift company. It was floated on the London Stock Exchange in March 2000, and capitalised at £850 million. This floatation took place in the full glare of the media spotlight. Brent Hoberman and Martha Lane-Fox became business celebrities. In April 2000 Martha Lane-Fox was described by *Management Today* magazine as the fifth most powerful woman in Britain.

For all the huge capitalisation, and volume of money raised, the company was unable to translate its internet activity into viable levels of sales. By the end of the year 2000, the company had generated just £1.6 million in turnover. In March 2001, it announced that it was going into partnership with Thomas Cook, the high street travel agency, so that each company would be able to benefit from the other's expertise.

Over the period 1996–2002, the value of the internet as a business medium has generated a great deal of financial, academic and commercial speculation. The ability of organisations and their managers to turn the vast amount of information and access available on the internet into sustainable commercial or public service activities remains unproven. To date, the most successful companies trading on the internet are those that have established an internet branch alongside their mainstream activities: for example Tesco.com and RyanAir.com. These companies, and others like them, are able to sustain commercially viable internet activities only because of their physical presence and identity elsewhere.

influence; the enormous potential of Africa, South America, and China as areas for commercial development.

- **Expectational:** in which the changes may be expressed as from stability to a state of change itself, a state of flux; the change from the expectation of working for one company or organisation to working for many, and the realisation that the former is increasingly unlikely.

In order to achieve the degrees of permanence, order and stability essential for the sustenance of long-term commercially viable products and services, and effective public services, the turbulent and changing environment has to be accommodated. In particular, change has to be considered from the following standpoints.

- Markets, their size, scope, scale and nature are ever changing.
- Technological advance is ever-more pervasive, and ever-wider uses and adaptations are being found for technology.
- Work patterns, expectations and methods are constantly being altered and adapted while operations and activities are being globalised.
- Competition, and this includes recognising that competitive pressures can come from any organisation, anywhere in the world, as well as understanding that consumers have a much greater choice in most areas as to where to spend their money.

Barriers to effective change

Barriers to effective change may be classified as either operational or behavioural.

Operational barriers

These are:

- **Location:** this is a barrier when, for whatever reason, it becomes impossible for the organisation to continue to operate in its current premises. Relocation has consequences for the resettlement of families, retraining and organisation development. Even where the new premises are close by, it may affect access, work and attendance patterns. For greater distances, the consequences of widespread disruption have to be addressed. As well as personal consequences, this includes attention to organisation culture and structure.
- **Tradition:** this is a problem where there has been a long history of successful work in specific, well-understood and widely accepted ways. This may be underlined where a whole community has grown up around a particular industry or organisation and where this is a major provider of employment and prosperity (for example, coal mining, iron and steel, shipbuilding, engineering). If this has been steady for long periods, there are strong perceptions of stability and permanence.
- **Success (and perceived success):** if the organisation is known or perceived to be successful in its current ways of doing things then there is a resistance based on: 'Why change something that works?' This is especially true if there is a long history of stability and prosperity. It is often very difficult in these circumstances to get workforces to accept that technology, ways of working and the products themselves are coming to the end of their useful life.

- **Failure:** this is a barrier to change where a given state of affairs has been allowed to persist for some time. The view is often taken – by both organisations and the staff concerned – that this is 'one of those things', a necessary part of being involved in a given set of activities. Resistance occurs when someone determines to do something about it – again, upsetting an overtly comfortable and orderly status quo.

- **Technology:** this is a barrier for many reasons. It is often the driving force behind jobs, tasks, occupations and activities. Their disruption causes trauma to those affected by the consequent need for job and occupation change, retraining, redeployment – and often redundancy. Technological changes may also cause relocation to more suitable premises. Technological changes, in turn, cause changes to work patterns and methods. Technology has been one of the driving forces behind the increase in home working and part-time working. In the former, employees can be provided with all the equipment necessary to work without the need to come together at the employer's premises. The latter increases where demands for maximisation on investment in technology and increases in customer bases have led to extended opening and operational hours. Technological change disrupts patterns of identity. It has led to flexible working, away from traditional job titles, restrictive practices and demarcation. It has also disrupted traditions of representation and belonging to trade unions, and professional and occupational bodies. This has occurred as jobs and occupations have become obsolete, causing both the individuals and the bodies concerned to seek new roles.

- **Vested interests:** needs for organisational change are resisted by those who are, or who perceive themselves to be, at risk. Vested interests are found in all areas. They include senior managers threatened with loss of functional authority, operational staff faced with occupational obsolescence, people in support functions no longer

---

EXAMPLE BOX 2.2   Vested Interests

At this stage, it is useful to define those lobby groups and vested interests that may be present in all organisations. These have to be managed whatever the present state of the particular organisation. It is essential to recognise the nature and extent of their influence, and where, why and how they are able to exert this.

- **Management groups:** as stated in the text, especially where their own interests and priorities are threatened.
- **Trade unions:** especially when faced with loss of influence in workforce representation.
- **Shareholders' representatives, stockbrokers and other financial interests:** when, for example, a change of ownership or direction is mooted or strongly indicated.
- **Customer, consumer and environmental groups.**
- **Over-mighty and over-influential individuals, groups, departments, divisions and functions:** especially where organisational restructuring or changes of direction mean that this influence is to be diluted or lost.

considered necessary, and those on promotional and career paths for whom the current order represents a clear and guaranteed passage to increased prosperity and influence (see Example Box 2.2).

- **Managerial:** the managerial barrier is a consequence of 'the divorce of organisation, ownership and control', where there is a divergence between the organisation's best interests and need for long-term survival, and the needs of individuals and groups of managers to preserve their own positions. Existing patterns of supervision may again provide both general order and certainty, and specific career and promotion paths.
- **Bureaucracy:** the bureaucracy barrier occurs where patterns of order and control have grown up over long periods in the recording and supervision of activities and in the structuring of organisational functions. The problem is worst where the bureaucracy is large and complex, and a significant part of the total range of activities.
- **Redundancy and redeployment:** this is referred to above. It is a barrier in its own right because in the current context any proposed change may imply redundancy and redeployment, and because these have so often been a consequence of other changes.

Behavioural barriers

The main barriers are as follows.

- **'It cannot be done':** this is a barrier both to confidence and understanding and is based on a lack of true, full and accurate information concerning the matters which the organisation is proposing.
- **'There is no alternative':** this comes in two forms. First, it may be adopted by the workforce, and the interest groups in and around it (for example trade unions) that have a vested interest in the maintenance of the status quo either because it is familiar or because any change will result in loss of influence. This is especially true where business has been conducted in an effective and productive steady-state for a long period of time. The other side of this is where directorates and managers adopt the maxim as the one and only explanation for a change that is to take place. Conducted in isolation 'there is no alternative' simply becomes a challenge for others to think of alternatives. The matter requires explanation and communication in order to demonstrate to all those affected that alternatives have indeed been considered and that what is now proposed represents a carefully chosen strategic direction.
- **Lack of clarity:** if organisations have not sorted out the basis of the changes that are proposed, neither staff nor customers will go along with them with any degree of confidence or understanding. Aims and objectives must be clearly understood as the prerequisite to successful and effective change, and communicated to those concerned in their own language.
- **Fear and anxiety:** these are human responses to concepts and situations that are unknown or uncertain. They are the initial response (or part of it) to any change that is proposed; if allowed to get out of hand, they can become an exercise in the devising and promulgation of hypothetical scenarios that could in certain circumstances become problems on the changing landscape. Not only does this

constitute a waste of organisational resources and a diversion from actual purposes, but such interaction among the staff feeds on itself, generating negativity and unnecessary internal turbulence.

- **Perfection:** at the point at which change is proposed suddenly everything concerning the status quo becomes 'perfect'. Anything that is proposed as an alternative has therefore to address this barrier. It is another manifestation of familiarity and comfort, and when people face the loss of them, such elements become highly desirable.

For all barriers, the main issue is to avoid leaving a vacuum. Organisations have therefore to understand where the proposed changes are to lead and what their consequences are. Early communication is essential for the benefit of all concerned. The best employers give every opportunity to their workforce to be a part of their future before casting around outside for new staff and expertise.

In most cases most of these barriers, operational or behavioural, are present.

The influence of each barrier depends upon the particular situation, the nature and extent of the changes to be made, and whether they are strategic, operational, locational, attitudinal, structural or cultural. Whichever is present, the keys to effective and sustainable progress are the following.

- integrity and directness, coupled with a clarity of direction (above all, people always suspect a partial interest when phrases such as 'economies of scale' or 'synergies' are used)
- clarity of purpose, strategy, direction and priority, easily understood by all affected
- clarity of communication, which includes sustaining the directness of communication over the period of change
- clear monitoring, review and evaluation processes, enabling problems and teething troubles to be addressed as soon as they become apparent
- consultation, counselling and support for individuals and groups that know, believe or perceive themselves to be most at risk from particular changes
- a capacity for addressing specific problems, issues, quirks and anomalies as these become apparent.

Changing cultures and structures

Effective, lasting and operationally successful change is achieved only if attitudes, values and beliefs are addressed and the same universal importance placed on change as on operational and technological factors. They all impinge on each other: for example, the introduction of an automated production line leads to new job requirements, which leads to new job descriptions, which lead to new ways of working, which lead to revised staff handbooks and work agreements, and so on. Consequently, the attempts to introduce an operational change in isolation (for whatever reason; a common one in the UK used to be trade union pressure) simply results in the old stance being conducted less effectively on the new machine. While there may be a short-term gain in terms of expediency in the avoidance of a labour dispute, in the longer term, both operation and production will suffer.

For change to be effective, it has to be recognised that what is currently in place is

TABLE 2.1   Unfreezing–transforming–refreezing

Unfreezing	Transforming	Refreezing
• Consultation • High quality open information • Getting people used to the idea	• Introduction of new technology, work patterns, products, services, attitudes	• The new becomes the steady-state and familiar • Note the danger of becoming rigid or set anew

undesirable for a variety of reasons. The desired state of affairs must be articulated; and a strategic approach adopted to ensure that the required conclusion is reached.

There are two standard approaches as follows.

- Unfreezing–transforming–refreezing (see Table 2.1). It is important to recognise that the idea of 'refreezing' incorporates aptitudes of flexibility, dynamism and responsiveness.
- Force field analysis (see Figure 2.1). This is where the forces that drive change and those that restrain it are separated out. The drivers are then energised and pushed on; the restrainers are either removed, neutralised or else re-energised in ways productive to the required outcome.

The key problems with both the unfreezing/refreezing and the force field approaches are as follows:

- The history of organisation development indicates that structures are easier to put in place than they are to change, dismantle or rearrange.
- The need for change, as we have seen, may neither be apparent nor recognised.
- The structure has often provided a career progression path through the organisation that has been one of the attractions of working in it and staying in it.

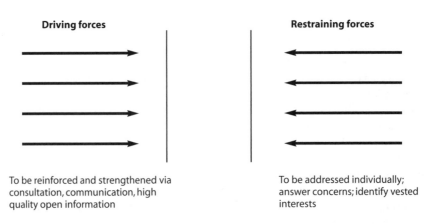

Driving forces

Restraining forces

To be reinforced and strengthened via consultation, communication, high quality open information

To be addressed individually; answer concerns; identify vested interests

FIGURE 2.1   Force field analysis

EXAMPLE BOX 2.3 Consultants

Consultant-bashing is huge fun. The incomparable Stanley Bing, a real executive at a real, but unnamed, large US company, recently wrote his regular column in *Fortune* magazine on: 'Why consultants generally suck. It's nothing personal. It's just that we know you are out to kill us'.

Whenever I write about management consultants, readers send me their anti-consultant stories and very entertaining they are too. If I attempt to redress the balance and say something positive, I am told not to be so silly.

'They are snake-oil merchants. Their only strategy is slash and burn. They get between top management and the rest of the workforce spreading fear and mistrust. They do not know the first thing about the businesses they are trying to advise. They cost too much.'

The tirades make not a whit of difference. Consultancy remains impervious. The latest quarterly survey from the Management Consultancies' Association, which represents the largest consulting firms in the UK, shows a rise in the number of consultants employed, higher fee rates and growth in new business. Confidence is high; clients are buying as never before.

Moreover, management experts and consultants have created a culture of reliance and dependence. Too many companies seem afraid to help themselves, with too many senior managers preferring to abdicate responsibility rather than face difficult issues themselves. This has been encouraged by the consultants themselves who have created proprietary brands of management voodoo, of which business process re-engineering (BPR) is perhaps the best example.

BPR's message is that organisations need to identify key internal processes and 're-engineer' them to become more efficient. That is, to strip out unnecessary steps in organisation structure to streamline operations. This requires hard work and attention to detail with no black art involved, but consultants would have us believe that this requires the help of expensive outsiders. BPR has consequently been a prodigious money-spinner for the big consultancies, and they have grown fat on advising companies about how to implement it.

Moreover, consultants will sell you only what they know. They latch on to the latest high profile fad, and persuade their clients that this is the one true approach. When re-engineering was first defined by Michael Hammer and James Champey in *Re-engineering the Corporation* (1994), they stated unequivocally that the alternative to re-engineering was to close the doors and go out of business. The choice, they stated was 'that simple and that stark'.

For all the hype, fad-based management, based on consultants' recommendations, usually fails to deliver. Quality programmes are launched with great fanfare, then fade away. Cutting management layers often disrupts internal communications. Moreover, the overwhelming impression is given that any manager who fails to follow the latest fad – regardless of its relevance to his or her own organisation – risks being thought unprofessional. Beyond this, management gurus encourage firms to believe that all fixes are not just easy to implement but quick to take effect: quality programmes will produce rapid declines in defect rates; re-engineering will

Example Box 2.3 (continued)

clear clogged production lines. Then, when the promised benefits fail to appear, managers – especially senior managers – quickly lose heart, and this is why most re-engineering and quality initiatives eventually break down.

Sources: Alison Eadie, 'Management Matters', *Daily Telegraph,* 15 June 2000; Des Dearlove, 'The Changing Business', *The Times,* 5 November 1998; 'Instant Coffee as Management Theory', *The Economist,* 25 January 1997.

Change catalyst and change agent

The concept of the change catalyst and change agent must be addressed. They may constitute one and the same thing; or they may be different sides of the same coin – the catalyst for change may be the need to reform workplace industrial relations (for example) and the change agent the person given the responsibility of doing this (see Example Box 2.3).

The catalyst may be a person, event or factor, internal or external to the organ-

EXAMPLE BOX 2.4   The Seductive Power of Management Gurus

'Many people in business have probably been surprised by the extent to which a clever, clear-headed colleague has come under the seductive power of management consultants. Some become dependent, seemingly unable to make even banal decisions without checking with their favourite guru. Others appear to turn their back on received wisdom and MBA training to pursue wacky, modern, airhead ideas favoured by the more alternative consultants.

   Cynics suggest two causes for this sometimes bizarre behaviour. First is the old favourite "cognitive dissonance" or buyer's nostalgia. This is about reconciling two contradictory facts.

   At great expense you hired consultants but they did not produce the results you wanted. One solution is to redefine the result and point out how good the consultants were at diagnosing the real problem and helping a long-term solution.

   The more they cost and the greater the disappointment, the stronger the need to rationalise the mistake.

   Others point out that stressed, bewildered, workaholic managers need a confidant, part confessor, part friend, part sounding board, a second opinion – in short a psychotherapist. Someone outside the business to whom they can talk about a range of issues.

   This is a formidable cocktail to the rejected, ignored, despised business manager. And it gets better and stronger over time. A good business consultant knows that he/she is in the relationship business and that it is the support that gives the courage for business people to act decisively'.

Source: Adrian Furnham, University College London, 15 June 2000.

isation. Whichever it is, it is that which brings the organisation to the realisation that 'we cannot go on as we are'. It may be a very uncomfortable or even debilitating or destructive process in which the organisation and its managers are faced with unacceptable or unpalatable truths – the catalyst here is that which forces this out into the open. The catalyst thus provides the initial energy that sets the change of process in hand (see Example Box 2.4).

The agent is the person (or event, or phenomenon) that drives change. This may again be internal to the organisation (for example, an increase in the priority of marketing will become effective if the marketing director appointed to achieve it comes with a high reputation and track record in the field). Or it may be external; a common use of management consultants by the organisation is to get them, as external advisers, to articulate to organisation stakeholders (especially staff and shareholders) what may be unacceptable coming from within the organisation and from its top management team.

Changing attitudes and approaches to quality, value and expectations

It is necessary to recognise the conception of quality as part of a corporate state of mind, a core element of prevailing attitudes and values, rather than as an adjunct to existing practices. It follows from this that the organisation's true commitments to quality will be reflected in the capabilities of staff employed; the tenor of sales and marketing efforts; levels of investments in plant, machinery and equipment; types of plant, machinery and equipment; induction, attitude formation, training and development programmes; and the style of IR and staff relations, supervision methods and managerial approaches that are adopted.

'Organisational obsessions with quality'

These include the following.

- Obsession with customer satisfaction, in terms both of the products or services offered, and the ways in which they are delivered by the organisation. This must cover the whole process from the acceptance of orders, through delivery and dispatch to after-sales service. In many cases, this is instrumental in the generation of repeat business. There is thus a strong element of long-term investment inherent in any true, genuine approach that has quality at its core.
- Obsession with staff excellence, in terms of their expertise, skills and knowledge. This must be underpinned, however, by a commitment to them that ensures that they are instilled with the attitudes necessary to deliver this expertise in the ways in which the organisation and its customers require. They must be paid and rewarded adequately. They must have their expectations and aspirations accommodated in the intention and pursuit of excellence. Again, this is regarded as a long-term, mutual investment and commitment between staff and organisation. It is not regarded as a purely instrumental or functional approach, or concept of employment.
- Obsession with constant improvement, the recognition that each and every

aspect of the organisation – its products and services, its practices, procedures and operations – can be made to work better and more effectively in the pursuit of quality and excellence. Levels of investment in production methods and capacities, standards and life span of production plants and equipment will also be the subject of this commitment. Only the best equipment will do: that which has all the attributes required to meet the output levels required in terms of speed, reliability, perfection, regularity and universality.

The maintenance of operations at a continuing high-quality level is underpinned by both procedures and processes. The procedures include inspection, random sampling, testing and monitoring of products as they come off the line, and of the lines themselves during planned maintenance periods. The processes reflect the concept of continued improvement and must include work improvements and quality improvement groups addressing both product and production methods (see Example Box 2.5).

Lessons from Japan

The concept, practices and approaches adopted by managers in Japanese companies are of interest for a variety of reasons. First, and most important, is clearly

---

EXAMPLE BOX 2.5 Quality Circles

Organisations in all sectors now operate their own versions of 'quality circles'. These groups may be called quality improvement groups, work improvement groups, product and service improvement groups, or factory improvement groups.

The concept of quality circles was American and post-war in origin. It was exported to Japan which, in turn, made it an integral part of the continuous quality improvement process in organisations. A quality circle is a group of staff who meet on a regular basis to review the whole area of quality at the workplace. This involves identifying and clarifying problems, selecting issues from among these for resolution, organising and prioritising them, setting deadlines, timetables and target dates, and setting aims and objectives by which the improvements in the quality of the organisation's operations can be measured. To be effective, they require accommodation, resourcing and support from the organisation and a commitment to back the judgements of the quality circle. Organisations have to recognise that there is a pay-back, not only in improvement in quality or, at least, in problem identification, but that this is also instrumental in promoting the desired attributes of greater commitment, achievement, identity and participation by all concerned. Quality circles are voluntary, generating and selecting their own leadership, frequency and timing of meetings, and precise agenda format. Where they have worked, especially in Japanese companies, it has been because there is a greater cultural pressure to participate, together with an environment that is both conducive to and expectant of a full measure of involvement (whether something is actually designated as being voluntary or not).

that concerned with commercial success; the post-war Japanese 'economic miracle' is of critical global importance. However, there are other matters, both cultural and practical, which merit careful study and understanding.

Gambara

There is a work ethic traditionally imbued by society that is manifest in a number of ways. A basic concept is *gambara*, which means 'don't give up, do your best, be persistent, put in a great effort'. This lies at the core of the Japanese work ethic. There is also a high concept of service, which is much more widely regarded than elsewhere in the world; service is regarded as important not only at the customer interface, but also over the lifetime of the products provided, and also for new products and models and their lifetime to the customer. The Japanese work for the good of their group and their company above all; the view adopted is that the whole only functions effectively when all its component parts are, in turn, functioning to full effect and capacity.

The relationship between work and society is vital. Bad business is regarded as a waste of society's resources. Service to society is performed through the high industrial, commercial and managerial virtues of fairness, harmony, cooperation, and continuous betterment of quality, courtesy, humility, adjustment, assimilation and gratitude. Responsibility in all these spheres is fostered through managerial arrangements at the workplace; and the inherent requirement for obedience, conformity and respect is combined with an enlightened and egalitarian view of society that is the equivalent of 'from each according to his means, to each according to his needs'.

The concept of interdependence also runs through Japanese companies (see Figure 2.2). This also is viewed in the widest context. As well as relationships between organisation and customer, regard is given to those relationships between the individual and his work group, interrelationships between groups, the concept of self-restraint, cohesion and harmony, senior/junior and mentor/protégé relationships. The individual is valued for his contribution on all fronts: team, group, divisional and corporate.

Japanese management practices are designed actively to prevent problems from arising. This is distinct from elsewhere in the world where great store is often set by the ability of the manager to resolve problems. While the Japanese manager is expected to resolve these as and when they do occur, the need for this should be kept to a minimum, and organisation and managerial style reflect this.

The decision-making process is a combination of *nemawashi*, which means 'binding the roots' and has come to mean 'thorough preparation'; and *ringi*, which is the outcome of this. In practice, the process involves full consultation before a decision is taken, and engaging the cooperation of all those who are to be affected by it. Preparation and pre-preparation time and effort is everything and, to those who do not come from within the culture, the process may appear inert for a very long period. However, once *ringi* is reached, once everyone's support is engaged, it is understood that the matter in hand will go ahead at full speed from that point onwards, because there is nothing further to consider. The provision of information and the means for full participation, involvement and consultation on the part of all is critical to the success of operations if this style

a)

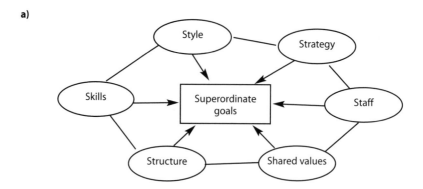

This is based on the management summary by R.T. Pascale and A. Athos, *The Art of Japanese Management*, and is a variation on the 7S model of excellent organisations. It illustrates the centrality of long-term commitment.

b)

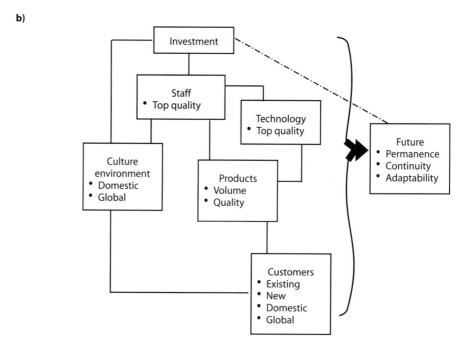

A systems approach to Japanese management. The key input is **investment**: the key output is a 'secure' **future**.

FIGURE 2.2   Japanese management

of management is to be adopted successfully and effectively. Japanese companies adopt a philosophy of 'management of the whole organisation', not a series of components. It is the effective functioning of the whole that is critical to operational success, not some of the parts only. To this extent adequate and effective communication and consultation systems are essential.

Kaizen

Kaizen refers to the constant progress of humanity, and the continuous striving for perfection. In management terms, this has become 'constant continuous improvement'. It refers to all aspects of all organisations:

- continuous staff training and development
- continuous product improvement
- continuous production and output improvement
- continuous attention to procedures and administration to make this as simple and clear as possible
- continuous attention to the 'whole': the Japanese organisation is seen overwhelmingly as one entity, rather than a collection of parts and divisions.

At its best, the result is continued output of high volumes of high-quality products, often at premium (that is, high) prices. This is supported by adaptation and innovation rather than creativity. The Japanese have no particular reputation for invention and creation; they are experts at taking existing products and improving each and every aspect. This is, in time, supported by an absolute commitment to high levels of investment in all aspects of staff, business and technology. It is reinforced by the high expectations placed on staff, the high degree of conformity required, and the high levels of pay offered. Japanese companies set out to offer lifetime employment to their staff, and lifetime service to their customers. This can only be achieved if the company exists for a lifetime, and ensuring this is the required result of *Kaizen*.

Mu

Related to *Kaizen* is *Mu*, or 'complete openness'. This constitutes a refusal to be hidebound by policies, constraints, directions and structures. It means being receptive to ideas, innovations, opportunity and potential; it also means engendering the qualities of vitality, flexibility, and adaptability to organisations and their staffs. The guiding principle of the company is to 'live for a long time', rather than to be 'the best airline' or 'the best car company'. It was this approach that enabled Mitsubishi to transform relatively easily from shipbuilder to car maker. Purposes and goals are set according to the demands and opportunities of the business sphere rather than preordained internal strategies; indeed, corporate strategy consists of having the staff, capital, technology and capability to respond to these demands and opportunities.

In the pursuit of this, the Japanese company sets great store by creative, innovative and extensive research and development activities. Only by investing and prioritising heavily in these areas is a continuing run of fresh offerings for the markets ensured. In addition, different applications for existing technologies may be found in this way, as are capacities for introducing a hitherto exclusive product to mass markets.

In the pursuit of this also, the Japanese company takes a very different view of failure from that elsewhere. Failure is when a commercially offered product fails to satisfy the customer. It is not a judgement generally made at the research or inception stage. Any product or idea which does not progress to the output stage is nevertheless retained as the subject for the research or prudent activity, or else is kept in storage until market perceptions change and it can be commercially developed at a later date.

Finally, while it may come to nothing in itself, the creative spark that engendered it may come up next with a market leader.

The stakeholders in an organisation and their relative positions of importance may easily be inferred from this. Staff come first; success is only possible through top-quality, secure employees. The major Japanese corporations adopted philosophies of lifetime employment and have managed to practise this up to the present day (though there are signs of current difficulty in some organisations). Customers are next. Third comes the shareholder, very often one of the large banks (companies are often also underwritten by the Japanese exchequer). In addition, shareholders are often customers of the companies that they underwrite. The emphasis on continuity, performance, satisfaction and the customer is therefore underlined again, in contrast to the concentration on dividends and shareholder benefits found elsewhere. Japanese consumers want the best. They expect this to extend across the entire range of consumer goods and services, based on principles of continuity, service and quality enhancement.

The other reasons for the initial and continuing success of Japanese companies are as follows.

- **Conformity** and the harnessing of this characteristic of Japanese society to the requirements of profitable business; for this to be successful requires vision and direction from the top of companies that is both profitable and worthy of respect from the staff and customers.
- **Adaptation and adaptability:** very few of the products made by Japanese companies were invented in Japan; Japanese technologists, researchers and business developers have rather seen the potential of inventions from other parts of the world adapted to existing products for other purposes. They have been able to standardise production both to a high level of quality, and to a price that makes the products available to mass consumer markets, and been willing to promote and develop a full range of related products, after-sales and back-up services to ensure a high level of repeat business.
- The emphasis placed on the **long term**, rather than the immediate, return. There is an advantage in the financial system of Japan, which basically consists of the underwriting of Japanese business and industry by the government (at least over the short to medium term). This in turn allows flexibility and confidence on the part of the industry to experiment, to pioneer, and to develop new products and initiatives in the expectation of long-term success and profitability, without having short-term financial products or targets as priorities.
- **Investment in staff training at all levels of the organisation:** for example, Nissan spent millions of pounds and dollars training production operatives at Washington, Tyne and Wear, UK, and Smyrna, Tennessee, USA, *before* a single car was produced. As well as the high quality of the finished product, the returns are measurable in terms of employee commitment, positive attitudes, identity (rather than alienation), and minute levels of absenteeism.
- Concentration on, and commitment to, the **development of managers and supervisors:** especially in the areas of staff management and problem-solving there is great pressure on managers in a Japanese company to resolve issues successfully themselves, rather than refer them through 'channels' (as in a more traditional Western bureaucracy). There is also a great cultural pressure not to get into institutionalised disputes and, above all, not to lose them.

- **Single workplace status:** there is a strong social hierarchy in Japan. It is reflected to an extent at the workplace, in that the senior is worthy of respect. However, the workplace requires that this is translated into business needs only, and in this situation everyone is important in their role, whatever that may be. It is usual for everyone to wear the same uniform, to go through the same basic induction and orientation programme, to use the same facilities (e.g. canteen, restaurant and recreation), and to be on the same basic terms and conditions of employment.

- A strong **identity** on the part of all staff with the company is insisted upon. In managerial and professional occupations within the organisation this may involve, for example, working very long hours, and taking an active part in corporate hospitality and business-related activities in the evening. Similarly, activities designated 'voluntary' are not voluntary to such staff in Japanese companies (see Example Box 2.6).

EXAMPLE BOX 2.6 Konosuke Matsushita (1892–1989)

Matsushita founded what is now the largest consumer electrical and electronic goods company in the world, and was also a much respected Japanese management guru.

He embodies all the principles outlined here. The three qualities that he required of his production processes were high volume, high quality and low prices. Staff were taken on for lifetime employment and the company accepted any obligation inherent in that for retraining and development as new technologies came on stream and had to be used.

Matsushita was an advocate of different management styles in different parts of the organisation. This should also apply in organisations of different size, technology, sophistication and complexity. Finally, management style must also change as the organisation itself changes, grows and diversifies; it is not possible to find a single successful formula by which it would work. He summarised this as: when to lead from the front; when to lead from the middle; and when to lead from behind.

He adopted the painstaking and deliberate expansion, development and diversification policies of the concept of *nemawashi* and *ringi*, so that risk was eliminated as far as possible from such initiatives and business success was, for a long period of time, assured.

He was a proponent of the business relationship between society and industry, advocating that it should be mutually profitable. Business operations that were not profitable should be closed down.

His leadership style was that of benevolent, enlightened and commercially orientated paternalism. He kept in constant touch with his senior managers and also regularly visited all of his plant and production areas. He commissioned a company song that all employees had to sing at the start of each working day. He preached the virtues of self-sacrifice and self-discipline in the pursuit of company permanence and excellence. By doing this, all would benefit: company, customers, staff and Japan.

Current managerial issues

At present, and for the foreseeable future, the major issues facing organisations and their managers are as follows.

Technological advance

This brings opportunities in terms of increased potential for production, quality and durability; speed and flexibility of response to customer demands; and the capability to organise and develop workforces in ways that were simply not possible beforehand. In addition, organisations have been under both operational and cultural pressures to develop e-business and internet activities wherever they can; there is a widely held perception that not to have a website or internet activity is demeaning to the particular organisation.

Investment

The best organisations are increasingly taking the view that much greater attention is required in this sphere. Investment in technology is viewed as a continued commitment, together with the need to change technology almost overnight if and when radically new approaches are invented. Investment in the production and maintenance of high-quality staff is a prerequisite to long-term and continued customer service and satisfaction and, therefore, to long-term organisational well-being (see Example Box 2.7).

Culture, attitudes and values

The best organisations are increasingly adopting and requiring their staff to adopt distinctive ways of doing things that:

* support the organisation's own distinctive and considered view of how it should conduct its affairs

---

EXAMPLE BOX 2.7 Investment

The apocryphal tale is told of two groups of managers, one British and one Japanese, who each ran a production line employing 20 people.

A machine was invented that could do the work of this line but which only needed one person to operate it.

The British managers went home with heavy hearts because they knew they would have to make 19 people redundant.

The Japanese managers went home with glad hearts because they were going to get 20 new machines, they were going to expand output by a factor of 20, all the staff were going to get retraining and a fresh place of work, and they would not be adding to the wage bill.

- are capable of accommodating the differing, and often conflicting, interests of the employees and other stakeholders
- transcend local cultural pressures, meaning that both products and the ways in which they are produced and offered must be of a fundamental integrity, so that they are acceptable wherever business is conducted
- create a basis of long-term mutual commitment serving the interests of the organisation, its customers, the wider community and its staff.

Business across cultures

This especially applies to organisations operating in global markets, but also to a lesser extent to smaller organisations operating in a variety of localities. It constitutes the capability to 'play away from home': understanding what is important to people in those areas and developing the capability to operate in those conditions and under other legal, social, political and economic constraints.

Strategy

The capability to develop long-term clarity of purpose in all areas of activity, and taking the organisational steps to pursue it effectively. This means:

- reconciling a range of conflicting pressures
- learning global and general lessons from successes and failures
- investment and commitment to the long term in terms of technology, markets, customers and employees
- flexibility and responsiveness in the immediate term in the face of changing customer demands
- generating staff loyalty and commitment through a determination to invest in their long-term future. Above all, this means attention to training and development. It constitutes a mutual and continuous obligation. The view is also increasingly taken that long-term customer satisfaction can only be achieved through a commitment to staff excellence.

Flexible patterns and methods of work

This requirement is based on a combination of the demand to maximise and optimise investment in production and other technology, together with changing patterns of customer requirements. This has led, for example, to longer factory, shop, office, public and private facility opening hours, based in turn on the recognition that customers will use organisation services when it suits them. As organisations have extended their activity times, so they have found that extra customers have come to them, and also that there is a great demand for short hours and other forms of part-time working and job opportunities on the part of employees and potential employees.

Ethics

There is a realisation that consumers are much more likely to use organisations in which they have confidence and that they can trust. This is based on the expectation of a long-term and continuously satisfactory relationship, and on the knowledge that, if this is not forthcoming with one organisation, it can be found with many others. There is also a much greater demand for work and staff relationships based on honesty and integrity rather than bureaucracy, barriers, procedures, and in many cases duplicity. If an organisation promises lifetime job security, then its first duty is to remain in being for that lifetime: and to do this, it must take a view of itself based on integrity rather than expediency.

Concern for the environment

This is a matter of universal, political, economic and social priority at present, and is likely to become more extreme in the future. It has direct implications for business and managers. It is also plainly related to the investment concept detailed above. It affects ultimately all aspects of the business sphere. Globally, there is a balance that must be struck between, on the one hand, developing economic and business activities in order to support a world population that is expanding at a great rate (the population of the city of Cairo goes up by a million every seven months, for example), and that has short-term needs and, on the other hand, preserving the world so that it may support life and a quality of life further into the future.

At an organisation level it is necessary to consider the effect of operations on the environment in relation to all business aspects. Marketing policies and activities, for example, may demand levels of packaging to preserve the product, to demonstrate it to its best possible advantage and to meet public and sectoral expectations. On the other hand, both the packaging itself and the technology used to produce it may themselves consume resources and also create high levels of pollution or waste. Production and operations and the technology related to this also create drains on the world's resources. They create waste and effluent that also have to be managed and disposed of. Human resource policies in certain parts of the business sphere (for example the UK) provide high-quality, prestige cars to go with particular occupations; these cars are very often resource-intensive in production and have high fuel consumption.

The net result is that strategies and policies for managing the environment have to be devised globally, sectorally and organisationally. This requires organisations and their managers to place the environment at or near the top of their list of priorities. It requires them to take a much wider view of the true cost of operations. Related activities may therefore include reorientation of marketing and product presentation and a parallel re-education along these lines as part of the total strategy aimed at changing customer expectations in this way (and reconciling this with positive, persuasive wider marketing activities). It also requires organisations to take a longer-term view of production processes. The approach required is that which relates both to responsibility for, and the adoption of, procedures and practices which truly address the problems of the disposal of waste and effluent and for which the organisation must make provision in strategic, operational and investment terms.

The changing nature of public services

The restructuring of municipal, public and health services requires a mention here, as do the related concepts and realities of service level agreements and arrangements (we have made reference above to the privatisation which often accompanies these). The strategic conception relates to the stated need to revitalise and regenerate these services, to restructure them, to improve the quality and effectiveness of their management, and to make them more efficient. This is all based on the premise that it can be achieved only if the organisations responsible are freed from bureaucratic, state or other authority control. Managers will in turn be free to conduct and provide and order these services in the ways in which their expertise directs. This is of a special importance when the nature of these services is considered; they are the primary, critical, health, social and education activities that are ever more in demand, ever-expanding and the object of ever-higher social and public expectations. The same thinking has been applied to public utilities and strategic state industries. In the UK, gas, electricity, water, transport and telecommunications and some research have all been privatised or transferred from government to shareholder ownership. Others, especially postal services, are set to follow in the near future.

Conclusions

All of the factors and issues raised in this chapter concentrate on the drive for business and organisational quality, effectiveness and excellence. They reflect the fact that these constituted the major concerns of the business sphere in the last decade of the twentieth century. They are further underlined by the relationship that is drawn between the existence of these qualities in organisations and the success, effectiveness, growth and profitability that are considered to arise from the fact that either they operate in these ways or they exhibit these qualities.

The greatest mistake that anyone could make however, is to believe that these qualities constitute an end in themselves; that, once they are achieved, an organisation is guaranteed permanence and eternal profitability. This is not so. At their highest level (if one is preaching perfection) these concepts represent threads and strands that ought to run through the core of any organisation or undertaking; they constitute a standard of ethic, aura, belief and pride in the organisation that is increasingly recognised as the sound foundation on which business success must be built. They also represent the obsession with top quality of products and services, the central position of the customer in the activities of any undertaking and the critical importance of this. Such foundations require constant attention and maintenance, as do the organisations, structures, cultures and practices which are built on them. This is also the basis from which the next developments of the business and management sphere, and of managerial expertise, are to come. It has taken the composition of the expertise and reality of management that is currently recognised thousands of years to develop this far; and this includes the globalisation of experience and practice.

CHAPTER SUMMARY

The processes, qualities and expertise of business and management outlined here, and their interaction and interrelationship both among themselves and with the wider business sphere and environment, are having great and lasting effects on business practices. The transformation is to generate the creative and energetic aspect in the business sphere and to develop the nature and level of expertise in as many ways as possible. Management is thus no longer a straitjacketed or bureaucratic process; above all, it is not the equivalent of administration. Both business and management are ever-developing concepts, phenomena and realities. Their progress and transformation are limited only by the capacities and capabilities of those who work in them in whatever the sector or aspect.

Finally, these constitute global and universal activities and it follows from this that 'good practice is good practice wherever it is found'. It is ever more evident that this is so and that any true expertise, whenever it is found and from wherever it is drawn, provides an increase both in understanding and in the fund of knowledge, skills and capabilities of the expert manager. The professional and expert manager has therefore above all to bring to his chosen profession a willingness, openness and capacity to learn and develop, and preparedness to draw lessons from wherever they may become apparent and to assimilate them in regard to his own expertise. This covers the whole spectrum of business and managerial activity, with opportunities afforded in all sectors across the whole world. This is the scale and scope of the range and potential offered to the truly expert manager. The whole field therefore opens up opportunities that are truly exciting, challenging and adventurous for anybody who wishes to take advantage of them and who has the qualities, capacities and personal attributes to do so.

DISCUSSION QUESTIONS

1. For the organisation of your choice, identify: a) a change that was particularly successful; and b) the main reasons for this. What steps could or should have been taken in order to build on the successes and minimise the failures?
2. Identify and discuss the cultural barriers that have to be overcome by retail and banking organisations when they establish activities in countries other than those of their origin.
3. What steps should organisations take to ensure that their managers and staff do not constitute a barrier to change as a vested interest?
4. Under what circumstances would you recommend that organisations use external consultants as change agents; and under what set of circumstances would you recommend that they do not use external consultants as change agents?

CHAPTER CASE STUDY

THE HOLLYOAKS HOTEL, MARGATE

The Hollyoaks Hotel is situated on the cliff tops at Margate in Kent overlooking the sea. It is about 100 years old and has always enjoyed a reputation for peace and tranquillity. Its core business is the provision of weekend breaks for couples. It has 80 rooms, each with full facilities, a swimming pool and fitness centre, and a large dining room where the food is consistently good. It is highly recommended by the English Tourist Board; both the AA and RAC have accorded it three stars.

For the past 50 years, the hotel has been owned by the Casper family. It was bought by Brian Casper; and he has subsequently handed it on to his son Colin who has run it with his wife Beryl for the past twenty years.

The hotel has always been prosperous and enjoys a consistently high reputation among its visitors. However, Colin and Beryl have noticed a gradual decline in bookings, and especially a lack of young people coming to Margate for weekend breaks. As well as declining, therefore, the clientele is also ageing. This has meant that over the past five years, while the hotel has continued to enjoy a good living, desirable refurbishment work has not taken place. Some of this is now beginning to become essential, and the gentility of the hotel is beginning to fade.

The hotel employs 60 staff: waiters and waitresses, chamber and room cleaning staff, chefs and kitchen staff, and maintenance staff. Unemployment in the area remains high, and were the hotel to go out of business they would have little prospect of work elsewhere.

Ever mindful of this, Colin and Beryl have recently been to meetings with the Chamber of Commerce and the County Council to explore ways in which the business might be developed. The local Chamber of Commerce was not so promising; other than undertaking to consider the possibility of holding conferences and meetings at the hotel, it was able to provide little in the way of business prospects. However, the County Council was much more helpful, and suggested to Colin and Beryl that they look into the possibility of turning the hotel into a major conference centre. The person from the County Council suggested that up to £50 000 might be available for refurbishment by way of grant support, provided that jobs could be guaranteed for an unspecified period.

The Caspers have always taken a pride in the business and are keen to ensure that it continues if at all possible, and they wish to increase the level of turnover so that they can hand it on to the next generation when their children grow up. At the back of their mind, however, is the knowledge that they could sell the site for redevelopment (subject to planning permission) into retirement flats.

One afternoon, during a quiet period, they sit down, determined to work out their options.

QUESTIONS

1. Conduct a force-field analysis for the hotel, identifying drives and restraints, barriers and opportunities, for the hotel in its situation as described.
2. Identify the vested interests that have to be satisfied by the direction that they ultimately choose.
3. On the basis of your answers to 1 and 2 above, outline the advantages, disadvantages, opportunities and consequences of each course of action open to them.

3 Measuring Business and Managerial Performance

'No more than 7.5 prisoners per 1000 are to be allowed to escape.' Performance target, Scottish Prison Service, 1993.

'If we put up prices to first class, business class, and club class passengers, we will take more revenue.' Performance target, British Airways, 1999.

Interviewer: 'So then – you don't make mistakes. You get everything right first time, every time?' Response from UK Managing Director, Panasonic Electronics: 'Of course we make mistakes. I make them – lots of them – every day. The important thing – the reason why we are so successful – is that we acknowledge them and learn from them.' Radio 4, *The Today Programme*, 26 June 1999.

CHAPTER OUTLINE

The context of business and managerial performance

Establishing priorities, aims and objectives

Quantitative methods

Qualitative methods

Summary.

CHAPTER OBJECTIVES

After studying this chapter you should be able to:

understand the range of performance measures that are available to managers in particular circumstances

understand the need to choose, justify and apply specific measures to specific sets of circumstances

understand the advantages and shortcomings of relying on quantitative methods alone

understand the advantages and shortcomings of relying on qualitative and contextual measures.

Introduction

In general terms, all organisations in every sphere of activity are concerned with the same things:

- maximising customer, client and user satisfaction of their products and services over the long term

- maximising the confidence of everyone involved with or affected by the organisation over the long term
- maximising long-term owner/shareholder value: that is, getting the best possible return on investment over the long term (and this applies to public services as well as commercial undertakings)
- securing the long-term future and well-being of the organisation
- working within this context and environment, with especial recognition of functions inside and outside the organisation's control.

This all applies to private and commercial companies, public sector and service organisations, and the not-for-profit sector.

- For example, people buy cars from a garage on the basis that any faults can be put right in the future, and that the garage will maintain and service the car during the period of ownership. People buy groceries from a supermarket on the basis of its reputation for selling good food, and their knowledge that if for some reason an item is not good, it can be taken back and replaced. People would not buy from either the garage or the supermarket if they knew or perceived that neither would last long into the future, or if they had no general feeling of confidence in their ability to sustain themselves.
- In public services, for example, people do not willingly send their children to school where there is no confidence in the quality of education being offered. If it is announced that a school is to close, even if this is not to take place for a year or two, there is a rush to find alternatives with a more secure future. If there is no confidence that a hospital can treat a particular condition effectively, or if there is to be a long wait before it is able to do so, people will again seek alternatives, as witness the burgeoning UK private health care sector.
- In the not-for-profit sector, people give to the causes represented by individual charities because they want their money to go to those whom they represent, or in whose interest they operate. They find other outlets for their giving if they have no confidence that particular charities have a future, or that their money is being spent directly on the cause or client group. This is reflected in the ways in which the larger charities – Oxfam, NCH, NSPCC, RSPCA – have spent heavily resources on strengthening their institutions and identity (not always to the satisfaction of long-term regular supporters). Nevertheless, they are securing their long-term existence in order to be able to operate more effectively in the future.

Prerequisites for successful and effective performance

All of this is only achievable if some basic elements are present.

- **Clarity of purpose and direction:** knowing where you are going and how to get there; understanding the full implications and commitment necessary to achieve this.
- **Adequate levels of resources:** investment; information; technology; staff capability; expertise; willingness and commitment.
- **Knowledge and understanding:** of the markets in which activities and operations

are to take place and what customers and clients want and expect from them; of what the organisation's total capacity is; what it can and cannot achieve; and any operational implications arising; of the total environment in which activities are to take place.

This gives the broad context in which performance is measured. It cannot be measured effectively if this is not fully understood.

Components of successful performance

Organisational and managerial performance is measured in the following areas.

- **Market standing:** overall organisational reputation; reputation of products and services; reputation of staff and expertise; size of market served; location of market served; specific needs, wants and demands.
- **Market position:** actual market position in relation to desired position; the costs and benefits of maintaining this; opportunity costs; returns on resources; returns on investment.
- **Innovation:** capacity for innovation; desired and actual levels of innovation; time taken for new products and ideas to reach the market; attitudes to innovation; percentages of new products and ideas that become commercial successes.
- **Creativity:** expertise of staff; versatility and ability to diversify; capability for turning ideas into commercial successes; new product/service strike rates; attitudes to creativity; other related qualities, above all flexibility and responsiveness.
- **Resource utilisation:** efficiency and effectiveness; balance of resources used in primary and support functions; wastage rates; resource utilisation and added value.
- **Managerial performance:** total managerial performance; performance by function, department, division, group; performance at different levels of management: director, general manager, senior, middle, junior, supervisory, first line (see Example Box 3.1).
- **Management development:** areas of strength and weakness; progress and improvement; desired expertise and capability; actual expertise and capability; development of specific skills and knowledge; desired and actual attitudes and behaviour; priority of training and development.
- **Staff performance:** areas of strength and weakness; progress and improvement; attitudes and willingness to work; degrees of commitment; desired expertise and capability; actual expertise and capability; development of specific skills and knowledge; desired and actual attitudes and behaviour; attention to work patterns; commitment; extent and priority of training and development; targeting of training and development; attitudes to staff suggestions; specific positive and negative features.
- **Workforce structure:** core and peripheral; flexibility in attitudes and behaviour; multi-skilling; work patterns; general employability; continued future employability; relations between organisation and workforce; relations between managers and staff; length and strength of hierarchies.
- **Wage and pay levels:** relationships between pay and output; relationships between

---

EXAMPLE BOX 3.1 Managerial Performance: The Paddington Rail Disaster

On 5 October 1999, two trains collided outside Paddington railway station in West London. Thirty people were killed.

It quickly became apparent that the disaster was caused by a combination of inadequate maintenance of the track and signalling systems, and signals that did not work properly. The company responsible, Railtrack plc, undertook to put everything right.

However, continued media interest in the state of the railways ensured that the actions of Railtrack were kept constantly in the spotlight. Accordingly, on 21 October 1999, the Commercial Director of Railtrack, Richard Middleton, said to the media: 'It is time for the hysteria around rail safety to be calmed down. Rail is a safe mode of transport.'

This provoked outrage among the families of the 30 victims. Furthermore, on 6 November 2000, there was another serious accident, when a train travelling at high speed was derailed at Hatfield, to the north of London. It quickly became apparent that the cause of this crash was a faulty stretch of track, and that in spite of the fact that the company had known for months that it needed replacing, no action had been taken.

---

pay, profits and performance; local factors and conditions; industrial factors and conditions; relationships between pay and expertise; pay as incentive; economic rent; known, believed and perceived areas of over and underpaying.

- **Organisational culture:** the extent to which this is positive/negative; identifying and removing negative factors; accentuating the positive; motivation and morale; staff policies; industrial relations; staff management; aspects of organisation culture that are designed, emergent, strong, weak, suitable, unsuitable, acceptable, unacceptable.
- **Key relationships:** with backers; with staff; with suppliers; with distributors; with customers; with community (see Example Box 3.2).
- **Public standing:** the respect and esteem in which the organisation is held in its markets, the community, among its staff, customers and suppliers; confidence and expectations; general public factor coverage.
- **Profitability:** levels of profits accrued; timescales; means of measuring and assessing products; scope for enhancement and improvement.
- **Ethical factors:** the absolute standards that the organisation sets for itself; what it will and will not do; its attitudes to its staff, customers, clients, suppliers and communities; the nature of the markets served; standards and quality of the treatment of staff; management style; attitudes and approaches to customer complaints; attitudes and approaches to suppliers; quality of public relations; quality of community relations.
- **Other factors:** general efficiency and effectiveness; product and service quality and value; areas for improvement; areas where complaints arise; opportunities and threats; crises and emergencies (see Example Box 3.3).

EXAMPLE BOX 3.2 Stakeholders

A stakeholder is anyone who has a particular interest in any aspect of the organisation. Stakeholders include:

- shareholders, backers, financiers and financial institutions and their representatives
- stock markets, stockbrokers and financial advisers
- organisation directors and shareholders' representatives
- public service governors and those charged with responsibility for gaining finance and backing for public ventures and enterprises
- organisation functional directors, managers, staff and their representatives
- suppliers and distributors
- customers, clients and end-users
- industrial and commercial markets
- the communities in which activities take place
- the media, business, financial and management journalists and media analysts
- pressure groups, lobbies and vested interests
- dominant stakeholders.

Organisations inevitably have dominant stakeholders: those whose interests must be served above all else or, more insidiously, those whose interests are served as a priority, whether or not this is the correct course of action for the particular organisation. The financial interest is invariably to be found as a dominant stakeholder; the best organisations also place their staff, suppliers and customers at this level. It is also true that any group that has cause to raise legitimate concerns about the organisation and its activities should be treated as a dominant stakeholder until its problems have been resolved.

Serious problems can arise when the interests of the dominant stakeholders are served in spite of conflicting or divergent concerns from less influential sources.

Many of these areas overlap. In some cases the same phrases are used under different headings. Without doubt, different words and phrases could be used to convey the same meanings. The mix and balance varies between organisations. However, every element is present in all situations to a greater or lesser extent. Initial lessons can therefore be drawn.

1. There is no single effective measure of performance in any situation or organisation. Even if a supervisor is working to a single daily production target, he/she must have the right staff, adequately trained and motivated, the right volume and quality of components; and somewhere to put the finished items. And given the normal nature of work – all work – all this has to be available on a steady and continuous basis.

2. Many of the elements indicated are qualitative not quantitative. The main qualities necessary to evaluate such factors properly are therefore judgement and

---

EXAMPLE BOX 3.3 Crises and Emergencies

The following are examples of the management of crises and emergencies.

- In 1990, the Hoover Company offered vouchers that could be exchanged for airline tickets as part of its Christmas promotion. These vouchers were issued with every sale of a Hoover product during the period September–December 1990. For the price of an electric kettle, it was possible under the terms of the promotion to obtain an air ticket for the United States. When the scale of this marketing crisis became apparent, the company first tried to deny that it was a serious promotion, and then simply ignored requests from customers with vouchers for their airline tickets. It took the company six months to admit its mistake; indeed, it only did so after extensive adverse media and television coverage of the promotion. Not until 1997 did all those customers who were entitled to free air tickets get them.
- Pan-Am, the American airline, undertook a security operation after it became worried that its staff were stealing miniature bottles of whisky from its aircraft. The company wired up an alarm clock inside the drinks cabinet of one of the airliners. The clock was so arranged that it would stop whenever the door was opened. This, they said, would reveal the exact time of the theft. However, the company management omitted to tell the cabin crew. As the result, on a flight between New York and Dubai, one of the stewardesses heard the clock ticking and assumed that there was a bomb on board. She alerted the pilot, and the plane made a forced landing at Berlin. In the inquiry afterwards, it became clear that the thefts had amounted to little more than petty pilfering. The emergency landing cost the company £16 500.

---

analysis. Success and failure are value judgements placed on events and activities based on high levels of knowledge and expertise. Seldom, if ever, is success or failure self-evident except in the immediate or very short term.

3. It follows, in turn, that the main attributes of those who measure business and managerial performance are knowledge, expertise and understanding: of results; of the environment; of people; of customers and the market; of the product/services offered; of the organisation's general position.

Information and planning

None of this is possible without full, or at least adequate, information covering each of these areas, and this must be constantly gathered and evaluated. Markets, technology, expertise are all constantly changing and organisations that do not respond have at the very least to recognise the effects that such a lack of response will, or may, have.

Full information enables organisations and their managers to reduce uncertainty, analyse levels of risk, maximise chances of success, minimise chances of failure and assess the prospects and likely consequences and outcomes of particular courses of activity. It enables projections to be made for the organisation as a whole and for each

---

EXAMPLE BOX 3.4 Cock-ups Can Have a Silver Lining

Many organisations, and especially their top managers, find themselves unwilling to admit where, when or why mistakes are made. Invariably, they rather look for scapegoats, or else are inclined (if allowed to do so) to put failure down to 'factors outside their control' or 'volatile market conditions'.

Yet the theory of managerial cock-ups is the orphan of management studies. Innumerable books have been written on strategic triumphs and tragedies, but nearly all assume that the heroes or villains knew what they were doing. By contrast, the 'cock-up' theory holds that management moves, not from one considered coordinated ploy to the next, but by isolated lurches. These are governed, not by deep analysis and optimisation of resources, but by impulse and unguarded optimism.

The 'cock-up' theory holds that problems always prove much greater than anyone expects. Financially, the potential killer is cost. If actual earnings fail to cover the true cost of capital and other resources used in particular ventures, the value of the company becomes eroded. Cock-ups might well be fewer therefore, if top managements were penalised when acquisitions, changes of direction and other supposed brainwaves generated negative returns. Bonuses and long-term remuneration for directors and senior managers ought to be reduced in direct relationship to these negative returns. That is, after all, how many chief executives use remuneration systems to pressurise subordinates. What is sauce for the geese should surely apply to the ganders. But the 'cock-up' theory holds that this is where the whole bungling process begins: with the lack of checks and balances on over-mighty corporate rulers.

Cock-ups teach invaluable lessons. Management that has had its nose rubbed in the realities of the market and economic conditions tend to ensure that false assumptions are replaced by true facts. Necessary changes in people and policies are clearly indicated. Instead of indulging in corporate hand-wringing, there is a clear opportunity to assess why things went wrong, and from this, to take steps to ensure that specific, useful and practical measures of performance are instigated at the outset of any venture or initiative.

Source: Robert Heller, *Management Today*, October 1998.

---

of its activities. Summary positions are often established under the headings of **strengths, weaknesses, opportunities, threats**; these are most effective when related to the organisation as a whole, to its markets, to its backers and stakeholders, and to its competitors.

Effective planning is also based on full information. The value of planning is at its greatest when it allows organisations:

- to see the future as it unfolds, recognising possible, likely and (more or less) certain developments
- to assess the continued performance of all activities and operations
- to assess the ways in which other people and organisations, especially competitors, are operating.

Effective planning is a process, the purpose of which is to arrive at and retain continued clarity of direction. It involves the analysis of the information; thinking it through, testing ideas; examining what is possible and what is not.

More specific schedules, practices, operations, activities, aims and objectives all then come from this body of knowledge and the understanding which arises from analysing it. Implementation and execution are then handed on to different people, functions, divisions and departments within the organisation.

It should be apparent from this that there is a world of difference between planning and plans. Dwight D. Eisenhower, the United States General and President, once said 'Planning is everything, the plan is nothing.' At their best, corporate and organisational plans are statements of what is now proposed as the result of information available; they are subject to change, modification and, when necessary, abandonment as and when circumstances change.

At their worst, they are detailed statements covering the way that the world is certain to be extending into the far distant future. No such position is sustainable now; indeed, it probably never was in the past. This does not prevent large corporations – both public and private – and the policy units of public services drawing these up. At best, they are an irrelevance. More usually, they constitute a waste of organisational resources that would be better used elsewhere. At worst, they are indeed slavishly followed in the teeth of a changing world and competitive environment with immense adverse consequences for the organisation.

Responsibilities

Organisational responsibilities

Specific organisational responsibilities exist in the following areas.

- Anticipating the future in terms of the changing environment; anticipating changes in customer demands and perceptions; recognising changes in the nature of competition; recognising changes in production and service technology; recognising and anticipating changes in the nature of people attracted to work for the organisation and the sector; recognising and anticipating changes in the customer base.
- Investment as a continued commitment: in the areas of product development; quality improvement; management and staff training and development; production and service technology; the well-being of the customer.
- Organisation development: in terms of its skills, knowledge, capabilities, attitudes and expertise; in terms of customer awareness and satisfaction; in terms of processes and procedures; in terms of supplier and distributor relations; in terms of its culture and structures.
- Training and development: of both management and staff in the skills, qualities, attributes and expertise necessary to secure the future; and in the key attitudes of flexibility, dynamism, responsiveness, willingness and commitment.
- Recognition of the fact that all organisations currently operate in a changing and turbulent environment; that historic and current success, efficiency, effectiveness and profitability are no guarantee that success will extend into the future. From this comes an obligation to ensure that all staff are capable of

existing in this environment, and that they are equipped with the resources and capability to do so.

- Openness: people respond to uncertainty and turbulence much better if they understand its extent and why they must constantly update and develop. Organisations therefore have a clear duty to inform, consult and provide detail on all aspects of performance in general; and in more detail, concerning things which directly affect specific members and groups of staff.
- Ethics: long-term existence, the ability to secure the employment of staff, and establishing a regular and profitable customer base are enhanced by taking, accepting, and understanding a view of the world as it really is. There is therefore a moral, as well as commercial, commitment.

Managerial responsibilities

Specific managerial responsibilities exist in the following areas.

- To develop (and be developed in) capabilities and expertise required by the organisation; those required by the nature of professional management as it develops; and those which involvement in the particular business, industry or service requires.
- To take a personal commitment to organisational success as well as that of the department, division or function for which the individual is responsible. High levels of personal commitment are required of all professions and professionals in all spheres of activity and expertise, and this is also true of management and managers.
- To develop the full range of managerial skills and qualities required by the profession of management. This currently means being able to: solve problems; manage people; set standards of performance; understand where the manager's domain fits into the wider scheme of things and total organisational performance; use

---

EXAMPLE BOX 3.5 Internet Companies and Performance Measurement

Reflecting on the events of the past five years, and especially the capital volumes invested in internet companies, it becomes clear that very few ever considered in any detail the likely nature and level of returns on capital employed. Neither did most internet companies pay any attention to measures of managerial performance in relation to staff motivation and morale, customer service and satisfaction, or frequency, availability and accessibility to the people who worked at the company. As examples, Boo.com had no customer helpline until a fortnight before it was liquidated; LastMinute.com had nobody responsible for staffing matters for the first two years of trading.

Clearly, much of the fault lies with the companies. However, all of this also bypassed those backing the companies. In many cases, backers simply failed to ask where the returns would actually be coming from; they acted simply on an assumption that customer volumes would exist once the website was up and running.

resources efficiently and effectively; set and assess budgets; recognise the constraints under which operations have to be carried out; and generate a positive, open and harmonious culture and set of attitudes.

At the heart of all organisational and managerial responsibility is the need to produce goods and services in the required volume and quality, at the right price, in the right place (see Example Box 3.5). This can only be achieved through having top quality, expert and highly motivated staff. This is the critical factor by which the long-term future of the organisation is secured, and all effective measures of organisation and managerial performance have this at their core.

Stakeholder considerations

Both organisations and their managers have to recognise that their performance is going to be measured and assessed by a variety of different people and in a great range of different ways. Everyone who comes into contact with an organisation assesses it in one way or another. The assessors may be summarised as:

- **The staff:** all those who work for and in the organisation, and are therefore dependent upon it for their income and spending power; this also applies to subcontractors and other retainers and potential staff.
- **The customers:** for continued satisfaction and service.
- **The communities:** in which staff and customers live and work, and in which the organisation operates.
- **Social customers:** for example, charities, schools and hospitals which may approach the organisation for sponsorship and support.
- **Backers:** shareholders, contributors, bankers, loan makers, venture capitalists, sponsors, city institutions, stock markets, and public funds.
- **Suppliers of components and raw materials:** who have a vested interest in the success of the organisation in terms of their own continuity of activity and profitability.
- **The community sectors and markets:** in which the organisation offers its products and services for sale and consumption.
- **Distributors:** relying on their own position between the organisation in question and the end users of the products or services for their continued existence.
- **Trade unions, market and employers' federations and associations:** which are active in the particular field.
- **Competitors and offerers of alternative products and services:** as part of their own quest for knowledge and expertise in the given field.
- **Lobbyists and vested interest groups:** related to the location of activities, the nature of activities and the ways in which those activities are carried out.
- **Media:** especially business and financial journalists. Organisations and their managers also receive wider local and media coverage as the result of particular initiatives and ventures undertaken, and as the result of crises and disasters (see Example Box 3.3 earlier).

Performance is measured by each of these groups according to their own particular interest. For example, brilliant commercial performance may be rated very highly by consumers but not by shareholders if this brilliant performance does not result in rises in the share prices.

It is measured continuously by each of the groups indicated. It is punctuated by formal and semi-formal events: annual reports, interim reports, staff, production and service performance appraisal, production and sales figures, pay rises and pay rounds, activity levels, and budget efficiency and effectiveness.

Aims and objectives

All performance has to be measured against something and this is the reason for setting aims and objectives. Aims and objectives occur at different levels, and again, are set or inferred by each of the above groups to satisfy their particular points of view.

- **Corporate:** reflecting the overall scope of the organisation; how it is to be run in structural and financial terms; how resources are to be allocated.
- **Competitive/business level:** how the organisation is to compete in its different markets; which products and services should be developed and offered; the extent to which these meet customer needs; monitoring of product performance.
- **Operational:** how different functions of the organisation contribute to total organisational purpose and activities.
- **Behavioural:** related to the human interactions between different parts of the organisation; and between the organisation, its customers and the wider community.
- **Confidence:** the generation of confidence and reputation among all those with whom it comes into contact.
- **Ethical:** meeting specific standards that may be enshrined in policy; the ability to work in certain activities, in certain locations; the attitude taken towards staff, customers and others with whom the organisation comes into contact.

Aims and objectives should be a combination of the precise:

- **specific:** dealing with easily identifiable and quantifiable aspects of performance
- **measurable:** devised in ways so that success and failure can be identified
- **achievable:** striking a balance between maximising/optimising resources and output without setting standards so high that targets are unattainable and therefore unvalued
- **recognisable:** understood by all concerned
- **time constrained:** so that a continuous record of progress and achievement may be kept and problem areas identified.

and the imprecise, continuous and proactive:

- reconciling these differing and often conflicting pressures
- attending to all aspects of organisational performance
- providing distinctive measures of success and failure
- enhancing the total performance of the organisation
- where necessary, reconciling the different and conflicting demands of particular stakeholders and interested parties

- being prepared to adjust or alter direction and priority if the situation demands
- establishing procedures for monitoring, reviewing and evaluating all aspects of performance, and acting on the results.

No single set of generic objectives exists. All aims and objectives must be drawn up against the organisation's specific context and background if they are to have any meaning. Whatever they refer to, they must reflect the following questions.

- What contribution does this activity/set of activities make to total organisational performance? Where does this fit into the broader objectives of the department, division or function concerned? Where does this fit into the wider purpose of the organisation?
- What resources, equipment, information, technology and expertise are needed to carry it out successfully?
- What specific restraints are there? For example: can it be done straight away; are there other things that must first be done? How long does it/will it/must it take?

Aims and objectives therefore attend to both the broad and the precise.

This is the broad context in which measuring all aspects of organisational and managerial performance takes place. It is not possible to do this effectively or successfully in isolation, and the fact that some organisations nevertheless attempt this does not make it right. Unless this basis is understood, quantitative and qualitative performance measures alike have no meaning to those who are allocated more specific performance targets. Lack of any context is also one of the main reasons why staff, product and service performance appraisal and measurement schemes fall into disrepute. Whatever is done must be understood, acceptable and valuable to those involved. Acceptability springs from understanding and this is based, in turn, on the effective communication of the right and required information to those involved.

Qualitative measures of performance

Business and managerial performance measurement is largely qualitative (see Example Box 3.6). This is because organisations are created and staffed by people, and because their customers, clients and users are people also. Moreover, the most overtly mathematical and precise measures of performance have to be seen in the context in which they are established and then judged and evaluated by those responsible.

Priorities

Ideally, priorities are established to ensure concentration of organisational resources to best commercial or service advantage in the pursuit of long-term customer, client and user satisfaction. In practice, it is rarely possible to achieve everything desired or required. Two basic approaches are possible (see Figure 3.1).

There is nothing intrinsically right or wrong with either approach indicated in Figure 3.1. The main issue at the outset is to know which approach is being taken and the opportunities and consequences of that choice.

EXAMPLE BOX 3.6 Performance Measurement

To illustrate the point, a 35 per cent increase in sales is an overtly easy and straight-forward measure of performance. There is a precise target to aim for, and whether or not it is achieved is easily quantifiable. However, the following elements have still to be addressed:

- the time period over which the increase is to take place
- whether the 35 per cent increase is required across the board, or whether an overall increase of 35 per cent will do
- whether the 35 per cent would be covered by a one-off purchase or windfall
- whether, if the 35 per cent increase is fulfilled the following week, the target will be revised for the future
- whether this is a reflection of the capacity and capability of the rest of the organisation
- whether this is within the workforce's capability, whether overtime will have to be worked, or whether new staff will have to be taken on
- any questions of location: questions of specific market/localised constraints; the extent to which it is related to relative levels of prosperity in the market
- the wider state of the market; the activities of competitors; whether the market is capable of sustaining this (or any other level of increase)
- whether the 35 per cent increase represents an increase in the total market, or whether it means taking market share from competitors.
- Finally, where does the figure of 35 per cent come from; who decided it; and on what grounds?

Once this form of judgement and evaluation has been made, the behaviour of customers, consumers and clients has to be considered. For example, the buyer may come into the establishment, not receive instant service, turn round and storm out. Or a sales person may be so busy giving excellent satisfaction to one customer that other customers are delayed, leading to dissatisfaction on their part. Customers may be dealt with by a good salesperson who has nothing to offer them; or by a bad salesperson, who nevertheless persuades the customer to buy, leading to an instant sale but subsequent dissatisfaction.

The process cannot therefore possibly be completely objective or rational. Qualifying performance effectiveness and success therefore relies on recognising:

- the human signs of buyer behaviour and attitudes
- the human signs of organisational behaviour and attitudes
- the convergence and divergence of priorities and objectives
- the importance and influence of stakeholders and participants.

The best approach is to identify the most likely outcome in the most sets of circumstances, to concentrate primarily on this, and to deal with exceptions as and when they arise.

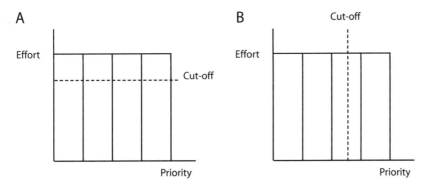

A Everything is attempted, but unsatisfactorily
B Those things which cannot be completed satisfactorily are not attempted

Establishing priorities

FIGURE 3.1

Objectives

The objectives are:

- **organisational:** reflecting the overall purpose and direction
- **departmental/divisional/functional:** reflecting the contribution that each is expected to make to the whole
- **managerial:** reflecting the contribution that different managers are expected/ anticipated to make to the overall direction
- **professional/occupational:** reflecting the need for professional and occupational satisfaction in different staff and work categories
- **personal:** reflecting more general needs, especially those of job security, enhanced reward and prosperity, and advancement
- **present priorities:** from whatever source they are driven
- **future priorities:** those that begin to become apparent as the result of knowing and understanding the organisation's preferred future direction.

Measuring and appraising organisational and managerial performance

The purpose of appraisal is to measure the performance of individuals, groups, operations, activities, production and output, projects and services at the place of work. Performance appraisal conducted in this way reflects the standard and quality of activity in each functional and occupational division and category. For performance appraisal to be effective and successful, the following elements must be present.

- Preset, pre-agreed aims and objectives, clearly understood by all concerned. These should be prioritised with deadlines for achievement. Performance targets should be realistic and achievable, balancing the need for effective and improved performance against effective resource utilisation. If targets are unrealistic they will be ignored; if they are too easy they set a wider agenda for the lowering of performance standards.

EXAMPLE BOX 3.7 Subjective and Prejudicial Convergence and Divergence of Objectives

It is essential to recognise the existence of these differing objectives. The best and most successful and effective organisations harmonise personal, professional and occupational objectives with those of the organisation as a whole. Where this is not possible, a certain amount of dysfunction/malfunction occurs.

For example, a manager charged with responsibility for introducing a new education policy knows that this will take several years to evaluate for success. The manager's political masters want tangible results within three months. The next promotion in the manager's career is dependent upon the satisfaction of the political masters with their performance. The manager has therefore to reconcile the following:

- delivering the initiative professionally
- advancing his/her own career
- doing the work to the satisfaction of the political masters.

It is clear that doing the job properly requires persuading the political masters that a three-month measure is neither feasible nor legitimate in the circumstances. It is also clear that, on the face of it, there exists a real discrepancy between doing the job properly and receiving personal reward, recognition and advancement.

The greatest success is achieved where the potential problems have been recognised and steps have been taken to harmonise and integrate these different forms of objectives.

Failure is likely where no/little recognition exists of the problem. Where it is not possible to integrate organisational and personal/professional objectives, recognition of the effects on performance (especially long-term pe rformance) is essential. Problem areas for the future can then at least be more clearly identified.

Moreover, levels of motivation and morale are normally much higher where objectives in each category are harmonised. Where objectives do diverge and conflict, people always pursue their personal and professional objectives rather than those of the organisation.

- Appraisal is a process which consists of a series of regularised formal reviews at which targets and objectives are discussed and assessed for success and failure. It entails a continuous relationship between appraiser and appraisee that builds both confidence and understanding, and also enables particular issues and problems to be identified early.
- Appraisal must be flexible and dynamic, and part of the wider process of ensuring that the organisation's purpose is being adhered to.
- Appraisal is a participative process at its best between appraiser and appraisee, which again helps to ensure a mutual confidence and commitment.
- Appraisal must be believed in and valued by all concerned; it must be adequately resourced and prioritised.

- Appraisal must provide a basis for action, so that whatever is agreed during the process or at a formal review, is acted upon by both appraiser and appraisee.
- Formal reviews should take place at least every 3 to 6 months. If they are more frequent than this, they tend to impose on the continuing process and relationship

---

EXAMPLE BOX 3.8 Performance Appraisal and Measurement Criticised

Human resource management performance appraisal schemes may seek to provide merit pay awards, identify potential, identify training and development needs, identify job–person match and mismatch, identify organisation development needs, identify poor and substandard performance, check achievement against agreed objectives and agree individual objectives for the future.

The measurement of production and service activities is designed to identify that everything remains on course and, where there are deviations, to identify these early, understand them, and either accommodate them and work within them, or else change direction to ensure that what is required, can still be delivered.

All performance measurement approaches fall into disrepute where it appears that:

- they are neither believed in nor valued
- they do not contribute to the wider success of the organisation
- they are bureaucratic or mechanistic
- it is the scheme and its paperwork that are important, and not the process
- the reviews are too infrequent or missed altogether
- what is promised in them (e.g. pay awards, training, promotion, development) is not delivered in practice.

Measurement approaches may also suffer from performance criteria being identified in general terms only. This leads to inconsistency in application; this leads in turn to unevenness and unfairness in the measurement of staff performance, and a lack of clarity and precision in the measurement of organisational performance.

The best approach to performance measurement is to be completely open. Monitoring, review and evaluation activities should be conducted on the basis of mutual understanding, trust and honesty. If staff are required to declare shortcomings in their own or departmental performance, they must be able to do so from the point of view of remedying matters, rather than punishment.

It therefore follows that there is a necessary body of skills and knowledge required of senior managers in the establishment of effective performance measurement. This has to be underpinned by the presence of positive attitudes and a determination to measure performance accurately, and make improvements where required, rather than finding fault. Communication, articulation, target and objective setting, consultation, counselling, support, trust, dependency and assertiveness are all clearly necessary. If this is the basis on which performance is to be measured, there is plenty of scope for picking up genuine poor performance, whatever its cause or source.

that should also be present. If they are less frequent, it becomes very difficult to conduct an adequate or genuine review of what has been done over the past period (see Example Box 3.8).

An ethical approach to performance measurement

There is a direct correlation between the taking of a strong moral/ethical stance and long-term profitability. Examples of this can be drawn from all over the world. The Japanese car and electrical-goods companies set high standards of probity and integrity, and through their published documentation place the onus on their managers to deliver. The Body Shop has made a strong and highly profitable feature of its concern for the environment and the standards that it has set in its dealings with the Third World. McDonald's have set absolute standards of quality, cleanliness, value and service across every operation, everywhere in the world (though the amount of refuse generated by the company's activities continues to give cause for concern).

These approaches can be broken down into the following components:

- disclosure of information in terms of volume, quality and honesty
- employment issues, pay, benefits and conditions; industrial democracy; equality of opportunity; information, participation and consultation
- the nature of community involvement and relations with the environment
- the nature of political involvement and donations to political parties, candidates, vested interests and pressure groups; donations and support for charities and 'worthy causes'
- the nature of products and services – with particular emphasis on contentious areas such as tobacco, alcohol, drugs, pharmaceuticals and military equipment
- marketing policies and attitudes to customers, consumers, client groups; the nature and quality of advertising
- a general respect for people and life
- the moral components of organisational strategy and purposes; categories of concern which may be divided into the **broad** – the world, the nation, the local community; and the **narrow** – industry, the organisation, the sector
- the range of concerns that **ought** to be considered by organisations
- public interest, public lobbies and pressure groups; specific interests including socio-political groups, lobbies and fringe interests
- ordinary common decency.

This is a highly qualitative and subjective checklist. However, organisations that enjoy high levels of esteem and respect always do so because their general conduct stands up to social and ethical scrutiny as well as commercial viability. It is very difficult to find examples where commercial success has been achieved without consideration of social factors or public acceptance except in the very short term. In the longer term, organisations have to operate in, and be acceptable to, their staff, customers and communities. For this to occur, a positive, mutual and continuing respect is necessary. This is always damaged, and often destroyed, when the general integrity of particular organisations is called into question. Organisations have therefore to have full knowledge and understanding of what is acceptable, both globally and locally. This extends to all spheres of business operation. Marketing initiatives strike a balance between being positive and exciting, while at the same time stopping well short of making claims for the product that are simply not true or presenting something in ways unacceptable to sectors of the communities. Successful staff management is based on mutual respect and trust, as well as effective work organisation. General management is always more successful where those involved understand why they are doing things in particular ways and can trust the organisation to lead them successfully and effectively in the proposed directions, and then deliver the desired results. The production of shoddy or inadequate goods is only feasible until another organisation comes along with improved, adequate and satisfactory products with which to replace them.

Administration

Administration exists to support primary functions. Administrative functions create and operate procedures that are used to:

- control expenditure
- provide information
- attend to the human side of enterprise
- monitor progress
- resolve problems.

Measuring the performance of support functions and administration refers first and foremost to the contribution that they make to primary activities. To preach perfection, no other position is sustainable. Any system or procedure that hinders or dilutes primary performance is to be abolished and replaced, or reformed.

The best procedures and systems are simple and clear to understand by everyone concerned. They attend to:

- **finance:** providing clear and adequate information as to how organisational resources are being used so that judgements may be made as to their effectiveness
- **human resource management procedures and functions:** in the areas of discipline and grievance handling, health and safety at work, consultation and participation, negotiation (where collective bargaining still exists), and procedures with a quick and effective resolution of problems and disputes
- **progress chasing and quantity assurance:** so that blockages, shortcomings and shortfalls can be identified early and addressed successfully; so that customer orders can be prioritised and reconciled
- **quality assurance:** picking up customer complaints early and resolving them quickly.

The main problems with administrative systems and procedures arise when they become too complex to be handled quickly and effectively. This leads to teams of staff being taken on in support functions that have then to be sustained by the primary activities. This is true for both public services and private sector activities. Any extensive recruitment and development of support functions is to be seen in this context. Again, no other position is sustainable.

Problems also arise when head offices of giant and complex corporations, public services, and multinational companies ask for performance targets, especially revenue targets, because of the cost of their own sustenance and maintenance.

More specifically, they arise in public services when cuts in primary services are made to accommodate requested expenditure on support functions.

Qualitative measurement of performance is dependent upon the expertise, knowledge and understanding of those who measure it. It depends for success on knowing and understanding each of the elements indicated above. Each element – objectives, motivation, appraisal, payment, and ethics or absolute standards – has to be reconciled with the others; and then in turn, reconciled with:

- the level of service that customers, clients and users desire
- the organisational form, structure, skills, knowledge and attitudes required to achieve this
- the collective and individual values, attitudes and behaviour required
- a detailed understanding and acceptance of the required nature of performance
- commitment to remedy failure, build on success and continuously improve.

Attention to these aspects is the key to sustained high levels of performance. Except in the very short term, high levels of high-quality output are not possible where morale is low, where staff are unvalued and under-rewarded, where standards of probity and honesty do not exist and where performance in all areas is not measured and appraised as effectively as possible.

How performance is measured

The most important fact is continuity in the assessment, measurement and appraisal of performance, drawing conclusions on a regular basis so that a full watching brief is maintained, and so that early warning is given of things that may be going wrong.

Ideally, this is punctuated with regular team, peer and organisational meetings arranged for the specific purpose of reporting on performance. Given that no activity takes place in total isolation, performance reporting must consider the effectiveness of working relationships and coordination of activities, as well as the legitimate interests of those both within the organisation, and outside it.

Organisations and their managers should also regularly review the actual measures and indicators and the ways in which they are used, to ensure that these continue to be valid, reliable and capable of demonstrating what they are supposed to demonstrate. This extends to received wisdom, generalisations and self-perceptions, from inside and outside the organisation, as well as more specific measures. As examples, the following questions may be asked.

- 'Why do we have performance related pay?' – 'Because it motivates the staff and targets performance.'
- 'Why do my staff complain that I am inaccessible? I am always consulting them.'

These questions, and others raised in exactly the same way, need full and careful analysis and consideration. Otherwise, the points raised simply become institutionalised.

One or two such features are likely not to be too damaging (though they should always nevertheless be remedied). Each feeds off others however, and too many such questions nearly always reflect complacency within managerial ranks. For these (and all other such questions), quantitative and qualitative approaches are required to gather real information, and they then have to be considered from the required managerial standpoint. In turn, it is consequently essential to identify the right points of inquiry for all managers and groups of managers as a check on their own performance, and on their contribution to that of the organisation as a whole.

Points of inquiry

These are treated from two different angles:

- functional issues that apply to each function
- considerations of confidence and expectations.

Functional issues

Human resource management

- The numbers of strikes, disputes and grievances; movements in the numbers of disciplinaries and dismissals; the extent and movements in the operation of disciplinary grievance and disputes procedures.
- Movements in the numbers of accidents and injuries; movements in the numbers of self-certificated absenteeism.
- Levels of disputes and grievances among those who enjoy perceived high levels of job satisfaction and job security.
- Movements in staff turnover; movements (especially decreases) in organisational, departmental, divisional and functional staff stability.
- Increases in administration and support functions at the expense of front line operations; increases in the administration and reporting workload placed on front line operations.
- Pay differentials between the top and bottom of the organisation.
- Pay increases are awarded to those at the top of the organisation at the expense of those at the bottom.
- Those at the top of the organisation receive benefits (e.g. cars, computers, mobile phones) based on status rather than operational necessity.
- Pay awards, promotion and other enhancements are given for administrative and procedural efficiency rather than direct performance effectiveness.
- Performance related pay is achieved by those in head office and other support functions, and not by those at the front line.
- Those at the top of the organisation are treated more favourably than those at the bottom in matters of discipline, grievance handling, disputes.
- Those in support functions are treated more favourably generally than those at the front line.
- Discipline, grievance and dispute problems are institutionalised and not resolved; and these procedures take a long time to work through.
- Pay awards are paid in arrears rather than on time.

Production

- Production targets, especially where production output bears no relationship to targets set; this is as much a cause for concern when targets are far exceeded as when they are not met.
- Production, volume and quality, especially where these fall short of projections.
- Increases in customer complaints about one aspect of product performance, for example, failure of one component.
- Increases in customer complaints about total product performance.
- Increases in customer complaints about packaging, delivery, appearance, durability and after-sales service.
- Increases in customer recalls because the organisation has found the product to be faulty.
- Increases in supply problems, access to components and raw materials.
- Increases in internal disputes between those responsible for gaining raw materials, those responsible for direct production, and those responsible for sales and distribution.
- Increases in unit costs and variable costs.
- Inability of fixed costs to sustain commercial operations and activities.
- Production and information technology is not or is no longer suitable for purposes for which it was bought or designed.
- Difficulties in use of production and information technology; lack of user-friendliness.
- Maintenance issues and problems with production and information technology; balance of preventative and emergency/crises maintenance.
- Extent and nature of training offered, demanded and available; extent of obligation to understand this/make it available.
- Identifying where blockages occur, and the cause (e.g.: component and raw materials supplies, availability of packaging); their effects on total effectiveness.
- New products and developments: proportion of new products that get to market; actual and required research, development capability and expertise; research and development as a percentage of total organisational activities/fixed costs.

Marketing and sales

- Currency and effectiveness of marketing information and research.
- Sources of customer satisfaction and dissatisfaction; the benefits that customers expect to accrue from purchase/ownership of the products and services; the benefits that actually accrue as the result, and where the differences between the two lie.
- Changes in customer perceptions – especially from positive to negative (though a change from negative to positive may cause increases in demand with which the organisation is unable to cope).
- Organisational perceptions of 'good value' that are seen by customers as 'cheap'.
- Benefits to customers perceived by producers are not or are no longer perceived to be benefits by customers themselves.
- Marketing and promotion campaigns do not have the desired/projected effects on sales.
- Marketing and promotion campaigns cause major problems due to lack of full investigation, assessment and analysis.

- Lack of full market knowledge and understanding, often based on market research that generates 'generally favourable impressions' (i.e. 'would you buy' rather than 'will you buy').
- Poor public relations that are usually symptomatic of organisational lack of sureness, capability or faith in what the organisation is doing.
- Required and desired images and identity, not generated by marketing and advertising campaigns.
- Marketing rebounds – unlooked for (usually negative) consequences of marketing, advertising and promotion activities; this may also be a problem when very high notes are scored and the organisation is unable to satisfy increased demand.

Communications

- Quality and volume of written, oral, formal and informal communications.
- Extent and content of grapevine.
- Extent and nature of communication blockages and misunderstandings.
- Frequency and value of team, group, department, division and functional meetings; their agenda; outputs and outcomes.
- Extent and use of formal communication channels; length of time taken; general effectiveness; effects on operations, administration, decision-making processes.
- Extent and use of informal channels; length of time taken; general effectiveness; specific effects on operations, administration and decision-making processes.
- Effectiveness of formal and established systems – especially of consultation, participation and access to organisation information.
- Nature and value of information to which different groups have access.
- Organisation and operational confidentiality; perceived organisational and operational confidentiality.
- Information systems: ease of access to information; capacity for the acquisition, storage, retrieval and analysis and processing of information.
- Visibility and accessibility of managers and supervisors.
- Language used: the simpler and more direct this is, the more likely it is that what is said will be understood.
- Integrity of communications: the extent to which they mean what they say and say what they mean.
- Hidden/secondary agenda: the messages that are actually received by those receiving them; the messages that the organisation is actually putting across; reflected in the nature and language of what is said and written.

Each of these elements is to be considered in relation to all stakeholders and interested parties; and this means assessing the quality of external communications as well as internal.

Organisational

- Poor quality and volume of communications.
- One way (or perceived one-way) style of communications where orders are handed down from on high.

- Lack of adequate consultation.
- Increases in awards against the organisation by industrial tribunals, the health and safety executive, trading standards.
- Increases in adverse publicity and media coverage; decreases in favourable publicity and media coverage.
- Increased psychological distance between levels of the hierarchy and between different functions.
- Presence of physical distance between managers and those at the front line; lack of recognition of the effects of this and of problems caused/inherent.
- Lack of autonomy on the part of those working away from head office; the constant need to refer back to head office.
- Bad/negative/adversarial management style: often compounded by priorities on administration and procedural efficiency rather than operational success.
- Lack of clarity of overall purpose; lack of attention to subordinate goals, aims and objectives.
- Poor organisational standing in its community: often caused by a combination of being a known or perceived bad employer, and using production processes which are known or perceived to harm or pollute the environment. This is, in turn, compounded when the organisation refuses to take its full place in its community.
- Inaccessibility of managers and supervisors; lack of communication and coordination between functional and operational groups, departments and divisions.
- Balances and proportions of front line with support and administration activities; and balances and proportions of resources allocated to each.
- Complexity/simplicity of procedures; accessibility and understanding of procedures; time taken and resources used in their operation.
- Extent of crisis management; the matters that fall into the 'crisis' category.
- Attention to work patterns and methods; extent of alienation, divisive work practices; attention to job and work improvement methods.
- Extent and prevalence of 'them and us' divides between: head office and outlying functions; primary and support functions; managers and staff.
- Organisational politics: identifying where the real power and influence lies; why; whether this is appropriate; the extent and influence of over-mighty subjects and over-mighty departments.

Confidence and expectations

Everyone who comes into contact with an organisation expects to have confidence in it – confidence in the strength and quality of the overall relationship; confidence in its products and services; confidence in its continuity, reliability and stability; confidence in its continuing success and effectiveness.

People join and work for organisations, make purchases and avail themselves of services, with certain expectations in mind. They anticipate that their expectations will be fulfilled. Problems occur when these expectations are not fulfilled. Levels of expectation are set by a variety of needs.

- **For staff:** there is the need to be well rewarded; to gain job satisfaction, fulfilment, development and achievement; to be associated with a positive and prestigious organisation or occupation; to be valued, respected and esteemed.

EXAMPLE BOX 3.9 Performance Targets in Public Services

The main problem to be addressed lies in the establishment of a valid standpoint from which to measure the performance of these services. This has to be reconciled with immediate short-term needs, drives and directions of politicians and service managers. There are also often historical bases, resource constraints and social pressures which all have to be accommodated.

The knowledge, expertise, judgement, attributes and qualities of the public service manager become critical. These form the context in which the following broad and narrow perspectives can be taken.

- **Broad:** the state of the work environment (the school, classroom, library, hospital ward, laboratory, prison); the availability, use, value, quality and appropriateness of equipment to service users and consumers; cleanliness, warmth and comfort; general ambience; professionalism of staff; currency of professional expertise; interaction of staff with consumers; prioritisation of activities; resource effectiveness, efficiency, adequacy and usage.
- **Narrow:** application of absolute standards of service delivery; speed of response to consumers; nature and content of response to users; nature and volume of complaints, failures and shortcomings; attitudes of service users to providers and vice versa; acceptance of professional responsibility for standards; acceptance of professional development; personal commitment.

This is the context for setting specific aims and objectives in public services. It requires concentration on the output of specific services, and has no reference to inter-functional comparisons or league tables. This is the best basis of judgement and evaluation of performance for such services. It is to be carried out by service experts and analysts (in the same way as commercial and business analysts and experts carry out the evaluation of private-sector company performance).

- **For shareholders and backers:** there is a need to receive regular positive returns on investment; to receive specific dividends and other benefits as the result of investment.
- **Customers, consumers, clients and users:** expect satisfaction and utility from the products and services; in many cases, they also expect esteem, respect and value to be enhanced.
- **Communities:** expect to feel pleased and proud to have certain organisations established and working in among them.

Problems arise when a lack of confidence sets in and when expectations are not met. Part of the wider assessment of managerial performance is therefore, to understand what the nature of confidence is and what the expectations of the particular stakeholders and interested parties are, and to take steps to ensure that, as far as possible, these are satisfied.

Conclusions

Each of these elements and factors is an essential and legitimate area for managerial inquiry when assessing either total organisation performance or parts and features of it. Most of these elements and factors are interrelated. Several appear under different headings. Others are directly consequential; for example, it is impossible to have good and positive organisational attitudes without having clear standards established by top management. Taken together they reflect the fact that the performance of every organisation – and every department, division and function within it – can always be improved.

This also underlines the complexity of measuring performance successfully. This is true even where supposedly simple or direct targets have been set: for example, a simple increase in the output of a production line. Before such a decision can be taken, it has to be ensured that adequate volumes of components and supplies are available (or can be made available); that they can be stored; that any additional staff or overtime can be paid for; and that the increased output can be packaged, stored, distributed – and sold. It may be that such an increase adversely affects morale (for example, the need for additional production may be the latest in a long series of crises); or it may send morale sky-high, and this may subsequently lead to complacency if a positive, yet realistic, approach is not maintained.

So the role of the professional manager – whether chief executive officer, director, top, middle, junior or front line and supervisory – is to understand this, and to continue to attend to each of the elements and factors indicated. This is equally important when things are going well, as the reasons why success is being achieved can be fully explained and understood. When things do go wrong, and problems begin to arise, they can be identified early and nipped in the bud. This, in turn, is best achieved if all managers understand the full range of inquiry that they need to make, and realise that nothing happens in isolation.

CHAPTER SUMMARY

The measurement of organisational and managerial performance is complex and requires a high level of contextual knowledge and understanding, as well as the capability to choose the right qualitative and quantitative measures, and the required points of inquiry.

From this, managers are able to identify what contributes to successful, effective and profitable performance for their own organisation, and that part of it for which they are responsible. They can also pinpoint:

- activities that contribute to effective, successful and profitable organisational performance; the extent and nature of those contributions; and their effects upon each other
- activities that do not make any direct contribution to performance
- activities that detract from successful and effective performance; that destroy and damage it; that dilute its effectiveness
- diversions from purpose; blockages and barriers to progress
- the proportion and balance of steady-state activities with crisis handling.

It is necessary to recognise the range of parties, both internal and external, who have a legitimate interest in the organisation, who measure it for success or failure, and the measures that they bring to bear from their own point of view. Long-term viability is much more likely where the concerns of each group can be addressed and reconciled successfully. One of the main tasks of top managers is to recognise the nature and legitimacy of the interests of the different stakeholder groups and interested parties, and to take steps to see that these are widely understood and satisfied as far as possible.

From this approach to performance, assessment and measurement comes a clear understanding of what the organisation and its managers can control and influence, and what they cannot. For example, it may not be possible to suppress a glut of bad or negative publicity and adverse media coverage. However, organisations can influence future coverage by responding as positively as possible in the circumstances, and by using this as a springboard to generate long-term positive interest.

Similarly, it is not possible to control particular social, legal, economic and political constraints; but it is possible to recognise and understand the extent of their influence, and to work within them. It may also not be possible, in the short to medium term at least, to influence the size or nature of markets served; but again, it is possible to recognise these specific constraints, and to provide products and services as successfully, effectively and profitably as possible within them.

DISCUSSION QUESTIONS

1. Outline the advantages and disadvantages of using performance league tables for schools and hospitals. What, in your view, are the right measures of performance for schools and hospitals? How should these be implemented, monitored, reviewed and evaluated?

2. Discuss the view that the shareholder and the financial interests are the only stakeholders with legitimate views on the performance of organisations.

3. For the organisation of your choice, choose a set of performance indicators. Measure the performance of this organisation using the company annual report and any other information that you are able to obtain. Compare and contrast this with the statement by the chairman or chief executive officer in the annual report. What conclusions can you draw?

4. Using a high profile public project as an example (e.g. the Channel Tunnel, the Millennium Dome, Concorde) state how, when, where and by whom this venture should be measured for success.

CHAPTER CASE STUDY

INTERIOR SERVICES GROUP PLC
'I am delighted to be able to report another busy, successful and fulfilling year for ISG with profits increasing from £2.9 million to £4.3 million.

The value of work performed increased from £200 million to £290 million, an increase of 39 per cent. Adjusted earnings per share increased by 48 per cent to 13.97p from 9.43p.

An interim dividend of 1.5p per share was paid in April 1999, and a final dividend of 2.5p per share has been recommended. Subject to its approval at the Annual General Meeting on Thursday, 2 December 1999, the final dividend will be paid on 6 December 1999 to all shareholders on the register on 12 November 1999.'

STRATEGIC DEVELOPMENT

'Growth of the group this year has been focused on three areas: to develop our facilities management capability by acquisition; to grow the interior fit-out and refurbishment business organically; and to establish ourselves as a credible force in the professional new build construction management market.

Starting in February 1999, we have made a number of significant acquisitions. This includes H. Waters and company, a northern based property management company specialising in the leisure, transport and health sectors. In May 1999, we acquired the London-based property management and advisory company, Walker, Sun and Packman.

Since the year end, we have made our largest acquisition yet of the multidisciplinary facilities management services provider, Care Services Ltd. Care is a national company employing over 1700 staff offering a broad range of facilities support services.'

TRADING

'Despite the global economic concerns of late 1998, demand for our services has been high. This has grown by over 25 per cent in volume, winning many of the largest and most prestigious fit-out projects available. These include the new HQ for West LB valued at £50 million, the new £12 million Mobil HQ and most recently, in joint venture, the expanded HQ of a global investment bank in London. In Europe, the new management team has been redefining the business and has identified a number of major opportunities. Since the year-end, a £10 million project for Level 3 Communications in Dusseldorf has been awarded.

We have therefore achieved critical mass with a number of major projects under way.'

STAFF DEVELOPMENT

'We measure the level and quality of service that we deliver. This has increased again this year. This is a measure of the level of commitment, positive attitudes and willingness of all the staff to continuously improve and embrace new ways of working. Their enthusiasm is a major asset to the business and once again, I want to thank them sincerely. Encouraging and maintaining the values-driven culture that has been so important in the development of the Group so far is a major priority. The Group's in-house training facility, the Academy, will continue to play its role in helping us integrate our culture and invest in our people.'

PROSPECTS

'With the acquisition of Care completed, we will be concentrating on the integration of new businesses and realising some of the considerable potential for cross-selling available within the group. We have started the new financial year positively with the order book at a new high. Fee income margin growth will be a key objective this year, as well as expanding into new sectors and territories.

With the economic outlook more stable than last year and with most of our acquisition work completed, we will now concentrate on improving the quality and visibility of our earnings. Fundamental changes are occurring in the delivery of total occupancy services and ISG is in a strong position to benefit from these changes and we look forward to the future with enthusiasm and optimism.'

David King
Chairman and Chief Executive (15 October 1999)

QUESTIONS

1. Study this statement from the point of view of all stakeholders. Which groups are likely to be encouraged by the statement and why? Which are not likely to be encouraged by the statement and why?

2. Identify the areas where performance has been measured precisely and where it has not. From this, identify a set of precise performance measures that you feel would be appropriate to this particular company.

3. What further information would you need in order to be able to arrive at a fully accurate evaluation of the company's performance for this year?

4 Ethics

'I only started the Body Shop because I could not get any of the department stores to take my idea seriously. Once we became successful, they have simply copied our ideas, and rebranded them themselves.' Anita Roddick, co-founder, the Body Shop (2000).

'Our staff are our greatest asset.' Tarmac plc, *Annual Report* (1995) – a year in which they had made 2200 members of staff redundant.

'What was wrong with Marks and Spencer was that its senior management, notably the man at the top, reported in the general press as regarded as a bully by some colleagues, failed to realise that they were the shareholders' servants.' David Thomas, *Writers' News*, March 2001.

CHAPTER OUTLINE

Introduction: the relationship between ethics, management and profitability

Relationships with employees, customers and suppliers

Responsibilities and obligations to staff

Conduct

Professional standards

Compliance with the law

Product and service integrity.

CHAPTER OBJECTIVES

After studying this chapter, you should be able to:

understand the relationship between ethical standards and business and public service effectiveness and delivery

understand the effects of ethics on all aspects of organisational and managerial performance

understand the personal, professional, occupational and human responses to variations in standards of ethics, morality and integrity

draw conclusions as to the relationship between ethical standards and sustainable organisational performance.

Introduction

Ethics in management is concerned with those parts of organisational, operational, occupational and professional conduct that relate to absolute standards and moral principles. More generally, it is concerned with human character and conduct, the distinction between right and wrong, and the absolute duties and obligations that exist in all situations.

Some views and perspectives on the relationship between ethics and business are now given.

- 'Business ethics applies ethical reasoning to business situations and activities. It is based on a combination of distributive justice – that is, the issuing of rewards for contribution to organisation goals and values; and ordinary common decency – an absolute judgement that is placed on all activities' (Sternberg, 1995).
- 'Ethical issues concerning business and public sector organisations exist at three levels.
  - At the macro level there are issues about the role of the business in the national and international organisation of society. These are largely concerned with addressing the relative virtues of different political/social systems. There are also important issues of international relationships and the role of business on an international scale.
  - At the corporate level the issue is often referred to as corporate social responsibility and is focused on the ethical issues facing individual and corporate entities (both private and public sector) when formulating and implementing strategies.
  - At the individual level the issue concerns the behaviour and actions of individuals within organisations' (Johnson and Scholes, 1994).

In their book *Changing Corporate Values*, Adams, Hamil and Carruthers identified a series of factors and elements as measures against which the performance of organisations could be measured in ethical terms. These factors are:

- the nature of business
- the availability and use of information
- participation, consultation, employment relationships, the recognition of trade unions, means and methods of representation
- relationships with the Third World (where appropriate)
- the nature of particular products – especially where these included armaments, drugs, tobacco and alcohol – and the means by which these were produced, marketed and sold
- connections with governments, especially where these were considered to be undesirable or where the regime in question was considered to be unethical itself (see Example Box 4.1).
- general approaches and attitudes to staff and customers
- attitudes to the communities in which they operated
- attitudes to environmental issues, especially waste disposal and recycling, and replanting
- the ways and means by which scarce resources were consumed
- business relationships with suppliers and markets
- product testing – again, especially where this involved the use of animals or parts of the environment (see Example Box 4.2).

EXAMPLE BOX 4.1 The Hunger Business

There is mounting evidence to suggest that much of the effort carried out in the Third World by charities and voluntary organisations (including the United Nations) is extensively manipulated by the governments of the people that they are supposed to be aiding.

General Michael Ojukwa, President of the Nigerian enclave of Biafra in 1967, stated:

> We were fighting a civil war with the Nigerian government. We needed support from the outside world, otherwise we would have been massacred. We therefore took a television news crew to a small enclave of the region where people were starving. These pictures were then transmitted around the world. The result was that donations from the Western public, and assistance from the big charities, came pouring in. As a condition of receiving this aid, we were able to insist that the big charities also flew in armaments and other military equipment that could be used in order to sustain our campaign.

In 1995 and 1996, there was a very brutal civil war in the African state of Rwanda. In 1999, trouble flared up again and there was a mass exodus of the people of Rwanda to neighbouring countries. Refugee camps quickly became unmanageable, and their population swelled to about two million.

Representatives of all the big international charities went on television to announce an imminent humanitarian disaster. Each spokesman tried to outbid all of the others in their description of the number of people likely to starve to death. One figure extensively used was that there were over one million persons at risk of starvation or disease.

In the event, 192 people died in the camps before there was a mass return by the people to their homelands in Rwanda. Of those who died, two were stillborn babies. One was killed as the result of a domestic dispute. The other 189 were all killed in inter-tribal and inter-gang fighting within the camp. There was no humanitarian disaster.

Source: *The Hunger Business*, Channel 4 Television, 2000.

Peter F. Drucker (1955) wrote:

> The more successfully the manager does their work, the greater will be the integrity required. For under new technology the impact on the business of decisions, time span and risks will be so serious as to require that each manager put the common good of the enterprise above self-interest. Their impact on the people in the enterprise will be so decisive as to demand that the manager put genuine principles above expediency. And the impact on the economy will be so far reaching that society itself will hold managers responsible. Indeed, the new tasks demand that the manager of tomorrow root every action and decision in the bedrock of principles so that they lead, not only through knowledge, competence and skill, but also through vision, courage, responsibility and integrity.

EXAMPLE BOX 4.2 Genetically Modified (GM) Crops

Scientists believe that they have found ways to improve the quality and durability of agricultural crops, through modifying the genes of the particular plants. This has caused extensive political, social and media debate and argument: on the one hand recognising the need to enhance global food production; on the other many concerns about long-term damage to the food, agricultural, and environmental infrastructure have been voiced.

The key problem here is lack of openness, quality and integrity of information. The companies responsible for producing GM crops have found themselves under attack from powerful consumer and environmental lobbies, and have therefore retreated within themselves, concentrating on their existing markets and those that they are able to dominate, rather than opening up a higher quality of debate. Politicians, while recognising the need to enhance the quality and volume of food production, have equivocated on the environmental issues. Environmental lobbies have sought to simplify the debate into a single issue: the general rights and wrongs of 'tampering with nature'.

The net result is an entrenchment of position, resulting in turn in a hysterical and ill-informed exchange of views, arguments and insults. The chief sufferers of this are the public at large, who to date have not been told the true merits and demerits of each part of the case.

Payne and Pugh identified the relationship between the absolute standards of the organisation and its 'climate'. They stated that: 'Climate is a total concept applying to the organisation as a whole or some definable department or subsystem within it.' It is descriptive of the organisation. There are four main aspects of climate:

- the degree of autonomy given
- the degree of structure imposed on work positions
- the reward orientation, either in terms of individual satisfaction or organisational achievement
- the degree of consideration, warmth and support.

There is clearly therefore, a variety of points of view from which the wider question may be addressed. At the core, however, lies a combination of:

- the long-term view (rather than the short or medium)
- absolute standards relating to organisational policies, aims and objectives
- common standards of equity, equality, honesty and integrity
- relationships between organisation standards and absolutes, the carrying out of performance and the distribution of rewards
- relationships between means and ends, and actions and motives
- reconciliation of conflicts of interest.

It is further necessary to identify the nature of those legitimate interests. If the organisation is not profitable and/or effective it will close (or be closed down). The first duty therefore, to staff and customers, is to ensure long-term permanence. This only occurs where there exists a fundamental integrity of relationships and activities, and where this extends to all dealings with every stakeholder. From this arises the confidence that is the foundation of the ability to conduct activities over the long term. Ethics therefore pervades all aspects of organisation activities and performance.

Survival

Survival therefore becomes the main ethical duty of the organisation, to its staff, customers, communities and other stakeholders. For this to happen over the long term, a long-term view must be taken of all that this means. For business and companies, profits must be made over the long term; for public services, this means effectiveness over the long term. This is the basis on which confidence and an enduring and continuous positive relationship with customers (or service users) is built and developed. This is also the only ground on which an effective and satisfactory organisation for the staff is to be created.

Short-term views, expediency, the need for triumphs – all detract from this. In particular, there is a serious problem in this area with some public services. For example, the output of education can take 15 or 20 years to become apparent. Health and social services have similar extreme long-term requirements and commitments. Yet those responsible for their direction (both service chiefs and cabinet ministers) need to be able to show instant results to be presented before the electorate or before the selection panel for their next job.

This problem is not wholly confined to services. For example, pressures from bankers and other financial backers in some sectors (especially loan makers) lead to companies being forced or strongly encouraged to sell assets during lean periods in order to keep up repayments or show a superficial cash surplus over the immediate period. This happened with the UK construction industry over the early 1990s when there was a great decline in work brought on by recession and a general loss of confidence. Short-term cash gain was made through the sale of assets (especially land banks). Long-term survival was threatened because these assets would not be present when any upturn in confidence and activity came about.

However, this again has to be balanced with matters of general confidence and expectation. If backers expect to see a series of short-term positive results then these have to be produced, especially if backing may be withdrawn if they are not forthcoming or do not meet expectations. This implies re-educating backers into the long-term view. It also means seeking out others who are disposed to take the long-term view.

Relationships with employees

This refers to the nature of participation and involvement, and the point of view from which this is approached. Basic integrity in employee relations stems from the view taken of the employees, their reasons for working in the organisation, their reasons for being hired to work in the organisation and the absolute levels of esteem in which they are held.

Confrontational or adversarial styles of employee relations are always founded on mistrust and reinforced by offensive and defensive positions adopted by the two sides concerning particular issues. The phrase 'the two sides' confirms and underlines this. Resources are consumed in this way to the detriment, both of organisation perform- ance and of resource utilisation; those used in these ways cannot be put to better use elsewhere (see Example Box 4.3).

This form of employee relations is therefore unethical. On the other hand, greater or full participation and involvement is only ethical if the point of view adopted is itself honest: if a genuine view of respect and identity is taken. This is made apparent – or not – in the continuity and enduring nature of this relationship. It is underlined by the volume, quality and relevance of information made available to the staff, the means by which problems are addressed and resolved, the prevalence of equality of treatment and opportunity, and the development of staff.

EXAMPLE BOX 4.3 Employee Relations and Problem Solvers

Many large industrial, commercial and public sector organisations have extensive human resource management departments and functions. In this context, an especial problem concerns those that have responsibility for employee relations.

These companies and organisations hire employee-relations specialists to devise policies for the effective management of staff and resolution of conflict, and to resolve problems when they arise.

Serious organisational problems can – and do – arise when these employee-relations staff are rewarded on the basis of the problems that they solve. If empha-sis is placed on the ability of employee-relations staff to solve problems, then they will find problems to solve. For example:

A large London radio station was going through a period of extensive restructur-ing. Two programme-producing departments were required to restructure their workforce, terms and conditions of employment, and hours of work. The manager of one of these departments saw the problem early and, by engaging in extensive consultation and discussion with the staff, avoided all problems; the matter was resolved smoothly and without any disputes.

The manager of the other department did nothing about the matter until the weekend before the changes were due to take place. In the period immediately preceding this weekend, staff morale plummeted, and there was an increase in the number of disputes and grievances. Accordingly, the manager commanded all of the staff to attend a weekend briefing, consultation and crisis resolution session immediately before the changes were due to take place. The matters were resolved at this weekend meeting.

The radio station's senior management, who were well familiar with the situa-tion and the mounting crisis, looked on with admiration as, at the end of the week-end, all of the staff trooped out and announced themselves satisfied with the new arrangement. Because of his crisis management skills, the latter manager was rewarded. The manager who had tackled the problems early received no reward or recognition for the ways in which she had managed the situation.

It also refers to the attention to the standards to which employees are expected to conform and the reasoning and logic behind this. It covers all aspects of the traditional personnel area: recruitment and selection, induction, performance appraisal, pay and reward, promotion and other opportunities for development and advancement. Above all, at its core, lies equality of treatment for everyone.

Responsibilities and obligations to staff

The general responsibilities and obligations to staff consist of providing work, remaining in existence, equality and fairness of treatment, compliance with the law and the specific regulations of training and development. The basis on which this is established consists of the following.

- Acknowledging the range of pressures and priorities that exist in everyone's lives, including health, family, social, ethical, religious, as well as those related to work. The outcome of this is understanding and not interference or imposition. It sets in context the relationship between work organisations and people. It indicates areas where stresses and strains are likely to arise. It indicates the relationship between organisation and individual priorities, where these coincide and where they diverge. It indicates areas for accommodation and for regulation.
- Acknowledgement of extreme human concerns. This refers to personal crises: serious illness, death, bereavement, divorce, drink and drug problems. The concern is to ensure that the organisation gives every possible support to people facing these issues so that a productive and profitable relationship is maintained even through such times. Individuals can, and should, be referred to outside professional support services and agencies for these matters with the full backing of the organisation (see Example Box 4.4).

EXAMPLE BOX 4.4 Organisational and Managerial Responsibilities and Staff Bereavements

One of the world's big oil companies had to manage two bereavements affecting members of its staff.

A senior finance executive, working at the company's London office, suffered the loss of his wife in childbirth. This was quickly demonstrated to have been as the result of medical negligence. He was given three months' paid leave of absence from the company in order to get over his bereavement, and to sort out childcare and domestic arrangements for the new-born baby, and for his other two children.

At about the same time, a female member of staff in her mid-fifties lost her 22 year old son, who died as the result of a drug overdose. The female member of staff worked as a forecourt cashier at one of the company's 800 filling stations. She was given three days' paid leave immediately following the death, and paid time off to attend her son's inquest and funeral only. Any other time off she was required to take either as annual or unpaid leave. The company held her job open for her until such time as she felt able to return to work.

In the last resort, however, organisations do not have the right to pry into people's personal affairs. Individuals may be referred for counselling or other expert help and advice if they give their consent. The organisation cannot justifiably go further unless the matter is adversely affecting the employee's work performance beyond a fair and reasonable extent, or where he/she constitutes a real or potential threat or danger to colleagues or the activities of the organisation.

Problems related to drug or alcohol abuse always fall into the latter category and are therefore always a matter of direct concern. Organisations set absolute standards of handling and using equipment, carrying out activities and dealing with the public. Addiction and abuse problems directly affect each of these. The individual is therefore to be removed from these situations and supported through rehabilitation.

- Confidentiality and integrity in all dealings with staff. This is the cornerstone on which all effective staff relationships are built. Where confidences are not kept, where sensitive personal and occupational information becomes public property, the relationship is tainted and often destroyed. Confidentiality also encourages people to be frank, open and honest themselves, and this leads to a genuine understanding of issues much more quickly. It also enables managers and supervisors to address their matters of concern – for example, a decline in standards of performance and behaviour – directly and immediately they are observed (see Example Box 4.5).

- Respect for individuals based on the value of their contribution to the organisation. If they bring no value, they should not be there in the first place. Ideally

---

EXAMPLE BOX 4.5 Integrity in Dealings with Staff

This incident happened to a senior and extremely capable bank employee. He was assigned an urgent project with a very high priority that involved designing a new product in a very short period. He worked 18-hour days for weeks. He treated weekends just like weekdays. He only went home to sleep. The project was completed on time, and the employee's boss was congratulated heartily by the bank's executives. The next week was time for the individual's performance review.

The review meeting took five minutes. The manager sat the employee down and said:

I think you may be a little disappointed with the rating I have given you. Generally speaking, you have been working well. However, there are two problems which you have that need to be addressed. First, I have never seen you go a whole day without unbuttoning your shirt and loosening your tie. Second – and this is more important – you have a habit of stretching out at your desk and kicking your shoes off. Frankly, that is offensive. If it weren't for these problems, you would rate a solid 'competent'. As it is, you are scruffy and I'm afraid that means you are 'developing'.

Source: Scott Adams, *The Joy of Work*, Macmillan, 1999.

EXAMPLE BOX 4.6   Staff Loyalty and Rewards

In the City of London, the nature and size of bonus payments comes in for criticism, because of the disparity that exists in the size of bonuses awarded, and those who receive them, and those who do not. A senior corporate finance manager stated:

> Some corporate financiers with as little as four years' experience are receiving between 300 and 400 per cent of salary as bonus, creating a considerable imbalance between them, and others in the banks who work within what are regarded as cost centres rather than revenue generators. This creates a highly remuneration-orientated culture that is not necessarily productive, and certainly over-values skills, especially in the current [2001] candidate-led market.

In many cases, high bonus levels have evidently become the crucial factor in decisions about careers. A survey carried out by CityPeople.com, a city online recruitment and remuneration consultancy, stated that this reflected the overwhelming supremacy of bonus awards when financiers chose companies for which they were going to work. One-third of those questioned said that if their bonus was less than expected, they would start looking for another job. With a key skills shortage at present, the City could be creating for itself a serious dilemma by paying big bonuses, in spite of the fact that these neither buy nor guarantee loyalty.

Similar problems abound in the football industry. One top international star at a wealthy London club had his salary doubled between the years 1998 and 2000, and still left in 2001 claiming that he was undervalued. Another joined a top Spanish club in 1996 on a guaranteed salary of £72 000 per week for a 3.5-year contract, and subsequently failed to perform to expectations. Another was transferred between English, Spanish and French clubs for a net value of over £50 million; at each club the particular individual criticised supporters for failing to show him the respect that he felt he was due. In each case, the clubs felt bound to pay the salary levels demanded, regardless of relationship to individual or club performance.

At the core of both examples is the (almost incredible) managerial dilemma, centring on whether loyalty can be bought, or whether it has to be earned.

Source: Wendy Ledger, 'The Bonuses that Create Millionaires Overnight', *Evening Standard*, 20 February 2001.

therefore, the fact of their employment (in whatever capacity) equates to high and distinctive value; where it does not, stress and conflict invariably occur.

This respect extends to all aspects of the relationship. It includes attention to the current job, future prospects, continuity of working relations, creation of suitable working environments, creation and maintenance of effective occupational and personal relationships, creation and maintenance of effective management and supervisory styles (see Example Box 4.6).

The traditional or adversarial view of this approach to responsibilities and obligations was that it was soft and unproductive, and diverted attention away from production and output. Organisations could not afford to be 'nice' to their employees while there was a job to be done.

The reverse of this is much closer to the truth. The acknowledgement, recognition and understanding of the full nature and range of complexities and conflicting pressures on individuals is the first step towards effective and profitable activities. By engaging on a basis of honesty, confidentiality, trust, support and integrity – rather than coercion, confrontation, dishonesty and duplicity – a long-term positive relationship can be established. The interests of organisation and individual are bound up with each other, especially over the long-term. Ultimately therefore, their interests coincide. A critical part of this approach is concerned with creating the basis on which this can be built.

Relationships with suppliers

There used to be a received managerial wisdom that it was good and effective practice to create 'a multiplicity of suppliers', because this would 'keep them on their toes', and 'keep them loyal'. In practice, companies that adopt this approach actually show no loyalty to suppliers; they simply shop around, taking either the short-term view that they will accept deliveries from the lowest-priced suppliers at the particular moment; or taking the expedient view that particular suppliers may be changed at will. This especially applies where there is an over-supply of particular commodities, components, and primary and raw materials.

By the same token, companies and organisations may know, believe or perceive themselves to be held to ransom by those who supply rare or highly sought-after primary resources and components.

Wherever either of these two extremes exists, the relationship has to be managed with integrity, if long-term security of purpose and business is to be achieved. Indeed, any business or managerial relationship where there are dominant and dependent partners must be considered from the business requirements, rather than the imbalance of power which exists.

It is also true that those organisations that secure themselves medium- and long-term contracts to supply large public and commercial institutions may take advantage of this security of relationship. For example, those supplying management consultancy services and medical supplies to the UK National Health Service have, in many cases, secured for themselves premium-priced contracts in return for stability and security of supplies. Organisations engaged in public–private partnerships and other forms of contracting out of particular activities normally found in the public service domain have been able to get themselves fully underwritten by the government, in case of changes in the business relationships, or strategic and political directions of particular services. Similarly, those organisations providing subcontracted specialist products and services to industries such as civil and mechanical engineering, building and construction, and information technology have also been able to charge premium rates at the times when their particular expertise is required.

This has caused many organisations and their managers to take a fresh look at the nature of the relationship they want with their suppliers. At the core of this must be attention to the short-, medium- and long-term organisational and business demands, and also the nature, value and frequency of the supplies required. This is certain to

---

EXAMPLE BOX 4.7 Relationships with Suppliers

Three years ago, as part of a schools–industry liaison project in south-east England, a small group of schoolteachers spent two weeks shadowing the staff of a large fruit and vegetable farm. During the course of their placement, the teachers found out that over 90 per cent of their produce was sold to a major department store chain. One of the teachers, a man in his forties, was perturbed by this. He asked the farm general manager:'Isn't that a bit risky?'

'What do you mean?' replied the general manager.

'Well – what if the department store chain were to go out of business? Or to stop selling food? Or to change its suppliers?'

'Oh, that will never happen', replied the general manager.'We have supplied this company for over 20 years. They know us and understand us; and we know and understand them. Why on earth would they want to change their suppliers?'

Some time later, the particular teacher was driving past the farm. The vegetable greenhouses were clearly not being used; and in one corner of a field, there was a huge pile of rotting apples. He drove on to the farm gate. At the gate was a 'for sale' sign. The farm was clearly closed.

The schoolteacher noted the name of the estate agents, and made contact. He asked them what had happened. He was told:'The company that bought all of the farm's produce changed its supplier at 24 hours' notice. They found themselves a supplier in France who would deliver the same quality and volume of fruit and vegetables at a lesser cost'.

---

change with technological advance, the opening up of new markets, and increased availability of supplies of components, materials and information from different parts of the world (see Example Box 4.7).

Relationships with customers

This is the basis of the commercial or service provision: the respect and value in which the customers and clients are held. From this springs the drive for product quality, presentation and offering; for public relations and other customer management and service activities; and for handling complaints.

It also impinges on the staff. Where staff know that high standards of customer service and top-quality products are being offered, the relationship between organisation and staff is also reinforced. The converse is also true: where these standards are low or falling, or where it is known that poor products and services are being offered, the integrity of the relationship between organisation and staff is also compromised.

This impacts on all production, output and sales activities, especially in terms of attention to product quality, the terms under which it is offered, its uses and availability and recognition of the levels of satisfaction that are required by the customers. In the long term, if this is not present, confidence is lost (see Example Box 4.8). While it is possible to identify areas where short-term gain has been made without integrity (for example, in the sale of building products, home improvements, life assurance and

> **EXAMPLE BOX 4.8 Product Quality, Integrity and Wholesomeness: Barbie**
>
> The Barbie phenomenon illustrates much of the complexity surrounding the quality and value of products to customers and consumers, and their fundamental integrity and wholesomeness.
>
> Barbie dolls are overwhelmingly played with – consumed – by urban and suburban small girls; they are bought for them, also overwhelmingly, by their mothers, grandmothers, elder sisters and aunts. The product is constantly being developed and enhanced; new doll designs, clothing and accessories are brought on-stream every week. The product and brand are further reinforced by extensive advertising campaigns and a range of complementary books, comics and films.
>
> The product has existed for 44 years. It is one of the most recognised products and brands in the world. A Barbie product – either doll or accessory – is sold every 11 seconds. In 2001, turnover of Barbie products exceeded £1 billion.
>
> A part of the success of the product development refers to the number of different jobs and occupations that Barbie has had. These include schoolteacher, doctor, nurse, dentist, astronaut, fashion model, show-jumper and financier. The doll has been presented in a variety of different ways, including walking, talking, disabled, dark-haired, fair-haired, shorthaired, longhaired, and from various perceived different ethnic origins.
>
> The core of the debate around the fundamental wholesomeness and integrity of the product, however, centres on the core presentation of the doll. It is deemed to enhance unethical and unacceptable perceptions of womanhood by the world at large, and to contribute greatly to the early attitudes formed by young girls of society's broad expectations of them.

pensions, or poor quality Christmas presents), there is no (or reduced) likelihood of repeat business occurring. This also fails to satisfy either the long-term criteria or the requirement of confidence on the part of the employees; above all, there is no integrity of relationship. This way of conducting business is therefore also unethical.

This also refers to attention to the marketing activities undertaken and the point of view adopted. Creative and imaginative presentation is highly desirable as long as this underlines (and does not misrepresent) the quality, desirability and image of the particular product or organisation. Again, where integrity is missing, the relationship is invariably short term and terminated by loss of confidence in the organisation, and loss of regard for its products and services. This applies to all aspects of marketing: promotion and advertising, packaging and presentation, direct sales and distribution (see Example Box 4.9).

Relationships with communities

The more general organisational and managerial relationship, between companies or public service bodies and the communities within which they operate, has also to be addressed. The factors that have to be considered are as follows.

EXAMPLE BOX 4.9 Marketing: Contentious Examples

The following are worthy of consideration.

- **Benetton:** in the mid-1990s, Benetton, the Italian clothing company, created its *United Colours of Benetton* advertising and marketing campaign. Two controversial images used were photographs of human foetuses and new-born babies – presented as stark images on white backgrounds, with the slogan *United Colours of Benetton* underneath – and wounded soldiers photographed during the Bosnian civil war of 1993–4, with the same slogan underneath. These were roundly condemned by advertising lobbies and pressure groups concerned with maintaining standards of probity and integrity. They were deemed by the Benetton company to have been a major contributory factor in doubling company turnover in the clothing market during the period 1993–8, and the campaign was revived again in 2001 with similar success.
- **Marlboro:** Phillip Morris Inc., the company which manufactures and distributes Marlboro cigarettes world-wide, has settled without contest many claims brought against it by persons who have contracted serious diseases, including heart disease and lung cancer, as the result of using the company's products. As the major sponsor of Formula 1 motor racing, the company is able to secure for itself a minimum of six hours multi-channel television promotional exposure each time a Formula 1 race takes place. Marlboro is the most universally recognised cigarette brand. It is also, of all the cigarette brands in the world, that which enjoys the greatest universal customer loyalty.

- The provision of long-term enduring work, and the prosperity that this brings to communities. One of the major problems that was not managed in the UK during the recessions of the 1970s and 1980s, and the job losses that accrued as the result, was the provision of substitute or alternative sources of work and, therefore, economic support for communities at large. This had an enduring social effect on attitudes to work in certain areas of the country. Moreover, there is plenty of evidence to suggest that this part of the transition process is seldom addressed. Examples include the extensive job losses and community deprivations that have occurred in the former East Germany as the result of reunification, and in countries such as Poland, the Czech Republic, and Vietnam, as the result of the fall of communist regimes.
- Community confidence incorporates the general feelings of social well-being that accrue as the result of having particular organisations located in specific communities. This may bring with it particular ethical dilemmas; for example, there is a conflict that has to be addressed in areas where nuclear power stations are located. These stations provide large volumes of high value and well-paid work to the communities, and this has to be reconciled with continuing concerns and perceptions about radiation pollution.
- Other concerns centre around pollution and environmental damage, especially

the disposal of waste and effluent, noise and lighting blight, and the effectiveness of waste and effluent management by organisations. Closely related to this are more general concerns surrounding the health and safety aspects of specific operations that are located in particular areas (see also Chapter 8). Much of this is compounded by a failure to pin down global and corporate responsibilities for particular activities, as well as legislative inadequacies and a lack of executive powers on the part of statutory executives.

- Community disruption is relevant especially to construction and civil engineering activities, which bring with them 'building blight' for the duration of their activities. They may also leave 'residual blight' if those responsible for drawing up the contract have not ensured that the particular construction or civil engineering firm concerned has been made responsible for the restoration and enduring quality of the broader environment in which the work was carried out.

- Exploitation may occur when organisations move into particular areas as the result of the cheapness and perceived plentiful supply of labour and other resources. This was a problem that successive governments tried to address in the 1970s and 1980s in the UK through the use of regional aid and other development grants in areas of high unemployment. This is less of a problem now in the UK; however, there are enduring concerns about the wholesomeness and integrity of those organisations that source their manufacturing operations in the poorest parts of the world, purely because labour is cheap, plentiful, and unregulated.

- Social dominance and dependence come in three main forms.
  - A large organisation moving into a particular location may be able to poach staff from others already working there, by virtue of its economic ability to provide substantially superior terms and conditions of employment.
  - Large firms are able to insist on specific development activities, to the known, believed or perceived detriment of the rest of the economic community. Of specific concern here is the development of out-of-town industrial and retail centres, which are believed to damage or destroy the economic viability of centre-of-town activities.
  - Large organisations may have the economic ability to transcend their central responsibilities, by ensuring that they have powerful political and economic support. In these cases, they are able to build and operate what they want from their own point of view and narrow self-interest, rather than what is in the wider interests of the particular community.

These are the main relationships upon which successful and effective organisational performance is built and developed. They are underpinned by the following.

Corporate governance and direction

This is the position adopted by the organisation that is apparent from its policies, aims and objectives and the means established by which these are to be achieved. In this context the extent of honesty and integrity are immediately apparent. This is reinforced by the clarity and realism of overall purpose, the basic approach taken to customers, markets and staff, and management style; and underlined by the rules, systems and procedures that are put in place to support all of this, and the ways in which these are presented, delivered and implemented (see Example Box 4.10).

Stakeholders

Attention to the relative position of stakeholders is based on the recognition that some – especially staff, customers and owners – are more critical than others, for example, the local community pressure groups and vested interests. Each has its own position and is worthy of being dealt with from the point of view of honesty and integrity, and worthy also of respect and esteem. However, organisations will not normally accommodate a peripheral interest at the expense of the core purpose, though they may do this if it can be successfully integrated. The best organisations seek ways forward which are capable of integrating the interests of peripheral groups with that of the core.

Resources

There are ethical implications for resource utilisation. Profligacy is wasteful and therefore wrong, even where constraints are not apparent. It is unsatisfactory, normally leading to a general loss of care and consideration. It is also off-putting to customers; for example, customers visiting luxurious offices may well come to the conclusion that a good part of the turnover is being used on expensive furnishings rather than business performance and effectiveness. In general therefore, it is bad business.

A useful equivalent in public service terms may also be drawn. This is the propensity – very often driven by managers and directors – to use up the year's budget in time for the end of the year (usually February and March because of the end of the financial year on 1 April). Resources that have been conserved for 9 or 10 months suddenly become expendable; this tendency is reinforced if there is no prospect of carrying the resources forward to the following year. The result is that departments affected in this way engage in any activities or purchases that will use up the resources.

On the other hand, resource constraints lead to choices and priorities. This leads, in turn, to the consideration of who should receive resources and who should not, and why. An ethical assessment will look at organisational aims and objectives. Other elements include establishing whether everything is to be attempted in the knowledge that this will probably fall short of full success and effectiveness (common in public services), or whether resources will be concentrated on that which can be completed fully at the expense of that which cannot.

Resource constraints also lead to resource battles in many cases and this compounds the issue. Problems especially arise when resources are seen to be distributed on the basis of favour and expediency as distinct from operational necessity, or to head office functions at the expense of outlying and often front line activities.

The ethical line is therefore to maximise and optimise resources in the pursuit of objectives. This is based on the judgement and integrity of those responsible, and on their taking the point of view of what is best for the organisation and its long-term future.

> ## EXAMPLE BOX 4.10 Ethical Policies
>
> Many organisations take a very strong, clear and distinctive ethical stance in their dealings with everybody. For example:
>
> - **The Body Shop:** is the twenty-first most highly regarded company in the world from this point of view. This is in spite of the fact that it operates to net profit margins of between 2 and 5 per cent, levels that would be commercially unacceptable in any other cosmetics company. It is able to maintain its high level of overall respect, and its enduring value in a niche market, because of the distinctive ethical stance adopted by the company's founders, Anita and Gordon Roddick. This refers overwhelmingly to the company's stated policy of buying its supplies at Western rather than local market values, and of placing the emphasis on everything that they do as contributing to the community at large, as well as to the narrow self-interest of the company. Even The Body Shop, however, was forced to change one of its core logos from 'This product is not tested on animals' to 'Against animal testing'. This was because many of the binding agents used in the manufacture of its cosmetics are required by law to have been tested on animals.
> - **Corus:** announcing its decision to cut 6000 jobs in the UK, Corus, the Anglo-Dutch steel corporation, stated: 'Our first duty is to our shareholders. Only by taking this action can we ensure enduring share values.' This at least states that the company was prepared to make clear where its priorities lay rather than mincing words about them, even if the wider effects on the staff, and the communities in which they lived, were to be disruptive and traumatic. This should be contrasted with the Tarmac quote at the start of the chapter.
> - **BP Energy:** from the year 2001 onwards, this company has sought to rebrand itself as an environmentally concerned oil company. In support of this, it produced a series of public relations announcements, supported by environmentally appealing television advertisements, declaring its aim to make the world a cleaner place to live. In no part of its environmental policy does the company make any reference at all to the enduring levels of pollution produced by its products via car and aero-engine exhausts. Nor does it make any reference to the fact that the company and its contractors both continue to dump oil drilling and refining waste and effluent in Third World countries and into the atmosphere.

Conduct

This is the basis on which all relationships are founded. The key is the attitude adopted by staff to each other and the organisation to its people. It is underlined by establishing standards of conduct and enforcing them so that a clear distinction is made between what is acceptable and what is not. Everyone is held in confidence, respect and esteem. This is, in turn, underlined by the nature, emphasis and application of the rules and regulations.

Professional standards

This category concerns attention to the quality of staff, the ways in which they apply their particular trades and expertise, and the expectations and requirements that are placed on them by the organisation. These standards are to apply to everyone. There is no reason why ostensibly unskilled or simple tasks should not be carried out to the highest possible quality. This is supported by the organisation's commitment to provide the correct working environment, equipment and style of supervision, and by the standards of respect, trust and esteem referred to above. Absolute standards are present and upheld where each of these elements is present, and where one falls short this may lead call into question the integrity of the relationship. Where the shortfall is allowed to persist, professional standards inevitably fall in all areas. There is, moreover, a loss of self-worth all round, and those with distinctive trades or professions retreat into being professional or expert practitioners (as distinct from organisation practitioners) and may seek employment elsewhere where these standards are known (or perceived) to be higher (see Example Box 4.11).

The law

Compliance with the law may or may not be ethical; this again depends on the attitude and standpoint adopted. Organisations are known to hide behind the law in certain circumstances, especially where legal standards are lower than the absolutes that are known to be required.

This applies especially to waste disposal and discharges, and the relationship between the organisation and its environment. It occurs also in all dealings with staff: rights to disclosure of information, to time off work, to breaks, to maternity leave, and to minimum levels of redundancy notice and pay. Organisations comply with the law because they have to and not because they know that this is the right approach to take.

Organisations should nevertheless comply with the law. Not to do so questions, and is likely to destroy, the total integrity and honesty, and the standards which they have set themselves. Condoning acts that are against the law (even encouraging them) also destroys integrity. The quality of the working relationship is also compromised when organisations take a calculating or expedient view of how far the law can be stretched without actually breaking it (see Example Box 4.12).

Health and safety

The field of health and safety at work is covered by the law and is also a distinctive element in its own right, simply because it is such a fundamental reflection of respect for people (and especially lack of respect for people). The key lies in the organisation's acceptance of its responsibility to take an absolute view of its environment, technology and other equipment, its procedures and practices, its staff and any other persons who visit or use its premises, in its acknowledging the entirety of things that can go wrong, and designing each element so that nothing can go wrong.

This is a continuous responsibility and requires reaction as and when new knowledge becomes available.

For example, asbestos was used during the period 1930–60 as an effective fire-proofing material in buildings, and construction workers worked with it in the same

---

EXAMPLE BOX 4.11   The Actions, Attitudes and Values of Key Figures

Organisational and professional standards are reinforced (both positively and negatively) or diluted by the actions, attitudes and values of key figures. If a company chief executive states that 'the staff are our most valuable resource', but actually hires and fires at will, he or she will be judged by actions, not words. Similarly, any company that is determined not to make staff redundant must use a phrase equivalent to 'we will not make staff redundant', rather than 'there are no plans for redundancies at present', because the latter statement has been widely used by dishonest and expedient companies and their managers in the past. Other examples that may usefully be noted are as follows.

- 'Riddled with the disease of sloppiness': verdict of Lord Justice Sheen on the then Townsend-Thoresen car ferry company following the inquiry into the *Herald of Free Enterprise* disaster in March 1987 at Zeebrugge.
- 'The mechanics refused to fly in these planes': the Chief Executive of Vietnam Airlines, addressing a travel trade conference in Saigon, September 1994. He was referring to the company's inability to maintain its fleet of Soviet built Illushyn and Tupolev airliners in an airworthy condition, and comparing these very unfavourably with the Airbus and Fokker airliners with which the company was beginning to be re-equipped.
- 'Jupp Heynckes has been dismissed as coach of Real Madrid, because we have had a poor season': Lorenzo Sanz, President of Real Madrid Football Club, announcing Heynckes' dismissal at a press conference, June 1998. The Club had just won the European Champions' Cup for the first time for 37 years; it had also reached the Spanish Cup quarter-finals, and had finished fifth in the domestic championship.

---

way as any other material. When it became apparent that it caused skin disease and that the dust it produced was harmful to the lungs, protective clothing, including breathing protection, became obligatory. The best organisations went out and bought the correct equipment and insisted that their staff used it; when the equipment was improved, they went out and bought it again. Other organisations either phased the equipment in, or made it available to the staff to use if they wanted to, or simply rejected the evidence (see Example Box 4.13).

Means and ends

Crimes are not annulled by altruistic motives even though they may arouse human sympathy. For example, where a hungry person robs a rich person just to obtain food, a crime is still committed. Robin Hood was a robber, whether or not he gave the proceeds of his robberies to the poor. The sale of cocaine on the urban streets of Europe and North America is wrong, even if it provides the means of economic survival to the people of South America.

EXAMPLE BOX 4.12 Shift Patterns for Medical Staff in the NHS

In UK hospitals at the start of the twenty-first century, nursing and other medical staff are regularly required to work 12.5-hour shifts. These are either days (from 7.30 am to 8.00 pm) or nights (from 7.30 pm to 8.00 am). A full-time working week consists of three of these shifts. However, the following problems occur which cause hospitals and their managers to operate right on the cusp of the law.

- Rosters are drawn up for four-weekly or monthly periods, and this can result in some staff working four, five or even six long shifts in succession. While, from the point of view of expediency, this may be achievable in the short term, in the medium to long term, it is certain to result in staff exhaustion, stress and loss of effectiveness. No clear guidelines exist as to what constitutes 'best practice' when working in healthcare and medical situations. Hospital ward managers are therefore free to use the rostering process as they see fit.
- Some staff work their regular shift patterns in accordance with their contracted obligations, and then pick up extra shifts through nursing and medical employment agencies, for which they receive fees vastly in excess of pro rata salary payments.
- In many cases, those working 12.5-hour shifts receive a break of only 30 minutes per shift. The collective corporate attitude within the NHS to this is: 'Medical needs must come first; staff needs have to be subordinated to patient demands.'
- No clear standards for day and night working are stated, nor are any enforced by statute. It is therefore possible for staff to be rostered on for days and nights without any pattern or structure at all; this also is very damaging to individual health and welfare.

All of this breaks the spirit of the law, and the attitudes required of managers in general to the hours worked by their staff. However, the letter of the law is not being broken, provided that those with managerial responsibilities within the health service are able to invoke 'patient demand' and 'service demand' as their primary drive.

This applies to organisation practices also. If a manager dismisses an employee to make an example, and if the employee did not deserve dismissal, then a wrong act is committed even if it brings the remaining staff into line. If the organisation secures its long-term future by offering a bribe to a major customer to secure a contract, then a wrong act is committed. In each of these cases, in practice, the stated ends are very unlikely to be secured anyway because there is no integrity in the relationship. In the first case, the staff will look for other ways of falling out of line (but without risking further dismissals); in the second case, the corruption may come to light and the relationship be called into question or cancelled as the result.

EXAMPLE BOX 4.13 Health and Safety at Work

Health and safety at work is both a corporate and collective responsibility. This means not only that organisations and their managers must know, understand and be able to implement what is healthy and safe in their particular set of circumstances, but that the staff must also be trained in the right procedures, attitudes and behaviour. Staff may not be asked to work in unhealthy or unsafe manners, and may refuse to do so without fear of discipline or dismissal.

Organisational integrity is compromised, if not destroyed, when staff are bullied, coerced, cajoled or bribed into working in unhealthy and unsafe ways. This is also the effect when staff are asked to do something that is legitimate at the time but, with hindsight, becomes known or believed to have been unhealthy or unsafe. When this becomes apparent, organisations and their managers should put the matter right immediately, and pay compensation or offer staff support where damage has been done.

This was the case at Chatham Royal Naval Dockyards before it was closed down as a military base. Staff were employed to clean the nuclear reactors of submarines, without adequate protection from radiation. When research demonstrated that damage to individuals had indeed been done, the Ministry of Defence first resisted this on the grounds of ignorance, and subsequently on the grounds of Crown immunity (a statutory instrument that meant nobody could be prosecuted for breaches of health and safety regulations if they were acting in the name of the government). When the matter came to Court, both defences were rejected, and the principle of Crown immunity was lost for all but a very limited set of circumstances.

The radiation damage was done to staff over the period 1950–75. The case finally came to Court in 1995. Judgement was delivered in 1996. The managerial attitudes that prevailed at that time have since made it very much more difficult and expensive for the Ministry of Defence (and other government departments) to get private contractors to carry out work in such circumstances.

Organisations must recognise and resolve conflicts of interest. The first step lies in acknowledging the legitimacy and certainty of these. From this, steps can be taken to ensure a resolution that benefits the long-term future of all concerned. Conflicts of interest arise between individuals, and within and between departments and divisions. These may be based on general professional and expertise disagreements as to the best interests of the organisation (as well as matters of in-fighting and operational and personality clashes).

The ethical approach is bound up in an integrity and visibility of management style and working relationships, and the early recognition of operational, professional and personal problems. These are then addressed when they arise and before they are allowed to fester and become a part of organisation folklore. What is to happen as the result of these matters arising can then be transmitted early, and it can be demonstrated why this is in the best interests of the organisation (see Example Box 4.14).

EXAMPLE BOX 4.14 Good Ethics is Good Business

Although ethical conduct is not sufficient to assure business success, and business success is no guarantee of ethical conduct, distributive justice and ordinary common decency do typically enhance long-term owner value. They do so in many ways. Chief of these is obviating the difficulties of operating without them. Stakeholders who doubt the good faith of companies and organisations, or of their colleagues, are more likely to spend time in protecting their backs than in performing their functions. Time, resources and energy that could be spent more productively and rewardingly are consequently diverted to basic self-preservation with a direct opportunity cost to the business. Decent treatment, in contrast, permits and encourages stakeholders to get on with the job and to conduct business effectively and profitably.

The costs of disregarding ordinary decency and distributive justice are far-reaching. In a business characterised by lying, cheating and stealing, this illusion of low morale typically replaces initiative and enthusiasm; teamwork becomes difficult at best, and long-term commitments counter-productive. When exertions on behalf of a business are rejected or penalised, rather than encouraged and rewarded, they are unlikely to be repeated. Distributive justice and a modicum of decency are therefore essential for any business to operate. Without them, the best business is unlikely to attract the best people or their best efforts. But when these principles are respected, the business will normally be characterised not only by responsibility and integrity, but by maximum long-term owner value.

Source: E. Sternberg, *Just Business*, Warner, 1995.

Conclusions

The ethical approach is not altruistic or charitable, but rather a key concept of effective long-term organisational and business performance. The commitment to the staff is absolutely positive. This does not mean any guarantee of lifetime employment. It does mean recognising obligations and ensuring that staff, in turn, acknowledge their obligations. These obligations are to develop, participate and be involved; to be flexible, dynamic and responsive. The commitment of staff to organisation and organisation to staff is mutual. This also extends to problem areas – especially the handling of discipline, grievance and dismissal issues, and redundancy and redeployment – and the continuity of this commitment when these matters have to be addressed.

Organisations must structure decision-making processes in ways that consider the range and legitimacy of ethical pressures. This also means understanding where the greater good and the true interests of the organisation lie, and adopting realistic steps in the pursuit of this. An ethical assessment will consider the position of staff, the nature and interrelationship of activities, product and service ranges, mixes and balances, relationships with the community and the environment (see Figure 4.1).

Organisations are not families, friendly societies or clubs. By setting their own

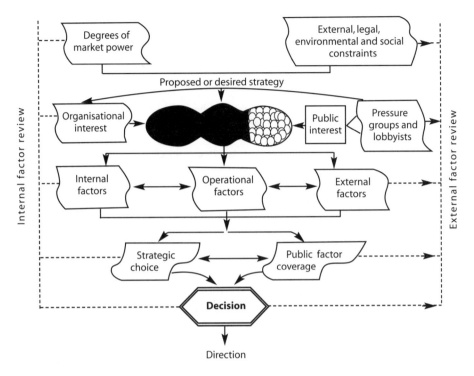

Decision-making model including ethical considerations

FIGURE 4.1

values and standards and relating these to long-term effectiveness they become distinctive. They are almost certain to be at variance from those that are, and would be, held by natural families and clubs. Problems that arise are clouded therefore, where the organisation does indeed perceive itself to be 'a big happy family'. Families are able to forgive prodigal children; organisations may not be able to afford to do so however, if they are to maintain long-term standards, or if substantial damage has been done to customer relations for example. Organisations exist to provide effective products and services for customers, while families and clubs exist to provide comfort, society and warmth. These elements are by-products, they are not the core.

Organisations are not obliged to provide employment at all except in so far as they need the work carrying out. They will select and hire people for this on the basis of capabilities and qualities. They have no obligation to take staff from the ranks of the unemployed (though they may choose to do so). They have no obligation to locate for all eternity in particular areas (though again they may choose to do so).

Organisations that pursue high ethical standards are not religious institutions, nor do they have any obligation to reflect any prevailing local traditions, values, customs, prejudices or, indeed, religion.

Japanese organisations setting up in the UK were, and remain, successful precisely because of this. Rather than trying to integrate their activities with the traditions of their locations they brought very distinctive and positive values with which people who came to work for them were required to identify.

Organisations must distinguish between right and wrong. Lying, cheating, stealing, bribery and corruption are always wrong and can never be ethically justified.

This has to be set in the context of the ways in which business is conducted in certain sectors and parts of the world. If a contract is only to be secured by offering a bribe, the relationship is corrupted and based on contempt. If and when prevailing views change, the total relationship between organisation and customer is likely to be called into question and any scandal or adverse publicity that emerges invariably affects confidence. It is in any case extremely stressful for individuals to have to work in this way or indeed to connive or conspire to any overt wrongdoing (though this may clearly be accommodated if the organisation institutionalises such matters, protects individuals who are caught or accepts responsibility for every outcome).

CHAPTER SUMMARY

The ethical approach to organisation and managerial activities is adult and assertive; it is not soft, religious or moral. It takes the view that continuous and long-term existence is the main duty of organisations to their staff, customers, suppliers, community and environment.

Above all, this requires a fundamental shift in corporate attitudes away from the short-term or expedient, from the instant approach to returns, from the needs of the influential figures, and from wasteful and inefficient budgeting control and production systems. These are to be replaced by active participation and involvement by all, in each of the areas indicated, in the pursuit of effectiveness and success. This requires placing a value on everyone with whom the organisation comes into contact – above all, staff, customers, backers, suppliers and communities. Organisations are only sustainable in the long term if adequate and continuous investment is made in technology, staff and staff development, research and development into new products and services, and in constantly improving and updating products, services, processes, systems and practices. This, in turn, is made most effective where everything is done with clearly stated aims, objectives, priorities, opportunities and consequences, and where these are understood, adopted and valued by everyone concerned.

There is a direct relationship between organisation success and organisational and managerial attitudes to the elements indicated in this chapter. High profile and notorious organisational failures – for example, BCCI and Maxwell – have demonstrated the consequences of this lack of basic integrity. The inefficiencies of some public services – for example, health, education and social services – arise from imposing short-term and expedient priorities on long-term, enduring and socially valuable services, priorities that chiefly arise through the dominant pressures of key players and political drives. Conversely, the results achieved by organisations that do adopt high absolute standards clearly indicate the levels of sustainable achievement possible, whatever the industrial, commercial or public sector considered.

DISCUSSION QUESTIONS

1. Under what circumstances, if any, may organisations legitimately be dishonest with their staff customers, markets, community and environment? What are the short-term and long-term benefits and consequences?
2. Outline the legitimate reasons for the existence of the armaments and tobacco industries. Of all their activities, which may be considered ethical, which may be considered unethical, and why?
3. Discuss the ethical implications surrounding the statement made by many organisations that: 'We are an equal opportunities employer'.
4. An individual is accused of theft. He vehemently denies the accusation. The organisation conducts an inquiry, and satisfies itself that he was indeed guilty. It dismisses him. The fairness of this dismissal is upheld at a subsequent employment tribunal hearing. Much later, it comes to light that the individual was indeed innocent. What action, if any, should the organisation take, and why?

CHAPTER CASE STUDY

SHANGRILA

The ShangriLa project envisages the construction of a hi-tech social, commercial and industrial community on a new site in southern India. The project has been devised by an American company, Catalytic Software, which has produced plans for a self-sustaining community of concrete domes that will house 4000 software engineers, as well as 300 sanitation, police, fire and other support personnel.

The chief employer in this new city will be Catalytic Software themselves. The company will supply contract software engineers for high-level technical projects around the world. They will also produce technology support systems, and industrial, commercial and leisure computer software.

The project is being driven by a directorate of three: Stefan Engstrom, Swain Porter and Christopher Phillips. The total cost is expected to reach £250 million. All aspects of the project – work, leisure and social – are to be housed within a series of giant domes. The site is to include multi-storey office domes, swimming pools, tennis courts, football and baseball pitches and an ice rink. As employees, members of the community will be entitled to live in shelters ranging from 800 to 2400 square feet in size. They will not be required to pay for their accommodation; they are to receive salaries competitive with these sorts of activities in the software and hi-tech consulting industries; they will also be entitled to share options in Catalytic Software.

The buildings have been designed to ensure that they are earthquake resistant, and this has gained especial currency in view of the disaster in north-west India in February 2001.

Building a techno-city in India is designed to save Catalytic Software from having to import workers to other sites, especially the United States. It is envisaged that the overall quality of life in ShangriLa may help the company retain job-hoppers. There are also broader social issues, which the company is determined to consider. On previous visits to India, Stefan Engstrom had witnessed barefoot women hammering rocks at construction and civil engineering sites. Catalytic Software are determined to change all this. Engstrom stated: 'We wouldn't feel good doing business in India if we didn't have a hand in raising the standard of living'.

QUESTIONS

1. Comment on the ethical approaches stated and implicit in the ShangriLa project. On balance, is the approach ethical and wholesome or not?
2. What other factors have to be in place in order to ensure the long-term success of this venture? From the material in this chapter, identify the key ethical considerations that have to be addressed; and the consequences should any of these fail.
3. What specific problems do you foresee for this project in the medium to long term?

5 The Organisation and its Environment

'We predict an inflation rate of no more than 5 per cent. We also predict an interest rate of no more than 5 per cent. It is therefore impossible that the Channel Tunnel will run over-budget.' UK Treasury Briefing Paper, 1986.

'The *Titanic* is unsinkable.' White Star Shipping Line press release, 1912, on the relationship between their flagship and its environment.

CHAPTER OUTLINE

Developing an understanding of the relationship between organisations and their environment

Identifying different forms and approaches of organisations to their environment, and the interactions between them

Decision-making processes and the context and limitations that affect them

Identifying the major environmental pressures and constraints within which organisations have to operate; and above all identifying those factors that can and cannot be controlled

Identifying the constraints placed on managers if they are to be able to operate effectively within the environment.

CHAPTER OBJECTIVES

After studying this chapter, you should be able to:

understand the main organisational and environmental pressures and constraints that have to be accommodated

identify specific organisational forms, and the particular constraints under which they have to operate

identify both opportunities and problems associated with decision making and organisational progression and development

understand the specific opportunities, consequences and pitfalls that are present in organisational and managerial attitudes and approaches to their environment – especially those relating to decision-making processes.

Introduction

Organisations are created on the basis that more can be achieved by people working in harmony and towards a stated purpose than by individuals acting alone. It is also more efficient and effective to specialise in seeking to serve or fulfil a given set of wants or needs. Resources – technology, expertise, information, finance and property – can then be commanded and ordered for the stated purpose. Activities can be determined, coordinated, directed and controlled.

The result of this is that society is more or less founded on a highly complex and all-pervading network of organisations, each of which serves a given purpose and all of which serve the entire range of purposes required. Organisations pervade all aspects of life – economic, social, political, cultural, religious, communal and family. They provide for needs – food, shelter, health, education, water, energy, transport and communications – as well as wants and choices such as cola, cinema or football. They serve these needs and wants from before the cradle, through every aspect of life until after the grave.

An organisation is any body that is constituted for such a given purpose, and which then establishes and conducts activities in pursuit of this. Managers are then employed to run them.

For those who work in them, organisations form a distinctive and significant of their part of society. Human beings generally need, want and enjoy the company of other people. Organisations fulfil social as well as technical, occupational and professional needs.

Also, those who interact with organisations – as customer, clients and suppliers – require a positive relationship based on satisfaction, expectation and value.

From this, it becomes apparent that there is a great complexity in the relationships between organisations, organisations and their place in the wider environment, among those who work within them, and between organisations and those who come to them for products and services.

This may be summarised as the range of relationships between organisations, people and the environment. It is now necessary to consider in more detail the factors and components that affect these relationships. These in turn form the basis of understanding the ways in which people behave in organisations and the creation of effective and successful behaviour in organisations.

Organisational considerations

Organisations may be considered from a variety of different points of view. These are:

- legal status and formal regulation
- primary beneficiaries for whom the organisation is especially important for some reason
- approach and attitude to staff
- psychological contract, or the nature and level of mutual commitment between organisation and staff.

Whichever view is taken, it is essential to recognise:

- the constraints under which organisations have to operate; especially legal, financial, social, traditional and technological
- corporate pressures, especially those imposed by financial backers, key figures and groups, and other influential stakeholders

- ethical pressures, including recognising and understanding the social, moral, religious and cultural traditions and pressures that exist in particular parts of society, industrial and commercial sectors, and locations.

Legal status

The main forms are as follows.

- **Sole trader:** in which an individual sets up as a going concern and provides his or her own resources. People who do this are entitled to receive any profits or surpluses accrued; and are also responsible in full for any losses.
- **Partnership:** in which two or more people establish themselves as a going concern as above.
- **Limited company:** in which the organisation is based on the private sale of shares which provides it with a financial and capital base. The company is given its own life and entity in this way; it receives any profits made and is responsible for making good any losses. The liability of shareholders for any losses is limited to the extent of their share ownership.
- **Plc or corporation:** as for a limited company, but shares are offered for sale to the general public on a recognised stock exchange.
- **Multinational or trans-national corporation:** able to locate and conduct activities anywhere that appears suitable; able to locate and produce corporate results in any country and currency that they deem fit.
- The project-and-finish companies established for specific purposes (TML, for example, was created by a consortium of five British and five French construction and civil engineering companies to build the Channel Tunnel).
- **Specialist subsidiary:** found increasingly, in both public service and commercial sectors, established to gain a foothold and reputation in specific areas of activity. For example, many construction and civil engineering companies are now establishing facilities management divisions in order to take advantage of opportunities in private finance initiatives and other government ventures.
- **Friendly or mutual society:** in which the benefits accrued by activities are distributed among members as agreed between them.
- **Cooperative:** usually constituted as a company or partnership in which everyone involved has a stake (financial, physical or psychological).
- **Public body/public corporation:** central, regional or local government organisation set up to provide essential public services and ensure adequate infrastructure, transport and communications for the society at large.
- **Non-governmental organisation:** autonomous entity funded by government grant and constituted for a particular purpose.
- **Charity:** funded by donations and other receipts for stated purposes; these funds are then distributed to the areas with which the charity is concerned. Charities must be registered with the charity commissioner in order to carry out activities in this way.
- **Church or other religious foundation.**
- **Social enterprise:** in which commercially viable activities are established in order to provide economic (and therefore social) regeneration for particular areas, sectors and groups within society (for example, The Prince's Trust, founded by the

Prince of Wales in 1986, whose primary purpose was to provide the means for those otherwise not able to do so, to establish their own commercially viable activities).

It is important to note that the legal status of organisations can, and does, change. This may be due, for example, to government privatisation, merger and take-over, withdrawal and divestment, change of activities or location, or changes in corporate and company law.

Primary beneficiaries

Primary beneficiaries are those people for whom the organisation is especially important or for whom it was constituted. A primary beneficiary approach requires organisations to be looked at as follows.

- **Business organisations:** where the primary beneficiaries are shareholders and staff, and where the benefits accrue from providing products and services required by customers and clients.
- **Utilities:** where the primary beneficiary is society at large. Utilities include gas, electricity, water, transport, post and telecommunications organisations.
- **Public service organisations:** where the primary beneficiaries are particular client groups drawn in because of their characteristics. Their functions include provision for the homeless destitute, elderly, disabled and handicapped (some of these roles are also carried out by charities).
- **Cooperatives:** where the primary beneficiaries are all those who work in them. Cooperatives coordinate their business from the point of view of this mutual commitment and identity.
- **Convenience organisations:** where the primary beneficiaries are those that avail themselves of the organisation's products and services on the basis of convenience. They includes village shops and amenities. A form of this is also to be found in those organisations that take a 'just-in-time' approach to the purchase of raw materials.
- **Institutions:** where the primary beneficiaries are those who avail themselves of the institution's services and facilities, or who are sent there (for whatever reason) by society. Examples include schools, colleges and prisons.
- **Mutual benefit associations:** where the primary beneficiaries are the members; they include trade unions, churches, political parties, clubs, friendly societies and cooperatives.
- **Service organisations:** where the primary beneficiaries are the clients who come to use services for stated reasons, or when they need them on particular occasions. Examples include hospitals and the fire service.
- **Bodies for the regulation of society:** constituted by government and given the means and wherewithal to act in the interests of members of the society. The main examples of these are the police, the judiciary and other arms of the law.
- **Bodies for the defence of society:** including civil and military defence, national banks (economic defence and protection), prison services.
- **Common general organisations:** where the primary beneficiaries are the general public. These include police services and education, health and social services (see Example Box 5.1).

EXAMPLE BOX 5.1 Primary and Other Beneficiaries

The primary beneficiary approach ought to indicate clearly the priorities and direction of the organisation, and the ends to which all resources should be concentrated. However, it is important to note the following.

- **Ultimate beneficiaries:** it is usual to define the ultimate beneficiaries as customers, clients, consumers and end-users of the particular organisation's products and services. This however, becomes lost in organisations and situations where there are other powerful, dominant – and therefore ultimate – interests. Political beneficiaries tend to disrupt the effectiveness of public services, in the interests of their own position and reputation. Short-term shareholder interests often disrupt the long-term effectiveness of commercially driven organisations.

- **Changing beneficiaries:** this becomes important when organisations change their status for whatever reason. For example, newly privatised public services have suddenly to operate under the financial regimes dictated by the new owners. Companies founded, developed and grown by individuals often lose their identities when they are floated on stock markets or sold on by the founder. Mergers and take-overs mean that staff and customers of the previous organisation have to get used to new ways in which they are to be dealt with, and the clarity of this may be lost as the new regime seeks to impose new directions and priorities.

- **Continuing beneficiaries:** this is overwhelmingly the staff interest. It is also essential to recognise the position and influence of a continued family presence through the generations following the foundation and development of an organisation by an individual (such as the Sieff family at Marks & Spencer, the Sainsbury family at Sainsbury's supermarkets), and long-term, established, and secure shareholder interests.

- **Non-beneficiaries:** this occurs where people do not receive the products and services that they expect from organisations in which they are overtly considered the primary beneficiaries. Of especial concern, at the beginning of the twenty-first century in the UK, are health, education, social and public transport services.

Approach to staff

Organisations may also be viewed from the standpoint from which they regard their staff. They may be viewed as:

- Unitary: in which the aims, objectives, hopes, fears, aspirations and ambitions of the individual must be harmonised and integrated with those of the organisation – and where necessary subordinated so that the overall purpose of the organisation remains the main driving force.
- Pluralist: in which the organisation recognises the divergent and often conflicting aims, objectives and drives of the people who work for it. Organisations that take

this view normally provide opportunities for personal and professional (as well as organisational) fulfilment. The basis is that by recognising this divergence and attending to all needs, organisation needs will be satisfied.

- **Radical:** in which it is recognised that there can be no long-term productive effort and harmony unless everyone involved is given a substantial and meaningful stake in the organisation. This used to be regarded as the Marxist approach, and has therefore fallen into some disrepute. However, many organisations take the view that by offering staff substantial shareholdings in the company for which they work, or substantial profit-sharing arrangements, they therefore engage the direct interest of the staff in their own future and economic prosperity. For example, John Lewis, the department store, divides 15 per cent of its retained profits between its staff; Semco assigns 23 per cent of its retained profits in the same way.
- **Mutual:** normally founded on the abolition of status and rank in favour of occupational and organisational effectiveness; however, this normally only works where there is full openness and availability of information, knowledge of activities and understanding of the value of every contribution.
- **Cooperative:** in which the organisation establishes a psychological and behavioural basis of partnership and involvement based on the value of the contribution that everyone is to make.
- **Confrontational:** an adversarial approach to staff. This is based at best on the recognition that harmony of objectives is impossible, leading to the creation of systems and processes for the containment and management of conflict. At worst it is based on mistrust and coercion, often stemming from a lack of genuine value placed on staff.

Psychological contract

Organisations may be viewed from the nature of the psychological contract that they engage in with their staff. This is the result of implications and expectations that arise as the result of given organisational, occupational, professional and personal relationships in specific situations. They vary between all organisations and situations, and may be summarised as follows.

- **Coercive:** whereby the relationship between organisation and staff, and also organisation and customer, is founded on a negative. An example of this is prison: the prisoners are there against their will. It is also present where sections of the community are forced or pressurised into using a monopoly or near-monopoly for an essential commodity or service; examples are electricity, telecommunications, petrol and fuel. It also can be present in institutions such as schools and colleges where the children or students attend because they are required to do so by the society.
- **Alienative:** whereby the relationship between staff and organisation is negative. This has traditionally applied to large and sophisticated organisations, and especially to those staff working on production lines and in administrative hierarchies where they have no or very little control over the quality and output of work.
- **Remunerative:** whereby the relationship between staff and organisation is clearly drawn in terms of money in return for effort and attendance. It is normally to be found as the dominant feature where there is also a low level of mutual identity between staff and organisation.

- **Calculative:** whereby the staff have a low commitment to organisation goals and high commitment to current levels of earning and satisfaction. This is again a key feature of the wage work bargain for production and administrative staff. For those with high levels of professional and technical expertise, the calculative relationship is based on the ability to practise, the need to find an employer and outlet for those skills, and individual drives to serve and become expert.
- **Normative:** whereby the individual commitment to organisational purpose is very high. This is found in religious organisations, political parties and trade unions. It is also increasingly found in some business organisations when a normative (i.e. committed quarrel) approach is taken to the wage–work bargain as well as the economic. It is effective as long as the wage–work bargain itself is sound and the organisation accepts a range of obligations and responsibilities to ensure that it is maintained.
- **Internalised:** whereby individual and collective commitment to organisation purpose, activities, attitudes and values is unquestioning.

Viewing organisations from a variety of positions in these ways indicates the background against which aims and objectives are to be drawn up. It also indicates the source of some of the limitations and constraints that have to be taken into account when considering the capabilities of organisations and the nature and relationship of these with the purposes that are to be pursued.

Management style

Each of these approaches – legal status, primary beneficiaries, psychological contract and approach to staff – indicates the ideal management style required for the particular situation. Problems arise with the suitability of management style where what is stated and what actually happens are out of synchronism. This also gives rise to conflicting and divergent aims and objectives, as those with managerial responsibility either seek to reconcile these divergences, or else prioritise some (often their own interests rather than those of the organisation) at the expense of others (see Figure 5.1).

Limitations

The limitations on both management style and organisation effectiveness begin where the context is not fully evaluated or understood. Further problems arise when the following are either dominant or not capable of being reconciled with overall purpose.

- The drive is for volume of work rather than quality or effectiveness. This is exacerbated where rewards are given for volume. This is satisfactory only as long as competitive position can be maintained on the basis of volume and as long as some level of profit is achieved. It is invariably unsatisfactory in the long term unless accompanied by drives for quality and effectiveness.
- Too little attention is paid to supposedly non-quantifiable aims and objectives, especially for managers, administrators and support functions. At its most positive this gives those categories of staff considerable latitude to exercise judgement, initiative, creativity and enthusiasm; this is the usual excuse cited by organisations that fail to address the problem of establishing effective aims and objectives for

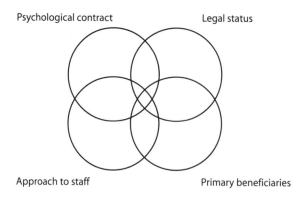

Psychological contract

Legal status

Approach to staff

Primary beneficiaries

Environmental pressures

FIGURE 5.1   The foundations of management style

these categories of staff. More usually however, it is a symptom of failure to structure and direct these activities in the organisation's best interests and harness the qualities indicated in this pursuit. The invariable result is that managers set and pursue their own agenda, achieving high rewards for themselves and minimum-to-satisfactory levels of success for the organisation.

- Displacement occurs where the work itself becomes the overriding aim. Attention becomes focused on length rather than effectiveness of attendance; volume rather than quality or purpose of work; day-to-day activities, clearing the in-tray and invariably the backlog; attention to immediate tasks and requests; attendance at meetings.
- Operational and political influence of interest groups increases at the expense of their productive output. This tends to put pressure on resources and stress on individuals and groups. Internal competition for resources becomes itself a resource-consuming process and an objective in itself.
- Adherence to, and operation of, procedures and rule books becomes a goal in itself. Focus is therefore placed on compliance and conformity rather than effectiveness.
- Goal conflict is not addressed or reconciled. Such conflicts often occur as the result of differing pressures and strains: for example, professional commitments, administrative requirements, production and maintenance, production and sales. They are compounded where more than two different elements are present.
- Compliance is not achieved. This is either because the required attitudes and standards are not recognised or valued, or because those working in the organisation place no value on the overall purpose and the work is not carried out in its pursuit.

Decision making

Whatever the size, nature or purpose of the organisation, and the management style adopted, effective decision-making processes are required. Decisions are taken at all levels: strategic and policy; operational, divisional and departmental; managerial and supervisory; and individual. Whatever the level, there are certain fundamental considerations to be considered if the process is to be effective and successful. There are also different stages that have to be understood and followed.

This is the context in which elements and process are considered as follows (see Figure 5.2).

Decision making, organisations and their environment

The key features are as follows:

Problem or issue definition

This is the starting point of the process. Once the issue is defined, the likely effects and consequences of particular courses of action can begin to be understood. Failure to do this may lead to considerable waste of time, effort and resource. This means establishing clear, achievable and acceptable objectives, and relating these to the full context (see Example Box 5.2).

Process determination

Much of this depends on culture, structure, and environmental and other pressures on the organisation or department involved. It also depends on ways of working and the

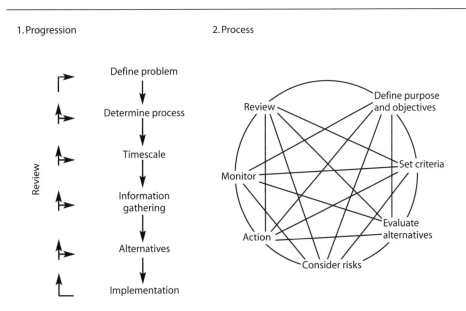

1. Progression   2. Process

Define problem → Determine process → Timescale → Information gathering → Alternatives → Implementation

Review

Define purpose and objectives · Set criteria · Evaluate alternatives · Consider risks · Action · Monitor · Review

Purpose: to draw the distinction between the two elements of progress and process. The former is a schematic approach; the latter is that form from which the former arises, and which refines it into its final format. Effective and successful decision making requires the confidence that is generated by continued operation of the process.

A decision-making model

FIGURE 5.2

EXAMPLE BOX 5.2 Management by Objectives

The concept of management by objectives grew out of the attention given by Drucker and others to the need for establishing means by which the success and failure of managerial performance could be measured. It also provided the means for focusing on results rather than activity, by translating corporate objectives into measures of individual, group and departmental performance. It concentrated on:

- Key tasks, key results, performance standards and area of activity. It also provided for control data, the availability and use of information against which task performance could be measured. These were established in both quantitative (measurable) and qualitative (not so easily measurable) areas.
- Work improvement plans, setting key tasks against action plans and target dates, again using control data to monitor performance.
- Regular performance reviews based on participation and agreement, concentrating on future directions as well as assessment of the present.
- Potential reviews and previews, based on concepts of career development and succession planning, concerned with the capability and likelihood of success in the next job (whatever that was to be). This included attention to training and development needs, as well as attention to performance outputs and requirements.

The main pitfalls and criticisms of the approach are as follows.

- It tends to cast activities in stone unless attention is also paid to the need for flexibility, dynamism, adaptability and responsiveness.
- It tends to assume a state of stability over the period; the process is easily disrupted in practice by changes in superior–subordinate relations, new work demands and priorities, operational constraints and crises, and changes in technology and work practices.
- It can be very bureaucratic and time-consuming to establish. This tends to reinforce the perception that once established, it is to be followed religiously because so much time and resource has been taken to set it up in the first place. People do not like to perceive that their time has been wasted.
- It focuses on objectives in ways that leave little room for judgement or initiative. It also does not address the key managerial issues of sympathy, empathy, identity and understanding of the broad context.

Tangibility

The tangible aspects of managing by objectives are as follows:

- market standing, reputation and position, sales performance
- innovation, enterprise, pioneering, research and development, general attention to the future
- productivity and output performance

Example Box 5.2 (continued)

- use of physical, human, premises, capital and other financial resources
- productivity, profitability and effectiveness.

Intangibility

The intangible aspects of managing by objectives are as follows:

- managerial performance and development
- worker performance and attitude
- public responsibility.

Attention is necessary in each area. While the balance will vary between organisations, neglect in any one area is likely to weaken the whole. It is also important to ensure that the organisation is not blinded by extremes of performance in one area to the detriment of the others. For example, excellent sales performance may lead to feelings of complacency and lack of attention to the need for new products when the current range becomes obsolete. Conversely, poor sales performance may be seen in isolation as a crisis; or, as long as the rest of the activities are considered to be fundamentally sound, this would lead to focusing managerial attention to bring this aspect of performance up to the standards of the rest.

---

personalities and groups involved. There may also be key groups – staff, customers, vested interests, pressure groups – who must be consulted on particular matters. Not to do this, in spite of the fact that the decision may be 'right', is likely to minimise or even nullify the whole effect (see Example Box 5.3).

Timescale

Time is involved heavily in process determination. There is also a trade off between the quality and volume of information that can be gathered and the time available to do this. The longer the timescale, the better the chance of gaining adequate information and evaluating it effectively. However, this also increases the cost of the eventual course of action. On the other hand, a quick decision may involve hidden extras at the implementation stage if insufficient time has been spent on the background (see Example Box 5.4).

Information gathering

Very few decisions are taken with perfect information; conversely, decisions made without any information are pure guesswork. Both quality and volume of information are required; means for understanding, evaluation and review of what is gathered are also essential.

EXAMPLE BOX 5.3 SPECTACLES Analysis

Cartwright (2001) takes a detailed approach to assessing the organisational, environmental and operational factors, features and constraints under which activities have to be conducted and decisions taken. He identified a ten-point approach under the acronym SPECTACLES as follows.

- **Social:** changes in society and societal trends; demographic trends and influences.
- **Political:** political processes and structures; lobbying; the political institutions of the UK and EU; the political pressures brought about as the result of, for example, the Social Charter or market regulation.
- **Economic:** referring especially to sources of finance; stock markets; inflation; interest rates; government and EU economic policy; local, regional, national and global economies.
- **Cultural:** international and national cultures; regional cultures; local cultures; organisational cultures; cultural clashes; culture changes; cultural pressures on business and organisational activities.
- **Technological:** understanding the technological needs of business; technological pressures; the relationship between technology and work patterns; the need to invest in technology; communications; e-commerce; technology and manufacturing; technology and bioengineering; technological potential.
- **Aesthetic:** communications; marketing and promotion; image; fashion; organisational body language; public relations.
- **Customer:** consumerism; the importance of analysing customer and client bases; customer needs and wants; customer care; anticipating future customer requirements; customer behaviour.
- **Legal:** sources of law; codes of practice; legal pressures; product liability; service liability; health and safety; employment law; competition legislation; European legal pressures; whistle blowing.
- **Environmental:** responsibilities to the planet; responsibilities to communities; pollution; waste management; farming activities; genetic engineering; cost benefit analyses; legal pressures.
- **Sectoral:** competition; cartels, monopolies and oligopolies; competitive forces; cooperation within sectors; differentiation; and segmentation.

Cartwright states that his intention is:

> to widen the scope of analysis that needs to be carried out in order to include a more detailed consideration of the environment and culture within which an organisation must operate, the customer base, competition within the sector, and the aesthetic implications, both physical and behavioural, of the organisation and its external operating environment.

This approach requires managers to take a detailed look at every aspect of their operations within their particular environment and niche. They need to understand

Example Box 5.3 (continued)

fully the broadest range of environmental constraints within which they have to conduct effective operations. The approach is also much more likely to raise specific, precise, detailed – and often uncomfortable – questions that many managers (especially senior managers) would rather not have to address.

Above all, the approach can be used by managers at any organisational level in order to make themselves think more deeply about all the issues and constraints present in their own particular domain, in order to be able to operate effectively.

Source: R. Cartwright, *Mastering the Business Environment*, Palgrave Masters, 2001.

EXAMPLE BOX 5.4 Timescales

Organisation and managerial time is viewed from a variety of points of view as follows.

- **Steady state:** the total time frame required in order to engage in, produce, deliver, develop and enhance activities.
- **Productive/non-productive balance:** the amount of time that is actually taken on productive activities; the amount of time that is taken on non-productive activities; the balance of this; and the reasons for this.
- **Maintenance time:** in which periods of equipment and technology maintenance are in-built to organisational activities.
- **Downtime:** in which activities are not taking place. It is again essential to establish the reasons for this.
- **Development time:** as a proportion or percentage of total time available to the organisation; and again, subject to continuous monitoring, review and evaluation.
- **The primary function/non-primary function balance:** in which organisations assess the volume of total time available to them, in terms of the amount of time spent on dealing with production, service and customer management activities; and the amount of time spent on administration and support.
- **Wasted time:** all organisations have this, and it is essential that this part of time management is assessed in order to understand the reasons for this, and where wastage can be reduced.

These act as a general discipline on the organisation and as specific performance constraints on groups and individuals. Timescales also have to be considered when specific decisions are being taken and implemented; whatever is considered must be capable of achievement and implementation in the time allowed.

The alternatives

The result of the process is that alternative courses of action become apparent. At the very least there is always the choice of doing nothing.

Implementation

This is the point of action. It arises as the result of working through each of the previous elements. The choice made affects future courses of action; the reasons for which it was made should be understood.

This is an attempt to provide a rationale for courses of action that often have to be taken in ways that are not fully logical. Part of the purpose is therefore to recognise where the non-rational elements lie and, in recognising these, how they can best be accommodated. It is not a prescription for providing perfect decisions. It is rather the means by which the opportunities and consequences of following particular courses of action may be understood, assessed and evaluated.

Other factors

Risk and uncertainty

Uncertainty occurs where no information exists. This in itself underlines the need to gain as much knowledge and understanding as possible, in advance of choosing a particular course of action. However, there is an element of risk in all decision taking. This is reduced by the quality and volume of information available, and the accuracy of its evaluation.

Participation and consultation

This is necessary where a wide measure of support from among the workforce, community or public at large is required. The purpose here is to generate understanding and acceptance of courses of action.

It may also be necessary to consider:

- legal constraints, affecting all aspects of business and organisation practice
- public interest, public pressure, lobby and special interest groups
- economic, social and political groups – including consumer groups, environmental lobbies, local and public authorities, public agencies and statutory bodies, industrial lobbies and staff representative bodies
- committees and other formally constituted boards.

Organisational adjustment

This is where the process is limited or constrained, based on each of the factors indicated. The normal result is that the organisation alters, adjusts or limits its activities in some way as the result. Sufficient time and resource must be set aside to deal with this adjustments, if what is proposed is to be supported and accepted.

Effective decisions are therefore arrived at through a combination of the preferred and chosen direction, together with recognising and accommodating a means by which this chosen direction can be made successful. Many of the consultation, participation, staff and public communication processes are directed at generating understanding and acceptance of particular courses of action. Organisations must accept that everyone is much more likely to follow a course of action if it is understood. If they do not understand what they are being asked to do, people tend either to reject the matter outright, or else view it with suspicion and uncertainty (see Example Box 5.5).

Problems are also caused when any of the following occur.

- Insufficient attention to the behavioural aspects of operations, above all in creating effective and suitable conditions and support systems as the basis for carrying out the work. This also includes insufficient attention to the need to motivate and value the staff engaged in it.
- Insufficient attention to the quantifiable performance requirements of management and to the establishment of proper aims and objectives in managerial, administrative and support functions.
- Prioritising short-term results at the expense of the long-term future together with the over-consumption of resources in this way. This normally occurs because the organisation can see easy results if it pursues the short term. It also occurs because of the need for triumphs on the part of a key figure or particular department.
- Artificial constraints and deadlines, driven by budget systems and reporting relationships, requiring energy and resources to be used in non-productive and often counter-productive activities, rather than as a check on continuous performance.

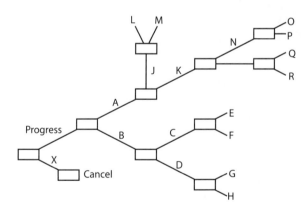

Purpose: to illustrate proposed courses of action, and likely and possible outcomes of them, from a given starting point.

In this particular example, option X – Cancel – is evidently not on the agenda, as the consequences of this are not extrapolated.

What are illustrated are the ramifications that accrue once the decision is taken to progress; and assuming two positive choices (i.e. other than cancellation) at each stage.

The tree is a useful illumination of the complexity and implications of the process, and of the reality of taking one decision.

The decision tree

FIGURE 5.3

EXAMPLE BOX 5.5 Satisficing

Many of these limitations were first identified by H.A. Simon (1967) as parts of the process of achieving satisfactory performance, or satisficing. Simon identified three levels of performance:

- **Excellent:** high achievement, output, and quality, leading to high levels of profit effectiveness and satisfaction. This was in reality achieved by very few.
- **Unsatisfactory:** low and unacceptable achievement, output, quality and volume, leading to losses, inefficiency, ineffectiveness and dissatisfaction. This would be remedied by training, development (disciplinary activities where necessary) and greater management focus on acceptable performance.
- **Satisfactory:** achieved by most and producing acceptable levels of output, volume and quality, and leading to steady, acceptable – and therefore satisfactory – levels of profit and effectiveness. In practice he found this was an acceptable and likely state of organisation performance. It included attention to volume rather than quality of work, and allowed the freedom of managers to set their own agenda as long as organisation objectives were met at least partly. It recognised that organisations would tend not to try and measure the overtly unquantifiable. Satisfactory performance was apparent where the organisation continued to exist for a long period of time.

Simon coined the word 'satisficing' to explain this. It is defined as 'the ability to achieve satisfactory performance'. This also influenced decision-making processes; managers would tend to take decisions based on the ability to achieve some measure of satisfaction rather than seeking high levels of performance which were not always achievable (especially where the latter had high attendant risks or requirements for increases in commitment that could not always be made).

Source: H. A. Simon, *Organisations and Performance*, McGraw Hill, 1967.

- Establishment of priorities for reasons other than performance effectiveness and especially for reasons of publicity, kudos, status and the demands of key figures for their own purposes (see Example Box 5.6).
- Setting unreasonable deadlines for the achievement of particular objectives.
- Casting plans, aims and objectives as 'tablets of stone'; once they are written they are never to be changed or modified.
- Failure to recognise that which cannot be controlled, and which may nevertheless have great effects on organisational activities. This includes changes in customer demands and expectations, legislative changes, the activities of competitors, loss of sources of supply, change in relationships with distributors and so on.
- Complacency, often based on a long history of success, continuity and achievement in the past, which tends to lead to feelings of infallibility and immortality. This leads to loss of commitment to purpose, loss of focus and of what constitutes truly effective performance.

EXAMPLE BOX 5.6 Influences on Priorities and Deadlines

- **Computers and information technology:** in the interests of having a quick, accessible and comprehensive database for the UK tax system, the Inland Revenue purchased an off-the-shelf package from an American company. This subsequently had to be discarded because it was not compatible with the demands of the UK tax system, nor were the specific operational features familiar to UK staff or compatible with existing approaches to computer and information technology training.
- **The Millennium Dome:** this was created as a monument to 2000 years of civilisation since the birth of Christ. It was established in the London Borough of Greenwich. It quickly became apparent that visitor access would be limited by transport and infrastructure problems, and that for this reason alone, the stated visitor target of 35 000 per day would not be achievable. This was driven by a governmental and political need for a monument. It quickly became apparent that this would be a monument to short-term political expediency and triumphalism. At the point of conception, guarantees were given by both the government of the day, and its successor, that it would at least break even. When it closed on 1 January 2001, it had lost £770 million.

In contrast:

- **Virgin:** the above examples should be contrasted with the approach adopted by Richard Branson when he determined to establish a Virgin airline. Knowing nothing about airlines, he surrounded himself with expertise in this field drawn from all over the world. He analysed the operating environment thoroughly. He understood the pressures– economic, social, legal and competitive – under which he would have to operate if he were to be successful. Above all, the view was adopted that in order to be successful, long-term continuing levels of investment were required, and that this could only be fully and effectively realised if the environment were fully understood, and the constraints within which operations would have to take place accepted.

- Attention to means rather than ends, and the confusion of hard work with productive work. Sheer volume of work therefore becomes the measure of performance rather than the purpose for which it is being conducted.

Systems

A system is a collection of interrelated parts and components that form a whole. Typical organisation systems are production, communication and electronic data systems. Systems may first be defined as either closed or open.

Closed

Closed systems are those that are self-contained and self-sufficient, and do not require other interactions to make them work. There are very few systems that are genuinely closed. Some domestic central heating systems are more or less closed. In these cases the components are assembled. The system is switched on and must operate continuously or else break down. Even in these cases the systems are dependent upon being fed a constant supply of energy to ensure continuity of operation. They are also dependent upon maintenance, both to prevent breakdowns and to make repairs when faults occur.

Open

Open systems are those that require constant interaction with their environment to make them work (see Figure 5.4).

Systems may also be:

- **Formal:** devised and developed by the organisation with specific purposes in mind and with the view that effective operations are dependent upon those that are put in place.
- **Informal:** devised by individuals and groups to facilitate their own place and well-being in the organisation and to fill those gaps left by the formal approach.
- **Networks:** the combination of the formal with the informal; networks are normally based on human interaction and information exchange (and sometimes information hoarding and trading). Their purpose is both to support the operations of the organisation and to ensure the continuity and stability of the position of individuals and groups.

Organisation systems may now be shown as in Figure 5.5. They convert human activity, energy, information resources and components of raw materials into products and services, usable information, by-products and waste.

Main systems

Main systems are those devised to ensure that the organisation can pursue its core purposes successfully. They are normally the production service and information systems essential to well-being and success. They may be largely:

- human or social, where achievement of the core purpose depends greatly on interactions between people
- technological, where achievement of the core purpose depends greatly on the output of large volumes of items
- socio-technical, in which the interaction between the two is critical.

In practice, a mix of the social and technical invariably occurs. The system itself therefore consists of the combination of technical and social components, as shown in Figure 5.6.

Inputs (External)	Process The system	Outputs
Expertise Supplies Components Resources Energy Demands ⟶	Technology Expertise Energy ⟶	Products Services Waste Exhaust ⟶

The characteristics are:

- The need to provide inputs and energy to make sure that the process – the system– is able to operate. Inputs and energy come from elsewhere in the environment
- The discharge of outputs – production waste and energy residue and exhaust – into the environment.
- The operation of the system itself as the conversion process.

An open system

FIGURE 5.4

Support systems

Support systems are devised in the same way in order to harmonise and order the rest of the work, to ensure that the prime activities are provided with the resources and sub-activities necessary to remain effective.

Maintenance systems

These are devised in order to prevent failures and blockages occurring and to put these right where they do happen. Maintenance systems require attention to both social and technical aspects. A part of organisation and individual development is concerned with maintaining the human resource. This includes attention to morale and commitment, as well as skills, knowledge and expertise.

Technological maintenance consists of regular servicing of equipment, depreciation

Input	Process	Output
Raw materials Energy Expertise Components Information Demand Ideas Invention ⟶	Technology Applied expertise Applied information Coordination Planning Control Supervision ⟶	Finished goods Services Waste Exhaust By products Niches Expertise development Potential opportunities ⟶

Organisation systems

FIGURE 5.5

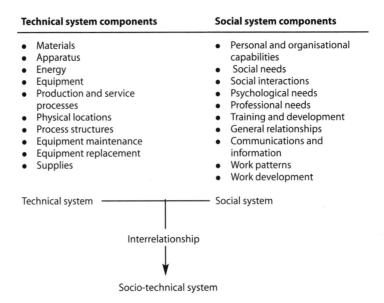

Technical system components	Social system components
• Materials	• Personal and organisational
• Apparatus	capabilities
• Energy	• Social needs
• Equipment	• Social interactions
• Production and service	• Psychological needs
processes	• Professional needs
• Physical locations	• Training and development
• Process structures	• General relationships
• Equipment maintenance	• Communications and
• Equipment replacement	information
• Supplies	• Work patterns
	• Work development

Technical system ———————— Social system

Interrelationship

Socio-technical system

FIGURE 5.6 Socio-technical systems

and replacement. It also includes the purchasing and introduction of new hardware and software – and the training and development of staff so that it can be used effectively.

Systems for the handling of customer complaints are also forms of maintenance and should have the purpose of putting things right and maintaining standards, and of making a general contribution to the development of the effectiveness of work.

Crisis systems

These are devised and put in place on the basis that they are seldom to be used but nevertheless when they are required they can be speedily energised. Emergency systems are clear examples of this. So also are systems for the handling of operational input and distribution breakdowns and hiatuses, and in these cases will normally consist of hot-line arrangements for emergency supplies, activities and distribution.

In this context, the specific concerns of systems are:

• production and service outputs and the management of operations and projects
• research and development, innovation and concern with the future
• maintenance functions
• attention to resource management matters and activities, including culture formation and development
• marketing, public relations and other activities concerned with building images and giving impressions of quality and confidence
• sales and distribution: the delivery of products and services to market
• purchasing and supply: ensuring regularity and required volume of inputs
• resource gathering, organisation and prioritising

- the means of conflict resolution, containment and management
- communication and information.

For all systems to operate effectively the following characteristics must be present.

- **Energy:** required to give the systems life, make them work and continue.
- **Returns:** part of the returns on output will be used to ensure the fresh flow of inputs into the processes.
- **Steadiness and stability:** most systems work best to a steady flow of work rather than having to accommodate peaks and troughs; if peaks, pressures and over-pressure do occur, steps should be taken to recognise these and establish the reasons for them; where possible remedial and modifying action should be taken.
- **Balance:** of input, process and output to ensure a steady flow of work and the avoidance of blockages and bottlenecks.
- **Flexibility and adaptability:** concerned with the ability to respond effectively to changes in the environment, markets, perceptions and tastes; and to structure the work so that speedy responses can be made when necessary.
- **Coordination and control characteristics:** to ensure that as far as possible steadiness and balance are maintained and to take remedial action where peaks and troughs start to become apparent; also to ensure the maximisation and optimisation of resources at each stage.
- **Equifinality:** the concept that similar outputs can be achieved from a variety of systems and processes; that there is no one right way of doing things; that there are many different routes to the same destination; that no one's system, process or approach will be right in all situations.

Managerial systems

At their best, these start with the performance of others. They are created to provide a process for evaluation of performance, organisation adaptation, coordination of activities and taking decisions.

- **Evaluation of performance:** the actual performance of the system will be evaluated through constant monitoring and review, and the results achieved analysed to show why success has been achieved, and where and why any failures have occurred. This will also indicate general areas for attention, capabilities for improvements and progress; it will include establishing the reasons for success so that these may be built on for the future in other areas.
- **Adaptation and change:** this is concerned with the future of the organisation, the development of structures, attitudes, values, skills, knowledge and expertise for the purpose of achieving aims and objectives and planning for longer term strategies and directions.
- **Coordination and control:** this is the harmonisation process, the ordering of the disparate and divergent elements, conflict resolution, balancing and ordering of priorities and resources.
- **Decision making:** this is attention to the processes by which effective decisions are made and the elements that contribute to this.

For effective performance in each of the processes to take place, a systematic approach is required. This is to ensure that sufficient attention is paid to all aspects, and examination of each area takes place on the basis of depth and breadth of knowledge, so that in turn a full basis of judgement, analysis and assessment is achieved and ensured.

Conclusions

As no organisation exists in isolation from its environment, the nature and extent of the relationship and interactions must be considered. Organisations are subject to a variety of economic, legal, social and ethical pressures which they must be capable of accommodating if they are to operate effectively. In some cases, there are strong religious and cultural effects, and local traditions that the organisations must also harmonise with effectively. More specifically, organisations need access to workforces, suppliers, distributors, customers and clients; and to technology, equipment and financial resources (see Figure 5.7).

Relationships between organisations and their environment may be simply summarised as:

* Environment domination: especially overwhelming legal, social and ethical pressures and also those that relate to any strong local histories and traditions.

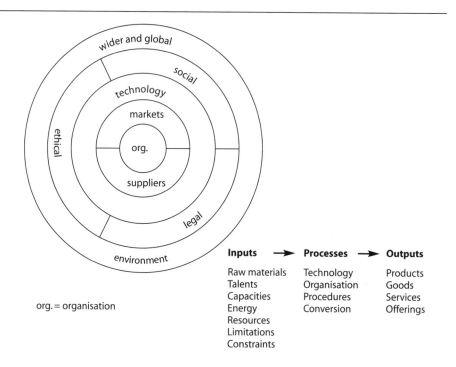

Inputs	→	Processes	→	Outputs
Raw materials		Technology		Products
Talents		Organisation		Goods
Capacities		Procedures		Services
Energy		Conversion		Offerings
Resources				
Limitations				
Constraints				

org. = organisation

FIGURE 5.7 Archetype model of the organsation in its environment

Source: D. Katz and R. L. Kahn, *The Social Psychology of Organisations*, Wiley, 1978.

- Organisation domination: where the environment is dependent on the organisation for the provision of work, good and services.

This must then be seen in the context that the best organisation–environment relationships are generated where measures of general responsibility are attached to each. If the environmental pressures are too great, or somehow otherwise unacceptable to the organisation, it will eventually relocate elsewhere. If the organisation takes an expedient or cavalier view of its involvement in the particular area, it will be rejected by those who live there. The picture is further complicated by the fact that all organisations interact with other organisations that are also part of their own environment, and they influence these and are influenced by them.

There is therefore a range of capabilities by which the organisation influences its environment and vice versa. A framework may then be put around this as follows.

- Those factors that can be controlled and those that cannot. The latter normally include global and international interactions, other political factors, the actions of government – and the effects that these bring to economic and social activities.
- Those areas where the organisation has greatest influence in the relationship and those where the environment has greatest influence.
- Those areas that lead to greatest cooperation between the two and those that tend to cause conflict.
- The degree of certainty and permanence of the relationship between the two, and the ways in which this is to be nurtured and maintained in order to ensure continuity and permanence.
- The degree of interdependence between the two, or the extent to which one is dependent on the other.
- The degree of stability and turbulence that exists in the environment, and the ways in which this affects organisations.
- The degree of sensitivity of the environment to the actions of organisations and vice versa.
- The nature and mixture of these and their relevant importance will clearly vary between organisations and their environments and between organisations in the same location; much of this is dependent upon the nature of the work carried out by particular organisations and the pressures and priorities of the environment.
- The overall attitude that the organisation adopts to its environment; and vice versa.
- Specific attitudes taken about specific issues: the wider role of the organisation in its community; attitudes to pollution; attitudes to employment practice.
- The view taken by organisations and their managers of what constitutes corporate social responsibility. This again requires considering both the operational and broader environment from the point of view of legal requirements and social expectations, as well as adopting a responsible, ethical and enlightened attitude to the full context.

Moreover, the environment has to be seen from a variety of points of view. It is likely to be a combination of markets, infrastructure, locations, activities, social and political pressures (and vested interests and pressure groups). This in turn varies according to context. For example, an environment may be Warwickshire, mining, Indonesia, the

Pacific Rim, Southern Africa, the south east, the computer sector, London, Oxford Street. It may be the health service, the school system, share shops, town centres. Each has its own validity and influence at different times. Organisations may further describe a variety of different environments with which they interact for varying reasons; the term 'catchment area' will mean different things dependent upon whether they are currently considering staff, supplies, customers, distributors, or backers and bankers.

Above all, the environment is overwhelmingly competitive. At different times organisations compete for staff, customers and resources. Competition may take a range of forms.

- **Overt:** the choice between two or more similar items at the same price, two or more similar items at different prices, or different items. The choice is made by organisations whether to hire one individual in preference to others to fill a particular post; the choice of an individual to take up one post and not others also constitutes a form of competition.
- **Covert:** choosing a particular item, job or activity because of feelings of well-being that the individual expects to accrue from owning it; the rejection of an item, job or activity because its possession is not valued; making choices as means to ends rather than as the end in itself.
- **Opportunity cost:** choosing one item, activity or job means that others on offer cannot be bought, taken up or fulfilled.
- **Rational:** buying something or doing something because there is 'a logical reason'. For example, buying a Picasso painting for £2 at a market stall knowing that it can be sold for £30 000 is logical in economic terms; taking up a job with a bank knowing that it will lead to the opportunity to work overseas also indicates a line of logical reasoning.
- **Irrational:** doing something for 'illogical reasons', such as buying a suit knowing that it is never going to be worn.
- **Socialised:** doing or buying something because of strong social pressures: becoming an army officer because that is what everyone else in the family/peer group has done, or working to particular standards because of the need for acceptance by the peer group rather than economic maximisation.
- **Something and nothing:** there is moreover, always the choice to reject. This is where for example, individuals turn down 'the perfect job', 'the perfect holiday' or 'the perfect car' on their own grounds, whims, 'reasons' and prejudices.
- **Demands:** organisations make demands on their environments and vice versa. These may be summarised as:
  - Organisational demands: for workforce, resources, access, transportation and distribution; education, training and development; primary resources – gas, electricity, water, telecommunications and fuel; there are demands for customers and clients; demands for confidence and continuity of relationship; and for security, health and maintenance services.
  - Environmental demands: for work or money to be spent elsewhere in the community; access, support and sponsorship for schools, clubs and other local institutions; demands for honesty and openness; for good relationships, for confidence, for continuity. The environment expects also that organisations will take care and trouble with the disposal of waste and with other aspects of

pollution such as noise and lighting. The environment expects relationships with organisations to be positive and beneficial.

There is therefore, a very broad and complex picture to be understood. Only if this is achieved however, can successful and effective organisations be designed and produced, and systems devised that enable them to interact efficiently and effectively with their environment.

CHAPTER SUMMARY

It is clearly essential that organisations, and their managers, understand the environmental pressures and constraints under which they have to operate. It is also clear that this is an extremely complex process, requiring time, energy, resources and commitment. Because of this, this aspect of managerial understanding is often not considered at all, or else not attended to in full. The position is further complicated when this part of management expertise is summarised as follows.

- There is clearly no best way to organise; as the environment changes so systems, aims and objectives must be flexible and responsive.

- The environment changes in both predictable and unpredictable ways; it changes in ways that can be controlled and influenced and in ways that cannot be controlled or influenced. The key for managers lies in the extent of their understanding of their environment and in their ability to anticipate the unexpected by building systems that are capable of accommodating these pressures.

- Because of the nature of the relationship with the environment, organisations need to spend time on external issues, assessing and understanding the environment, and the changes and turbulence within it. ⟩ *d·s*

- Decision-making processes have to be both structured and effective within the context and environment in which they are undertaken. No decision can be taken in isolation from either internal or external pressures.

- Each input–process–output cycle changes the nature of the organisation's social and technical resources, presenting an opportunity to strive for optimisation and improvement.

- Above all, the environment is dynamic, not static or rigid, allowing for limitless opportunities for change to occur. Thus investment in environmental adaptation and transformation is as essential to success as investments in capital, equipment and staffing. The more complex and turbulent the environment, the more essential this form of investment becomes.

- Environmental, technological, market and competitive pressures, as well as social changes, are the primary causes and inspiration for organisational improvement, development, enhancement and change.

- Social, legal and ethical constraints constitute the main limitations placed on the activities of organisations. They require specific approaches to be adopted to all aspects of activities in order to meet standards prescribed by law or laid down by the prevailing values and morals of society.

The purpose of this chapter has been to summarise and indicate the various forms of organisation, the different points of view from which they may be considered, and the wider context in which they operate. No organisation operates in isolation from, or without reference to, its environment. The environment provides staff, customers, resources, technology and equipment, and also confidence and expectations: the context in which successful and effective activities take place.

DISCUSSION QUESTIONS

For a city hospital, waste disposal organisation, airport, mass production car factory, internet-only bookseller:

1. Summarise the environment pressures and constraints that are imposed and have to be accommodated.
2. Identify the timescale pressures that are present in each case. What are the implications for managers in these organisations?
3. What steps should each of these organisations take to create, maintain and improve harmonious relationships with their community and environment? What specific problems may the managers of these organisations need to address?
4. To what extent does each of these organisations dominate its environment, and to what extent is each dominated by its environment?
5. Who are the ideal and likely primary beneficiaries of each? What specific pressures does this produce for managers in these organisations?

CHAPTER CASE STUDY

BURROUGHS-WELLCOME AND AZT

The prevalence of the HIV virus, and its increase throughout the world, has generated intense and highly pressurised activities among pharmaceutical companies to find an immunisation vaccine or other treatment for those who have contracted the virus, and in whom this has developed to full-blown AIDS.

Burroughs-Wellcome produced AZT in response to this during the 1980s. Huge levels of investment were generated, and initial results among users of the drug were encouraging in spite of the fact that it had serious side effects, including severe diarrhoea, dehydration, weight loss and skin rashes.

The drive to get it onto the market came from the usual areas of need to get returns on investment. There were also overwhelming social, political and community drives. Moreover, from the point of view of the industry, the company that could demonstrate itself the first to produce a vaccine or cure for this infection would generate a sustained long-term market advantage. Burroughs-Wellcome was besieged by patients' groups and AIDS and HIV charities, and subjected to a sustained period of media and vested interest group lobbying.

This was reinforced by the promotional culture and aspects of the healthcare industry. Promotional activities in healthcare, drug and pharmaceutical sectors are all-pervasive. They range from notepads and pens issued by drugs and medical equipment companies, to the medical equipment itself. Anything provided by the companies carries logo, brand

and other distinctive identity marks. This is all provided in hospitals, clinics and doctors surgeries. According to Eric Clarke (1988):

> Doctors are subject to the most intense sales promotions and pressures in the community. As much as 25 per cent of the sales effort may be spent on promotions. In the United Kingdom, each doctor is the target for over £5 000 worth of promotion a year... which falls better into place when another is added – the £58 000 worth of drugs that the average British GP prescribes each year.

AZT was promoted in exactly this way, and quickly gained a huge general familiarity as a supposed landmark in the fight against a disease that was – and remains – incurable. This was reinforced by extensive media coverage of drug trials, in which those with both the HIV virus and full-blown AIDS clamoured to take part.

Trials of the drug went on for an initial period of five years, and for a subsequent period of a further three. Then, in 2000, the results of the trials were finally published. The conclusions were as follows.

- There was no difference in the timescales in which the HIV virus developed into full-blown AIDS, whether the patient took AZT or not.
- It was more likely that the general state of health and well-being of patients who took AZT would be worse than those who did not, because of the severe side effects.

QUESTIONS

1. What were the effects of the environmental pressures on Burroughs-Wellcome to produce a cure for HIV/AIDS? Why do you think these pressures arose? What should the company have done to manage them?
2. On the basis of the information given, what was the company's absolute corporate responsibility in this situation? How should this have been managed?
3. What lessons are there to be learned by all organisations from this example?

Part II
Strategy, policy, direction and activities

6 Strategy, Policy and Direction

'What are we going to do Sir?' 'Why, soldier, we are going to advance and win the war. That is what we are going to do.' R.C. Sheriff, *Journey's End*, on the First World War military deadlock of 1916.

'I've always worked terribly hard.' Anita Roddick, founder, Body Shop.

'Unless you are motivated with determination to succeed, you will not be able to go past obstacles. When passion and desire become so strong as to rise out of the body like steam, and when the condensation of that which evaporated occurs and drops back like raindrops, problems will be solved.' Kazuo Inamori, quoted in Peter Senge, *The Fifth Discipline*, Century Business, 1990.

CHAPTER OUTLINE

Business policy and strategy

Sources and development of strategy

Internal and external factors

Core and peripheral activities

Strategic approaches: cost, focus, differentiation, withdrawal, acquisition, pioneering, incremental

Strategic analyses: SWOT, PEST, Five Forces, customers, competitors.

CHAPTER OBJECTIVES

At the end of this chapter, you should be able to:

understand the overall conception of organisational business and public service strategy, policy and direction

understand the opportunities and consequences that accrue as the result of pursuing particular directions and initiatives

understand the importance of relating desired and required directions and activities to what is possible in the context and environment

understand strategy, policy and direction as part of the process of securing long-term organisational viability.

Introduction

The overall purpose of strategy is to guide and direct the inception, growth and change of organisations as they conduct their activities (see Example Box 6.1). The purpose of this chapter is an introduction to the essentials of corporate policy and strategy; the form that it takes in different types of companies; the variations in strategy between companies, public services and other sectors; the issues involved in devising policy and strategy; and the development, implementation and evaluation of policy and strategy.

A clearly articulated, accurate and well-understood strategy is at the hub of all successful commercial and public activities; where success is not forthcoming it is often where this clarity of purpose is also not present. Specifically the need for strategy is based upon the overall requirement to manage resources effectively and efficiently. This process has been intensified by requirements for greater accountability in both public and private sectors. There is also a growing realisation among those responsible for directing organisations that these resources must be coordinated and controlled towards agreed policy objectives. Organisations need to plan ahead in order to ensure that they understand their required direction and are working towards it. Employees also need to know the purpose to which their efforts are being directed.

The development of strategy, policy and direction

Corporate strategy is based upon a series and pattern of decisions that determine the organisation's aims, objectives and goals; produce the plans and policies required to ensure that these are achieved; define the business in which the organisation is to operate; and establish how it intends to conduct this business and what its relations with its markets, customers, staff, stakeholders and environment will be (see Example Box 6.2).

Operational policies are based on the choices made within the overall strategic view. They are based upon a continuous appraisal of current and potential markets and spheres of activity; the ability to acquire, mobilise and harmonise resources for

---

EXAMPLE BOX 6.1 What Strategy Is Not

The aim of all industrial, commercial and public service sector organisational strategies, policies, purposes and directions should be:

> long-term existence in a competitive and turbulent world.

Anything that does not contribute to this should not be contemplated. Strategy therefore is not:

- a product of focus groups, contemplating what would happen in a hypothetical or imperfectly modelled set of circumstances
- a statement of blandness or general intention that binds nobody to anything
- an avoidance of real issues: failure to match opportunities with resources; ignoring the consequences of particular choices; concentrating on one group of stakeholders at the expense of others
- about prestige, triumphalism, vanity or image, except where these factors can also be translated into successful, profitable and enduring activities.

EXAMPLE BOX 6.2 The Internet Revolution

The inability to attract, retain and serve customers on an enduringly commercial basis is a fundamental, invariably fatal, weakness of the vast majority of internet companies at present. Overwhelmingly, the vast amounts of capital drawn into internet company start-ups were driven by:

- fashionability and faddishness, based on extensive media coverage and public relations activity surrounding what was perceived to be 'a new generation' of entrepreneurs
- the perceived technological supremacy of the internet
- environmental pull, in which those who were known, believed or perceived not to be at 'the cutting edge' of technology were deemed to be obsolete or boring
- failure to consider the customer, consumer, client or end-user aspect in any detail
- lack of analysis of how the levels of investment made in internet organisations were to generate returns, or where and when these would arrive.

The problem was also compounded by the attitude adopted by many of the new venturers and entrepreneurs when their companies ceased to trade. One virtual shoe retailer stated: 'It was a lovely place to work, and we still can't think of anything we have done wrong'.

Another, a virtual cookery and recipe production company stated: 'We assumed that further investment funds would be forthcoming, on exactly the same basis as they had been before'.

the attainment of the given aims, objectives and goals; and the actual means of conduct, including philosophical and ethical standpoints and the meeting of wider social expectations (see Example Box 6.3).

The focusing and determination of corporate strategy, policy and objectives is a process designed to ensure that the organisation knows: why it exists; its strengths and weaknesses; its position in its markets or service sectors is; what it can do and what it should do; what it cannot and should not do; and what its structure and style are to be in order to be an effective and profitable operator in its sector.

To do this, the following require accurate assessment:

- the level of finance and capital required in order for the operation to be established and maintained successfully
- the levels of income and profit that the organisation needs and wishes to make
- the structure of the organisation that is appropriate for those operations to be carried out
- the management style that is to be adopted and the style of leadership, direction and supervision
- the priorities that are to be placed on each of the operations; the markets and sectors in which business is to be conducted.

EXAMPLE BOX 6.3 The Rise of Social Entrepreneuring

Social entrepreneuring arose out of the high levels of unemployment that came about in the UK as the result of the collapse of traditional primary and heavy engineering industries in the 1970s and 1980s. The concept was adopted by the Prince of Wales, in which he sought to make a real contribution to the quality of life of those to whom this would not otherwise be available. He generated funds and business support, using his royal social position.

The success of projects generated and supported by The Prince's Trust caused others to pay attention, though the total economic output, as a percentage of gross domestic product, remains small. However, substantial contributions have been made to communities that have been encouraged to take responsibility for their own economic well-being, and to relate this to the social, ethical, cultural and traditional elements with which they are surrounded. Initiatives supported by the singer Bob Geldof, and the sportsmen Duncan Goodhew and Geoff Thompson, have led to substantial regeneration of small parts of south-east and north-east London. Elsewhere, similar activities have been generated in seeking to turn parts of south Wales, the south-west of England, and central Scotland into tourist attractions, using the previous historical heritage as the base.

- the timescales involved, especially where these are long-term, and therefore difficult to predict (see Example Box 6.4).

Figure 6.1 models the sources and development of organisation strategy. Figure 6.2 shows the stages in the strategic planning process.

Internal strategies and policies

Effective and successful organisation strategy is dependent upon supportive and complementary internal policies as follows.

- **Financial, investment, budgeting and resourcing** strategies, concerned with both the underwriting and stability of the organisation, and also the maintenance of its daily activities.
- **Human resource** strategies designed to match the workforce and its capabilities with the operational requirements of the organisation. Related policies must ensure the supply of labour, effective labour relations, and the maintenance and development of the resource overall.
- **Marketing** strategies, designed to ensure that the organisation's products and services are presented in ways that give them the best possible impact and prospects of success on the chosen markets.
- **Capital resource and equipment** strategies, to ensure the continued ability to produce the required value and quality of output to the standards required by the markets. It will also be necessary to replace and update these resources in a

EXAMPLE BOX 6.4 Strategic Development and Timescales

The long-term nature of strategic development, essential to the overriding aim of long-term viability and existence, is in direct conflict with financial and other stakeholder drives for short-term, indeed immediate, financial results and advantages. The problem has nevertheless to be addressed. For example:

- **The UK Berlin Embassy:** this project was conceived in 1997 and designed by Richard Rogers, the top UK architect, and was to be built under a public–private partnership. The government required a 37-year lease on the Embassy building before the commercial value of the activity could be fully realised. It was impossible to find a UK (or for that matter a European) building contractor to accept this length of term. Consequently, the project was built by Nomura, a Japanese construction and finance giant, because it was the only company prepared to adopt the extreme long-term view required.

- **The airline industry:** it was not until the 1930s, a generation after the first manned flight took place, that anyone was able to produce a sustainable, commercially profitable airline operating on a regular schedule of routes. The concept of flight as a means of mass travel took 35 years to develop into something that was commercially viable (there is a lesson here for those currently involved in internet and other high-tech start-up activities).

- **Mergers and take-overs:** when organisations are taken over by others, there is normally an instant financial advantage to shareholders and other backers. For those concerned with strategy development and long-term business activities, there are additional pressures to get results out of the newly acquired 'asset', and these are very often not realisable in the immediate future.

planned and ordered fashion (that includes research and development, and commissioning of new products and offerings).

- **Communication and information** strategies, both for the organisation's staff and its customers/clients, designed to disseminate the right quantity and quality of information in ways acceptable to all.
- **Organisation, maintenance, development and change** strategies, for the purpose of ensuring that a dynamic and proactive environment is fostered, along with a flexible and responsive workforce, and an environment of continuous improvement and innovation.
- **Ethical factors** including establishing overall standards of attitude and behaviour; absolute standards in dealings with customers, suppliers and the community; specific approaches to the environment; corporate citizenship; the nature and quality of leadership.
- **Subjective elements** reflecting collective and individual preferences and priorities. One must also acknowledge matters of expediency and organisational politics, including the need for triumphs, and the pursuit of individual whims and fancies.

Core and peripheral activities

Core activities

Core activities reflect primary purpose and may be assessed in terms of:

- **volume of activity:** what most people do, or where most resources are tied up
- **profit and income:** where most of the money comes from
- **image and identity:** that which gives the organisation its position, status and prominence in the sphere in which it operates.

Peripheral activities

These are the other activities in which the undertaking gets involved. They must not be at the expense of the main or core activities, nor should they be a drain on

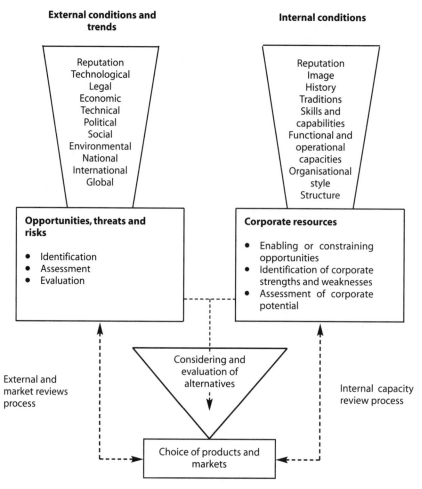

External conditions and trends

Reputation
Technological
Legal
Economic
Technical
Political
Social
Environmental
National
International
Global

Internal conditions

Reputation
Image
History
Traditions
Skills and capabilities
Functional and operational capacities
Organisational style
Structure

Opportunities, threats and risks

- Identification
- Assessment
- Evaluation

Corporate resources

- Enabling or constraining opportunities
- Identification of corporate strengths and weaknesses
- Assessment of corporate potential

Considering and evaluation of alternatives

External and market reviews process

Internal capacity review process

Choice of products and markets

FIGURE 6.1   Source and development of organisation strategy

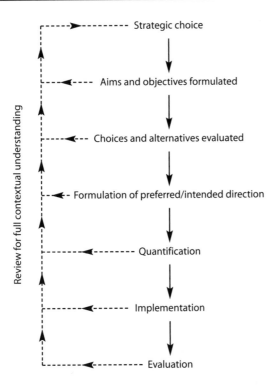

Purpose: the translation of strategy into direction and activity. Full contextual understanding requires the following.

- The **true nature** of the product or service, the functions that it serves, could or should serve; how it could be adopted, adapted, extended or improved.
- The organisation's main **strengths** and **weaknesses**, whether there are any overriding or dominant strengths or weaknesses; and what the main strengths and weaknesses of the organisation's competitors are
- The **demands** of the customer group for the sectors that are to be served
- The **opportunities** and **threats** that exist; the risks and uncertainties that can be identified; and the scope there is for improving the position of the organisation in its markets.

Consideration will able be given to other wider factors – social, economic, political, technological and ethical – that need, or may need, to be taken into account; and the extent to which the organisation is at mercy of factors that it cannot control.

The planning process

FIGURE 6.2

resources. Rather they should enhance the core activities, or reflect niche or segment opportunities that exist as the result of the core business. Such activities may nevertheless be essential, expected and extremely profitable. A hospital is not 'in business' to sell food, sweets, newspapers, books, cards, fruit or flowers; nevertheless it is essential for a variety of operational and social reasons that these activities be undertaken. Similarly, a car company will invariably make additional parts for the replacement, service and spares sectors; these simply require some form of repackaging or 'differentiation' to generate additional business, in an obvious and profitable area of activity.

Risk

The purpose of identifying and studying the components of risk and uncertainty from a strategic point of view is to ensure that anyone in a managerial or executive position understands the full range of issues that must be considered for any situation in the devising and implementation of strategy, and in the management of operations, if they are to stand the best possible chance of success, and minimise the chances of failure (see Example Box 6.5).

In straightforward and familiar situations this will be a simple process and easily carried out. Otherwise, it requires a full recognition and assessment of a variety of factors.

1. **Sectoral trends:** whether growing or declining, either in size or prosperity; whether this is likely to continue; factors affecting this at present, likely to affect it in the future, and that could possible or remotely affect it.
2. **Substitutes:** what else people could buy or do as an alternative to their current set of activities; what else they might buy or sell or make; where else they might locate.
3. **Social, political and economic issues:** major drives and restraints. This also includes ethical and environmental considerations and attention to fundamental values and standards.
4. **Strategic aspects:** relative to the organisation's position in its sector; its preferred direction; its size; its ability to dominate or take control of its niches; the balance of its proactive, steady-state, responsive, and crisis activities.
5. **Operational aspects:** in relation to precise goals and objectives, especially over the short and medium term, and balancing proactive, steady-state, responsive, and crisis activities (see Example Box 6.6).
6. **The constitution of the organisation:** its directorate, executive and management. The style and attitude and capability of these, and the extent to which they are stable or changing, or open to reform or take-over, must also be taken into account. This is especially true at present of civil, health and public utilities and services in the UK, which are increasingly subject to privatisation and a profit motive, as well as service delivery.
7. Identification of the **critical requirements of success** of the operation: this is truly dependent upon the executive capabilities of the managers and directors involved in projects. Above all, this part of the process requires a full consideration of the questions: 'What can possibly go wrong?' and 'What is the single most important factor for success?' (See Example Box 6.7.)
8. A **monitoring and evaluating and projection process** that covers the following:
   * identification of the best, medium and worst outcomes
   * analysis of any critical path or critical incident
   * ability to extricate oneself from the situation (or not) and the consequences of this
   * assessment of the full range of cost and benefits.
9. Factors **outside the control** of the organisation and its managers.
10. **Behavioural and perceptual issues:** the extent of these in the organisation; their nature; and their influence on strategy and operations.
11. **Early warning systems:** based on collective, individual, management and staff awareness of changes in the environment, markets, customer and consumer behaviour, and the lifecycle of products and services.

EXAMPLE BOX 6.5 Strategies for Failure

While it is impossible to predict with absolute accuracy where success and failure are likely to occur – especially if a rigorous approach is not taken – it is possible to indicate likely causes of failure. The usual ways of expressing this are as follows.

- **Increased price/standard value:** risks loss of market share, especially where lower price, undifferentiated alternatives are available to the same quality and value.
- **High and increasing prices/low value:** this is unlikely to be sustainable in the long term in anything but a monopoly situation. Where perceived quality and value for money are not forthcoming from organisations, customers and clients will change from using them if they have any choice in the matter at all.
- **Low value/standard price:** in these cases, customers and clients perceive that they are over-paying for a reduced or basic level of benefits and satisfaction. Especially where there is no cost advantage possible, organisations finding themselves in this position are at immediate risk from either others who improve quality and value levels, or from those that reduce prices in order to reflect existing levels of quality and value.

A strategic approach that is based on any of these is sustainable only so long as there is a relatively captive medium- to long-term customer and client base. For example, petrol retailing manages to secure medium- to long-term advantages under the heading of 'increased price standard value' simply because their product is such a fundamental commodity of the present state of civilisation. Some privatised health and social care organisations are able to sustain themselves under 'increased price/low value' and 'low value/standard price' because of the political drive to place clients of these organisations, and because the activities are underwritten to some extent by government policy and willingness to pay. Nevertheless, there will certainly be serious disadvantages if there is ever a political drive to improve the quality and value aspects.

In recent years, as the result of the internet revolution, a further indicator of likely failure has become apparent.

- **Standard price/low convenience:** in which customers and clients are required to search for products and services on the internet. Even assuming that the correct company website can be found, problems are often compounded by the fact that while this is technologically brilliant, it is customer and end-user unfriendly. It is also increasingly apparent, at least in commercial-consumer transactions, that it is essential that the virtual presence is reinforced by help lines or, increasingly, access to a physical presence alongside.

Source: G. F. Johnson and K. Scholes, *Exploring Corporate Strategy*, Pearson, 1999.

Within this broad managerial frame, quantitative, statistical and mathematical approaches may be used to project likely results and possible outcomes. These approaches include:

- accounts, profit and loss modelling to assess commercial and cost liabilities; cost apportionment; minimum income levels
- statistical modelling, to assess probability and likelihood; averages, frequency and mid-point; standard distribution; the critical path of a given project; time factors; space usage
- the inclusion of given variables to project changes in circumstances; changes in possible outcomes; and to address the effects of these variables on other components
- market size and product/service usage projections to infer initial and long-term demand and income.

This is then considered by managers, executives and experts in the light of the real situation in which they must operate. All of this will therefore, in turn, be limited or influenced by the following:

- workforce capacity and potential
- technological capacity and potential
- market capacity and potential
- deadlines

EXAMPLE BOX 6.6 Sandals Weddings

Sandals, the top of the range tour operator, operates a luxury wedding service for those wishing to get married in an exotic location.
  The nature and level of resources required are as follows:

- availability of wedding clothes in a variety of fashions, shapes and sizes, to suit all tastes, for hire or purchase
- availability of all of the 'component features' including clergy, registrars, wedding cakes, canapés, champagne and other drinks, iced water, tea and coffee
- capability among staff to combine and present these at the required time, in the mixes required by customers and clients
- attitudes among staff, based on the understanding that this is the most special day in the life of the couples involved
- the ability to create an environment of harmony, respect, peace and quality
- the availability of support services, especially photographers and video equipment.

All of this has then to be combined in such a way that the day remains special for the customers involved, whether the weather is good or bad, hot or cold, wet or dry. This also has to be achieved so that the couples involved have their own special day, without detracting from the requirements and expectations of those other customers staying at the particular resort.

EXAMPLE BOX 6.7 The Generally Favourable Response

The 'generally favourable response' is based on an assumption that because people have a general understanding or liking for something, they will therefore buy and use it. A useful illustration of the ways this is arrived at is as follows.

- Potential customers, clients and end-users may say that they like a particular product or service, and that they would use it, but are then not asked how often they will use it, nor how much they would be willing to pay for it and under what set of circumstances.
- Business projections and forecasts are accepted as a statement of truth rather than possibility by directors, divisional chiefs, and other senior managers.
- General interest is assumed to translate into specific customer and client activity.

This last is another key contributor to the failure of many consumer-based internet companies. The internet has generated a vast amount of general interest. Internet companies measure the effectiveness of their website in terms of the number of hits or visits. This is the virtual equivalent of window-shopping only, yet it was mistaken for genuine commercial interest and potential during the dot.com start-up boom of 1998–2000.

- particular ways of working
- where executive power, authority and influence lie
- key characters
- local factors and political and institutional aspects
- particular strengths, weaknesses, opportunities and threats
- aspects of difficulty, value, frequency, importance and presentation
- the decision-making process
- culture, values and ethics
- the balancing and accommodation of all these.

The end result is thus that an accurate or informed assessment of the risks involved in any activity or proposal is produced in advance. This does not mean that risks are not taken, but rather that an informed judgement has been made before going ahead. If this is done, a truer range of outcomes can be assessed; more accurate contingency plans can be drawn up; and any future matters arising from the issues in hand can be proposed from a position of relative strength and certainty.

Strategic approaches

Both business and public policy and strategy must have the following components.

- **Performance targets:** in whatever terms these are to be measured (e.g. income, volume or quality, but set against measurable, understandable and achievable targets).

- **Deadlines that are achievable:** these will have been worked out in advance, and represent a balance between commitment, resources and contingencies.
- **Contingencies** built in, to cover the unlikely, and the emergency.
- Consideration of the **long-term effectiveness** of the organisation.
- Consideration of the organisation's **products and services** in terms of value and quality, and utility to customers, clients, consumers and end-users.

Generic strategies: M.E. Porter

Porter (1981, 1985) identifies three generic positions from which all effective and profitable activities arise.

- **Cost leadership:** the drive to be the lowest cost operator in the field. This confers the absolute ability to compete on price where necessary. Where this is not necessary, higher levels of profit are achieved both in absolute terms and in relation to competitors. To be a cost leader, investment is required in 'state of the art' production technology and high quality staff. Cost leadership organisations are lean form, with small hierarchies, large spans of control, operative autonomy, simple procedures, and excellent salaries and terms and conditions of employment.
- **Focus:** concentrating on a niche and taking steps to be indispensable. The purpose is to establish a long-term and concentrated business relationship with distinctive customers, based on product confidence, high levels of quality, utter reliability and the ability to produce and deliver the necessary volumes of product to customers when required. Investment is necessary in product technology and staff expertise. It is necessary to understand the nature of the market and its perceptions and expectations. It is also necessary to recognise the duration of the market, where developments are likely to come from, and the extent to which requirements can continue to be satisfied.
- **Differentiation:** offering homogeneous products on the basis of creating a strong image or identity, as outlined earlier. Investment is required in marketing; advertising; brand development, strength and loyalty; and outlets and distribution. Returns are generated over the medium to long term as the result of cost awareness, identity, loyalty and repeat purchase.

Porter argues that the common factor in all successful strategies is clarity and that this stems from adopting **one** of these positions. Organisations that fail to do this do not necessarily fail themselves; they do however fail to maximise and optimise resources. They lay themselves open to loss of competitive position from those who do have this clarity. They tend towards a proliferation of management systems and processes that dilute effective efforts.

Outcomes

Outcomes should be pre-evaluated in terms of the following (see Figure 6.3).

- **Best:** what is the greatest level of success that we can possibly gain by following this course of action?

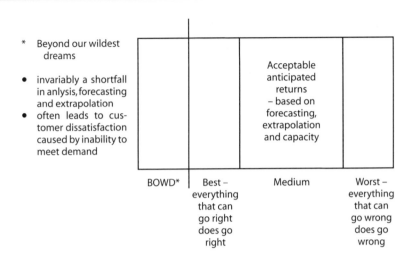

* Beyond our wildest
  dreams

• invariably a shortfall
  in anlysis, forecasting
  and extrapolation

• often leads to cus-
  tomer dissatisfaction
  caused by inability to
  meet demand

Acceptable
anticipated
returns
– based on
forecasting,
extrapolation
and capacity

BOWD* | Best –
everything
that can
go right
does go
right

Medium

Worst –
everything
that can
go wrong
does go
wrong

Pre-evaluation of strategy, policy and direction   *FIGURE 6.3*

• **Worst:** what is the worst level of failure that can be achieved (if that is the right word) if everything that can go wrong does go wrong?

• **In between:** a range of outcomes under the general heading of 'medium' or 'acceptable'.

In particular, the level of bare acceptability of the outcome of a particular strategy should be assessed at the stage of devising strategy.

Outcomes should be extrapolated from each of these positions to try to envisage the next stage of the organisation's activities and the wider implications for the short, medium and long term.

Within this context, the main approaches are now to be considered in turn.

Growth strategies

Growth is measured against preset objectives, whether in terms of income, profit margins, shareholder value, reputation enhancement, income per customer, income per location, income per product, market share, sales volume or new products and services. Required, expected or anticipated measures of growth, and the reasons and timescales for these, must be stated in advance. How such strategies are to be supported, financed and resourced, and the implications of this, must also be clearly stated and understood. The staff concerned must know this, and how it affects them.

Acquisitions, mergers and take-overs: are all variations on the theme of growth. Again, these approaches must be against preset objectives, and with an overall view to enhancing the profitability and/or quality of the business (see Example Box 6.8). In support of this, developments may serve to introduce the organisation into new geographical areas, to increase the sectoral position; the process may also help to defend and protect the organisation's own position.

EXAMPLE BOX 6.8 Acquisitions: Sony and Matsushita

In 1989 the Sony Corporation paid $3.4 billion for Columbia Pictures, a Hollywood TV and film studio. In 1990, Matsushita paid $6.1 billion for MCA, the American music, video and entertainment company.

The lessons to be drawn in both cases stem from an assessment of the strengths and direction of the organisation in question. In general, any growth, diversification or acquisition strategy will be based upon an estimation of what the new business will bring to the existing one and how this will strengthen both the overall portfolio and its operational capacities.

Thus the rationale behind each was that they had expertise and capabilities in electrical and electronic technology that could usefully and profitably be translated into the new spheres, and that there would be returns on the amounts paid measurable in commercial terms. The acquisitions would also lead to new market opportunities in the USA and in the entertainment sectors, and would give each of the companies a further foothold and reputation in the West.

Both decisions were criticised at the time as being acquisitions for their own sake, pushed on by the desire of the company's ownership to gain a stake in a glamorous and high-profile industry, and by companies that had more cash than they knew what to do with. There was also perceived to be a competitive element between the two organisations, and especially their chairmen (Akio Morita of Sony and Konosuke Matsushita of Matsushita).

The flaws both in this particular example and in the wider consideration of mergers and acquisitions have subsequently been extensively researched. Reports published by the London Chamber of Commerce and Industry (1998) and the American Management Association (2001) strongly support the view that almost 90 per cent of mergers and acquisitions lead to increased costs, declining performance in the short and medium term, and extensive staff and customer uncertainty, dissatisfaction and stress. This is because mergers and acquisitions are almost exclusively driven by a short-term dominant stakeholder interest, or reasons of prestige and triumph, rather than in order to secure long-term commercial or public service advantage.

Such activities may also include the acquisition of suppliers and distributors and sources of raw materials; this is known as 'vertical integration'.

They may additionally represent niche opportunities, the ability to get into new and profitable market sectors, or a chance to purchase the client list, resource or base of a competitor or parallel operator.

Retrenchment

This entails the withdrawal from niche or peripheral activities, or the sale of assets, in order to concentrate on the core activity. It need not have negative connotations; for example an organisation may sell off its lorry fleet, and lease lorries, at the time of credit squeezes and high interest rates. On the other hand, where there are negative connotations, effective retrenchment will have the overall purpose of protecting the core business and the certain markets (in so far as there are any), at the expense of the niches in which the organisation has been operating.

Retrenchment activities in public services are very often the cause of operational crisis, because there has to be every attempt to maintain the level of service against a declining budget provision.

Diversification

This is where organisations take the conscious decision to move into new markets and activities, very often in spite of the fact that they have no particular expertise in the new chosen field. Expertise in the new field, and the assimilation of its modus operandi, must he acquired by the organisation, if it is to be successful.

In practice, most effective and successful diversification strategies follow the vertical integration patterns, moving into new sectors that are clearly indicated by the current core business. For example, the Murdoch organisation moved into satellite television; it had no particular expertise in television or satellite technology but, looked at from a different standpoint, was a major player in mass media and communications. Consider also Example Box 6.9.

Price leadership

The organisation in this case sets out to gain the position of being the market player with the lowest prices, and to ensure that everyone who purchases from the organisation knows this. This will not be entirely at the expense of quality; products and services still have to be good enough to attract people to buy them in the first place.

Some price leadership activities are spectacularly successful, such as the sale of petrol by British and European supermarket chains, but the concept is most widely developed as 'loss leadership', rather than as price leadership. Supermarkets in Europe and North America do adopt 'pile it high, sell it cheap' strategies, and 'do-it-yourself' chains will generally have some products at good prices for the consumer, but these are generally limited to certain products. The IKEA furniture chain, however, is making attempts at present to expand across the countries of the EU, on the premise and image that all its prices are low, and represent better value than the indigenous competition.

Branding strategies

Branding strategies concentrate on using a combination of marketing, operational, technological and professional activities in order to fix an instant perception of the company product or service in question in the mind of customers or clients (and also the community at large) as soon as they see the brand name. A strategic approach to branding usually considers one or more of the following points of view.

- **Global branding:** of which the prime examples are McDonald's and Coca Cola, whereby a set of core business drives – in McDonald's case, quality, value, cleanliness and convenience – are presented in ways that will generate the maximum response from locations anywhere in the world.

EXAMPLE BOX 6.9 The Virgin Group

The move by the Virgin Group into the business of airline operation, financial services and railways from music, video and record distribution was spectacularly successful. However, it required extensive research, projections, expertise acquisition, and market understanding on the part of what was hitherto essentially a chain of shops. There were certain assets perceived by the group, of which it could take advantage as it moved into other areas: a large customer base, strong UK image, reputation for quality, and public confidence. In practice, however, these were qualities that had to be refashioned by the new airline for itself. Moreover, any failure on the part of the new venture would have had serious consequences for continuing and future confidence in the rest of the group's activities.

The Virgin Group's approach to involvement in new ventures is based on the following premises.

- The proposed new sector of activities is already well established and served by other providers.
- The service provided by other organisations falls short in some way, especially perceived customer satisfaction.
- There must be commercial and profitable potential for engagement in 'the Virgin way'.
- There must be potential for developing the sector using the existing Virgin customer base.
- There must be a sense of fun and adventure.

Provided that any proposal meets at least four of these points, the company will consider it seriously.

- **National:** in which particular marketing strategies are devised to generate the required responses among particular nations of the world.
- **Organisational:** in which the organisation seeks to attach organisational values to any line of business or activity into which it chooses to go. For example, Virgin attaches a single name – its own – to its airline, music, bridalwear, publishing, and high-tech activities; Heinz attaches a single name to its food products, whether they are for babies, children or adults, and whether they are standard, good value, healthy option or high value. Supermarkets also offer extensive ranges of their own brand products, though with very few exceptions they sell these alongside other branded goods thus offering the maximum range of consumer choice.
- **Organisational diversity:** in which organisations adopt different brand names according to different product lines and/or different markets served. For example, Sony offers high-quality, high-value, premium-price ranges of electrical goods under its own name; in order to serve medium-quality, medium-value, medium-price ranges it has devised the name AIWA for its products. Similarly, Matsushita offers commercial electrical goods under its own name, and consumer electrical goods under the name Panasonic.

- **Local:** in which smaller organisations seek to gain a local presence and reputation through being corporate citizens, model employers, or high-quality, high-value servants of local markets.

Market domination

Strategies aimed at market domination normally adopt and adapt components from each of the above to ensure a dominant position. Domination may be by sales volume, assets, derived income, largest number of outlets, or outlets in the most places (or a combination of these). It may also arise as the result of being the majority supplier (holding more than 50 per cent of the market); or the largest single player, though with less than 50 per cent; or one of an oligopoly of operators (in some countries and sectors, this may be organised into a cartel, though in many others this is illegal).

In practice, it is rare to find massive majority dominators of sectors, though British Airways handles about 40 per cent of internal British air traffic by passenger volume. This has declined from 70 per cent in 1996, and to offset the increased competition on specific routes from low priced operators, the company created its own subsidiary, Go (which it has subsequently sold on in order to concentrate on what it now perceives as its core business: medium- and long-haul international travel). Otherwise domination in this way is limited to gas, electricity, water, telecommunications, and public road and rail transport. Oligopolies may be found in media, newspaper, oil and car companies among others.

Incremental strategies

The view of strategy as being incremental is popular with those who argue for a rational approach to long-term business and public service sustenance. The reasoning is that a genuine long-term strategy is actually impossible to achieve given the sophisticated structure of organisations, and the turbulence and instability of markets and sector activities, without paying constant attention to direction and purpose. A successful approach to long-term viability has therefore to be seen as being constantly influenced by changing environmental, social, political and economic circumstances.

The starting point for future strategies is therefore the position of the organisation today. From this, the organisation moves forwards in small steps or increments. As each of these steps is successful, the next becomes apparent. If a mistake is made, it is easy to retrace the step and seek other directions from the previous position. The status quo, and present levels of performance, are both taken as correct. If costs are reduced or if profits have gone up in relation to last year, this is a good general measure of performance. If costs have risen or profit has declined in relation to the previous period, this becomes a cause for concern.

Opportunities arise from the fact that the organisation is moving slowly enough to recognise and evaluate those situations that present themselves before rushing in headlong, or rejecting measures out of hand.

Measurement and evaluation

Measurement and evaluation are carried out against pre-set aims and objectives. These must be quantifiable wherever possible. Areas of particular success or shortfall then become easily apparent. This in turn contributes to the organisation's expertise in the field, and ensures further improvement in strategic development and planning processes.

Beyond this, evaluation is both a continuous process and the subject of more formalised regular reviews at required and appropriate intervals, thus setting a framework against which the strategy is to be judged.

The following can then be assessed:

- To what extent is the strategy **identifiable** and clearly understood by all concerned, in specific and positive terms? To what extent is it unique and specifically designed for its given purpose?
- Is it **consistent** with the organisation's capabilities, resources and aspirations, and with the aspirations of those who work in it?
- What levels of **risk** and **uncertainty** are being undertaken, in relation to the opportunities identified?
- What **contribution** is the proposed strategy to make to the organisation as a whole over the long term?
- What will be the market **responses** and **responsiveness**, and what will be the effects of market captivity or choice?
- What will be the effects – **positive and adverse** – of dominant stakeholders, driving and restraining forces, and product, service and project champions?

These questions can be answered as part of both the continuous evaluation and the regular review process.

Implementation of strategy

The determination of strategy is therefore a combination of the identification of the opportunities and risks afforded by the environment; the capabilities, actual and potential, of the organisation, its leaders and top management; and issues of ethical and social responsibility. Turning this into reality requires that the following are addressed.

- **Key tasks** must be established and prioritised, effective decision-making processes drawn up, and systems for monitoring and evaluation of strategic process devised.
- **Work and workforce** must be divided and structured into a combination of functional and hierarchical aspects, designed to ensure the effective completion of the tasks in hand; this must include relevant and necessary committee, project co-ordination, working party, and steering group activities (see Figure 6.4).
- **Information** and other management systems must be designed and installed; control and constraint systems must be a part of this, to include financial, human resource, production, output and sales reporting data.
- Tasks and actions to be carried out must be **scheduled** and **prioritised** in such a way as to be achieved to given deadlines. As well as establishing a background for precise work methods and ways of working, scheduling provides the basis for setting standards against which short- and medium-term performance can be measured.
- The **required technology** must be made available, and staff trained to use it.
- **Maintenance** and **repair** schedules must be agreed and integrated with other activities.

- **Research** and **development**, improvement and enhancement schedules must be incorporated with the rest of activities. This includes making financial, techno-logical and staff resources available as a key part of organisation product and service development.
- **Monitoring, review** and **evaluation mechanisms** and **procedures** must be estab-lished, to attend to hard aspects of market responses, sales figures and product and service usage; and soft aspects of meeting customer, client, consumer and end-user satisfaction and expectations.
- The **measurement** of **actual performance** against forecasted, projected or budgeted activities must be arranged.
- **Staff management** and **human resource** polices must be assessed for: effectiveness and quality; the extent and prevalence of conflict, communication blockages, dis-putes and grievances; the effectiveness of pay and reward systems; the application of rulebooks and specific procedures.
- **Financial returns** must be assessed in line with projections and forecasts. A key feature of strategy implementation is the ability to compare overall returns, costs of sales, product and service delivery, with projections; and to gauge the effects of unforeseen circumstances on particular activities.

Each of these aspects provides a critical element for effective monitoring, review and evaluation activities (see Figure 6.5).

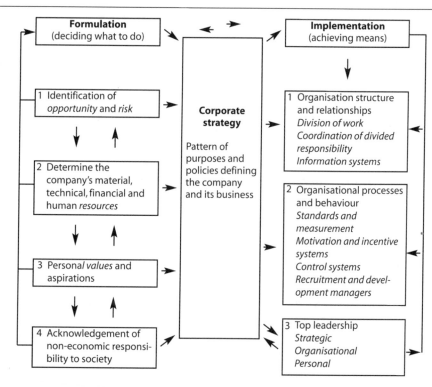

The implementation of strategy

FIGURE 6.4

Strategic analyses

Strategic analyses are conducted to ensure that each aspect of the organisation, and its competitive and general environment, are clearly understood. The approaches used are as follows.

Strengths, weaknesses, opportunities, threats: SWOT analysis

The purpose of SWOT analysis is to help organisations learn, clarify issues, and identify preferred and likely directions (see Figure 6.6).

In this activity, issues are raised, highlighted and categorised under four headings.

- **Strengths:** the things that the organisation and its staff are good at and do well; that they are effective at; that they are well known for; that make money; that generate business, and reputation.
- **Weaknesses:** the things they are bad at, or do badly; that they are ineffective at; that they are notorious for; that make losses; that cause hardships, disputes, grievances and complaints; that should generate business, but do not. This aspect requires a degree of candour.
- **Opportunities:** the directions that they could profitably take in the future that may arise because of strengths or the elimination of weaknesses.
- **Threats:** from competitors; from strikes and disputes; from resource and revenue losses; from failing to maximise opportunities or build on successes. This also includes matters over which the organisation has no control.

Opportunities and threats are representations of the external environment and its forces. The information raised and presented by analysis of these factors is then developed, researched or investigated further. It can be done for all business and managerial activities, and to address wider global and strategic issues. It is an effective means of gathering and categorising information, of illustrating or illuminating particular matters, and for gathering or articulating a lot of information and ideas very quickly.

Social–technical–economic–political: STEP analysis

The purpose of STEP (or, sometimes, PEST) analysis is also to help organisations learn, but the material arising is much more concerned with the analysis of the wider strategic situation, and the organisation in its environment.

- **Social:** the social systems at the workplace, departmental and functional structures, work organisation and working methods. Externally, this considers the relationship between the organisation and its environment in terms of the nature and social acceptability of its products and services; its marketing; and the regard with which it is held in the community.
- **Technological:** the organisation's technology, and the uses to which it is put, and its potential uses; and the technology that is potentially available to the organisation and others operating in the given sector.
- **Economic:** the financial structure, objectives and constraints (e.g. budgets and

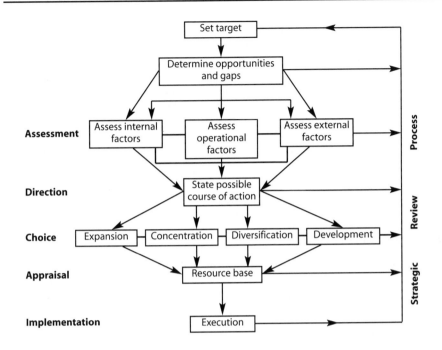

The monitoring, review and evaluation of strategy and direction   *FIGURE 6.5*

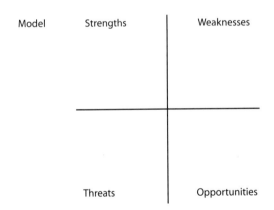

The method by which the ideas are generated and compartmentalised is a creative discussion, OS, 'brain-storming'. The end result of this is a list of items under each heading.
From this a full discussion and development of the idea is concluded.
There are no 'holds' or 'taboos' in a SWOT analysis: the purpose is to be creative, not restrictive.

SWOT analysis   *FIGURE 6.6*

budgeting systems) at the place of work. Externally, this considers the market position, levels of economic activity, and the commercial prospects and potential of the products and services offered.

- **Political:** the internal political systems, sources of power and influence, key groups of workers, key departments, key managers and executives. Externally, this considers particular considerations in the establishment of markets, by product, location, ethics, and values.

Again, the information thus raised can be further analysed and evaluated. It establishes in more detail the wider background against which particular product or service initiatives are to take place, and raises wider issues or concerns that may in turn require more detailed resource and analysis.

Industry structure analysis

This is based on Michael E. Porter's 'five elemental forces of competition' (1981). In this analysis focus is directed at each of the five distinctive elements that are present to some extent in all sectors. Again, the purpose is to clarify the position of the organisation in its chosen sphere of operations, and also to signal any likely or obvious issues for concern. The five elements are:

1. The industry competitors: the nature and extent of rivalry among those organisations currently operating in the field and the implications of this for the future (e.g., reduced profit margins where price wars occur; reduction in capacity where there is over-provision).
2. Suppliers: the extent to which they dominate the sector. This may relate to: their supply of a key, critical or rare component; their ability to integrate forwards into the market itself; the range of choice of suppliers available; the ability to use alternative supplies; and the overall bargaining position of the suppliers.
3. Buyers: the extent to which they dominate the sector. This may relate to their purchase of high volumes from it, or their control of the final outlet of the product in question; their ability to integrate backwards into the market itself; the number and type of operators in the buyer group; the ability to generate and supply alternative buyers; the overall bargaining position of buyers.
4. Potential entrants: the extent to which organisations operating in other sectors have product, technology and staff capacities to gain entry to the sector in question; and the extent and nature of the entry barriers that surround the sector (see Chapter 7).
5. Substitutes: the extent to which the organisation's product is a matter of choice on the part of the buyer; the extent to which equivalent benefits can be gained from a product that is similar, but not the same (see Figure 6.7).

Competitor analysis

This involves an assessment of the other players in the field. It considers the initiatives that they may themselves take to promote their own strategic advantage and also to measure their likely responses to such initiatives on the part of the organisation in question (see Figure 6.8).

The components of a competitor analysis are:

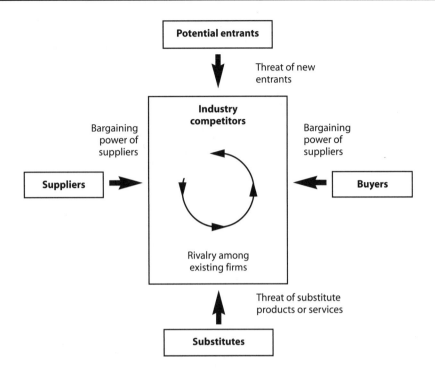

Porter's five elemental forces of competition

FIGURE 6.7

Source: C.R. Christensen *et al., Business Policy: Text and Cases,* Irwin, 1987.

- the strategy of the competitor, its driving and restraining forces
- its current business operations, capacities, strengths and capabilities
- the assumptions held about both the competitor and the industry itself
- a detailed profile of the competitor, its current satisfaction with its current position; its likely moves and responses to moves; its position in the market; its under- or over-capacity.

This constitutes a detailed discussion to be devised and conducted by sectoral, corporate and strategy experts and to be used as the basis on which both offensive and defensive strategic moves are made. Presentation to an organisation's top management and directorate will normally be limited to the matters arising, the results of analysis, and the conclusions and recommendations drawn from a detailed competitor analysis.

Customer and client analysis

The purpose of conducting customer and client analyses is to ensure that the business or public service relationship is considered from the point of view of customers, clients, consumers and end-users. It should form a major component of strategic analysis. This is necessary in order to:

- test assumptions and received wisdom concerning the attitudes of customers and clients to the particular organisation, its products and services

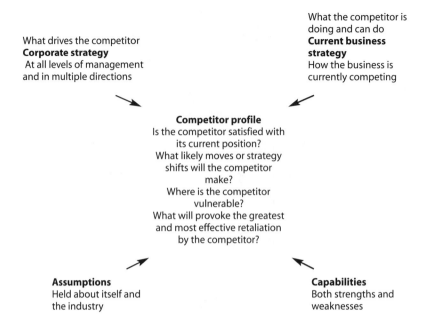

What drives the competitor
Corporate strategy
At all levels of management
and in multiple directions

What the competitor is
doing and can do
**Current business
strategy**
How the business is
currently competing

Competitor profile
Is the competitor satisfied with
its current position?
What likely moves or strategy
shifts will the competitor
make?
Where is the competitor
vulnerable?
What will provoke the greatest
and most effective retaliation
by the competitor?

Assumptions
Held about itself and
the industry

Capabilities
Both strengths and
weaknesses

FIGURE 6.8 **The components of a competitor analysis**

- ensure that these assumptions are not being taken as absolute fact
- assess the extent to which organisational direction is being based on generally favourable responses and attitudes, rather than real customer and client demands
- ensure that customer behaviour is not being taken for granted.

In order to build up as much understanding as possible, it is necessary to make detailed enquiries along the following lines.

- Why do customers and clients use us/not use us?
- Why have customers and clients increased/decreased the value or volume of business that they conduct with us?
- Why have customers started/stopped using us?
- Where does our product or service come in the customer's order of priority? Do we serve wants or needs?
- What causes customers to use us/not to use us?
- Under what circumstances would customers use us more/less? Under what circumstances would customers increase/decrease the value and volume of their business with us?
- What are the alternatives available to customers if they do not do business with us?
- What do competitors provide that is better than us/worse than us?
- Why do customers use us/use our competitors?

These are direct and precise questions, requiring accurate answers. In particular, if the answer to any question is either available in general terms only or is simply not known, then lines of enquiry should be opened as a matter of urgency.

Customer types

Cartwright (2000) defines the following customer and client types.

- **Apostles:** apostles demonstrate ultra-loyalty. They are delighted with the service or product, and delighted to be associated in any way with the particular organisation. They identify very strongly with the organisation and its products and services. Apostles carry out part of the marketing function for the organisation. They are highly loyal and satisfied, and they tell their friends and relations.
- **Loyalists:** loyalists form the most important component of any customer base. All organisations require to be able to identify accurately where their loyalist customer base lies, and to take all steps necessary in order to preserve, maintain and enhance it. Cartwright states: 'Loyalists are akin to the cash-cows outlined by the Boston Consulting Group to describe those products that form the basis for organisational success'.
- **Mercenaries:** mercenaries are the hardest customers to deal with as they are basically a-loyal. They tend to go for the cheapest or most convenient option. They are difficult to deal with because they may well be satisfied but are not loyal. Or they may demonstrate product loyalty but brand a-loyalty; or brand loyalty but supplier a-loyalty. They may move from brand to brand or supplier to supplier. If asked why they moved, the answer may be in terms of cost or convenience, but the real reason may be just a desire for change.
- **Hostages:** hostages are the individuals that make up 'captive markets'. They are overwhelmingly the customer base of public utilities, public services and public transport. Hostages are also found in isolated communities where, for example, there is only one convenient shop, garage, pub or restaurant.
- **Defectors and terrorists:** these are customers who once used a particular organisation, but now do not do so. Defectors may move from a position of loyalty, simply because there is now a much better or more convenient alternative source of supply; or they may move because they are actively dissatisfied with what has previously been on offer, but have simply said nothing about it.

  Terrorists, however, tend to have been extreme loyalists or apostles, and so, when they switch their allegiance, are determined to make sure that everybody knows. Cartwright states that: 'Many of those who appear on consumer affairs television programmes have been previous apostles. On being let down, they have no problem in letting the world know about it.'

To this list others may be added, as follows:

- **Browsers and window-shoppers:** those who have a general interest in what particular organisations have to offer, and who may make unconsidered occasional purchases from time to time.
- **Passing trade:** in which particular customers and clients find themselves confronted by chance with something they are interested in purchasing.
- **Convenience customers and clients:** who use a particular organisation purely

because of its overwhelming convenience to them in their own terms. This is especially important in the case of business-to-business activities, when organisations become the clients of suppliers purely because of the quality of relationship between themselves and the suppliers' representatives (see Example Box 6.10).

This approach provides an easy-to-understand explanation of where and why customers and clients come to particular organisations, and why they cease coming,

---

EXAMPLE BOX 6.10 Customer and Client Types

It is possible to distinguish the following types of customers and clients, and customer and client behaviour.

- **Passive loyalists:** those who think very highly of particular organisations, but who seldom or never use their products and services.
- **General loyalists:** those who think very highly of particular organisations, but who use those organisations very, very infrequently (this is a particular problem in the luxury goods and services industries, and also in the medium-, high- and top-quality holiday package industry).
- **Passive apostles:** customers and clients who in the past always used an organisation, its products and services, but who do so no longer – either because they have ceased to need them, or because the organisation is not easily accessible. They nevertheless continue to praise the organisation, often years after they have last used it. (N.B. this was an especial problem in the decline of Marks & Spencer; when the organisation asked about the reasons for declines in sales, everyone continued to speak very highly of the company as an entity, and so the problems of product sales were never addressed.)
- **Loyal mercenaries:** customers who come to an organisation for the first time as mercenaries may be translated into loyalists, so long as the product or service quality can be demonstrated. This was the basis on which the Japanese car and electrical goods manufacturers built their industrial base in the UK, USA and Western Europe in the 1970s and 1980s. Customers and clients had no particular affinity for the Japanese (indeed many still had vivid memories of brutal treatment at the hands of the Japanese military during the Second World War). Nevertheless, when the product and service quality was demonstrated, they were persuaded to change their buying habits.
- **Anticipatory terrorists:** this is an enduring present problem for those needing to avail themselves of public services. Because of media coverage that gives the overwhelming impression of a decline in quality of healthcare, education and social services in the UK, clients of these services use them with the assumption that they are going to receive poor quality service, badly delivered. They therefore tend to look for the bad rather than the good in the service, and this gives rise to a culture of client complaint and compensation. So far the strategic management of these services has not begun to address this issue.

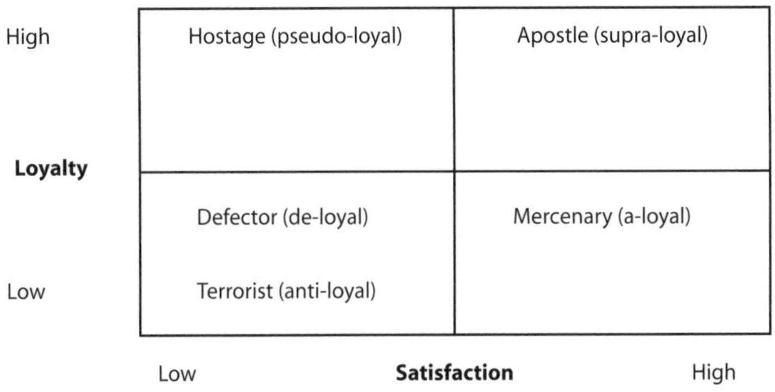

	Low	Satisfaction	High
High	Hostage (pseudo-loyal)		Apostle (supra-loyal)
Loyalty	Defector (de-loyal)		Mercenary (a-loyal)
Low	Terrorist (anti-loyal)		

The loyalty matrix

FIGURE 6.9

and change their attitudes and behaviour. The approach may be shown as a matrix as in Figure 6.9.

Customer and client analysis is a key task of strategic management, and a critical component in the determination of policy, direction and priorities. It is also more complex than organisational or environmental analysis, because it requires the use of time, energy and resources in understanding the precise nature and requirements of those with whom the organisation is to do business. It therefore becomes very easy to neglect this, to take customer and client attitudes on trust, or to understand them in general terms only. Specific points of enquiry are required as follows, in order to establish precise understanding of:

- the price customers are willing to pay for particular products and services
- the value and quality they expect from particular products and services
- how to make products and services as convenient as possible to the customer and client bases served
- length, frequency and intensity of usage
- depreciation/appreciation and resale aspects
- maintenance, repair, replacement and upgrade elements
- personal feelings of esteem and worth that accrue from ownership and usage
- fashionable and faddish elements (especially important in clothing, cars, computers and furniture)
- feelings of exclusivity, luxury and desirability
- returns on financial and emotional investment
- particular demands and requirements of individual customers.

Much of this is therefore clearly subjective. Purchases made by different customers of the same item, for the same purpose, for the same price may result in widely differing levels of satisfaction.

Conclusions

The devising of corporate policy and strategy must identify and reconcile a complex range of matters if it is to be effective. This chapter has attempted to illustrate the main issues.

Devising and implementing strategy is a continuous process, one that is subject to constant analysis, evolution and review. It must be clear and strong enough to give a universally understood clarity of purpose, but this must not be mistaken for rigidity. All organisations must combine this with the qualities of flexibility, dynamism, opportunism and responsiveness if they are to survive into the future.

Strategy has also to be seen as operating in different ways over different time periods. A strategy articulated for a period of up to a year may be very clearly defined, easy to assimilate and follow, and something to which everyone can subscribe. The same may be true to an extent for a period of between one and two years. In relation to the business sphere and wider environment however, anything projected over a period longer than this requires careful and constant re-evaluation at all times. The nature of the environment makes it extremely difficult to predict anything that may happen anywhere in it, or even what its nature will be in, for example, five years' time. Consequently, the best and most valuable use of long-term plans and strategies is as a guiding light; they should be used to illuminate the pathway chosen, rather than as a set of rigid directions that are to govern the organisation for the period stated.

CHAPTER SUMMARY

A successful strategic approach can only be achieved if the ways in which the particular sector operates are fully understood and analysed. This analysis must also depend on gaining as full an understanding as possible of customer and client behaviour, demands, wants and needs.

Ideally, the main outcome of these analyses is an informed base for those responsible for organisational direction. This should consist of a full understanding of the wider environment and general pressures that exist, as well as the more specific aspects indicated.

It is important in the process of educating and informing all managers, and especially top managers, to think strategically, as well as operationally, and to relate the two directly. All of the approaches and models indicated should cause managers to look beyond their operations, activities and areas of responsibility to the wider context, and from the short to the long term. They also act as initial indicators of opportunities and threats. Areas of risk and uncertainty should start to become apparent, and points of stress and strain that may be created by following certain directions should also be indicated, especially if the full environment has not been analysed.

These activities are not ends in themselves. The key to successful strategic management lies in how the information gained is evaluated and used, how accurately the particular position of the organisation is assessed. Organisations must be able to translate this into effective activity based on their own strengths of flexibility, dynamism, responsiveness and commitment. They must also be able to recognise potential weaknesses and pitfalls, and take whatever steps are necessary to address these.

DISCUSSION QUESTIONS

1. Analyse the state of the market for petrol in the UK, using the SWOT and STEP models. What conclusions can be drawn from this? What are the likely effects on car companies, the oil companies and consumers of: taxing motorway driving; doubling the price of crude oil; the production of medical evidence proving that both petrol and diesel fumes are potentially lethal health hazards to car users?

2. Conduct a customer analysis for the top UK football club of your choice. Identify: who the customers and clients of the club are, and their place in the order of priority in the club's interests; the nature of satisfaction expected and anticipated as the result of buying the club's products and services (including tickets to matches and season tickets); the reasons why apostle and loyalist customers become a-loyal or even terrorists in this industry.

3. Choosing a particular strategic initiative with which you are familiar and which is deemed to be a failure, identify the reasons why it failed. Identify the points at which failure could have been reasonably anticipated. Identify the remedial action that could, should or might have been taken to ensure its success, and the circumstances in which the particular venture should have been cancelled.

4. Addressing the particular questions of price, quality, value and convenience, identify the actions necessary for an internet venture, if it is to stand any chance of success.

CHAPTER CASE STUDY

MARKS & SPENCER AT THE BEGINNING OF THE TWENTY-FIRST CENTURY

In 1998, Lord Marcus Sieff retired from the company's board of directors. This represented a severance of the last link between the company's founding fathers and the present day (Lord Sieff was the great-grandson of Michael Marks). At the same time, the beginnings of decline in the company's fortunes began to be apparent. The company, which had prided itself on high-quality, high-value sales of clothing and food products to middle-class customers, began to build a reputation for being out of touch with present customer demands. The company went through various short-term initiatives. These included:

- changes in top management (the company had two chief executives in nine months)
- changes in the supply chain, shifting sources of clothing away from traditional suppliers in England and Scotland, to perceived better-value operators in the Third World
- attempts to 'modernise' the ranges of clothing for women.

Business analysis carried out over 1999 and 2000 identified the following.

- Sales of underwear (especially female underwear) by the company remained buoyant; customers found that these were both of high and enduring quality, and also sufficiently fashionable to suit a wide range of tastes.
- Sales of food remained buoyant; again, the quality was perceived to remain high.

The company also recruited fashionable designers including Julien Macdonald 'to add some much needed glamour to its clothing range for both men and women'. The company also introduced the designer range, Autograph, to drive up perceived product quality and durability, and again, to give a more fashionable and current image.

However the Autograph range has consistently under-performed since its introduction in October 2000. The new menswear range also under-performed. The overwhelming problem was that of customer perception. A survey carried out at the company's Kensington store in March 2001 concluded that there was neither product nor price differentiation between what Marks & Spencer had on offer and what was offered at specialist designer stores.

The company therefore determined upon the following courses of action:

- an internal campaign called 'fight back' which expressed a corporate will to counter the current bad publicity and adverse media coverage
- bonus and incentive scheme to motivate all store staff
- job cutting in the company's head office: the loss of 300 jobs, mainly in the information technology, administration and financial management areas
- closure of the company's twenty stores on mainland Europe.

QUESTIONS

1. Produce a customer analysis for the company, based on the details given above.
2. To what extent do you think that the strategic approach indicated at the end of the case study above is appropriate? What are the problems faced by the company? How should these be tackled?
3. Assuming that the company is to go into the designer clothing market, what further strategic initiatives are necessary in order to ensure that this is successful?

7 Marketing

'All this marketing is such a bore.' Alec Douglas-Home (1963), during the run-up to the general election of that year. He lost.

'I will make Britain great again.' Margaret Thatcher, Conservative leader, during the 1978 election campaign. She won.

'Mother, I'm second in my class.' Sam LeFrak, New York property developer. 'Then go back to work. You still have one to beat.' LeFrak's mother. Quoted in L.E. Shefsky, *Entrepreneurs are Made not Born*, McGraw Hill, 1998.

CHAPTER OUTLINE

Introduction to marketing and its importance in all sectors and activities

The marketing process

Marketing mixes

Marketing strategies

Product and service lifecycles

Public relations.

CHAPTER OBJECTIVES

After studying this chapter, you should be able to:

understand what marketing is, and why it is so important to managers and organisations

understand managerial priorities and responsibilities to the integrity and presentation of products and services

understand the importance and value of marketing and market research

understand how the different marketing strategies and activities may best – and worst – be applied.

Introduction

The purpose of this chapter is to introduce the background and concepts needed for an understanding of marketing and its importance in the business sphere. In addition, there are related aspects to do with both the internal management of organisations, and the presentation and delivery of proposals, initiatives, and ideas, that must also be understood. There is a fundamental business relationship between a product, invention, or service, and the way in which it is presented both to the world at large, and to market sectors in particular, which is critical to overall commercial success.

The marketing process

Marketing is the competitive process by which goods and services are offered for consumption at a profit. This definition should be seen in the broadest possible terms. Marketing combines product and service substance with effective presentation,

---

EXAMPLE BOX 7.1 Effective Marketing: Some Initial Examples

The quality of marketing very often makes all the difference to the viability of particular organisations, and industrial and commercial sectors. For example:

- **Nuclear electricity generation:** in the face of enduring public uncertainty and lack of overall confidence in the long-term safety of this industry, its managers have concentrated the presentational side of their activities on what they can do well. The marketing of nuclear electricity therefore concentrates on two key features: the bringing of work into remote and isolated communities (in the UK all of the nuclear electricity generating stations are situated on the coast, away from centres of population), and education – above all for schoolchildren, but also for anyone who is interested; this has led to most stations opening up visitor centres. These are supported with archive material, brochures, and a general publicity programme that emphasises the enduring benefits of an industry that nevertheless has a very uncertain future in the long-term management of its waste effluent and radioactive residue.

- **The tobacco industry:** this industry has managed to secure for itself major sponsorship of high profile global sporting events in order to counteract the bans that exist throughout most of Western Europe and North America on direct advertising and sales efforts. Concentrating especially on Formula 1 motor racing, and the Indie circuit in North America, tobacco companies have created for themselves a position in which the global sport of motor racing cannot exist in its present form without them. This gives them a television audience of between six and ten hours per channel per country every fortnight for ten months of the year. To counter this, government-sponsored anti-smoking promotions consist largely of small and under-produced leaflets, distributed in schools, public libraries, and doctors' surgeries. This marketing is so ineffective that the commercial producers of products that counteract the effects of smoking have had to assume direct marketing responsibility for their own products, rather than coordinating their efforts with government anti-smoking campaigns.

convenience and acceptability to engage the interest and commitment of customers, consumers and clients, and the public at large (see Example Box 7.1).

The fundamental concept of marketing is thus that all business activities are, in some way, the relationship between oneself and one's clients. This applies as follows.

- Consumer marketing: which comes in two basic forms:
  - unconsidered purchases, leading to instant satisfaction (or dissatisfaction)
  - considered, high value purchases, leading to enduring satisfaction (or dissatisfaction).
- Industrial and business-to-business marketing: unconsidered purchases (e.g. the office coffee), and considered purchases (e.g. capital goods, access to information); this is based on the development of relationships so that considered purchases carry trust and confidence, as well as enduring utility.
- Public services marketing: an area in which substantial development is required, particularly in response to political drives to engage commercial interests in these activities.
- The not-for-profit sector: advantages gained by engaging interest, sympathy and, above all, action from those targeted.
- Internal marketing: activities designed to build mutuality of interest and confidence, and enduring workplace relations, across organisations.

Every interaction between the organisation, its staff and its environment, has some input on these enduring relationships. For example, when members of an organisation address a school prize-day or appear on the television to give a point of view, they contribute to its marketing. When they are in trouble with the police or involved in an affray or other problems, they also affect the organisation's marketing.

Organisations therefore devise strategies and carry out a range of activities designed to assess and satisfy customer needs and wants. They gather market intelligence, conduct market research and obtain customer responses. They organise product packaging, promotion, sales and distribution. They generate product awareness through advertising, image formation, differentiation, promotions, sales methods and techniques, and presentations (see Example Box 7.2).

Finally, purchasers of goods and services buy them for the value benefits and satisfaction that they afford, rather than for their own sake (although possession of an item for its own sake may afford satisfaction).

Marketing strategies

As stated in Chapter 6, all organisations require a generic strategic position; and all the strategies they adopt will ultimately reflect the strengths, capacities, inclinations, technology and size of the organisation in question. Within this broad constraint marketing strategies fall into the following seven categories:

- **Pioneering or 'first in the field':** opening up new markets or new outlets for existing products, or new products for existing outlets; taking an original and distinctive view of the marketing process and devising new methods and campaigns.

EXAMPLE BOX 7.2 Customer Needs and Wants: The Packard Approach

Vance Packard carried out extensive work in the 1950s to try to define the relationship between product, presentation and image, on the one hand, and customer and consumer motivation on the other. His conclusions were that the most successful marketing of products and services arose when both the product and its presentation engaged one or more of the following responses among customers, clients, consumers and end-users.

- **Emotional security, comfort and confidence:** related to bulk purchases of food, safety features in cars, domestic security and insurance. The comfort, confidence and security needs of the customer are satisfied because within their purchase there is security, survival and stability.
- **Reassurance of worth:** purchases must make customers feel good. They have to satisfy themselves both in their own eyes and in those of their friends, acquaintances and colleagues. This applies both to small-scale domestic goods – Packard quotes research carried out in the 1950s by soap powder and detergent companies, which found that unsuccessful marketing was directly related to those campaigns where no self-worth or achievement on the part of the user was evident – and to the purchase of major items. Domestic appliances and cars are required to have a long and useful life. They are also required to have a long 'behavioural' value. Their styling and presentation has therefore to reflect this.
- **Ego gratification:** anything that is sold successfully must include a measure of perceived personal achievement. For example, instant coffee would not sell purely as a convenience; it has to be good enough to present to friends and colleagues either as a mid-morning break, or at the end of a good meal. Another example quoted by Packard was the success of vanity publishing, which promised (and continues to promise) immortality rather than riches, and which therefore remains a huge industry.
- **Creativity:** a variety of the ego-need is creativity. For example, cake mixes that required the addition of eggs were found to be more successful than those that simply needed water. The perception was that there was a greater input on the part of the user or consumer, while at the same time maintaining the benefits of convenience.
- **Love objects:** this aspect may be summarised as: 'cuddly toy', 'dear little child', or 'sweet/cute little animal'. Andrex, the major supplier of toilet tissue to the UK retail sector, has used labrador puppies as the central feature of its commercials since the 1970s. Children are used extensively in television commercials to engender this sense of love and warmth; this extends to the marketing of washing powder, groceries, fast food, cars, holidays, central heating and double-glazing.
- **Power**: the power of the product or offering is reflected in the person who uses it. Nearly all automobile advertising and marketing is on the basis of power, performance and speed as well as security. Power and strength are also strongly

---

Example Box 7.2 (continued)

related to cigarette marketing, especially in Formula 1 motor racing but also the sponsorship of cricket, rugby league, sailing and power boat racing.

- **Traditions and roots:** this relates 'the good old days' to the modern era. For example, food promotions use phrases such as 'just as good as mother used to make'; Rolls Royce cars maintain the traditions of fittings and furnishings, reliability and exclusivity on which their original reputation was built. Politicians exploit perceptions and visions of a golden age with calls for 'returns to traditional values' and 'back to basics' because there is a very strong perception of 'the good old days' and their association with historic success, order, stability and prosperity.
- **Immortality:** this follows on from ego gratification, and traditions and roots. Stability, order and control, and eternal personal prosperity are all associated with longevity, and are important in the presentation of long-term offerings such as housing, life assurance, other insurances, loans and other financial products. Those that are successful are presented alongside images of steadiness, increased prosperity and value, and also alongside a stable, happy and successful domestic situation. Even in societies where there are high levels of divorce and the consequent traumas of family break-up, these remain powerful and positive images. By association, reassurance of worth, value and emotional stability are also very positive.

Packard carried out his work during the industrial, commercial and consumer boom that followed the Second World War. It retains its currency because it is almost unique in that it concentrated a managerial approach to marketing and product and service presentation on the subjective (rather than the perceived or pseudo-rational) needs of customers, consumers, clients and end-users.

Source: Vance Packard, *The Hidden Persuaders*, Penguin, 1958.

- **'Follow the leader':** the great benefit of being second in the field is to learn from the mistakes and experience of the pioneer, and make informed judgements about the nature of the involvement to be taken based on their experience. Or it may be that the second organisation can see opportunities that were not exploited by the first.
- **'Me too' or 'all-comers':** entry to and exit from the market are relatively easy where the market is wide open, where the products and services in question are universal or general, and where there are many suppliers but more buyers than suppliers.
- **Supply led:** the product is produced because the organisation has complete faith in it and knows that, once made, it can be sold at a profit.
- **Technology led:** the organisation finds itself in a particular line of business because it has at its disposal a particular type of technology which can be turned to productive and profitable advantage in a variety of sectors.
- **Staff led:** the drive comes from the skills, qualities and preferences of the staff of

EXAMPLE BOX 7.3 The Leisurewear Sectors

The provision of products for the leisurewear sectors of Europe, Australia, New Zealand, South Africa and North and South America constitutes the ultimate in fast-moving consumer goods. The benefits that accrue to the customer from their ventures into this area are to do with image, impression, distinctiveness, lifestyle, identity, the imitation of film, pop or sports stars, and personal esteem and comfort. Having gained all this for themselves, customers wish to be held in positive and popular esteem by their peers, and to carry a wider label of status and prominence in the society in which they live. Niches for leisurewear may therefore additionally be identified by:

- **Age:** which ranges from birth virtually through to death and is often very precisely targeted in the areas in between. For example, the teenage (13–19) sector can be further defined at each of – and any combination of – these ages; this applies also at sectors such as pre-teen or tween (8–12) and post-teen (early 20s and even beyond).
- **Sex, gender and sexuality:** and associated images.
- **Location:** regional, local and national variations on the particular products; this is compounded by that which is perceived to be either a leading location or one to be avoided at all costs.
- **Branding:** the quest for distinctiveness mirrored in the desire and ability on the part of the consumer to wear the badge and distinction with the given qualities of pride, identity and esteem and to gain the esteem, real or perceived, of others; this goes with the ability to charge high prices.
- **Transience:** the new is not new for long. The moment the next distinctive offering comes along the previous one is first passé, and then obsolete.

These aspects must be reflected in both strategies and ways of working adopted by companies that seek to operate in this field. In particular, at the beginning of the twenty-first century, the leisurewear sector is dogged by ethical issues, particularly allegations of slave labour in the garment manufacturing factories. Nike, Reebok, The Gap, have all had to counter these allegations; and it remains an enduring problem for all those companies that draw supplies from the Third World. Marketing and market research are therefore required to cover everything if the establishment of a profit-base is to be created. In particular, many companies that have relocated manufacture in the Third World, are increasingly required to adopt a practice of close supervision of factory activities, in order to secure the total integrity of product manufacture and presentation. Staffing policies will ideally mirror this, drawing upon a range of qualities and levels of commitment that represent expertise, familiarity, understanding and a fundamentally ethical approach, as well as the ability to forecast developments in the area and to produce new, effective and targeted products quickly. Design is a critical facility in such companies. Marketing strategies concentrate on differentiation aspects and use all media sectors, mainstream and niche alike, in the pursuit of this. The leisurewear sector is

> **Example Box 7.3 (continued)**
>
> saturated, yet entry and exit barriers are low, affording plenty of opportunities in a business area in which the consumers of the entire world wish to participate, and will participate in provided that they have sufficient disposable income. This is the strategic base from which all players in this sector must operate.

an organisation who happen to be gathered together, and the products or offerings reflect these; this is very prevalent in the small business sphere.

- **Market led:** the organisation looks first at a range of markets, then assesses their requirements, and finally decides which of these it can most valuably and profitably operate in and fill (see Example Box 7.3).

The organisation may also adopt its commercial position based on a strong moral or ethical stance. This, in turn, becomes the initial strong or overriding attraction of clients to the business and gives a firm additional impression (usually of honesty and integrity) in addition to its commercial and business capabilities.

Marketing strategies may be offensive or defensive. Offensive activities seek to make inroads into the competitive position and client base of others. Defensive and responsive activities are taken with the object of at least preserving the original position in response to the offensives of others.

Segmentation

Those involved in marketing categorise society by means of 'social segmentation', based on the occupation of the head of the household as follows.

A: Aristocrats and upper middle class, directors, senior managers, senior civil and public servants.
B: Middle class, lawyers, doctors, senior managers.
C1: Lower middle class, teachers, nurses, doctors, engineers, technologists, managers.
C2: Skilled working class, including some engineering and technology activities.
D: Working class.
E: Subsistence, including the underclass and unemployed.

Clearly, this is not exact; the inclusion of some occupations in more than one category is deliberate and illustrates the imperfections present. It is, however, a useful means of defining society for the purpose of understanding and evaluating it for a variety of reasons. It enables a relationship to be drawn between sectors of the population, and income, tastes, aspirations, spending patterns, product and service purchase and usage, and related matters. It is also universally recognised in the UK. (For an alternative categorisation, see Example Box 7.4.)

Segments may additionally be defined by age, sex, status, aspiration, values, location, occupation and expectations. These are then underpinned by image, identity, differentiation, branded and visual qualities and presentation. This is done to identify:

EXAMPLE BOX 7.4 A New Approach to Market and Social Segmentation

In 1998, the National Office of Population, Census and Surveys produced a new framework for social structure. This is as follows.

- **Class 1A:** large employers, higher managers, company directors, senior police, fire, prison and military officers, newspaper editors. Top football managers and restaurateurs are also included in this section.
- **Class 1B:** professionals – doctors, solicitors, engineers, teachers. This section also includes airline pilots.
- **Class 2:** associate professionals, journalists, nurses, midwives, actors, musicians, military NCOs, junior police, fire and prison officers. This section also includes lower managers (with fewer than 25 staff).
- **Class 3:** intermediate occupations – secretaries, air stewards and stewardesses, driving instructors, telephone operators. This section also includes 'employee sports players', such as footballers and cricketers.
- **Class 4:** small employers, managers of small departments, the non-professional self-employed, publicans, plumbers, farm owners and managers. This section also includes self-employed sports players such as golfers and tennis players.
- **Class 5:** lower supervisors, craft and related workers, electricians, mechanics, train drivers, bus inspectors.
- **Class 6:** semi-routine occupations: traffic wardens, caretakers, gardeners, shelf stackers, assembly-line workers.
- **Class 7:** routine occupations: cleaners, waiter/waitress/bar staff, messenger/courier, road worker, docker.
- **Class 8:** the excluded. This includes the long-term unemployed, those who have never worked, the long-term sick, and prison populations.

This structure has not yet gained national currency. It is also perceived to be full of anomalies, especially because it is less directly related to earnings, disposable income, or the propensity to spend than the earlier A–E categorisation.

It is, however, extremely useful to those with managerial responsibilities for marketing in that it illustrates further the impossibility of absolute social or market segmentation.

Source: OPCS, *A New Social Structure*, HMSO, 1998.

- the types of buyers
- the class of buyers
- the size of the customer base in given niches
- the balance of quality that buyers expect
- the value of the product relative to other items available for consumption
- patterns of spending among the members of the niche or sector, and the extent to which they use credit, credit cards, cash, or cheque books

- their propensity to spend or save
- ease of access to product and after-sales outlets
- ease of access to facilities and services
- the frequency with which a given item is likely to be used.

Competition, rivalry and the competitive environment

Competition and rivalry exist wherever there is choice. The market is an environment in which competition and rivalry take place. Rivalry is the process by which a company establishes its position in particular sectors, using the marketing tools and techniques at its disposal. The main features are as follows.

- **Competition with whom:** it is very easy to assume that there is genuine competition between large organisations in particular markets: that McDonald's and Burger King compete in the fast food market, for example, or Coca Cola and Pepsi in soft drinks. It is true that individual branches and outlets compete when they are located close to each other. However, market size and share is determined to a large extent by the numbers and locations of outlets provided by each. This also applies to many other sectors: for instance, supermarkets, department stores, oil and petrol sales.
- **Competition for what:** competition for the business of customers and consumers means that, on specific occasions, competition is between organisations that have no direct relationship to each other. For example, there is competition between car and holiday companies when customers make the choice to have either a new car or a good holiday. Competition exists between fast food retailers and transport companies when the consumer is faced with a choice of either having something to eat and then walking home, or else taking public transport and forgoing the meal. In industrial markets, competition may exist between capital goods providers and construction companies, as when an organisation takes the decision either to replace its photocopier or to refurbish its premises.
- **Degree of market captivity:** whether customers and consumers have to buy from a particular source or whether they have a choice.
- **The state of the market:** whether expanding, static, stagnant or declining; this may be measured in sales, financial and volume terms; in terms of numbers of customers; in terms of the reputation of product or service offered.
- **Social and ethical aspects:** for example, the use of animals for product research; sexual images in advertising campaigns; exploitation of cheap labour; working in areas where employment legislation is lax or non-existent; and environmental pollution (see Example Box 7.5).
- **Entry barriers:** consisting of necessary levels of capital investment; staffing volumes; expertise and technology; market location; protectionism and size; legal constraints; economies of scale; access to distribution channels; the loyalty of customers to those organisations supplying substitute or alternative products; and the costs incurred in switching from the current to the proposed activities, or of starting up and making entry as the first initiative of a new business. Barriers may be very low if the products, buyers and markets are easily accessible, and the production technology freely available.
- **Offensive and defensive capability:** the ability of existing players to defend their

---

EXAMPLE BOX 7.5 The Complexities of Ethical Marketing

- **Barbie:** the Barbie doll is an enduringly successful commercial product, having been in existence for nearly 50 years. This is in spite of the fact that it has been very heavily criticised as projecting unacceptable social, ethical and sexual images of young girls and reinforcing particular stereotypes. This did not prevent an exhibition 'The Art of Barbie' being mounted to raise funds for the Elton John AIDS Foundation in 2000. For this exhibition, world celebrities were asked to lend or donate their Barbie dolls. In addition, a collection of 50 Barbie figures were dressed by artists and fashion designers including Stella MCartney, Alexander McQueen, and Phillip Treacy. Some of the dolls were dressed in high fashion items; others were dressed as Princess Diana, punks and the homeless.

- **Charities marketing:** there is no question that at the core of the activities of all major charities is the fundamental drive to alleviate problems that exist in different parts of society, and different parts of the world. However, the drive for ever-greater access to sources of funds, together with overall increases in funding, has led to questionable marketing and promotional activities on behalf of these charities. Many charities now blitz town and city centres with teams of subcontracted public relations staff. These teams stop passers by in the street, engage them in conversation and then ask for covenanted or credit card donations in support of the particular cause. This is a clear direct sales approach and would probably be unacceptable if it were for consumer or capital goods and services. However, the large charities point to the financial results of this approach; for example, in 2000, donations to War on Want rose by 27 per cent.

Both of these examples illustrate the complexities that have to be considered when seeking to adopt an ethical approach to marketing, and in marketing for ethical causes.

---

position, or to engage in activities devised to prevent the entry of new competitors. They may possess substantial financial resources, and also more nebulous perceptual advantages to do with image, confidence, quality and reliability, which any organisation wishing to break into the market would first have to overcome. Because of its position and reputation also (apart from any reasons to do with size and influence, or financial resources), an existing player may be able to cut its prices low enough for long enough to force a new competitor out.

- **Legal constraints:** most markets and sectors have specific legal regulations and constraints, quite apart from the wider considerations of the laws of the country concerned. Governments may also regulate organisations by various requirements: to obtain licences for particular activities; to operate to given legal minima in employment, marketing and production practices; and in conform to quality standards for certain products and services.

The law also extends to imitation and copyright; organisations have the right

---

EXAMPLE BOX 7.6 The Loss of a Major Player

The major players in every sector have achieved this position because they either command high levels of customer loyalty or exert some other form of dominance (see above). The result is that, whenever a major player does withdraw from a particular sector, this becomes destabilised, and may lead to enduring loss of customer, client and consumer confidence in the products and services of the sector as a whole. For example:

- Were McDonald's ever to cease trading, it is not easy to gauge the effect on the fast food and convenience restaurant industry. There would be an initial swamping of competitors and other equivalent outlets, leading to substantial price rises, and shortage of supplies among the remaining players. The effect of this is likely to be a withdrawal by consumers until such time as the sector re-stabilised itself. Thus the removal of the largest player would result in the decline in fortunes (rather than an increase) of those companies that remained.
- When the UK domestic car industry collapsed, it took between 10 and 15 years for Ford, Vauxhall, Nissan, Toyota and the large European manufacturers to fill the gap. Over the period 1970–90, as the indigenous companies declined, there were substantial price rises in the sector. At present, in spite of the fact that the global car industry now has substantial over-capacity, car prices in the UK have not come down into line with what is on offer in the rest of the world.
- The decline in regional house building in the UK, brought about as the result of building recessions in the early 1980s and early 1990s, mean that there is still a shortage of good quality, affordable housing in and around centres of commercial, economic and public service importance. This is because expertise has gone out of the industry, and is taking years to restore. This, in turn, has led to industrial, commercial and consumer pressures on prices; and the charges available to successful and effective construction, building and property companies are very high.

---

not to have their pioneering or profitable ideas stolen and represented as their own by an imitator.

- **Confidence and expectations:** of organisations in terms of the returns on investment from their particular activities; in terms of assured product and service quality on the part of customers, consumers and clients.
- The number of **competitors** in the sector, especially where there are many companies of equivalent size and capacity in the sector, and the products and services are undifferentiated; there is then no particular brand loyalty or identity, or at least this is not the overriding factor.
- **Sector dominance:** who or what dominates the sectors, who the market leaders are, whether by reputation, income, sales volume, customer volume, location or command of resources.
- **Sectoral growth:** where growth is slow or steady, companies that wish to expand will precipitate marketing wars. Related to this is the expectation of high rewards

to be gained by the 'winning' player or players. Where growth is rapid there is a threat of entry when existing players cannot cope with increased demand.

- **Sectoral stagnation and decline:** where the present range of products or services are no longer valued by the customer, client and consumer groups in question.
- **Sectoral transience and faddishness:** where customers, clients and consumers have gone into the sector because it has for some reason become attractive in the short term; it is essential to recognise that this only endures until the next fashion or fad comes along.
- **Exit barriers:** where exit barriers are high, companies may remain in business in the sector even if they are not making profits because the costs of total withdrawal are greater than continuing to produce. Companies facing this use it as an opportunity to seek other markets, sectors and niches. A company can also engage in wider marketing activities with the purpose of differentiating its products and services, generating new images, identity and loyalty. Where exit barriers are low, companies normally withdraw (see Example Box 7.6).

The mixture and balance of these elements change as the sector and market environment changes, and as the marketing activities of all players in it have effect. Ultimately, there will be company collapses, shakeouts, mergers and take-overs, as the weaker players go to the wall, and the stronger seek to consolidate their positions.

- **Buyer groups:** these have the greatest influence where they are in the position of being able to force down the price to be paid to suppliers; or to demand higher quality, volume or service from the supplier group. They may also play one supplier off against others. The power and influence of the buyer group depends on the following.
  - If there are few entry barriers or critical switching costs on the part of potential suppliers, especially to do with capital or legal constraints; in such cases, buyers are able to approach anyone they choose.
  - Where products are undifferentiated, where there is no brand loyalty, buyers also have greater influence.

  The level of profit in the buyer group's business is also critical; where this is low, there is great pressure on the sector to lower its costs.
- **Supplier groups:** these exert pressure on participants in a sector by raising prices or reducing the quality of products and services offered. They squeeze profitability out of any sector unable to recover its costs through price rises. The supplier group is particularly powerful if it is dominated by a few companies, and is more concentrated or organised than the sectors to which it sells (an example is oil, which is dominated by the major multinationals of Shell, BP, Texaco, Aramco, and Gulf). The same also applies in other industries; for example, diamonds are dominated by de Beers, and the defence electronics industry by Plessey Marconi.
- **Internal marketing:** the application of the wider principles and practices of marketing to in-organisation activities as follows.
  - Credibility and confidence of particular departments, in relation to their interaction with others: creating a positive or productive working environment, and inter-departmental harmony, mutuality and trust; dependence of one department or function on another for its expertise is well-founded; the results of inter-departmental cooperation are positive and productive.

- The ability to approach internal functions for expert and high-quality advice, service, support and direction, in the knowledge that this will be forthcoming.
- Internal marketing also creates the aura, harmony and general mutuality within which the organisation works; it is a contributor to the motivation of individuals, and the morale of the total organisation; it helps in the setting of modus operandi, performance standards, attitudes and values.
- Management style, the relations between different levels of staff, the identity with and adoption of the purpose, vision and core values of the organisation, also owe much to the organisation's ability to market itself to its staff.

Marketing mixes

Marketing activities are based on mixes of all the elements present. They are conveniently defined as follows.

The 4Ps

- **Product:** variety, branding quality, packaging, appearance and design.

EXAMPLE BOX 7.7 Product and Service Classifications

Ford, the car manufacturer, used this model approach as follows.

- **Cars to advertise:** high performance (e.g. RS Turbo); high specification (e.g. top of the range Granada, off-road, Ford Probe).
- **Those that sell:** Ka, Fiesta, Bonus, Mondeo, especially the mid-range; the high specification at one end of the scale, and the basic model at the other end of the scale, both sell less well than the mid-range.
- **Areas that make money:** accessories, servicing packages, trade-in value, and finance plans.

Sony, the electrical goods manufacturer, classifies its product range as follows:

- **Yesterday's breadwinners:** the Walkman, sales of televisions, other electrical goods, video, audio and computer equipment and accessories.
- **Today's breadwinners:** music catalogues, the Walkman, DVD and other advanced computer, audio and video equipment.
- **Tomorrow's breadwinners:** mini-disc, Playstation 2, Columbia-TriStar Pictures, music and video production.
- **Twinkles and sparkles:** Playstation 3, commercial computer software, minidisc potential.
- **Dead-weights:** very little: the company takes the view that even if something is a commercial failure, the knowledge and expertise gained as the result of its development should not be lost, but rather retained within the organisation.

- **Promotion:** advertising, sponsorship, selling, publicity and mail-shots.
- **Price:** basic, discounting, credit, payment method and appearance.
- **Place:** coverage, outlets, transport, distribution and accessibility.

The 4Cs

- **Customers:** directing marketing and presentational activities at the needs and wants of customers.
- **Convenience:** a combination of establishing the required and desired outlets; and of educating customers and clients to access the available outlets.
- **Cost:** the equivalent of price in the 4Ps; with the additional management discipline implicit that requires the balancing of cost and price with value and benefits.
- **Communication:** the production of advertising, sponsorship, sales publicity, mail-shot and internet material that is customer, client and consumer-friendly, rather than technically or visually brilliant *per se*.

Marketing mixes arise from combinations and interactions of each of these elements. Consumers of products and services – offerings – will normally hold one of the elements more important than the others. In turn, the forces and pressures of the markets in which the offerings are made also reflect their relative importance.

There are legal and ethical restraints placed on marketing activities in the Western world. In general, spurious or misleading claims may not be made for products, nor

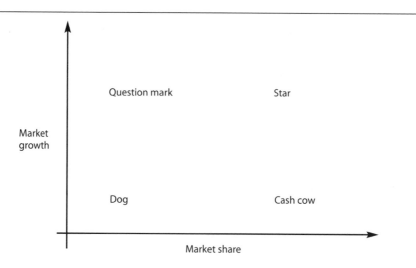

Cash cows: high share of low growth market; today's breadwinners; the main source of income.
Stars: high share of high market growth, today's and tomorrow's breadwinners from which future cash will come; normally need high investment and support to maintain position.
Question marks: low share of high market growth; today's potential breadwinners; not all will succeed.
Dogs: low share of low market growth; normally only kept if they have some distinctive feature (e.g. something on which a traditional or enduring reputation has been built, and without which, the present reputation may be diluted).

FIGURE 7.1   The 'Boston Group' matrix

should misleading impressions be deliberately fostered; apart from anything else this is very bad for repeat business. Actual products must reflect the reality or impression given by both promotion and packaging. Products must also not be harmful or detrimental to their consumers; minimum standards of performance, manufacture, quality and safety have therefore to be met.

We will now consider each of the elements in turn.

Product

'Product' in this context is the term habitually used to describe anything that is offered to a market sector for consumption, and includes commercial and public services. The product mix is the range of products offered by an organisation. This is determined by matching the organisation's capabilities and capacities with the markets and niches to be serviced and by the scope and scale of its operations. People buy the benefits that they expect to accrue from a product or service as follows.

- **Quality and durability:** product and service quality and durability must be considered from the point of view of the balance required, and also in terms of customer demand (there is no point in offering a highly durable product to the stated market sector if that is not what the customers want).
- **Branding:** which gives credence and confidence, especially where the brand is well known and the consumer is content with what is offered and comfortable with the appearance of the name on the product.
- **Packaging:** used to present the product to its best advantage and to protect it up to the point of consumption. Packaging also reinforces the identity of all products and services: for example, Barbie (toys); Persil (soap powders); brochure presentation (e.g. package tours).
- **Product and service benefits:** these should be seen in their widest context. The full offering often includes after-sales service, spare parts, help and emergency lines, call-out facilities, and product and service advice and familiarity sessions.
- **Product and service ranges and portfolios:** reflecting the total range of offerings. Ideally, the confidence and reputation of each feeds all the others. When one product or service is perceived to be bad or unreliable, it is likely to have a knock-on effect on the others. There are various different ways of looking at product and service portfolios and ranges. Examples are:
  - those which are advertised; those which sell; those which make money
  - yesterday's breadwinners; today's breadwinners; tomorrow's breadwinners; sparkles and twinkles; dead weights (see Example Box 7.7 and Figure 7.1).

The product lifecycle

All products have a beginning, middle and an end (see Figure 7.2). The concept of product lifecycle defines more precisely these stages and identifies the points at which specific marketing initiatives and activities might usefully be generated.

There are four stages.

- **Introduction:** the bringing in and bringing on of the new product; this is the

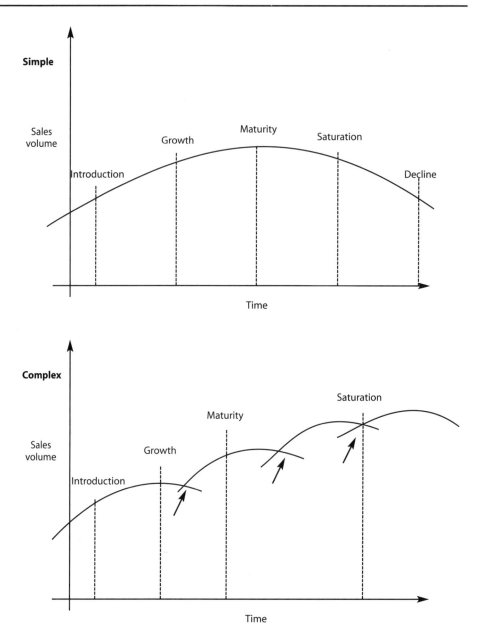

FIGURE 7.2 Product lifecycles

culmination of a period of both product and market research, the point at which the offering in question first comes on to the market.

- **Growth:** this is where the product takes off and its true potential (rather than that projected by research and modelling) begins to become apparent; sales and demand both rise where this is successful; unit costs decline.
- **Maturity:** the product is now a familiar and well-loved feature on the market; people are happy and confident with it, and unit costs are low. The last part of the maturity stage is that of saturation; this is where the company seeks to squeeze the last remaining possible commercial benefits from the item before it loses its commercial value.
- **Decline:** where the product is deemed to have run its course and no more value or profit is to be gained from it; it will then be withdrawn from the market.

Marketing interventions are made at each stage to ensure that the product potential is maximised. The product must take off so that the full range of benefits to be gained from the consumers of it are realised by the sector at which it is aimed. Then, as it reaches maturity, initiatives are taken to breathe as much new life into it as possible using the whole range of promotional and advertising media; very often this means one advertising campaign too many before the product declines.

Products may also be rejuvenated through repackaging, re-presentation and changing the quality or value emphases.

Price and cost

In simple terms, the price of an item covers at least the variable costs incurred in producing it. It also reflects the levels of perceived quality and value held by the customers, clients and consumers. Beyond this, organisations set price levels that enable them to generate sufficient income to keep shareholders and other stakeholders happy. They must further set prices to ensure that sufficient income is generated to ensure continuity of operations and to provide sufficient general cash flow to meet the needs of the organisation (above all, it must be profitable).

The price of an item must reflect both the willingness and capability of the customer to pay. If one is offering in niches where the customers and consumers always pay cash (as distinct from cheque or credit or debit cards or finance plans) then prices must reflect the volume of cash carried and must be sensitive to the competing demands on it. Example Boxes 7.8, 7.9 and 7.10 demonstrate crucial aspects of price setting.

Organisations need both an understanding of the full range of constraints on price, and also a measure of flexibility in its determination, enabling them to respond to competitive moves elsewhere in the market.

It is also necessary to consider what is actually included in the total price of an item or commodity. When a car is bought, for example, the consumer achieves personal transport and mobility. However, the price may also include the concept of the 'lifetime of the car', including regular servicing, after-sales arrangements, emergency cover, insurance policies, and finance plans that cover the purchase of the car, as well as the other accessories that may go with it. In addition, a relationship with the garage or dealer may be bought that takes all the worry out of motoring, provided that the customer continues to patronise the establishment, to have the servicing and after-sales conducted by them, and possibly also to replace the car through them in

---

EXAMPLE BOX 7.8 Legend of the Razor

The legend of the razor carries a series of primary marketing lessons.

In hypothetical terms, the razor costs £1.00 to make but customers will only pay 20p for it. However, the razor blade costs 0.1p to make but customers will pay 20p each for them.

A distinction is therefore drawn between offering a razor for sale and the ability of the customer to shave. If the organisation concentrates on the razor, it cannot conduct profitable business. By concentrating on the 'shave', however, and additionally ensuring a steady and continuing supply of blades, profit is made on the offering to the customer's continuous satisfaction.

---

due course. Customers and consumers may also be prepared to pay for convenience of access to products and services, provided that quality and satisfaction are assured.

Promotion to customers

Promotion is a combination of methods used to generate public awareness, identity,

---

EXAMPLE BOX 7.9 Airline Tickets

People travelling on the same airline flight will almost inevitably have paid widely differing amounts for their seat.

The offerings by the airline are: first class, business or club class, tourist and economy class, and charter. However, the variation in price will depend on a much greater number of matters.

- **When** the ticket was purchased: airlines give discounts for purchases well in advance or right at the last minute (standby).
- **Where** it was purchased: through travel agent, discount house (bucket shop), at the airport, direct with the airline; or which country it was purchased in, and what currency was used.
- **Who** purchased it: whether it is a corporate or personal expense.
- **Why** it was purchased: for business, pleasure or holidays.
- **Other factors:** especially concerning whether the trip is part of a package holiday, fly-drive or reciprocal arrangement with a hotel chain, for example.

Airlines arrange their schedules with the prime purpose of ensuring that their planes travel as full as possible as often as possible. The price range thus ensures both a variety of offerings and also many sources of passengers. More importantly from the airlines' point of view, they thus maximise their chances of achieving their prime purpose.

EXAMPLE BOX 7.10 The 99p Syndrome

The first use of price as a means of marketing in itself is ascribed to Marks & Spencer plc of the UK in the 1970s. Instead of charging £5, £10 (5 or 10 local units of currency) the amount is reduced by one currency unit, to £4.99 or £9.99.

There is a strong perceptual message inherent in this, which must be considered at this stage. The customer receives change as well as the goods or service that they desire, assuming that they pay with the single currency unit. The message that they consequently receive is that they are paying less than a particular amount for the product. In addition, the price is related to the currency units where possible: £4.99 is related to the UK £5.00 note, for example, and 99p to the £1.00 coin.

The price label thus becomes a feature of the presentation of the product or service itself, and becomes incorporated into the mainstream marketing activities.

This also acts as a check on the integrity of both staff and customers. It is very unusual to pay the exact price in such cases. This means that the staff have to use the till, and that the customer must be given a receipt.

---

confidence, desire and conviction in a product, and ultimately its adoption and usage by the general public. The methods used in the pursuit of this are:

- advertising in all mass media including newspapers, television and radio; sponsorship of events, other products and activities
- sales calling by organisational representatives to generate new business and general awareness, and to maintain and service existing business
- brochures designed to generate the image required for the product and to demonstrate that it has the features and benefits its consumers are perceived to require
- product placement, by which producers of films, brochures, magazines, novels, stories and television series are persuaded to adopt distinctive brands of product such as cars and clothing to be used and worn by their heroes and heroines, thus assisting in the generation of positive images and high-level identity
- other publicity features such as general awareness-raising articles, news items and general interest stories, featuring particular products and services
- price, which may also be integrated into the promotional campaign adopted, and which is of critical importance in marketing at the extremes of luxury/high value products and services; and cheap/good value products and services (see Example Box 7.11).

Image and identity

In the early twenty-first century, in spite of all the social and ethical pressures to the contrary, the strongest, most enduring and effective promotional images remain as follows.

- Sex, especially female sexuality.
- Glamour and opulence, especially in relation to clothing, lifestyle, cars and holidays.

EXAMPLE BOX 7.11 Cheap and Good Value

All those with responsibility for marketing should understand that very few customers, consumers (or for that matter commercial clients) buy anything purely on
price alone. Even mercenaries (see customer analysis, Chapter 6) who state that
they buy simply on price very often spend a lot of other resources (especially time
and energy) in finding the perceived, cheapest or best value option.

There is also a serious behavioural issue to address. Feelings of self-worth are
affronted if consumers believe they are being forced into buying the cheapest
option. Anything that is pitched at the low-price market should carry enduring perceptions of 'good value' because this is a reinforcement of self-esteem and self-
worth ('I am getting excellent value for money'), rather than cheap, which gives
negative feelings ('I am forced to buy this because I haven't any money').

In the capital goods and major projects sectors, where competition is overtly
on price, very often the cheapest tender carries with it all sorts of hidden extras. In
construction and civil engineering, there is a long history of claims processes at the
end of contracts. The companies that have successfully tendered for the work have
offered a superficially attractive price up front to the client, and have then sought
to build on this by seeking to claim for extras that were either not built n to the
original tender, or else have become apparent as the contract has been completed.

- Sunshine and brightness, as the backdrop to the sales of any product or service. These images are both socially and professionally perceived to be positive.
- High-tech, to demonstrate the association between human brilliance and product and service usage.
- The use of famous people and stars to endorse products and services, though this has in recent times proved to be a doubled-edged sword. For example, Madonna and Michael Jackson both had to be dropped from lucrative advertising contracts with Coca Cola, following scandals in their private lives; the use of John Cleese by the Sainsbury's supermarket chain gave him extensive recognition, but did not increase the general public awareness of Sainsbury's as 'the best' supermarket at which to shop.
- Strong colours, especially black, red, crimson, purple and deep blue. The use of green in advertising and promotion is widely perceived to reinforce perceptions of ecological and environmental awareness, but there is no research to suggest that this enhances interest in, or desire for, consumer products and services, except in small niches of the population.
- Enduring safety and security. Again this is a double-edged sword, as customers and consumers at large expect products and services to be fundamentally safe and secure; and in any case, nobody likes to be reminded of their own vulnerability or mortality.

There has been extensive creative activity within the advertising and marketing industries to try and break the mould, or at least to use it differently. However, given that
the overall purpose of these activities is to ensure that products and services have a
high profile for actual and potential customers, consumers and clients, it remains

absolute that, all other things being equal, images based on these factors are the most likely to carry out this function effectively.

Place and convenience

The fourth element of the marketing mix is place: getting the products and services to the customers and clients. This means knowing who they are, where they are, how they want the products and services delivered, what the nature and level of their expectations are, and how these may best be satisfied. Part of the creative process involved in marketing is concerned both with meeting the customers' requirements and generating an expectation that if they go to a particular place then their particular needs will be satisfied.

The concept of place derives much from the segmentation process (see above). The other main feature that must be considered is that of location. This reflects the nature of distribution networks, especially those concerned with getting the product or service to the point at which consumers buy it or take delivery of it. There is thus currently a tendency among manufacturing and retail organisations in Western Europe and North America to locate on the edge of towns in order to have convenient access to road distribution networks. Organisations that use railway, sea and air distribution will consider the rest of their own specific marketing mixes in relation to this.

The question of location also relates to the traditional view that an organisation would locate near the sources of raw materials if the items that it produced lost weight during the production and manufacturing processes. Conversely, they would locate near the markets if their processes resulted in the products gaining weight (see Example Box 7.12).

Location also reflects any sectoral or regional demands, desires or constraints. Hitherto, for example, there has been an expectation that each community would have its own school, library and hospital; these have become limiting factors in the offering of education and health services. The same is true for certain sports facilities. There are thus an onus on those responsible for providing these services, and constraints within which they have to work. If this is not the most efficient or effective way of providing the service, then part of the process of changing it must include a raising of the understanding required of the public: promotion of the benefits of the new proposed arrangement. People will go along with this if they see that it is in their best interests to do so, and if they can see the benefits that will accrue to them (see Example Box 7.13).

This has been achieved by the supermarket and shopping mall sectors in Europe and North America. A whole process of behaviour and expectation reform has been completed in the pursuit of this. People now go to out-of-town mega-stores in the UK and France, and to shopping malls in North America. The benefits of ease of access and 'everything under one roof' have been successfully demonstrated to those niches of the population that use them. Those responsible for the hypermarkets and the generation of business for shopping malls took steps to understand the requirements of those that were expected to use them, what products and services they would require from them; they designed a consumer environment where both could be satisfied. This has had a major impact upon the location of commercial activity, and those who continue to do business in the centre of towns have had to consider much more precisely the attractions of their particular location to the consumers that continue to come to them.

EXAMPLE BOX 7.12 The Internet as Location

The use of the internet as a marketing and organisational location has to be seen from a variety of often conflicting points of view, as follows.

- From the organisation's point of view, it means it has a presence – a location – on every computer screen in the country.
- From the point of view of customers and clients, the particular organisation has a general presence on computer screens. However, this location is convenient to customers and clients only if the organisation website is easily accessible, and then customer-friendly once accessed. This has especially to be borne in mind when it is remembered that speed and convenience of access (and perceived speed and convenience of access) are a key marketing function.
- If the great strength of the internet as a location is its potential presence on every computer screen, its great weakness is the lack of a physical or human presence. This has to be seen in the context that the enduring success of all marketing activities is built on the expectations of customers and clients. This, in turn, is universally reinforced by the human interaction that also takes place in every traditional transaction: whether consumer, industrial, commercial or public service.

The other matters that concern the 'place' element of the marketing mix are principally to do with the nature and style of distribution adopted. The product or service in question may go straight from the organisation to its customers; conversely, it may go through a highly sophisticated channel of distribution. Whichever it is, it must be borne in mind that the customers' key requirements of flexibility, responsiveness, ease of access and general convenience remain the key to conducting continuing and effective business.

EXAMPLE BOX 7.13 Marketing Professional Services and Location

The marketing of professional services is carried out according to the norms and expectations of the particular sector. In these cases, those providing professional services – for example, private medical services, private education, architectural and other construction and civil engineering services, or for that matter marketing and public relations consulting – have to make themselves accessible to their potential customer and client bases. A major part of the investment in these cases is therefore the creation of communications links, public relations functions, customer and client services, management functions, and marketing and sales teams, in order to ensure that the 'location' is taken to existing and potential customers and clients.

Individual marketing mixes

The precise nature of individual marketing mixes will depend upon the product and the ways in which it is to be offered in the particular sectors; the rationale for this depends upon the key marketing strategies and standpoints adopted by the organisation. Organisations may seek to vary their marketing mixes in the interests of generating or regenerating new business initiatives. For example, organisations will bring down the price of commodities that are principally sold on the basis of quality rather than price, if by doing so they consider that an advantage can be gained. Conversely, a manufacturing organisation may release its products for sale in a supermarket, thus trading off the exclusivity of its product in return for the ability to generate a much wider accessibility and acceptance.

Marketing research and development

The purpose of such research is to identify and maximise opportunities that the product and marketing mix of the organisation affords. Essentially, this combines the need to seek alternative outlets for products and the technology that the organisation has at its disposal with that of finding out what customers' wants and needs are. Initiatives can then be proposed and generated with a view to satisfying these needs, and to devising and initiating further business opportunities. Properly structured market research also addresses the 'generally favourable response'. Once a generally favourable response is identified, the customer or client group can be targeted. It then becomes essential that this is followed up in detail to establish exactly how often the product or service is to be bought, used and consumed, how much the particular segments are prepared to pay for this, and how often they are willing to pay it (see Example Box 7.14).

EXAMPLE BOX 7.14 Customer Perception

Research conducted by the tobacco industry demonstrated that brand loyalty was almost entirely based on image and identity rather than the taste of the product. Tests were conducted on those who stated categorically that they only liked their own brand. In blind tests, they could not differentiate between their own brands and others of equivalent strength and similar tobacco.

Research carried out by the Coca Cola company on the blind tasting of its own cola products and those of competitors gave initial cause for alarm. In the blind tasting sessions, Virgin Cola was found to carry what the testers perceived to be the best taste. Initially alarmed by this finding, the company soon became comfortable with its products, when it was realised that, whatever the results of *blind* taste, the customer base at large would buy the Coca Cola product anyway.

This applies to other soft drinks: tea and coffee; bread, cakes and biscuits; butter and margarine; beer, wine and spirits.

People are also more positively disposed towards any of these products if they are told that it is of their preferred brand, whether it is or not.

Source: E. Clark, *The Want Makers*, Corgi, 1988.

The process undertaken is concerned mainly with an understanding of the capabilities and capacities of the organisation on the one hand, and the requirements of the market and environment on the other. This will address matters concerning general levels of confidence on the part of the market, customers' purchasing power, their needs and wants, their priorities and any other seasonal aspects, and relate these to the capabilities and capacities of the organisation. Other factors to be taken into account will include a more general assessment of the market and the products in question, and the extent to which these are in expansion, decline or stability. Research will include competitor analyses and the availability of alternative and substitute products in the broadest sense. It will consider the reputation of the organisation in question from a universal and general standpoint, as well as in the particular case of its own relationship with its own market sector. Customer assessments will also be conducted in order to gain a general understanding of their motives, desires, preferred images and identity with the particular product, or range of products, that is to be offered. Finally, modelling activities will need to be commissioned or conducted by the organisation with a view to assessing the extent of the profitability or effectiveness of the range of activities in question. Marketing research and development is thus an integral part of wider strategic aspects, and critical to the determination of the organisation's future direction.

Public relations

The public relations or PR function is to ensure that the marketing wheels are kept oiled and that the organisation's marketing machine works smoothly and positively in order to fulfil the purposes for which it was designed. It has a maintenance and development function that mirrors the operational equivalent. Planned PR concerns identifying in advance suitable initiatives and items that will generate good publicity, and placing them in the media where they will have the greatest positive effects. There is also remedial PR, which is where the organisation has to take responsive or other action to put right something that has gone wrong or to address a negative story that has appeared somewhere in the media (see Example Box 7.15).

Similarly the handling of the press, television and radio must be conducted in ways that ensure that an overall positivism is maintained and that, when problems arise, the last and most enduring note of the story is of the progress that is now to be made.

Organisations will also engage in the placement of stories favourable to themselves in the media, and in those parts of it where the greatest benefit to them will accrue. This is both as a counter to those occasions when problems do arise, and also as part of the more general process of building confidence, and projecting positive images and an aura of 'good corporate citizenship'.

Organisations may also engage in more general customer and market liaison activities as part of their PR effort. This usually takes the form of sending staff on high-profile and sectoral seminars and conferences, and taking stands at trade fairs and exhibitions. Part of the effort of the sales force may also be simply to ensure that customers, and potential customers, are kept aware of the organisation's continued existence and activities. The sponsorship of events also contributes to this general effort.

EXAMPLE BOX 7.15 Public Relations and Politics

The UK Labour government that came to power in 1997 fully understood the value and effectiveness of positive public relations. Before it was elected, the Labour party leadership gave the overwhelming impression that there would be a revolution in public services, infrastructure, and social well-being. This was reinforced with regular, extensive, structured press releases and other media activity that ensured that the political agenda was of prime importance in newspaper and television coverage.

The Labour government kept this up throughout the period of its first term in office. While it quickly became apparent that this was a complex approach, sometimes resulting in messages that were either conflicting, or else downright wrong, the overwhelming impression, among both the media and the public at large, was that the government was continuing to do a good job, and that the political opposition found itself unable to respond in either substance or presentation. At the margins, those who study the substantial political situation in the UK identify groups that are known or believed to be disenfranchised, and groups that are known or believed to be disillusioned or uninterested in the whole process. However, the core public relations drive concentrates on those who are known or believed to be enfranchised and interested; this is perceived to more than address the issues raised by those at the margins.

In 2000 and 2001, there was an extensive national protest against the high price of petrol and diesel. Caused by the real concerns of farmers and hauliers, who could see themselves being priced out of business as the result of these charges, the protests quickly spread to the entire population. There were petrol shortages for days at a time, and serious concerns about the movement of both people and goods. Initially caught unawares, the Labour government engaged its public relations machine.

Through the national television and newspaper media, it promised consultations with the farmers' and hauliers' groups, and gave the strongest possible indication that it would discuss the matter of high fuel prices with the oil companies. Alongside this, the public relations campaign gave the overwhelming impression that if the fuel protests continued, services – especially health and police – would begin to break down.

Accordingly, the protesters called off their action. Some consultations did indeed take place. In March 2001 the Chancellor of the Exchequer, Gordon Brown, reduced the duty on fuel by 2p per litre. Petrol companies matched this, reducing their own prices by 2p per litre also. No further protests took place.

The original demand from farmers and hauliers had been for a reduction of 25p per litre.

Conclusions

Marketing has to be seen as permeating the entire organisation and all its activities. While all products and services must have substance and integrity, they also require effective presentation. Without a marketing stance, the organisation has no reason for existence. This also extends to the provision of public services; in absolute terms the consumers or users of these services are the clients of the public service organisation.

Marketing is at the core of the strategic purpose of the organisation. The organisation will have no impetus or clarity of direction without a clear concept of the nature of the operations that it is going to conduct, the business that it is going to be in and the markets in which it is going to operate. Further to this, there is a range of organisational and managerial activities that has to be conducted in the successful devising and implementation of marketing initiatives.

Marketing is an all-pervasive business concept. It is there to ensure that what is done is both effective and profitable. Any activity that is undertaken should be in accordance with the strategic aims, the technology, the capacities and capabilities of the organisation, its staff and resources. Marketing is also concerned with seeking and generating improvements in the organisation's business activities. It provides the impetus for the devising, development and implementation of new products and services. It is concerned with seeking new business opportunities in fields with which it is familiar and also in new areas. Marketing sub-strategies, plans and objectives will be devised in the pursuit of this.

Effective marketing is also concerned with the gathering of effective and suitable information concerning the organisation's products and their impact on customers, competitors, suppliers and the market place, and the environment at large.

The final part of marketing activity is concerned with the continuity of the organisation. It is the generation of, and bringing on stream of, a steady supply of new products, suitable in both operational and quality terms for the markets in which the organisation operates or seeks to operate. More generally, organisations will seek to identify market opportunities, devise strategies and then implement and develop them. Marketing is thus both a process and a reflection of the corporate state of mind in relation to its business as well as a combination of functional activities and expert and specialist understanding.

CHAPTER SUMMARY

Effective marketing management stems from the successful identification of a core or generic strategic position, and then relating this to the distinctive marketing strategic approach: whether first-in-field, me-too, all-comers, product or service-led, staff- and expertise-led, or market-led.

From this, it is essential to develop effective marketing mixes of all products and services on offer, targeted at customer and client perceptions, expectations, and connotations of quality, value, and convenience.

Alongside this, it is essential to develop images and impressions of the organisation as being safe and steady, full of confidence and strength. This is directly related to the current range of offerings, and also has implications for new products and future activities, and for the organisational culture and management style.

Effective marketing depends on determining the sectors in which products are to be offered, so that the benefits and satisfactions to be accrued through ownership and usage may be presented in ways that reflect customer and consumer needs. Activities created in support of this – including advertising campaigns, sales teams, brochures, information, help and support lines, websites, public relations activities, product placement and sponsorship – must reflect the hopes and aspirations of those targeted, as well as concentrating on the benefits of the specific products and services. Increasingly popular also are perceived and real relationships between organisations, their markets, and communities at large; this element includes support for local groups and clubs, and philanthropic and charitable activities, as well as precise attention to concerns about the particular products or services in question.

Market research and development are essential to ensure that high levels of mutual satisfaction and advantage continue to accrue. This is particularly important in assessing likely and potential demand, opportunities to be gained and possible consequences of failure.

Product and service lifecycles have also to be continually assessed. This needs to be done for both individual items and the total range. It is also essential to consider the effects of general organisational and management practice on the confidence in which particular products and services are held. For example, the Ratner's jewellery and gift shop chain was extremely well regarded by customers and consumers, until Gerald Ratner, the chain's owner, ruined the company at a stroke by describing the product as 'crap' at a private luncheon. Conversely, Gordon and Anita Roddick have been able to maintain extensive confidence in the Body Shop by consistently drawing attention to the ways in which they conduct business, and what their expectations of it are, in spite of the fact that the profit margins are much lower than those available elsewhere in the department store, cosmetics and gift shop sectors.

Finally, the management of marketing requires continued attention to all aspects. Activities that are acceptable and effective today have to be maintained, developed and improved in order to ensure that their currency is retained into the future. The development of marketing strategies must be entwined with the wider aspects of organisational direction, purpose and priorities. Marketing, as with all functional activities, has to be directed and managed in support of this, in order to ensure that the presentation of the organisation, its products and services, remains as effective as the substance.

DISCUSSION QUESTIONS

1. What steps should those responsible for public services management take to enhance the reputation and standing of these services?
2. Why is cigarette marketing so effective? What are the main lessons to be learned from this by those working in sectors where marketing activities are less well developed (e.g. construction and civil engineering, the internet, health promotion)?
3. What are the main factors to be taken into account when deciding to use:
   • a major celebrity
   • controversial images
   in the marketing and promotion of goods and services?
4. Why does everybody consider themselves so familiar with the Virgin organisation? What are the implications of this for any change of ownership in this and other similar companies that may occur in the future?

CHAPTER CASE STUDY

ETHICAL INVESTMENTS IN FINANCIAL SERVICES: FRIENDS PROVIDENT

Friends Provident, the mutual life insurer and financial services company, launched the first ethical financial services lobbying unit in the UK in October 1998. The purpose of this is to put pressure on FTSE companies to amend their environmental policies, to include investments in:

- 'wholesome industries', rather than the safe and generally assured sectors of international infrastructure investment, defence, oil and energy, and gas and chemicals
- those that took active responsibility for waste and effluent management and disposal
- those that engaged in 'fair trading policies', both with Third World governments and with the companies that managed the commodity output produced in those countries
- those that took active responsibility for infrastructure development in order to provide social, as well as narrow economic, benefits for those areas.

The company stated that its ethical investment unit would employ six researchers and cost up to £1 million per year to run. This is estimated to be at least ten times the sum spent on ethical research by other companies in the industry. The unit will also lobby companies with whom it places investments, to improve their stance on pollution, human rights, equal opportunities and broader responsibility to the environment.

Through these activities, the company hopes to attract a greater share of individual pension and unit trust savers. It has also set its sights on targeting the lucrative niche of occupational and personal pension schemes in the UK. Friends Provident already runs a range of 'ethical' unit trusts, life assurance and pension funds under the brand name 'stewardship'. Stewardship manages £1 billion of individual investments and £100 million of institutional funds, and is seeking to double this level by 2005.

The premise for this is that investors in each of these sectors, and especially occupational pension schemes, are looking at ways of giving members a choice over where their money is invested. However, the company has sought to reassure traditional investors by stating that the new range of activities would not alter the investment performance of any of the existing funds, and that the company would remain competitive, and with all of its products.

GENERAL DISCUSSION QUESTION

To what extent is a genuinely ethical approach to investment possible?

QUESTIONS

1. In your view, how should such an ethical approach to investment be marketed? What are the benefits and pitfalls of the approach you have chosen?
2. What is going to cause investors to:

(a) be drawn to ethical investments

(b) be drawn away from ethical investments

in the medium to long term?

3. What other general marketing and public relations activities are required in order to make a venture such as this

8 Managing Operations and Projects

'I always wanted to manufacture real products from real assets to be sold world-wide.' Sir Denys Henderson, former Chairman, ICI, 2000.

'The key to effective company and operations launches is to refine your plan and assemble your team with care.' Matthew Lynn, *Management Today,* May 2000.

'What in the world is a time clock? All we want is successful products and happy staff.' Shigeru Kobayashi, Sony, commenting on the highly successful operations management style at the Company's main factory in Japan, 1986.

CHAPTER OUTLINE

The complexity of operations and project management

Scales of production and services output

Universal factors: location, safety, quality of the working environment, scales of production and output, managing the supply side, maintenance, coordination and control

The application of technology and expertise

The distinctive combination of expertise necessary for effective operations and project management

Similarities and differences between operations and project management

Healthy and safe working practices.

CHAPTER OBJECTIVES

After studying this chapter, you should be able to understand:

the implications and demands made on managers in different sized operational activities

the need for a wide range of skills, aptitudes and expertise when managing projects and operations

the need for absolute universal standards in health and safety at work

and be able to apply simple and universal scheduling methods.

Introduction

The primary concern of operations and project management is the translation of strategy, policy and direction into productive, effective and profitable activities. To do this requires attention to internal and external demands and constraints, and to design work activities so that the desired returns on investment are achieved.

The nature and mix of operations and project activities varies between, and within, organisations. The purpose here, therefore, is to concentrate on those aspects that are universally found. These are:

- location
- safety
- quality of working life and environment
- scales of production and output
- managing the supply side
- maintenance
- coordination and control.

Location

The following considerations affect location.

- Sources, frequency and regularity of input deliveries, especially where these include physically heavy or bulky resources. There must therefore be adequate access to transport and distribution infrastructures.
- Virtual location: location is less of a problem where the delivery of everything critical can be guaranteed through computer networks and via the internet. However again, it is necessary to ensure that the staff required do have access to places of work. Conversely, where the 'place of work' is at home, in business centres, or on the road, managers and supervisors require convenient access to staff working in these ways.
- Just-in-time inputs and deliveries effectively mean that a lot of physical storage takes place on the road; again, the 'location' aspect has to ensure that there is sufficient infrastructure capacity for this to remain effective and profitable.
- Location is also affected by political, social and cultural factors. For example, many transport, distribution and haulage companies, and multi-activity companies with transport, distribution and haulage fleets, are now looking at the best places to locate from the point of view of optimising their corporation and capital taxation allowances, as some countries load these elements much more heavily than others.
- Location was traditionally influenced by the nature of production processes. Industry traditionally tended to locate near its markets if the production process added weight to the product, and conversely at the sources of materials if the processes detracted weight from the products.
- Location is affected by wider environmental support. For example, communities expect to have their own schools, social, health and hospital services, as well as commercial services, including supermarkets and banks.
- For project work, location is dictated by where the work is required. The constraints of the environment have to be reconciled with demands of the project. Building and civil engineering require consideration of effective access and egress. Information technology projects have to reconcile the

demands placed on the particular system with the constraints of their physical location and the size of the environment in which they are to be implemented.

- Organisations must choose their location on the basis that there is a sufficient volume of staff available; where this is not possible directly, those employed must be able to get to work through the use of commuter routes and public transport (see Example Box 8.1).

EXAMPLE BOX 8.1 Access to Work

Access to work is becoming a serious problem for those responsible for the delivery of public services. Solutions have to be found to problems caused by the inability of those in public services to live in some areas because of the high prices of homes in relation to salaries offered. This is also an enduring problem for those on career paths in public services. In the overwhelming majority of cases, frustration and stress are caused by conflicts between strong and enduring levels of commitment to the service itself, and to the client groups in question, against the inability to afford to remain in the sector; or if do remain, then coping with the high levels of fixed charges that accrue as a consequence of remaining in the profession.

This has led to highly publicised, long-term and enduring shortages of teachers, nurses and social workers. However, this is not confined to the high commitment, low salary occupations; there is also a long-term enduring shortage of those coming into the medical, legal and military professions, which enjoy high salaries and high levels of job security. The location of these activities, together with the enduring levels of stress and social dysfunction faced as the result, mean that:

- a better quality of life can be enjoyed in other occupations for the same level of qualification, salary, and expertise
- equivalent levels of personal, professional and occupational satisfaction can be gained without the locational dysfunction.

For example:

- A lawyer working within the military establishment had to stay in London during the week for a period of two months. This was due to a combination of particular work pressures at the time and the uncertainties of public transport. This meant that he was only able to return home at weekends, and this caused domestic stresses and strains, in spite of the fact that he had been married for over 15 years.
- A country GP in the south-west of England found himself working from six separate locations. This was because he was required to cover his own surgery, a cottage hospital, two clinics, and two out-of-hours call centres and emergency surgeries. While this was a clearly stated and understood precondition of the job, it took nearly three years for the local health authority to agree to provide a mobile telephone or a substantial medical emergency travelling kit.

Health and safety

'It is the duty of every organisation, so far as is reasonably practicable, to provide a place of work that is both healthy and safe' (Health and Safety at Work Act, 1974: Preamble).

The great strength of taking this approach to health and safety at particular workplaces is that it requires organisations to be fully aware of the contextual, environmental and operational pressures. From this, organisations are required to provide a place of work that is both healthy and safe, and to take an active responsibility for this, rather than to respond to a detailed set of legally stated criteria.

Health and safety at work in the UK are inspected and monitored by the Health and Safety Executive (HSE). The HSE is responsible for ensuring that standards are set and maintained, and for investigating accidents and emergencies.

This is underpinned by specific legislation in particular areas. Both the EU and the UK government have legislated to address particular operational issues, especially in the following areas.

- **Working time:** the establishment of a basic level of maximum hours that may be requested without employees' further consent. In the UK at the beginning of the twenty-first century this is 48 hours per week. This may be varied in particular cases according to the nature of the work being carried out; where longer hours are required in some weeks, time off must be given in others to ensure that the average of 48 hours per week, over a reasonable period of time, is not exceeded.
- **Substances hazardous to health:** these must be registered, monitored, recorded and, when not in use, kept under lock and key. Such substances may normally only be used under supervision, or with the knowledge of someone else on the premises.
- **VDU screens:** it is normal practice not to allow anyone to work for longer than 2.5 hours at a VDU screen without giving them at least 15 minutes away.
- **Breaks:** it is usual to ensure that everyone who works for a continuous period of four hours is then given a break of at least 30 minutes. Anyone working longer than eight hours per day must be given a break of at least one hour.
- **Emergency procedures:** all organisations must have stated emergency procedures. These must be in written form, and made available to all staff and visitors to the premises, regardless of size of the organisation, or complexity of operations.
- **Road haulage and transport:** anyone driving for more than four hours at a time is required by law to take a break of at least 30 minutes; anyone driving for more than ten hours is required by law to take a break of at least two hours.
- **Waste and effluent disposal:** all organisations are responsible for disposing of any waste or effluent that their operations and activities produce.

The penalty for breaches in each of these areas is a fine. At the beginning of the twenty-first century, plans exist to introduce the offences of 'corporate negligence', 'corporate harm' and 'corporate manslaughter'.

The effectiveness of these statutory approaches to the management of health and safety in operations activities lies in:

- the acceptance of corporate responsibility, as well as the one-dimensional duty to work within the law

- the powers of the HSE, and levels of fines, in order to act as deterrent to corporate malpractice
- the relationship between being a known healthy and safe employer and levels of positive operational activity; the effects of being a known unhealthy and unsafe employer, and the detrimental effects on business and service operations.

Overall responsibility for health and safety at the place of work rests at the top management level in terms of setting standards and producing formal policies. However, all individuals at every level have a joint degree of responsibility to ensure that their own role and work environment is kept as far as possible both safe and healthy. The organisation's policy will identify any instruments for monitoring and assessment such as safety representatives and the election or appointment of safety committees. It may also include training for both managers and operative staff. Finally, particular hazards will be indicated, as will the requirements to wear particular types of clothing, use particular types of equipment and follow particular procedures in dealing with particular hazardous substances or potentially unsafe practices at the place of work. This includes the storage, handling and usage of restricted or supervised goods, chemicals and other equipment.

Quality of working environment

The work environment must be organised in such a way as to be healthy and safe as far as possible, and to provide the required and acceptable standards of comfort and humanity. This includes:

- **Temperature** levels; proper training and clothing must be provided for those who have to work in extreme heat or cold.
- **Lighting,** which must be adequate for work without strains on the eyesight of the workforce.
- **Ventilation** of all work premises, where necessary through air-conditioning and filtration procedures.
- Suitable and sufficient **sanitary accommodation** for all, including separate conveniences for each gender and the disabled; related provisions of washing and drinking-water facilities.
- **Machinery** must have in-built guards and cut-outs, and training must be given in operation; these guards must be maintained in an effective state, and not be removed during operations.
- **Offices** must also be **maintained** in a safe way: telephone and computer wires must not be left trailing; fire doors must not be propped open or locked shut; passages and corridors must be clear and unobstructed.
- **Floors, stairs and passages** must be soundly constructed and maintained, and railings put on stairs and raised walkways.
- Specific **training** must be provided for all those who are required to lift **heavy weights**, or to work with **toxic or dangerous fumes or substances** (for example, in laboratories, chemicals and radioactive substances).
- **Records of accidents** must be kept; all accidents that result in fatality, loss of limb, or absence from work of more than three days must be notified to the Health and Safety Inspectorate.

- **Technology** provided must be capable of safe, effective, productive and profitable use; where necessary, training must be provided. This applies to upgrades as well as the installation of new equipment (see Example Box 8.2).
- **Toxic and hazardous substances** must be kept locked; access to them must be via designated persons only.
- **Access and egress** must enable everyone to get to work and be accommodated; and where necessary, or required, make adequate provision for visitors and deliveries.

Scales of production and output

Woodward (1961) defined the following scales of production.

- **Jobbing or unit production:** the production of single, unique or specialist items; unique quality of service delivery; the ability to customise or make unique products and services according to customer and client demands (see Example Box 8.3).
- **Mass production:** organising work in order to produce high volumes of standard quality products and services. Traditionally, mass production is the cornerstone of all consumer goods; the same principles apply to the output of consumer services (e.g. holidays, travel and transport, banking and financial services).
- **Process and flow production:** traditionally applied to oil, petrol, chemicals, plastic extrusion, steel and paper manufacturing: the output of commodities in a continuous stream or flow. This approach also applies to commercial and public services (see Example Box 8.4).
- **Batch production:** the output of medium volumes of products and services, normally based on the ability to re-jig production and service technology so that different inputs, processing and production methods can be accommodated, and different outputs produced. Batch production is the standard form used in the manufacture of drugs and pharmaceuticals. It is also found in the package holiday sector, where companies buy up in advance volumes of hotel bookings, airline seats and other facilities that are then combined into distinctive batches of offerings.
- **Project production:** a combination of technology, expertise, information, resources and components for the purposes of producing substantial, unique, finished items. Project work is a major concern in all sectors, both internally (e.g. the installation of information systems), and externally, where market testing and feasibility may be conducted on a project basis. This is quite apart from those sectors that operate on a project basis: information systems, civil engineering and construction, defence, and electronics and robotics.

Production capacity

Whatever the form of production capacity undertaken, attention has always to be paid to the following.

- **Equipment and technology,** which must be commissioned, designed, installed and used so as to ensure that there is always a steady stream of products and outputs to the required quality and volume. In some cases this means having equipment

EXAMPLE BOX 8.2 Technology and Staffing

Logically, all technology should be provided on the basis that it is useful, valuable, effective, profitable and productive in the terms demanded by the organisation, as it produces products and services for the enduring satisfaction of its customers and clients. There are however, other points to be considered.

- No technology is ever effective on its own. Its value to the organisation is entirely dependent upon the capability of those operating it.
- The purchase of generic technologies – especially in production and information technology – must always be considered from the point of view of their precise suitability for the particular organisation. In particular, many off-the-shelf personnel information management systems have been found to be less than effective because they do not address the precise questions required by the particular organisations that have purchased them. Similarly, many financial management information systems purchased by central government for the management of public services, and by multinational corporations for the management of international operations, have been found not to address the substantial and priority questions required by these institutions.
- Many technologies are produced to demonstrate the technological brilliance of the inventors and designers, rather than meet the requirements of the end-users.
- Many technologies have insufficient capacity for upgrade, maximisation, or changes in product and service specification.
- Many perceived revolutionary technologies have failed to deliver the benefits promised or strongly indicated. This, above all, applies to commercial usage of the internet; and this is not confined to dot.com companies. Many organisations have websites, purely because it is perceived that they must: that not to have one represents a lack of modernism, lack of current awareness.
- Many individuals, groups, departments, divisions and functions are fitted out with technology (especially computer technology), effectively as part of the reward package. For example, for managers or other perceived experts not to have a personal computer in their office or individual place of work is perceived as a loss of status, or an implication that the particular individual does not know how to use it.

specifically designed and commissioned for particular jobs; in others this will mean the use of generic or flexible technology that can be adjusted to suit a variety of purposes as and when necessary. The onus is on those responsible to ensure that what is required is available. This means ensuring, in turn, that a realistic and practical view of the nature and volume of demands on the organisation is undertaken in the first place (see Example Box 8.5). It also means reconciling the balance between getting adequate returns on the technology (all other things being equal), with having the flexibility and spare capacity to undertake special activities when required. These include special orders, opportunities for new

EXAMPLE BOX 8.3 Customised Production at Levi Strauss

Levi Strauss conducted a project to test the feasibility of offering a customised service allowing customers to choose from a set of features, enabling them to have jeans adapted to their choice. The company has created a website page offering the range of features, including colour mixes, measurements around the hips, waist, thighs and ankles, choice of waist fasteners, and belt buckle options. Customers simply log on to the website, choose their precise requirements from the range on offer, and arrange to collect their jeans or have them delivered when convenient. For those wanting more precise made-to-measure, a body scanning service is available. This comes through either:

- indicating precise measurements, where the individual customer knows these, on the website
- attending a Levi Strauss outlet that has the body scanner facility
- attending another outlet which has the scanner facility available by arrangement with Levi Strauss.

First piloted in the United States in the summer of the year 2000, the facility is set to spread to the UK, Western Europe and the Far East, so as to be fully available by the end of 2003.

Source: Costas Pringipas, *Individual Customisation of Mass Offering Products*, UCL, 2000.

market and new activity entry, a creative and enlightened view of the business of the organisation, and the capability to produce and pilot new products.

- **High quality staff**, capable of using the technology to its full capacity in all circumstances. This, in turn, means attention to workstation and work environment design and training in the understanding, use and operation of the equipment itself. The organisational view must be that this is an absolute commitment; and this is to be transmitted to the staff so that they are in no doubt that they also are committed to being trained in the full, effective and continuous use of the equipment (see Example Box 8.6).

Confidence and feasibility

Projects, products and services must be the subject of wider assessment. This is to ensure that what is proposed fits in with all aspects of the nature and level of activities. If it is decided to proceed down a particular line in support of a new product, it must both have the support of the staff and be complementary to the organisation's current range. If the new product is to replace an old one, the process must ensure that this is indeed so. If it is to tap into a hitherto unexploited sector, the same criteria, of confidence and feasibility, will also have been tested.

Schedules and timetables can then be drawn up. Project work requires establishing the earliest point at which all materials, resources, equipment, technology, staff, information and supplies can be gathered together for the particular purpose stated.

EXAMPLE BOX 8.4 Process and Flow in Commercial and Public Services

Problems in both commercial and public services become apparent when managerial attention is concentrated on operational efficiency rather than quality of service, and customer and client satisfaction.

For example:

- **Banking:** one major clearing bank went through a process of closing hundreds of small branches. The defining criterion was simply the volume of money held in each account. Accordingly, a tiny rural branch in which one or two wealthy people held accounts was kept open, while branches with a larger volume of accounts were either closed down altogether, or opened on a part-time basis only, because they did not serve a sufficient number of more opulent customers. The programme was subsequently rescinded, costing the bank a total of £170 million. Paradoxically, the bank was the same one that greatly improved the effectiveness of service in the eyes of customers by introducing the single queue, in place of individual queues at each desk. This innovation was copied by post offices, large estate agencies, and travel agents, among others. Some banks are, however, diluting the effectiveness of this part of their operations, by restricting the nature of services which can be provided through the cashier and customer service, and insisting that customers use machines for particular service requirements, whether or not they wish to do so.

- **The National Health Service:** the single operational criteria in the provision of hospital services is frequency of bed usage. Extremely efficient in narrow terms, in that it is most unusual to find a bed unoccupied for more than an hour between patients, this has nevertheless led to ward closures and reductions in hospital capacity. This, in turn, has led to: increases in waiting lists for hospital treatment that is deemed to be non-emergency or non-urgent; increases in times between admission through casualty, accident and emergency departments, and being found a ward bed; and, in extreme cases, the stacking up of patients on trolleys in hospital corridors, canteens, and other non-operational areas. In some cases, it is possible to observe a queue at the entrance to wards, where patients are waiting to go in before the previous bed occupant has actually been discharged.

Operations management requires that each of these is organised in order to meet the schedules demanded by production and service output processes.

Proper running timetables, charts, work flows and other processes can then be determined. Each includes the maximum and minimum completion and acceptable periods determined by the particular work in hand. This then forms one part of the basis for work arrangements and methods, and a key element of monitoring, review and evaluation processes. Actual timetables and schedules are compared against ideals; and remedial action taken where the two are out of harmony. Schedules must

---

EXAMPLE BOX 8.5 Measuring Productivity

- **McDonald's:** McDonald's calculate that the average stay per customer in each of their restaurants is 12 minutes. This can lead the unwary into thinking that every seat in the restaurant can be filled five times an hour.
- **The National Health Service:** in the mid-1990s, the NHS entered into extensive calculations designed to work out: costs per patient across the entire service; costs per patient in particular regions; costs per patient in particular hospitals; costs per patient in other activities -- clinics, day care centres, doctors' surgeries, district nursing, and midwifery. This led to a system of service budgeting that was flawed from the outset.
- **Further education:** a further education college calculated the costs of using its classrooms at £130 per hour. A nearby hotel offered conference facilities at £80 per hour. It was not until extensive discussions had been held between the college authorities and the hotel management concerning the feasibility of renting rooms on a regular basis from the hotel that the college realised the fundamental flaw in its comparisons: the calculation of costs and the payment of charges are only tenuously related in complex activities.
- **Semco:** 'One sales manager sits in the reception area reading the newspaper hour after hour, not even making a pretence of looking busy. Most modern managers would not tolerate it. But when a Semco pump on an oil tanker on the other side of the world fails, and million of gallons of oil are about to spill into the sea, he springs into action. He knows everything there is to know about our pumps and how to fix them. That's when he earns his salary. No one cares if he does not look busy the rest of the time' (Semler, 1992).

---

also be related to precise targets and sub-targets along the way so that work appraisal, operations and project development may take place at regular intervals and in relation to critical activities.

Managing the supply side

The key point here is to ensure that all materials, resources, and information required are in place when necessary, while at the same time striking a balance against unnecessary storage costs and charges.

The main elements for consideration are:

- convenience of access, frequency and reliability of sources and deliveries, the flexibility or otherwise of production and project scheduling
- speed of obsolescence of components and information
- whether to bear the price of stockpiling as a comfort or necessity
- any specific demands of the particular range of operations, or project requirements
- the extent to which it is necessary to do things in accordance with the demands of suppliers

EXAMPLE BOX 8.6 The Human Factor and Managerial Responsibilities

It is important to recognise that neither job enlargement, nor the overtly glamorous nature of particularly industrial, commercial and public service activities, are an end in themselves. Managerial responsibility still has to be assumed on a continuous basis to ensure that staff continue to enjoy the benefits of a good quality of working life. Examples of responsibilities that have to be addressed by managers in particular situations are as follows.

- **Railways:** because of technological advances, many present-day trains only require one member of staff to operate them. However, the removal of the second and sometimes third members of the train crew results in feelings of isolation on the part of the driver. While automation therefore leads to a greater potential for service effectiveness, the human factor has still to be satisfied.

- **Financial services:** the practice of 'hot desking' – occupying work space on a first-come first-served, essentially user, basis, as opposed to having one's own designated work space – is operationally efficient in terms of reducing the need for extensive office premises. This is especially true when all members of staff are given their own comprehensive packages of information technology to support their activities. It nevertheless remains true that organisations that have switched the culture of their operations from 'cultural and territorial' to 'technological and flexible' have experienced behavioural problems with their staff where transition has not been managed effectively from a human relations point of view.

- **Football:** a study carried out at Hellas Verona, a top Italian football club, concluded that, in spite of the very high level of wages and salaries paid, the players found themselves isolated. From the pure footballing point of view, the 'automation' and 'high quality production output' consisted of: completely predictable training schedules, exercises and routines; completely predictable diet patterns; completely predictable lifestyles; and a complete lack of personal responsibility. For all the perceived glamour, and very high financial rewards available, young players especially perceived themselves to be cosseted, removed from the real world, and removed from general contact. Accordingly, the only time in which the 'tedious, repetitive, alienating and debilitating' aspects of being a top professional footballer were relieved were on match days. Of especial importance were the four hours of freedom accorded immediately after the end of games. Once press conferences were over, the players were released for the rest of the evening, before reporting back for training and other club duties the following day. The players also found themselves affected by whether they had been selected for the teams or not, and whether the team in which they played won or lost. From a behavioural point of view however, the most important and valued part of their working time was their ability to phone their families and friends outside football during the evening immediately after matches.

- specific issues on the supply side, especially the scarcity of expertise or raw materials
- storage costs and charges
- the need for specific storage facilities; large storage facilities become expensive in terms of land and capital resource usage; information may require storage in specific formats.

The sourcing of raw material, components, information and other supplies is based on the required balance of each of these elements.

Just-in-time

The just-in-time (JiT) approach to purchasing is attractive because it removes the need to use expensive premises for the storage of components and supplies. JiT is based on the ability to engage in relationships with suppliers requiring regular deliveries to be made (daily and in some cases, many times a day). This form of supply has always been the norm in the fresh foodstuffs industry. It has now been extended into many industrial and commercial areas, and public service activities.

When they are delivered, supplies go more or less straight into production areas. As long as it works well and supplies can be more or less guaranteed, JiT is both efficient and effective. Its success depends entirely on the reliability of the suppliers. In practice, it also depends on the ability and willingness of the supplier (or suppliers) to vary the volumes, normally at short notice, to cope with sudden up-flows and down-flows in production.

Further developments are as follows.

- Only when required: the supplier has the capacity and willingness to provide what is required, when required, at instant or very short notice, in response to individual requests from purchasers.
- Only when provided: the supplier establishes a set pattern of frequent deliveries. This enables suppliers to schedule their own activities with a degree of certainty, and requires entering into relationships with purchasers to establish the enduring convenience of the 'only when provided' approach. From this it is possible to plan hourly, daily, or weekly schedules by arrangement (see Example Box 8.7).

Dominance and dependency

Dominance and dependency relate to a behavioural view of the relationship between purchaser and supplier.

Suppliers tend to dominate the relationship when they are the key or major source of a particular component or material, or when they are the only organisation able to respond to specific needs in the ways required by a purchaser. It also occurs where they control a rare and much sought-after primary source of raw materials.

Purchasers tend to dominate the relationship when they are the major user of the materials or components, or when they are so important that the loss of their business would be a threat to the well-being of the supplying organisation.

In the short term on either side, an advantage may be gained through dominating

---

EXAMPLE BOX 8.7 'Just-in-time'

- **DHL:** DHL is a fully flexible, high-quality, instant-response mail, delivery and courier service provider. The company undertakes to take and deliver anything, anywhere in the world, within three hours (local), six hours (regional), ten hours (national) and twenty-four hours (international), subject only to the vagaries of long-haul air flights. The only leeway that they allow themselves in setting their standards concerns long-haul air deliveries; in these cases, specific terms of business are drawn up with particular clients, in order to establish reasonable parameters around scheduled air services. In return for this quality assurance, reliability, and flexibility of delivery, the company charges extremely high prices.

- **Harrods:** Harrods and other perceived exclusive providers of goods and services insist on full flexibility of response when dealing with those who supply them with exclusive, unique or customised goods and services. Again, the charges incurred in such a relationship are very high; and again, this is reflected in the price paid by individual customers for this quality of service.

- **Sandals:** Sandals, the exclusive travel and tour operator, had to change its West Indies weddings package from 'only when provided' to 'only when required', and accept any increase in costs that this brought about. This was because, on some days, couples to be married found themselves being rushed through due to the numbers being married on the same day, while on other days it was impossible to provide the full range of services (e.g. video packages, priests of particular religious denominations) because the lack of volume demand meant that those subcontracted to provide these found it economically unviable to turn out.

It is important to recognise that each situation brings its own advantages, disadvantages, opportunities and consequences. If a durable and high-quality working relationship is to be established between suppliers and purchasers, then any potential pressures brought about by instant demands, short-term changes in quality and volume, or changes to production and service specifications are addressed by those managers responsible.

---

the relationship. In the longer term, whichever side is dependent will seek to reduce its dependency. Suppliers seek alternative outlets for their products and alternative uses for their technology. Purchasers seek alternative sources of components or may redesign their products to avoid having to use the particular components or materials.

Maintenance management

The core purpose here is to ensure that all resources and equipment are in a state suitable for use when required and to provide a swift and effective remedy when things break down or go wrong. It is thus essential that maintenance activities are planned, scheduled and organised in the same way and from the same standpoint as anything else.

Two distinct factors emerge from this: that of **planned maintenance** and that of **emergency response**. Planned maintenance requires the ordering and rescheduling of activities designed to prevent things from going wrong; indeed it is often called 'preventive maintenance'. By conducting regular audits and checks of equipment, signs of wear and tear can be detected. Parts that are beginning to wear out can be replaced before they break down or cause malfunction; equipment that is reaching the end of a production or operational period can be planned to be out of productive action while it is being remedied (see Example Box 8.8).

Coordination and control

Operational and project systems, procedures and processes must be both sufficiently well ordered and flexible enough to be improved where necessary. This is necessary to ensure the task in hand is addressed effectively, and to make it possible to improve every aspect.

The following key points have to be addressed.

*   **The slowest part of the process:** where this occurs; why it occurs; what if anything should be done about it; how it might be speeded up; the consequences of this on other activities.
*   **The quickest part of activities:** together with any consequences; this especially becomes a problem if it results in staff or equipment operating to less than full capability.

EXAMPLE BOX 8.8 Railway Maintenance

Since the privatisation of railways in the UK, maintenance contracts and schedules have presented an enduring problem. This has centred around:

*   requirements for extensive investment in improvements and upgrades to the 'permanent way' (the railway tracks)
*   the demands of train operating companies to keep their trains running
*   the strategic priorities of Railtrak plc, the owners of the permanent way.

It was only late in the year 2000, following a spate of serious crashes, that a clear maintenance strategy began to emerge. Prior to that, maintenance operations consisted purely of 'repair response', in which no action would be taken unless a fault was discovered. Preventative maintenance took place only as a matter of coincidence, where the 'permanent way' was in any case being refurbished or upgraded.

Problems were also caused by the incomplete nature of maintenance contracts, and the inability to find sufficient contractors to carry out the sheer volume of work required. This led to gaps in schedules and specifications for particular operations. For example, one maintenance contract failed to specify a requirement to replace the third electric conductor rail, and this led to the particular stretch of line being shut for a further 48 hours during a busy operating period. Others have failed to include provisions for delays caused by bad weather or a lack of access to supplies.

- **Blockages:** where, why and how these occur; how often they occur; and the range of possible responses. Blockages occur as the result of the nature of production, service, and output processes; shortage of specific facilities; stockpiling at the input and output locations. They causes stresses and strains on other parts of the process (see Example Box 8.9).
- **Volume, quality and time issues:** consideration of what is available, what is possible and what the customers, clients and consumers require.
- **Wastage rates:** these should always be attended to, and constantly assessed for acceptability or otherwise; the expense incurred requires calculation and evaluation; this may also increase concerns for, and volume of activities in, waste and effluent disposal.
- **Customer complaints:** traditionally, this is not regarded as being part of the sphere of operations management. However, it is essential to recognise that all customer complaints originate during production and output processes, and that therefore production and service functions require designing with this in mind. As stated elsewhere, many organisations now make their production functions responsible for managing customer complaints. Even where this is not the case, production and output processes require assessment for the potential for dissatisfaction and complaint.
- **Workforce morale:** there is a direct relationship between a good quality working environment and sustained levels of volume and quality output. Attention to the working requirement requires:
  - a full assessment of the working environment, its strengths, weaknesses and shortcomings
  - a full assessment of the expectations of individuals and groups, and what they require to do the jobs properly and effectively

---

EXAMPLE BOX 8.9 Blockages in the National Health Service

Regular, enduring and frequent blockages occur in the provision of effective patient services in many parts of the NHS. Specific blockages occur in:

- casualty, accident and emergency departments, where patients often have to wait many hours for treatment
- admission delays, often of many hours, to the correct hospital ward; in extreme cases, where an urgent condition becomes an emergency, this has resulted in the need for high speed transfers to other hospitals
- bed-blocking, when it becomes difficult to pass patients on to the form of care required next, or back into the community; this is an especial problem with elderly patients.

Each of these has a compounding effect on activities in the immediate future. They are caused by a combination of staff, equipment and bed shortages that have resulted from a lack of full understanding or attention to the broader medical environment.

- prioritising areas that require attention
- identifying factors inside and outside the control of those involved
- identifying accurately staff pressures brought about by the requirement to work, for example, in untidy, dirty, damp or draughty conditions; and recognising that these conditions may exist in any form of activity
- recognising the particular health and safety constraints inherent, and taking all steps necessary to ensure that accidents, injuries, emergencies, and illnesses, are kept to an absolute minimum.

- Recognising the particular constraints caused by engaging in different **patterns of work**. Specific professional and occupational groups also require particular attention. Those with high degrees of specialisation or expertise, or who work away from the organisation, or to non-standard patterns of work, require full organisational and managerial support if they are to remain effective for the long-term. This applies to many occupations, for example:
  - professional health-service staff working nights and weekends
  - sales staff working in the field for long periods of time and, in many cases, also working evenings and weekends
  - those who work twilight shifts, at times when senior management are likely not to be present
  - those on job and finish activities
  - those working for agencies, subcontractors, consultancies and other distinctive specialisms that are only required for short periods of time.

Measures of success and failure

Projects and operations are measured for success and failure as follows.

- **Specific aims and objectives:** whether these were met; the reasons why and why not; areas for improvement.
- **Derived aims and objectives:** the ability to take advantage of specific opportunities that occurred along the way.
- **Timescale:** whether the deadlines were achieved and if not, the reasons for this.
- **Budget and financial performance:** and the reasons for variances in these.
- **Acceptability:** of the finished project to those who commissioned it, and again the reasons for this (especially if it is not acceptable).
- **Durability:** of the finished project to those who use it; the durability and continuing utility of the finished project to the community at large; the specific durability of information management projects to those now required to implement them.
- **Effects:** on the organisation (or organisations in the case of joint ventures) that has agreed to carry out the work; these will be seen in terms of general changes, cultural effects and special effects upon the rest of the work (e.g. the extent to which one project is dominating the whole of an organisation)
- **Side effects and spin-offs:** opportunities, inventions and openings that occur as the result of carrying out the core activities or main project (see Example Box 8.10).

EXAMPLE BOX 8.10 Concorde

Concorde was developed in the 1960s as an Anglo-French joint initiative that was going to show the way forward to universal supersonic airline travel.

As a project and product it fell far short of this success. It did not succeed in generating large-scale supersonic travel; the only supersonic airliners currently in use remain the Concordes of British Airways and Air France.

In marketing terms, however, it has been turned to great advantage. Concorde is both a monumental technological achievement and a highly photogenic flagship for the two airlines and the two nations. Furthermore, the service developed around it is designed to be first class in every sense. As well as the speed of travel the quality of facilities and service, hospitality, food and refreshment is very high. All those who travel by Concorde are made to feel especially important, part of an elite. The aura thus generated is similar to that which surrounded the 'pullman' class on the railways in the first half of the twentieth century.

In July 2000, one of the French Concordes crashed, killing over 100 people. The remaining planes were grounded for over a year while tests were carried out. British Airways and Air France started flying them again in October 2001, citing the enduring appeal and operational profitability of the service, together with the fact that the accident is overwhelmingly likely to have been caused by a random set of circumstances rather than any technological fault.

The complexity of operations and project management

Other matters relating to operations and project management must be addressed.

- information flows, worked out in advance and evaluated for effectiveness
- establishing the means of dealing with crises and emergencies
- management of the financial aspects of the work, based on accurate high-quality information available to, and understood by, everyone involved
- management of the work and task schedules inherent in the work, including the establishment and acceptance of work methods, timescales, resource gathering, problem-solving, maintenance and development functions
- management of the personal and professional aspects, including identifying and addressing barriers to understanding and progress
- managing communications between everyone involved, with especial reference to organisational, occupational, professional, cultural and language difficulties
- attention to the demands of key individuals
- attention to all individuals, making constructive use of talent and expertise of all those involved
- creation and adoption of a positive and dynamic management style, with especial concentration on the coordination and communication aspects; ensuring effective staff, supplier and customer liaison
- agreement of common aims and objectives, understood, valued and accepted by

all those involved; or at least capable of being harmonised in pursuit of the ultimate outcome
- establishment of key and specific areas of responsibility and accountability, with procedures established for the resolution of any conflict of dispute.

The mix of this varies. In the management of a computer or information systems project for example, ultimate responsibility for its effectiveness lies with the clients and their ability to communicate their precise requirements to the contractor. For civil engineering and building projects, responsibility lies with the contractors to translate the project requirements into something that is acceptable, using their design, building and environmental management expertise.

In certain public projects it may be necessary to develop the liaison process into a non-executive but highly authoritative steering group, because of the requirements or demands of the commissioning bodies, for example where these are municipal health authorities or instruments of national, regional and central government.

Operations management requires the design and implementation of production and service output processes to ensure that the end result is their availability to customers and clients on demand. This involves coordination and harmonisation of all the related activities. Managers and supervisors must be capable of engaging in progress chasing, and in varying the speed, quality, quantity and timescales of delivery so that targets can be achieved as far as possible. Particular blockages and barriers to progress must be addressed. Responsibility lies in ensuring that there are effective channels of communication and access to the resources required, in order to prevent these problems from arising as far as possible, and to take speedy and effective remedial action (see Example Box 8.11).

Joint ventures and other cooperative efforts

These occur when two or more organisations come together for a stated business purpose or project. Such ventures are overwhelmingly related to strategic business reasons to do with the pooling of expertise, sharing of risk, building of confidence and playing to expertise, capacity, resources, specialisms and strengths that make the joint venture a sounder approach than an attempt on the matter in hand by an individual organisation.

In this context, from an operational and executive standpoint, there is a requirement to establish a commonality of purpose among those drawn together from the different organisations in the joint venture. What is necessary is the reconciliation of organisational rivalries and propensities for conflict through means of focus on the precise purpose of the joint venture. Within this, it is also necessary to reconcile the often differing and divergent sub-objectives that the individual organisations have for becoming involved in the first place. This is exacerbated if one organisation is the senior partner or another has been brought in simply to fulfil a small but critical part of the project. Qualities of trust, harmony and openness between organisations that may be competing for work elsewhere may need to be fostered. Reporting relationships, lines of communication, and management structure and style have to be adopted that achieve all of these matters and provide a basis for positive and harmonious activity. Any network planning or project scheduling is complicated by the need

---

EXAMPLE BOX 8.11 Creativity and Innovation

It is essential that creative and innovative attributes are present if organisations, their departments and their staff are to progress and develop. A key feature of project and operations management training is therefore the requirement to concentrate on these elements. Some occupations, business sectors and organisational and management styles lend themselves better to this than others. Above all, those activities that engage people with formal, technical or professional qualifications are more or less certain to require professional and occupational development as a condition of a continued capability to practise.

Activities and approaches are therefore undertaken with the view to progressing and developing the organisation and its activities, in order to solve problems, bring new ideas and ways of working, as well as developing new products, projects, initiatives and services.

A key concern therefore is to foster the energy, enthusiasm and drive that those in managerial positions must have. A personal, as well as professional, commitment to the work in hand is required. This can only be achieved if there is full organisational support for the approach, and resources are made available. The attitude to problems must be that they are there to be resolved; the attitude to known or perceived failure must be based on full assessment, combined with ensuring that everybody involved learns lessons.

Both operations and project management require the capability and willingness to undertake, when necessary, feasibility studies, projections, pilot production, models and mock-ups. Extrapolation and 'what if?' exercises should also be undertaken when required. Misconceptions and misunderstandings about the nature of the work to be carried out can then be ironed out. Any necessary external constraints that become apparent must be addressed; this includes attention to public perceptions, and the attitudes of lobbies and vested interests, as well as the technical, operational and organisational feasibility of the work proposed.

---

to reconcile inter-organisational as well as operational factors. In summary, the 'project approach' is complicated by the need to create both a distinctive identity and clarity of purpose within the situation as outlined and implied. This will be underwritten by a form of contract at the point at which the work is commissioned and the venture agreed.

Projects and operations constraints

All work is carried out within particular constraints. These are as follows.

- **Sectoral economics:** activities in every sector are limited by the rates of return available, and by the costs of technology and expertise required.
- **Schedules:** the speed at which operations and projects progress is, in part, dictated by the speed at which supplies, expertise and information can be made available.

- **Operational and project lifecycles:** relating to the length of useful life of the finished item; fashionable and seasonal goods and services, for example, have to be provided at very short notice; project work often requires substantial redesign in order to meet changing social, economic and technological pressures.
- **Resources, expertise and technology:** project and operations work is always affected when resources, technology and expertise suddenly become available due to matters outside the organisation's control. For example, finance may suddenly become unavailable because of wider economic changes (especially downturns); expertise may no longer be available when required (e.g. due to the UK recession in building and civil engineering in the early 1990s, much expertise was lost to these sectors altogether).

Conclusions

The nature and complexities of operations and project management outlined in this section should serve as an illustration of the managerial tasks necessary in these activities. They cover all manufacturing and service activities, and all forms of project work: construction and engineering projects, urban regeneration, power stations, irrigation schemes, transport and traffic activities (such as highways, motorways, bypasses and the Channel Tunnel). Such projects have their own external and distinctive entity, life and manifestation, often bringing work, resources and inward investment to the communities in which they are located.

Managerial functions also cover academic and commercial research, medical research, computer and defence projects, as well as wider social issues (see Example Box 8.12). Such activities normally trigger off research and development initiatives all of their own, and sub-project, related and contributory activities and the teams that go with them are generated in response to the main matter in hand and in support of it. Such projects and activities inevitably have a 'blossom' effect: that is, due to their very nature and complexity, inventions, technological advances and new opportunities are made or come to the fore.

Projects may be developed because there is a ready and known market or use for the prospective outcome. This is especially true of defence activities, and also research commissions concerning drugs, medicine and health care. Pressure is on university research departments and companies operating in this field to find the means of curing AIDS, motor neurone disease, muscular dystrophy and cancers. Successful project activity in these fields leads to the creation of steady-state and assured operational activities.

CHAPTER SUMMARY

The effectiveness of the management of projects, operations and activities lies in the ability to understand, and apply to particular situations, the extremely complex set of principles indicated in this chapter. There is no absolute set of rules that applies to all circumstances, and the balance and mix of these principles varies between organisations (even those in the same industrial, commercial or public service sector) and projects (even those concerned with the same ultimate output, such as a new motorway or a new information system).

EXAMPLE BOX 8.12   The Big Issue: Commercial and Social Drive

The Big Issue was founded in 1996 by John Bird, a journalist. It is a foundation for the homeless, raising funds to purchase commercially accommodation, food, shelter and clothing for people in the UK who either have no home or live in sub-standard accommodation. The Big Issue is a company limited by guarantee, and accorded charitable status. It raises money through lobbying, covenanting and philanthropic donations. It employs homeless persons to sell its magazine – also called *The Big Issue* – as a means of getting them back into work, and away from the problems of homelessness.

Originally campaigning on the single issue of homelessness, it quickly became apparent that *The Big Issue* magazine would have to appeal to a much wider audience if it was to be commercially successful in the long term. It was accordingly revamped at an early stage to include feature articles on controversial and campaigning issues. Some pages in each issue are devoted to the creativity of the homeless. There is also an extensive entertainments section.

The original project was designed to find an alternative route to tackling both the causes and effects of homelessness. However, it quickly became apparent that the operational side had to be enduringly successful. The homeless people employed to sell the magazine have to be convinced that they are a newsagent by any other name, otherwise the work itself would have no intrinsic value. The operational side of the project is run on standard lines. Emphasis is given to those wishing to get into news media, journalism, and other creative activities; otherwise the structure is exactly equivalent to that operated by mainstream magazines. The initial project has therefore developed into a long-term and enduringly viable operation. Regional issues are produced in different parts of the UK, and the magazine is sold in most towns with a population of over 10 000. It has attracted a strong following of loyal customers, especially in the major commuter areas, and also continues to attract a large amount of interest from browsers and passers-by.

Operations and project managers therefore need as full an understanding of their particular environment as quickly as possible. Currently, it is becoming increasingly the norm that anyone responsible for a set of activities or project must become an enthusiast in the particular field in which they are being asked to work. For example, the project manager who was responsible for the completion of the Twickenham rugby stadium in 1996 had never been to a rugby match, or had anything to do with the game until he was asked to build the stadium; he subsequently became – and remains – an enthusiast and committed follower. For all the failings of the Inland Revenue database in 1999, the project manager responsible made it his business to understand the legal, social and operational intricacies of the UK tax system. All those who work on The Big Issue adopt personal commitments to the problems of homelessness, whether or not they have had any involvement before.

It is also essential to recognise that the understanding and application of these principles requires constant development. For example, production and operational processes can be speeded up; blockages and barriers can be removed, and effective attention to these requires that managers are creative and visionary, as well as rigorous and focused. This applies to all aspects of activities.

Effective project and operations management requires the ability to coordinate this level of application with a detailed understanding of the following in every particular set of circumstances.

- A strategic approach to operations and project management.
- Operational planning in detail; operational efficiency; operational effectiveness; each of these applies in project, as well as mainstream, activities. Each requires full attention. It should be noted that attention to one at the expense of all the others is certain to result in long-term operational and general management decline, to the detriment of customers, clients and end-users. For example, in the NHS attention to operational efficiency – bed management, in which hospital beds are left unoccupied as little possible – has contributed greatly to the declining fortunes and reputation of the service. Narrowly efficient though this undoubtedly is, it is flawed because it is based on a perfect set of calculations, rather than human demand, and has also caused other factors to be neglected.
- Whether in operations or project management, the importance of relationships cannot be overstated. Relationships with contractors, suppliers, expertise, customers and clients must be developed and maintained on a personal as well as professional basis in order to establish the effectiveness of activities and mutuality of interest. Where this is not possible, or not seen as a priority, there is a loss of understanding of the precise requirements on the part of those involved. This leads to medium and long-term performance declines – especially when purchasers feel themselves able to switch suppliers at short notice, when subcontractors feel themselves able to produce substandard work for project managers, and when specific expertise is capable but not willing.

Finally, it is essential to recognise the broader context of operations and project management. It is perfectly possible to do this from the point of view of both the satisfaction of a narrow self-interest and key stakeholder drive. Anything that requires a more enduring basis must, however, be managed with the wider environment, other stakeholders, and long-term effects of particular activities in mind.

DISCUSSION QUESTIONS

1. A new management information system is to be installed into an organisation. What operational activities immediately become necessary as a result?
2. A medical research company has spent 20 years and £600 million developing a

cure for cancer. It now thinks it has the results, and these are positive. Identify the operational drives and restraints that now exist, stating where the overwhelming pressures are coming from, and the implications for those responsible for the management of operations.

3. A pottery production line can produce 500 mugs an hour. A blockage then occurs at the decoration stage, because each has to be painted by hand (except where simple patterns and designs are required). Each member of staff responsible for painting mugs can do six per hour. What is the nature of the blockage that exists, and what action, if any, should the managers of this situation take and why?

4. When it was commissioned, a motorway project was expected to cost £63 million, and be completed in nine months. To date, it has cost £93 million, has taken 15 months, and is not expected to be ready for a further six months. What actions should those responsible for the project design, inception, management and delivery now be taking, and why?

CHAPTER CASE STUDY

EDINBURGH AT CHRISTMAS

The City Council, the Health Service, and the Scottish Office have been taking part in discussions about a proposal to develop the site in Chalmer's Street, at the side of the Edinburgh Royal Infirmary (ERI). At present, the site largely consists of substandard housing, under-utilised space, car parks (owned by NCP) and depots and storage facilities for the university and ERI.

In outline, it is proposed to clear the site and redevelop it to include:

- a ten-storey block of offices in which 3500 of the City Council's officials would be relocated
- an eight-storey block in which the ERI management and administration would be housed
- underground car parking beneath the two blocks for 700 cars, to be shared jointly by the City, ERI and the university
- the development, jointly between the university and the ERI, of an acute and serious injuries centre of excellence, adjacent to the two office blocks.

The development is to take place under a PFI/PPP arrangement. A preferred lead contractor, Cazeries Sarl (a large French civil engineering company based in Toulouse in southern France) has been approached. Cazeries are very keen to participate, because they need to expand into new markets, and they want to build up their own experience in this kind of work. They propose an arrangement as follows.

- The clearing and building work is to commence in February of next year, and to be completed in 30 months; this Cazeries estimate to cost £93 million.
- The facilities are to be finished and ready to use after a further six months; Cazeries estimate that this will cost £63 million.
- The facilities are to be leased by Cazeries to each of the clients for an estimated £260 per square metre per annum for a minimum term of 25 years. This rental is to rise by 2 per cent per annum after an initial period of three years; this figure may be revised upwards to reflect commercial pressures on Cazeries

brought about by inflation, interest rate changes, and any changes in value to the site itself.

- At the end of this period, either the site will revert to Cazeries to be redeveloped yet again, or it will be transferred to the clients for 'a fee that reflects the commercial value, factor utilisation elements, and general relationship' of the project.

Everyone involved is very keen to proceed. A skeleton organisation, Erigate plc, has been created to coordinate efforts. Erigate is to be the formal client of Cazeries for this project. It has hired a top executive, Anthony Hague, from a small political consultancy in London, to be the venture's CEO and project leader. His deputy is to be Michael Brown, another Englishman. Hague and Brown have a high professional respect for each other, and do not socialise.

Hague is very keen to go ahead, and proposes to call a press conference for 3 January, in order to be able to announce that the venture will go ahead, that it will commence on time in February, and to sign the agreement publicly. Also if the project does go ahead, he is to hold a massive firework party and celebration on the open ground at the back of the project site, at which he will appear, introducing some of his many English pop-star friends.

Brown however, would like to know more about what he is letting himself and the clients in for. He accordingly asks you to address the following questions.

QUESTIONS

1. Briefly evaluate the assumptions and information that you have; identify gaps in the information, and what needs to be done about them.
2. Briefly summarise the environmental pressures and arrive at an initial view of the viability of the proposal as given.
3. Identify the broader issues that have to be considered if the strategic and operational approaches are to be successful.
4. Briefly identify the pressures, drives and restraints on the proposal; stakeholder positions and requirements; and the main elements that are likely to contribute to the overall success or failure of the venture.

9 Financial Management

'If we owed our backers £1 million, we would have a problem. Because we owe them £10 billion, they have a problem.' Alistair Morton, Chief Executive, Eurotunnel, 1998.

CHAPTER OUTLINE

The relationship between financial management and accounts; the distinction between financial management and accounts

Assets and liabilities; the valuation of assets and liabilities; the assessment of assets and liabilities from a managerial point of view

Measuring and assessing returns on capital and other assets employed

Managerial measures of financial performance.

CHAPTER OBJECTIVES

After studying this chapter, you should be able to:

understand the complex relationship between finance, accounts, and financial management

understand how accounts are constructed, and how managers should make use of these

understand some of the different approaches used by organisations in the management of their finances

understand and apply the simple measures of finance to particular activities and operations, and evaluate these for success and failure.

Introduction

Finance is the lifeblood of all organisations, in whatever sphere they operate. Companies in the private sector are required to make profits, to generate a surplus of income to expenditure over a period of time that supports the continuation of the business and provides an adequate return to the backers. Public, social and health services, working to targets allocated by governments and other authorities, must use these resources to best advantage to satisfy the sectors that they serve, and reconcile any constraints under which they may be placed.

Accounts are kept and produced for three main reasons.

- An essential check by the organisation on the state of its activities, income and expenditure in financial terms. This enables it to identify where resources are being consumed, in what volumes and the reasons behind this.

- The presentation of its financial state to stakeholders: staff, stock markets, stock and shareholders, banks, suppliers, customers, the community at large and the sectors in which it operates.
- Compliance with the law. Across the Western world, the law requires organisations to produce 'a true and fair' statement of their activities in financial terms, normally once a year, indicating the performance and state of the organisation in this way. This must be subject to external scrutiny and audit. Organisations have to pay tax and the extent of liability for this arises as the result of these accounting activities.

The context of financial management

Accounts are produced by qualified and professional accountants, and other experts in accordance with legal requirements and their own rules, codes of conduct and conventions which govern the ways in which they carry out the work and produce results. Explanations and translations of these are often given in organisational, annual and other public reports, together with how these have been applied. Detailed explanations of these are available from the professional bodies of the accounting industry.

The managerial approach to accounts and financial aspects is concerned with the use, evaluation, interpretation, analysis and judgement of the financial data, and what it means for the present and future of the organisation. It is one of the points of information used as the basis for effective decision making. It enables a managerial assessment of current and recent performance in financial terms.

More specifically, effective and accurate accounts enable managers to pinpoint the following:

- **Costs:** these can be assessed from an informed view of the extent to which costs are justified; whether or not they represent effective usage of the organisation's resources; whether these constitute activities worth pursuing; whether improvements could/should/must/might be made in the given area.
- **Income:** this can then be assessed on the basis of adequacy overall. It also makes it possible to build a picture of income per product, per product range, per outlet; per region, and overall.
- **Returns:** attention to returns enables the organisation to assess the extent to which the income being generated represents an excellent, adequate, satisfactory or unsatisfactory return on investment, activities and cost. This is seen, in turn, from a variety of points of view: the organisation's own desired levels of return, the time period over which the returns are to be made, and the performance of products, services and activities in their pursuit.
- **Timescales and deadlines:** all financial performance has to be seen in terms of how long it takes to achieve particular aims, objectives, goals and targets. This can then be evaluated in terms of whether returns desired are feasible in the circumstances, and the lessons that need to be learned as the result. It is also essential to realise that:
  - where desired or required returns were anticipated, the actual returns need to be monitored, reviewed and evaluated

- where they were met more or less exactly, in order to understand the reasons why things were successful
- where returns were seriously under target, in order to understand what went wrong or had not been considered
- where returns were seriously over target, in order to be able to understand why this particular set of circumstances had not been considered in advance.

- **Wider expectations and perceptions of satisfaction:** based on sectoral norms and the interests of stakeholders. Specific attention needs to be paid to:
  - shareholder and backer demands: for dividends on their shareholdings; repayments; other financial returns; to be paid on the deadlines anticipated and agreed
  - staff: the demand for steady and increasing levels of wages and salaries; the capability to earn commissions and bonuses where these are stated or clearly implicit in reward patterns
  - suppliers: the ability to establish a pattern of financial management that ensures that their cashflow management is adequate and effective
  - customers, clients, consumers and end-users: the hub of all financial management lies in the ability to charge prices for products and services that ensure the volumes of business necessary to sustain the organisation's financial requirements in the medium to long term, and to provide adequate returns on the capital and other resources employed (see below)
  - media and financial analysts: unless carefully managed, the media and financial analysts are likely to arrive at their own view of the performance of a particular organisation, partly on their own judgement, and also on the demands of their own particular professions, especially if there is a potential for a controversial or sensational news story
  - vested interests, pressure groups, and lobbies that require a proportion of organisational finance to be spent in addressing their own particular concerns; of especial currency are the needs to put a proportion of resources into maintaining and improving the environment, quality of life, and quality of working life.

- **Comparisons:** with the achievements of other organisations in the same or related sectors and activities. It is important to note, however, that all organisations are ultimately required to stand alone. While comparisons along these lines make easy reading, they do not always convey a total understanding of organisational financial performance, nor do they give anything other than a single and non-contextual means of comparison. For example, a company that had overtly under-performed others in its sector by 90 per cent may have done so because the majority of its contracts were in a sector of the world that had suddenly become volatile; or because one of its key suppliers had gone bankrupt; or many customers in a key market had suddenly lost their jobs due to closure of their own place of work. The list could be more or less endless.

- **Departmental, divisional, functional and sectional performance:** in the same terms. Again, it is important to recognise that it is very unusual to allocate resources purely on departmental headcount or nature of activities. Assessment is required according to specific needs. From a financial management point of view however, managers should be seriously concerned when it becomes evident that support functions are consuming increasing volumes of resources and primary activities, especially where it is also apparent that the primary activities are declining as the result.

Sources of finance

Companies and commercial organisations draw their financial resources from the following.

- sale of shares, either to family, friends and colleagues (if the company is small and private), or to the general public and other institutions on the stock markets of the world if the company is 'public'
- sale of loan notes and debentures, which may be described as short-term or fixed-term capital, and which must be repaid on the date specified
- government and EU grants and incentives issued either in the form of a company guarantee, or else in return for undertaking government and EU contracts, including private finance initiative and public–private partnership work
- retained income and profits from activities carried out
- bank loans on which interest is repayable over the period of the loan; the loan itself is normally arranged under a form of contract and, again, must be repaid at the stated time (or times).

Note: gearing

Gearing is the relationship between bank loans and other sources of finance. The convention in the West is that gearing should be as low as possible, meaning that the balance of financial resources should depend as little as possible on bank loans. Conversely, Japanese companies tend to have very high gearing, though it should be noted that the majority of their loans come from nationalised banks underwritten and effectively guaranteed by the government; this is seen as less of a problem in these circumstances.

Assets and liabilities

Assets

Assets may be defined as follows.

Capital and tangible assets

Capital assets consist of premises, technology, equipment, expertise and machinery to be used in the production of the organisation's offerings. They are sometimes referred to as fixed or tangible assets. Their acquisition is based on a combination of what the organisation can afford, the projected length of the assets' useful life and the uses to which they are best suited.

Capital expenditure is also undertaken on supplies (and suppliers) and the means of distribution including vehicle fleets, containers, retail and other points of public contact outlets.

Intangible assets

Intangible assets consist of reputation, goodwill, confidence, identity and expectation levels. They reflect the basis on which people come to do business with a particular organisation. High levels of goodwill and expectation are normally expected to translate into high levels of repeated business, increased reputation, and the enlarging of customer demands and customer bases.

This may, in particular, be applied to brand names and images. Strong brand names (such as Coca-Cola, Nescafe, Barbie) carry high and continuing levels of value. They each also have a commercial value in their own right, and the owning companies could (if they so wished) put them up for sale.

Customer bases, the regularity and frequency of business, and the general perceptions in which customers hold particular organisations, may also be said to be intangible assets and are often referred to as 'goodwill' in company accounts. This holds true for other major stakeholders, especially suppliers, the media, and the community at large.

Key figures

Also, somewhere in the asset base, account should be taken of the contribution of key figures. For example, the 'value' of Richard Branson to the Virgin Group is clearly considerable; yet it is very difficult to put a precise figure on this. It is also possible to infer from this that other stakeholders will write down the value of the group once he leaves it, or should anything happen to him.

Other organisations employ key figures to support their total assets in similar ways. For example:

- **Once-family businesses:** some businesses previously owned by founding families but now in the hands of shareholders' representatives continue to keep a family member on the board of directors. This is to ensure that the original identity is not completely lost, and to retain the sense of purpose with which the business was first built up. For example, there are still family members on the board of McAlpine (civil engineering), John Lewis (department store) and Pichetsreider (BMW), even though overall control has long since passed out of the hands of the families.
- **Football:** many top clubs continue to employ former great players as consultants, advisers and directors. For example, Franz Beckenbauer (Bayern Munich), Gianni Rivera (A.C. Milan) and Bobby Charlton (Manchester United) are all executive directors of the clubs for which they used to play, and this gives an impression of continuity to both backers and club supporters.
- **Financial services:** someone who has made a real or perceived major contribution to the commodity performance of financial products, stocks and shares may be hired by a rival organisation in order to enhance their own prestige and confidence among their client base. For example, Nicola Horlick became an extremely valuable commodity in her own right once it became known that she was a very successful fund manager. She became even more valuable from an intangible/behavioural point of view when she became famous for also being a working mother with five small children.

Short and medium-term assets

These take the form of acquisitions made specifically for a purpose. Building companies acquire land banks on the basis that they will be able to build on these in the near future. Glassware and china companies acquire designs to be used in future product development. Travel companies and agencies acquire banks of hotel rooms and airline seats to be sold on in the next season.

Long-term assets

These are acquired on the basis that the organisation is always going to need them. This especially applies to property and some forms of capital goods and production equipment. However, at present production technology in all fields is being improved with such rapidity that it also may be necessary to discard expensive equipment even if it is only a fraction of the way through its useful life, if to continue using it would render the organisation uncompetitive. In the particular case of information technology, the demands from management information systems may be predicted with a fair degree of certainty; the capability of organisational websites certainly cannot. While the former are therefore clearly an asset, the latter have to be seen from a much broader perspective: on the one hand it may be psychologically damaging not to have a website at all, while on the other hand it may be commercially unviable to retain one.

Managerial assets

The concept of managerial assets takes the view that all elements of the organisation should, be viewed as assets. This especially concerns:

- Staff: especially where they have distinctive expertise and high and enduring reputation for quality, value and service, or excellence in innovation, research and development activities; or rare and highly prized skills and knowledge.
- Markets, customers and client bases: especially those dominated by the particular organisation in terms, either of volume of business conducted or high levels of reputation. However, this should be acknowledged in all areas in which the organisation operates, especially as even a bad reputation acquired in a small niche market may have substantial knock-on effects for the rest of activities.
- Command of commodities, components or other valuable and highly sought-after scarce resources; command of key expertise; command of key outlets and points of distribution.
- Excellence and expertise of management and direction (see Example Box 9.1).

Liabilities

Liabilities are the obligations and charges that are certain to be incurred or that are present as the result of the company's current activities. They are as follows.

- **Regular and continuing costs and obligations.** Of these the most regular and continuing is staff; all staff incur costs and have to be paid. Other regular liabilities include capital repayments; interest charges; supply, production and

EXAMPLE BOX 9.1 Management as an Asset

Many organisations can confuse the value of management as an asset, and that of particular managers, with the price (i.e. salary, share options, bonuses, and perks) that they place on them. The value of management as an asset is something about which it is difficult to be precise; it is a reflection of a combination of:

- the relationship between the results required and those achieved
- the difference that managers as individuals have made to the performance of a particular organisation; again, this is something about which it is very difficult to be precise
- the value to the organisation of their name and past reputation; again, very difficult to measure
- the value accrued as the result of the consequences of particular actions; for example, managers who employ high-profile management consultants to make recommendations for business restructuring may accrue a short- to medium-term increase in the share price, but this has also to be seen in terms of the long-term performance of the organisation
- the relationship between courses of action prescribed by managers, and opportunities foregone; which again are very often the subject of supposition or extrapolation only.

The problem is further compounded by the perceived need to pay high salaries for perceived key individuals, particularly when senior figures and others are known, believed or perceived to be over-compensated for failure. Examples include the following.

- Announcing a salary package of £145 000 per annum for the Chief Inspector of Schools in 1999 at the Labour Party Conference, the Education Secretary, David Blunkett, stated, 'It is necessary to pay the market rate for key executives' (though he did not state what the market rate actually was, nor why he had arrived at that particular figure).
- One major clearing bank doubled the pay package available to its chief executive officer in order to secure the right person. This person subsequently left the company after three months because of cultural differences and boardroom in-fighting.
- Robert Ayling received a severance payment of £2 million when he left British Airways, in 2000, following a poor period of sales.

From this, it is clear that organisations which are genuinely concerned about their long-term future are going to be required to take a much more precise view of what constitutes the relationship between the value of particular managers (and indeed others) and the price that ought to be paid for them. It is another clear indication that in the future there are going to be far fewer managers in organisations, with far greater precise expectations placed upon them, and levels of reward commensurate with achievement, rather than presentation.

distribution costs; and other bills and charges incurred – especially fuel, electricity, rent, rates, heating and lighting.

- **Activity-related charges:** these vary according to the nature of the organisation. The most universal are marketing activities, maintenance charges, research and development and other pioneering and prospecting work.
- **Short-term liabilities:** incurred, for example, by hiring extra or specialised staff or equipment to get over a particular problem, for which a long-term benefit is expected to accrue.
- **Intangible liabilities:** of which the most common is a bad reputation based on poor production, quality and volume; inability to meet deadlines; poor presentation; wrong and inappropriate images; or the loss of reputation or presence of a key figure.
- **Sudden liabilities:** that occur based, for example, on the sudden obsolescence of products, sudden price drops, increases in the price of supplies or components, of or production and other technology. When this occurs, the organisation has to decide very quickly whether it is going to try to rejuvenate what it is already doing; or whether to remain in the sector or not. If it decides to do so, then it must meet the sudden liability as a consequence of this (see Example Box 9.2).

EXAMPLE BOX 9.2 Sales of Assets

The item 'sales of assets' very often appears as a line in corporate balance sheets and profit and loss accounts. From a managerial point of view, this has to be viewed in one of two ways.

- The assets being sold are genuinely assets, but there is an overriding organisational reason for selling them on which is normally to get over a short-term crisis.
- The sale of assets is actually a sale of liabilities: the organisation is divesting itself of things that it no longer wants.

Once it becomes apparent that an organisation is divesting itself of a substantial volume of property, goods, databases or expertise that it no longer requires, it is important to recognise that the value of these on the market always declines. Other organisations know that these items are required to be sold, and are therefore prepared either to wait for the price to drop, or to name their own lower price in order to secure the particular item at an advantage.

From a managerial point of view also, it is essential to recognise that the sale of items that genuinely are assets is certain to do short- and medium-term damage to the continuing viability of the organisation, and that some way is going to have to be found of replacing these assets as soon as operating conditions allow. The sale of liabilities should be conducted as quickly as possible in order to remove the necessity to consume resources on their continued upkeep and usage.

The relationship between assets and liabilities

Something that is bought as an asset can quickly turn into a liability. Production and information technology, bought as a long-term investment, may be rendered obsolete at any time by new inventions. Building companies that have bought land banks find that these become a liability if the demand for buildings dries up or if the price of land falls. Projects for which capital goods have been bought may be cancelled if other costs or unforeseen problems make the project no longer worthwhile.

Depreciation

Depreciation is an accounting convention that shows the period of time over which an item is gradually paid for, paid for in instalments, or written off altogether. It is important to remember that it is purely an accounting convention and not a managerial tool.

For example, a piece of equipment may have cost £100 000. The organisation's accounting function may set out to depreciate it, quite legitimately from their point of view, at £20 000 per annum for five years. If it becomes obsolete after two years, then the managerial stance must be to scrap it and replace it, whatever the accounting convention may say (see Example Box 9.3).

Investment appraisal

Investment is a continuous commitment, a condition and consequence of being in a particular sector. The specific nature of investment varies between sectors and between the organisations operating within them. Generally, however, this continuous commitment always covers the following.

- staff expertise, training, improvement and development
- organisational capability, capacity, improvement and development
- systems improvement, development and refinement
- brand and other marketing asset reinforcement, development and enhancement
- reputation, confidence and expectational enhancement
- technology improvement, development and replacement.

A managerial approach to investment appraisal enables fully informed financial decisions to be taken by managers, especially for the long term. These include the following aspects.

- whether to buy, rent or lease premises, staff, equipment and technology (see Example Box 9.3)
- whether to buy up stocks of supplies; whether to stockpile or to rely on frequent deliveries (just-in-time)
- whether to buy up or lease transport and distribution fleets and other vehicles
- whether to employ or sub-contract specialist staff and expertise
- the vagaries surrounding the useful life of each of these elements and necessary actions that may have to be taken concerning them at any time.

EXAMPLE BOX 9.3 Products, Services and Equipment: To Make, Lease or Buy?

This part of financial management is specifically concerned with whether organisations choose to:

- make their own products from components and raw materials, or buy them ready-made and then repackage them and sell them on
- lease or buy capital goods and other equipment
- construct, own or lease their own databases
- employ or lease their own expertise.

It is a complicated series of decisions. However, overriding considerations will include:

- expenses, liabilities and charges incurred as the result of going down each path
- the relative availability of equipment, expertise, products and services should they only be leased or bought in when required
- the nature of any contractual and other legal obligations that may have to be met each time the product, service or expertise is used.

It is also essential to recognise that even where there is an overtly clear financial advantage, the decision will ultimately be taken on the basis of managerial choice. Whatever the financial advantage, some organisations prefer to own their own assets so as to have full control over them; while others prefer to lease or charge out as much as possible in order to reduce their fixed cost base. It is therefore not possible to arrive at a decision on the basis of any 'rational' approach.

The purpose of investment is to gain a return, and this is normally expressed in financial terms. This then needs further development in order to establish:

- boundaries of acceptability
- timescales.

This is so that, if things do not go according to plan, a full assessment of the reasons can be made (see Figure 9.1).

This can be dealt with, to an extent, using computer simulations, critical path analyses, or performance, evaluation and review techniques. However, it needs broader consideration at the outset because timescales can be changed, extended or contracted as the result of political pressures in public investment, commercial pressures in business investment, or fluctuations in the value of money and interest rates.

Attention is also required to the following which may be desired, or required, returns on investment.

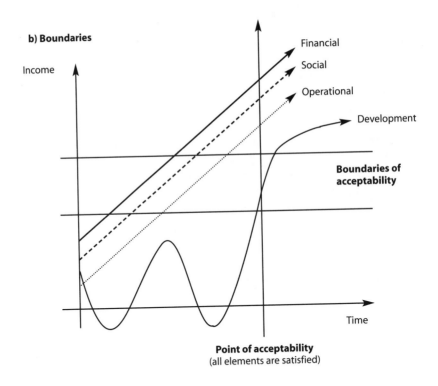

a) Purpose

FInancial	**Operational**
• Returns • Commitment • Contingencies	• Investment relations • Dominance and dependency • Future potential
Social	**Development**

• Acceptability
• Concerns, e.g. waste
  disposal
• Reputation
• Ethical factors
	• Future opportunities
	• Technology and
	  expertise
	• Reputation
	• Value

b) Boundaries

Notes:

- The outcomes of all investment decisions should always be assessed and evaluated and this applies to both success and failure.
- Failure is often easier to assess than success.
- Where the upper boundary is greatly exceeded, this is often put down as 'We have succeeded beyond our wildest dreams'. If nothing else, the phrase illustrates just how much investment is, in reality, little more than inspired guesswork or a shot in the dark.

FIGURE 9.1 The purpose of investment

- **Reputation:** to enhance existing reputation; to gain a broader reputation; to change reputation; to gain reputation in new and unfamiliar areas.
- **Foothold:** to consolidate a foothold in a particular market that now is perceived as being attractive; to gain a foothold in new markets.
- **New markets:** to establish a presence in new markets; to find new markets for existing products; to find and develop new products for existing markets; to find and develop new products for new markets.
- **Prestige:** this is where, for example, organisations make investments in building the biggest buildings, tallest towers, the largest ships, the fastest aeroplanes or the most destructive military equipment; and where politicians and others invest in real and perceived triumphs and achievements.
- **Command of resources:** where organisations invest in a scarce or valuable resource, commodity, expertise or technology. This may be because they need it themselves and it is very expensive, or they may aim to buy up the resource so that it can then be rationed and sold on to others requiring it.
- **Market expansion and dominance:** in which investment is made either to expand existing markets in volume or returns, or else to drive other players out of a finite market.
- **Desire:** especially the desire to be in a particular sector, market or location. For example, Virgin became an airline because of Richard Branson's desire to be in the airline industry.
- **Association:** this is often a feature of sponsorship investment or joint ventures. For example, for twenty years the Japanese electrical goods manufacturers Sharp invested by association in Manchester United Football Club. Ten of the largest construction companies in the UK and France invested in the Channel Tunnel project.

In each of these cases, a financial gain was expected. However, this will be seen as running parallel to the stated reason; and returns available are limited by what the investment in these areas can bring with them.

Organisations also invest in their own time, resources, staff, expertise, technology, quality and volume of products and services, markets and marketing in the same ways. This approach enables a fully informed view to be taken of the opportunities and constraints of continued involvement in the sector and gives the complete context for the following:

- the levels of return that the sector is providing at present
- the levels of return that the sector may be expected to provide in the future
- the levels of return desired by the organisation
- pay-back periods on particular activities
- identification and evaluation of alternatives available to the organisation, and the uses to which its resources could be put.

It is also necessary to look at costs specific to the particular sector. All sectors have their own particular cost and economics mixes. For example, the construction industry has extensive pre-project commitments, including gaining planning permission, permission to build, design times, public enquiries, arranging sub-contractors and arranging equipment. All this must be funded as a condition of being in the sector.

The level of investment and funding necessary must also take into account project completion, fitting out and refurbishment, and after-sales facilities. This is the time and cost frame against which those in the industry must work, and all sectors each have their own equivalent.

All investments must take full account of the following.

- **Environmental pressures:** especially those factors inside and outside the control of organisations and their managers.
- **Stakeholder demands, drives and pressures:** especially those from dominant stakeholders (which in practice normally means the financial interest of key customers and clients).
- Assessing the quality and quantity of **economic and financial information** available; and especially making sure that this is tested for accuracy as far as possible, rather than being based on assumptions and expectations.
- Ensuring **conformity** with **strategy, policy, direction and priorities**; ensuring too that when something is proposed it does not dilute resources away from other organisational activities or, if it does, that the likely and possible consequences are properly understood.
- Attending to the **behavioural aspects** of making investments. This especially applies to investment in new technology, which staff groups are then going to have to be trained to use; ventures into new markets, in which case customers are going to have to be made familiar with the particular products and services through marketing activities; and in project-based activities, in which effective liaison between those involved in the particular venture has to be established.
- **The measurement of risk,** which involves understanding all the pressures of the particular environment in relation to the investment proposed, and understanding the key elements of risk that have to be assessed and minimised as far as that is possible. Risk must be measured in terms of the likely relationship between anticipated and actual rates of return, and also from the broader point of view: for example, the effects on long-term investment performance if a key component suddenly becomes unavailable, or a key member of staff suddenly leaves.
- **Implementation of investments,** which is normally aimed at medium- to long-term results; it is essential to maintain confidence among all those involved, if there are initial teething troubles or problems that were not apparent at the pre-investment stage. If a decision is ever taken to withdraw from an investment because of matters that were not apparent at the planning stage, it is essential that a full evaluation is carried out to ensure that:
  - whatever lessons necessary are learned
  - all factors possible were taken into consideration, and not simply ignored because they were inconvenient at the time
  - anything that did go wrong is in-built into organisational processes and managerial expertise so that this can be avoided next time.

If short-term returns are required, the organisation in question will move out of areas where returns are only available over the long term. If long-term returns are required by companies working in retail and consumer goods sectors, the commitment is to ensure that a sufficient volume and quality of current products and a steady stream of innovations and improvements for the future are present.

More generally, any organisation requiring specific rates of return on investments must work in or move to those sectors where these rates are possible. It is no use requiring a 35 per cent annual return on investment if the best return afforded by the sector is 10 per cent. The organisation has then to decide whether it wishes to continue in the sector or not, to accept and try to maximise the returns based on the norms and possibilities, or to move elsewhere.

Financial data has therefore to be collected by the organisation to establish how this resource is being used, and to enable a managerial evaluation of this usage to be made. There is a control element in this, the ability to measure the costs of particular activities, as well as the whole. It enables the organisation to see where its money is tied up – for example, in stocks and storage, work in progress, raw materials, and goods in transit – and provide the basis of an assessment of this. It enables any slack, or stresses or strains to be identified. It is part of the wider necessity to provide a full range of management information.

Profit and Loss Account and Balance Sheet

Once the data is collected it has to be made available to both the internal and external environments. The external environment in the UK requires the annual presentation of a Balance Sheet, and Profit and Loss Account. These are governed by accounting conventions, and must be subject to scrutiny and audit. The Balance Sheet is a financial snapshot of the company on a stated day. It shows assets and liabilities in balance, and what the components of each are; this enables the wider business and financial world to make an informed judgement on the company's inherent strength and stability. The Profit and Loss Account is a representation of income and expenditure, showing a surplus or deficit on it (see Figure 9.2).

Company accounts must be countersigned by an externally appointed auditor as giving 'a true and fair reflection' of the financial state and performance of the organisation.

Profit and Loss Accounts and Balance Sheets are normally presented as part of the Annual Report. As well as the figures, the Annual Report also includes statements by the chairman and other top managers and directors concerning the well-being of the organisation, the nature, content and volume of activities, and future plans.

It is then possible to compare one year's performance with another, both overall and line-by-line. This is useful up to a point.

To gain a more complete picture, however, it is much more useful to take the same view over a longer period of time, often five years. This approach is the same: to take overall and line-by-line comparisons. Taking this longer view enables identification of more genuine trends and directions. It also enables 'blips', extraordinary items of sale and expenditure, share issues and special loans, to be set in context.

The Balance Sheet and Profit and Loss Account are primarily for external consumption, though much useful information can be gathered by anyone.

From a managerial point of view, it is much more useful to be able to observe trends over longer periods of time than simply to compare the current year's figures with the previous. Comparisons of performance over five years, both total organisational performance and line by line, give a much clearer indication of what has been changing in the long-term. The reasons can then be investigated in much more detail. One year's figures compared against another's give little more than the percentage

Profit and Loss Account

	2001 £ million	2000 £ million
Income	3188	3097
Operating cost	(2736)	(2771)
Operating profit	452	326
Interest	(27)	33
Profit before tax	425	359
Tax	(140)	(117)
Profit after tax	285	242
Dividend	(82)	(72)
Retained profit	203	170

(brackets indicate subtraction)

Figures are then normally given for earnings per share and dividend per share

Balance Sheet

	31 December 2001 £ million	31 December 2000 £ million
Fixed assets	2106	1996
Current assets	1109	1043
Short-term creditors	(771)	(890)
Net current assets	338	153
Total assets	2444	2149
Long-term creditors	(475)	(325)
Liabilities and charges	(299)	(359)
Net assets	1670	1465
Capital and reserves		
Share capital	1470	1000
Capital reserve	150	265
Other reserves	50	200
Total equity	1670	1465

Notes:

It is usual to give current and previous years' figures for purposes of comparison. Thus, the overall performance can be compared, and also the line-by-line movements and charges.

FIGURE 9.2 Profit and Loss Account and Balance Sheet example

increase or decrease; while this might be satisfactory to some managers, it is unlikely to give a complete picture.

Moreover, the availability of this much more extensive information means that it is possible to assess whether something is truly effective. At an organisational level, trends in turnover, profit levels, costs and overheads can be assessed, and enquiries made when it becomes apparent that these are changing steadily and substantially over periods of time. At a departmental level, the availability of financial information over such periods gives a much truer indication of whether, for example, budget and resource levels are adequate, where resources are being consumed, and the extent to which this is contributing to the effectiveness or otherwise of departmental performance. Consider Figure 9.3.

Costs

From a managerial point of view, the following cost breakdowns are required.

Fixed costs (FC)

These are the costs incurred by the organisation whether or not business of any sort is conducted. They consist of capital charges, premises costs, staff costs and administrative, managerial and support function overheads.

Variable costs (VC)

These are the costs incurred as the result of engaging in direct business activity. They consist of raw materials, packaging and distribution costs. A price established for the items will, as stated above, normally seek at least to cover these; additionally it may make a contribution to the fixed cost.

Marginal costs (MC)

These are the costs incurred by the production of one extra item of output, and reflect the extent to which the production capacity of the organisation may be extended without incurring additional fixed costs in the forms of investment in new plant, staff, equipment or machinery. There comes a point at which the production of an extra item does require these expenditures.

Sunk costs (SC)

These are the costs incurred by any organisation on which there is no further return. Sunk costs include for example the costs of organisational restructuring; the costs incurred in purchasing technology and equipment which has no residual or resale value; and the costs incurred in putting things right when these have been allowed to go wrong because of negligence, ineptitude, or error.

Hidden costs (HC)

Hidden costs are those that are either unnoticed, unrecorded, or actively ignored. They may not be easily measurable in pure financial terms. For example, a company that takes the decision to dispose of toxic waste by dumping it in a river, because the cost of paying the fine is less than disposing of the waste products properly, may nevertheless lose enduring long-term reputation because of this action. The company that engages management consultants to restructure its organisation may enjoy a short-term rise in its

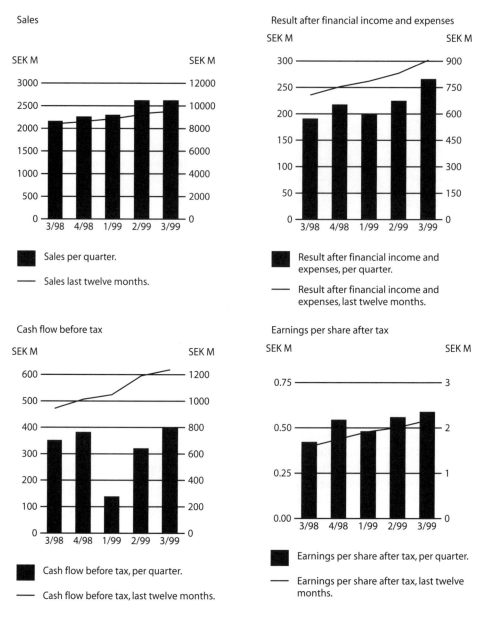

FIGURE 9.3 Trends example

share value, but long-term problems with staff motivation, morale, recruitment and retention. A company that seeks perceived economies of scale by merging with another may lose its customer base, because customers have no identity with the new merged organisation.

Coercive costs (CC)

Coercive costs are those that organisations are for some reason compelled to pay. These include statutory charges for electricity, gas, water, energy and communication infrastructure. They also include legal costs that arise as the result of being in a particular line of activity. Companies also incur costs and charges that they are forced to pay as the result of negligence or misconduct; examples include fines for pollution, engaging in victimisation and harassment, breaches of competition rules and regulations. Coercive costs have been incurred by organisations engaged in private finance initiatives and public–private partnerships with government. For example, Balfour Beatty, the present owners and operators of the Skye Bridge in Scotland, were forced to go to court in order to try to make users of the bridge pay for the facility, after they had initially refused to do so.

Switching costs (SwC)

These are the costs involved in switching from one area of activity to another, or of changing some substantial organisational initiative such as production and information technology, or engaging in a new marketing campaign. Especially in the case of changing production and information technology, the switching cost that has to be considered is that of retraining staff. Relocation of premises also invariably incurs substantial switching costs.

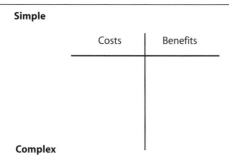

	Costs	Benefits
Simple		
Complex		
Action choices	Priorities	Initiatives
Short Medium Long term	Strategic aspects	Risk
Relative valuation	Income Expenditure	Value

Costs and benefits and cost–benefit analyses   *FIGURE 9.4*

Withdrawal costs (WiC)

Withdrawal costs are those incurred when an organisation withdraws from a particular market, location or type of activity. The intangible element of withdrawal costs is extremely hard to measure; however, this is especially important when trying to assess the effects on wider reputation and enduring viability, of a high profile withdrawal from a particular sector.

Opportunity cost (OC)

Opportunity costs represent the opportunities forgone as the result of being involved in another area.

Total cost (TC)

Total cost is the summary of all costs incurred by organisations as the result of engaging in particular activities. Total costs can then be balanced and assessed against the returns and benefits required (see Figure 9.4).

Cost–benefit analysis is a straightforward ready-reckoner method of establishing a basis on which particular initiatives might be feasible or profitable, and of identifying those elements that require further, more detailed consideration before implementation. The simple approach is to establish each anticipated cost and benefit or advantage element in two columns (the simple example in Figure 9.4); a more complex approach requires a detailed itemisation (the complex example).

Cost apportionment

Fixed and variable cost apportionment

These are the processes devised by the organisation for the purposes of identifying where costs should be charged and apportioned. This is often known as the process of 'cost centring', and the activity thus identified is called the cost centre.

Many organisations are increasingly taking the view that the apportionment of fixed costs is both operationally unnecessary, and also misleading when trying to assess the true costs of activities. The fixed cost base – overheads, staffing costs, interest charges, and shareholders' obligations – are taken as an organisational bill that has to be paid as a condition of being in the particular line of activities at the time. Cost apportionment is limited to assessment of variable costs: those incurred as the result of the volume of activities conducted.

Profit apportionment

This is the converse of cost apportionment and is the organisation's method of ensuring the nature and sources of income generated by its various activities. This constitutes the identity of profit centres in the same way as cost centres.

Similarly also, while it is useful to be able to identify those activities that make the greatest contribution to organisational viability, it is increasingly recognised that there are limitations in assessing each activity narrowly as a profit centre. It is much more usual to take the total range of activities as being the basis on which profits are earned, even if some of these are much higher for some products and services than others.

Break even

This is the point at which the balance between costs and income is established (see Figure 9.5).

Asset valuation

The purpose of identifying, assessing and valuing the activities and resource as assets is to help measure their total contribution and worth to the organisation. Example Box 9.4 shows the method adopted in such evaluation in response to the human resource. Equivalent approaches can be taken to 'hard resources' (production technology, capability, expertise, production volumes), and to 'soft' assets (reputation, goodwill and quality).

Ratio analysis

Ratios are used in financial management to identify, establish and measure particular performance aspects. The results and outcomes of the analysis of the ratios, and the level and quality of performance that they indicate, contribute to management knowledge and information and become part of the process of assessment and evaluation. These ratios include those shown in Figure 9.6.

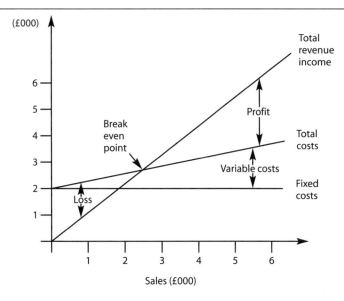

A break even diagram   *FIGURE 9.5*

EXAMPLE BOX 9.4   A Model of Human Asset Valuation and Accounting

1. The 'base' to be adopted is employment costs, which are measured (a) in total, (b) by staff category, (c) by operational division, (d) in terms of the added value that each contributes, and (e) by sectoral factors.

2. Return on these bases may be measured and assessed in the same way as for any other asset. The concept of the human liability must also be addressed. This must include occupational obsolescence and consequent depreciation of the asset, the full occupational liability, turnover and terminal losses, replacement costs, and refurbishment (that is, training and development) costs. It is also necessary to include a full assessment of expenditure on human resource management, industrial relations and organisation and employee development.

3. The value that organisations place on collective and individual expertise requires careful assessment. Questions of profitability, effectiveness, and organisation and market development have to be assessed as the result of having this expertise present, and as the consequence of not having it. It is also necessary to consider the effects on organisational reputation and confidence, and therefore value, of key figures and expertise, and the goodwill that occurs as the result. This is of especial concern for owner/chief executives such as Richard Branson, and also Stelios Hadjoannou (EasyJet), Michael O'Leary (Ryan Air), and Julian Metcalfe (Pret-à-Manger). It is essential that the consequences of not valuing reputation are assessed. During the initial phase of the dot.com revolution, little account was taken of reputation or durability; it was simply 'established wisdom' that dot.com companies would be successful. Any reputation that the entrepreneurs had was driven by the media, rather than by business viability and longevity. While it remains true that most dot.com entrepreneurs have fought very hard to make their businesses successful, the question of reputation was taken very much on trust.

4. The economic rent – very high value – placed on particular expertise has also to be assessed. In professional sports, players are bought and sold for a more or less 'pure' market value: the price at which one club is prepared to sell a player and another to buy him/her on a particular day. This again, bears no relation to enduring capability, willingness or effectiveness. This is also true of top executives at shareholder dominated companies, where chief executive officers are hired on the same basis as professional sports players, and again without any regard for their enduring future value.

5. Gains and losses in organisational value as the result of acquisitions and divestments of particular expertise have also to be assessed. Again, whether the particular expertise is kept or allowed to leave may be driven by short-term expedient or political motives. However, when assessing the enduring financial viability of the organisation as a whole, it is essential to take a strategic view of the required expertise, and of the specific individuals. Where it is likely that specific individuals will leave to the detriment of organisational value, the transitional period has to be extremely carefully managed.

The ratios provide distinctive measures of particular activities. The information gained has to be seen in context however. For example, while a 'quick ratio' may show that a company could not easily cover its current liabilities, this does not matter if the liabilities are not to be called in. Similarly, different commercial and public sectors will have their own norms and expectations that have also to be taken into account; a 2 per cent return on capital employed may sound low, but it may be twice the usual rate in the industry concerned. There is also the wider environment to be considered, and any opportunities, or difficulties, such as boom, or recession.

The main purpose of identifying the nature of these costs and their extent in given situations is to provide the basis of managerial assessment and decision making. Costs should never become straitjackets outside which a department or function may not budget. It should always be remembered that the driving force of any organisation is its products and services and relations with its markets; costs and the management of these should never take the place of market imperatives. This is essential if a true assessment of the nature and extent of the effectiveness (in financial terms) of the organisation's activities is to be made (see Example Box 9.5).

Profit ratio	$\dfrac{\text{Net profit}}{\text{Total sales}}$	x 100 indicates percentage return
Selling costs	$\dfrac{\text{Selling costs}}{\text{Total sales}}$	x 100 indicates percentage consumed on sales costs

The same approach can be taken for energy, production, marketing, staff distribution, research, development and capital goods as a percentage of sales

Assets and liabilities	$\dfrac{\text{Assets}}{\text{Liabilities}}$	A general ready-reckoner

This may then be broken into:

a)	$\dfrac{\text{Long-term assets}}{\text{Long-term liabilities}}$	
b)	$\dfrac{\text{Current assets}}{\text{Current liabilities}}$	
c)	A quick ratio or 'the acid test'	$\dfrac{\text{Quickly realisable assets}}{\text{Current liabilities}}$
d)	Debtors and creditors	$\dfrac{\text{Debtors}}{\text{Payments}}$ — Indicates whether an organisation is paying out its bills more quickly than it is receiving
e)	Return on capital employed (ROCE):	$\dfrac{\text{Profit before tax}}{\text{Capital employed}}$ — Gives rate of return on the investment Depends on what is included in 'capital employed' and 'returns'

Ratio analyses

FIGURE 9.6

Internal markets

Internal markets are present in holding company structures, multinational organisations and health and public services. They are a combination of the following elements.

- The distinction between **purchasers** and **providers** for the purposes of establishing internally contracted arrangements as the basis on which the relationship between the two is to be carried out in the future.
- The establishment of a **price–service return** and the ways in which everything is to be paid for, including the agreement of quantity/volume, quality and timescales/deadlines criteria. In multinationals this will generally be on a system

---

EXAMPLE BOX 9.5 Financial Measures of Performance from a Managerial Point of View

The following are useful managerial financial measures of performance. Their application and emphasis varies between organisations.

- **Income/profit**
  - per product, per product group or cluster, per product range, per activity, in total
  - per employee: front line staff, support staff, in total
  - per square metre, per outlet, per location, per region, per country
  - per customer
  - per hour/day/week/month/season/year
- **Fixed variable and total cost:** for each of these costs, calculations may be made
  - per employee, per function, per activity, per department/division/section, per outlet, per location, per region, per country, per square metre
- **Marginal cost:** marginal cost is usually best calculated
  - per product, per outlet, per employee (if overtime or time off is given).

Notes:

1. Fixed and variable costs per customer can be calculated, but this is not normally very useful unless all customers are receiving the same regularity and level of service.
2. Cost per function can be developed into a full cost–benefit analysis (see below). This is especially valuable when assessing the contribution of support functions and the effectiveness of primary (i.e. production and direct service) activities.
3. Cost per customer is especially futile in assessing public services, health care and transport because the cost of providing given levels of service is more or less fixed. A hospital must be able to cope with maximum volumes of patients at all times and be able to provide the maximum range of services stipulated. Trains, buses and aeroplanes must stick to their schedules. One view is that, especially for trains and planes, there are no variable costs; they must follow their schedules and it is even necessary to move empty on one route or between two destinations, given that increased volumes of business are present further down the line.

of transfer pricing, using the most advantageous currency available to it; in other situations, a system of internal invoicing may be devised.

The emphasis placed on each element will vary; the overall constitution of any organisational internal market, however, must be to ensure effective operation, together with efficient resource identification, allocation and evaluation on the part of the control, administrative and support functions of the organisation.

Budgets

The budget is a plan (with sub-plans) that constitutes part of the process of managing the organisation, department, project or initiative. It aims to provide an accurate picture of where resources are being used, the speed and frequency of use, and the basis for making future judgements on the levels of finance required to meet particular targets (in terms of volume, quality and time).

The budget enables specific analysis and evaluation of the accuracy of the resource allocation process, and variances from it, and explanation of such variables.

Budgets normally identify the fixed costs associated with a particular department, division, function or activity. They must identify the variable costs, relating these to given volumes of activities and providing sufficient resources to ensure that the desired volume and quality of activities can be carried out. It is usual also to identify the marginal costs incurred by getting involved in one-off special and additional activities.

There is normally some form of time constraint imposed. The work of accountancy and resource allocation often requires an annual statement of budget/resource utilisation even if the budget is not being operated to the same deadlines.

There is also certain to be some form of budget reporting required from a managerial and directional point of view, to enable judgement on the effectiveness of this form of resource allocation and utilisation to be made (see Example Box 9.6).

Managers should be aware of the three main prevailing corporate attitudes to budgeting.

- Where there is a close relationship between the resources required and the resources budgeted.
- Where there is some relationship between the resources required and the budget allocated.
- Where there is no relationship between the resources required and the budget allocated. This is an especial problem in the provision of frontline public services.

Two forms of budgeting should be noted.

- **Historic budgeting:** where the previous year's (or activity's or project's) budget is taken as the starting point for the current allocation of resources. To be fully effective, it assumes that everything was correct and adequate in the previous period.
- **Zero-based budgeting:** the opposite of historical budgeting. This assumes that a fresh approach and consideration is required for current and future activities and periods. It requires a proper examination of the current and future activities, proposals and time periods, rather than reliance on historic figures as the starting point.

EXAMPLE BOX 9.6   Budgets: The Public Sector Example

This is an illustration of the shortcomings of the budgeting process and of what happens when budgets, rather than activities, become the driving force.

In UK public services, resources are allocated on an annual basis to support various activities. At the end of each 12-month period, the last budget is cancelled and a new one put in place. Any resources not used up over the period are lost and returned to whoever is responsible for providing them. There is therefore no incentive to conserve resources for a time when they might become useful in the future. There is every incentive to spend the resources, whether or not the activities are useful. There are two further effects.

- **The budget cycle:** this works as follows. For the first three months of the cycle, activities are constrained while assessment of the resources in relation to activities is carried out. A steady state based on this is generated during the next three months. Further restraints are applied during the third period of three months. The final quarter consists of a frantic attempt to use up everything not so far consumed because otherwise it will be lost.
- **Closures and shutdowns:** under this system these occur when the budget is used up due to pressures outside the organisation's control before the end of the cycle. Under this system it becomes 'more cost-effective' to have premises closed and staff and equipment idle, than to have them at work.

The very best that can be said for the system is that it can show where stated amounts of money have been spent. Apart from this, in virtually all circumstances, it is the wrong way to budget. It fails on all other counts, especially on that of devising budgets in support of real and desired levels of activities.

There are prescriptive, consultative and participative elements involved in establishing and implementing an effective budgeting process. There should be not only a means of effective resource allocation, and wage monitoring, but also the means of ensuring that all those involved in its implementation understand fully the resource obligations and constraints under which they have to work. Even in areas of severe constraint a better operational response will be generated if everyone concerned understands the nature and range of resource limitations (see Example Box 9.7).

One must also be able to reconcile control with flexibility, and divergent and conflicting demands for resources. This, in turn, requires a measure of leeway for an otherwise productive initiative that needs a small extra resource in order for it to be fully successful, without letting such leeway destroy the credibility of the budget process. It follows from this that all budgets and budgeting systems must be specifically designed for the organisations, initiatives, operations, projects, staff and facilities in question. While general principles and standpoints hold good, these must be applied as required to particular situations; a universal set of precise rules is therefore not appropriate.

Conclusions

The main conclusion to be drawn is in recognising the difference between the work of professional accountants, in producing figures, and that of managers in using, interpreting, analysing and evaluating them. In many ways, therefore, the work of the manager starts where that of the accountant finishes. Having said that, the manager

---

EXAMPLE BOX 9.7 Symptoms of Declining Financial Performance

Whenever it becomes clear that 'the figures' are not going to be 'right' for the particular financial year, organisations require their managers to make budget cuts. This normally involves tackling the variable costs which have been incurred as the result of engaging in activities, rather than assessing the fixed costs that are likely to be contributing much more substantially to decline in performance, or placing the overall burden on the organisation. For example:

- A hospital faced with a £2.5 million deficit sent a memorandum to all its nursing and medical staff asking them to be 'especially careful' with the use of medical resources. Staff were especially exhorted not to use too many dressings, bandages or toilet rolls, in order to maximise efficiency of resources. A 'back of the envelope' calculation conducted by a senior registrar came to the conclusion that the hospital would have saved more money had the memorandum not been sent out in the first place than it was possible to save by 'using bandages wisely'.

- Faced with constraints from its parent company, a financial services organisation cut its training budget from £600 000 to £40 000. It then spent a substantial amount of the 'saving' on staff time; this became necessary in order to manage the large volume of grievances that occurred as the result. In particular, the parent company never explained to the financial services subsidiary how it was supposed to handle £500 000 worth of training that it had contracted to provide to its employees.

More general symptoms of declining financial performance are observable in peripheral activities. Peters states:

> You can always tell an organisation that is in difficulties. The free tea trolley stops coming round, and staff are asked to pay for their drinks out of machines. Flowers disappear from the reception areas. Corporate subscriptions to business and trade press are cancelled. Senior managers go to expensive locations for weekend think-tanks, and emerge with the news that staff have got to up their productivity, with no additional resources. Bonuses for all but senior staff are cancelled. Expense claims are either capped or rigorously checked.

Source: T. Peters, *The World Turned Upside Down*, Channel 4 television, 1986.

must have the knowledge and understanding of how figures are produced, what they mean and what they state about the condition of the organisation as a whole and its particular activities.

It is necessary to recognise that, because of legal constraints, professional accountants tend to work in annual cycles. Managers should not be hidebound by this. Some managerial cycles are much shorter, others much longer. In particular, the establishment of annual budgets needs extremely close attention; this is not to say that annual budgets are necessarily wrong, but they must be seen in an operational as well as financial context – and the operational drive must be paramount. The archetype public sector approach indicated above is wrong and should be avoided.

It is also necessary to recognise the nature and content of investment. Investment is a long-term and continuing commitment on which is based the long-term continuity of the organisation. Profitability, profit maximisation and profit optimisation are to be seen from this point of view. Long-term viability should never be sacrificed for immediate gain except where there is a crisis (and even then, if it is sacrificed, it is as likely to perpetuate the crisis as not). Long-term profitability means investing in all of those things that are to ensure that it does indeed happen: top quality staff, top quality products and services in the volumes and locations demanded by customers, reinforced by high levels of quality, customer confidence and reputation, and, in turn, leading to repeat business. That is the context in which financial management is ultimately to be seen.

CHAPTER SUMMARY

The purpose of this chapter has been to illustrate the key financial concepts, and the complexities involved in assessing and using them as a part of managerial (rather than accountancy) activity. This requires a high level of contextual knowledge and understanding, as well as the capability to choose the right approach to finance in a particular set of circumstances, and the right financial performance measures, and the right means for the assessment of the financial aspects of management in particular situations. This also means ensuring that the right points of enquiry are identified and addressed. Only by doing this can those responsible identify what contributes to successful, effective and profitable performance; and what contributes to failure.

Taking a narrow view means that the range of activities that contribute to effective, successful and profitable performance is never considered in its entirety; narrow decisions are made about specific activities that are either overtly profitable or loss making in narrow terms.

It is also essential that managers understand the nature and levels of financial resources that they require in order to carry out effective and successful performance. They should be able to do this from at least two points of view:

- the nature and levels of finance required 'in a perfect world'
- the nature and levels available in the real world, and the pressures and constraints that these bring.

It is also true that the financial aspects of management are often not helped by the resource allocation process that occurs within organisations. At its worst, this consists of lobbying and bargaining for the levels of finance necessary in order to perform even a barely adequate job. For some reason, many senior managers find this to be an acceptable and useful way of 'ensuring that resources go to the right department'. In absolute terms this is unacceptable; in term of the real world, there is a clear duty on shareholders' representatives and other dominant stakeholders to ensure that, where this practice becomes apparent, it is cancelled forthwith.

There is also an enduring problem for those responsible for managing finance in public services. The point is made above that many budgets are set without any relationship to the levels of finance required, or what they are to be spent on. This is likely to endure until political dominance is removed from public services, and budget holders and other with financial management responsibility at the frontline of public services are allowed to use resources for the primary purpose of serving their clients.

It is also true that those who command financial resources are often under great pressure to divert these away from mainstream, steady-state activities, into those that have a perceived instant, high-profile, expedient and triumphal return. The long-term integrity of steady-state activities is therefore compromised in pursuit of instant returns.

DISCUSSION QUESTIONS

1. A departmental manager with a staff of 20 has suddenly received an additional budget of £40 000, which he is only allowed to spend on training for his staff. He has three months to spend it. What actions should he take: when, why and how? What overall courses of action are open to him?
2. For the organisation of your choice, obtain a copy of the Annual Report. Without reading the chairman's statement, study the five-year organisational trends. Draw your own conclusions from these. Then read the chairman's annual statement, and compare and contrast your findings with his/hers.
3. A department store chain is thinking of creating its own website-based virtual retail facility. What is the nature of the investment appraisal and cost benefit analysis that it should carry out prior to establishing this facility?
4. How in your view should organisations manage sudden downturns in overall business performance? Identify as full a range of actions as possible that are open to them; and from this, identify those which are likely to be most cost effective, and those which are likely to be implemented in the real world.

CHAPTER CASE STUDY

WHEATFIELDS AND THEIR TROUBLE WITH HOLIDAYS

Wheatfields is an independent department store located in the city centre of Canterbury, Kent. It has always enjoyed a good reputation for customer service, employment practice, and community contribution.

Last year it was taken over by a holding company located in London.

Prior to the take-over, and in spite of the vast tourist trade in the city, the shop was always shut for bank holidays, and also Christmas Eve and New Year's Eve. Now however, the new owners want to change this. As a consequence, the following directive was issued to the store's general manager three weeks before Easter.

It has been decided to bring all areas of activity into line concerning the Easter trading period. In order to alleviate the excessive pressure on profit margins, Wheatfields will consequently remain open all day Good Friday and Easter Monday. All staff will be compensated by an increase of 1 per cent (from 15–16 per cent) in the staff discount allowance scheme. Moreover, please note that in future all staff will be required to work on Christmas Eve and New Year's Eve.

A week later, the holding company's personnel director heard from Wheatfields' general manager that she had been inundated with staff complaints. She cited the following information.

- 20 per cent of staff complained on religious grounds.
- 15 per cent complained that their families would not enjoy the unique benefit of having Good Friday and other historic 'special days' together.
- Skeleton public transport and consequent congestion on the roads created difficulties for 20 per cent of staff, who commuted in from the outlying villages.
- Part-time staff who did not receive the staff discount would not benefit, but would still be required to work if their hours came up on these particular days.
- Whenever staff had been asked to work on other bank holidays, they were normally paid double time; would this still apply?
- Staff also wanted to know whether the requirements to work on these extra days of the year would be compensated by being able to take additional days as part of their annual leave allowance.

Neither Wheatfields' general manager, nor the holding company's personnel director, had been consulted on the decision. Each independently fed the results back to the chief executive of the holding company. He was astonished at the reaction.

Wheatfields employs 200 staff. Of these 140 work on the shop floor in contact with customers. A further 40 work in the store room area, unloading goods inwards and arranging for deliveries of goods to customers where required. The other 20 are all managerial, dealing with staff supervision, customer liaison (including complaints), and attending to specific requests from top value clients. Purchasing, sales and marketing is now carried out centrally at the holding company.

The average wage on the shop floor is £7.00 per hour. The average daily sales value is £120 000; the average profit margin is 4 per cent.

QUESTIONS

1. Conduct a full cost–benefit analysis for the proposal to open on Good Friday and bank holidays. Identify the intangible assets and liabilities present, and the likely effects of these on the financial performance of the store.
2. What is the volume of business that the store will need to conduct in order to

break even for the bank holiday periods assuming: that overtime is paid; that the days now worked are given as part of the annual leave allowance?

3. Identify a package of benefits designed to alleviate the concerns indicated above. Calculate as accurately as possible the cost of offering these to all staff in order to address their particular concerns. What other actions might it be necessary for the holding company management and Wheatfields' manager to take, and why?

10 Quantitative Methods

'Lies, damned lies – and statistics.' Spiro T. Agnew, US Vice President, 1971.

CHAPTER OBJECTIVES

After studying this chapter, you should be able to:

understand the range of mathematical and statistical approaches required by expert managers

understand and apply specific and precise forms of enquiry to particular situations

understand the forms of enquiry that particular situations demand

understand the need for accuracy of data, and the limitations where this is not possible

understand the contextual features of statistical and mathematical approaches.

Introduction

The purpose of this chapter is to introduce and outline the importance, use and value of the quantitative tools and methods that are available to the manager, and to indicate and illustrate their uses in different situations.

From the point of view of the manager, it is the ability to interpret and use statistical and financial data (rather than being a specialist in statistics or mathematics) that is important. It is this standpoint, therefore, that is taken.

As well as the ability to use and analyse material thus gained, there are behavioural and perceptual issues that must be addressed, and these are indicated also. The chapter additionally focuses on the particular quantitative, mathematical, statistical, financial and accounting elements that are important to the manager, and of general value in the identification of the 'complete management task'.

The importance of this basic understanding is critical to the manager, providing a quantitative basis for the evaluation of situations, and a sound basis for qualitative decisions. Gathering information and producing accurate statistics and other figures is not therefore an end in itself. It is the use to which these are put that is important.

Statistics

This is the discipline that deals with the preparation, collection, arrangement, presentation, analysis and interpretation of quantitative data. The discipline can be divided into the study of probability (or mathematical statistics); and descriptive statistics, which deal with the compilation and preservation of data to provide information on which to base decisions, and to assist in forward planning and forecasting.

Primary and secondary data

Data can initially be categorised as primary or secondary data.

- **Primary data:** is that obtained directly by organisations and individuals through observation, surveys, interviews and samples, and using methods and instruments drawn up specifically for the stated purpose.
- **Secondary data:** comes from other data sources, such as official statistics provided by government sources and sectoral data gathered by employers' associations and federations, and marketing organisations.

Uses of data gathered

The use of secondary data always involves taking information that others have gathered, and interpreting, analysing and using it for purposes different from those which the original gatherers designed or intended. There may also be variations in definition or coverage that have to be taken into account.

The decision to gather primary data or use other sources will depend on the nature of the information required, its availability from sources other than primary, its range and coverage, the field of enquiry and its size and scope, the accuracy of the data required, and the date or deadline by which it is required. It will depend also on the purpose and aims of the enquiry to be made and the uses to which the information is to be put. Finally, the reconciliation of all of these points may not be easy (for example, where wide-ranging, precise data is required urgently).

The data thus gathered is then classified into groupings, or classes, with a common element, for the purposes of analysis, comparison and evaluation.

As far as the manager is concerned, the main purpose of this gathering and assessment of data is to provide background information that is accurate and quantifiable. This is a basis in turn for accurate planning, forecasting, projected activities and decision making in whatever the discipline involved; or at a strategic level, providing a sound basis for accurate general direction.

It is useful, therefore, to identify the different statistical sources, methods and techniques that are available to managers in organisations, and their particular uses in this context.

Sources of information and data

The manager will consult six main sources:

- **Government statistics**: highly publicised in the media, and useful as general indicators of the state of the national, business and economic confidence, direction and activity, and the direction the economy is likely to take in general over the foreseeable future.
- **Sectoral statistics**: produced by trade federations, employees' associations and professional bodies for the support and enlightenment of member organisations, and to contribute their knowledge and awareness of the global aspects and overview of their own sectors. This information may contribute in great measure to policy formulation in particular sectors, in the setting of minimum and maximum wage, price and output levels, for example.
- **Market research organisations**: these hold data on vast ranges of issues that they promulgate and sell on a commercial basis to those requiring it. The main initial value of this is to indicate the general state of business, and range of business opportunities that may be available, again as a prelude to organisations either conducting or commissioning their own future investigations.
- **Local government**: this holds a wide range of general data on the composition, social state, occupational range and population structure of those who live in the UK; this is published in general terms by local government and municipal departments, and again is a useful precursor to more rigorous investigation.
- **Public enquiries and investigations**: these generate a great amount of information concerning particular initiatives (e.g. on urban development, by-passes or power stations) that are often a useful initial point of reference for those planning to go into similar ventures in the future.
- **Organisational statistics**: gathered internally for specific purposes (see Example Box 10.1).

Presentation of data

Data must be presented in ways that are easily understood by those on the receiving end. This is true both in the generation of overall impressions, and in the presentation of precise findings. The method of presentation must take into account the relative interest and capability of the audience, the time that is to be spent on it, and the purpose for which it is being presented.

It is essential that this is understood at this stage, because statistical surveys and information systems now hold, and can generate, vast amounts of data on all aspects of business in relatively short periods of time. The data is of value, however, only if it can be understood and assimilated. For this to be effective, presentation must be in 'audience-friendly' or 'user-friendly' terms, meeting their expectations as well as getting the required message across.

There are five main methods available (see Figure 10.1):

FIGURE 10.1 (opposite) Presentation of data

(a) Tabulation

YEAR	SALES £	PROFIT £
1986	3430	114
1987	3560	119
1988	4740	240
1989	5862	650
1990	4711	350

(b) Bar chart

(i)

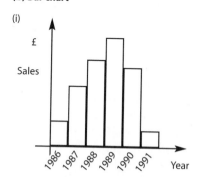

(ii)

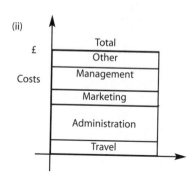

(c) Line graph

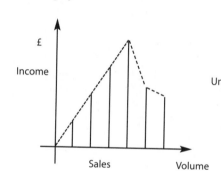

(d) Scatter diagram

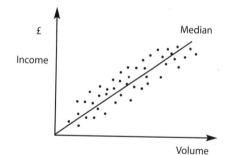

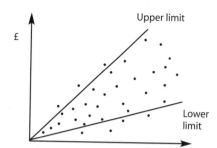

(e) Pie chart

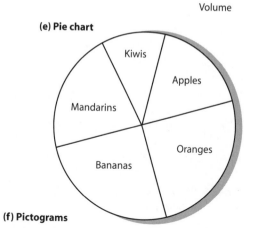

(f) Pictograms

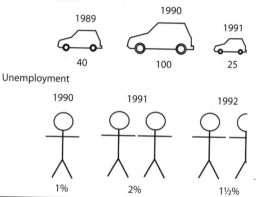

EXAMPLE BOX 10.1 Organisational Statistics and Management Information

This may be classified as follows.

- **Human resource management:** wage levels (individual, departmental, divisional, functional total); staff turnover (overall, individual, departmental, divisional, functional or occupational); absence and absenteeism levels (individual, departmental, divisional, functional and total); strikes and disputes; levels of disciplinary and dismissal activity; grievances and other staff problems; ability/inability to recruit; qualifications and capabilities; training and development records; identification of potential; succession; variety of work and experience; total experience.

- **Public relations:** nature and volumes of complaints; sources of complaints; nature and volumes of media inquiries; general requests; dealings with the community and its institutions (schools, colleges, evening classes, clubs and societies); nature and volume of organisational coverage in the community and media; proportions of time spent on general public relations activities; proportions of time and resources spent on specific issues.

- **Marketing:** market assessment information; gathering of marketing information; use of information; information for using and evaluating the effects of marketing campaigns; effectiveness of the targeting of marketing activities; effectiveness of general marketing activities; effectiveness of the total marketing position.

- **Sales:** by product; by product cluster; total range of product; by outlet; by location; volume and quality; demands for returns; after-sales demands; the number of times that guarantees are invoked; complaints; blockages.

- **Production:** deliveries; product output volumes; product to market; time factors; quality factors; volume factors; number of complaints per site/factory/batch/unit/production run/location; blockages; supplier factors; distribution factors.

- **Financial:** total costs; cost breakdowns by site, division, department, function, location, occupation; fixed costs; variable costs and causes of variability; marginal costs; budget and budgeting processes.

- **Administration:** staff records; financial records; budget usage; balance of activities; technology usage; technology life span; technology obsolescence; replacement programmes.

From this it is apparent that there is a vast range of information available for the organisation's use. How effectively it is used depends both on the organisation's ability to gather and store this information, and on the capabilities of individual managers to identify what they want and when they want it, and to evaluate it in particular situations.

- **Tabulation:** where data is presented in tables devised against two or more axes or criteria.
- **Bar charts:** a more visual representation of tables, usually presented against two axes or variables.
- **Pie charts:** where the data is represented in a circular or 'pie' format, with the slices representing the quantities or percentages given.
- **Graphs:** on which data is plotted, also against two variables (e.g. dates and volume; timescale and sales figures).
- **Pictures (pictograms):** such as the use of a small picture of a person to represent a small number of unemployed and a larger picture to represent an increase in the figure recorded.

Accuracy of data

The accuracy of any data depends on the way in which it was gathered, the quality of the actual data gathering, and any rounding at the end of it. If a survey took a sample, rather than dealing with everyone or everything concerned in a particular activity, the results may indicate particular conclusions very strongly, but they will only be proven if the entire sector is surveyed. If there is a flaw in the statistical methods used, or if the wrong questions are asked, the results will also be flawed, and inaccurate. Finally, rounding of numbers is widely used and has also to be seen in context and as a limitation; balance sheet figures for multinational companies are given to the nearest hundred thousand pounds, or even million pounds.

Social survey and market research organisations consequently go to a lot of trouble to make their surveys both valid and reliable through the establishment of proper objectives, the design of questionnaires and other survey instruments, the provision of high-quality and rigorously trained surveyors, and the recognition and promulgation of limitations on the research to be carried out. Any findings, analysis and conclusions are thus seen in context (see Example Box 10.2).

These lessons should be translated into the business sphere and its related managerial activities. The disciplines of accuracy of data and information gathering hold relevance in those management activities to do with:

- personal interviewing and assessment
- policy formulation
- business assessment
- marketing activities
- output
- the merits and demerits of particular initiatives
- the success or failure of recruitment campaigns, advertising initiatives
- image formulation
- the success or failure of particular technologies, production methods
- the ability of organisations and their specialist departments to plan, forecast, formulate policy and devise and implement strategies.

Other elements which impinge on the accuracy of data gathered and available are to do with: time lapses between the gathering, promulgation and interpretation of data; sampling errors; analytical errors; inexplicable inconsistencies; and the compounding

EXAMPLE BOX 10.2 Statistics and Proof

Taken in isolation, statistics can be used to prove everything and anything. In the wider context, they seldom prove anything, especially in the managerial sphere.

Example: government statistics

Government statistics are used by politicians in support of their own vested interests. For example, one political party may say, 'Crime figures are at an all time record high'. The other responds with 'Spending on policing and prisons is at an all time record high'.

Or, one party say, 'The economy is growing at the fastest rate of any in the world/Western world/civilised world/EU/Third World' – without taking into account or making clear that the lower the base from which measurements are taken, the higher the percentage growth rate is certain to be.

Product portfolios

The legend of the razor (see Example Box 7.8, Chapter 7) must never be forgotten. In practice the ability to buy satisfaction is what draws customers and consumers to organisations. If organisations withdraw given items because they do not of themselves make money, they may find customers going elsewhere; and they will consequently lose sales of items that are profitable.

This also applies to the concept of having product ranges that can be divided into those that are attractive and presentable, and those that make money and sell. A mathematical approach to sales figures in isolation would 'prove' that, in many cases, the attractive product was a loss maker. This again, has to be seen in the context that withdrawal of the attractive product would adversely affect sales of the main consumer offerings.

This is a useful illustration of the shortcomings of the use of statistics in isolation from context; and of the managerial approach required if understanding is to be achieved.

of these, where inaccurate extrapolations are inevitable if the gathering or analysis was inaccurate or flawed in the first place.

Managers must therefore develop a positive and healthy scepticism, questioning technique and enquiry into any data presented to them. This is not to promote managerial inertia; quite the opposite. Managers should ensure, however, that they do question and consider all aspects, and the full implications, of statistics, as the basis for accurate decision making and initiative formulation. The ability to do this in the light of accurate and wide-ranging data thus gathered is an aid to effective management and decision making.

This particularly applies to specific problems that come to their attention. Customer complaints, production recheck rates, staff complaints, and information database deficiencies, all require full logging and accurate analysis to establish:

- the nature and frequency of the occurrence of defects and complaints
- the source of these defects and complaints; whether for example, they are all coming from one source, from one region, or spread across the entire board
- the time period over which the complaints have arisen, and any trends within these time periods; for example, whether complaints have suddenly started to be made, or whether they have risen or fallen on a regularised basis, or whether the methods of logging them have changed (see Example Box 10.3).

Index numbers

Index numbers show at a glance the overall direction of changes in a variable over a period of time. These variables can be virtually any regularly produced statistic. Those most frequently referred to are: the retail price index (RPI); wholesale price index; unemployment rate; national output; the Financial Times Stock Exchange Indices of the top 30 and top 100 shares; (FTSE 30 and 100); and exchange ratios. Industrial and commercial sectors also produce their own indices.

Bases are established, against which subsequent movements are measured, in order to give accurate statistical variations. These bases are normally time (a base year or date), percentage relatives (the most common of which are price, quantity or value), and weighting (where more than one item or variable is used on one index). In the expression of indices, the base year, base percentage relative and any base weighting

---

EXAMPLE BOX 10.3 Customer Complaints and the Railway Industry

The railway industry in the UK at the start of the twenty-first century has a bad reputation. While it is true that service levels, reliability, and quality have all declined at the same time as prices have risen, there is no doubt that the volume of complaints received by the railway and train operating companies has been exacerbated by extensive negative media coverage and a series of high profile disasters.

This reinforces the need for structural investment, repositioning of services, short-term attention to specific complaints, and long-term strategic approaches to ensure that when the industry is renovated these complaints are removed altogether.

The railway operating companies have a great deal of data about the things that cause customers to complain the most. In many ways, they have ignored this statistical evidence and chosen to concentrate on what they can do. In the face of demands for reliability and services, and a basic standard of comfort on the trains themselves, they have chosen to do nothing until the railway infrastructure is renovated. This is likely to cause further upturns in the complaint volumes, and downturns in the perceived quality of service.

In linear terms, this may well be the right answer. In managerial terms, the problem is certain to be compounded by declining staff morale, the loss of good and committed members of staff, and the inability to attract the next generation to come and work in the industry.

are combined together and given a numerical value, a base number, against which future variations are to be expressed (see Figure 10.2).

The index thus published represents in a single figure the characteristics of a group of items.

Managers will tend to use the indices produced by their own sectors more than those produced nationally. These will be of greatest value to them in preliminary enquiry and assessment of their own sphere, and its component parts: wage rates, and the going percentage and composition of pay rises; market and marketing aspects, concerning such matters as price and price variations, trade volumes, the relationships between supply and demand; variations in related or substitute sectors (e.g. if the organisation is a seller of Spanish holidays, and sales are falling, it is necessary to know whether sales of holidays to other destinations are also falling, or whether their company is losing out at the expense of a substitute); and wholesale, warehouse, energy and transport indices and indicators. They are a useful source of information for raising causes of possible concerns and 'early warning' systems. They may also indicate opportunities (such as the emergence of a highly competitive energy source, for example, which may indicate the opportunity to invest in a real fixed-cost advantage, and provide the seed for a full business investigation into the matter).

Managers use the various national indices as general sources of data and information. In particular, the annual rise in the RPI may give an indication of the level of wage rise likely to be demanded by the staff. Indices of wholesale price may be used as a starting point for a full investigation into the likely costs to be incurred over the coming period in the purchase of raw materials; or of inflationary pressures (usually) or sectors with which the organisation has trading and other commercial relationships. More generally still,

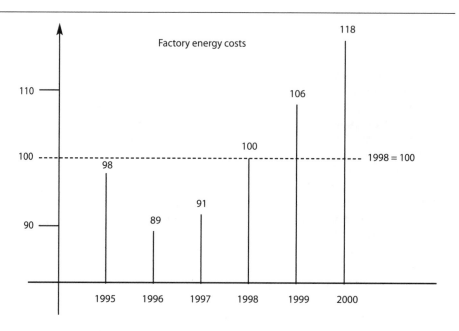

FIGURE 10.2 An index number

the indices may indicate or imply such things as national or market confidence, recessionary pressures, or even 'green shoots' of recovery. Though widely used in the media, they are of very limited true value to the manager in this way (see Example Box 10.4).

Probability

This concept provides a basis for assessing whether or not something is likely to happen. It requires the assessment of one or more variables against a constant, or the assessment of two or more variables against each other. By doing this, possible, probable and likely outcomes of particular initiatives can be assessed and pre-evaluated. In such exercises the true and exact outcome will not be predicted; it is not a certain exercise. It is a valuable way of identifying the components of risk and uncertainty that may be endemic and unavoidable in a particular situation or initiative; and more generally, it is part of the 'early warning' system that all managers should have in regard to their operations.

Accuracy and approximation

All data must be considered in the context of its collection, and any other pressures or constraints (such as time and resources) that are placed on this. The accuracy of the final data depends upon the soundness of the criteria on which the original

---

EXAMPLE BOX 10.4 Indices

Indices are used in general as 'evidence' to advance and support particular points of view. These points of view are usually partial, and the indices therefore misrepresented in support of a particular point of view. For example:

- **'The going rate':** the going rate for pay rises is normally a reflection of the prevailing retail prices index; those who work normally require compensation for loss in value of their earnings caused by inflation. The overwhelming impression is given by employers that employees and their representatives are using the RPI as a vehicle for driving pay levels up unduly; it is much more usual that the RPI is used by organisations to keep pay levels down to the minimum level possible.
- **Marketing:** many advertisements use phrases such as 'in tests, 9 people out of 10 preferred product x …' without ever saying what the tests were, with whom they were conducted, where, why and how; nor do they state how large the sample was. Anadin, the high brand pain relief, was forced to change its use of statistics from '9 out of 10 said they preferred Anadin', to '9 out of 10 who expressed a preference said they preferred Anadin'.
- **The internet:** websites draw attention to their perceived popularity by quoting the number of 'hits' or 'visits' over particular time periods. From this, it is easy to make a spurious connection between the interest in the website – clearly indicated by volumes of hits and visits – and its commercial or intrinsic viability.

collection was based, whether it was from primary or secondary sources. Other factors to be considered are time lag and rounding.

Time lag

This is the difference between the time when the information was collected and when it is to be used; some statistics are soon out of date; business and public initiatives are often planned to resolve future issues based on today's statistics.

Rounding

Whereby figures are rounded to the nearest manageable or usable element. An organisation's net profit for a particular year may be £56 203 459.52; for presentation and convenience this may be rounded to:

- £56 203 450
- £56 203 500
- £56 204 000
- £56 200 000
- £56.2 million
- £56 million
- £50 million
- £60 million

all depending on who is to use the figure and for what purpose.

Sampling

In relation to most business activities it is impossible to gain perfect information; sound methods of sampling must be used if data of meaning and value is to be gathered. Effective sampling may be used to gain valid impressions of markets, products, volume and quality of work, the nature of the work being carried out, the complexities of it, the intensities of work activities, staff turnover and absenteeism, and the regularity and severity of accidents.

The purpose of sampling is to learn information about the whole from the study of a part, providing results that would mirror those if a full survey were to be carried out.

Sampling methods

Any sample must be representative of the population, activity or product under consideration. This may be ensured by a variety of sampling methods.

- **Regular:** whereby each nth product is chosen for testing; each nth person is chosen for survey of their opinions.
- **Random:** whereby each person or product has an equal chance of being selected or tested. If a sample is chosen at random from a larger group or collection, it will exhibit the same characteristics as the whole provided that both are sufficiently

large collections in the first place. Random numbers may be used either as the starting point for this, or to select samples at each stage.

- **Stratified:** the grouping of populations and products into state or subgroups, according to the needs of the data being gathered. This may be by age, location, occupation, street, town, country, urban or rural environment, for persons; or by date, time, shift, and line, in the measurement of products.
- **Multi-stage:** the purpose of this is to provide a measure of checking on one sample; and to identify where bias and inconsistency may arise. In the normal course of events, the stages are:
  - piloting, to establish the fundamental soundness or otherwise of the methods to be used
  - the main survey, in which the main data will be gathered
  - a follow-up survey among those initially surveyed, to establish any inconsistencies, perceptual failings, anomalies and bias that may be present.
- **Non-random and the use of quotas:** this is most prevalent in street surveys whereby an interviewer may be required to get the responses of 50 people on a particular day to a particular set of questions. It is subject to a substantial degree of error, being additionally limited by the perceptions of the interviewer, external pressures on interviewees, and other variables (e.g. was it a Sunday, was it a town, city or village, where did the people interviewed come from?).

Validity, reliability and bias

At the outset of any proposed quantifiable or qualitative research, these elements must be considered. Research will be generally limited by additional constraints placed: accuracy, size of sample and populations, time and resource pressures. Within these constraints however, data gathered must be:

- **Valid:** that is, a measure or version of the truth; accurate (or a version of accuracy); and usable in the format in which it is presented.
- **Reliable:** that is, the data gathered would be the same, or equivalent, if either a different sample were used, or if the sample had been surveyed at a different time in the same way.

Bias arises from a variety of sources, and while it is virtually impossible to eliminate (except through a full census), its origins and limitations can be recognised and accommodated. It comes from the perceptions of the surveyors, the imperfections of the questionnaire and sampling methods, and any preconceptions or secondary agenda that has been included. Consideration must also be given to the sampling frame: the list, population or product range from which the sample is to be taken; partial response or non-response, misperception of the questions; and personal perceptions of the ranges indicated on such things as rating scales.

Census

A census is effectively a 100 per cent sample. A full survey of the population is carried out in the UK every ten years (1971, 1981, 1991, 2001). A census may also be carried out on particular sub-groups; for example, all those exposed to radiation or poison may be surveyed for lasting effects. For business purposes census will normally be limited to attitude surveys at the workplace; or interviewing all leavers to find out why and where they are going; or getting all potential employees to fill in standard application forms. In terms of market research and product quality and reliability, census is not possible, and samples have to be taken.

Questionnaire

This is an instrument for gaining information from an informant for a particular purpose. Any such instrument must therefore be designed with specific and understood purposes, aims and objectives; and if possible, it should be piloted or tested to check that it does fulfil these purposes, or is likely to do so.

With this proviso, however, questionnaires provide a most valuable format for gaining equivalent information from a variety of sources, all for use in a variety of managerial situations. They are used, further, either as the means for structuring an interview, or as a more precise instrument in which specific questions are asked in the same way to each person (either orally or by presentation of the questionnaire to the subjects for completion in their own way).

The questions used may be open (see Example Box 10.5) where the subjects are invited to expand their own response in their own words or style on given matters. Such questions are led by words such as 'who', 'what', 'where', 'why', 'how' and 'when'. The responses to these may be limited by the use of rating scales which may be either numerical:

EXAMPLE BOX 10.5 Open and Closed Questions

Open

What do you like about Sweden?

Closed

(a) What I like about Sweden is: (tick box)

- the scenery   ☐
- the public transport ☐
- the food   ☐
- other   ☐ (please specify) ....

(b) Do you like Swedish scenery?   Yes   No

This illustrates the range and limitation that can be placed on responses. The ways in which information is asked for can thus be varied according to overall need, and in order either to give the respondent maximum opportunity for self-expression, or to limit this into preset and predetermined areas.

How important is it? 1 2 3 4 5
(please circle)

or verbal:

How important is it? Very   Quite   Reasonably   Not   Not at all
(please circle)

It is normal also to ascertain some background information on the respondents for the purposes of classification, and to indicate any bias or external factors that may be affecting responses. Otherwise, the questions will be closed, eliciting precise and definite answers from the respondents (see Example Box 10.5).

Operational research

Operational research is the use of quantitative methods in problem solving. It is usually conducted by 'think tanks' and quantitative analysis units within organisations. Problems are considered and conceptual/mathematical/statistical/economic models are constructed to represent the system to be studied. The approach is to produce a model or simulation or 'mathematical game' version of what could/should happen in a particular set of circumstances. A rational model of the likely consequences of particular courses of action may then become apparent.

Operational research was originally used to solve military problems. Mathematical, statistical, economic and information sciences were applied to military situations; one of the most famous (and notorious) developments was the modelling of optimum shipping convoy sizes in the Second World War. It was also used to assess the logistics of moving large amounts of people, equipment and supplies around the battlefields of Western Europe towards the end of the Second World War. After the war, it was applied to industrial and commercial problems.

In industrial and commercial situations, this form of approach may be used in all aspects of organisational performance.

- **Blockage analysis:** blockages occur because organisational systems operate at the speed of the slowest part. Operational research is used to assess the effects on the total process of the removal or repair of the blockage.
- **Production:** operational research is used in ordering the sequences of work, tasks, jobs, machine pressures and loading, and order scheduling. It may also be used to model for profit maximisation, volume maximisation, income maximisation and market dominance.
- **Marketing:** the relationship between organisations and their markets; the consequences of introducing or reducing the volume and range of products available; the effects of steady-state activities; distribution; vehicle and mail shot scheduling; direct marketing activities. In more extreme cases, operational research may be used to model the effects of market saturation or, at the opposite extreme, red-lining.
- **Queuing:** modelling the effects of increased customer flows; increased operations to reduce queues; and the effects on financial and other resources, and on the operations of the rest of the organisation. It is used to produce 'perfect models'

of the optimum size of a particular part of the workforce concerned with managing and serving the queue.

- **Purchasing:** used to assess economic purchasing quantities; to assess the differences between stockpiling and frequent regular deliveries; also used to assess the continuing relationship between the organisation and its sources of supplies.
- **Research and development:** used for example to produce analysis of the frequency with which new inventions become commercial products; the effects of research and development on other activities; the priority of research and development activities.
- **Communication:** used to analyse the relationship between quality, volume and effectiveness of communications, and other aspects such as strikes and disputes, absence and turnover, accidents and misunderstandings. It may also be used to analyse the effectiveness of committee systems, meeting groups, and general quality of information dissemination.

The greatest problem with operational research methods and techniques is that it produces perfect models.

Managers must understand that in practice this is never going to happen. A perfect model is only an indication of what would happen if everything was orderly and rational. In practice, nothing ever is. Again, therefore, the information thus produced is to be used, analysed and evaluated; not adopted as a certain prediction for future activities.

Forecasting, extrapolation and inference

Forecasting, extrapolation and inference are concerned with facing the future with as much certainty as possible in the circumstances. Each depends upon the availability of high-quality and usable information for its accuracy and reliability. Each brings a slightly different point of view to the same problem.

Forecasting is a prediction of the future based on: knowledge and analysis of the present; knowledge and analysis of the past; and relating the two to the set of circumstances immediately foreseen. Forecasting further into the future is less certain. In managerial terms, it requires acknowledgement that business and commercial circumstances change and that operations and activities are affected by factors outside the managers' and organisation's control. Examples include changes in customer behaviour and confidence, government activities, the entry of new players into the sector, exit of players (especially a key player) from the sector, changes in production technology and changes in technology.

Extrapolation is the linear projection of the future based on current and historic statistics. It is a key output of operational research. Its value lies in identifying linear trends, which are produced by statisticians, economists and information scientists for use by managers in their decision-making processes. Extrapolation is not a decision-making process in itself.

Inference is the assessment of the likely state of the future based on a lack of complete (sometimes a lack of adequate) information. Inference leans heavily on relating the experience of previous similar situations to the present, and using this as the basis to make judgements and choose directions for the future.

Situational analysis (the basis of forecasting), the projection of statistics (extrapolation) and inference together form the quantitative basis for qualitative evaluation and analytical judgements to be made by managers when they consider future directions and activities. It follows from this that information must be as complete as possible and that managers must know how to use it. They must know what the information proves and what it indicates, the difference between the two and the strength of that indication.

Above all, managers must recognise that just because something is forecast or extrapolated, this does not mean that it will indeed come to pass. Serious problems always occur where forecasts are taken as future statements of absolute fact. Unwary managers – and this includes senior managers – are always caught out when they allow themselves to be drawn into this way of thinking. Forecasts and extrapolations should constantly be updated and changed in the light of changing circumstances and, especially, environmental pressures.

Network analysis

This is the term used to embrace a range of organisation, scheduling, planning and control methods used in the ordering of complex projects and operational activities. The purpose is to identify in advance the shortest possible time in which such activities or series of activities or projects may be completed, or a new product brought on stream. From this, sub-schedules and activities can be worked out to establish the nature of resources, staff, equipment and other inputs that need to be present at given stages in order for this efficient and effective main schedule to be adhered to (see Figure 10.3).

The shortest and most effective route through such a schedule is called the 'critical path'; that is, the one that determines the speed of operations within it. Non-critical paths – flows of activity that have more flexibility in their inception, execution and timescale – will also be identified so that resources can be optimised at all stages of the work.

Critical incidents within the network will also be identified in advance. Each incident will be related to a set of criteria that contributes to the nature and extent of its critical configuration. Such criteria relate to matters concerning the difficulty, frequency, importance and value of the activity itself; scarcity and balance of resources; availability and conflicting demands on resources, expertise and equipment; and the consequences of delays on the critical incident to the rest of the schedule.

Such a network will then be used as a control mechanism, progress monitor, progress chaser (where desirable or necessary) and as a continuing means of monitoring and evaluating the whole series of activities and each component of the series.

Proof and indication

Effective managerial use of information must distinguish between proof and indication. At one level, statistics can prove anything (see Example Box 10.2). This takes no account of the wider context or of the interrelationship between one set of figures and others.

- **Cars:** a car dealership which sells 10 per cent of its expensive models and 100 per cent of its cheap models must take into account the likelihood (and the extent of

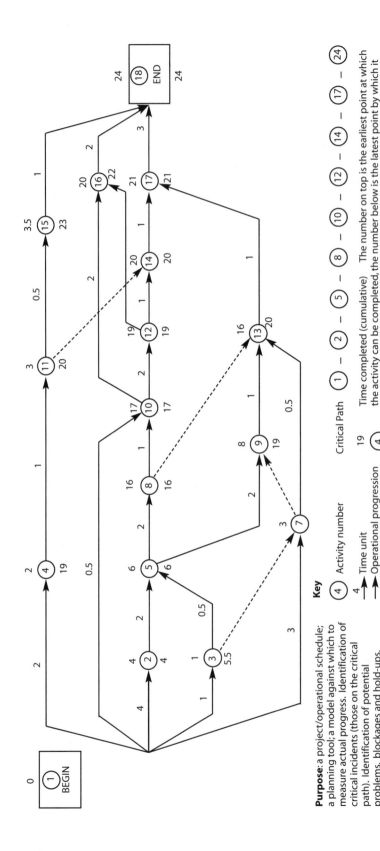

Purpose: a project/operational schedule; a planning tool; a model against which to measure actual progress. Identification of critical incidents (those on the critical path). Identification of potential problems, blockages and hold-ups.

Key

④	Activity number
4	Time unit
→	Operational progression
⤏	Operational tie-ups

Critical Path ① – ② – ⑤ – ⑧ – ⑩ – ⑫ – ⑭ – ⑰ – ㉔

Time completed (cumulative) The number on top is the earliest point at which the activity can be completed, the number below is the latest point by which it must be completed.

19
④
19

FIGURE 10.3 A network diagram

the likelihood) that it has only sold all of its cheap models because the customers were first attracted by the expensive ones.

- **Hospitals:** an indication of hospital workload is likely to be the number of patients treated. If this rises by 20 per cent it proves increased workload. Again, this cannot be seen in isolation, and factors which would always have to be considered include: the number of patients returning for extended courses of treatment or for retreatment following unsatisfactory treatment the first time round, and the number of patients attracted to the hospital following closure of other facilities elsewhere in the region (see Example Box 10.6).

From a managerial point of view, information and statistics are not therefore to be seen in isolation. They complete (or help to complete) a broader picture which consists at least in part of qualitative and behavioural aspects. Information, however complete, does not of itself make decisions or solve problems. Problems, especially, are always bounded by a combination of information, deadlines and consequences; it is therefore certain that the solution to problems will normally be 'the best answer available on the day'. Information provides a basis (indeed part of the basis) for this approach. This is ultimately carried out based on the manager's judgement, analysis, evaluation and choice. It follows that the greater the volume of relevant and useful information available, the greater the propensity, rationally, for effective and successful analysis – and therefore accurate decisions and effective solutions to problems.

Management information systems

The purpose of such systems is to 'oil the wheels' of the organisation, providing means for the effective transmission, reception and general communication of information.

EXAMPLE BOX 10.6 Health Authority Management

There is a great range of information on all aspects of healthcare available to those responsible for the direction of health authorities. This creates problems when the statistical evidence supports senior managers in choosing particular priorities in spite of the fact that other things need doing more urgently (as is invariably the case).

For example, local statistics that indicate pressures on accident and emergency departments often lead to the choice to extend this facility by purchasing more trolleys, so that a greater volume of patients can be accommodated, even if this means putting them in corridors and other non-medical areas. The fact that this is done, and needs doing, demonstrates 'managerial activity'.

However, the overwhelming statistical evidence is that the problems of the health service are simply being shifted from one location to another. No overall improvement is possible until the structural problems caused by declining levels of professional staff, bed shortages, and the lack of other hospital facilities and expertise are addressed.

Source: National Audit Office (1999–2000); East Kent Health Authority *Annual Report*, 2000.

This must be in terms and formats that are efficient and effective, presenting information in ways that are understandable, relevant, and above all usable. Such systems provide the basis for effective general business practices and are specifically aimed at enabling sound decision making.

Information systems and technology

Information systems are normally physical (at least in part), based on the retention of papers and documents recording the nature and volume of activities and providing material for internal and external consumption in all spheres: production, sales, marketing, staff management, finance and administration. Almost universally, this is supported, and in many cases driven, by technology used to produce, store, retrieve, analyse and present information in a variety of different ways in order to meet divergent demands, and according to the nature of the information and the purposes for which it is to be used.

Usage

Usage means addressing and analysing the organisation's needs for information, and the capabilities, capacity and durability of the systems that are being considered. It particularly concerns the volumes of information that are to be stored and processed and the nature and means of access required. It is especially necessary to pay attention to system design, workstation content and context, and location and hardware. In many cases, it is also necessary to consider integration with existing systems, both physical and electronic.

It is necessary to consider the nature and content of the relationship between the particular organisation and the system and software suppliers. This is likely to include after-sales and attention to teething troubles, training for all those who are to use the system, software upgrades, and replacing and servicing the hardware when necessary (see Example Box 10.7).

System activities

Six specific business and management activities that impinge upon information systems may be identified.

- planning and organising of all work and support functions
- control mechanisms
- identification of blockages, either organisational or operational
- provision of linking elements and forums between departments and functions
- motivational aspects
- functional aspects: the ability to gain and gather accurate information from all functional and operational areas.

System data

Certain types of data required by the organisation may next be identified. Such data will take its format from the following elements:

> **EXAMPLE BOX 10.7 User-friendliness**
>
> User-friendliness is the term used to describe the extent to which the needs of the system users have been taken into account. Problems always occur when access and usage of the technology is complicated and when computer programmes have complex and convoluted access and instruction systems.
>
> The best information (and production) technology is simple to understand and access, and straightforward to operate. It requires initial familiarisation and practice. This is normally provided by the supplying company. It also provides a variety of failsafe systems so that human error does not cause programmes to be wiped and large swathes of information and production capacity to be lost as the result.
>
> This is a particular problem with website companies and operations. The vast majority were designed without customer or user input. Technically excellent though they are from the designer point of view, in many cases they are inaccessible to the average user, who is neither a computer nor information systems specialist. The best websites (and for that matter the best management information systems) are always supported by instantly accessible customer and user help lines, so that the technology and the access to expertise complement each other.
>
> User-friendliness is therefore a summary of the needs of the user. Lack of attention to each area normally results in a lack of willingness to use the system. This leads to a failure of the system to be operated to its full capacity and, in turn, to incomplete information, inadequately stored, maintained and retrieved. The end result is to affect the quality of decision making of those using the system. It becomes discredited. Above all, it becomes extremely expensive and inefficient.

- long, medium or short-term nature
- the extent of the accuracy required
- the volume to be stored, processed and retrieved, and the formats required for this.
- what it is to be used for
- who is to use it, and how they are to gain access
- how often it is to be used.

System design

Next must be considered matters to do with the design of the system or systems themselves.

- whether to have one system or a set of related and interlocking sub-systems
- modes and methods of access
- frequency of access
- questions of urgency of access, the value of access, and general matters of speed, accuracy, and methods of information processing
- the nature of the staff who are to use the system or systems, and their levels of quality, qualifications and trainability.

This is a fundamental consideration. If the system is too complex for the staff, and they are not capable of being trained to use it, either the system must be redesigned or staff hired who can use it in its current format.

System responsibilities

There are wider implications also to be considered. The most basic of these is to establish where overall responsibility for the system lies, and also where the devolved functional responsibilities are. There may be specific as well as legal constraints (apart from anything else) which it is critical to pin down; this is quite apart from questions of operational necessity.

System technology

Then there is the technology itself. Many organisations, functions and managers have been so carried away by the brilliance and capacities of both hardware and software that they have lost sight of their own specific requirements for it. This has to be balanced against the genuine lifespan of equipment in an age of constant technological revolution, update and obsolescence. As with other operational aspects therefore, a strategic approach is required to the design, organisation and purpose of information systems. A system thus arrived at will invariably operate more productively for longer than one that is technically more modern, but which has not had the same overall approach to its purchase.

Alongside this is the option of purchasing 'off the shelf' information systems and software that can be installed and made operational very quickly, as opposed to the design and implementation of something that is tailor-made. The former will always be cheaper at the point of purchase; the true cost, however, has to be measured and evaluated over the full operational life of the system. There is also the wider question of the ability of complex organisations to accommodate satisfactorily the vagaries of something not specifically designed for them.

System security and control

Questions of control and security of information must be considered. Again, this must be done from the global or strategic point of view; a balance must be struck between use and value, questions of access, operational factors, and the power and influence of those who are responsible for the outputs. There are also more general elements of power and influence to be considered in regard to the information itself, its volume and quality and its ultimate destinations and users.

System installation

There are behavioural aspects especially to be addressed. Lack of understanding of the technology, or a more nebulous disquiet or feeling of being threatened by it, will invariably mean that the systems are not used fully or at all.

The installation of any system must therefore be accompanied by programmes of staff and management training, briefing, familiarisation, and overall appreciation, designed to ensure that the system does indeed 'oil the wheels' of the organisation, rather than becoming an adjunct to it.

There are wider considerations for such matters as recruitment and selection processes, job design, and workplace layout, structure and design. The end result must extend to the whole organisation, so that the information system is fully integrated with all other organisation systems and activities, ensuring that those employed can use them and are comfortable with them, and that the organisation as a whole has systems that contribute to its overall effectiveness, rather than detract from it.

System outputs

The data outputs from any system must be such that they are usable by those who receive them. Managers, in particular, do not normally require volumes of raw data; or if they do, they also require synopses and summaries and analyses indicating what the data itself indicates, and giving pointers to the likely and suitable ranges of activities that the data implies. In this way management information systems are essential adjuncts to decision-making processes and the outlining, formulation and determination of strategic choices. They also give particular functional information in regard to the operational area in question.

Management information systems and the data that they generate must themselves be managed if they are to continue to remain effective and serve the organisation and its managers and fulfil the functions indicated above.

Conclusions

From a managerial point of view, statistics, information and the systems used are concerned with value and contribution. Statistics, mathematics and economics produce figures and information; it is the ability to analyse and evaluate that is the concern of the manager. For this to be successful and effective, specific concerns must be addressed.

Validity and reliability

The methods by which the data is gathered must be consistent. It should be gathered by one of the methods indicated above. Where this has not been possible, or where the information gathering was incomplete or biased or skewed, the defect must be acknowledged. Ideally the data should be free from bias and subjective judgement. In most cases, where this is not absolutely possible, defects must again be acknowledged. Where this is, as happens in many cases, virtually impossible, the data is to be treated with great degrees of scepticism (see for example, Example Box 10.8).

As far as possible, the data gathered should be reliable: capable of validation in all equivalent situations and circumstances from which it was gathered. Again, if this is not possible, the fact should be acknowledged.

Managers therefore need to know and understand the basis or bases on which the information has been gathered if they are to use it effectively. It is necessary therefore to have an understanding of the statistical and mathematical methods, and the ability to use the figures in the pursuit of managerial effectiveness. For this to happen, managers need to know and understand a range of factors.

• The basis on which the information was gathered and any specific constraints

EXAMPLE BOX 10.8 The Generally Favourable Response (2)

It is very easy to generate a generally favourable response (GFR). This is achieved as follows.

Example: marketing (upon the launch of a new product)

Interviewer:	Do you like this product?
Subject:	Yes.
Interviewer:	How would you rate it on a scale of 1–10, where 10 is the most favourable response?
Subject:	About 7.
Interviewer:	Would you use it?
Subject:	Yes, I would.

Asking questions in this way is comfortable and reinforcing. But it is fraught with danger. Not enough follow-up information is demanded. It is certain to be clouded by: perceptions of what the rating scale means (different to every individual); the likeness (the subject will not wish to offend the interviewer); the question: 'Would you use?' (very different from: 'Will you use?' and 'And if so, how often?').

Example: staff references

Many organisations send out pro-forma questionnaires to previous employers of potential employees. A common question on these is: 'Would you re-employ?', to which there is a range of GFRs, including: yes; yes if a suitable vacancy were to arise; probably; possibly; maybe; and so on.

The question is never asked as: 'Will you re-employ?' or: 'Will you re-employ if a suitable vacancy comes up?'

The problem is bad enough in the staff-reference case. In the interview situation, the question is incapable of validation as it is based entirely on a set of personal perceptions (on the part of the responder) to a future hypothetical situation.

Example: questionnaire structuring

More insidiously still, GFRs are achieved through careful combinations of ostensibly direct, but actually leading, questions. It is for example, used by political parties in the pursuit of a vested interest as follows.

- **Question 1:** Do you believe that crimes against children should be stopped?
- **Question 2:** Do you believe that those who carry out crimes against children should be punished?
- **Question 3:** Do you believe that society should clean up those who carry out these crimes?

Example Box 10.8 (continued)

- **Question 4:** Will you support the death penalty?

The effect is at least threefold. It leads people down a particular direction involving them in the desired train of thought. It produces (in fact) subjective answers to (overtly) rational questions. It makes overtly rational, but actually spurious, connections between questions 1–3 and question 4. And it is the answer to question 4 (not 1–3) that is then used by the vested interest.

that were imposed such as time pressures, size of samples and access/lack of access to sources of information.

- The context in which the information was gathered: the extent to which it was directed or prescribed; what information has not been taken into account (for whatever reason); who requested the information and why; what, if anything, it is intended to prove or indicate; what it actually proves or indicates.
- Expert conclusions drawn by statisticians, mathematicians and information systems experts, and their impact on managerial judgement, evaluation and analysis.
- Uses to which the information may legitimately be put; uses to which it may not legitimately be put; the extent to which it is legitimate to use for other purposes information that was gathered for one purpose.
- The wider context: the general extent to which the information may be used; its place in the overall scheme of things; the effects – both positive and negative – of taking one piece of information in isolation from others.

It is also important to recognise the difference between what can and cannot be controlled. Where organisations have to deal with factors outside their control, the

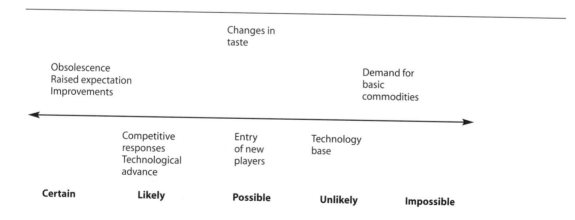

Factors outside the organisation's control   *FIGURE 10.4*

best approach is to gather as much information as possible, to know as much as possible about those factors that are outside its control, and to cover the range of possible outcomes on the basis of the spectrum shown in Figure 10.4.

Currency

The other main issue to be addressed is the currency of the information. In general, circumstances change rapidly and information quickly becomes obsolete. To be effective, systems have to be kept up to date so that whatever is extracted and analysed is current also. This applies in all spheres. Production design, capability and quality may be superseded by others in the field and the organisation needs to know this in order to be able to respond. Human resource systems must be kept up to date concerning qualifications, length of service, employee history and staff capability. Marketing information must reflect current, not recent, states of the segments and niches in which activities are carried out. Sales information must reflect the current state of activities if there is to be any chance of effective forecasting, extrapolation and inference for the future.

Otherwise, the main conclusion to be drawn here relates to the managerial constructs that are to be placed on the quantitative data and information. Managers must ensure that both the information and the methods used to collect, store and present it are suitable for the purposes of the organisation and the needs of the managers. Quantitative data is only of value if it is available in ways that the organisation and those within it can understand and use. This must include the behavioural and perceptual aspects of it as well as the quantitative material itself. Above all, managers must have faith and confidence in both the budgeting information that they receive and the systems that produce it if these are to have in themselves any credence or organisational value.

CHAPTER SUMMARY

Hannagan (1998) states that 'the principal function of statistics and quantitative approaches to management is to narrow the area of disagreement that would otherwise exist in a discussion, and in that way help in decision-making'. The key areas are:

- the rigour with which data is gathered
- the purposes for which it is gathered; this is a particular problem when using secondary data and non-specified sources of information
- the uses to which the data is to be put once it is analysed.

The problem for managers lies in their ability to coordinate each of these elements. If they are required to use data that is flawed, the first step must be to acknowledge its imperfections. This need not necessarily be a basis for not going ahead, but it should reinforce the need to constantly review and update data, as well as progress once the decision is taken.

The context in which data is gathered is also important. If people are asked what is wrong with something, they will tend to respond by seeking and reporting faults. If people are asked for their comments on something, unless they know the precise nature of the comments required, they will stick to blandnesses rather than present a notion with which they are not entirely confident. If people want a particular result from statistical and quantitative analysis, they tend to ignore that which dilutes or disproves the point. If statistics indicate a tiny flaw in a line of reasoning, this is often ignored. If the flaw is tiny but critical, this can be fatal (for example, in 1944, the Arnhem landings in Holland were a disaster because the evidence of three photographs was ignored: these photographs showed the presence of large numbers of German troops precisely where the landings were to take place).

Managers do not need to be mathematical experts. However, they are required to be experts in the analysis and evaluation of information, and in questioning that which they do not fully understand or recognise. They must also be receptive to those who are expert in these disciplines, when they explain the results. Above all, when statistical and quantitative analyses indicate the need for particular courses of action, managers should be prepared to engage in them.

DISCUSSION QUESTIONS

1. What statistical measures should be used by a department store to indicate that it had: serious customer complaint problems; serious problems with suppliers; serious staff morale problems?
2. What primary research should be carried out in order to assess the reasons for reject rates on a food production line?
3. What statistical measures should be used to assess the commercial viability of an organisational website? What would these measures show; and what would they not show?
4. What are the dangers of having either too little or too much information available in any set of circumstances?

CHAPTER CASE STUDY

LEVI STRAUSS

In recent years, Levi Strauss have looked at ways of diversifying away from their heavy dependence on a jeans market that they perceived to be saturated, and have tried introducing shoes, shirts and socks. These sold quite well among people who were already buying Levi jeans. A more recent initiative was to move into the market for higher priced clothes, in order to attract a new type of customer to the Levi Strauss brand. As menswear had always been their biggest seller, it was decided to concentrate on the male market first.

Social segment Class B (see Chapter 7, page 171) was known to be a primary customer group with a high propensity to spend in this market. A research company was engaged and asked to computer analyse the behaviour and attitudes of this specific group. The large total number of interviews made it possible to have confidence in the reliability of the data from this sub-sample. It emerged that Class

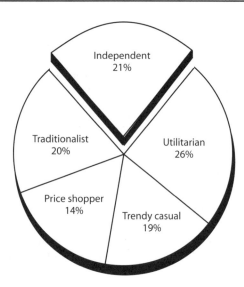

FIGURE 10.5 Menswear market segmentation

B men wanted traditionally styled, perhaps pin-striped, suits, that they liked to buy through independent clothes shops or tailors, rather than at department stores, and that they liked to shop alone (whereas others liked having their wives or girl-friends with them).

To tackle this segment of the market, Levi decided to introduce 'Tailored Classics', a range of high-quality wool suits, trousers and jackets. The research showed that Class B buyers valued quality and fit above low prices, so the company decided to price their range 10 per cent above that of the competition. To avoid direct product comparisons – and to ensure that not too large a sales force was needed – Levi chose to distribute through department store chains and their own outlets.

Having decided on this strategy, its acceptability to the target market was tested via a series of group discussions. These were conducted by a psychologist who was to look for the real motivations behind respondents' opinions or behaviour. The psychologist reported that the Class B men had two misgivings: first, they were concerned that the garments would be in standard fittings, and so would not provide the tailoring they wanted; second, although they could believe that Levi could make a good suit, they still felt uncomfortable about the Levi name. They also expected individual attention when buying high-quality suits, and Levi were under-stood or perceived as being unable to provide this. It also had to be considered that, if the company became known as a suit tailor, core product sales – denim and fashion clothing – might be diluted.

Marketing executives responded by deciding to concentrate on the core, and let the new range 'slipstream': it would be advertised alongside the jeans, and avail-able close by in the stores. The range of outlets would be limited, and retailers would be obliged to charge prescribed minimum prices in order to protect and reinforce the brand's exclusivity. This, it was reasoned, would lead to targets being at least met, if not exceeded.

Soon after this decision, salesmen started contacting retail buyers. After months of selling to the trade, it was clear that the range's sales targets would not be met. Even a price cut did little to redeem the situation, and Tailored Classics achieved only 65 per cent of its modest sales targets. The line was cancelled after two years.

Levi could only find consolation if they could learn why they went so badly wrong. They need to know especially why things went wrong at the design and forecasting stage.

Sources: Channel 4, *Commercial Breaks,* 2000; Ian Marcouse, *Business Case Studies,* Longman, 1990; Financial Times FT.com/Levi Strauss, *Levi Strauss Annual Report,* 2000–01.

QUESTIONS

1. What primary research should Levi Strauss have undertaken before deciding to go down this particular line? What questions should they have asked, to whom, when, where and why? How should the data thus gathered have been analysed?
2. What mistakes did the company make in its forecasting and extrapolating? How might these have been avoided?
3. What are the strengths and shortcomings of the market segmentation method used for this particular activity? What other form of segmentation might have been used?
4. What preconceptions are apparent, and how should these be tackled?

11 Innovation and Enterprise

CHAPTER OUTLINE

Innovation, enterprise and self-employment; innovation and enterprise in existing organisations

The importance of heart and soul in the management and execution of innovation

The need for innovation and enterprise in coping with change and uncertainty

Clarity of purpose and direction

Long-term enduring commitment

Organisational, managerial and business heroes and heroines.

CHAPTER OBJECTIVES

After studying this chapter, you should be able to:

understand the position, priority and value of generating new ideas, products and services

understand the nature of investment required to do this, both in financial terms, and also with reference to the commitment of other resources, including personal energy and commitment

understand the position of research and development in terms of long-term organisational profitability, effectiveness and viability

understand the importance of developing innovating and entrepreneurial attitudes in all organisations.

Introduction

All innovation, development and enterprise is dependent upon the combination of creativity, inventiveness and imagination, with professional knowledge, understanding and expertise, and the availability of, or potential for, sufficient resources to be gathered together. This applies equally to:

- new business start-ups, created by individuals as entrepreneurs and pioneers
- new product and service developments in existing organisations
- new ventures and changes of market conducted by existing organisations
- organisational regeneration by those taking on moribund and under-performing companies and making them work effectively once again

- research and development experts working in all fields, whether in start-up companies, existing organisations or university research departments
- think-tanks and project groups charged with developing new initiatives and ventures
- visionary activities
- technological and market transformations.

It is also essential to recognise that all managers and supervisors are at least implicitly expected to improve ways of working in their own particular areas of responsibility. To this extent therefore, all managers are required to have a measure of innovative and/or entrepreneurial expertise. They are also increasingly expected to be able to analyse and evaluate new ideas, proposals, initiatives – and daydreams – for potential, feasibility, and commercialisation (see Example Box 11.1).

It is also the case that new ideas and potential innovations and developments are the beginning of hard, targeted and thorough work, not an end in themselves. This, in turn, is certain to lead to financial and other resource commitments. For example, Sony have always taken the view that once an idea is adopted it is to be pursued with 100 per cent commitment. If for any reason the venture is not fully realisable or a commercial success, nevertheless lessons will have been learned, expertise and technology developed, and these provide a greater body of knowledge and understanding on which the next set of ventures and therefore the long-term future, will be built (see Example Box 11.2).

For all innovation and enterprise, whatever the organisation and sector, the following are required:

- dreams and imagination
- research and development activities
- market and marketing research and development
- product and service development, innovation, improvement and enhancement; including the more nebulous concept of 'idea development'
- business planning, to combine the disciplines of strategy, marketing, finance and operations
- administration planning, to combine the need for speed and quality of operations and processes, with deliverability to market
- champions, product, service and project leaders, and the drive, energy, leadership, enthusiasm and vision necessary to transform ideas into reality (see Example Box 11.3).

Dreams and imagination

All ideas, great and small, start with imagination, or 'what if?' approaches – from 'What if I could reduce each task in the office by five minutes per day?' to 'What if I could operate my own shipping line?'

Most ideas are rejected at this stage, yet interest and creative processes have been aroused. The point is to ensure that all managers are encouraged to think like this as a part of the pursuit of overall business organisational and operational excellence, and their own contribution to this. All managers should also be encouraging their staff to think in these ways.

EXAMPLE BOX 11.1 Heroes and Heroines of Business

It is always useful and valuable to study the actions and behaviour of both those who are demonstrably successful, and also those less so.

> His supreme courage and unshakeable faith outshone all physical weaknesses and conquered. His path could never be a smooth one – he was to make many enemies, find himself in many more tight corners, but he was always driven to further effort.
>
> Norman Wymer, *The Father of Nobody's Children: The Story of Dr. Thomas Barnado*, Arrow, 1954.

These words could have been written about any individual who has either started his or her own organisation, or contributed extensively to an existing corporation. Barnado's great and enduring contribution was that he transformed the whole attitude to poor, homeless and uncared for children. His organisation still exists today.

Current mainstream business heroes and heroines include:

- Gordon and Anita Roddick and Richard Branson, who began respectively The Body Shop and Virgin Group. Each of these organisations come into being at a time when there was recession in Western markets, and when people were looking much harder at what they bought and consumed. People were attracted to them, not just because of what they did, but also the ways in which they operated. Each brought a very distinctive ethical approach, supported by high-profile publicity and public relations. It was also apparent that they brought a large measure of humanity to their business activities.

- It is also important to note that perceptions can, and do, change in line with events. In the 1960s and 1970s, Robert Maxwell was regarded as the epitome of business acumen and expertise. This changed during the period immediately before, and also after, his death, when it became apparent that he had been stealing from his organisation's pension fund. Many others have also suffered this fate – John Blume, for example, whose Rolls Razor washing machine empire was set to transform the white goods industry in the 1960s; Freddy Laker, whose cut-price transatlantic airline failed because he was unable to sustain a price war; and Mark Goldberg, who was unable to transform Crystal Palace Football Club into a viable business concern.

- This also applies to new companies and industries. For example, with the launch of LastMinute.com Martha Lane-Fox exploited the media demand for young, glamorous entrepreneurs; perceptions quickly changed when the City and other investors failed to get the returns anticipated, while Brent Hoberman, Martha Lane-Fox's co-founder, attracted publicity only when he took a fortnight's holiday in the south of France.

- This applies to process as well as product and service innovations. 'Business process re-engineering' (BPR) has come to be regarded as a management fad, and has been further discredited because it is now used as little more than a

Example Box 11.1 (continued)

sales pitch by high-brand, high-cost, management consultants. Yet the message – that all business processes should be investigated to see where improvements and transformations can be carried out -- remains valid; and that any process that can be reduced, enhanced, speeded up or made more efficient, contributes positively to the cost base of the particular organisation.

Source: M. Hammer and J. Champy, *Re-engineering the Corporation*, Free Press, 1998.

EXAMPLE BOX 11.2   A Note on the Dot.Com Revolution

Investment in internet companies is driven by the real or perceived opportunity to take advantage of the huge volume of information available on the world-wide web on the one hand, and the equally vast potential access afforded by computer and telecommunications technology to customer bases on the other. Consequently, internet companies operating over the period 1998–2000 were able to attract both corporate and individual investors to make substantial investments. For example LastMinute.com, the online travel and airline ticket sales company, was able in March 2000 to attract investment of £850 million at a time when its annual turnover was £1.6 million with an annual operating loss of £24 million.

Anyone seeking a business-related return on investment in internet companies is overtly committed to a period of anything up to ten years before they begin to get their money back. In practice, many investors are unwilling to wait this long, and have therefore sought to look for real, rather than potential, markets and customer bases. This has led to a repositioning of the commercial potential and viability of internet activities. LastMinute.com, for example, are now effectively in partnership with Thomas Cook, who sell LastMinute.com products and services at their travel agency outlet, while Cook's products and services are made available through Last-Minute.com's website.

Yet the pursuit of real customers, spending real money on real products and services, came late to the internet revolution. In March 2000, Anthony Impey, General Manager of Touchbase plc, stated:

> Investment in internet opportunities and the dot.com revolution represents 0.5 per cent of total investment volumes only. Of the first wave of companies floated on the stock exchange, 97 per cent are expected not to exist in their present form in five years' time. Many will fail; others will merge; others still, will be taken over. Of those that do still exist at the end of the period, a similar shake-out is expected over the following five years.

He also went on to put forward the view that when – not if – a fall in values came around, it would be the entrepreneurs themselves and small private investors, not big institutions, who would lose their investment.

EXAMPLE BOX 11.3 The Little Things

At first glance, much of this appears extreme. This is especially so if all that is being considered are minor changes to existing ways of working. Even with small things, however, it is essential that they are fully considered, capable of making the changes anticipated, made acceptable and understandable to all those affected, and seen through to completion. Moreover, if a small change is not properly managed, then the credibility of the individual and organisation involved is called into question when larger ventures are being considered.

Entrepreneurs think like this all the time, from the point when they decide what they are going to do, why and how they are going to do it, who they are going to serve, and the activities necessary as the result. They then attend to each element of whatever it is they are starting up, and this includes concentration on processes and functions, as well as invention and pioneering.

Dreams are also an extremely effective trigger when trying to convince others of the value of new ideas. Small changes in office procedures are certain to be acceptable if they respond to the staff's dream of a less stressful or more useful working day. At the other extreme, Elaine Vaughan of Sandal's Resorts Ltd, the exclusive holiday company, states that she is 'selling dreams to people' (see above, Chapter 1).

This form of approach then becomes the basis for brainstorming activities, serious analysis and evaluation, projections and forecasts, leading to acceptance in principle, or rejection (see Example Box 11.4).

Myths and legends

Peters (1996) states that 'all new ideas come from the wrong people, in the wrong location, in the wrong line of business, at the wrong time. If you thought about this rationally, you would never start.' It is certainly true that far too many organisations

---

EXAMPLE BOX 11.4 Acceptance and Rejection

Within all organisations, and whatever the idea, this first part of the process has to be conducted with absolute integrity. It is extremely damaging to motivation and morale, as well as long-term organisational commitment and operational well-being, if ideas are overtly rejected but actually stolen by those in higher authority and claimed as their own.

Many organisations run extremely successful suggestion schemes. These only work well if there is a tangible return when they are implemented to the person or group that dreamed them up. This encourages others to adopt the same approach. Properly managed, this is an extremely valuable and effective method of organisation development and enhancement, because it involves everyone as a matter of course.

---

preach empowerment and development without practising it. Any attempt at genuine innovation is smothered by rank, status and hierarchy, or put into the corporate mill and never heard of again. At the other extreme, those with status and influence are known, believed or perceived to get pet schemes off the ground on the basis of being seen to have the ability to command resources, or because they have the need for a political triumph.

Breaking free of organisational myths and legends requires courage for those who have genuine ideas that they wish to try and develop. The only ways to do so are:

- to adopt an intrapreneurial stance: that of an enterprising individual within an existing organisation; and if the present organisation cannot, or will not, accommodate this, then find one which will
- to establish the idea as a business: either at first as a hobby on evening, weekend and free time activity until it becomes clear that the idea does have commercial potential; or to establish a company straightaway, the purpose of which is to commercialise the idea (and which will clearly fail if the idea is not, or cannot be, commercially viable).

In either case, the main pitfall at the early stage is that of 'fool's gold' or the 'absolute certainty'. Once an idea has been given life, it becomes 'an absolute certainty' that it will work, and that it will make a fortune. Those contributing to suggestion schemes avoid this problem altogether, because their ideas are evaluated elsewhere. In practice, there is never an absolute certainty, foolproof scheme, or product and service without which people cannot do. The world existed before the new idea, and will continue to exist after the particular venture has run its course.

This did not prevent many would-be entrepreneurs starting up internet businesses in the late 1990s, and small investors from backing them. All this was supported and fuelled by extensive media coverage, and for a time in 1999 and 2000 it became a business legend that:

- all you needed to do was design a website and people would queue to buy it for millions
- if you were not in the internet industry, you were nobody
- the collapse of traditional ways of conducting business was both certain and imminent.

Many small investors consequently pulled funds out of investments in traditional enterprises at the time. By going into the internet, they lost most of their investment. One exception to this over the period 1998–2000 was Warren Buffett, the US investor. Though hardly a small or uninfluential player, he showed a net return of 15 per cent per annum on his own investments over this period by placing his funds in companies that produced kitchen furniture, tiles and carpets.

Failure

The fear of failure is a strong cultural and behavioural barrier, especially in the UK. This is quite apart from the fact that it clearly has economic consequences. People collectively do not like having to admit to failure, and will seek excuses for it, above all to absolve themselves from any responsibility or contribution when things do go wrong (see Example Box 11.5).

Yet all organisations and their managers, not just new venturers or innovators, operate in their own wider environmental context, and this has to be clearly understood as a precursor to further progress. For it is certain that anything will fail that does not take account of those factors that cannot be controlled, and of the competitive, operational and cultural pressures present; or that fails to recognise that these can, and do, change in influence and importance.

Research and development

Research and development comes in many forms. It is an essential feature of all innovation, progress and enhancement as follows.

- Pure research and development strives to find out what exists, how and why things work, how and why they could be made to work better, and the opportunities and consequences for combining elements, materials, matter, information and process in an infinite number of ways. The purity of this kind of research is maintained by ensuring that it is 'untainted' by any commercial or personal gain. It is up to others to decide what the various different results can be used for, whether they can be used at all, or whether they simply add to the fund of knowledge. This approach to research and development is becoming increasingly rare. Even university postgraduate and postdoctoral

---

EXAMPLE BOX 11.5 Attitudes to Failure

Following the success of the London Millennium celebrations on 31 December 1999, it was determined to have a giant New Year's Eve party every year. However, during the autumn of the year 2000, it became apparent that there would be difficulties both with transport and with the provision of medical emergency and policing services. On 1 December 2000, the government minister for London Transport, Keith Hill, announced that the party would have to be cancelled. Ken Livingstone, the Mayor of London, stated that the only reason that the festivities would have to be cancelled was the government's dislike of him personally; Keith Hill then responded by saying that Livingstone was using his own personal popularity to whip up support for something that could not be carried out properly.

In this case – and in many others – blame is apportioned to events or personalities outside the individual's control, and thus people seek absolution for being associated with failure. This should be contrasted with the Arsene Wenger's explanation on Radio 5 Live for the failure of Arsenal Football Club to progress beyond the first phase of the European Champions' League in 1999 and 2000:

> I got the team wrong, the selections wrong. That was why we failed. It was nothing to do with playing at Wembley. And even if it was, it was still my decision to go there.

students are being increasingly steered in the direction of research that has a real or potential commercial spin-off.

- Applied research and development is funded where, at the very least, a commercial spin-off is anticipated. Applied research and development is now undertaken widely because there is a known or believed direct opportunity to commercialise the results. The consequence of this is that the broader approach is often lost. For example, medical research is heavily concentrated on curing diseases rather than health promotion, because there is a ready and tangible market for the products that emerge as the result, rather than one that is nebulous and intangible, if still essential. Computer consulting is driven by the ability to solve particular problems, rather than concentrating on improved software design and capability. Management consultants depend heavily on their ability to sell business process re-engineering, total quality management, and other branded tangible solutions, rather than conducting nebulous organisational research to assess where problems truly lie.

This kind of understanding must be applied in all sectors.

Market research and development

Anyone wishing to commercialise anything that is genuinely or perceptually new must take whatever time and steps are necessary to ensure that there is an enduring market, and that customers and clients will buy it because of the utility and benefit that it brings to them.

Most business and innovations that fail at an early stage do so because they do not fully assess their markets or the capability and willingness of customers to pay adequate price levels. The vast majority of dot.com company failures are directly attributable to the fact that entrepreneurs mistook genuine interest in the internet for market certainty; yet they would be the first to understand that people who take a genuine interest in old steam engines seldom actually buy one.

This applies to all sectors. There is always room for those who bring real and differentiated alternatives to that which exists already provided that certain conditions are met.

- The benefits and utility offered must be those that customers want and are prepared to pay for.
- The location must be sufficiently convenient to the proposed or target market.
- The wider behavioural issues must be understood, especially in terms of the relationship between price, real and perceived quality and value, expectations and satisfaction.
- Customers must get at least what they expect (even if they do not quite know what this may be until they get it).
- The product or service envisaged must be capable of being presented and marketed in a real or perceived differentiated way. If this is to be done on price alone, then the particular organisation has to be absolutely certain that it can if necessary sustain a long-term price war with large, well established existing players. If this cannot be done on price alone, then other approaches have to be taken (see Example Box 11.6)

EXAMPLE BOX 11.6 Market Research and Innovation

When John Gray was made redundant from his job in the City of London, he and his wife Jane took a holiday in the New Forest. They loved the location, and with John's redundancy money, could afford to move there. On the first day of their holiday, they drove around the area, and resolved to have fish and chips for their supper.

They found only one fish and chip shop. They queued for hours, only to receive a small, over-priced and poor quality meal. Discussing the matter later, they decided there was a potential business opportunity. Accordingly, for the rest of their holiday, they worked: researching the market, alternative provisions, and above all, the cost of premises. They found that there was indeed an insatiable demand among regular visitors, as well as locals, for high-quality convenience food of this kind. The only problem was that the price of property made it prohibitively expensive to open this kind of venture to any sort of quality.

However, further research strongly suggested that the product, though highly quality sensitive, was not at all price sensitive. Holidaymakers had a high propensity to spend, provided that the quality could be assured.

Accordingly, some months later, John and Jane opened their fish and chip shop in a small town in the centre of the New Forest. Because of the need to make returns on their investment, the prices that they charged were substantially higher than those offering alternatives in the area. However, they compensated for this by serving huge portions, well presented, and cooked to a high quality. During the main holiday seasons at Easter and the summer, people would drive from all over the New Forest, and were prepared to queue, just in order to receive an excellent meal.

Not long afterwards, the Grays were visited by a deputation from the local Chamber of Commerce. These people wanted to know how it was possible for such a business to 'buck the trend' at a time when all their market research had suggested that everything was price sensitive.

- The customer volume must be sufficient in itself to allow the development of a loyal, active base capable of sustaining long-term, profitable, effective activity. Where a loyal base is not available, then others have to be considered. If passing trade is all that is available, then passing interest must be capable of development into active interest. If mercenaries are sought then the price advantage must be capable of sustenance, without compromise on quality or value. If repeat business is sought or assumed, then the regularity, frequency and income volume per customer must be assessed on the basis of: what is required and essential; what is likely; what is possible; what circumstances may cause this to change. If one-offs only are being provided (e.g. once in a lifetime holidays) then there must be sufficient volume of potential customers in this situation who can be turned into real customers with the regularity required.

All this is only achieved through sustained general and precise marketing activities and research. It is no use having the best new product or service in the world if no one ever gets to hear of it. If word of mouth is to be ultimately the most highly desired form of marketing, then the new venture has to attract those whose words and mouths are sought in the first place (see Example Box 11.7).

New product and service development

Alongside marketing research and development is conducted new product and service development. This consists of the following.

- Existing products, differentiated by new organisations in the same and other sectors.
- New products and services for existing markets and sectors.
- Existing products and services for new markets. These may have to be differentiated in some way in order to preserve the satisfaction levels of existing customers and clients (see Example Box 11.8).
- Product and service extension, to include:
  - in products, for example, after-sales, maintenance and finance plans; guaranteed trade-ins and upgrades; the ability to buy add-ons and accessories
  - in services, the provision of peripherals as standard and all-inclusive
  - demonstrable improvements in quality, value, convenience and price; this has to be supported by precise market targeting, so that customers and clients know in advance that what they are to receive in the future is better than in the past (see Example Box 11.9).

Once at least one of these developments has been decided on, then a precise and rigorous

---

EXAMPLE BOX 11.7 Word of Mouth Marketing

- **Concorde:** British Airways do not market Concorde. 'It speaks for itself'. Knowledge and familiarity are maintained by the continued media coverage and interest in the airliner. This has continued even following the 1999 Concorde crash. The plane is assured of its own continued self-generated media interest because it was relaunched in a flurry of universal newspaper and television coverage in October 2001.
- **Marks & Spencer:** this is a contrasting case. Like BA, the company did not market, and for many years its own mix of quality and value did indeed 'speak for itself'. However, when the downturn in its fortunes came, it had no marketing or public relations strategy to put in place to counter adverse coverage in the financial and economic press. It was therefore forced into a range of what were effectively innovative, enterprising and entrepreneurial marketing activities; because of this, some were successful, some failed, some led to other things, some promised false hopes. It took a very long time for the company to come round to the point of view that it should concentrate on the enduring quality and value – and presentation – of the strengths of its core businesses: underwear and food.

EXAMPLE BOX 11.8 New Product and Service Development

- **Virgin:** Virgin has chosen to put its own brand name on everything that it does, whether music, air travel, bridal wear, publishing, financial services, or mobile telecommunications. This has laid the company open to the charge of 'brand stretching': trying to put the Virgin brand on so many different products that its intrinsic value is lost. This is refuted by Richard Branson, who states that the strength of everything that they do, in whatever sector, lies in the distinctive Virgin corporate approach.

- **Sony and Aiwa:** the approach taken by Sony to get into perceived lower-value markets was to rebrand those offerings pitched at non-premium customers. The company took the view that if they put the Sony name on lower-price, good-value products, it would dilute the expectations and perceptions of those who continue to buy the premium offering.

- **British Airways and Go:** as a perceived global high-quality and premium-price operator, British Airways took the view that to develop a large range of short-haul, lower-price, routes would call into question the integrity of its core business. It therefore created the company 'Go' which it operated as an independent, though wholly owned, subsidiary.

- **Manchester United:** the whole UK football industry was transformed in the early 1990s by the introduction of large and hitherto unimagined amounts of television money. This transformed the asset values of the top clubs, which became potentially global television entertainers as well as competitors in their sport. Manchester United, together with many other top and perceived top clubs, took the view that they would drive themselves upmarket. Market research had made clear that there was a sufficient volume of 'higher value' customers who, if targeted successfully, would provide a much greater return on investment. The club therefore took the decision to go upmarket. Traditional supporters could stay with them if they chose, but they would be required to pay a much greater volume of their disposable income in order to remain demonstrably loyal to the club. In part at least, both Manchester United and other big football clubs have been able to do this and sustain it on a long-term basis because their customer base – the supporters – are apostles rather than loyalists or mercenaries.

evaluation of the proposal, product or service needs to take place. Again, this applies to new companies and ventures, new products and services from existing companies, and improvements to processes, procedures and functions. The initial line of enquiry consists of answering as many of the following questions as positively as possible.

- **Fit with the market.** Is there a real customer need? Are prices available that give good margins? Will customers and clients buy this product or service from this company? Do the products and services produce customer benefits that are clearly much greater than what is currently being offered? Are there cost-effective ways to get the presentation and the product or service across to customers? Is the

---

EXAMPLE BOX 11.9 Chiltern Railways: 'The Future is Better'

As part of the improvements in the UK railway system following privatisation, Chiltern Railways promised 'improved quality of service and attention to customer needs and wants'. What customers needed and wanted was comfortable, reliable trains. What they got was improvement in the quality and variety of on-board refreshments, while the regularity, frequency and reliability of the train services themselves declined.

More generally, new ventures in all public services are invariably at least partially driven by political expediency. (Chiltern Railways was no exception to this.) The total quality of what is required is therefore compromised, so that political rather than service advantage is achieved. Moreover, when new initiatives have to be undertaken using existing resources, both the new initiative and the existing services are diluted still further. Chiltern Railways were required to achieve what the previous nationalised railway network had failed to do.

---

customer and client base convenient? If not, can it be made so? If it cannot, do the benefits outweigh this lack of convenience?

- **Implications.** Are there good reasons to believe that the company will be excellent at the business? What is the nature of the profit required? What is the nature of income volume that has to be generated? Over what time period? How much money does the company want/need to make from this particular venture? Will this dilute or enhance other products, services and offerings?

  Where else may this lead? What if the company succeeds beyond its wildest dreams? What if the product or service fails? What are the consequences of each? Will this lead to larger markets and higher growth? Will this lead to enhanced volumes of business from existing customers?

- **Those involved.** Do they believe in the product or service? Do they have personal, professional and occupational commitment? Do they understand the potential customers and clients? Do they like, respect and value them? Are they committed to serving them?

- **Circumstances.** Do the prevailing set of circumstances lend themselves to the commercialisation of this particular idea? Can a set of circumstances be envisaged in which this commercialisation could fail? If the product or service feels right, but the timing feels wrong, or if market research and evaluation suggests that it is wrong, can a set of circumstances be envisaged in which this may become effective at some time in the future?

- **Business processes and organisation structure.** Can these accommodate the idea as it exists? Do they need to be adjusted or changed? What are the consequences of each?

- **Business process innovation.** If changes in the ways in which things are carried out are being envisaged, what are the tangible benefits? What are the cost advantages? Are these effective in terms of: pure cost, derived cost, and 'cultural and behavioural cost'? Is staff comfort and effectiveness enhanced or diminished? What are the consequences of each?

- **Support.** Is the idea institutionalised? On whose support does it depend for success or failure? What are the consequences of this, especially if the supporters change their priorities or move on?
- **Resources.** Is capital available? On what conditions? For how long? What are the consequences and advantages of this? Is expertise and technology available? If so, for how long? If not, does it have to be sought? If so, from where? Internally or externally? What are the consequences of this?
- **Benefits.** Are the benefits tangible or intangible? Instant or long-term and enduring? Who are the primary beneficiaries: staff, customers, backers, the innovator? What are the consequences of this? Are there social as well as commercial benefits? What is enhanced and diminished as the result of the venture? What are the consequences of this?

This may then be represented graphically as shown in Figure 11.1.

Innovation planning

The innovation planning process crystallises the particular proposal as follows:

- by answering each of the above questions as accurately and positively as possible

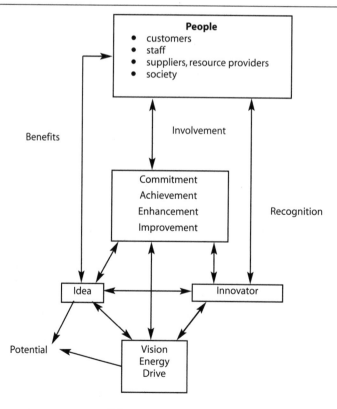

FIGURE 11.1 The development of innovation and enterprise

- by attending to the questions of strategy, marketing, finance and operations that have to be engaged as the result
- by harmonising these two aspects.

The nature of the venture, and how it is to be perceived and classified by others as well as those involved, is then ideally apparent.

Beyond this, any plan for the introduction of an innovation or advance must have the following attributes, and these must be made clear.

- It must be easily understandable, and capable of acceptance, on the part of all others involved.
- It must make clear the benefits that are to be achieved as the result.
- It must make clear that alternatives have been considered.
- It must be capable of withstanding sceptical questioning; this above all, refers to any assumptions that have been made, or any steps proposed that are based on less than accurate or perfect information.
- It must pay particular attention to the question of finance. In the case of commercial innovations, this must include cash flow and profitability considerations. In the case of internal process innovations, this must include attention to cost savings, greater efficiency, and better returns on existing activities.

   Where these conditions cannot be satisfied fully, there must be a substantial alternative reason for proceeding.

It is then necessary to:

- detail cash and other financial requirements and timing, in both the short and long term
- indicate accurately the extent of managerial, organisational and individual commitment
- indicate where assumptions have been made, and be prepared to justify why these have been found to be reasonable in the particular set of circumstances
- indicate wherever possible the range of best, medium and worst outcomes that have been considered, and the consequences of these
- indicate by name who is to be the innovation driver or champion.

Innovation and new product and service drivers and champions

Drivers and champions are those people who put their heart and soul, as well as expertise and acumen, into the particular venture. It is essential that everything that is proposed has a single named and identified individual who holds ultimate responsibility and authority for the venture, and is accountable as it unfolds, and also upon completion, success or failure. In these cases, committee structures do not work. For example, when Virgin went into the airline business for the first time, the company bought in expertise from all over the world to ensure that it was successful – but ultimate responsibility and accountability rested with Richard Branson.

   The champion's job is to energise, enthuse and motivate, as well as coordinate and control. Champions must ensure that resources and expertise are gathered and used as required. This invariably means creative use of time, energy and existing technology as well as developing and enhancing the new product or service along the way as opportunities for this become apparent (see Example Box 11.10).

Potential problems arise whenever the driver or champion moves on. They may do this for a variety of quite legitimate reasons: career moves, further opportunities elsewhere or the fact that they have taken the venture as far as they can. In these cases, somebody else must be available to take up the reins.

More insidiously, drivers and champions may be removed because the overall backers of the new venture have lost confidence in it, or the champion, or both. Drivers may be removed because new pressures and priorities have simply replaced the particular venture. Whatever the case, when this happens, it normally leads to at least a temporary loss of energy, vision and drive – and therefore confidence is called into question (see Example Box 11.11).

EXAMPLE BOX 11.10 Product and Service Champions as Project Managers

The roles of product and service champion and project manager are very similar. Each is required to call on different resources and expertise as and when required, and do everything possible to schedule these into some sort of priority or critical path order.

For each also there is a very fine line that divides healthy commitment from unhealthy obsession. It is not always easy to see where the line is. Brian Dennehy, who developed the Post-It, only took up the challenge so that he could mark the pages in his church hymn book without the pieces of paper falling out. The whole process took twelve years. Because the end result was the transformation of the office stationery industry, this clearly represents healthy commitment!

There are problems also when organisational authorities pressurise the champion to produce results. This leads, in many cases, to corners being cut, or a lack of attention to finer detail. This lesson was learnt many years ago. The thalidomide drug was produced with the objective of reducing morning sickness suffered by women during pregnancy. Because it was not fully tested, and the total range of side effects was unknown, it led to the birth of several hundred babies with malformed legs and arms, and extensive social distress. The project was shortcut in this way because of pressures from the Distillers Company, the owners of the research, to get tangible commercial returns to satisfy their own financial interest. Elsewhere, a major reason why the loss of life on the *Titanic* in 1912 was so great was that there were insufficient life boats on the ship. In spite of the fact that she was thought unsinkable, they should have been provided.

Both the particular drug and the particular ship were supposed to transform the totality of their markets, and produce greatly enhanced social benefits. Because of the lack of attention to detail, and the perceived commercial drives and pressures, each failed.

EXAMPLE BOX 11.11   Problems with Driving Forces

When innovation is being driven in these ways, and when problems do arise, one or more of the following is likely.

- A period of limbo or vacuum occurs, during which no one quite knows where they stand, and so they consume valuable time, energy and resources in trying to find out.
- Powerful or dominant individuals and groups try to take the project on themselves with varying degrees of success. They may also try to use it for their own ends, for example to build their own reputation, or to have a high profile triumph.
- When confidence is called into question, the driver or champion may be removed on spurious or political grounds. For example, a person in charge of a major research initiative into the consequences of the private finance initiative at one of the 'new' London universities was removed after the initial phase on the grounds of 'cultural incompatibility'. This was a euphemism for 'we don't like you, and in any case, you are not producing the results we wanted'. Elsewhere, a man in charge of a computer software development at a plastics factory was removed on the grounds that 'he did not smile enough'. In each case, the particular innovation (both hitherto considered vital, pioneering and farsighted) was dropped shortly afterwards.

More generally, when it becomes known, believed or perceived among top managers that the particular drive is going to cost more than forecasts and projections indicated, they seek cuts elsewhere to pay for it. These are invariably demoralising, petty, inadequate and drawn from other frontline activities, rather than from the support, administrative and head office functions. An early symptom of this is the removal of newspapers, magazines and flowers from reception areas. Other examples may be cited.

- A hospital manager had to fund a £2 million shortfall caused by the requirement to follow political drives to cut waiting lists. Accordingly, he wrote to all nursing managers and staff asking them to be careful about the number of bandages that they used.
- An internet bookseller cut out the free Friday night champagne for all staff (cost approximately £80) as a step along the way to filling a £33 million shortfall.
- A London clearing bank lost £110 million on a corporate venture. It therefore took the decision to set a level of charges aimed at recovering £110 from each of one million private customers.

Keeping up the momentum

The hardest part of all innovation and enterprise is maintaining it – from the initial creative, positive and optimistic burst through the period of dogged determination, the crises of confidence, problems and issues that become apparent – and dealing with the many unforeseen or unplanned circumstances as the venture comes to fruition. All this is necessary if the matter is to be brought to a successful conclusion, so that the venture gains real life, and the initiative gains full acceptance.

John Firth, a Sussex farmer, speaking to a group of local businessmen at a Business Link Kent meeting in May 2000 summed this up as: 'I always work on the premise that everything will take twice as long as I planned, cost twice as much, and that I will have to work twice as hard.' Tom Peters, also addressing an audience, called the drive to maintain momentum 'irrational expectations based on inadequate evidence' (BBC2, *The Money Programme, 1994*).

From a slightly different perspective, the first Boeing 747 was demonstrably certain to fly, according to computer simulations and calculations. However, the project took a lot longer than envisaged, and a major aid to momentum was the constant building and modification of models and mock-ups. This led to what one Boeing executive called 'the longest minute in the world' when the prototype eventually taxied into position, put its engines into full throttle, roared down the runway – and flew. Even at Boeing, there were many who slightly doubted whether anything so big could be made to fly until it actually happened, whatever the computers may have said.

Each of these examples demonstrates the need for somebody to maintain enthusiasm, commitment and a positive attitude, whatever the circumstances. Inevitably, people start to doubt the viability of anything that is undertaken once problems and issues start to become apparent; and from this, it is a very short step to seeing failure, rather than hurdles that have to be overcome.

Using networks and alliances

Everyone involved in any kind of venture needs support, help, assistance and reassurance from time to time. Everyone who drives any major enterprise or innovation needs networks: organisations and people they know who can be called upon for advice, expertise and resources as and when necessary, often at very short notice and on a semi-formal or informal basis. Such contacts become necessary as well as invaluable when genuinely unforeseen circumstances arise, and when some of those who had planned to be involved at a later stage have in practice moved on, or somehow otherwise become unavailable.

The result of this is a kind of 'shadow virtual organisation' which exists as a form of safety, security and emergency net. It tends to work because those who avail themselves of favours when they need them effectively commit themselves to providing their expertise when it is needed elsewhere; and the more they are able to do both, the stronger the network or alliance becomes. Moreover, those who turn someone down, even for the best of reasons, will generally not be asked again, and they effectively deal themselves out of the network.

Attention to detail

It is also important to recognise that success or failure, in many cases, hinges on the attention paid to detail (see Example Box 11.9 above). Other examples include:

- The 1944 Arnhem paratroop landings, mentioned in Chapter 10, failed because nobody in authority paid sufficient attention to three photographs that clearly showed fresh and well-equipped German troops in the designated landing zone.
- The Canary Wharf project took 12 years (rather than the projected 30 months) to become fully successful, because nobody considered the enduring problems with transport to and from the area to be a significant factor.
- Workforce restructuring at the Orion Insurance Company failed because no one took account of the public transport timetables from the places where many of the staff lived, and nobody thought to provide sufficient car parking or company transport as an alternative.

Monitoring, review and evaluation

Processes should also ensure that even the slightest detail receives attention. The drivers or champions of particular ventures must ensure that, if they are unable to pay sufficient attention to details, then they have someone available who can do this on a daily basis. The adoption of a management style based on visibility, integrity and high-quality communication goes a long way to ensuring that when particularly adverse issues arise they can be addressed and dealt with immediately. Beyond this, all monitoring, review and evaluation must be punctuated with regular formal meetings involving all those concerned, so that those whose resources are being invested or consumed in the particular activity are satisfied that their own particular contribution is being used effectively.

Conclusions

All organisations depend on innovation and enterprise for their advancement. Much of this is dependent upon the imagination, creativity – dreams even – of individuals within organisations; and this extends to changes in business processes as well as the creation of new products and services.

It is equally clear that imagination is not enough. Once the decision has been taken to implement a particular initiative, then hard work is required. This in itself indicates one of the main reasons why many organisations are so resistant to change and advancement. Faced with the prospect of the level of commitment and energy required, they seek alternatives. For large complex organisations, and those that have substantial market share and capital resources, it becomes overtly straightforward to take over smaller organisations so as to acquire their technology, customer base, inherent imagination and creativity and expertise. This is all very well provided that the acquiring organisation uses the new purchase for the purposes that were initially attractive. All too often, the innovative zeal (such as it is) is lost as it becomes easier and more straightforward to subsume the whole under the existing culture. Innovation and progress therefore become by-products, rather than the driving force.

It is also essential to ensure that the person put in charge of any innovation or development is given sufficient authority and responsibility, as well as resources. Again, in practice, it becomes expedient to find fault with developments when these are starved of resources and therefore given little strategic chance of success at the outset. This does not prevent organisations from choosing to pick on innovations and developments in times of crisis rather than tackling the root causes, which are normally to be found in existing steady-state activities and organisation culture rather than new ventures.

Innovation, enterprise, development and enhancement are dependent upon energy, ambition, enthusiasm, drive and commitment. This must extend to the organisation as a whole, as well as to particular individuals. In cases of entrepreneurial and pioneering development, it must extend to backers and investors. There is no point in going down such a route if the particular innovation or development does not command the full support of those who control finance and resources. Above all, where difficulties and problems arise (and this is universal in all circumstances from time to time) there must exist a forum in which such matters can be discussed at whatever length required. On the one hand, the driver or champion must have sufficient confidence to be able to tell backers when serious problems are arising; on the other, when backers and investors are told that a particular problem is a hurdle only, they must have sufficient confidence to accept that this is indeed the case. It is the responsibility of all concerned to create the conditions in which this level of confidence can be sustained and developed itself.

This lesson is not always easy for corporations and their top managers to learn. In very many cases, there is an institutional unwillingness to accept responsibility or accountability, especially for failure – though everyone is obviously eager to attach themselves to successes! In the past (and this remains the case today) many organisations and industrial sectors have sought to absolve themselves from blame for things that have gone wrong through spurious references to global conditions. For example, manufacturing industries blame the Japanese for destroying their markets, while forgetting that the only reason Japanese manufacturing industries ever took a foothold in any market anywhere in the world was because they delivered product quality, durability, value and service. The same was found among those drawn into internet ventures; one investor, seeing the value of his backing of LastMinute.com fall to a fraction of its original level, blamed Martha Lane-Fox for being both a woman and also too glamorous (*Management Today*, May 2000). Banks that committed themselves to investments in the Channel Tunnel project blamed political projections of inflation, interest rates and currency values when they did not get the anticipated returns. From a business and managerial point of view, it is much better to accept the following facts:

- The need for innovation, enterprise, enhancement and development remains constant, and it is a universal organisational, managerial, occupational and professional responsibility.
- This commitment is certain to bring hard work; it is also certain to bring problems, uncertainties and imperfections; it will inevitably bring failures, as well as successes.

Both the direction and the process need to be managed with the same attention to long-term outcomes as to short-term operational factors.

CHAPTER SUMMARY

Innovation and enterprise are key elements of long-term organisational and managerial sustainability and performance. They are also key elements of the core functional activities of strategy development, marketing effectiveness, operational cohesion and the management of financial resources, including the maintenance of cash flow, and enduring profitability. In order for this to be effective, the conditions in which innovation and enterprise can flourish have to be created. This is an enduring responsibility for those in positions of responsibility.

- The most influential people in society, including financiers, backers and politicians, have to help create the macro-conditions in which positive attention, respect and value are accorded to those with ideas for products and services that provide an enduring and positive contribution to society in general, and customer and client bases in particular.
- Directors and senior managers in organisations are required to take an enlightened view of what constitutes the best use of the resources available to them. Not to take an enlightened view of the benefits of innovation and enterprise means that organisations are invariably left behind by those that do.

When all is, or appears to be, going positively within organisations, it is very easy to lose sight of the need for innovation and development. In truth, however, success is only sustainable if full attention continues to be paid to what made the particular organisation successful and effective in the first place, and this, in itself, is a form of innovation and development. In its heyday, Marks & Spencer (the organisation that had 'no need to carry out marketing activities') ensured that its steady state was maintained by having a regularly updated range of food and clothing, products and services available to the customers, who in turn knew that these would be made readily available to them. The company only ran into problems when it lost sight of the commitment necessary as the result of 'carrying out no marketing or innovation'. It also remains true that those organisations that starve innovative activities as the result of economic or financial constraints gain only a short-term or inadequate advantage at best; present problems are certain to remain, and problems for the future are equally certain to be compounded by the fact that there is a reduced basis on which to develop the organisation and its activities.

DISCUSSION QUESTIONS

1. Under what circumstances would it be right to withdraw organisational resources from innovations and development?
2. An organisation has employed a firm of management consultants to look at its business processes. They have come up with a series of recommendations for streamlining these; however, the proposed new way of operation will lead to substantial job cuts, and the need for extensive retraining of those staff that remain. What actions should the organisation now take? If it follows the recommendations

of the consultants, how is the proposal to be measured for success and failure, when, where and by whom? How should it structure the implementation of this innovation in order to ensure that the minimum possible disruption is achieved?

3. Why do organisations blame anyone but themselves when innovations go wrong? How might these attitudes be tackled?

4. What problems are faced by organisations when they need to 'rebrand' themselves? Outline an effective strategic approach to get over the problems that you have identified.

5. Why do some organisations take the view that it is better to keep all new ventures under the same heading, brand or logo, while others choose to rebrand or rename each new product or service?

6. Identify the lessons that may be learned from industrial and commercial companies by the public services, as they seek to enhance and improve the quality of health and education services.

CHAPTER CASE STUDY

St George's Farm Shop

Many farmers are finding it increasingly difficult to continue supplying many of the large chains of supermarkets where prices are kept to the absolute minimum for the supplier (though without any financial benefit being passed on to the end consumer). Moreover, with competition from air freighted imports produced more cheaply abroad, it is not surprising that many producers are looking for alternative markets that not only remove these problems, but also have the advantage that their customers are buying only the freshest locally produced goods.

Where once farmers and growers sold their produce at their local market, a growing number of them now see the farm shop as a reasonable alternative. By selling direct to the public locally, not only are the logistics of transporting goods long distances eliminated, the producers no longer need to be totally dependent on a market that does not operate in their favour economically. The farm shop also goes a long way to recreating the atmosphere, if not of the market of bygone days, then at least of the fast-disappearing village store.

When Susan and Edward James inherited their farm from Edward's parents in the early 1980s, they had already come to terms with the fact that in order to make the farm survive as a commercially viable concern they would need to diversify. As cattle farmers, Edward's family had farmed the land for over a hundred years selling produce locally in East and West Sussex.

During the 1940s, a transport café known as the Union Jack had operated on land adjoining the Jameses' farm. When the café and associated land came on the market in the early 1960s, the family bought it with the long-term view of selling produce direct to the public. It was not until 1984 however, when Edward inherited the land, that he and Susan were able to push ahead with their plans to diversify, little realising that it would take them twelve years to gain planning permission from the local council.

'We initially applied for planning permission in 1984 but our application was declined,' explained Susan, 'and we also lost on appeal. Even alterations to the plans so that the farm shop did not exceed the café's original size were at first rejected.'

It was only on further appeal that the Jameses were finally granted planning permission and the St George's Farm Shop opened its doors for business in December 1996. There was however one stipulation: that 90 per cent of all the goods sold had to be home produced. How 'home produced' was to be defined was never clarified, causing further bureaucratic nightmares. An enforcement officer from the local council's planning department gave them just two days in February 1997 to remove any goods that had not been produced on their own farm.

Susan found that she had to close the farm shop every Monday to find the time needed to resolve this latest issue with the council. Local support though, including the signing of a petition, encouraged her to continue the battle. She is particularly grateful to the monks at the local monastery, St Hughes Charterhouse, who kindly offered to buy all her unsold produce at the end of each weekend to help her stay in business during this period.

Now, several years further on, Susan and Edward have a thriving farm shop that sells fresh produce from the family farm, and also provides a retail outlet for other local products, ranging from cheese, fresh vegetables and organic cream, to chutneys and home-baked cakes and biscuits. They also sell both fresh meat and meat products: sausages, bacon, ham, pate, lard and dripping. The advantage to the local consumers is that while producers and growers are paid the weekly recommended market price, any reduction in that market price is automatically passed on to the customer. As Susan says:

Not only is it now rather like a small scale village cooperative, it is also helping to make shopping locally the social event it once was and this particularly appeals to my older customers. After all, how often do you see people chatting to each other, let alone smiling, in the supermarket?

Source: taken from 'The Union Jack Farm Shop, Chates Cottage, Henfield Road, Cowfold, West Sussex', *Prime Health* magazine, February 2000.

QUESTIONS

1. Why did the negative attitudes to the farm shop on behalf of the local council exist in the first place? In general, how are such attitudes overcome?
2. What actions should Susan and Edward James now be taking in order to develop their customer base?
3. What circumstances outside the control of Susan and Edward James could conspire to place this particular venture at risk? How should they respond to these?

Part III
Management, organisational and human behaviour

12 Culture

'The Body Shop is a tribe, a movement. It is a revolution in business.' Anita Roddick, founder and chief executive, The Body Shop, 1996.

'The Wimbledon spirit used to be worth 30 points a season. We would look at the people that we were playing against, international stars, household names, the lot. And I would say to Vinnie Jones, "This lot don't fancy it today. We're going to win easily," and usually, we were right. We would beat the big clubs because we had spirit.' John Fashanu, interview, *Talk Sport,* 1999.

CHAPTER OUTLINE

The meaning of organisation culture, its inception, growth and development

Key cultural pressures

Cultural studies and analyses

The importance of effective organisation culture; and the destructive effect of ineffective, inadequate and unacceptable cultures

Managerial responsibilities in developing organisation culture.

CHAPTER OBJECTIVES

After studying this chapter, you will be able to:

understand the sources and effects of cultural and behavioural pressures in organisations

identify the steps necessary in order to be able to manage effectively these cultural and behavioural factors

understand the relationship between what is to be done, and how it is to be done

understand the consequences of not attending to the behavioural aspects of management.

Introduction

Organisation culture is an amalgam and summary of the ways in which activities are conducted and the standards and values adopted. It encompasses the climate or atmosphere surrounding the organisation, prevailing attitudes within it, standards, morale, strength of feelings towards it and the general levels of goodwill present.

It is an essential feature of effective organisation creation and performance. It arises from:

- **History and tradition:** the origins of the organisation; the aims and objectives of the first owners and managers, and their philosophy and values; the value in which these are currently held; the ways in which they have developed.
- **Nature of activities:** historical and traditional, and also current and envisaged; this includes reference to the general state of success and effectiveness; the balance of activities – steady-state, innovative, crisis.
- **Technology:** the relationship between technology and the workforce, work design, organisation and structure; alienative factors and steps taken to get over these; levels of technological stability and change; levels of expertise, stability and change.
- **Past, present and future:** the importance of the past in relation to current and proposed activities; special pressures (especially struggles and glories) of the past; the extent to which the organisation 'is living' in the past, present or future, and the pressures and constraints that are brought about as the result.
- **Purposes, priorities and attention:** in relation to performance, staff, customers, the community and environment; and to progress and development.
- **Size:** and the degrees of formalisation and structure that this brings. Larger organisations are much more likely to have a proliferation of divisions, supervisory structures, reporting relationships, rules, processes and procedures tending to cause communication difficulties, interdepartmental rivalries and problems with coordination and control.
- **Location:** geographical location, the constraints and opportunities afforded through choosing to be in, for example, urban centres, edge of town or rural areas. This involves recognising and considering prevailing local, national and sectoral traditions and values.
- **Management style:** the stance adopted by the organisation in managing and supervising its people; the stance required by the people of managers and supervisors; the general relationships between people and organisation and the nature of superior–subordinate relations.

This is the context of organisation culture. A simple way of defining organisation culture is:

The ways in which things are done here.

Culture is formed from the collection of traditions, values, policies, beliefs and attitudes that prevail throughout the organisation (see Example Box 12.1).

Specific pressures are also present.

Pressures on organisation culture

External pressures

These stem from the particular attitudes, values and ethics of the locality in which business is to be conducted and from where the organisation staff are to be drawn. In many parts of the world this includes religious pressures. Forms of prejudice may also have to be taken into account; for example, some people do not readily accept direction from women or members of particular racial or ethnic groups (see Example Box 12.2).

EXAMPLE BOX 12.1 Characteristics of Culture

Culture is:

- **Learned:** rather than genetic or biological.
- **Shared:** members of groups and organisations share culture.
- **Continuous:** cumulative in its development and past on from one generation to the next.
- **Symbolic:** based on the human capacity to symbolise, to use one thing to represent another.
- **Integrated:** a change in one area will lead to a change in another.
- **Adaptive:** based on human qualities of adaptability, creativity, innovation and imagination.
- **Regular:** when participants interact with each other, they use common language terminology and recognised and accepted forms of behaviour.

It is based on or affected by:

- **Norms:** distinctive standards of behaviour; the ways in which people interact with each other; relationships between, and within, ranks and hierarchies; the general patterns of behaviour, familiarity, habits, dress and speech.
- **Dominant values:** advocated by the organisation and expected by participants.
- **Philosophy:** policies concerning beliefs and standards of performance, attitude, behaviour and conduct.
- **Rules:** the formal rules that underline the constitution of the organisation; the informal rules that govern the interaction of individuals on a daily basis.
- **Organisational climate:** conveyed by the environment, the physical layout, the ways in which participants interact, and the relationships with the outside world.

Local working practices and customs, especially relating to hours of work and ways of working, have also to be considered. In some regions, activities close down for several hours in the middle of the day; in others, people start and finish early, for example.

In some cases also, strong pressure is placed on people to accept invitations to dine out with colleagues and groups drawn from the rest of the organisation. What is presented as an invitation may actually be an instruction, and rejection of this is likely to be detrimental to the career or prospects of the individuals concerned and the general respect in which they are held.

Physical distance affects culture. The inability to see and meet with others, for example when working in a foreign or remote location from the main organisation, has effects on the structuring and ordering of tasks and activities, relationships among the staff at the location, and relationships between the location and head office. It also affects decision-making processes, and the attitudes and approaches to local

---

EXAMPLE BOX 12.2 Human Prejudices

It is important to recognise that 'prejudice' – the subjective and unfounded attitudes adopted towards particular people, products and services – is a fact of human existence and behaviour. Most prejudices are harmless. For example, people who choose only to wear blue clothing are exhibiting a form of prejudice, as are those who always vote for a particular political party. Supporting a football club is a form of prejudice, as is always using the same supermarket for shopping.

Prejudices against particular members of the community are abhorrent and unacceptable in organisations, however. It is repugnant, and also illegal, to treat people with less respect on grounds of gender, race, disability, membership or non-membership of a trade union, or spent criminal convictions. It is also abhorrent to treat people differently and with less respect on the grounds of age, sexual orientation, marital status, physical appearance, the way they speak or the place in which they live. It is both repugnant and illegal to allow bullying, victimisation, harassment, and physical and verbal assaults.

Organisations that allow these forms of prejudice invariably suffer from low morale and declining levels of output. Organisation cultures become weak and divided, as people gang up on the particular oppressed group; and as the oppressed group seeks the means to fight back.

A key feature of the management of organisational behaviour is to ensure that all behavioural patterns are well known, and immediate steps taken when these become unacceptable.

---

problems and issues. Those at the location, and especially the person with overall responsibility and control, are likely to experience feelings of isolation from time to time, and they may need to be supported if the overall effectiveness of that part of the organisation is to be sustained.

Psychological distance is also important here. This is likely to exist as a feature of physical distance even if there is a full range of electronic and telecommunications systems available. Psychological distance is also certain to be present to a greater or lesser extent between the organisation and the local community at least at the outset, and it is also likely that this will never quite be removed.

The organisation's own culture and the interaction of its prevailing attitudes, values and beliefs with those of the locality have also to be considered. Strong prevailing practices and standards may have to be reconciled and harmonised between organisation and community. This is best achieved if a high level of mutual understanding, respect and interest is developed quickly, and if high overall standards of probity and integrity are established.

Standards of living and wider expectations of the community have also to be considered from the point of view that there is no point in offering high levels of material reward if these are not valued by the people of the location. There is no point in offering promotion and advancement prospects if people do not want to move from the area.

The organisation's success in a particular location therefore involves understanding its expectations, and presenting and harmonising its own objectives and interests in ways compatible to all.

Reputation

This must be seen from all points of view. The organisation may go into a given location for commercial advantage but with preconceived ideas or prejudices (which may be positive or negative). The organisation may bring with it a particular reputation (again, positive or negative) and a more general reputation either about itself or the sector which it represents and within which it operates. There may be wider questions of prejudice, fear and anxiety to be overcome as the organisation tries to live up to (or live down to) its reputation. Areas that have had bad experiences of multinational activities in the past for example may be anxious about the next influx.

The activities of stock markets and the changing values of shares bring pressure from time to time. This becomes acute when questions of confidence, possible take-overs and mergers – and therefore changes – are raised.

Legal constraints

All organisations have to work within the laws of their locations. These exert pressure on production methods, waste disposal, health and safety, marketing and selling, contractual arrangement, staff management, human resources, industrial relations and equality (or otherwise) of opportunity and access, community relations, organisational and professional insurance, and the reporting of results.

Pressures are compounded when the organisation operates in many countries and under diverse legal codes. Balances have to be found in these cases to ensure that, as far as possible, everyone who works for the organisation does so on terms that transcend the varying legal constraints. Organisations are therefore obliged to set absolute standards that more than meet particular legal minima. Moreover, the phrase 'we comply with the law' invariably gives the message that 'the only reason that we set these standards is because we have to' and that the organisation has therefore been pressured into these standards rather than achieving them because it believes that they are right. It calls into question not just the organisation's attitude to the law, but also its wider general attitudes, values and standards (see Example Box 12.3).

Ethical aspects

Ethical pressures arise from the nature of work carried out and from the standards and customs of the communities in which the organisation operates. There are also general ethical pressures on many activities that are covered by the law; examples of these pressures are given in Example Box 12.4.

Again, the ideal response of any organisation is to put itself beyond reproach so that these pressures are accommodated, and leave the way clear to developing productive and harmonious relationships with all concerned.

Internal pressures

- The interaction between the desired culture and the organisation's structures and systems. Serious misfit between these leads to stress and frustration and also to customer dissatisfaction and staff demotivation.
- The expectations and aspirations of staff, the extent to which these are realistic

EXAMPLE BOX 12.3 The *Independent's* Global Sweatshop

Sweatshop labourers in some of Britain's small garment factories are routinely paid less than the minimum wage but are too frightened to complain, the Low Pay Commission has been told. Evidence to the Commission from the textile workers' union says that they fear reprisals if they ask for the £3.60 an hour legal minimum. Most are scared of losing their jobs, and some have suffered physical abuse. 'The workers have told us that non-payment of the minimum wage is common practice in every company they know', the National Union of Knitwear, Footwear and Apparel Trades told the commission.

The union is now bringing tribunal cases on behalf of several workers, all of them Asian. The lowest pay it found was about £1.50 per hour. The union says that because small garment factories are usually found in Britain's ethnic minority communities, workers often speak little English and, although they know their rights, they do not always know how to demand them.

One woman who was sacked because she asked her boss for the minimum wage told the union:

> Many women are scared, especially those who have worked for the same employer for 10 years or more and have even more to lose. I told my friend to come forward, but she said that because her husband is out of work she cannot risk losing her job.

Union officers took the *Independent* on a tour of Leicester's garment factories, where 80 per cent of the manufacturing units employ fewer than 20 people. We saw blocked fire exits, machines without safety guards and workers sewing garments behind padlocked doors. In a former typewriter factory that contained dozens of small garment units, we were told work stopped for the day when health and safety inspectors were expected. Off each damp, dark stairwell we found groups of workers huddled over antiquated machines amid piles of cloth and debris. We spoke to workers here and elsewhere, some of whom said they were making goods for big high-street stores and who were earning less than £3.60 an hour. Haroun Khan told us he made jeans and leggings for a well-known store at rates as low as £2.50 an hour. During a quiet period this summer he had been laid off without pay. 'There is no guard on my machine and when a needle flies out anything could happen', he said. 'I told the boss there was supposed to be a guard. He said he knew what I meant but he didn't do anything. I'm thinking of avoiding factories in the future.'

He and several others confirmed that they were paid piece-rate and their bosses simply divided their weekly earnings by £3.60 to come up with a fictional number of working hours for their pay slips. In many cases, no record was kept of what hours they worked.

Source: Fran Abrams, *Independent*, 27 September 1999.

EXAMPLE BOX 12.4   Ethical Pressures

- **Activities:** most activities carry some form of commitment, and others are imposed on their staff by organisations. For example, medical staff have commitments to their patients; community services staff have commitments to their customers; public servants have commitments to their clients.

- **Sectors:** again, there is a universal commitment not to supply shoddy goods and service, but rather products of integrity. Some sectors have additional problems with this: for example, tobacco, alcohol, armaments and medical research.

- **Waste disposal:** the onus is clearly on organisations to make adequate arrangements to clear up any mess made by their processes. Some areas and countries have lower standards for this. Organisations assess the convenience of easier dumping of rubbish and balance this against absolute standards of right and wrong and any loss of reputation that might occur in the future if their waste leads to some form of contamination.

- **Equal opportunities, staff management, industrial relations and health and safety:** high standards of practice in each of these areas are marks of respect and care to staff, customers and communities. Their absence or variations in them lead, apart from anything else, to feelings of distrust and loss of confidence and therefore, to demotivation of the staff.

- **Results reporting:** the pressure here is in the presentation. Ideally, this should be done in ways that can be understood by anyone who has an interest or stake in the organisation and, indeed, anyone else who would like to know how it is performing. Again, obfuscation tends to lead to those taking an interest to look for hidden meanings and agenda.

---

and can be satisfied within the organisation. This becomes a serious issue when the nature of the organisation changes and prevailing expectations can no longer be accommodated. Problems also arise when the organisation makes promises that it cannot keep.

- Management and supervisory style, the extent to which this is supportive, suitable to the purpose and generally acceptable to the staff.

- The qualities and expertise of the staff, the extent to which this divides their loyalties. Many staff groups have professional and trade union memberships, continuous professional development requirements and career expectations, as well as holding down positions and carrying out tasks within organisations. In many cases – and especially when general dissatisfaction is present – people tend to take refuge in their profession or occupation, or their trade union.

- Technology and the extent to which it impacts on the ways in which work is designed, structured and carried out.

- Working customs, traditions and practices; including restrictive practices, work divisions, specialisation and allocation, unionisation and other means of representation; and the attitudes and approaches adopted by both organisation and staff towards each other: flexible and cooperative, adversarial, degrees of openness.

- The extent to which continuity of employment is feasible; or conversely, uncertainties around future prospects for work and employment. This includes degrees of flexibility, the extent and prevalence of employee and skills development, learning subcultures and the wider attitude of both staff and organisation to this. It also affects reward packages.
- Internal approaches and attitudes to the legal and ethical issues indicated: the extent of genuine commitment to equality of opportunity and access for all staff; whether or not different grades have different values placed on them; standards of dealings with staff, customers, communities, suppliers and distributors.
- The presence of pride and commitment in the organisation, its work and its reputation; standards of general well-being; the extent of mutual respect.
- Communication methods and systems, the nature of language used, the presence or absence of hidden agenda.
- Physical and psychological distance between functions, departments, divisions and positions in the organisation and its hierarchies.

The cultural web

The cultural web is an alternative way of looking at the internal pressures upon organisation culture. People draw heavily on points of reference which are built up over periods of time and which are especially important at internal organisational level. The beliefs and assumptions that comprise this fall within the following boundaries.

- The routine ways that members of the organisation behave towards each other, which link different parts of the organisation and comprise 'the way that things are done'. These at their best lubricate the working of the organisation and may provide distinctive and beneficial organisational competency. However, they can also represent a 'take for granted' attitude about how things should happen which can be extremely difficult to change.
- The rituals of organisational life such as training programmes, promotion and assessment point to what is important in the organisation, reinforce 'the way we do things around here' and signal what is actually valued.
- The stories told by members of the organisation to each other, to outsiders and to new recruits embed the present organisation in its history and flag up important events and personalities.
- The more symbolic aspects of organisation such as logos, offices, cars and titles, or the type of language and terminology commonly used.
- The control systems, measures and reward systems emphasise what is actually important and focus attention and activity.
- Power structures are also likely to be associated in so far as the most powerful groupings are likely to be the ones most associated with what is actually valued.
- The formal organisation structure and the more informal ways in which the organisation works are likely to reflect these power structures and again, to delineate important relationships and emphasise required levels of performance (Johnson and Scholes, 1992).

Cultural influences

Geert Hofstede (1980) carried out studies that identified cultural similarities and differences among the 116 000 staff of IBM located in 40 countries. He identified basic dimensions of national cultural and the differences in their emphases and importance in the various countries. The four dimensions were.

- **Power–distance:** the extent to which power and influence are distributed across the society; the extent to which this is acceptable to the members of the society; access to sources of power and influence; and the physical and psychological distance that exists between people and the sources of power and influence.
- **Uncertainty–avoidance:** the extent to which people prefer order and certainty, or uncertainty and ambiguity; and the extent to which they feel comfortable or threatened by the presence or absence of each.
- **Individualism–collectivism:** the extent to which individuals are expected or expect to take care of themselves; the extent to which a common good is perceived and the tendency and willingness to work towards this.
- **Masculinity–femininity:** the distinction between masculine values (the acquisition of money, wealth, fortune, success, ambition, possessions); and the feminine (sensitivity, care, concern, attention to the needs of others, quality of life); and the value, importance, mix and prevalence of each.

Power–distance

The study looked at the extent to which managers and supervisors were encouraged or expected to exercise power and to take it upon themselves to provide order and discipline. In some cases – for example, Spain – this expectation was very high. Relationships between superior and subordinate were based on low levels of mutual trust and low levels of participation and involvement. Employees would accept orders and direction on the understanding that the superior carries full responsibility, authority and accountability. Elsewhere – for example, Australia and Holland – people expected to be consulted and to participate in decision making. They expected to be kept regularly and fully informed of progress, and had much greater need for general equality and honesty of approach. They would feel free to question superiors about why particular courses of action were necessary rather than simply accepting that they were.

Uncertainty–avoidance

People with a high propensity for uncertainty avoidance – that is, those who wished for high degrees of certainty – tended to require much greater volumes of rules, regulations and guidance for all aspects of work. They sought stability and conformity, and were intolerant of dissenters. Uncertainty caused stress, strain, conflicts and disputes. Stress could be avoided by working hard, following the company line, and adhering to required ways of behaviour. Where uncertainty avoidance was lower these forms of stress were less apparent, and there was less attention paid to rules and less emphasis on conformity and adherence.

Individualism–collectivism

The concern here was to establish the relative position of individual achievement in terms of that of the organisation, and also the wider contribution to society and the community. In the UK and USA, for example, overwhelming emphasis was placed on individual performance and achievement. This had implications for membership of teams and groups and the creation of effective teams and groups in such locations. It also indicated the likelihood of divergence of purpose between the organisation and individuals. Where collectivism was higher, there was also a much greater emphasis on harmony, loyalty, support and productive interaction. There was also a much greater attention to organisational performance, to the position of the organisation and its wider environment, and its contribution to society as well as the achievement of its own desired results.

Masculinity–femininity

This considered the value placed on different achievements. Cultures with high degrees of masculinity set great store by the achievement of material possessions and rewards (see above). Those with high degrees of femininity saw success in terms of quality of life, general state of the community, individual and collective well-being, the provision of essential services, the ability to support the whole society and to provide means of social security.

Hofstede's work emphasises the importance of cultural factors and differences in all areas and aspects of organisational behaviour. It indicates both the strength and inter-action of cultural pressures. It indicates the source and nature of particular values, particular drives, barriers and blockages, and behavioural issues and problem areas that all organisations need to consider. Above all, it illustrates the relative strength of some of the main cultural and social pressures that are brought to bear on all organisations in all situations.

All this indicates the context in which organisation culture is founded and developed. A form of culture is clearly present in all organisations. It is either positive, which tends to attract, and with which people can identify; or negative, which tends to repel, and which people reject (see Table 12.1).

It is especially important to understand the value of designing organisation culture, rather than allowing it to emerge.

Designed culture

This means that the culture is shaped by those responsible for organisational direction and results, and created accordingly. This involves setting standards of attitudes, values, behaviour and belief that everyone must subscribe to as a condition of joining the organisation. Policies are produced so that everyone knows where they stand, and these are underpinned by extensive induction and orientation programmes and training schemes. Procedures and sanctions are there to ensure that these standards continue to be met. Organisations with very specific cultures are not all things to all people; many indeed, make a virtue of their particular approach of 'many are called but few are chosen'. High levels of internalisation of shared values are required.

The context of organisational culture

TABLE 12.1

Designed	Emergent
Strong	Weak
Positive	Negative
Productive	Unproductive
Unifying	Divisive*
Harmonious	Discordant*
Cooperative	Conflict*
Constructive	Destructive

* Note: in practice, some organisations design these elements in. This is most prevalent in large corporate head offices in industrial, commercial and public service sectors. Where this happens – for example, when departments are required to compete for resources at each other's expense – the effect is always destructive.

Other perceptions emerge from this. Feelings of confidence, trust and respect are created. Individual response to the level of organisation commitment that is evident in this approach tends to be high.

Emergent culture

This is where the culture is formed by the staff (and staff groups) rather than directed by the organisation. The result is that people think, believe and act according to the pressures and priorities of their peers and pursue their own agenda. This is clearly fraught with difficulties and dangers; organisations that allow this happen will succeed only if the aims and objectives of the staff coincide absolutely with their own.

It leads to the staff setting their own informal procedures and sanctions, or operating formally in ways that suit their own purposes rather than those of the organisation. Individuals and groups, again, are not all things to all people; they may and do reject those who refuse to abide by the norms and values that they have set for themselves.

Informal elements and subcultures

Subcultures exist in all organisations. They relate to membership of different groups and vary between these, for example in the state of openness of dealings between members. Subcultures become more destructive when they operate contrary to absolute standards. Forms of this are:

- **The canteen culture:** whereby the shared values adopted are those of groups that gather away from the work situations in such places as the washroom or canteen.
- **Elites and cliques:** whereby strength and primacy is present in some groups at the expense of others. This leads to over-mightiness. It affects operations when the elites and cliques are able to command resources, carry out projects and gain prestige at the expense of others; to lobby effectively for resources at the expense of others; and to gain favour at the expense of others.

- **Work regulation:** whereby the volume and quality of work is regulated by the group for its own ends rather than those of the organisation; when it sets and works to its own targets which are at variance with those of the organisation.
- **Informal norming:** whereby individuals are pressurised to adopt the attitudes and values of those around them rather than those of the organisation. This occurs most when the organisation's own norms are not sufficiently strong or structured to remove the local or group pressure.

Archetype cultures

The following archetypes may be distinguished.

Power culture

This is where the key relationship exists between those who wields power and influence, and those work for them. It depends on the figure at the centre, the source of power. Everyone else draws their strength, influence and confidence from this centre and requires its continued support to ensure prosperity and operational viability. The relationship is normally terminated when people at the centre of power lose confidence in those who work for them. Individuals generate power cultures when they attract those who have faith in them and who wish to be involved with them.

The main problem that a power culture must face is that of size. As it grows and diversifies, it becomes difficult for the person at the centre to sustain continued high levels of influence. There is also the problem of permanence, of what happens when the person at the centre of power passes out of the organisation. In situations where they have generated the ideas, energy, identity and strength of the situation, a void is left when they leave or die.

The structural form of the power culture may be seen as like a spider's web (see Figure 12.1). The main relationship between the subordinates is with the centre.

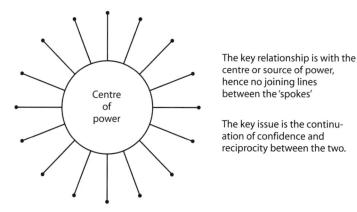

The key relationship is with the centre or source of power, hence no joining lines between the 'spokes'

The key issue is the continuation of confidence and reciprocity between the two.

FIGURE 12.1 Power culture + structure: the wheel

People/person culture

People/person culture exists for the people in it: for example, where a group has decided that it is in its own overriding interest to band or form together and produce an organisation for its own benefit. This may be found in certain research groups, university departments, family firms, and companies started by groups of friends where the first coming together is generated by the people involved rather than the matter in hand. The key relationship is therefore between people; what binds them is their intrinsic common interest. Hierarchy and structure may evolve, but these too will be driven by this intrinsic common interest (see Figure 12.2).

Task culture

Task cultures are to be found in project teams, marketing groups and marketing-oriented organisations. The emphases are on getting the job completed, keeping customers and clients satisfied, and responding to and identifying new market opportunities. Such cultures are flexible, adaptable and dynamic.

They accommodate movements of staff necessary to ensure effective project and development teams and continued innovation, and allow for concurrent human activities such as secondments, project responsibility and short-term contracts. They are driven by customer satisfaction. They operate most effectively in prosperous, dynamic and confident environments and markets. They may also generate opportunities and niche activities in these and create new openings. Their success lies in their continued ability to operate in this way (see Figure 12.3).

Role culture

Role cultures are found where organisations have achieved a combination of size, permanence and departmentalisation, and where the ordering of activities and preservation of knowledge, experience and stability are both important and present.

The key relationship is based on authority and the superior–subordinate style of relationships. The key purposes are order, stability, permanence and efficiency.

Role cultures operate most effectively where the wider environment is steady and a degree of permanence is envisaged.

Other forms may also be identified.

The key relationship is between the people; what binds them is their intrinsic common interest. Hierarchy and structure may evolve incidentally; they too will be driven by this intrinsic common interest.

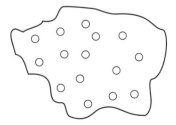

People/person culture + structure: the mass   *FIGURE 12.2*

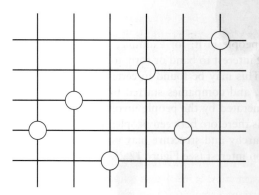

The key relationship here is with the task. The form of organisation is therefore fluid and elastic. The structure is often also described as a **matrix** or **grid**. None of these gives a full configuration: the essence is the dynamics of the form, and the structure necessary to ensure this.

FIGURE 12.3 Task culture + structure: the net

Focal elements

This is where the organisation identifies one key element as its cultural base. These are to be found in such areas as safety and learning cultures, whereby the particular point – safety or learning for example – is placed at the centre of the organisation's commitment to standards. Examples of safety cultures are airlines and the oil industry, whereby everything is designed, built, structured and organised so that accidents cannot happen. Examples of learning cultures are to be found across all sectors and are instigated by companies as integral to continuous change and improvement, drives for flexibility and dynamism, the development of potential, quality and organisation behaviour transformation (see Figure 12.4).

Tribes

This is where organisations create a tribal concept. This is usually accompanied by a strong vision from the top. Its purpose is to unleash strong creative forces and generate

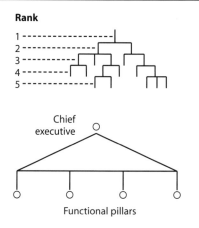

The key relationship is based on authority and the superior–subordinate style of relationships.
The key purposes are order, stability, permanence and efficiency

The 'Greek temple' format delineates function as well as authority

FIGURE 12.4 Role culture + structures: the pyramid or temple

high levels of enthusiasm, ethics, energy and fun. This is the stated position, above all, of the Body Shop. It is also to be found in some people cultures. It may also be found as a feature of other creative and dynamic pockets of organisations. Regular brainstorming groups also produce this among themselves, especially where their activities are successful.

Pioneering culture

Pioneering cultures are the extension of the process of continuous improvement and innovation into constantly questioning the ways in which things are done, continuously seeing new markets, projects and opportunities. It involves attention to processes and practices, technology, organisational form and structure, customers and staff.

The objective is the equivalent of 'getting the response in first': anticipating and responding to changes in customer needs, improving the organisation as a whole, developing and enhancing productive and staff quality. This is a part of the thrust of business process re-engineering and total quality management.

Entrepreneurial culture

Entrepreneurial cultures are based on the creativity, dynamism, vision, energy and enthusiasm of the entrepreneur who may nevertheless lack the organisational and behavioural expertise necessary to sustain a permanent and continuing enterprise. Richard Branson, for example, always recognised that he lacked this expertise and so, as the Virgin Group grew and diversified, he surrounded himself with top-quality managers, as well as industrial and commercial experts from the sectors in which he sought new business opportunities.

Entrepreneurial cultures may be found in all industrial and commercial sectors. Both Ryan Air and EasyJet have grown to the point where they can offer an alternative to the large national and international airlines on specific routes, as a result of the entrepreneurial acumen of the founders (Michael O'Leary of Ryan Air; Stelios Hadjoannou of EasyJet). In retail, the Next and Habit-Mothercare chains grew up where opportunities were identified and acted upon by individuals who then hired experts and managers in order to develop the next stage of the business. The factor common to each of these was the recognition by the company founders that genuine commercial opportunities existed in particular niches, provided that:

- the product and service quality was at least comparable with those already existing
- a distinct advantage could be placed in front of a customer: price on the airlines, and differentiation in the other examples
- a form of organisation could be created that, so long as the two above points were satisfied, customers would actively prefer to use.

It is also worth noting that, while an entrepreneurial culture existed in the great majority of internet businesses, none of the above points was genuinely satisfied.

Intrapreneurial culture

Intrapreneurs – enterprising individuals who work within organisations rather than creating their own – are hired by organisations as change and development agents;

they gravitate to those places that give the space and direction for their qualities of creativity, dynamism, vision and energy. They act as internal pioneers constantly questioning the status quo, seeking ways of improving products, services, processes, quality and satisfaction, and enhancing the effectiveness of the organisation as a whole. The most successful intrapreneurial cultures are those that combine an overall clarity of vision and purpose with the ability to enable high-quality individuals to operate with the freedom and space that they need.

These archetypes are very seldom found in isolation. In practice, most organisations (except for the very small) have features of each. Some conclusions may be drawn however. Whichever the dominant culture, the main concerns are:

- relationships between people, hierarchies, authority, reporting, attention to task and interaction during work
- standards: of behaviour, attitudes and performance; of integrity, honesty and openness; of mutual respect and regard
- values and shared values; the basis on which these are established; the gaining and maintenance of commitment; the creation of a strength and identity of purpose
- management and organisation style that is suitable both to effective work and to underpinning the standards and values that ensure that this can take place
- expectations and aspirations, ensuring that what the organisation offers is clearly understood at the outset by all who come to work in it and reconciling these with those of the people concerned
- being positive and dynamic rather than negative, emergent and inert
- working within the pressures and constraints present in particular situations, locations and types of work; and devising means by which these two can be reconciled with organisational purposes, aims and objectives
- establishing universal interest in the success and future of the organisation; reconciling and harmonising the divergence of interests, personal and professional aims and objectives within the organisation's overall purposes
- establishing a strength of identity between staff and organisation; a common bond; pride and positive feelings in belonging to the organisation; and a team, group and organisation spirit (see Example Boxes 12.5 and 12.6).

Other aspects of organisational culture

Other features of organisational culture may be distinguished.

- **Relationships with the environment:** including the ways in which the organisation copes with uncertainty and turbulence; the ways by which the organisation seeks to influence the environment; the extent to which it behaves proactively or reactively.
- **History and tradition:** the extent to which the organisation's histories and traditions are a barrier or a facilitator of progress; the extent to which the organisation values and worships its past histories and traditions; key influences on current activities and beliefs; the position of key interest groups, such as trade unions.
- **The internal relationship balance:** the mixture and effectiveness of power, status, hierarchy, authority, responsibility, individualism, group cohesion; the general relationship mixture of task/social development.

EXAMPLE BOX 12.5 Identity

A telecommunications giant ran a series of culture-change programmes for all its people in 1991–2. The purpose was to generate a new feeling and high degree of identity and commitment among those working for the company in the wake of recent privatisation, restructuring, job losses and redundancies.

Senior staff were flown to locations in Spain, Portugal and the South of France for a week to be put through the programme. For the same purpose middle and junior management and supervisory staff attended two-day programmes at 2, 3 and 4-star hotels around the UK. Skilled, semi-skilled, unskilled, operative and clerical staff attended half- and one-day programmes at village halls, colleges and company training centres.

At the end of the programme each member was given sets of papers and hand-outs to take away with them, packaged in distinctive bags with the company's logo printed on them.

Consultants and trainers who carried out the work in the village halls and training centres reported that most people either left the bags behind or else turned them inside out before leaving the venue.

- **Rites and rituals:** these are the punctuation marks of organisation operations. They include: pay negotiations; internal and external job application means and methods; disciplinary, grievance and dismissal procedures; rewards; individual, group, departmental and divisional publicity; training and development activities; parties and celebrations; key appointments and dismissals; socialisation and integration of people into new roles, activities and responsibilities.
- **Routines and habits:** these are the formal, semi-formal and informal ways of working and interaction that people generate for themselves (or which the organisation generates for them) to make comfortable the non-operational aspects of working life. They develop around the absolutes – attendance times, work requirements, authority and reporting relationships – and include regular meetings, regular tasks, forms of address between members of the organisation and groups, pay days, holidays and some trainee development activities.

EXAMPLE BOX 12.6 Joint Ventures

Organisations involved in joint ventures normally create a company or entity with its own distinctive identity for the duration of the project. This is to generate positive feelings of commitment towards the matter in hand and override the view that would otherwise continue on the part of those involved that they are still part of their old organisation. A fragmented and disordered – and negative – approach and identity would thus otherwise ensue. By creating the separate and new identity, the negative is overcome and a distinctive focal point for the work in hand is established.

- **Badges and status symbols:** these are the marks of esteem conferred by organisations on their people. They are a combination of location (near to or away from the corridors of power for example); possessions such as cars, technology, personal departments; job titles that reflect a combination of ability, influence and occupation; and position in the hierarchy pecking order.

The effects of rites, rituals, routines, habits, badges and status symbols all lie in the value that the organisation places on them and the value in which they are held by the members of staff. There is no point in offering anything or in undertaking any form of cultural activity if a negligible or negative response is received. In general therefore, these forms of culture development both anticipate people's expectations and seek to reinforce and meet them.

Stories, myths and legends

All organisations have their fund of stories, myths and legends. The nature and content of these reflects the current state of organisational culture and well-being (see Example Box 12.7).

The grapevine

All organisations also have their own grapevine; this is the means by which stories, myths and legends become circulated and gain currency. In simple terms, the grapevine is the difference between what people want to know and what they do know; in particular, where communications are bad, a lot of personal time and energy is wasted on informal clusters, talking through particular scenarios and wondering what the future is to hold for them. In the worst cases, this is very destructive of motivation and morale.

Power and influence bases

In cultural terms, this refers particularly to the reasons why measures of influence are found in particular places. It also refers to matters of organisation politics: the means by which people interact in order to facilitate their own position.

Ideal culture

The ideal culture is one that serves the organisation effectively. It may be summarised as the shared patterns of attitudes, values, beliefs and behaviour – covering strategy, operations, decision making, information flow and systems, managerial and supervisory behaviour, the nature of leadership and the general behaviour of the staff. It involves setting absolute standards and ensuring that these are achieved. It also requires reference to each of the elements and factors indicated above.

The relationship between the ideal and the actual culture should be a matter of constant concern because both develop (see Example Box 12.8). Specific attention is paid to those gaps in culture that cause problems where, for example, people follow the leads, values and norms of their work or professional group rather than those of the organisation. Technological advances and changes may mean that

---

EXAMPLE BOX 12.7 Stories, Myths and Legends

- 'I knew I'd made a mistake, and I knew that the senior consultant was in a towering rage. I could hear him coming. So I borrowed a patient's dressing gown, wrapped it around me so that my uniform was not showing, and sat on a commode next to one of the beds until he had gone' (staff nurse, south-eastern general hospital at an RCN branch meeting 2000) on inter-professional relations).

- 'We took an incredible risk going into the airline business' (Richard Branson, keeping up the adventurous image of the Virgin Group). In fact the venture was meticulously planned and the subject of extensive investment, before Virgin Atlantic ever flew (*The Money Programme*, BBC2, 2000).

- 'McKinsey consultants used to be brilliant, creative and interesting – they were eccentrics. Now they all look the same, say the same, and have the same thing to offer – whether or not this is what the client requires' (Tom Peters, *Masters of the Universe*, Channel 4, 2000, on the development of McKinsey Management Consultants since his departure).

- 'Everybody is harking back to the good old days. They speak and reminisce fondly of bygone times, a golden era – in fact, an era that never was' (John Major, *John Major: The Autobiography*, Harper Collins, 1998).

---

suddenly the ideal hitherto striven for has to be changed in order to accommodate new divisionalisation, patterns of work, retraining, regrouping and so on.

Sub-cultures, parallel cultures, covert cultures are all bound to exist in organisations. The problem is to ensure that they do not damage or detract from total organisational performance. They must be capable of harmonisation within the overall standards; any sub-cultures that do not conform to this should be broken up. The purpose is to arrive at something that is dynamic, adds value to operations and energises the people positively. This affects attitudes and values and the ways in which people regard themselves, each other and the organisation as a whole. It affects customer relations and relations with the wider community. It contributes to perceptions and images and wider feelings of general confidence.

Culture management and attention to culture

As stated above, both the actual culture and the perceived ideal are subject to constant development. With this in mind, the best organisations therefore pay this constant attention. There are some basic assumptions here.

- Culture can be changed and developed. There are too many examples where this has happened to think otherwise. Nissan UK transformed a population of former miners, shipbuilders and steelworkers into the most productive and effective car company in the UK. Toyota at Derby is following suit with former railway staff. British Airways transformed a bureaucratic nationalised monopoly into a customer-orientated multinational corporation. British Steel transformed itself

EXAMPLE BOX 12.8 Culture Development

The basic approach is not to allow culture to emerge to form itself at the whim of the staff, but rather to create that which is desired by means of predetermined and targeted interventions.

- Strategy and direction, to ensure that everyone understands that their place is in the pursuit of the organisation's purpose whatever job they are carrying out. For example, a cleaner at NASA interviewed on TV in 1967, when asked what the job entailed, replied 'I am helping to put the first person on the moon'.
- Reorganisation, to ensure that old ways, procedures and practices are consigned to history. Anything may act as a lever for this: new technology, new premises, work and job redesign, training and development. For each new store that it opens at out-of-town sites for example, the Tesco supermarket company provides extensive job training for all the staff who are to work there, whether or not they have worked for the company in the past. This is to ensure that they know the new and absolute standards to which they are required to conform.
- Induction, to ensure that the required attitudes, values, beliefs and standards are understood by all at the outset. Re-induction is required where the prevailing standards are no longer satisfactory.
- Other human resource activities, targeted to give impetus to the new. This includes everything: rewriting job descriptions (and the retraining that is then required for new job holders); changing recruitment advertising; attention to the qualities and capabilities of new and existing staff; repositioning and reorientation of performance appraisal, industrial relations and staff management activities.
- Use of fashions and fads such as total quality management, customer service training and business process re-engineering as the means of doing that which is required. The main contribution of these to all organisations is to challenge existing thinking and to act as the means by which desired developments can be introduced.
- Use of dramas and crises to get people to think. Where necessary this may involve overstating the case. For example, the entry of the Virgin group into the cola market had business analysts and pundits wondering publicly if this was to be the beginning of the end for Pepsi and Coca Cola. This plainly was a vast exaggeration. However, the volume of attention given was quite sufficient to ensure that everyone at both Pepsico and Coca Cola continued to pay positive attention to their own activities.
- Use of new language, which is ideally both more direct and also sufficiently different from the old. This both drives and reinforces development. It also reinforces understanding and acceptance as long as the language is more direct. In addition it is a general underlining of the fact that there is a general new way in existence.
- Use of project work and cross-functional teams, to breakdown existing barriers and fiefdoms, as well as generating expertise and potential among employees,

from a loss-making national corporation, riddled with demarcation and restrictive practices, to a profitable, effective and flexible operator.

- Culture should be changed and developed. The constant development of operations, technology, markets, customer bases and the capabilities of the human resource make this inevitable. Current ways of working and equipment, and current skills, knowledge and qualities serve current needs only. The future is based around the developments and innovations that are to take place in each of these areas. Therefore, the culture must itself develop in order that these can be accommodated.

- Culture change is long and costly. It is certainly true that where stability has existed for a long while, change is traumatic at first – and therefore costly in terms of people's feelings and possibly also in terms of current morale. It is made easier for the future if new qualities and attitudes of flexibility, dynamism and responsiveness are included in the new form, and if this reinforced through ensuring that people understand that the old ways are now neither effective nor viable.

- Culture change need not take forever. Indeed, people who are told that there are to be lengthy periods of turbulence lose interest and motivation. The reality of change and development can quickly be conveyed through critical incidents, such as the gain or loss of a major order, the collapse of a large firm in the sector, the entry of a new player into the sector, radical technological advances and so on. Once this is understood, the attitudes, behaviour and orientation of the staff are given emphases in a particular direction and the general positioning of their aspirations, hopes and fears is changed.

Conclusions

Effective organisation cultures are positive and designed rather than emergent. They must be capable of gaining commitment to purpose, the ways in which this is pursued and the standards adopted by everyone (see Example Box 12.9). Cultures are a summary and reflection of the aims and objectives, and values held. Where these are not apparent, different groups and individuals form their own aims and objectives and adopt their own values; and where these are at variance with overall purpose, or negative in some way, they are dysfunctional and may become destructive.

For this to be effective, a strong mutual sense of loyalty and acceptance between organisation and people is essential. Employees exert positive effort on behalf of the organisation, making a personal as well as professional or occupational commitment.

The reverse of this – the organisation's commitment to its people – is also essential. A strong sense of identity towards the organisation's purposes and values is required, and this happens when these are clear and positive. Any commitment made by people to organisations (or anything else) is voluntary and personal, and can be changed or withdrawn. The best organisations produce cultures that are capable of generating loyalty. They create the desire among their people to join, remain and progress, recognising their mutuality of interest and the benefits available to everyone.

CHAPTER SUMMARY

If strategy, policy and direction are concerned with what organisations do, then organisational culture is about how they do it. The culture of an organisation is the basis for its management style, and individual and collective attitudes, values, behaviour and beliefs. It is therefore essential that the ways in which things are required to be done are clearly established, and accepted by all concerned. Distinctive standards of behaviour and attitudes must be established, rather than be allowed to emerge; they must not be tolerated where they are legally, socially or morally unacceptable.

It is essential also to recognise the influence of different aspects of work layout, the working environment, and management style on the behaviour of organisations. The main points are as follows.

- Technology influences work arrangements and groupings, physical layout and the nature of the people employed.
- Structure and hierarchy influence personal and professional interactions, personal and professional ambitions and aspirations.
- Rules, regulations and systems influence attitudes and behaviour (positive or negative) depending on how they are drawn up and operated and on their particular focus.
- Leadership provides the key point of identity for everyone else, from which people establish their own perceptions of the organisation's general standards.

EXAMPLE BOX 12.9 Excellence and Culture

Without exception the dominance and coherence of culture proved to be an essential quality of the excellent companies (the 62 American companies studied by Peters and Waterman). Moreover, the stronger the culture, and the more it was directed to the market place, the less need there was for policy manuals, organisation charts or detailed procedures and rules. In these companies, people way down the line know what they are supposed to do in most situations because the handful of guiding values is crystal clear.

Source: from T. Peters and R.H. Waterman, *In Search of Excellence*, Harper and Row, 1982.

- Management style influences the general feelings of well-being of everyone else, and sets standards of attitudes and behaviour as well as performance.
- Managerial demands and the ways in which these are made influence attitudes and behaviour.
- Hierarchical and divisional relations and interactions influence the nature of performance, attention to achievement and the value placed on achievements; this also applies to functional activities.

Where the need for culture change or development is apparent interventions can be made into each or all of these.

The conclusion of this is an organisation culture that has the following elements.

- A positive aura, one to which people can subscribe and identify with confidence, pride, feelings of well-being. This in turn encourages positive views of the organisation and its work, and positive and harmonious working relationships.
- Shared values and standards, capable of being adopted and followed by all concerned. This includes attention to high standards of integrity and morality, mutual concern and interest, and equity and equality.
- High levels of individuality, identity, motivation and commitment; high levels of group identity and mutual respect and regard.
- An organisation and management style that is supportive of everyone involved (whatever the style, whether autocratic or participative) and which concentrates on results and output, effectiveness and quality of performance, and also on the development and improvement of the people.
- Regular flows of high-quality information that reflect high levels of respect and esteem for the people on the part of the organisation.

Again, these can provide a useful point of reference for those concerned with the general well-being of the organisation, not least when it becomes apparent that things are going wrong.

Much of this is clearly concerned with setting high standards and creating a positive general environment and background. This is to be seen in the context that where these elements are either not present or not attended to – or where the converse is present, a negative aura to which people do not subscribe, a lack of shared values, or an unsupported management style for example – there is no identity or common purpose. People seek refuge in groups or in their profession or technical expertise. Absenteeism and turnover increase, performance declines. There is an ever-greater concentration on self, on individual performance, often at the expense of the purposes of the organisation. Interpersonal and inter-group relationships also suffer.

Both the positive and the negative are self-reinforcing. Striving for a positive and ideal culture tends to reinforce the high levels of value placed on the staff and the more general matters of honesty and integrity. Similarly, allowing the negative to persist tends to mean that relationships will get worse, aims and objectives become ever more fragmented or clouded, organisation purpose ever more obscured.

DISCUSSION QUESTIONS

1. Outline the benefits and drawback of offering status symbols – for example, personal offices, car parking spaces, job titles – as marks of progress. What steps should be taken to ensure that overall benefits prevail and not the drawbacks?
2. What steps should organisations take to maintain and develop their culture in periods of rapid expansion and of rapid shrinkage?
3. What does the work of Hofstede indicate about cultural similarities and differences? Why are some multinational organisations so much more successful than others when operating away from their main locations and country of origin?
4. What changes are required in skills, knowledge, attitudes and behaviour for all groups of staff when moving from an archetype role culture to an archetype task culture? Produce an outline culture change programme to achieve this, indicating the timescale that you are prepared to allow for this change to take place.

CHAPTER CASE STUDY

ROBERT ARCHER'S NEW JOB

Robert Archer has recently been appointed manager of the information systems office at a large firm of business technology consultants. He has taken over from Jack Jarvis, who retired six months ago after working for the firm all his life. In between, there was a period of eight weeks when the office was run by Malcolm Shipman, another long-serving employee who made it his business to impose himself and his ways of doing things on the rest of the staff. Most of the staff evidently fear and hate him, and there have been rumours that he has hit two individuals in recent weeks.

There are twenty staff, eight men and twelve women, each of whom has a separate cubicle and workstation. Individuals may leave their workstations at any time provided that it is for no more than five minutes. Everyone gets half an hour for lunch; the manager is entitled to one hour.

Morale is low. Two members of staff, Shenaz Ali and Rachel Ling, have recently had a stand-up argument over a 'personal matter', and it is clearly only a matter of time before they come to blows. Some of the other staff are quite looking forward to this, and seem to be egging them on. Another member of staff, Paul Frencham, is awaiting investigation over the alleged sending of obscene e-mails; notes have been sent from his address, but he alleges that someone has cracked his password and is out to make trouble.

Because of the delay in Robert's appointment, all staff have failed to receive productivity bonuses and commissions to which they are entitled for the past nine weeks. The longest serving member of staff, David Smith, has quite openly given up altogether; he feels very strongly that he should have been given the manager's job when Jack retired, so that his own pension would be enhanced when he retires in two years' time, and so that he could have his own office and a bit of peace and quiet. Things were never like this in the old days!

Robert has now been in post for two months and has been wondering what to do. His own manager, Harriet Blumen, now wants to know what he is going to do, when and how.

QUESTIONS

1. What is the state of the culture of the department? What steps should Robert take to remedy this?
2. How should Robert go about getting at the core of the morale problem; and what steps should he take to raise this? How should this be measured for success or failure, when where and by whom?
3. What steps should be taken to address the problems and attitudes of the individuals, as indicated in the case study?
4. What other steps does he need to take in order to develop the ways in which things are done in the department?

13 Perception, Attitudes, Values and Beliefs

'You don't have to be mad to work here but it helps.' Workplace notice.

'Quality, value, cleanliness, friendliness.' The core values of McDonald's.

'High levels of pay can be very rewarding. However, when everything else about the job is wrong, they act as a shackle.' Jenny Hirschkorn, *Daily Telegraph*, 23 March 2000.

CHAPTER OUTLINE

The position of perception, attitudes and values in managerial understanding and expertise

Behavioural and managerial approaches to perception, attitudes, values and beliefs

The importance and value of understanding perception as part of managerial expertise

Shaping and forming positive attitudes; the consequences of negative attitudes

The relationship between attitudes, values and management style.

CHAPTER OBJECTIVES

After studying this chapter, you should be able to:

understand the main behavioural aspects and features with which managers have to deal

understand and influence behaviour and attitudes

understand the source of shared positive attitudes and values

understand the source of negative and divisive attitudes and values; and be able to identify steps required to influence

understand the general basis of human behaviour in organised situations.

Introduction

The purpose of this chapter is to introduce the more nebulous aspects of human behaviour with which managers have to be concerned. It is therefore necessary to deal with the main elements of perceptions, attitudes and values in turn. Each of these is then developed from the particular point of view of management requirements and understanding.

Perception

Perception is a primary human activity, the process of limitation by which everyone manages their views of the world. Perception is essential because of the amount of information, signals and cues with which the senses are constantly assailed. The total is not capable of assimilation because it is constantly changing and developing and because of the constant nature of human activity. A process of some sort is therefore clearly necessary by which this is first limited and then transformed into something that is useful and usable.

The processes by which individual and collective perception are developed are both learned and instinctive. Some come from the senses – sight, hearing, touch, taste and smell – and some from instinct; one's view of what is edible is clearly coloured by how hungry one is. Some come from socialisation and are based on levels of understanding of what is expected of individuals in particular situations (see Figure 13.1). Some come from civilisation, and an understanding and awareness of the norms of particular parts of society. This gives rise, above all, to moral and ethical codes by which behaviour is regulated. Perception also forms the basis for concepts of fashion and desirability and the need for achievement (see Figure 13.2).

Perceptions are heavily influenced by media and business activity. Marketing is directed in a large part to the formulation of positive and acceptable impressions. Measures of success and failure are determined by key and influential figures as much as product and service performance. Much human resource activity is taken up with influencing people's perceptions of others as they interact in work situations. Control functions are desirable in order that organisations may understand the state of their status and progress. Primary activities such as manufacturing or service provision must be undertaken in such a way that those conducting them understand as far as possible what is being done, how and why (see Example Box 13.1).

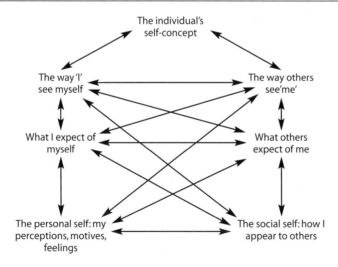

The basis of interpersonal perception　　　　　　*FIGURE 13.1*

Source: C. Rogers, 'Observations on the Organization of Personality', *American Psychologist* vol. 2, 1947.

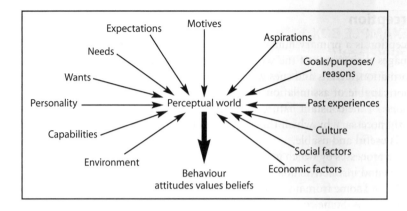

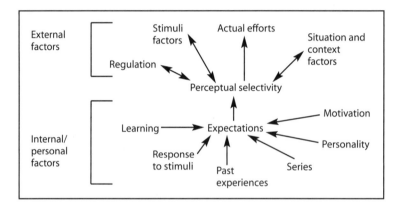

FIGURE 13.2 Relationships between perception, behaviour, attitudes and values

Source: from A. Huczynski and D. Buchanan, *Organisational Behaviour*, Prentice Hall, 1993.

Comfort and liking

Comfort and liking occur when elements and features accord and harmonise with each other. Instant rapport is achieved when initial perceptions – strong characteristics, halo effects – coincide, meet expectations and lead to an initially productive relationship. This is developed as people become more knowledgeable about each other and about situations and circumstances.

The greater the continuing coincidence, the greater the harmony and accord, and the more flexible the boundaries of this become. For example, if the initial impression of someone is that they are a 'smoker', this may lead to discord; if the relationship then develops in strong and positive ways, the smoking becomes less and less relevant and easier to accommodate.

Discomfort and dislike occur when the elements are in discord. This is usually founded in strong and contradictory initial and continuing impressions. For example, in

---

EXAMPLE BOX 13.1   Wages at Nuclear Power Stations: A Good Deal?

In the 1960s the UK Central Electricity Generating Board built nuclear power stations in remote parts of the UK. Many of the staff, especially the technical, semi-skilled and unskilled, were to be drawn from rural, coastal and often remote communities. Stations brought additional income and work to these areas.

The first attempts to recruit people from these communities consisted of offering a high salary (about £18 000 at present levels) in return for which the staff concerned would work rosters determined by the station directorate. Hours would be flexible and extensive time-off arrangement in lieu would be afforded to those having to work nights, weekends and public holidays.

Take up of this arrangement was so low that the company returned to the drawing board. It came up with a basic wage of £10 000 per annum (also at present values) and extensive and complicated rostering arrangements that required overtime, shift pay, attendance, inconvenience and call-out allowances. The total to be earned by the staff concerned was to be between £15 000 and £18 000 provided that the overtime and so on continued to be forthcoming. Without exception the demand for jobs in the communities involved exceeded supply, in spite of the fact that the offer was worse than the original. But the perceptual barriers had been overcome and those involved felt themselves to be getting a better deal. This was the reason for the success of the latter approach.

---

response to a job advertisement, a beautifully prepared and overtly substantial CV may arrive but, when called for interview, the individual turns out to be scruffy; discomfort and dislike occur because expectations are not met. To the unwary the person has turned from a potential employee into someone to be got rid of as quickly as possible. In practice, everyone has contradictory characteristics and those with whom they come into contact have to reconcile these in order to build up a comfortable picture (see Example Box 13.2).

Inference

People infer or make assumptions about others and about things, situations and circumstances, depending on the information available and their interpretation and analysis of it. This may be straightforward or contradictory (see Figure 13.3).

It becomes more complex when these effects cannot be seen in isolation (see Example Box 13.3). It is not possible to define attitude from behaviour or performance from attitude; it is only possible to infer them. This means that while it may be possible to predict performance to a certain extent, there are always many uncertainties; a wide range of actual results remains possible and available and should be considered.

Extreme forms of inference are jumping to conclusions and 'gut reactions', in which quantum leaps of supposition are made about the outcome of something from a limited range of information available. In such cases, individuals select those elements

EXAMPLE BOX 13.2 Perceptual Errors

The sources of error in person and situational perception include:

- not collecting enough information
- assuming that enough information has been collected
- not collecting the right information; collecting the wrong information
- assuming that the right information has been collected
- seeing what we want and expect to see; fitting reality to our view of the world (rather than the reverse)
- seeking in others what we value for and in ourselves
- assuming that the past was always good when making judgements for the future
- failure to acknowledge and recognise other points of view
- failure to consider situations and people from the widest possible point of view
- unrealistic expectations, levels of comfort and satisfaction
- confusing the unusual and unexpected with the impossible

The remedies are:

- understanding the limitations of personal knowledge and perception; that this is imperfect and that there are gaps
- deciding in advance what knowledge is required of people and situations, and setting out to collect it from this standpoint
- structure activities where the gathering of information is important; this, for example, should apply to all interviews, research activities, questioning, work organisation, use of technology
- avoiding instant judgements about people, however strong and positive, or weak and negative the first impression may be
- avoiding instant judgements about organisations, whether as customer or employee
- building expectations on knowledge and understanding rather than halo effects, stereotypes and self-fulfilling prophecies
- ensuring exchanges and availability of good quality information
- ensuring open relationships that encourage discussion and debate and generate high levels of understanding and knowledge exchange
- developing self-awareness and understanding among all staff
- recognising and understanding the nature of prevailing attitudes, values and beliefs – and prejudices
- recognising and understanding other strong prevailing influences, especially language, nationality, culture and experience.

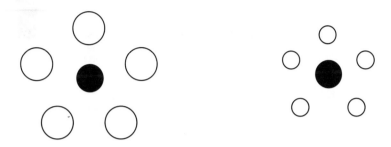

(a) Which black dot is larger?

(b) Old lady or young girl?

(c) A farmer was asked how many animals he had on his farm.
   'Well', he replied, 'I have 233 heads and 843 legs. Work it out from that'.

Perception: illustrations

FIGURE 13.3

with which they are familiar and place their own interpretation of the likely or 'logical' (in their terms) outcome, based on their knowledge of what happened before when these elements were present. The range of misunderstandings possible is virtually limitless. There may be three elements out of six present with which the individual is familiar; or there may be three out of ten, three out of forty, or three out of a hundred. In each case it is the familiar three which form the basis of judgement (see Example Box 13.3).

Characteristics of perception

The key elements and characteristics to be aware of are the following.

Halo effect

This is the process by which a person is ascribed a great range of capabilities and expertise as the result of one initial impression of an overwhelming characteristic. This may be either positive or negative.

The negative is called the 'horns effect' (the halo apparently comes from heaven; the horns therefore clearly originate elsewhere). A negative connotation

---

EXAMPLE BOX 13.3 Jumping to Conclusions and Gut Reactions

- The old school tie: if from the same school, familiar and positive; if from a different school, subject to instant interpretation.
- You play golf; I play golf; therefore you are like me.
- You play golf; I play golf; I am a successful manager; therefore you are/will be a successful manager.
- Football has hooligans; you like football; therefore you are a hooligan.
- Mick Jagger has long hair; you have long hair; therefore you are like Mick Jagger.
- Men with beards are hiding something; Richard Branson has a beard; therefore he is hiding something.
- He has a firm handshake; I have a firm handshake; therefore I like him.
- Kim Philby was a member of the establishment; he worked in the establishment; therefore, he could not possibly have been a Soviet spy.
- All Marks & Spencer products are good; Marks & Spencer sell these apples; therefore, they are good.

---

is put on someone or something as the result of one (supposedly) negative characteristic. Thus the person with the soft handshake and lisp is perceived to be soft and indecisive. Anyone who wears fashions from a past era is deemed to be eccentric or old fashioned.

Stereotyping, pigeonholing and compartmentalisation

It is a short step from the halo effect to developing a process of stereotyping, pigeonholing and compartmentalisation. This occurs at places of work where, because of a past range of activities, somebody is deemed forever to be a particular kind of a person. This may either enhance or limit careers, activities and organisation progress, dependent upon the nature of the compartmentalisation. In either case it gives specific and limited direction. A person who has worked overseas for a multinational corporation for a long time may have difficulty getting a job back at Head Office because they have been pigeonholed as 'an expatriate' and may be perceived to have difficulties should they be required to conform to the Head Office norms and practices.

Self-fulfilling prophecy

Self-fulfilling prophecy tends to occur when a judgement is made about someone or something. The person making the judgement then picks out further characteristics or attributes that support his or her view and edits out those do not fit in (See Example Box 13.4).

Perceptual mythology

This occurs where myths are created by people as part of their own processes of limiting and understanding particular situations. A form of rationale emerges, usually spurious.

Thus, for example, people will say such things as 'I can tell as soon as someone walks in the door whether they can do this job', or 'I always ask this question and it never fails', or 'I never trust people in white shoes/white socks/with moustaches/with tinted glasses' – in order to give themselves some way of understanding and therefore 'mapping' the person who stands before them.

People also use phrases such as 'in my opinion' and 'in my experience' for the same general reasons. Others use lines of argument such as 'X did this and it worked and so we should do it and it will work for us'; or 'it happened like this in 1929 and so this is the way to do it now'; or, more insidiously, 'we had to do things like this in my day and it never did us any harm, and so this is how it has got to be done now'.

On a broader scale, industries publish league tables of company performance by business volume, business value, wage and salary levels, numbers employed and so on. These are then used to justify and explain a range of other issues of varying degrees of relevance and substance. Companies for example say 'we are sixth in the league', or 'we are in the same boat as the rest of the industry', or 'we are no worse than anyone else' without attaching any rationale to any of the points made. This develops a comfort zone which, in many cases, leads to feelings of complacency, immortality and infallibility.

Above all, this part of the process illustrates the difficulties involved. On the one hand each of the examples given in this part is flawed at best and spurious at worst. On the other hand, people have to limit their intake of information, stimuli and cues in some way and provide themselves with a means of understanding. At this stage therefore, the main lesson to be drawn is in the recognition of this and limitations attached.

Personal mapping and constructs

In this process people, situations, activities, images and impressions are being fitted into the perceptual map of the world in ways which can be understood, managed and accommodated. The information thus gathered is broken down into constructs or characteristics which may be categorised as follows.

EXAMPLE BOX 13.4 Self-Fulfilling Prophecy

- 'If you want people to be trustworthy, trust them. If you want people to accept responsibility, give them responsibility' (R. Semler, *Maverick, 1992*).
- 'People will behave as they expect those in charge would behave in the same situation. The *Herald of Free Enterprise* sank because the staff perceived that it was important to set sail in spite of the fact that the bow doors were not closed. When the ship turned over the hunt was for scapegoats, not mistakes' (*Brass Tacks*, BBC2, 1989).
- Many universities have adopted systems of numbered exam papers. This is so that those who mark the papers see what is actually written rather than what they expect to see written by particular students to whom they can put a name and therefore a set of perceptions.

- **Physical:** by which we assume or infer the qualities of the person from their appearance, racial group, beauty, style, dress and other visual images.
- **Behavioural:** whereby we place people according to the way they act and behave, or the ways in which we think they will act and behave.
- **Role:** whereby we make assumptions about people because of the variety of roles they assume; the different situations in which they assume these roles; their dominant role or roles; and the trappings that go with them.
- **Psychological:** whereby certain occupations, appearances, manifestations, presentations and images are assumed to be of a higher order of things than others (part of this is also sociological). This reflects the morality, values and ethics of the society of the day as well as the environment and organisation in question.
- **Situational:** whereby collective and individual confidence increase as the result of becoming familiar with physical and psychological environments, and the ways in which they work. Repetition of patterns of behaviour, forms of address, and ways of working also contribute to situational perception.

This part of the perception process aims to build up a picture of the world with which the individual can be comfortable. Comfort is achieved when people and situations are perceived to have complementary characteristics or constructs. Discomfort occurs when characteristics and constructs are contradictory. For example, there is no difficulty placing an individual as kind and gentle in the perceptual map. There is difficulty, however, in being comfortable with an individual who is both kind and violent.

Closure

Closure occurs where an individual sees part of a picture and then completes the rest of it in their mind; or hears part of a statement or conversation and then mentally finishes it off. It also occurs as part of the process of exclusion, halo effects and stereotyping, so that the picture is completed around the strong trait and everything else is omitted or excluded.

Attribution

Attribution is the explanation put by individuals on behaviour or activities. Attribution may be:

- rational: 'you burnt your hand because the plate was hot'
- pseudo-rational: 'he is a bully at work because he has a difficult home life'
- empathised: 'in her place I would have done the same thing'
- mythological: 'this was how we always used to do it and it worked then'
- insidious: 'he is a bully at work; he has a difficult home life; therefore, I am not going to do anything about his bullying'
- excusing: 'he is an expert and so is entitled to behave like a brute'
- fearful: 'he is an expert so I do not know how to approach him, therefore I will not approach him'
- inert: 'I must be even-handed in dealing with complaints, disputes and grievances'.

Whether rational or not, attribution gives people a point of reference for their actions and for those of others. It also helps in the attaining of comfort and satisfaction, enabling people to explain – to themselves at least – why they continue to work in particular occupations, ways, situations, or with particular people.

Other influences on perception

The following more general influences may also be distinguished.

Emotions

Feelings of anger, antagonism, mistrust and disregard emphasise the tendency to reject. At the very least therefore, any such feelings present or potentially present in a given situation need to be recognised at the outset and at least neutralised where possible.

The greatest of all emotional barriers in organisations is pride. Nobody likes to lose face or to have it made plain that they were wrong. Nor do others wish to be associated with someone who is seen as defeated or forced to back down from a given position.

This is especially important in the understanding of the conduct of workplace disputes and grievances. It is important in the understanding of why projects that are plainly doomed to failure are nevertheless allowed to proceed. In each case the alternative – withdrawal – is an admission of failure. It is seen as such and is therefore unacceptable from a variety of points of view.

Visibility

Visibility is the cornerstone of managerial effectiveness, style and communication. It greatly helps in the generation of confidence, familiarity and interaction. It underlines levels of honesty, trustworthiness and straightforwardness. It helps develop both professional and personal relationships between those involved. There are therefore both general and specific benefits to be gained from an effective face-to-face relationship.

Visibility reinforces the perceptual elements of proximity, intensity and confidence. Proximity is the tendency to empathise with those people and pressures that are physically visible rather than generally known or understood. Intensity is a reflection of the physical and psychological elements present in working (and other) environments. Confidence is generated by feelings of familiarity and contribution; and each of these is reinforced by physical visibility and access.

The converse is also true. Lack of visibility is both a perceptual barrier in itself and also compounds others that are present: general feelings of disregard, distrust and dishonesty for example. Misunderstandings occur least, and are most quickly and easily sorted out, face-to-face. Without personal contact, such misunderstandings invariably take longer to resolve and may quickly become disputes and grievances.

Comparison

Some comparisons are precise and exact: this glass is fuller than that; she is better qualified than he is, for example. Others are less so and may be based on a range of opinion – informal or otherwise – expectation and prejudice. Some comparisons are valid, others not.

Comparisons have the added value of helping to meet the expectations of people in certain situations. If a company has a bigger percentage pay rise than elsewhere, staff tend to be happy. If the pay rise is lesser staff tend to be unhappy. Organisations therefore tend to seek out and emphasise those comparators that present them in their best light.

The standpoint from which the comparison is made must also be considered. For example, the statement that bankers earn more than teachers is valid only if a simple comparison of earnings is being considered. It does not prove or disprove that one job is better or worse than the other. For other aspects therefore, other equivalent comparators have to be identified and addressed.

It is also usual to put weightings on different comparators when trying to arrive at satisfactory, complex and valid comparisons. The process at least recognises the difficulties involved and proposes steps towards addressing them, even if it is unlikely that they can be entirely resolved.

First impressions

First impressions count. They are plainly misleading – prima facie you must know less about someone after 30 seconds than after 30 minutes – yet they are overwhelmingly influential and this should be understood.

Above all, the first impression gives a frame of reference to the receiver. The appearance, manner, handshake and initial transaction is the writing on a blank sheet. Before there was nothing, now there is something on which to place, measure and assess the other. The impact is therefore very strong. It is essential to recognise this. The consequence of not doing so is that a one-dimensional view of the individual is formed and everything that is contrary to that dimension or indicates complexities, other dimensions and qualities is edited out (see Table 13.1).

Expectations

People go into every situational transaction with a purpose. The fulfilment of this is their expectation. Expectations are measured in hard material terms, soft behavioural terms, and a combination of the two.

- **Hard:** goods for money.
- **Soft:** courtesy, honesty, trustworthiness, value.
- **Combination:** value for money – that is, a combination of the measurable (the money) with the immeasurable (value).

Meeting expectations

When expectations are met people are satisfied. This applies to all those who come into contact with a particular organisation: staff, customers, clients, the community, the media and other stakeholders.

The community also expects a general positive response to itself from playing host to particular organisations. The output of expectation is therefore satisfaction in whatever terms that is to be measured.

Other expectations may be distinguished.

First impressions

TABLE 13.1

People
- appearance, dress, hair, handshake
- voice, eye contact
- scent, smell
- disposition (positive, negative, smiling, frowning)
- establishing common interest/failure to do so
- courtesy, manner
- age

Service
- friendliness (or lack of)
- effectiveness
- speed
- quality
- confidence
- value
- respect
- ambience
- appearance

Objects
- design
- colour/colours
- weight
- shape
- size
- materials
- purpose/usage
- price, value, cost

Organisations
- ambience
- welcome
- appearance
- image and impression
- technology
- care
- respect for others
- confidence
- trust

This is a useful (but by no means perfect or complete) means of compartmentalising the cues and signals which are present when coming into any situation or into contact with someone for the first time. There are certain to be contradictions and contra-indications. It is essential to recognise and understand this in order to understand, in turn, the impact and influence of first impressions.

- **Expectation as customer:** of value for money; of utility and reliability of products and services; to be treated with courtesy and accuracy.
- **Expectation as shareholder or stakeholder:** of the longevity, stability and profitability of the organisation; of steady and increasing returns on investment; of strength of positive reputation.
- **Expectation as staff member:** to be treated well and fairly; to be paid well and on time; to have prospects for advancement; to have pay and rewards increased; to participate in the success of the organisation; to be treated with respect; to receive accurate and up-to-date information.

Fulfilment of expectations is a key feature of the motivation of the individual. This is the basis of expectancy theories and motivation (see Chapter 20). Marketing activities generate the expectation that particular needs and wants will be satisfied through the use of products and services indicated. Part of the recruitment and selection process is concerned with setting out a range of expectations that may be satisfied if the individual is to come to work for the organisation. Much of what is usually called industrial relations is concerned with meeting the more general and universal human expectations, and having access to information and being kept abreast of developments in the particular situations in which individuals find themselves.

Exceeding expectations

Generally expectations are exceeded only in the very short term. This occurs when the outcome of a particular situation, performance or product, or the result of a transaction, is more positive or brings a greater level of satisfaction than was anticipated at the outset. The invariable result of this is the setting of a new level of expectation in regard to the particular activity in question. This becomes the norm by which events will be measured in the future; if there is then a reversion to the original level of performance or output, dissatisfaction will be engendered.

Failing to meet expectations

This occurs where satisfaction is not achieved. The outcome is shown in loss of business, increased customer complaints and loss of reputation. It is also revealed in heightened levels of disputes, grievances, accidents and absenteeism.

Perceptual defence mechanisms

People build defences (blocks or refusal to recognise) against people or situations that are personally or culturally unacceptable, unrecognisable, threatening or incapable of assimilation. Perceptual defence normally takes one or more of the following forms.

- **Denial:** refusal to recognise the evidence of the senses.
- **Modification and distortion:** accommodating disparate elements in ways which reinforce the comfort of the individual.
- **Change in perception:** from positive to negative or from negative to positive, often based on a single trait or characteristic becoming apparent which was not previously so.
- **Recognition but refusal to change:** where people are not prepared to have their view of the world disrupted by a single factor or example. This is often apparent when people define 'the exceptions to the rule'.
- **Outlets:** where the individual seeks an outlet (especially for frustration or anger) away from its cause. For example, browbeating a subordinate offers a sense of relief to people who have previously been browbeaten themselves by their superior.
- **Recognition thresholds:** the greater the contentiousness or emotional content of information, the higher the threshold for recognition (i.e. the less likely it is to be perceived readily).
- **The use of the messenger:** organisations use external consultants and experts to deliver messages that are known, believed or perceived to be unacceptable if they come from within the organisation. Perceptual credibility is therefore given to proposed initiatives and ventures, and also to the negative aspects of business process re-engineering, if delivered by somebody who is not a member of the particular organisation.

Adaptation

This includes the following.

- When people exhibit strong and conflicting characteristics, the general response on the part of the rest of the world is to reject or mistrust them, as accommodation and acceptance require an understanding of the limitations of perceptions at the point of meeting and dealing with them.
- A combination of the various perceptual processes is to be found in the 'preconceived idea' and 'pre-judged case'. What invariably happens is that a situation arises to which the individual can bring different familiarities and experiences to different aspects of it. Individuals then reconstruct these for good or ill to the matter in hand, and jump to a conclusion and solution to it.
- It is possible, through the observation of an individual's activity and behaviour, to **infer** that person's attitude. It is **not** possible to prove it; and if this is the over-riding requirement of the moment, further action must be taken in this regard to overcome these inferences and gain a true picture.
- The adaptation process is constantly in action. People over-respond to someone who is polite if the last six others that they have met have been rude. People driving home in a rush from work may fear the wrath of their partners if they are late; if they crash the car in their haste to be on time, they immediately feel lucky to be alive; the feelings of the person waiting for them change from anger to anxiety and then relief.
- There is also the question of 'construct reconciliation' to be addressed, where one encounters a person at different times in different roles. Examples of this include reconciling the brilliant performance of actors with their own personalities; the radical politician or religious leader who is also familiar as a next door neighbour or travelling companion; the children's matinee idol who refuses to sign autographs.

In general, a grasp of the basic principles of perception on the part of those in managerial roles at least enables the questioning of certain supposed 'rules' and 'facts'. It should be part of the process of generating a healthy scepticism and genuinely enquiring mind, when faced with such perceptual 'absolutes' (see Example Box 13.5).

Attitudes and values

Attitudes

Attitudes are the mental, moral and ethical dispositions adopted by individuals to others and the situations and environments in which they find themselves (see Example Box 13.6).

The following elements are present in all attitude formation and development.

- **Emotional:** feelings of positivity, negativity, neutrality or indifference; anger, love, hatred, desire, rejection, envy and jealousy; satisfaction and dissatisfaction. Emotional aspects are present in all work as part of the content, working relationships with other people, reactions to the environment, and the demands placed on particular occupations.
- **Informational:** the nature and quality of the information present and the importance that it is given. Where this is known or widely understood to be wrong or incomplete, feelings of negativity and frustration arise.
- **Behavioural:** the tendency to act in particular ways in given situations. This leads

---

EXAMPLE BOX 13.5 Adaptation

A passenger survey carried out by one of the world's leading global airlines was rendered virtually useless because those who commissioned it overlooked one simple point. The survey questionnaire was given to passengers to fill in during long haul flights and to be handed in at the end. It covered the service offered by the cabin staff, range of goods on sale, quality of the food, comfort and general feelings about the flight.

Because the survey was carried out on the actual flight, the airline received average feedback only when everything had gone more or less smoothly. The feedback was highly negative when small things had gone wrong. Twenty minutes' discomfort in flight was reported as a major negative implying a threat to life and limb. Lack of instant response to demand for service was regarded as sloppy and symbolic of a poor attitude. One item in the food offered would colour the entire perception of food quality, especially if this was poor or not to the liking of the individual passenger.

In summary, the results were based on the constant adaptation of the passengers to each occurrence rather than their wider perceptions and feelings of satisfaction.

---

to the formation of attitudes where the behaviour required can be demonstrated as important or valuable; and to negative attitudes where the behaviour required is seen as futile or unimportant.

- **Past experience:** memories of what happened in the past affect current and future feelings.
- **Preconceptions:** especially where those coming to work in the organisation have past histories as customers, clients or users of its facilities. These are key issues when going to work in education, health, social services or the travel industry; they require addressing at the outset of employment through effective induction programmes.
- **Visibility, proximity and intensity:** these are reflected in attitudes that cause people to deal with present problems rather than the most important issues; and to value staff with whom they interact everyday above those working elsewhere.
- **Over-mighty and over-influential individuals and groups:** the assumption that particular groups and individuals may not be approached, managed or directed, because of the power and influence that they are known or perceived to wield.
- **Specific influences:** especially those of peer groups, work groups and key individuals: managers and supervisors. These influences also include family and social groups, and in some cases religious and political affiliations.
- **Defence:** once formed, attitudes and values are internalised and become a part of the individual. Any challenge to them is often viewed as a more general threat to the comfort of the individual.

Values

Values are the absolute standards by which people order their lives. Everyone needs to be aware of their own personal values so that they may deal pragmatically with any

> ## EXAMPLE BOX 13.6 Conveying Real Attitudes (1): Language
>
> There are a great variety of words and symbols that define the actual view held by those that use them in regard to those about whom they are used.
>
> - 'These people': different and inferior groups, classes, tribes and families. It is a favourite phrase of politicians describing groups that they would rather not have to deal with (such as the poor, the homeless the socially disadvantaged).
> - 'Workers, workforce': always used by directors. A variation of this is to be found in the Annual Report: 'Staff are our most valuable resource'.
> - }'If you don't want this job there are x million unemployed who do': this phrase is never used in a satisfactory, or productive, or harmonious situation; the question of whether the person has a low level of value simply does not arise.
> - 'We conform to legal requirements: we meet legal minimum standards; we meet particular directives': this is manifested is where the organisation concerned is hiding behind the letter of the law rather than assuming absolute responsibility for its own activities.

situation. This may extend to marked differences between individuals or between an individual and the demands of the organisation. Conflicts of value often arise at places of work. This must be recognised when setting standards which people are required to follow; if they are to be effective, they must be capable of harmonisation with the values of the individual. Individual and shared values may be summarised as follows.

- **Theoretical:** where everything is ordered, factual and in place.
- **Economic:** making the best practical use of resources; result orientated, the cornerstone of people's standards and costs of living.
- **Aesthetic:** the process of seeing and perceiving beauty; relating that which is positive and desirable or negative and undesirable.
- **Social:** the sharing of emotions with other people.
- **Integrity:** matters of loyalty, honesty, openness, trust, honour, decency; concern for the truth.
- **Political:** the ways and choices concerning the ordering of society and its sub-sections and strata.
- **Religious and ethical:** the dignity of mankind; the inherent worth of people; the morality – the absolute standards – of human conduct, including the specific beliefs and requirements of particular religions.
- **Prejudicial:** individual and collective preferences for colours, clothing, design or cars are all subjective influences on values, and contribute to feelings of conformity. These are legitimate subjective elements, and not at all to be confused with repugnant gender, race and other social prejudices.

Attitudes and values are affected by:

- the prevailing present climate, whether positive or negative

- past experiences and interactions with the given person or situation
- continuing experiences and interactions
- perceptions and levels of general understanding
- presence of, and understanding of, the particular rules, regulations and other limitations with which these are bounded
- particular mental and physical aspects
- levels of identity with the others involved and with the situation
- the extent to which the people/situation are known or unknown
- aspects of risks and uncertainty
- levels of active or passive involvement
- positive aspects: the extent to which something good and productive is certain or expected to come out
- negative aspects: the extent to which something negative and unproductive is certain or expected to come out
- any strong or prevailing moral, ethical or social pressures
- general degrees of comfort: usually again based on levels of knowledge and understanding (see Example Box 13.7).

Formation of attitudes

The elements indicated are adopted by individuals in their own unique ways to form their own distinctive attitudes. The main factors that are involved are as follows.

EXAMPLE BOX 13.7 Conveying Real Attitudes (2): Symbols and Differentials

- **Job titles:**
    - A.   Typist, clerk, worker, operative.
    - B.   Assistant manager, manager.
    - C.   Crew, gang, cast.
- **Status:** hourly, clock, salary, levels and nature of supervision, industrial relations, management style, job titles, location, manuals and procedures.
- **Trappings:** cars, car phones, personal computers, offices, personal assistants, personal departments, staff officers, furniture and furnishings, personal facilities (fax, toilet, lift).
- **Behavioural differentials:** forms of address, separate canteens, designated car parking spaces, executive dining rooms, workers canteens, location by floor.
- **Procedural differentials:** dependent upon: occupation, job title, department, division, location, etc.
- **The cover-up/openness syndrome:** dealing with mistakes and errors, scapegoating, use of (and failure to use) phrases such as: 'we have made a mistake'; or: 'I was wrong'.
- **Dress codes:** dress allowances, the use of uniforms, overalls; universality or differential.
- **Address codes:** referring to staff by first and last names, job titles and rank.

- Their propensity to accept rather than reject the attitudes of the group (including the organisation) to which they seek to belong; this gives a high degree of potential compliance.
- Their perception of the future relationship as being productive, effective, profitable and harmonious; people do not willingly enter a situation if they do not expect this; their willingness to enter situations is proportionate to the likelihood of this being achieved.
- Relating past experience to current and future situations, relationships and environment; positive experiences tend towards the formation of positive attitudes, and negative experiences towards the reverse.
- Availability and completeness of information; availability includes access and clarity; completeness includes reference to key and critical gaps; and also to the value and usefulness of that which is available.
- The general state of organisational well-being, the general state of the individual, and the relationship and interaction between the two.
- Other pressures, including the views of peers, co-workers, superiors, subordinates, family and friends; economic, social, legal, moral and ethical pressures. These are likely to include sweeping generalisations, received wisdom, opinions and prejudices (opinions formed without full reference to available facts); again, these come from the variety of sources indicated.
- Any myths and legends present in the particular group or situation. For example, the statement that 'the person who holds job x or sits in office y always gets promoted first/never gets promoted at all' puts behavioural and psychological pressures on each situation.
- Other environmental aspects, especially management style and communication forms that are known, believed or perceived to contribute to the general organisation climate (see Example Box 13.8).

Each part of the process is present in the promotion and development of all attitudes, though the mix varies between particular situations and individuals. The mix also changes as people join and leave organisations and their groups. Also, by seeking to move individuals may need (or perceive themselves to need) to change their attitudes in order to stand any chance of being successful. The attitude may change again, depending on whether or not they were able to make the move, and if they did, whether or not this was successful (see Table 13.2).

Beliefs

Beliefs are the 'certainties' of individuals and groups. They may be:

- **Absolute:** based on such things as mathematical fact; night following day; mortality and taxation.
- **Near absolute:** based on seasonal changes; the continuous development of knowledge and awareness; continuous technological and social development.
- **Acts and articles of faith:** based on the certainty of God; often underpinned by religious allegiance and the following and adoption of the teachings of those who pronounce in the name of God; this may also extend to the adoption of social and political creeds.

EXAMPLE BOX 13.8 Conveying Real Attitudes (3): Managerial Job Adverts

- '. . . you should be self-motivated, imaginative and able to persuade and influence at all levels . . .'
- '. . . our innovative and proactive approach in all areas of HR means we are introducing new policies and systems. . .'
- '. . . the competitive salary is pitched at a level attractive to the highest calibre individuals and you will receive the excellent company benefits you would expect from a leading financial services organisation. . .'
- '. . . you must be a professionally qualified graduate with at least five years relevant experience. . . creative, commercially driven and self-motivated, you are capable of designing and implementing original solutions to business issues. . .'
- '. . . highly visible, highly challenging and highly rewarding, this position requires at least five years experience in a significant personnel function, gained in a fast-moving environment. . .'

It is very difficult to pin down any precise quality actually required. Each of those indicated in such job advertisements is open to purely subjective interpretation, spurious justification and rationale. The perception and attitude generated is therefore that the organisation is entirely free to appoint whomsoever they wish, regardless of the true demands of the situation.

Source: Samples taken from *People Management*, 30 July 2001.

- **Other strong ethical and moral standpoints:** relating to honesty, trustworthiness, right and wrong.
- **Strong illusions and perceptions of order, permanence and stability:** often founded on long steady-state factors.

Beliefs are the psychological cornerstone of people's lives. They provide the foundations and framework upon which people order and structure the rest of their existence. They are internalised to the heart and soul of the individual, providing the basis for other attitudes, values and chosen behaviour.

Forcing and imposing belief changes on people is very traumatic for those who are to be affected. Religious persecutions and the willingness of people to die for their beliefs indicate the extent of this. People would rather lose their life than their beliefs. (Frederick Forsythe describes this trauma as being akin to 'a china vase hit by an express train').

From an organisational behaviour point of view it is clearly possible to make the rational case that as there is no such thing as an eternal organisation, there is therefore no question of individuals believing in it. However, individuals may create a relationship very akin to belief, especially if they work in the same situation for a long time and the relationship is mutually productive, effective and harmonious. Any

Influences on attitude: summary

TABLE 13.2

Positive

- Equality of opportunity and treatment
- Saying what is meant, meaning what is said
- Identifying and solving problems
- Clarity of purpose
- Unity of pupose
- Reward for achievement, loyalty and commitment
- Openness of management style
- Particular standards set at outset
- Absolute standards for everyone
- High and equal value placed on all staff
- Recognition of every contribution
- Pride in the organisation
- Identity with the organisation
- High levels of esteem and respect for staff
- Clarity of communications
- Harmony
- High quality information

Negative

- Inequality of opportunity and treatment
- Expendiency
- Victimisation, scapegoating
- Lack of clarity
- Fragmentation of purpose
- Rewards based on favouritism and infighting
- Remoteness and distance of management style (both physical and psychological)
- Standards allowed to emerge
- Different standards for different groups, departments, divisions and individuals
- Different levels of value placed on different staff groups
- Lack of recognition
- Lack of pride in the organisation
- Lack of identity; rejection of identity
- Low levels of esteem and respect; variations in levels of esteem and respect according to occupation, department, division and function
- Lack of clarity of communications
- Hostility
- Low quality information

change in this (especially sudden change) is therefore in turn akin to the trauma indicated above. Moreover, people internalise particular aspects of the organisation, coming to believe (or nearly believe) in given standards of honesty, trustworthiness, high ethical and moral standpoints. In these cases when it becomes apparent that they are illusory the same degree of trauma is felt (see Example Box 13.9).

The nature of the relationship, if it is to be truly honest and effective, therefore needs to be contextual. This means creating a relationship which satisfies the need for some degree of permanence and at the same time setting out the boundaries of this, which normally means addressing questions of flexibility and dynamism and the willingness to change, develop and adapt. Permanence therefore becomes something in which individuals have their own direct and active contribution to make. It is not solely dependent on organisation provision.

Above all is the need to recognise the difference between attitudes and values on the one hand, and beliefs on the other. Organisations may have a legitimate

EXAMPLE BOX 13.9 Beliefs

Bank of Credit and Commerce International (BCCI)

BCCI collapsed in 1991 after a long history of allegations of fraud and participation in money-laundering. This was so extreme that most of the staff working in the bank simply shut it out. They could not accept that their organisation could possibly be corrupt in this way. When the closure of the bank came around following the removal of great volumes of its money and assets, many of the staff went into (and remain) in deep shock that this could have happened to them.

Maxwell

When Robert Maxwell drowned in September 1992 it became apparent within days of his death that he too had left behind a lasting legacy of fraud and corruption. Many of the staff of the *Daily Mirror*, the newspaper that he owned, simply left, taking jobs anywhere else to put behind them the knowledge that they had worked for a thief and the trauma this involved. Until his death, Robert Maxwell had gone to a lot of trouble to cultivate an image of being a larger than life character, an image based on his past history of having escaped from the Nazi invasion of his homeland Czechoslovakia, his arrival in the UK as a refugee, the brilliant military record that he had gained during the Second World War, his creation of a global publishing empire, and his subsequent election as a Labour MP.

In more general terms, much trauma has been caused to individuals who joined organisations on the basis of permanence and, after relatively long periods of stability and order, found themselves suddenly surplus to requirements during redundancy and reorganisations. The problem lay with the fact that the illusion of permanence had been shattered, and that most organisations did little to prepare their people for the fact that the relationship was not permanent and that changes would occur. In effect, they did nothing to generate any understanding of the fact that the illusion of permanence was just that: an illusion.

The lesson for organisations and individuals therefore lies in the necessity and ability to create and maintain a working relationship based on honesty, integrity and clarity. This means above all, recognising and reconciling:

- that individuals have beliefs
- that they seek a set of certainties in their lives and tend towards belief when the illusion of certainty and permanence is fostered
- that the organisations in which they work, and to which they commit a substantial part of their time, energies, expertise and talents (and therefore forgo the opportunities to use these elsewhere and in other ways), tend to give a measure of certainty and permanence.

role in the shaping and influencing of attitudes and values, but any requirement to adopt and internalise the organisation as an act of faith is undesirable and potentially devastating for the individual.

Socialisation

Socialisation is the process by which individuals are persuaded to behave in ways acceptable to their society, family, social groups and clubs. This also applies to work organisations and their groups, departments, divisions and functions. Effective socialisation results in compliance and conformity with the values, beliefs, attitudes, rules and patterns of behaviour required. While this does not necessarily mean that individuals must adopt all these to the point of total faith and commitment, successful integration only occurs if they can at least acknowledge and respect them as boundaries and constraints within which they can work and operate.

For this to occur the group's attitudes, values, beliefs, behaviour and rules must be capable of being accepted by the individuals that seek (or are required) to join. They tend therefore to reflect the prevailing customs of the wider society and be in harmony with general ethical and social pressures.

On the other hand, socialisation should also leave enough space, latitude and freedom for individuals to express themselves in the given setting. Too great a restriction leads to frustration. At the other extreme, a lack of clear understanding of these standards leads to lack of focus and purpose leaving the individual in a void, and this can be just as harmful and stressful as over-restraint.

Socialisation takes place from the moment of birth. It is conducted in the early years by parents and family, schools and colleges, religious institutions, sports and leisure clubs. By the time individuals arrive in work they therefore have been subject to a great variety of pressures and influences. The problem for organisations lies in their ability to build on this and create conditions that are acceptable to individuals, and also ensure that productive and effective work can take place.

This problem is greater with mature employees who may arrive at an organisation after experience in many others. They will therefore have formed their own ideas about high standards, best practice and optimum ways of working, and this in turn leads to the need for effective orientation at the outset of the new job. Where an employee comes to a new organisation after a long stay in a single place of work, the problem is greater still because that organisation forms the new employee's only recent (perhaps only other) point of reference. For whatever reason, positive or negative, the person is coming into a new situation for the first time in a long while and great care is needed to ensure that he or she settles in quickly and effectively. This also applies to those returning to work after long periods of absence, because of previous job loss or family commitments for example.

Effective organisation socialisation processes tackle this by addressing the organisation's needs from the perspective of the individual. By bringing comfort and warmth to the situation the organisation engages positive feelings in the new employee. By setting its standards and expectations out clearly at the start, it leaves no doubt about its expectations and the ways in which individuals are to use their talents and qualities. This also generates the beginning of a relationship based on mutual respect and identity (see Table 13.3).

This underlines the importance of adequate and effective induction and orientation

TABLE 13.3 Social needs

Organisation	Individual
• Productive effort	• Comfort
• Effective workforce	• Warmth
• Effective individuals	• Belonging
• Effective groups	• Contact
• Continuous development	• Success
• New talent and energies	• Fulfilment
• Work harmony	• Achievement
• Expectations	• Professionalism
• Job proficiency	• Expectations
• Professionalism	• Rewards
	• Training and development

The lists represent two sides of the same coin. Organisation socialisation is designed and devised to bring them together, match up and harmonise the pressures. Some of these pressures are convergent, others divergent; all must be integrated and interrelated as far as possible.

programmes. Too many organisations and their managers still neglect this, believing it to be a waste of time, cutting into their other priorities; or else they have simply never learned to see it as an investment, the return on which is a committed and effective employee; if this is really successful much of the process is achieved over a relatively short period of time.

Conclusions

Perception is the basis on which everyone forms their understanding of the world. People make interpretations of others that they meet, and places and situations they encounter, by combining each of the elements indicated to produce their own individual picture, which they can then understand and be comfortable with.

Perceptions, attitudes and values are affected by repetition and familiarity. Something or someone who is always present gives the illusion of permanence. Routines and habits are formed by organising activities and interactions into regular patterns based on a combination of expectation and near certainty, and this too, reinforces attitudes.

Perception, attitudes and values are affected by the context in which individuals are placed.

Perceptions, attitudes and values are affected by the personalities and characteristics of those present.

It is essential, therefore, that all managers have this basic level of understanding of human behaviour, and how it is shaped, formed and developed. Only by doing so is it possible to understand the conflicting characteristics, aspirations, motivations, drives and desires of people in work situations. Above all, this also helps to limit the chances of value judgements being made on the basis of preconceived ideas or imperfect understanding.

CHAPTER SUMMARY

All managers must understand the basis of human perception, and the major ways in which this is shaped and influenced. This is for two reasons:

- so that they understand and acknowledge their own perceptual approaches
- so that they understand and acknowledge those of the people with whom they come into contact, especially staff, but also superiors, peers, suppliers, customers and clients.

Forming and nurturing the required attitudes and values clearly requires a broad knowledge and understanding of all the factors and elements indicated. If this is to be effective, the following must be present.

- Identification of the required attitudes and values, together with the reasons why these are desirable; ensuring that these can be supported and adopted by all those concerned.
- Taking positive steps to reinforce them through the ways in which the organisation and its departments, divisions and functions operate, and penalising any shortfall.
- Recognising the effects of all training and development activities on attitudes and values, whatever the training and development is overtly concerned with. Attitudes and values are shaped, developed and reinforced by all learning activities, as is the general mutual relationship and commitment between organisation and individual.
- It is also necessary to recognise that attitudes, and especially negative attitudes, emerge whether or not they are shaped and influenced by the organisation. Where the organisation has no influence on attitudes, these are formed by other pressures, especially peer, professional and social groups.
- Positive attitudes help to provide a harmonious and open working environment, and increase general levels of motivation and moral. Negative attitudes tend to reinforce any stresses and strains: poor working relationships, lack of trust and value.
- Attention to workplace attitudes, especially at the induction stage, helps employees to adopt and find the place required of them in their environment. It helps to provide a clear mutual understanding between organisation and employee, and is one of the cornerstones of the working environment. Above all, as organisations strive for ever-greater levels of flexibility and responsiveness, building these characteristics as positive and valuable attitudes is essential.

DISCUSSION QUESTIONS

1. To what extent have the initial impressions that you formed about your current colleagues and/or organisation remained the same? To what extent have these altered and why?

2. Identify the main aspect of your own perceptual mythology. Identify examples that both confirm and deny your perceptual mythology. What conclusions can be drawn from this? Now repeat the exercise for well known public figures – e.g. politicians, actors, actresses, sports and media personalities.
3. Consider Example Box 13.8 (page 344). What assumptions and inferences are made by those who write these advertisements and those who read them? Given that nobody would make up their mind about anything on this quality and volume of information, what other information would you need and how would you go about gathering and validating it? What questions would still have to remain unanswered?
4. To what extent can shared values be said to be genuinely present at your organisation/college/university? What are the reasons for this? What steps does the particular institution take to ensure that everyone has the same basic attitudes and values? What further steps could be taken?

CHAPTER CASE STUDY

YVON CHOUINARD: THE MAN FROM PATAGONIA

'Take a young person and ask them to name the man behind their favourite fashion label. Many will offer Ralph Lauren, Calvin Klein or Tommy Hilfiger. But an increasing number of young people will tell you about a balding, weather-beaten 61-year old French-Canadian called Yvon Chouinard.

Now ask a class of ambitious business degree types to nominate a corporate Chief Executive they admire. Richard Branson, Michael O'Leary and Bill Gates are all obvious choices. But some will also opt for Chouinard. And who was it that inspired an ever-increasing number of young city dwellers to head for the hills in pursuit of the wilderness experience? Again, Chouinard's your man. Ask an environmental activist who helps fund their activities . . . well, you get the picture.

Yvon Chouinard is little known in Britain, but in the United States he is an icon. As the founder and head of Patagonia, the brand that ignited the craze for technical outdoor clothing – clothes that are all about functional simplicity – he can claim to be one of the most influential fashion forces of recent years.

But his appeal goes far beyond that of an expert marketer of fancy pants. Chouinard is perhaps unwittingly the point of convergence for any number of lifestyle trends – a reluctant guru of fashion, business and lifestyle. And ironically the more successful he becomes, the more he tortures himself over what he has created. He may be a hero but he is a complex and unwilling one.

Chouinard was born in 1938 and lived in Maine until he was seven when his parents moved to Burbank, California. Speaking only French-Canadian, the young Chouinard became something of a loner, spending much of his time surfing. An interest in falconry led him to climbing which became his major passion. By the early sixties he was roughing it at Yosemite National Park's legendary camp four – to this day, the place that any rock climber dreams of pitching his tent. Chouinard pioneered a number of routes up Yosemite's celebrated peak El Capitan and the valley's other massive rock faces. In doing so, he became a hero of the emerging beatnik climbing scene – reading Jack Kerouac, listening to jazz and delving into Zen Buddhism. Along the way, he supported himself as a blacksmith, producing climbing hardware on a portable forge. An ice axe he designed in 1968 became a permanent exhibit at New York's museum of modern art.

Yet Chouinard was already concerned about the effect of his sport on the environment. Aged 19, he had revolutionised climbing by creating pitons that could be removed from the rock rather than just left to rust. Throughout the seventies and eighties the Patagonia label grew and grew. It became the leading name in outdoor clothing and started to find its way into urban fashion. In 1986, he started to contribute 1 per cent of sales or 10 per cent of pre-tax profits, whichever was the larger, to a wide range of environmental groups, many of them small, local projects. And still Patagonia kept growing. By 1991, sales had reached $100 million.

Then recession hit hard. Chouinard had to lay off 120 of his 620 staff, many of them friends. This set back caused him to have a radical rethink. He began to remodel the company. He began to formulate an idea of sustainable development – natural organic growth. He still limits the Patagonia range and encourages customers only to buy what they absolutely need.

After an environmental audit of the company's production, Chouinard started making fleeces out of recycled plastic bottles. In 1996, he decided to use only organic cotton in Patagonia clothes even though this added 25 per cent to the production costs. Sales dropped 20 per cent but he held steady, even loaning money to organic growers to keep them in business. Everything in the world-wide chain of stores was checked for environmental impact. If he is a man with a moral mission, he also has a faith that what he does will be repaid in profits and that the corporation can be a force for good. 'If you want to change government', he says, 'change the corporations and government will follow. To change corporations, change the consumers. Perhaps the real good that we do is to use the company as a tool for social change.'

Patagonia's sales now stand at around $200 million. Chouinard it seems can do no wrong with the Patagonia model being used by any number of companies who have realised that brand honesty and environmentally responsible production can translate into long-term security and profitability. 'If you focus on the goal and not the process', says Chouinard, 'you inevitably compromise. But for me, profit is what happens when you do everything else right. A good cast will always catch a fish.'

This is not enough for Chouinard of course. He is still tormented by the company's success. Patagonia now reaches an audience far beyond the active outdoors types. The Patagonia zip-up jacket is part of a uniform for many young Brits and much of the range has been widely copied. Yet he has a strangely ambivalent attitude to those who use his products for the purpose for which they were intended.

'Part of the process of life is to question how you live it', he explains. 'Nobody takes the time to do things right. With mountain climbing, people are only interested in reaching the top of the peak so that they can tell others that they did it'.

However, there is a discrepancy here. The Patagonia catalogue is a glorious call to the wild. Can he really blame stressed out city dwellers for trying to get a bit of fresh air, especially if he allows them to look good and keep warm doing it? Chouinard proposes that the great American wildernesses should be the preserve of a dedicated few, yet his company encourages an exodus of the many. If the surf is crowded and the rock face cluttered, then Patagonia has had a big hand in making it so.

So the question arises: if Chouinard believes that we are consuming ourselves to destruction then why does he dedicate his life to making thermal underpants? It's a matter of compromise and Chouinard acknowledges his own weaknesses.

'We are an incredibly damaging species and we are pulling all these other beautiful species down with us. May be ought just to get out of here. You do what you can. Then, even if you are burning petrol to get there, you just have to say "forget it, let's go surfing."'

Chouinard's contradictions reflect those of our age. We want to heal the planet while stocking up with as many consumer goods as our credit cards will allow. We want to be outdoors but only if we get there in an air-conditioned, four-wheel drive and stay in rose covered cottages with modern central heating. Chouinard is a contradictory hero for contradictory times but he is still a hero.'

Source: Nick Compton, *Orange* magazine, Spring 2000.

QUESTIONS

1. Identify and discuss the conflicting attitudes present. In your view, which are the dominant attitudes and values and what are the effects of these on the performance of the Patagonia company?

2. How does the company develop the attitudes and values of customers in its dealings with them?

3. What potential for damage to the company is there in the divergent attitudes exhibited by Yvon Chouinard

14 Communication

'Pay attention to the direction signage.' Instruction at the entrance to BBC Headquarters, Wood Lane, London – requiring visitors to 'follow the arrows'.

'A picture paints a thousand words.' Anon.

CHAPTER OUTLINE

The processes of communication

Specific tools and techniques that can be used effectively by managers to make their communication effective

The behavioural aspects of communication

The relationship between organisational and managerial effectiveness, and effective and successful communication.

CHAPTER OBJECTIVES

After studying this chapter, you should be able to:

understand how communication processes work, and what makes them successful or otherwise

understand some specific approaches that aid effective communications

understand where barriers and blockages to communications may arise, and take steps to overcome these

understand how communication processes are manipulated and corrupted, and why this occurs.

Introduction

The issue of communication is vital for the successful functioning of any organisation. All organisations normally establish formal mechanisms and processes of vertical and lateral lines or channels of communication to provide the means by which information – facts, ideas, proposals, emotions, feelings, opinions and problems – can be exchanged. They also normally create integrating activities such as groups, committees and other meetings, and the means of consultation to improve the all-round quality and understanding of this information.

Effective communication is based on information:

- the volume that is available
- its quality

- the means and media by which it is transmitted and received
- the use to which it is put
- its integrity
- the level of integrity of the wider situation.

Communications and information feed the quality of all human and operational relations in organisations. Good communications underline good relations and enhance the general quality of working life, motivation and morale.

Bad and inadequate communications lead to frustration and enhance feelings of alienation and lack of identity and unity.

Communication structuring

Communications may be:
- **One-way:** edicts issued by organisations to employees, usually without any regard for their effect, especially negative. One-way communication may also occur where the workforce and its representatives issue ultimatums over disputes and grievances. The effect in both cases is to stoke up any fires of conflict that may be inherent. Some website material is one-way in that there is normally no choice in how it is presented and how it interacts.

  More generally, one-way communication is also found with some advertising and public relations though these are normally supposed to produce at least a generally favourable response, if not active acceptance.
- **Two-way:** the ability to engage in active and productive dialogue, consultation, participation and involvement. This is the basis of all effective staff management and industrial relations, as well as customer, client and supplier management.
- **Downward:** some downward communication is essential because overall standards and direction have to be communicated from those responsible to those

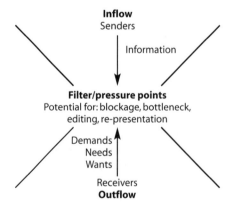

Note: may be upwards, downwards, lateral.

FIGURE 14.1 Principles of communication

who have to carry things out. Written rules, procedures and handbooks also require the backing and support of top managers. To be effective, downward communication requires active participation and consultation. It must be delivered in ways capable of acceptance by the staff and others at whom it is directed.

- **Upward:** upward channels of communications are those that provide access to top management for the rest of staff. Their effectiveness is enhanced or limited by:
  - organisation culture that sets the boundaries of openness, integrity and honesty
  - physical and psychological distance between top managers and the rest of the organisation
  - attitudes of top managers to the rest of the staff.
- **Lateral:** between different professional and occupational groups and locations, departments, divisions and functions. In many cases, this is especially hard to manage because of in-built and historic barriers that exist between:
  - primary functions, administration and headquarters
  - doctors, nurses, ancillaries and managers (healthcare)
  - air crew, ground crew and headquarters (airlines)
  - managers and backers (dot.coms and telecommunications)
  - production and sales; production lines and maintenance (factory work)
  - sales staff, branch managers and headquarters (retail).

All this is underpinned by policies, procedures and practices governing standards of attitudes, behaviour and performance; the management of conflict and specific issues such as customer, client and supplier management, public relations and other aspects of organisation presentation. The style and format of communications in each area set the overall standards required and underpin the formal, institutional and informal channels.

- **Formal:** the hierarchies, systems, procedures and committee structures established to underpin management style and organisation effectiveness (see Figure 14.2 and Example Box 14.1).
- **Institutional:** less formal channels that nevertheless carry both validity and influence; these include professional, occupational and managerial cluster groups, work improvement groups, quality circles (see Example Box 14.2).
- **Informal:** ad hoc gatherings, scribbled notes and the grapevine (see Example Box 14.3.)

EXAMPLE BOX 14.1 The Cascade Effect

This is attractive to hierarchies. Those at the top delude themselves that it works as an effective communication mechanism. It takes its name from the cascade appearance caused by pouring champagne into the top glass of a pyramid of glasses. The pouring is continued until the wine overflows and eventually fills all the glasses of the pyramid (see Figure 14.2). The effect of this – for champagne and for communication – is the same. The quality of both is lost and there is a good measure of wastage by the time the bottom of the pyramid is reached.

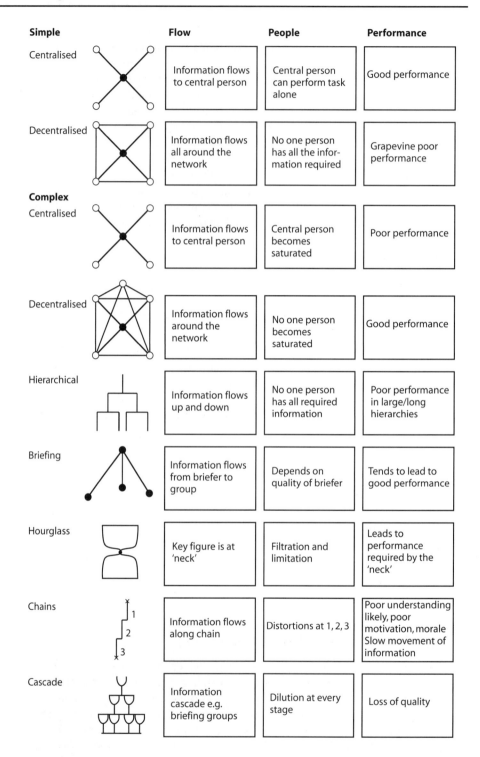

Simple		Flow	People	Performance
Centralised		Information flows to central person	Central person can perform task alone	Good performance
Decentralised		Information flows all around the network	No one person has all the information required	Grapevine poor performance
Complex Centralised		Information flows to central person	Central person becomes saturated	Poor performance
Decentralised		Information flows around the network	No one person becomes saturated	Good performance
Hierarchical		Information flows up and down	No one person has all required information	Poor performance in large/long hierarchies
Briefing		Information flows from briefer to group	Depends on quality of briefer	Tends to lead to good performance
Hourglass		Key figure is at 'neck'	Filtration and limitation	Leads to performance required by the 'neck'
Chains		Information flows along chain	Distortions at 1, 2, 3	Poor understanding likely, poor motivation, morale Slow movement of information
Cascade		Information cascade e.g. briefing groups	Dilution at every stage	Loss of quality

FIGURE 14.2 Chains of communication

EXAMPLE BOX 14.2 Cascades in Action: Ford UK

This problem of communication cascades arose at Ford UK at the beginning of the twenty-first century. For years, the company had struggled with the problems of institutionalised racism; above all, the knowledge, perception and belief that it was very difficult for members of ethnic minorities to gain promotions to managerial and supervisory positions. Over the same period of time, the company's head office in Detroit, USA, had been fed assurances that the situation was improving. The company described itself as having 'the best race relations policies in the business', yet this did not prevent increases in complaints being upheld over the period 1987–2000.

In late 2000, Ford took the decision to scale down car production at Dagenham, and to concentrate only on engines at that location. The result of this was industrial uproar, led by the company's trade unions. Allegations of racism were restated. The government also became involved in consultations with the company to see if the effects on employment could be mitigated.

Only at that point did the company Chief Executive, Jacques Nasser, come over to the UK from Detroit to see the problem at first hand for himself. The widely held conclusion was that most of the problems would have been resolved much more satisfactorily, if only senior officials from head office had come over earlier.

The effectiveness of the direct approach, and the ineffectiveness of the cascade or chains of communication method, were summarised by Dale Carnegie as follows: 'The only thing that should ever be passed on is simple messages. Otherwise, if you want someone to know something, tell them directly.'

Communication policies and priorities

Communication policies are based on the extent to which organisations and their managers are prepared to engage in consultation, participation and effective committee work.

EXAMPLE BOX 14.3 Grapevine

All organisations have a grapevine, consisting of gossip, half-formed opinions and general chatter about the present state of affairs.

It is an important indicator of general organisational well-being. If the grapevine is concerned with personal gossip and the mythical activities of individuals, all is more likely to be well than if the primary topic of conversation is the future state of the organisation, uncertainty over job and work security, and the spreading of rumours about redundancies.

Consultation

Organisations consult with their staff on the implementation of decisions and policies. The purpose is to ensure that everyone understands what is required of them and why, and to give them a full understanding of a particular situation. It also reflects the need for mutual confidence and unity of purpose among everyone in the organisation. Effective consultation also helps to ensure that what is proposed has been well thought out and tested, as well as providing a means for staff input (see Figure 14.3).

Genuine consultation also helps to ensure that any flaws in decision-making processes or the implementation of particular proposals may be raised. However well or thoroughly an issue has been overtly thought through, it must be capable of wide general scrutiny and examination.

Participation

Participation is where all those involved take part in the decision-making process as well as its implementation. In order to do this, full information must be made available to all involved, and effective means of involvement – works councils, staff committees – must be engaged. Genuine participation requires effective and clear decision-making processes that satisfy both openness and cooperation, but without analysing and stifling everything to the point of inertia.

Model

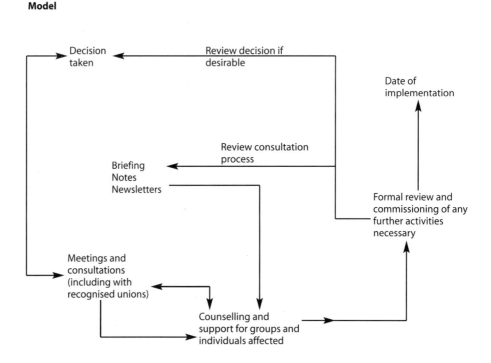

FIGURE 14.3 Consultation process following a decision

Committees

Committees are constituted for a variety of reasons. From the point of view of communication, it is essential that they enhance both quality and value rather than act as a blockage. To ensure this, their purpose, scheduling, size, composition, agenda, control and recording must be managed. The ultimate test of the value of any committee is its output. If this is not forthcoming, then alternative means should be found to tackle the issues that the committee or committee system is supposed to face.

Committees may be used to render inert something that is threatening to a particular vested interest. They are used to filter and edit information. They are used to draw the teeth of lobbies or pressure groups, and to advance particular desired points of view. In many cases, there is a pecking order. Committee membership may be subject to patronage or favour. Membership of certain committees is often a mark of status or achievement.

Committees should therefore be constituted for a purpose, and when this purpose is satisfied, they should be disbanded. They satisfy human needs for association, belonging, participating and contributing, and it is important that they do this in the interests of advancing the total quality and effectiveness of the organisation.

Principles of effective communication

These are as follows.

- **Language:** of sender, receiver, and anyone else who may read or listen to the message. The greater the clarity of language, the greater the likelihood that what is transmitted will be received and understood; the reverse – when language is not clear – always dilutes effectiveness. It also leads to feelings that things are being hidden or not stated fully.
- **Conciseness:** in which everything that needs saying is said simply and directly. This is not to be confused with lack of full coverage or leaving things out.
- **Precision:** language that addresses points directly will reinforce total confidence in the communication. Language that is not direct tends to reinforce feelings of dishonesty or mistrust (see Example Box 14.4).
- **The positive/negative balance:** people respond much more actively to positive communications. Where negative messages have to be transmitted, these should be given the same clarity and precision; at least then bad news is quickly, clearly and completely understood.

The selection of the correct media is essential and many communications go wrong because the wrong choice is made. The basic rules are as follows.

- Say what needs to be said; write what needs to be written; make best use of all the senses of those affected and of all media available.
- Say what needs to be said and confirm this in writing.
- Operate on a fundamental basis of openness, honesty, integrity and trust in terms of access to, and provision of, information.

EXAMPLE BOX 14.4 Language Barriers

Forms of words and phraseology are used extensively to give off coded messages and to reinforce the real agenda that is being followed. Examples are as follows.

- With the greatest respect, I respect your views, I am sure that you are a person of great integrity = you are wrong, you are talking rubbish, I don't value you at all.
- We will take all steps, we are doing everything possible, we are complying with the law, we are complying with specific regulations = we are doing as little as possible in the circumstances, we are doing the least we can get away with in the circumstances, you cannot tough us.
- We do not have the resources/money/staff/equipment = we do not want to do it, we are not going to do it.

Non-verbal communication

Non-verbal communication gives an impression of people to others without anything being written or said, and reinforces what is said or written. It also tends to give the real message: the non-verbal message is usually much stronger. The main components that must be understood are as follows.

- **Appearance:** this includes age, gender, hair, face, body shape and size, height, bearing, national and racial characteristics, clothing and accessories. Each of these items and their combined effect have great implications for interviewing, public images, creating impressions, advertising, public relations, salesmanship, presentation, design brand, marque, layout, comfort and familiarity.
- **Manner:** indicating behaviour, emotion, stress, comfort, formality/informality, acceptability/unacceptability, respect/disrespect.
- **Expression:** expression, especially facial expression, becomes the focus of attention and that is where people concentrate most of their attention.
- **Eye contact:** regular eye contact demonstrates interest, trust, concern, affection and sympathy. The depth of expression in the eyes generates deeper perception of feelings: anger, sorrow, love, hatred, joy.
- **Pose:** this may be static or active, relaxed, calm, agitated, nervous or stressful. It reinforces the overall impression conveyed. Different parts of the body – especially arms and legs – are used for expression, emphasis, protection and shield.
- **Clothing:** especially in work situations, clothing provides an instant summary of people. Technicians are instantly recognised by their overalls, police and traffic wardens by their distinctive uniforms and so on. Many organisations whose staff deal regularly and consistently with the public insist either on a dress code or a uniform; this helps reinforce organisational image and the trust and confidence of the public.
- **Touch:** this reinforces a wide range of perceptions. Consider the difference between different people's handshakes and the impressions that these convey.
- **Body movement:** this may be purely functional and fulfil certain requirements,

for example cleaning the car. Movements may be exaggerated, conveying anger or high emotions; languid, conveying comfort, ease or indolence; or sharp and staccato, conveying forcefulness and emphasis. They can also reinforces role and sex stereotypes: the chairman/chairwoman banging a fist on the desk for example.

- **Position:** this reinforces formality/informality; dominance/dependency; superiority/subordination. People use position to enhance feelings of control and influence. For example, people may face each other across a large desk; this conveys a sense of security and defence to the person whose desk it is and a barrier to be crossed by the other. Chat show hosts sit without tables and ensure that their guests do not have recourse to this prop either. This puts the professional at an advantage and ensures that the guest is sufficiently alien to the environment to be subservient to the host.

- **Props and settings:** props and settings can reinforce impressions of luxury and formality. They are designed to ensure that whatever happens does so to the greatest possible advantage of the instigator. They either reinforce or complement perceptions and expectations; or else they contrast perceptions and expectations, so that the person coming into the situation is impressed for whatever reason.

- **Discrepancy:** this occurs where the body conveys one message while what is spoken or written conveys others.

- **Social factors:** people are conditioned to preconceived ideas and general expectations of particular situations. For example, people do not generally attend promotion panels or job interviews unshaven or dressed informally. There is no rationale for this other than the expectations of society and the general requirement to conform.

- **The other senses:** other aspects of non-verbal communication include the use of scent and fragrance, the use of colour and coordination of colours, matters of social and ethical importance and expectation, the design and use of materials.

- **Listening:** listening can be both active and passive. Passive listening may be no more than awareness of background noise, or limited to a general awareness of what is going on. Active listening requires taking a dynamic interest in what is being received. While the message is received through the ears, it is reinforced through eye contact, body movement, pose and through the reception of any non-verbal signals that are given by the speaker.

- **Reinforcement:** non-verbal communication tends to reinforce relative and absolute measures of status, value, importance and achievement; relative and absolute measures of authority, power and influence; confidence and well-being; and psychological barriers.

Barriers and blockages

Barriers and blockages arise either by accident, negligence or design.

Accident

The wrong language, timing or method of communication may be chosen with the best of intentions. In such cases, those involved can simply step back from the situation and rectify it as quickly as possible. This is the only sure remedy. The worst thing that can happen is that the organisation instead takes on a defensive position so that a simple misunderstanding quickly becomes a major dispute or dysfunction.

Negligence

This is where barriers and blockages are allowed to arise by default. The organisation and its managers perceive that things are at least 'not too bad' or 'going along pretty well'. In such cases communication dysfunctions are seen as 'one of those things'. Specific problems are ignored or treated with a corporate shrug of the shoulders. From the staff point of view however, these are the first signs of corporate melées and neglect. If allowed to develop, they give the overwhelming perception to the staff that the organisation does not care for them or what happens to them.

Design

This is where the barriers and blockages are created and used by those within the organisation to further their own ends. They are used also to bar the progress of others. In these cases above all, information becomes a commodity to be bought and sold, to be corrupted, skewed and filtered in the pursuit of the sectoral interest in question. This is endemic throughout the middle and upper echelons of the military, civil and public service institutions, multinational companies and other multi-site organisations with large and complex head office institutions where an active and negative form of realpolitik exists (see Example Box 14.5).

Within this context the following barriers are identified.

- **Departmental, divisional, hierarchical and functional boundaries:** the problem is compounded when expertise or information held in one department is used as a bargaining chip, or else filtered out in its own interest.
- **Language:** use of bureaucratic and imprecise phrases acts both as a barrier to effective communication and as fuel to the fires of any inherent discontent.
- **Distance:** both physical and psychological. Physical distance acts as a barrier when people working away from particular locations simply do not receive information. The filtering, editing and presentation of information also reinforce any

---

EXAMPLE BOX 14.5 Errol Flynn

'Errol Flynns' are so called because they exhibit all the characteristics of the great film star. In organisational terms they are glamorous: blue-eyed persons, clearly favoured, on upward career paths, with histories and track records of successes. They attract followers and courtiers. They have a series of triumphs (real and overwhelmingly imaginary) that gain organisational recognition. They are their own best publicists.

Above all, their greatest characteristic is to be, in organisational terms, just the right side of the draw bridge as it comes up – to escape their own disasters by the skin of their teeth.

other psychological barriers (e.g. status, hierarchy, modes of address) that may be present. Also, some managers put up physical barriers between themselves and the rest of the world in the form of secretaries, switchboards and information filtering systems.

- **Trappings:** some trappings exude fear. For example, the person who has a car parking space, two personal assistants and a personal washroom puts up psychological barriers to communication with more junior staff. The junior, in turn, is both physically and psychologically discouraged from making any approach.
- **Control mechanisms:** where requests for specific information (e.g. output figures and costs) are made in ways that are inappropriate or that may be misunderstood. The problem is compounded when those who are required to produce such information do not fully know its purpose or the standpoint from which it is being requested (see Example Box 14.6).

EXAMPLE BOX 14.6 The Need to Know

This barrier occurs where organisations decide that information is to be issued in different ways – or different information is to be issued – to different groups and individuals. It is a process of limiting the availability of information. On the face of it there is some sense in this; most organisations have far too much information for any one person to understand, analyse and internalise.

The barrier arises from the reasoning behind 'the need to know'. As long as this is for operational reasons, it is sound. Otherwise, the message given is one of:

- a lack of capability to understand what is being said, and especially that the organisation (or an individual superior) does not think or believe that the subordinate has this capability
- lack of value or different levels of value placed on different groups of staff, especially those who are excluded from the 'need to know' list
- access: in order to be privy to certain information it is necessary to have reached a particular level of the organisation; communication therefore becomes a trapping of personal status and importance
- general disrespect: operation of this form of approach to the giving of information gives off an overall signal of lack of respect to those affected
- psychological distance: again, this emphasises the differences and divisions that exist in organisations and between their functions, departments, divisions and individuals.

Operating a 'need to know' approach also leads to distortions in the presentational style and use of information media. What is issued is for the purposes of the issuer rather than the receiver, emphasising their distance and supremacy rather than imparting valuable and useful information.

More generally, any restriction on information leads to reductions in the capabilities of those who need to take decisions and make judgements. Even if operated from the highest and most positive standpoint, this approach is restricting in this way.

- **Confidentiality:** which becomes a barrier when it is used as a means of attracting or acquiring status rather than for operational effectiveness. Confidentiality should normally be limited to people's personnel files, technological advances, marketing initiatives and research, development and pioneering inventions.
- **Lack of visibility or access:** which leads to the feeling that problems and issues cannot quickly be resolved.
- **Information systems:** combinations of communications, people and technology all have imperfections and therefore the potential to be a blockage or barrier. Information technology especially acts as a barrier where there is a lack of training for the staff, a lack of full understanding of the systems capabilities, where there are different and incompatible systems and formats present, and where not all staff have access.
- **The nature of work:** the greater the intrinsic interest in the work, the greater the volume of reasons that the staff have for being there, the greater the likelihood that effective communications will exist. Where work is boring and alienating there is normally a more general background of lack of respect and trust. Problems are compounded where there are extensive and complex rule and regulation books and committee management structures (see Example Box 14.7).

EXAMPLE BOX 14.7 Rules and Regulations

Rules and regulations are a barrier in all situations because they order and restrict people's activities. The problem arises when these are:

- Long, drawn out and complex, consisting of volumes of procedures that are designed to cover every possible eventuality or foible. This increases perceptions of restriction and negativity. It also indicates a more general negative view of the people: that if they need this amount of regulation, they are regarded as potentially lazy or dishonest.
- Written in language that is not simple and direct. The impression of restriction is compounded by the use of particular phraseology that seems to leave those in superior positions free to impose any restriction, or interpret the rules as they see fit. While recourse to grievance procedures is always available to staff affected in this way, this requires energy and commitment on their part. It is also in itself very negative and consumptive of resources that could be better used elsewhere.
- Operated unevenly, where standards vary between different managers, supervisors, departments, divisions and functions. Some of this will be the fault of the individuals concerned; much always arises because of the nature and complexity of the rules themselves and the ways in which they have been written and applied.
- Contradictory: the more complex the set of rules, the more likely contradictions are to exist. In these cases again, time and energy is spent on resolving individual issues when they do arise and in working out which of the contradictions is to be applied in the circumstances.

Other factors

These include the following.

Reinforcement

Reinforcement acts as a barrier where it and the given message are at variance. In these situations, it is always the reinforcement that is received and believed.

- Where what is said is positive, but the reinforcement is negative. The most common form of this is in using positive language without underpinning the communication with absolute commitments or objectives. This lack is the reinforcement and is that which is believed, acted upon and reacted to, and which becomes the focus for analysis.
- Where what is said is negative, but the reinforcement is positive. This works well when for example, the message is that 'We are in a crisis and we have to get out of it, and this is how we are going to go about it'.
- Where what is said is unclear and so is the reinforcement (see Example Box 14.8).

EXAMPLE BOX 14.8 Language and Messages
Negative

The use of words such as but, only, never.

Negative	Positive
It is excellent but it is very expensive	It is excellent and it is very expensive
He/she is only a secretary	He/she is a secretary
You will never get to the top unless …	You will get to the top if or by …

Acronyms

Two people engaged in a construction industry research project conducted a positive, happy and ostensibly productive conversation around the acronym WIRS. Only when one party wrote up a note at the meeting did it become apparent that at the core of the conversation was the construction sector's 'whole industry research strategy'. The other party had thought that it was about the workplace industrial relations survey.

Over-praising

Over-praising always gives a negative message because it reflects either a lack of sincerity or a lack of understanding on the part of the praiser. The only exception to this is where the subordinate has resolves a crisis or problem for the supervisor which could not otherwise have been achieved.

Example Box 14.8 (continued)

Ambiguity

This often occurs because of the simple human failing to order thoughts before speaking or writing (for example, school teacher to class: 'Watch the board while I go through it').

There may also be punctuation errors:

- She said 'she didn't mind what I did'.
- She said, she didn't mind what I did.
- 'She', said she, 'didn't mind what I did'.

Errors of emphasis

- *Long* may you run.
- Long *may* you run.
- Long may *you* run.

Confusion

The word 'solutions' means different things to management consultants, information technologists, chemists, doctors and nurses.

Dishonesty

More insidiously, phrases such as 'there are no redundancies planned at present' and 'there are no plans for reorganisation at present' give off a dual meaning; what is not said is whether there are future plans, and how long the present actually lasts. Reinforcement in these cases centres around 'at present'.

More generally, the usual justification offered by managers and supervisors for over-emphasis on negativity, to the exclusion of all forms of positive language, is to the effect that 'if my staff do not hear from me, they know they are doing a good job'.

It is a barrier when the organisation takes time and trouble to over-emphasise the positive or to set it in the wrong context. Consider the effect of sectoral league tables indicating that a particular organisation is:

- tenth in a field of 70 in terms of profit/losses/costs/charges
- third most productive in the same field (in whatever terms that is measured)
- twenty-third largest in the same field
- no worse than anyone else.

Such tables can and do lead to feelings of complacency and introversion on the part of the organisation at large and individual members of staff.

Media

Medium and message should reinforce each other. When the format and language are not appropriate there is a barrier to effective communication. This applies to the spoken and written word and to any visual or pictorial information. It is important to recognise the needs of the receiver as well as the objectives of the presentation. Distortion occurs when one or the other is not met. It is especially prevalent when the following kinds of presentation are used.

- Statistics and trends are presented using figures and performance that are taken in isolation or used out of context.
- Strong visual and pictorial images are used to project a narrow view that is at variance with the wider picture.
- Discussion and debate are not genuine but conducted from the point of view or vested interest of the protagonist.
- Essential information is put out in ways that ensure that not everyone can gain access (e.g. through e-mail and intranet systems).
- Different media are used by vested interests to advance and promote their point of view to best advantage (see Example Box 14.9).
- The delivery – especially written and oral – is accidentally or deliberately unclear. This also applies to the visual, when the pictures used are at variance with the overall message or are not recognised as reinforcing it.
- A protagonist has to put on some form of show for the benefit of someone else who is assessing him or her, where this assessment is based on reasons other than organisational effectiveness. The organisation may require particular managers to present issues in ways that are deliberately unclear and may reward them for this. Junior members of staff may make strident or controversial responses in order to gain a reputation among their peers, or to bring themselves to the attention of those in authority for their own future advancement.
- There is a party line to be followed and the presentation needs do not easily match this. A trade union, for example, may have great sympathy with an organisation's need to restructure, but have to reconcile this with its own need to be seen to be representing the interests of its members. This is compounded if the restructuring has effects and implications for their long-term future, especially redundancy, retraining or redeployment. The union may therefore be forced into a position of opposition in spite of its own careful analysis of the situation.

Realpolitik

In this context this is where the organisation's way of working is defensive. It follows from this that information becomes a commodity to be guarded, filtered and fed into systems, including the grapevine, for managerial or departmental advantage as well as (or rather than) used in the organisation's best interests. In these circumstances cluster groups and networks become the places where real messages get around the organisation. Managers are also known to make informal contacts in other parts of the organisation (the equivalent of having their own spy network). They will also tend to attract information just in case they missed something that might be to their advantage (or the absence of which might be to their disadvantage).

EXAMPLE BOX 14.9 Use of Media

Those with influence, power and authority choose the media that they believe they can use to best advantage.

This is especially true of political debate. For example, one party persists with the view that 'not enough resources are being given to a particular area (for example, roads, education, health, social services and social security)'. The other party counters this by saying that 'more resources are being spent in the given area than ever before'.

This is reinforced by the production of statistics, again for the end being pursued. On the question of health for example, one party will say that 'waiting lists for treatment are longer than ever'. The other counters with 'we are treating more patients than ever before'. Each produces statistics to back up its point of view.

The result is a stalemate. It is compounded by the overwhelming impression that:

- there are only two possible points of view to hold: the one or the other indicated
- aligning others to the point of view depending upon their own vested interest, personal and political preference and conviction
- producing subsequent 'evidence' to 'prove' that waiting lists have got longer/shorter; or that resources have gone up/down.

Equivalent distorted forms of debate and discussion potentially exist in all organisation situations. The protagonists again either take refuge in their own vested interest, seeking statistics to underpin it, or else produce counter arguments to the opposing point of view. No productive debate and discussion takes place. This dissipates any feelings of shared commitment and involvement, reinforcing the differences between various departments, divisions, functions, groups and individuals. It is compounded where one view is seen to be that of the organisation as a whole, or where the protagonist gains advantage or favour as the result of holding or presenting a particular point of view.

Very few organisations really value openness of information and the responsibility of the individual to do his/her own filtering and editing. Invariably the approach taken is based on a perceived (usually spurious) conception of need to know, as discussed above. Other than trade secrets and genuine inventions there is very little that should be truly confidential.

Messages also lose their effect if and when nothing is seen to happen as the result of their being issued. This is true, above all, where action is promised but not forthcoming; when promises are made but not kept; when people's opinions and views are asked for but then ignored. In each of these cases it is best to give a clear and unambiguous statement of what is to occur, rather than engaging in spurious consultative and participative efforts if there is no intention of acting upon them. They will in any case be construed as dishonest at the time and will colour the opinions of any such activities in the future.

Other forms of dishonesty and duplicity should also be recognised. The first is where information is sought from members of staff for one purpose and then used against them for others. A common version of this is to ask people during selection and appraisal interviews what they think their weaknesses are and then to use these as excuses for not appointing, developing or giving pay rises. This also occurs in forms of organisation-speak, whereby messages are couched in terms such as: 'There are no plans at present to close/make redundant/sell off', 'We are considering a range of options', and: 'Training and development and excellent prospects are available to the right person'. Such phrases are always subject to sceptical scrutiny.

The volume of information issued may also itself be a barrier. This occurs where one is told more than one wishes to know about a particular subject, or where one receives huge swathes of written information that are both incomprehensible and unusable in the form in which they are presented.

Organisational toxicity

All organisations have communications agenda. These include:

- **Stated:** where what is said is precisely what happens.
- **Primary:** which concentrates on priorities.
- **Secondary and hidden:** in which messages are given out dishonestly, using lack of clarity to distort and undermine what is being said. Secondary and hidden agenda are forms of organisational toxicity.

Organisational toxicity and toxic communications exist in organisations that have acquired malady or disease. The concept is akin to the presence of toxins in the human body, or to a toxic or poisonous substance.

Toxic communications demotivate and demoralise staff, and dissipate the volume and quality of organisational effort and effectiveness. Their outward manifestation is found in clusters of staff conversing endlessly on the general state of the organisation, high levels of grievance and discipline procedures, complicated and duplicated rules and procedures, and remoteness of managers from their staff.

This arises from negative views held and promulgated by the organisation and its managers about the staff, the situation and the activities (rather than a recognition that each negative should be the springboard for positive actions). Specific communications that are to be found in toxic situations are as follows.

- **Blaming and scapegoating:** the organisation finds individuals to carry the can for its corporate failings. Sales departments get the blame for falling profits. Personnel get the blame for disputes and grievances. Individuals are blamed for specific failures (for example, the failure of a particular promotion campaign or work restructuring). They are often also named in this respect and their failure publicised around the organisation.

  A more insidious version exists whereby the scapegoat is not official but is named on the grapevine and the organisation does nothing to deny the rumours or rehabilitate any individuals that are so named.
- **Accusation and back-stabbing:** this is a development of blaming and scape-goating. It exists where it is allowed to exist: that is, where the organisation either

actively encourages, or at least acquiesces in, departments and individuals making accusations and allegations about each other. This is an integral feature of any blame culture.

- **Departmental feuding:** this is where forms of internecine warfare exist between individuals, departments and functions. This is a derivation of both blame and accusation, where both become institutionalised. Again, some organisations either actively encourage this or at least acquiesce in it. An outcome of this is that individuals and departments gain favoured status, power and influence based on their ability to do others down. This is one of the prerequisites to gaining the status of an over-mighty subject or an over-mighty department.

- **Meddling:** this is where persons meddle outside their legitimate areas of activity. One of the most extreme forms of this is where powerful individuals promise favoured customers that special activities and deals can be done on their behalf and where, as a result, production, sales, marketing, finance and human resource functions are seriously disrupted. Meddling also includes the promotion and appointment of family and friends on the basis of their relationship rather than capability, as well as other forms of favouritism and patronage and the use of organisation resources for personal gain and benefit.

- **Secrets:** in a toxic situation information (as we have seen) becomes a commodity to be used as a source of influence and as a bargaining chip. Control, editing, filtering and presentation of information then becomes a departmental and managerial priority. Information becomes graded and classified. There emerges a culture of need to know on the one hand, and an overactive and destructive grapevine on the other.

- **Corporate self-deception:** the other major feature of a toxic situation is where the organisation creates its own view of the world and its place within it. This usually occurs in one of two ways. The first is where an elite is created (or where a group is encouraged or comes to see itself as such). Securing its unassailable excellence, it produces plans, proposals and outputs that must necessarily be correct and excellent. Where for example this is the output of a corporate policy unit, overwhelming pressure is put on the rest of the organisation to follow and conform to this. The group becomes unassailable; indeed, people who do question its excellence, legitimacy and output may themselves be marginalised or scapegoated. The blame for the failures of initiatives and policies derived by such groups is inevitably placed on functional departments and not the policy unit.

  The other form of this occurs where the organisation is in decline. Rather than dressing the decline, it lives on past glories. It retreats into itself and creates its own view of the world. This has come to be known as the 'bunker mentality'. The expression comes from the last days of the Third Reich in 1944–5. The Nazi leadership created its own triumphal view of the world within its operations bunker in Berlin rather than facing the reality of defeat and invasion that was going on outside.

- **Negative labelling:** we have referred elsewhere to negative connotations that are associated with particular jobs and occupations, especially those that are deemed to be of lower grades (for example, clerk or operative). The negative aspects of these differentials are always exaggerated and exacerbated in toxic situations.

- **Toxic communicators:** related to all of this is the toxic individual. This person, for a variety of reasons, issues toxic communications. These may be general and may be no worse than putting a negative or pessimistic construct on any form of information that he or she is required to transmit.

A more insidious version occurs where, for example, people concerned have to communicate contentious organisation policy or courses of action. They do so with the rider that 'It's not my fault' or 'It's nothing to do with me' or 'I didn't want it'.

The worst version is clearly the individual who introduces toxicity however. This occurs where information is disseminated in particular ways, knowing the effect that this presentation will have or with a particular effect clearly in mind. Major examples of this are the use by organisations of trade union representatives and over-mighty subjects as the channels of information in particular situations.

- **Toxic communications:** these are the outputs of toxic organisations and toxic communicators. The key features are bland and undirected offerings, hidden agenda and mismatch between message and media use. They take place in the context indicated above.

Transactional analysis

Transactional analysis (TA) is a system for the analysis of personal and interpersonal communication and behaviour. It was defined and evolved by Dr Erik Berne (1984), whose thesis was that there existed in everyone three quite clearly distinguishable sets of attitudes and behaviours. He called these ego states. These are readily recognisable by the things that we say, the ways in which we say them and the support that we give them by way of body language, gestures and mannerisms. For example, the question:

'Where is my pen?'

has a range of possible responses depending on the way in which the question is asked, for example:

'I don't know.'
'It's on the table.'
'I haven't had it.'
'Where you left it.'
'Am I to always be running round after you?'

and so on. The tone of voice gives the clue as whether or not the pen is to be found, or whether an argument is to follow.

Ego states

Transactional analysis involves using knowledge and skills to recognise ego states; and from this, to adopt an ego state that will decide whether the transaction is to be effective, ineffective, business-like or crossed, leading to misunderstanding and argument. The ego states defined by Berne are parent, adult and child. The parent is further modified into parent nurturing and parent critical. The child is further modified into free child and adapted child. Their importance lies in the fact that there is nothing in human communication that cannot be attributed to one of these. People talk and write from different states, and it is possible to identify this in most cases. From this a method of choice of response and an appropriate ego state can be adopted so that the transaction proceeds in an orderly and effective way.

Transactions

Transactions may be:

- **Complementary:** from adult to adult, parent to child, or child to parent.
- **Crossed:** any other variation – parent to parent, child to child, child to adult, adult to child, adult to parent, parent to adult.
- **Ulterior:** where the message that is stated is not the one that is implied. The ulterior is that which is intended to be received; for example, when one person says to another 'I respect your views', what they actually mean is: 'I do not respect your views'. When this is the case, the ulterior transaction is inevitably that which is acted upon; indeed, the initiator will probably have intended this.

This is summarised in Figure 14.4.

Games

Berne also identifies a number of games that arise principally from ulterior transactions. He suggests that people spend a large proportion of their time and energy in these games, and that the main reason for this is to gain recognition or 'strokes': units of recognition. Examples of these are as follows.

- **Why don't you – Yes but:** the initiator states a problem and seeks the advice of others. They offer solutions based on the 'Why don't you' which the initiator then rejects with 'Yes but . . .'. The initiator ends up feeling self-righteous and thinking that he or she knows best; the real message that comes from 'Yes but' is that the responder is not going to do anything.
- **Now I've got you:** the initiator of this game contrives a situation whereby somebody makes a mistake. At the appropriate moment the initiator steps in and confronts the offender to make him or her feel bad while the initiator enjoys feelings of superiority and dominance.
- **Kick me:** in this game, the initiators constantly do things that provoke criticism or punishment; they get negative recognition that is more important than getting no recognition at all.
- **I'm only trying to help:** this is where advice or aid, usually unsolicited, is constantly being offered. When it is eventually rejected the initiator can say: 'But I'm only trying to help you'.

Scripts

Scripts are developments of games. They are created by individuals to form work, social or life scripts. They represent a form or summary of the way in which individuals choose to lead their lives. People make their plans around these in response to the range of messages – critical, prohibitive and negative, and also nurturing and supportive – that is received from both the workplace and the wider environment.

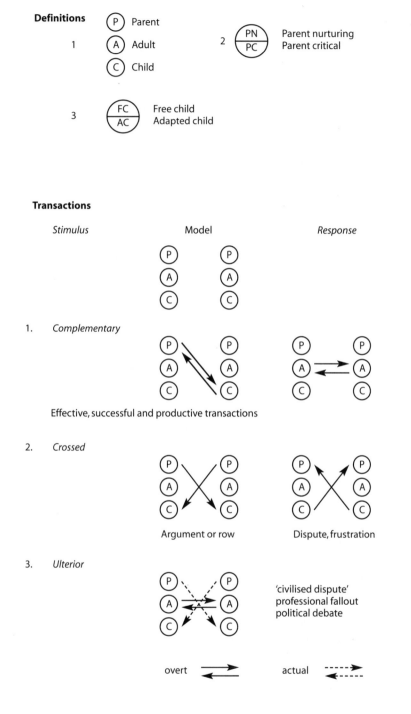

Transactional analysis: configurations

FIGURE 14.4

Source: E. H. Berne, *Games People Play*, Penguin, 1984.

Assertiveness

Another approach to producing effective communications has come to be known as assertiveness. It takes the point of view that communication can only be effective if it is well thought out, its effect is understood in advance, and the message is delivered clearly and directly to the recipient.

The following forms of behaviour and demeanour with negative effects on communication quality are identified as the background to this.

- **Aggressive:** characterised by shouting, swearing, table thumping, arguments (cross transaction). The matter in hand is forgotten as the aggressor strives to impose his or her point of view. Winning the argument becomes everything.
- **Hostile:** where the main emphasis is on the personalisation of the matters in hand, often also characterised by shouting and table thumping. The outcome is normally a personal attack (sometimes in public on an individual or group).
- **Submissive:** characterised by saying or doing anything that the other party wants so that they will finish the argument or transaction and remove themselves.
- **Inconsistent:** characterised by according people different levels of quality and value, applying different standards to different individuals and groups. This also extends to treating the same individual or group in different ways according to mood or the environment.
- **Non-assertive:** characterised by the inability of individuals to put their message across. This is because they either are not sure what to put across, or else have not used the correct words or media.

In order to resolve the problems caused by these forms of approach an absolute standard of behaviour, demeanour and language is used. This is called assertiveness. Assertive behaviour, demeanour and communications consist of the following.

- **Language:** clear, simple and direct; easy to understand and respond to on the part of the hearer or receiver; the words used are unambiguous and straightforward; request and demands are made in a clear and precise manner and with sound reasons.
- **Aims and objectives:** precise and clear; considered in advance; recognising the effect that the message is likely to have on the recipient.
- **Delivery:** in a clear and steady tone of voice or, where written, in a well presented and easy to read format. The tone of voice is always even, neither too loud nor too soft, and does not involve shouting, threatening or abuse.
- **Persistence and determination:** where problems or issues are raised by the recipient, the sender sticks to the message, aims and objectives without being side-tracked; any problems that are raised are answered without diverting from the main purpose.
- **Positive and negative:** the general thrust of the message is always clear and apparent, whether the overall tone is positive or negative. This approach is especially important in handling general staff problems, especially matters concerning grievances and discipline.
- **Face and eyes:** the head is held up. There is plenty of eye contact and steadiness of gaze. The delivery is reinforced with positive movements that relate to what is

being said (for example, smiles, laughter, nodding, encouragement; or a straight face when something has gone wrong).
- **Other non-verbal aspects:** the body is upright; hands and arms are open (in order to encourage positive response and productive transaction; there is no fidgeting or shuffling; there are no threatening gestures or table thumping, or other similar forms of behaviour.

Situational factors

Assertive delivery is based on an inherent confidence, belief and knowledge of the situation, and confidence in people. Openness, clarity, credibility and personal and professional confidence all spring from this.

Clarity of purpose or delivery is always spoilt through having to operate from a weak position or one which is not fully known or understood. This weakness or lack of clarity leads to other forms of behaviour and communications, as indicated above.

Negotiations

Effective negotiation requires the application of communication skills in addressing and resolving individual and collective problems. It requires undertaking discussions with a view to establishing agreements; and arranging and delivering those terms of agreement. All managers should be able to do this. The keys initially are:

- knowing what you want from the situation, and the requirements of the others involved
- knowing what you do not want from the situation, and what others involved also do not want
- knowing what is acceptable, and unacceptable, both to yourself and to the other parties.

Successful negotiations are based on:

- having the authority to make and deliver the agreement
- having the resources to deliver and implement the agreements
- paying attention to detail
- attention to the ability of everyone concerned to make sure that it continues to work.

It is also important to consider:

- the question of setting precedents: implications for future dealings along similar lines
- internal and external pressures, especially pressures from subordinates, superiors and backers
- the opportunities and consequences of agreeing to something; and the opportunities and consequences of not making an agreement
- what is open to negotiation and what is not.

The negotiating process has three elements.

- **Substance:** the matter in hand.
- **Process:** how it is to be addressed and resolved.
- **Presentation:** how the end result is to be perceived and received.

Negotiations may be conducted from two points of view.

- **Trust:** those involved trust each other to do their best by the particular situation and to resolve a particular matter in ways acceptable to all concerned.
- **Lack of trust:** managers do not trust staff members or their representatives; and staff and their representatives do not trust their managers or the organisation's owners.

dis

In many situations, negotiations are an integral part of the process of the management of conflict. It is essential therefore that both negotiating expertise, and understanding of the demands of the environment, are present.

Where there is a basis of mutual trust, matters can be discussed openly and honestly with a view to resolving them. Where this basis does not exist, the following aspects have to be understood.

- The opening position is always stated with the assumption that it will be rejected.
- There then follows a process of counter-offer and counter-claim with each party working its way gradually towards the other.
- The content of the final agreement is usually clearly signalled before it is made, as is the basis of what is genuinely acceptable or otherwise.
- Serious disputes occur when one side is determined not to settle or where there is genuine misunderstanding or misreading of the signals.
- Settlements are normally couched in positive terms in relation to all concerned to avoid the use of words such as 'loss', 'loser', 'climb down' and 'defeat', which have negative connotations and tend to store up resentment for the future and to polarise attitudes.

Behavioural aspects of negotiation

theory

The following must be understood.

- **The distributive effect:** opportunities and consequences of settling with one group at the expense of others.
- **Integrative drives:** opportunities and constraints of settling everything to the satisfaction of all involved.
- **Influencing attitudes:** in which attitudes are formed, modified and developed as follows:
  - confrontation: whereby the parties are motivated to defeat the other or win them over to their own point of view
  - individualism: in which the parties concerned pursue their own self-interests without any regard for the positions of others
  - cooperation: whereby each party is concerned about the others, as well as its own position

- collusion: whereby the parties concerned form a coalition in which they pursue a common purpose, possibly to the detriment of other groups within the organisation or to the organisation as a whole
- use of language: which may be confrontational or cooperative
- the formality–informality balance: especially the need for informal systems of communication between the parties involved where the formalised ones are presenting barriers.
- **Individual and collective expectations:** based on what people know, understand, believe and perceive that they are likely to gain from a particular situation. Serious misunderstandings occur when individuals and groups have been misinformed, or else have failed to read the fact that substantial changes in a particular situation have led to radically altered expectations.

These processes must be understood and engaged in according to the demands of the particular situation (see Figure 14.5).

Negotiations are required in resolving issues concerning the following.

- Issues between staff and management, in the pursuit of individual and collective grievances; also concerning pay rises and improvements in terms and conditions of employment. In traditional UK organisations, this process is known as collective bargaining.
- Disputes between organisations and their customers.
- Interdepartmental issues: addressing, managing and resolving misunderstandings; gaining cooperation and agreement.
- Internal issues: handling discipline, grievance, disputes and dismissals, resolving personal and professional disputes.
- Customer and client relations: handling and managing complaints.
- Contracting agreements: on supply and output sides; in the engagement of temporary, specialist and subcontracted staff.
- Gathering resources, especially where this is known, believed or perceived to be a competitive or distributive issue.
- Managing barriers and blockages, especially resolving crises and hold-ups on the supply and distribution sides.
- Managing the concerns of stakeholders and influential figures.

Conclusions

This chapter has concentrated on:

- the importance of communications as a critical factors of effective organisations
- the extent and prevalence of barriers to effective communication
- means by which the processes of communication may be understood.

Understanding these provides the ability to produce effective communications capable of being received, accepted and responded to. This is an organisational and individual issue requiring recognition at all levels, and remedial action where communications are poor or ineffective. It reinforces the need for clarity of purpose and language to which constant reference has been made. As many channels as possible or necessary

(a) Steps in the negotiating process

	Substance and process	Other factors
→	Initial offer and response claim	Strategic nature of offer
→	Adoption of postures	Strength and validity of cases
→	Ritual: movements and processes	Strength of each party
		Morale of each party
		Attitudes of each party
→	**Negotiations**	Public sympathy and support
←	Further offers/responsibilities	Government sympathy and support
→	**Basis of agreement**	
	Final offer/response	Media coverage

Each of these activities must be undertaken in these circles.
Each of the other factors must be acknowledged and understood.

(b) Process operation

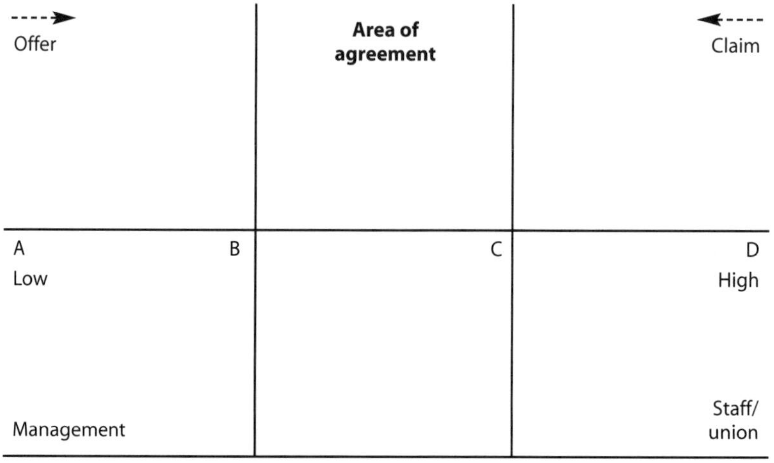

----→		**Area of**		←----
Offer		**agreement**		Claim
A	B		C	D
Low				High
				Staff/
Management				union

The collective bargaining process: offers between A and B rejected by staff; between C and D instantly accepted by staff; claims between A and B instantly accepted by managment; between C and D rejected by management; B–C is basis for negotiated settlement; normal first offer is around A, which leads to instant rejection; normal first claim is around D, but engages the process.

FIGURE 14.5 The negotiating process

should be used, giving the same message through each so that the message received is complete and not subject to editing, interpretation or distortion. Where communications are not direct, they will occur indirectly and people will search for hidden agenda and meanings.

Organisations are therefore responsible for creating the conditions in which effective communications can exist. Managers and supervisors must be trained in both the content and processes. All staff must be made to understand the importance and value of their contribution and how this is best made. This only happens when there is a high-quality working environment and a suitable general management style is adopted. Effective communications are an integral part of this. More generally, this is the foundation of all effective interpersonal, professional and occupational relationships between departments, divisions, functions and levels in hierarchies and throughout organisations.

CHAPTER SUMMARY

Effective communication is vital for the successful functioning of any organisation. It follows from this that all managers must be effective communicators, and all organisations must have effective formal methods, mechanisms and processes of communication, and suitable and effective means to make sure that what they wish to say is transmitted effectively.

Effective communication is dependent on the volume, quality and accessibility of information; the means and media by which it is transmitted and received; the use to which it is put; its integrity; and the level of integrity of the wider situation.

Understanding and being able to apply the rules, principles, skills and techniques indicated are universal managerial skills. They result in the ability to produce effective communication capable of being received, accepted and acted upon. All levels of communication should be monitored. Remedial action should always be taken where communication is poor or ineffective. Concentration on barriers and blockages to effective communication should be designed to reinforce the clarity of purpose and language. As many channels of communication as possible should be used, each giving the same message, so that the message received is complete and not subject to editing, interpretation or distortion. Wherever toxic, expedient or dishonest communications take place, it should always be clearly understood that the wider message received by those at whom the communication is aimed will always be read as such.

Organisations and their managers are therefore responsible for creating the conditions in which effective communications can take place, and ensuring that their managers understand the full effects of what they say, write and present. It is therefore essential to understand the broad context, as well as being able to apply specific skills and techniques.

DISCUSSION QUESTIONS

1. Of all the barriers to effective communication, which in your view are the hardest to overcome and why?

2. For an organisation with which you are familiar, produce a communication strategy that addresses the problems that you know to exist, and which takes positive steps to conquer them. How will you know whether your strategy has been successful or not?

3. Discuss the view that, because of the nature of organisational hierarchies and the differing aims and objectives of those within them, effective communications are not possible within organisations.

4. Identify the main strengths and weaknesses of television, radio and newspaper news and current affairs coverage. What lessons may be learned from this by organisations and their managers?

CHAPTER CASE STUDY

'WHO WANTS TO KNOW? WHO NEEDS TO KNOW?'

In September 2000, 752 employees at a Thames Valley computer chip manufacturing company took strike action over the company's proposals for major restructuring and organisational reform. Because of declining prices in the sector, and the consequent effect on profit margins, the company had called in management consultants who had proposed:

- 230 redundancies
- a restructuring of the workforce in order to allow for maximum flexibility of working
- a proposal to transfer a further 200 staff from permanent status to 'as and when required'; in other words, that there would only be work for them when production demands required them.

The staff, with the full support of their trade union (the AEEU), accordingly went through the full legal process required, and then called an official strike.

The independent Advisory Conciliation and Arbitration Service (ACAS) initiated regular contact with the parties during the strike. Neither side was initially prepared to ask for its direct involvement. After seven weeks of strike action however, both sides accepted an invitation to a series of informal meetings aimed at breaking the deadlock.

Management reiterated their argument that declining world markets, cutthroat pricing policies and successive years of falling profit margins had made it necessary to restructure the organisation in order to remain competitive. Surplus labour had been identified and, while the lay-offs and restructuring were regretted, there was little that could be done to alleviate this.

The AEEU rejected the company's arguments. The union claimed that management had accepted the consultants' proposals purely because they had been forced to pay heavily for them, and that there had been no consultation with the staff, or with anyone else. They also contended that pushing the staff down the path of confrontation had simply compounded the losses. Customers were being lost every day that the strike was going on. The union declared itself prepared to cooperate on a wider consultation. It stated that it fully understood the company's basic position, and the problems of the business environment. However, it was not prepared to accept any compulsion, either in the matters of redundancy or in the move to fully flexible working.

After full and frank exchanges of views over four days, agreement was reached that compulsory flexible working and redundancies would be withdrawn, in consultation with the unions and staff as a whole. This discussion would be subject to a strict timetable. At the end of this, if no agreement was reached, management would take whatever action they then deemed necessary. A timetable for transition to fully flexible working would also be agreed, and this would be extended to new staff joining the organisation in the future.

As the result of this, the union balloted the staff on the agreement that was reached. The staff voted, by a four-to-one majority, to accept the decision and arrangements were made for a full return to work the following day. Most staff were in any case anxious to get back to work, because they were in the situation where bills were not being paid, and it was also getting extremely close to Christmas.

QUESTIONS

1. What communications should have been put in place to ensure that this situation never arose in the first place?
2. What communications now need to be put in place? How should these be managed? How should they be delivered, and by whom?
3. What communication processes should be set up to ensure that the problem is not going to blow up again in the foreseeable future, and over the particular period of the consultations?
4. On the basis of what you have been told in the case study, identify the effects of this failure to communicate effectively on:
   a) profitable and effective business activity
   b) staff relationships.

15 Organisation Technology, Structure and Design

'Rubbish in – rubbish out.' Universal comment on the dysfunctional relationship.

'Everything that can be invented, has been invented. We have all the technology possible.'
Howe M. Weiss, US Presidential Adviser, 1898.

CHAPTER OUTLINE

The relationship between organisation structures, designs and technology

Managing the relationship between technology and activities

The creation and maintenance of good-quality working environments

The principles of organisation design.

CHAPTER OBJECTIVES

After studying this chapter, you will be able to:

understand the complexity of the relationship between organisation design and technology

understand the pressures that technology brings to bear on the activities of organisations, and understand some of the steps that may be taken to address these pressures

understand the opportunities and constraints present in particular organisational forms

understand the need to develop and advance the structure and design of organisations.

Introduction

Organisation structures reflect the aims and objectives, the size and complexity of the undertaking, the nature of the expertise and technology to be used, the desired quality of the working environment, the desired management and supervisory style, and means of coordination and control. Whatever arises as the result must be flexible and dynamic and responsive to market and environment conditions and pressures. It must provide effective and suitable channels of communication and decision-making processes; and provide also for the creation of professional and productive relationships between individuals and groups. Departments, divisions and functions are created as required to pursue aims and objectives, together with the means and methods by which they are coordinated and harmonised.

Structure also creates a combination of permanence and order. This is required to provide continuity for the organisation itself, and to generate the required levels of confidence and expectation in customers. It is also necessary to provide staff with (as far as possible) a settled and orderly working life. Means must also be found of ensuring the permanence and continuity of the organisation itself as people join or leave.

There are problems with structures. The history of organisation design indicates that structures are easier to put in place than to change, dismantle or rearrange. Longstanding organisations give the illusion of permanence to both staff and customers. Staff become accustomed to their position, and base their hopes and aspirations for the future on opportunities that are apparent within the structure. Many organisations have traditionally consciously provided career paths through the structure, and this becomes one of the attractions to stay rather than seek opportunities elsewhere. Customers become used to dealing with a particular department or official; if they have problems the structure traditionally provides a clear point of reference as to whom these should be addressed.

Pressures of economic turbulence and change, increased competition, diminishing resources and technological and expertise advances have all combined to cause a rethink of the ways in which organisations should be structured. The problem is to reconcile the qualities of flexibility, dynamism and responsiveness, and the technology and expertise present, with the need for permanence, order and stability. This is the context in which the question of organisation structure and design should be seen.

Technology

All organisations use forms of technology in pursuit of their business and this has a critical impact on the nature, design, structure and conduct of work. Technology also has implications for compartmentalisation, functionalisation and specialisation. Departments and divisions are created around the equipment used, whether for production, communications, information or control. It impacts on the physical environment: particular processes determine the layout and format in which work is conducted, and the proximity of individuals and groups to each other. It therefore becomes a factor to be recognised in the creation of supervisory and managerial functions and activities.

Again, there is a historic background. Forms of technology and equipment were used in the construction of the great buildings, temples and monuments of the ancient world. Most of this was unmechanised, often requiring armies of people to move heavy blocks of wood and stone into place. Roman war galleys – fighting ships – used slave-driven banks of oars for propulsion and direction and to manoeuvre into fighting positions. In each of these cases a basic technology existed and was exploited – but using human, rather than mechanised energy, to make it effective. In each case also, the task requirements meant that forms of organisation were required; and while in many cases the labour force was composed of slaves, these nevertheless had to be sufficiently interested, motivated and directed to ensure that the product or output was both effective and of the required quality.

From a strategic point of view, the following considerations are essential.

- **Approaches to production:** scientific management and its effects on production and behaviour; studies of groups in different working situations; the use of work groups in production.

- **Levels and types of technology:** the effects of the size, scope and scale of operations; the use of production lines; the effects of mechanisation and automation on individuals and groups. This extends to information technology. It also applies as much to commercial and public services as to manufacturing activities.
- **Organisational requirements:** the maximisation/optimisation of production; attention to standardisation, quality, speed, reliability and consistency of output.
- **Human and behavioural implications:** boredom and alienation; health and safety and occupational health; stresses and strains; job and task division.

Organisational technology consists of:

- **Hardware:** the capital equipment – computers, screens, robots, process machines.
- **Software:** the packages needed to energise and direct the hardware profitably and effectively.

It also includes the following interrelated elements.

- **Production and service technology and equipment:** which may be mechanised or largely manual, requiring human expertise, energy and input to make it effective and productive.
- **Largely automated mechanisms:** designed to produce products (or components of products) to uniform standards of quality, appearance and performance. In these cases the human input is often largely combined to switching the process on and off and monitoring (watching) the output flow. This has direct consequences for job and work design. These systems include production robotics and computerised manufacturing, as well as commercially-driven technology-centred services such as finance, travel and telecommunications.
- **Support function technology:** included computer-aided design, desk top printing and publishing, purchasing, stock room, storage and ordering systems.
- **Information systems:** for the input, storage, retrieval, output and presentation of data in ways suitable to those using it; and the production of data for purposes of control, monitoring, evaluation and decision making.
- **Specialised:** for example health equipment includes scanners, monitors, emergency equipment, laser technology for surgery and healing, heart, lung, organ and pulse monitoring equipment.
- **Generic:** off-the-shelf computerised production and information systems that are of value to a wide range of organisations and activities.

All organisational technology is developed and improved along the following lines.

- That which is to be used in future is known, believed or perceived to supersede that which was used in the past, either by improving quality or volume of output, or by reducing the time and resources (including human) taken to produce the existing levels.
- That which is to be used in the future has a greater variety of uses and applications than what currently exists and may give access to new markets and sectors, thus helping to secure the future of the organisation.

- Fashion: everyone else in the given sector is using a particular form of technology and there is pressure to conform.
- The organisation itself has an accurate assessment of the nature of the technology required to produce its products to the required volume, quality and deadline, and commissions the design and manufacture of the equipment to do this.
- Organisations and the technology that they use must be capable of harmonisation with the given culture, values, attitudes, skills and qualities.
- Items of technology must increasingly be capable of integration and inter-relationship with each other.
- Technological expertise brings implications for employment patterns, and pay and reward structures.

Expertise

The effective management of expertise requires addressing and reconciling the following.

- The scientific management and organisation of activities demands the standard-isation and ordering of work in the interests of efficiency, speed and volume of output.
- The scale and scope of production dictate that the flow, mass and (to an extent) batch types of activities require this standardisation.
- Professional and technical staff require variety, development and the opportunity to progress and enhance their work and expertise.
- Everyone, whatever their occupation, has basic human needs of self-esteem, self-respect and self-worth.

The specific effects of developments, improvements and automation of technology seen in isolation are:

- to remove any specific contribution made by operators to the quality and indi-viduality of production, whether real or perceived
- to dilute or remove understanding of the production processes used and to remove any direct individual contribution that is made
- to de-skill operations: operators become button pushers, machine minders and (when breakdowns occur) telephone users summoning specialist assistance
- to create feelings of distance – alienation – between the work and the people who carry it out
- to create frustration which occurs, either when equipment is available but the expertise to use it is not; or when the equipment is not available but the expertise is; or when both are available but the organisation chooses not to to use them.

The result is again to underline feelings of low self-esteem and worth, to encourage boredom and dissatisfaction, and sow the seeds of conflict (see Example Box 15.1).

Effects of technological advances

The following points must be understood.

EXAMPLE BOX 15.1 Alienation

Alienation is the term used to describe feelings such as the following.

- Powerlessness: the inability to influence work conditions, work volume, quality, speed and direction.
- Meaninglessness: the inability to recognise the individual contribution made to the total output of work.
- Isolation: which may be either physical or psychological. The physical factors arise when people are located in ways that allow for little human interaction or feelings of mutual identity and interest. The psychological factors are influenced by the physical. They also include psychological distance from supervisors, management and the rest of the organisation.
- Low feelings of self-esteem and self-worth arising from the lack of value (real or perceived) placed on staff by the organisation and its managers.
- Loss of identity with the organisation and its work; the inability to say with pride, 'I work for organisation x'. This is reinforced by the physical and personal commitment made by the individual to the organisation in terms of time, skill and effort that does not bring with it the psychological rewards.
- Lack of prospects, change or advancement for the future: feelings of being stuck or trapped in a situation purely for economic gain.
- General rejection: based on adversarial, managerial and supervisory styles and lack of meaningful communications, participation and involvement. This is increased by physical factors such as poor working conditions and environment.
- Lack of equality especially where the organisation is seen or perceived to differentiate between different types and grades of staff to the benefit of some and detriment of others.

Alienation is the major fundamental cause of conflicts and disputes at places of work. It is potentially present in all work situations. Those who design and construct organisations need to be aware of it in their own particular situations, and to take steps to ensure that it can be eliminated or at least kept to a minimum and its effects offset by other advantages.

- Pay, at whatever level it is set, does nothing to alleviate any boredom or monotony inherent in the work itself. It may make it more bearable in the short to medium term. In many cases, also, bonus systems are not within the control of the individual operator. Operators may work to their full capacity, only to see their bonus lost because of factors further down the production process.
- Insecurity and, related to this, the threat of insecurity and job loss may be used as a coercive management tool to try and bully the work out.
- Poor working conditions, especially those that include extremes of temperature and noise, discomfort, lack of human content and warmth, all contribute to poor morale.

- Low esteem is generated through feelings of being 'only a cog in the machine'. This leads to feelings of futility and impotence on the part of the operator. It is from this that feelings of hostility towards the organisation start to emerge. This also leads to increases in strikes, grievances and disputes.
- Mental health was identified as a feature by the 'Kornhauser' Studies, the results of which were published in 1965. Arthur Kornhauser studied car assembly workers at Ford, General Motors, and Chrysler. A major conclusion was that basic assembly-line work led to job dissatisfaction which in turn led to low levels of mental health. This became apparent in the low self-esteem of the workers who also exhibited anxiety, life dissatisfaction and despair, and hostility to others.
- Adversarial and confrontational styles of work supervision also contribute to alienation and dissatisfaction. This style of supervision tends to be perpetuated, even by those who have been promoted from among the operators. This is partly because it is all that they know and partly because of the pressure to conform that is exerted by the existing supervisory group. It is also apparent that supervisors themselves become alienated because of pressures from their managers, and also because of feelings of hostility towards them from the workers.

Approaches to the problems of dissatisfaction and alienation have taken three basic forms.

- Attention to the work.
- Attention to the working environment.
- Attention to the people.

Attention to the work

Attention to the work has taken a variety of forms.

- Job enrichment and enlargement, in which operators have their capabilities extended to include a range of operations. In some cases this has meant becoming responsible (with a group of others) for the entire production process in autonomous work groups.
- Job rotation, in which operators are regularly rotated around different work stations and activities making a different contribution to the whole.
- Empowerment, in which the operator accepts responsibility for supervision of quality control as well as for the work itself.

Each of these also partly addresses some of the psychological and behavioural aspects of dissatisfaction and alienation (see Example Box 15.2). It is worth noting also the experience of an electronics firm quoted by Handy (1993) as follows:

Production went up only slightly but, more important from their point of view, quality was very high without the need for quality control experts, absenteeism and turnover went down to low levels, production flexibility was greatly increased and the job satisfaction of employees was higher.

> **EXAMPLE BOX 15.2 Problems with Job Enrichment, Job Enlargement and Multi-Skilling**
>
> ### *Expectations*
>
> Where the expectations of staff are raised, they must be capable of being met. For example, people expect that when they are trained for something they will be able to practise it and that this will lead to increased levels of performance, prospects and reward.
>
> Conversely, people must have the potential for this increased level of performance and variety of occupation. It is stressful for the individual and counter-productive to the organisation to place demands on the staff they simply cannot meet.
>
> ### *Management*
>
> It is counter-productive if people are chopped and changed about too often; flexibility needs integration and coordination with the operational demands of the organisation. The requirement is to produce both work interest and effective output.
>
> It therefore becomes necessary for managers and supervisors to be trained in both behavioural and operational approaches to job enrichment if these approaches are to be effective.

Autonomous work groups

The general attraction of autonomous work groups is that they appear to address both the operational and psychological factors. The giving of autonomy in deciding the allocation of work, organisation and production, attention to quality and output based on broad performance targets (for example, to produce x amount of product y by deadline z) leaves the group itself to arrange and determine how these are to be achieved. This involves:

- participation in determining and allocating the work, scheduling of priorities and activities, meeting preferences, and gaining commitment to meeting the targets
- responsibility in ensuring that the broad targets are met and that stages along the total schedule are reached also
- esteem, in that a complete output is seen at the end of activities with which the individual member of staff can identify
- spirit and harmony, in that the contribution of everyone involved can be seen and valued
- developing fully flexible attitudes and capabilities through continuous individual and group development.

For autonomous working groups to be successful, high levels of skill and flexibility are required. Production technology and processes must be structured to meet behavioural as well as operational needs. Individual and group training and development is essential in all aspects of the work. The process is also greatly enhanced if the group is able to participate (or at least be consulted) on the target setting activities and to set its own means of quality control and assurance.

Attention to the working environment

The problems inherent in working environments were recognised by the Gilbreths and Gantt, who took steps to organise basic comforts such as rest rooms, canteens and chairs at the places where they worked.

Attention to the work environment is now a vastly wider field. It stems from the recognition that people bring their full range of needs to work with them and that the more of these that are met, the lower the levels of personal dissatisfaction likely to arise (see also Herzberg). Basic and adequate levels of comfort are required. The opportunity to sit down at the workstation, unless this is impossible for overriding operational reasons, should always be offered. Temperature is to be controlled and extremes of heat and cold avoided or managed. Good-quality furniture, decor and furnishings in all places of work reinforce the perceptions of value that organisations place on their staff; low-quality or decrepit furnishings and tatty decor tend to lead to low feelings of perceived value (see Example Box 15.3).

Attention to the people

The main features include the following.

- There must be absolute standards of honesty, integrity, expectations of perform-ance, quality of output, attitudes, values and ethics to which all those coming to work must aspire and conform.
- It is recognised that problems are inherent in all jobs, and work is organised around a philosophy of fairness and evenness that requires everyone to share in the problem areas and unattractive tasks.

EXAMPLE BOX 15.3 Attention to the Work Environment: Mars Chocolate Ltd

A former Mars manager recounts the tale of Mr Mars visiting a chocolate factory in mid-summer. He went up to the third floor where the biggest chocolate machines were placed. It was very hot. He asked the factory manager why there was no air conditioning. The factory manager replied that it wasn't in his budget and he had to meet that budget, which Mr Mars acknowledged was true. However, he asked the maintenance people to get all the factory manager's furniture and other items from his office and put them next to the big hot chocolate machine. A Mars under-manager said, 'The guy figured out that it was probably a pretty good idea to air condition the factory sooner rather than later. Mr Mars told him that once that had been completed he could move back to his office at any time he wanted.'

Source: T. Peters and N. Austin, *A Passion for Excellence*, Collins, 1985.

- There are absolute organisational standards for managing the staff. These are based on high levels of integrity, support, equality, training and development. Pay and reward levels tend to be high in return for high-quality work. Pay and reward methods are honest, clear and unambiguous. Communications between organisation and staff, and the general information flows, are regular, continuous and open.
- Everything that is done must contribute positively to the quality and volume of work required.
- The work environment is designed to support the output required and provide good standards of comfort and harmony, as well as integrating technology, operations and output.

The approach therefore is that, rather than addressing the causes of alienation, or taking action to minimise their effects, these are removed altogether. Also removed are factors that differentiate between levels of employee – for example executive dining rooms and individual car parking spaces – to emphasise equality in both personal and occupational terms.

In some cases, this has extended to the structure and ownership of the organisation. For example, employees have become part owners through company equity schemes (in the case of US Air, the majority shareholding is held by the staff). In others a proportion of pay is linked to the organisation's financial performance and a percentage of profits is paid out to the staff. In the best cases this is paid as a percentage of individual salary so that everybody receives the same proportion of reward. This again underlines equality of treatment, contribution and value.

Whichever view is taken, the desired outcome is the reconciliation of the organisational and operational drives with the technology and equipment that is to be used, and the effects of these on the staff. The ability to do this stems from a recognition and understanding of the influences of the technology, both operational and behavioural. Each approach addresses this issue from differing points of view. It also provides a level of understanding of the underlying causes of conflict and dissatisfaction inherent in any work situation.

Organisation design and structure

Organisations are designed and structured in order to:

- ensure the efficiency and effectiveness of activities in accordance with the organisation's stated targets
- divide and allocate work, responsibility and authority
- establish working relationships and operating mechanisms
- define patterns of management and supervision
- establish the means by which work is to be controlled
- find the means of retaining experience, knowledge and expertise
- indicate areas of responsibility, authority and accountability
- meet the expectations of those involved
- provide the basis of a fair and equitable reward system.

The general factors affecting organisation structure include the following.

- The nature of work to be carried out and the implications of this; unit, batch, mass and flow scales of production all bring clear indications of the types of organisation required, as do the commercial and public service equivalents; job definitions, volumes of production, storage of components, raw materials and finished goods; the means of distribution, both inwards and outwards; the type of support functions and control mechanisms.
- Technology and equipment; the expertise, premises and environment needed to use it effectively; its maintenance; its useful life cycle; its replacement and the effect of new equipment on existing structures and work methods.
- The desired culture and style of the organisation and all that this means. This affects the general approach to organisation management; nature and spans of control; the attitudes and values that are established; reporting relationships between superiors and subordinates and across functions; staff relationships.
- The location of the organisation; its relationships with its local communities; any strong local traditions, such as unionisation (or not); particular ways of working; specific activities, skills and expertise.
- Aims and objectives strategy; flexibility, dynamism, responsiveness, or rigidity and conformity in relation to staff, customers and the community; customer relations; stakeholder relations.

Organisation structures

Organisations may be structured as follows.

- **Tall structures:** in which there are many different levels or ranks within the total (see Figures 15.1 and 15.2). There is a long hierarchical and psychological distance between top and bottom. Tall structures bring with them complex reporting relationships, operating and support systems, promotion and career paths, and differentiated job titles. Spans of control (see below) tend to be small. The proportion of staff with some form of supervisory responsibility tends to be high in relation to the whole organisation.
- **Flat structures:** in which there are few different levels or ranks within the total. Jobs tend to be concentrated at lower levels. There is a short hierarchical distance between top and bottom, which may or may not reduce the psychological distance. Lower-level jobs often carry responsibilities for quality control, volume and deadline targets. Spans of control tend to be large. Career paths by promotion are limited; but this may be compensated by the opportunity for functional and expertise development, and involvement in a variety of different projects. Reward structures may not be as apparent as those offered alongside progress through a tall hierarchy. Reporting relationships tend to be simpler and more direct. There is a reduced likelihood of distortion and barriers to communications in a flat structure than in a tall one simply because there are fewer channels for messages to pass through.
- **Centralised structures:** in which centralisation is generally an authority relationship between those in overall control of the organisation and the rest of its staff. The tighter the control exerted at the centre, the greater the degree of centralisation. Even where organisations operate in wide ranges of activities and locations, top management may still seek to retain tight control over the ways in which activities are conducted.

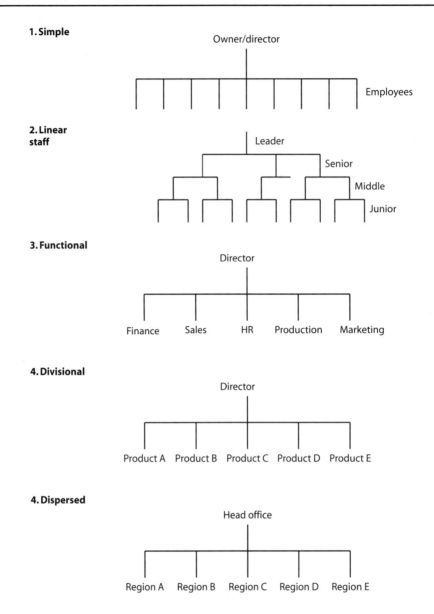

FIGURE 15.1 Organisation structures

- **Decentralised structures:** in which the role and function of the centre is to maintain a watching brief, to monitor and evaluate progress, and to concern itself with strategic rather than operational issues. The operations themselves are designed and allocated in accordance with overall aims and objectives, and the departments, divisions and functions given the necessary resources and authority to achieve them. The advantages of decentralisation are:
  - it speeds up operational decisions, enabling these to be taken at the point at

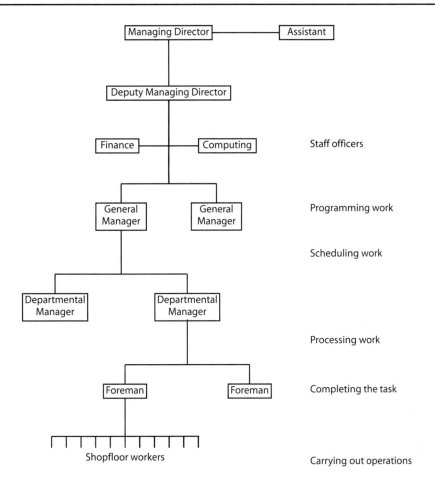

		Staff officers
		Programming work
		Scheduling work
		Processing work
		Completing the task
		Carrying out operations

Traditional organisational model   *FIGURE 15.2*

which they are required rather than having constantly to refer back to head office

- it enables local management to respond to local conditions and demands, and to build up a local reputation for the overall organisation
- it contributes to organisation and staff development through ensuring that problems and issues are dealt with at the point at which they arise. This helps organisations to identify and develop potential for the future; it also contributes to motivation and morale, as well as expertise development.

The role and function of head office

Head offices in all but the simplest structures have the responsibility for planning, coordinating and controlling the functions of the rest of the organisation; of translating strategy into operations; and of monitoring, reviewing and evaluating performance from all points of view: volume, quality, standards and satisfaction.

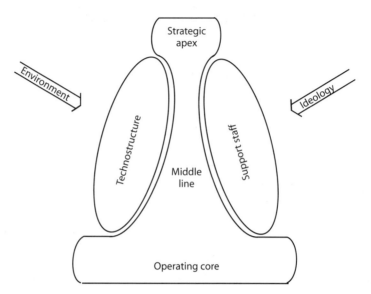

FIGURE 15.3 The Mintzberg model of organisations

In large, complex and sophisticated organisations – public, private and multi-national – the head office is likely to be physically distant from the main areas of operations and this brings problems of communications systems and reporting relationships. Equally important, however, is the problem of psychological distance and remoteness. This occurs when the head office itself becomes a complex and sophisticated entity. This often leads to conflict between personal and organisational objectives, in-fighting, concentrations of resources on head office functions rather than operational effectiveness. This is exacerbated when jobs at head office are, or are perceived to be, better careers and more likely to lead to personal opportunities than those in the field. In many cases the head office becomes so remote, that it loses any understanding of the reality of activities. Cocooned by the resources that it commands for its own functions, it may often preserve the illusion of excellence and dynamism in the face of overwhelming evidence to the contrary (see Example Box 15.4).

Spans of control

Spans of control relate to the number of subordinates who report directly to a single superior, and for whose work that person is responsible.

Spans of control are defined in a broad-to-narrow spectrum. The narrower the span, the greater the number of supervisors required by the organisation in total. A workforce of 40 with spans of control of four (one supervisor per four staff) needs ten supervisors (see Figure 15.4). The same workforce with a span of control of ten only needs four supervisors. If the principle is then developed as a hierarchy, it can be seen that in the first case additional staff are needed to supervise the supervisors.

The matter does require additional consideration, however. Narrow spans of control normally mean a tighter cohesion and closer working relationship between

Principles of organisation structure: a summary
TABLE 15.1

	Operational constraints		Key features	
	Environment	*Internal*	*Structure*	*Activities*
Simple structure	Simple/dynamic Hostile	Small Young Simple tasks CEO control	Direction + strategy	Direct supervision
Technocracy (*nadure*)	Simple/static Conformist	OM Large Regulated tasks Technocrat control	Technostructure	Standardisation of work
Professional bureaucracy	Complex/static	Complex systems Professional control	Operational expertise Professional practice	Standardisation of skills
Divisionalised bureaucracy	Simple/static Diversity Hostile	Old Very large Divisible tasks Middle-line control	Autonomy Reporting relationships	Standardisation of outputs Sophisticated supervision
Ad hocracy	Complex/ dynamic Committed	Often young Complex tasks Expert control	Operational expertise	Mutual adjustment
Missionary	Simple/static Committed	Middle-aged Often 'enclaves' Simple systems Ideological control	Ideology Standards	Policy, norms, standards
Network organisation	Dynamic Committed	Young Reformed	Operational expertise Technostructure	Networking

Source: H. Mintzberg, *The Structure of Organisations*, Prentice-Hall, 1979, and E. F. Johnson and K. Scholes, *Exploring Corporate Strategy*, Prentice-Hall, 1993.

supervisor and group. They also give greater promotion opportunities. There are more jobs, more levels and more ways of moving up through the organisation, and this may be a driving force for those within it and one of their key expectations.

If this principle is followed in larger organisations, layers of management and hierarchy can be removed by increasing spans of control. An organisation of 4000 staff would remove about 800 managers and supervisors by changing its spans of control from 4–1 to 8–1 (see Figure 15.5).

On the other hand, the complex structures created by narrow spans tend to act as barriers and blockages to communications: the greater the number of levels that messages have to pass through, the more likely they are to become distorted and corrupted.

EXAMPLE BOX 15.4   IBM

In 1992 IBM declared the highest-ever corporate loss in business history and John Akers, the Chief Executive Officer, was forced to resign.

The basis of the problem lay in the organisation's utter faith in its own excellence and infallibility. This was promulgated by head office in support of the company's main thrust of activities: mainframe computers and business operation systems. This was in spite of the fact that the emphasis of the computer world had switched to personal computers for both business and private use.

Belatedly, during the 1980s, the company started to develop its personal computer division, but sales were disappointing (due to the long lead times on delivery and the high prices charged) and the market continued to be dominated by those organisations that took the fast-moving consumer goods approach to computer sales. These companies produced equipment that was compatible with IBM business systems and effectively removed IBM from the market as the supplier of hardware.

The company failed to respond. It had been lionised in the 'Excellence' studies. It was a huge, multi-billion dollar corporation. Its technology and expertise were respected and held in awe the world over. Unfortunately, although this awe was a mark of technological respect, it was no longer being translated into the levels of sales necessary to support such an organisation. In particular, the company was slow to respond to the personal computer and software markets.

Subsequently, IBM has had to restructure and reposition itself. The priorities currently are:

- Development of industrial, commercial and public service management consultancy across North America, Asia and the countries of the European Union. The company also has fledgling operations in the former communist states of Hungary, the Czech Republic, Slovakia and Poland.
- Software development: working with subcontractors and small design houses to produce universal and globalised software packages compatible with both hardware and software. A key priority is the development of software packages for laptop and portable computers.
- The development of integrated organisational information systems, offered to organisations on the basis of 'one stop shopping', in which IBM effectively acts as the on-site permanent contractor for the maintenance, development and operation of integrated electronic information systems.

The crisis arose because the organisation and its Head Office had lost direction and contact with its markets. To date, the company restructuring has taken nearly ten years; alongside this, it has been necessary to institute flexible and dynamic attitudes and values, designed above all to make sure that never again will a centralised, institutionalised, and cocooned executive management cause such a crisis.

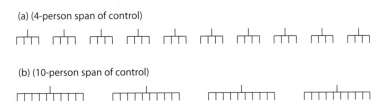

(a) (4-person span of control)

(b) (10-person span of control)

Spans of control: 1

FIGURE 15.4

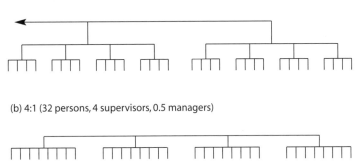

(a) 4:1 (32 persons, 8 supervisors, 2 managers)

(b) 4:1 (32 persons, 4 supervisors, 0.5 managers)

Spans of control: 2

FIGURE 15.5

On the face of it there is therefore, a trade off between the effectiveness of the organisation and the satisfaction of staff expectations through the availability of promotion channels. Assuming that the effectiveness of the organisation is paramount, it must seek ways to enable expectations to be set and met in ways that contribute to this. The absolute effectiveness of the promotion channels is therefore to be measured in this way, and where necessary different means of meeting staff expectations must be found.

Attention is then to be paid to operational factors. These are:

- The ability of management to produce results with spans of a certain size.
- The ability of the subordinates to produce results within these spans; in general, the greater the level of expertise held, the less direct supervision is required.
- The expectations of relative autonomy of the subordinates. For example, professional and highly trained staff expect to be left alone to carry out tasks as they see fit, while other types (such as retail cashiers) need to be able to call on the supervisor whenever problems, such as difficulties with customers, arise.
- The expectations of the organisation and the nature and degree of supervision necessary to meet these, or the ability of the staff concerned to meet these without close supervision.
- Specific responsibilities of supervisors that are present in some situations which give the supervisor a direct reason for being there other than to monitor the work

that is being carried out. The most common examples are related to safety – on construction sites and in oil refineries, for example – and to handling customer queries and complaints in shops and supermarkets.

- The nature of the work itself, the similarity or diversity of the tasks and functions, its simplicity or complexity.
- The location of the work, whether it is concentrated in one place or in several different parts of one building or site, or whether it is geographically diverse. Sub-spans are normally created where the location is diversified, even if ultimate responsibility remains with one individual, and boundaries of autonomy are ascribed to one person or group in the particular location.
- How far it is necessary and possible to coordinate the work of each group with all the others in the organisation; to coordinate and harmonise the work of the individuals in the group and to relate this again to the demands of the organisation.
- The organisation's own perspective: the extent to which it believes that close supervision, direct control and constant monitoring are necessary and desirable.

Hierarchies

Spans of control create hierarchies. These reflect the level, quality and expertise of those involved and also the degree of supervision and responsibility of those in particular positions. These are underpinned by job titles that indicate both levels of position held in hierarchy and also the nature and mix of expertise and responsibility.

Problems with hierarchies

The main issue is reconciling the need to divide and allocate work efficiently and effectively without the creation of blockages and barriers that the process of division tends to create.

Other areas include the following.

- Divergence of objectives; for example, the marketing department may be asked to create marketing initiatives with which it has no sympathy, or it may create marketing initiatives at variance with the products, style and image of the organisation. It may seek to enhance its own reputation, yet to pursue organisation objectives may be perceived as detrimental to this.
- If one of the functions of hierarchy is to provide career paths, then these may be blocked by long-serving officials in particular jobs. Vacancies may be filled by people who do not yet have the required expertise, or where this is recognised by the organisation, be filled by outsiders. Sudden departures in particular may leave a void which it is impossible to fill in the short term and which is then likely to lead to loss of departmental or organisation performance. In these cases outsiders may be brought in, again tending to lead to frustration for those already in position.
- Compartmentalisation: units and divisions tend to pursue their own aims and objectives as part of the process of competing for resources, prestige and status within the organisation rather than the overall purpose. Similarly, individuals pursuing career paths take whatever steps are necessary to get on to the next rung of the ladder; and again this may be detrimental to overall requirements.

- Responsibility: specific responsibilities are not always apparent. Things may not get done because nobody knows quite whose responsibility the matter in question is, or everyone involved thought that it was somebody else's area of operation. This is also a problem for the organisation's customers and clients, who may find it difficult to gain contact with the person specifically responsible for dealing with their problem.

- Rigidity: hierarchies can be very difficult to move once they are established. They may continue to exist in a given form after the purpose for which they were specifically created has been served. They often hinder the organisation development process and may act as a barrier to the introduction of new technology, project activities and culture and behaviour change.

Those responsible for the creation of organisation structures have therefore to recognise that whatever is done must satisfy the organisation's purposes and reconcile these with the problems and difficulties inherent. Any organisation form that arises must be capable of flexibility and responsiveness as well as creating order and stability.

Core and peripheral organisations

These forms of structure are based on a total reappraisal of objectives and activities with a view to establishing where the strategic core lies, what is needed to sustain it, and where, when and why additional support and resources are required.

The essential is the core. The rest is peripheral and may be seen as a shamrock or propeller (see Figure 15.6). This can be seen in the following ways.

- Professional and technical services and expertise, drawn in to solve problems, design and improve work methods and practices, and to manage change and act as catalysts and agents for change. All of these functions are conducted by outsiders on a contracted basis. Areas include marketing, public relations, human resource management, industrial relations, supplies, research and development, process and operations management and distribution.

- Sub-contracting of services such as facilities and environment management, maintenance, catering, cleaning and security. These are distinctive expertises in their own right, and therefore best left to expert organisations. This form of sub-contracting is now very highly developed across all sectors and all parts of the world as organisations seek to concentrate on their given expertise and minimise areas of non-contributory activity.

- Responses to operational pressures, in which staff are retained to be available at peaks (daily, periodical or seasonal) and otherwise not present. This has contributed to the increase in part time, flexible and core hours patterns of employment, and also to the retention of the services of workforce agencies, who specialise in providing particular volumes of expertise in this way.

- Outworking (often home working), in which staff work at alternative locations including home, avoiding the need for expensive and extensive facilities. This also enables those involved to combine work with other activities: parenting, study, working for other organisations. For this, people may be paid a retainer to ensure their continued obligation of loyalty. They may be well paid, even overpaid to compensate for periods when there is no work.

(a) *The Shamrock model*

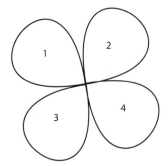

1. The core
2. Specialist
3. Seasonal staff
4. Staff on retainers for pressures and emergencies

(b) *The Propeller model*

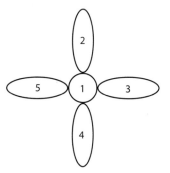

1. The core
2. Specialists
3. Subcontractors
4. Research and development
5. Seasonal staff

FIGURE 15.6 Core and peripheral

They may be retained on regular and distinctive patterns of employment: normally short-term or part-time.

The benefits lie in the ability to maximise resources and optimise staff utilisation. Rather than structuring the workforce to be available generally, the requirement for expertise and the nature of operations is worked out in advance and the organisation structured from this point of view. All activities that are to be carried out on a steady-state daily basis are integrated into the core. The rest are contracted or retained in one of the forms indicated.

Federations

Federations are extensions of the core and peripheral format (see Figure 15.7). They tend to be more or less regularised between organisations with their own specialisms that are then harmonised and integrated in the pursuit of overall stated objectives. Within this, each organisation has its distinctive identity and full autonomy to pursue and conduct other work as long as it meets its obligations and makes its contribution to the federation.

The main problem lies in integrating, coordinating and controlling the relationships and activities required of each contributor. The critical factors are ensuring mutuality of interest, continuity of general relationship, communications and

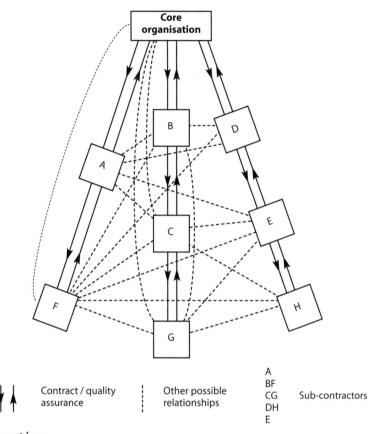

Contract / quality assurance   Other possible relationships

A
BF
CG   Sub-contractors
DH
E

Federation   *FIGURE 15.7*

harmony. The reporting relationship is based on a combination of work contract (or contract for services) and measures of integrity, rather than on a bureaucratic or legal/rational format.

Operationally, the critical factors are meeting volume and quality requirements and deadlines. A much simpler and clearer form of direction and purpose is likely to emerge as the result and this is focused on performance overall rather than procedures and functions.

The likelihood is therefore that organisations will seek to simplify all of their features as they become involved in this form of activity. As well as clarifying purpose, it also frees up resources that otherwise have to be used in accommodating staff and their equipment, supporting rules and procedures and the sub-functions that operate them.

Structures and expectations

Reference has already been made to the need for matching people's expectations with the opportunities that the organisation can offer. The traditional way of making progress through the ranks of organisations is well understood and has hitherto been a strong driving force especially for those in administrative, professional and technical grades. This has also opened up expectations for those in less skilled, front line and clerical jobs. As organisations drive towards simpler forms, federations, reduced hierarchies and scalar chains, and increased spans of control, there are fewer of these avenues available and competition for each position becomes greater. There is also, therefore, likely to be an increase in the quality of candidates from which to choose as each seeks to maximise his or her chance of gaining the particular position.

On the one hand, therefore, there is a great opportunity for organisations to choose excellent staff for key positions. On the other, there is the question of what to do with those who do not achieve these positions, bearing in mind that this may affect a large number of staff and lead to wider general dissatisfaction.

The matter is partly resolved by ensuring that expectations are set at realistic levels at the outset. The nature of avenues available must be made clear, whether these are based on promotion or variety, development, location and project work. The rewards to be gained through the pursuit of each should also be made clear. Organisations must also recognise that if these are higher for one path than for others, then individuals will gravitate towards this in preference to the others.

Structure and career development

In terms of organisation structure, the purpose is to translate the combination of expectations and anticipation for advancement that the individual brings with the prospects that the organisation can offer into a productive and positive relationship. For this to happen the position of each must be set clearly at the outset. There is no point in the organisation expecting loyalty and long service from the individual who anticipates rapid progression through the ranks if promotion channels are not open to all or very restricted. Similarly, there is no point in the individual expecting this form of progression if the organisation has made it quite clear that this is not open and that progress is based on variety and development rather than promotion through the ranks.

Organisations have therefore to establish the basis on which variety and progress is to be offered, what they expect of their staff in this context and where they place value on them.

Other points may usefully be made. Programmes of organisation and professional development must be seen as leading to goals and objectives. Staff who are given training and development normally expect to be able to practise their new skills and qualities and to attain some reward or enhancement as a result. In very few cases at present can organisations be certain that people have reached the absolute pinnacle of their potential, education, training or development and be sure of a particular niche for a long period of time. Even if this is the case, the niche is invariable subject to pressures of continuous improvement and development and this again places obligations on the long-term post holder. Successful people at all levels both raise their own expectations and have raised expectations placed on them by their organisation.

Structure and reward

A traditional driving force of the promotion path was normally that increased pay and therefore standards of living accrued as the result of progression upwards through the hierarchy. This was also a means of ensuring general measures of organisation talent and potential development, and of meeting the general expectations of enhancement of the staff. It was also seen to reward loyalty and commitment.

Today, two assumptions are regularly challenged. The first is that those at the top of the hierarchy should receive greater rewards than those lower down (see Example Box 15.5). The second is that this is the only way of developing and rewarding loyalty. Certainly, adequate means of reward have to be established. The organisation structure must be capable of doing this so that the contribution of everyone is seen to be valued. Once the connection is removed between rank and reward however, opportunities become available to assess this on the basis of whatever is of absolute value to the organisation, whether this is loyalty, output, professional development, invention, creativity or whatever.

The overriding concern is to ensure that rewards are targeted, paid out for achievement, give satisfaction and meet expectations. Rewards are not ends in themselves. People expect both continuity and improvement. In steady-state and rank-structured organisations especially, people forgo measures of instant or short-term reward in return for and expectation of this continuity and enhancement. In more turbulent organisations, the expectations is for shorter-term and enhanced levels of reward.

EXAMPLE BOX 15.5 Rewards

There are lessons to be learned from many sectors. The best-paid people in the entertainment sector are the entertainers themselves. Professional sports men and women earn more than tournament and competition managers and promoters.

In many cases labourers on construction sites earn more than site managers and supervisors. This is partly because of the hours that they have the opportunity to work and partly also because supervision is likely to be divided between several persons.

Productivity and output bonuses are often made available to factory and retail workers, enabling them to earn more than those on equivalent or higher (but non-front line) grades.

This has implications for promotion and development structures. People do not wish to lose money as the result of change (especially promotion) unless they know this will be only a short-term loss and that the prospects over the long-term are greatly improved.

Rewards must also meet basic expectations and be seen to be placing adequate levels of value on the efforts of the staff. A mail-order company based in Stoke-on-Trent, UK, asked its telesales staff to promote a distinctive range of kitchen products as part of their general workload. The initiative was highly successful and the 22 women involved sold £1 000 000-worth of products. The staff received a letter from the managing director of the company thanking them for their efforts. Enclosed with the letter was a small bar of chocolate. All of the staff felt insulted by this gesture; none found it to be an adequate expression of their efforts. Most said that they would rather have received nothing than such a slight gesture and token. The whole approach was perceived by the staff to be disrespectful and to belittle and denigrate their efforts.

Conclusions

Organisations are designed for particular purposes and circumstances and when these change the structure should move on also. The concept of organisation structure has come full circle: from the position of having a structure and seeking uses for it, to having a purpose and seeking the means to pursue it effectively.

The need for constant attention to the structure and design of organisations is reinforced by the speed of technological change, and the consequent effect on work patterns and priorities. Effective choice and use of technology requires attention to the volume and quality of production and output, the skills and qualities required for this, and also the wider effects on organisational functioning. Attention to investment in new technology and equipment has to be seen in this light. The best organisations concentrate on purpose, quality and suitability, as well as cost durability and returns. Investing in technology and equipment is a consequence of engaging in particular activities, and also has lasting implications for the future durability and viability of the organisation overall.

Related to this is the expense of carrying sophisticated support functions, hierarchies and administrative superstructures. It is also often very difficult to coordinate and harmonise these with the organisation's main purposes. They tend to generate lives of their own – aims and objectives, results areas, systems and reporting relationships – that are both time and resource consumptive, often out of all proportion to the actual purpose served or envisaged.

It is clearly necessary that organisations retain their permanence and their knowledge and expertise, in spite of the comings and goings of the staff. It is also necessary to coordinate and control activities, operations and resources. Most of the principles indicated therefore remain sound. However the creation of bureaucracies, human structures and pyramids, ranks and hierarchies, administrative systems and reporting relationships in the pursuit of permanence and order is not conducive to effective performance, clarity of purpose or optimum resource usage.

Overall therefore, it is very difficult to overstate the importance of attention to technology and its effects on organisational behaviour. In all circumstances, it affects organisation and work design and structure, and therefore working relationships, patterns of supervision, control and management style. It also affects the wider strategic and contextual views adopted.

The key lies in the choice and effective usage of technology. This involves attention to the volume and quality of production and output, the skills and qualities required to operate it effectively, and the quality of input and operation. Specific equipment must also be capable of harmonisation and integration with other technology that is used.

Attention to investment, levels and frequency of investment, and attitudes to investment have also to change. The best organisations concentrate on purpose, quality and suitability, as well as cost, durability and returns. Investing in technology and equipment is a consequence of engaging in particular activities.

Technological change, advance and innovation is also part of the equation. All organisations must be prepared to adapt, adjust, and even sacrifice, current equipment if and when others in the sector find better ways of doing things and better equipment to use. Again, there are implications for the skills, qualities and expertise required.

The impact of technology on organisational behaviour and performance is all-pervasive. This is both direct and indirect. It directly affects the size, nature and design of the environment and premises, the numbers of people required and their capabilities. It is also the focus around which support functions, processes and practices are devised and grouped, and directly affects the behaviour, motivation and morale of individuals and groups.

CHAPTER SUMMARY

There are clear complexities in trying to create and maintain organisational durability in the face of changing expertise and technology. It should be clear that problems are certain to arise when managers try to adapt their changing circumstances to the present organisational form, rather than seeking to create and maintain something that is capable of responsiveness and adaptation, as well as imposing its particular way of doing things on the environment and markets that it serves.

Approaches such as flexible working, multi-skilling, removal of demarcation lines, hot-desking, and virtual organisation have all been attempted in particular situations, with varying degrees of success. However, all too often, these fall into the trap of being perceived as 'quick fixes', and consequently

- are seldom given enough time to work
- are seldom fully thought out, with especial reference to the behavioural aspects
- are seldom fully evaluated in terms of what they are expected to achieve.

It is consequently essential that the behavioural aspects of structure, technology and design are addressed. As stated above, loyalties become divided: managers and others on career paths, as well as those with technological or professional expertise, find themselves retreating into the perceived safe world of group loyalties and occupational identity, rather than being engaged in addressing the real problems that organisations as a whole have to face. Such problems are very often compounded when top management of organisations take on consultants' recommendations without assessing the full implications. The pressure to do this is compounded if the particular consultancy is highly branded or extremely expensive.

There are also problems if career, professional and occupational paths are seen to be threatened. The groups of staff affected use their positions of influence to block developments in structure, design and technology, and this can lead to serious organisational dysfunction. Problems that arise in this way are then compounded if the organisation's top managers seek to impose changes by threat or force, rather than returning to the drawing board.

It is also essential that those responsible for designing and structuring organisations recognise that these problems and issues are certain to become very much more central to their future success and effectiveness. The speed of technological change renders present production, service and information output obsolete much more quickly; and the pressures are compounded, not eased, if a mechanistic approach is taken. Organisations must be designed to accommodate advances in technology and expertise, rather than considering them as professional, occupational or culture shocks. This requires a recognition and assumption by organisations of the broadest possible scope and scale of their responsibilities, and the creation of structural conditions that enable this to take place successfully and effectively. Investment in the structure and design of organisations is as essential as that required in expertise and technology.

DISCUSSION QUESTIONS

1. Discuss the view that truly rewarding and satisfying work is impossible to achieve because of the constraints placed on all occupations and organisations by technology and equipment.
2. Identify the opportunities and constraints placed on organisations by the establishment of formalised clocking-on procedures, and by the removal of such procedures.
3. Outline the nature, approach and attitudes required in order to establish effective, autonomous work groups. What broader responsibilities do organisations need to consider in order to ensure that these remain successful and effective in the long term?
4. What are the likely effects on the functional effectiveness upon those affected by a reduction in the number of levels in a hierarchy from twelve to three with no redundancies? What broader problems does this cause? What structural features should be created within organisations to keep these effects to a minimum?
5. Outline the main structural issues to be addressed when establishing a core and peripheral or federated working relationship.

CHAPTER CASE STUDY

CALL CENTRES

Call centres are in danger of becoming the dark, satanic mills of the twenty-first century as the industry gains a reputation for sweatshop practices and assembly-line methods. Centres already exist where staff sit in tiny pens and cubicles with high screens around them, or else in assembly-line rows. A report by the Merchants Group in 1997 said that 'in a survey of 106 call centres, morale was low, stress levels high, and absenteeism was running at 5 per cent, compared with the national figure of 3.5 per cent'.

Early in their development, call centres became a victim of their own success with response far outstripping projections. High stress levels were caused by the sheer volume of calls, wrongly forecasted levels of success, heavy pressure on achieving targets, and inadequate and cramped working conditions.

The call centre industry continues to expand rapidly. It employs about 200 000 people, and this is predicted to rise to five million in the next three years. Recent research by Incomes Data Services (IDS) into pay and conditions in call centres shows that their rapid growth has led to rising pay settlements, intense competition for staff, and high levels of turnover (up to 25 per cent per annum in some cases), and these are all attributed to competition between centres and the intensity of work. The speed of growth in the call centre industry has meant effective management strategies are often left behind. Organisations are not properly structured, and little consideration has been given to the enduring effects on morale, output, performance and profits of the relationship between staff and technology. Centres that do not invest in training, development and organisation design are bound to suffer from high rates of absenteeism, poor performance, and increases in labour turnover, according to the Chartered Institute of Personnel and Development.

Jim Parle, business personnel manager at Halifax Direct, which has 800 staff, agrees that stress is a symptom of poor management but argues that call centres are no different to any other working environment.

> Of course, there are pressures when an operation is based on bottom line cost figures, but it is important to balance the customer's needs with appropriate working practices. You have start from a premise that no one works a 7-hour day, and allow time for breaks, feedback, team meetings and training.
>
> *Management Today*

The industry has consequently gained for itself a reputation as a high stress area. However, there is some evidence that the environment is changing. As Phil Harris, sales director of the CallCentric consultancy, notes:

> Until recently, call centres were driven by productivity and keeping the costs as low as possible. Activities were largely functionalised so that people got bored or felt they were being driven to achieve numbers. The focus on productivity is giving way to a realisation that it costs a lot to win new customers. Staff therefore have to become more highly valued because they maintain the relationship with existing customers.
>
> *Management Today*

Far removed from the assembly-line image, Autobar, a catering wholesaler which handles 6000 calls a day, encouraged a fun environment for its call centre teams, with cartoons on the walls, and comic team identities such as the sharks and the bears.

Phil Harris forecasts that it will take five years for call centres to be perceived as career opportunities rather than short-term jobs at low wages. Some organisations are already introducing NVQs and job gradings so that staff can see that there is a career ladder.

Call centre work varies enormously. It ranges from telesales and marketing to technical assistance and emergency response. Before setting up a call centre, companies should be certain that they have the capability, technology, expertise, and structure of organisation; this must be related to capability and effectiveness in forecasting the projections of workload.

Source: adapted from *Management Today* 'One Minute Briefs', February 1999.

QUESTIONS

1. Comment on the view expressed that 'staff can see that there is a career ladder'. What form of career ladder is required in this industry in order to make career paths attractive to those coming into it?

2. Why do people get bored with this form of work? What can, and should, be done to alleviate this? To what extent do the 'cartoons on the walls' alleviate the sense of boredom and alienation in the short term and in the long term?

3. What form of management and supervisory style is appropriate to activities such as these, and why?

16 Human Resource Management

'We cannot have the monkeys running the zoo.' Frank Bormann, labour relations director, Eastern Airlines, 1984.

'Retention of key staff is too often dealt with by simply offering them more money. While it is important to reward people fairly for what they do, employees are far more likely to remain in an environment in which they feel valued and get real satisfaction from their work.' Mark Edelsten, human resources consultant, *Management Today,* February 1999.

'Better managed staff are happier, more motivated and more productive; and well managed companies often attract better staff than their competitors.' Mike Walmsley, Parker Bridge, *Evening Standard,* 24 November 1998.

CHAPTER OUTLINE

The context of human resource management

The coverage of human resource management: staffing planning; recruitment, selection and retention; performance measurement; pay and rewards; development; industrial and workplace relations

The relationship between effective human resource management practice and organisational profitability, effectiveness and viability

Fundamental principles of equality and fairness

Legal, social and ethical constraints in the management of people.

CHAPTER OBJECTIVES

After studying this chapter, you should be able to:

understand the importance and value of human resource management as a universal part of management expertise

understand the contribution made by effective recruitment, selection, retention and reward activities

understand the importance and value of establishing and managing effective workplace relations

understand the direct relationship between effective staff management practices, and sustained profitable and effective output.

Introduction

The concept and basis of human resource management (HRM) has moved from welfare concerns and a moral or enlightened attitude to the staff and workers of organisations, through highly structured and highly staffed personnel functions, to 'resource management'. This does have the initially disquieting connotation that the human resource is to be exploited in the same way as land, capital, technology and information.

However, this should be seen in a context of responsibility and obligations on the part of the organisation, its managers and its staff; the necessity to maintain and develop the resource (as with any other); and to see in true terms, the requirement to gain a return on the investment in the human resource (and all that truly means). It then sits easier from the moral standpoint, as well as making sound managerial sense. Effective HRM is a highly cost-effective, even profitable, aspect of management.

The main strategic areas of activity are as follows:

- devising a staff management style that sets the approach and standards of employee relations
- analysing and packaging work into jobs and occupations
- providing a service function, maintaining and improving management of staff at the workplace
- planning for the required staff; recruiting, motivating and developing
- industrial relations and staff management systems
- setting performance standards for everyone, providing the means of measuring and appraising performance, and supporting performance with procedures and practices
- devising and implementing fair payment systems
- providing and implementing strategies for change that address the organisational and 'human aspects'
- meeting general obligations to staff; there is a general duty of care, as well as legal and ethical requirements (in the UK and EU there is extensive legal protection for all workers).

All of these is best managed if they are fully integrated into general management practice and supported by specialist corporate HR functions. There is a direct correlation between the ways in which each aspect is addressed and approached, and organisation success, effectiveness and profitability (see Table 16.1).

Equal opportunities

Equality of treatment, opportunity and access is an issue of attitude, or corporate state of mind. It is a fundamental prerequisite to the creation of organisation and operation effectiveness. By law, managers and organisations must overcome the tendency to compartmentalise people by race, gender, religion, disability and membership of trade unions. Morally and ethically, it is also essential that marital status, location, postal address, non-essential qualification, school background, club membership, hobbies and interests are also discounted. The key standpoint is isolating the qualities essential and desirable to carry out work. People must be viewed in terms of their potential as staff members, as contributors to the success and prosperity of the organisation. Without this, true equality of opportunity cannot exist.

There is also a question of basic human decency that requires that all people be treated the same. This is a social as well as organisational concern. For organisations,

Human resource management summary

TABLE 16.1

Area of work	Corporate HR strategy	Managerial operations and direction
Work design and structuring	Principles, approaches, departmentalisation, organisation structure	Job descriptions, work patterns, work structuring
Staff planning	Systems appraisal, design commissioning	Systems usage
Recruitment and selection	Standpoint (grow your own, buy in from outside)	Training of recruiters and selectors, recruitment and selection activities
Induction	Policy, content, priority	Delivery
Use of agencies and external sources of staff	Principles, circumstances	Contacts and commissions
Performance appraisal	Purpose, systems, design, principles, aims and objectives	Systems implementation, training of appraisers and appraisees
Pay and rewards	Policy, levels, mix of pay and benefits, package design	Assimilate individual staff to policy
Occupational health	Policy, content, design of package	Operation of package in conjunction with functional departments
Equality	Standards, policy, content, context, ethics	Policy operation, monitoring of standards, remedial actions
Industrial relations	Standpoints (conflict, conformist), representation	Negotiations, consultation, participation, staff communications
Discipline	Policy, procedure, practice, design, standpoint	Implementation of policy and procedure, support for staff, training of all staff
Grievance	Policy, procedure	Implementation of policy and procedure, training of all staff
Training and development	Priority and resources	Activities, opportunities, accessibility
Dismissal	Standards of conduct, examples of gross misconduct	Operation of disciplinary procedures, operation of dismissal procedures, support and advice

/continued overleaf

TABLE 16.1 (continued)

Human Resource Management is divided into strategic and directional activities, and personnel activities. The role and function is:

- policy, advisory, consultative, supporting, a point of reference
- personnel practitioner
- establisher of policy content
- establishing standards of best practice
- creator of personnel activities
- monitor/evaluator of personnel activities.

all activities, management styles, policies, practices and procedures, publications, advertisements, job and work descriptions, and person specifications should be written in ways that reinforce this. This emphasises, formulates and underlines the required attitudes and beliefs.

Offering equality of opportunity to all sectors of the workforce is both cost-effective and profitable. By concentrating on (discriminating against) certain sectors of the population on operational grounds, organisations greatly limit their prospects either of making effective appointments or of maximising the human resource.

The lead therefore comes from the top of organisations and the attitudes filter down to all the staff. Organisational equal opportunities policies must be clear, unequivocal and easily understood by all concerned. They must be valued and adopted at all levels and in all sectors and departments. A genuine adoption of the principle of equality for all constitutes excellent marketing to the human resource of the organisation. Staff are known to be valued for their capabilities. It also underlines any high moral or ethical stance taken in other business and organisational activities.

Staff planning

This is a dynamic and continuous process of which all managers should have a good understanding. This is because of the increasing complexity of organisations and activities; legislation; the availability of required expertise; technological changes and advances; labour turnover patterns; the structure of the workforce; the changing nature of labour markets; imbalances between the skills available and those required; the nature of core and peripheral workforces. All of this is increasingly an expected and integral part of the task of any manager in every functional area and activity.

The key elements involved are as follows:

- **Work analysis** to order jobs and occupations in ways that are interesting, rewarding and fulfilling to the individual, and profitable and effective to the organisation.
- Assessing the **staff mix** by each of, and a combination of, the following criteria: age; length of service; jobs held; promotions; sex, race and ethnic origin; skills, knowledge and expertise in different categories; flexibility and transferability; building a comprehensive staff and workforce profile.
- Matching **supply** and **demand** of staff; matching actual with desired capability.

- **Future projections** for staff, based on accurate and informed projections of business activity and the HRM activities that are implicit in this.
- **Specific problems:** including absenteeism and turnover; sickness and accident rates; nature, location and causes of disciplinary problems, grievances and disputes.
- **Serious problems:** the nature, location and causes of bullying, victimisation, harassment, discrimination, vandalism and violence.
- **Staff and HR information and computer systems:** and the information that they contain. Managers are concerned not so much with the content and components of these systems as with the conclusions, use and value of the information.
- **Constraints:** especially resource constraints and those imposed by budget considerations and other operational factors. These include location and any consequent implications for the nature and type of workforce; the history and traditions of industrial and commercial activity in the area in question; and operational constraints that may be imposed by ways of working and industrial relations agreements.

With each of these elements, there is a corporate HR and general management responsibility to ensure that every aspect is addressed. Where problems are known, believed or perceived to be arising, remedial action is required.

Fitting the work to people; fitting the people to work

This process is abbreviated to FWP–FPW (see Figure 16.1).

The approach requires a full understanding of the critical behaviour, attitudes, skills, knowledge, expertise and technological proficiency required, and the ability to:

- match these with job and work requirements, prioritising them into essential and desirable categories
- understand the professional and occupational demands of those with these capabilities
- recognise the strengths and shortcomings of the present working environment in terms of attracting and retaining staff who have these capabilities
- understand the aspects of the work that are boring, dirty, dangerous or stressful, and therefore likely to put people off.

A full understanding of the FPW–FWP balance provides a sound basis on which to address each of the following.

- **Job and work descriptions:** parcelling up tasks into occupations and patterns of work.
- **Person specifications:** the behaviour, attitudes, skills, knowledge, expertise and technological proficiency required and asked for in job holders; these reflect the requirements of the job and work descriptions, and also provide the basis for selection.
- **Selection:** identifying how the critical behaviour, attitudes, skills, knowledge, expertise and technological proficiency aspects are to be tested in individuals for capability and willingness; identifying how best to test, observe and infer the particular qualities (see Example Box 16.1).
- **Induction:** the approach identifies those qualities required as a condition of

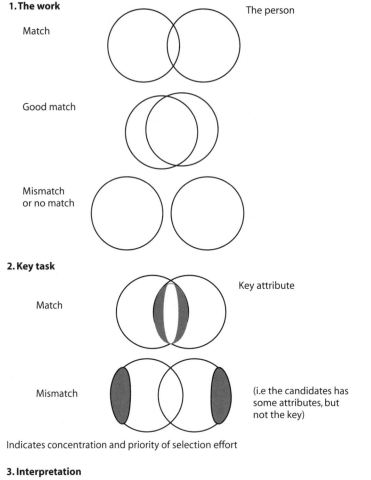

1. The work

The person

Match

Good match

Mismatch
or no match

2. Key task

Key attribute

Match

Mismatch

(i.e the candidates has
some attributes, but
not the key)

Indicates concentration and priority of selection effort

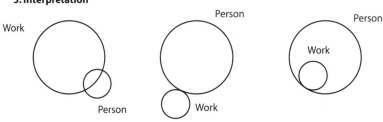

3. Interpretation

Work

Person

Person

Person

Work

Person

Work

Work

Job is too large for person,
leading to stress and
dysfunction

Person is too large for
job, but has no attribute
for it

Person is too large for job, has
attribute for it, but will soon
get bored

Purpose: indicates requirement to define personal attributes in relation to the job.
In all organisations, the process must be **validated.** The relationship between key tasks and key attributes
must be related to effective performance.
It must also be **reliable.** Any test used to predict performance from the process must demonstrate the
quality concerned, and relate it to performance, in all circumstances.

FIGURE 16.1   Fitting the work to people; fitting the people to
work

EXAMPLE BOX 16.1   Personality and Psychometric Tests

Personality and psychometric tests are extensively applied, especially by large organisations in the identification and selection of managers and others for key appointments. Candidates are asked a series of structured questions about their personality; the results are then fed into computer programs and 'personality assessments' are drawn out. Versions of these tests are now available on organisation and specialist provider websites, thus making the process even more impersonal.

Those responsible for the development and professionalisation of management and other technical, vocational and occupational expertise have long viewed these tests with suspicion. The Chartered Institute of Personnel and Development has produced at least three reports in which psychometric and personality tests are described as 'useless for predicting the future performance'. It is much more effective to concentrate on isolating specific occupational and other areas for testing, and then asking candidates to undertake tests. This also has the benefit of drawing attention to those areas that cannot be precisely tested, and consequently requiring managers, supervisors and HR professionals to think deeply about how they are going to observe or infer the specific characteristics required.

---

employment. Induction is required to ensure that people learn quickly and effectively how these are to be applied.

- **Employee and organisation development:** the approach identifies those areas where expertise and capability are either not present or else in need of improvement. It therefore contributes to defining collective and individual development requirements, and provides a basis for an orderly and structured approach.
- **Work patterns:** reflecting the demands for maximising and optimising returns on investment in technology and expertise, and ensuring that products and services are available to customers and clients at their convenience.
- **Pay and rewards:** balancing the demands of those coming into work with what is on offer; and recognising the actual and potential problems of retention.

Pay and rewards

The elements required in effective staff pay and reward schemes are as follows.

- **Expectations:** all systems must meet the expectations of the job holder to a greater or lesser extent if they are to be attract and retain staff in the required occupations.
- **Motivation:** within the constraints illustrated above, all payment and reward motivates to a greater or lesser extent; the levels of reward offered to particular job holders also carry implications for the nature, complexity and commitment to the work in hand that is required on their part.
- **Mixes of pay with other aspects:** much of also this relates to expectations; for example, the offer of a company car to professional and managerial staff is still very attractive in the UK, in spite of the diminishing tax advantage.

- **Occupational aspects:** part of the reward package may include the provision of specialist or expert training and equipment.
- **International, organisational and local variations:** these relate to the mix of payment and other benefits in the total reward package. In the UK, there is a wide variety of components; in Switzerland, on the other hand, only 2 per cent of managers receive a company car, preferring instead (collectively) a higher level of salary.
- **Respect and value:** levels of pay and other rewards on offer reflect the actual respect, value and esteem in which staff collectively, and also individual job holders, are held.
- **The nature of the work and working environment:** recognising that pay and rewards are one aspect only; these have to be matched against the opportunities and constraints of the working environment (see Example Box 16.2).

EXAMPLE BOX 16.2 Mass Production and Output Work

Food processing technology enables meat and vegetables to be frozen, dried and preserved for long periods of time. It also enables the wider production of all convenience foods and drinks. However the work itself, consisting mainly of watching the products being processed, and either picking out samples for testing or clearing up blockages when they occur, is extremely tedious and debilitating. For example, those who watch peas being freeze-dried frequently complain of nightmares (with the peas as the central feature).

Originally, the only HRM activity in use was the rotation of staff between different production lines. Each task quickly became equally disaffecting, and it was thus impossible either to motivate or retain the staff for more than very short periods of time. The food processing companies therefore concentrated their efforts on having a steady influx and supply of labour, rather than addressing the possibilities of reanalysing or redesigning the work that needed doing. Consequently, a substantial part of the cost advantage of mass production and technology was being lost in the constant pursuit of a pool of staff, and through staffing problems arising at the workplace.

This also applies to mass production, output and employment in the new industries. Call centres require a steady stream and influx of labour to compensate for the tedious, and often adversarial, conditions that are the cornerstone of their employment practices. Much VDU work is also boring, tedious and repetitive. In each case, problems are compounded by a lack of attention to the quality of working life or working environment.

The ways in which work is arranged and organised impinge on rulebooks, work practices, departmentalisation, divisionalisation, industrial relations, selection, training and development. If work is boring, there will be high levels of disputes, absenteeism, self-certificated sickness; high levels of managerial time and resources used up in the operation of procedures; and over-supervision of such things as time-clocks, work sheets, and meal breaks. It also has a great effect on the total atmosphere of the place of work, and 'canteen cultures' can easily take hold.

This form of work is both physically and mentally debilitating as well as expensive.

> **Example Box 16.2 (continued)**
>
> It has caused industrial and production organisations to seek alternative methods and patterns of employment and approaches to mass labour work.
>
> The Hawthorne experiments (see Chapter 1) demonstrated as part of their findings that work, in itself mundane, could nevertheless be conducted much more effectively by strengthening the personal and group identity of those carrying it out, while at the same time ensuring that management control was not lost to any potential informal system. The lighting experiments referred to, and the effects on both the experimental and the control group, underline this.
>
> Japanese manufacturing companies setting up in the West also go to a lot of trouble to remove some of the negative pressures. They instead create a positive atmosphere and culture based on valuing the contribution of everyone. Some companies have removed time-clocks and other forms of adversarial supervision practice. The quality of working life is maintained at all times. High levels of pay, in return for high-quality work, have caused a reduction in absenteeism and turnover. This is underpinned by offering development and advancement opportunities for all, and a greater personal responsibility for and commitment to work quality and achievement.

Components of wage, salary or reward packages

These are composed as follows.

- **Payment:** annual, quarterly, monthly, four-weekly, weekly, daily. Commission, bonus, increments, fees. Profit, performance and merit related payments (see Example Box 16.3).
- **Allowances:** attendance, disturbance, shift, weekend, unsocial hours, training and development, location and relocation, absence from home.
- **Benefits:** loans (e.g. for season tickets), pension (contributory or non-contributory), subsidies (on company products, canteen, travel), car, telephone/car phone, private health care, training and development, luncheon vouchers.
- **Chains of gold or super-benefits:** school holidays (teachers); cheap loans (banks); free/cheap travel (railway, shipping, airlines); pension arrangements (for older or longer-serving staff).
- **Economic rent:** high rates of pay for particular expertise (especially scarce expertise or that which is required at short notice).
- **Basic equality:** ensuring that the levels of pay, and other elements, are offered from a fundamental basis of equality; problems arise when benefits and allowances are awarded on the basis of status rather than work requirement.
- **Incentives:** relating pay directly to output (see Example Box 16.3).

Maintenance factors in human resource management

The basis of this approach is that the human resource requires maintenance in the same way as other aspects and resources of the organisation if it is to be maximised and optimised. Current issues are:

EXAMPLE BOX 16.3 Profit and Performance Related Pay: Ground Rules

The basis of any such scheme must be to relate as precisely as possible the rewards to staff with the effectiveness and success of their work. This is best achieved as follows.

- The scheme must be believed in, valued and understood by all concerned.
- Targets must be achievable. They must neither be too easy, or too difficult. Their purpose is to balance effective effort and effective output.
- Targets must be set in advance. If they are achieved, payments must always be made.
- The aim is to reward effort and achievement on the part of all the staff whatever their role or occupation.
- The language and presentation of the scheme should be positive and aimed at 'rewards for achievement'. The scheme's rules should not be couched in bureaucratic phraseology.

Notes

- Profit and performance related pay is not a means of cutting wage and salary bills. The purpose is to reward effective efforts not to penalise them. Profit and performance related pay normally increase wage and salary bills because people normally work much more effectively when their efforts are distinctively targeted.
- Effective profit and performance related pay ensures that all staff are focused on the purposes for which they are supposed to be working, and that they also assume a positive stake in operational success.
- Profit related elements: the allocation of percentage, or proportion, or amount from the surplus generated by the organisation to the staff. The means by which this is to be allocated should always be made clear in advance of any actual award in the interests of both fairness and confidence in the scheme. Some organisations offer shares and equity in the organisation to build staff commitment, public confidence and the market value of the organisation. Others offer cash bonuses. Cash bonuses should reward all on an equitable basis. This is often best achieved through giving everyone an equal percentage of their annual salary.
- Those assessing profit and performance related pay, and those being assessed, must have full confidence in each other.

- induction
- organisation and employee development
- work design and flexibility
- occupational and personal health.

Induction

The purpose of induction is to get the new member of staff as productive as possible, as quickly as possible. This consists of matching the organisation's needs with those of the individual as follows.

- Setting the **attitudes and standards of behaviour** required, ensuring that new employees know what is expected of them, and that they conform to these expectations and requirements. It is most important that the organisation assumes absolute responsibility for this, rather than allowing employees to set their own standards, or for these to emerge by default.
- **Job training and familiarisation**, mainly to do with the ways of working required by the organisation, and ensuring that these are matched with the new employee's expertise; and establishing the required standards and methods of work.
- **Introductions** to the team, work colleagues, and other key contacts as part of the process of gaining confidence, understanding and mutuality of objectives required for the development of effective working relationships and environment.
- **Familiarisation with the environment,** premises, ways of working, and particular obligations on the part of the employer; ensuring that new employees understand their position in this environment; emergency procedures and health and safety.

Commitment is vital. Many organisations go to much trouble to ensure that all this is adequately and effectively completed, recognising the returns on an excellent and well-resourced induction process in the production of a highly motivated and committed workforce.

The induction process will have been started in general terms by any vague impression that the new employee has picked up of the organisation; it will have been further reinforced if, for example, he or she has been a customer or client. Any correction of these impressions must also be addressed as part of the induction process, which will also be reinforced by the ways in which the selection process is conducted.

Organisation and employee development

This is designed in terms of the formation of attitudes and standards at the workplace, the division, regulation and allocation of the work, and the need to develop both. Each is undertaken with the intention of generating a greater measure of positive commitment, a reduction of workplace alienation, and enhanced quality of output. This normally involves initial and continuing job training, job rotation and progression schemes, project work, secondments, and fixed-term, action-learning placements. Related to this is the ever-increasing obligation on employees to maintain and improve their skills, knowledge and technical expertise in the interests of continuing organisation effectiveness. Conversely, the expectations of those at work have also changed, and part of the job design process increasingly includes improving the quality of working life.

Work design and flexibility

This involves a much greater awareness and willingness on the part of organisations to relate the hours of work that they offer to the non-work commitment and aspirations of potential staff members. This means having regard to:

- the use of flexitime, annual hours and other flexible work patterns
- job sharing

- working away from the organisation, and especially allowing staff to work at home and providing them with the means and workstations to do so
- the devising of shift patterns especially to fit around those with primary responsibility for looking after young children.

More widely, organisations may offer career breaks: extended periods of time off for employees in which they may go to do other things. Organisations may also offer 'returner schemes' pitched primarily at those who have had lengthy periods of time out of work, usually for the purpose of bringing up a family. The returner scheme tackles the issues of familiarisation, confidence-building and personal and professional comfort that are the concerns of anyone coming into a job after a lengthy break. Such schemes also provide specific job training and retraining where necessary. Organisations may also underline their commitment to these creative approaches through the provision of nursery facilities for very young children; canteen facilities that are open all day so that all work patterns are accommodated; and through the adoption of general ways of working and workplace attitudes that place the same intrinsic value on all members of staff regardless of any particular pattern of work.

Occupational and personal health

Organisations are increasingly assuming responsibility for the good health of their staff and taking positive steps to ensure this. This consists of determining that employees are fit and healthy when they first start work, and that this continues throughout the period of employment. For those who have persistent or regular time away from work there may be assessments by company medical staff as well as the employee's own doctor. This may require the employee, moreover, to take medical treatment at the behest of the organisation as a condition of continuing to work for it. Occupational health schemes at the workplace are, in the best cases, particularly strong and valuable in the early diagnosis of job-specific illnesses and injuries. They also provide a valuable general source of medical knowledge by which the organisation may assess the overall state of their workforce's health.

Particular matters related to the workplace have come to the fore and gained recognition and currency. Major issues of which any manager should be aware include the following.

- stress, its causes and effects and techniques for its management (see Example Box 16.4)
- repetitive strain injuries (RSI) which are caused by continuous use of certain muscles or the carrying out of certain activities, such as continuous keyboard working and process work
- back injuries, caused either by bad lifting practices or a continuous bad back posture
- the effects of VDU screens on eyesight
- industrial and commercial heating and lighting and the relationship between these and eye strain, coughs, colds and other minor, but recurrent, ailments
- smoking, both active and passive, and the effects of it on all staff (both in relation to health and also more general concerns as odours) (see Example Box 16.5)
- alcohol abuse (see Example Box 16.5)

> ### EXAMPLE BOX 16.4 Stress
>
> Stress may be either positive or negative. It essentially consists of the amount of pressure present in a given situation in which the individual finds himself. The sources of stress are occupational, role-related, organisational, hierarchical, social and personal; and stresses on the individual result from an imbalance of these.
>
> There is, in particular, a growing awareness of the links between work and stress and other illnesses such as nervous exhaustion, executive and professional burn-out, heart conditions and high blood pressure.
>
> Managers therefore have a threefold role: to recognise it as an issue; to prevent stress among staff; and to recognise it in themselves and take steps to limit it. The managerial role in this therefore consists of:
>
> - recognising stress as an issue
> - identifying the sources of stress in the particular situation
> - taking active steps to prevent stress among staff
> - taking active steps to recognise and limit it during the pursuit of managerial tasks.
>
> The best organisations institutionalise the recognition for the potential for stress, and are aware of its sources. Good occupational health schemes are designed so that its effects are addressed immediately they become apparent.

- HIV and AIDS, and the implications for particular workplaces and occupations (see Example Box 16.6).

Industrial relations

Industrial relations – or employee relations, employment relations, staff relations – is the system by which workplace activities are regulated, the arrangement by which the owners, managers and staff of organisations come together to engage in productive activity. It concerns setting standards and promoting consensus. It is also about the management of conflict.

Much of this has its roots in the economic and social changes of the industrial revolution and the urbanisation of the nineteenth century; the inherent conflict between labour and the owners of firms; the formation of collectives, combinations of groups of workers to look after their own interests; and the demarcation lines and restrictive practices that some occupations and trades were able to build up. The influence of these traditions remains extremely strong, particularly in long-established industries such as factory work, transport and mining. However, in recent years there has been a serious attempt to change the attitudes of all concerned in this field, and to generate a more positive and harmonious ethos. Companies and their managers have come to recognise the importance of positive industrial relations and the contribution that they make to profitable and effective organisational performance; some trade unions have seen this as an opportunity to secure their future, and to attract new members. Other

EXAMPLE BOX 16.5 Organisational Approaches to Tobacco, Alcohol and Drugs

These are dealt with because they are current, high-profile and contentious issues.

Organisations should make clear the stance to be adopted on each, giving a clear lead to managers and staff. Whatever the outcome it should reflect organisational requirements, and not simply be allowed to evolve unmanaged. Organisations may set any standard that they wish on each of these issues (provided that they also conform with the law).

Organisations that wish to exclude smoking from their premises may do so. In the implementation of this, they should consult with staff, and offer counselling and support to those who have to change behaviour fundamentally. They will follow the consultation process and timescale referred to elsewhere.

Staff who have addiction problems should be supported by organisations; they should be offered counselling, rehabilitation and reference to medical authorities except in the rare cases where this is impossible.

There is a moral as well as an operational imperative here that is increasingly being recognised as part of the organisation's total commitment, ethical stance and wider obligations to its staff. Levels of support for members of staff through programmes and periods of treatment will be directed both at treating the matter in hand and at rehabilitating staff, getting them back into productive and effective work.

EXAMPLE BOX 16.6 AIDS: Acquired Immune Deficiency Syndrome

Organisational policies towards AIDS and the HIV virus must address the following.

- They must include blood tests for potential members of staff, if necessary, as part of regular check-ups and other occupational health matters.
- They must include a continuing obligation to those members of staff who contract the virus while working at the organisation.
- They must include reference to customer contact, covering both clients and staff who have the virus.

The overall purpose is to ensure that all those who work in or deal with the organisation know where they stand in regard to this issue. In addition, the extent and nature of the organisation's precise obligations are thus at least defined for its own purposes, in an area where the extent and coverage of the law is not yet clear.

Operationally, there are problems of organisation and staff insurance that have to be addressed. From a cultural and perceptual stance, there are issues concerning the mystique, legends, and levels of knowledge of the matter that must be considered, with the purpose of generating understanding, enlightenment, and a suitable and effective way of working.

unions have lost influence because of the great numbers of jobs that have disappeared in the sectors that they represent.

Three distinct approaches may be clearly identified.

- **Unitarism:** which assumes that the objectives of all involved are the same or compatible and concerned only with the well-being of the organisation and its products, services, clients and customers. The most successful of unitary organisations (e.g. McDonald's, Virgin, IMG) set very distinctive work, performance and personal standards, to which anyone working in the company must conform. This is also inherent in the Japanese approach to the management of the human resource.
- **Pluralism:** admitting a variety of objectives, not all compatible, among the staff. Recognising that conflict is therefore present, organisations establish procedures and systems to manage it and limit its influence as far as possible. This is the approach taken especially in public services, local government and many industrial and commercial activities where diverse interests have to be reconciled so that productive work may take place.
- **Radicalism:** the view that commercial and industrial harmony is impossible until the staff control the means of production, and benefit from the generation of wealth. Until very recently, this was a cornerstone of the philosophy of many trade unions and socialist activists in industry, commerce and public services.

IR strategies

Industrial relations (IR) strategies ultimately depend on the industrial or commercial sector concerned, or whether it is public or government serviced. One of the following positions is normally adopted.

- **Conflict:** the basis on which staff are to be dealt with is one of mistrust, divergence, irreconcilable aims and objectives; disparity of location; divergence and complexity of patterns of employment and occupations; professional, technical, skilled and unskilled staff. In such cases as this, the IR strategy will be devised to contain the conflicts, and to reconcile differences; and to promote levels of harmony as far as possible.
- **Conformity:** where the diversity of staff and technology may be (and often is) as great as in the above scenario, but where the IR strategy rather sets standards of behavioural and operational aims and objectives that in turn require the different groups to rise above their inherent differences. To be fully effective, this requires openness and commitment all round so that the potential for conflict is minimised.
- **Consensus:** where the way of working is devised as a genuine partnership between the organisation and its staff and their representatives The consensus position in IR is rare in all but the simplest and smallest of organisations (and may not exist even in these).
- **Multi-unionism:** whereby several different trade unions may be recognised as having representation and bargaining rights for particular groups of staff. Where this is the case, an IR priority has to be established so that differences between the particular unions can be addressed and reconciled as far as possible. This is

the traditional form of approach in many multinational corporations, public and health services, which carry complex and sophisticated IR superstructures consisting of committees, subgroups, working groups and ad hoc groups.

- **Single-unionism:** this is a conformist approach, highly regarded by Japanese manufacturing companies operating in the West. IR agreements are made between the company and one trade union with the overriding concern of streamlining and ordering workplace relations to ensure that their operation is kept as simple and effective as possible. The IR policy is designed by the organisation, and the union invited along as a social and/or operational partner, into predetermined and pre-agreed areas.
- **Single table IR:** single table IR may allow for the recognition of different trade unions, but the same principles, practices and approaches are adopted by the organisation to each. All staff are on the same basic terms and conditions regardless of occupation. Staff may choose which trade union to belong to (or to belong to none), but no union will have a greater influence or rights than others.
- **IR without unions:** if this is to be effective, the reasons why people join unions must be removed. Trade unions grew to prominence to represent the employees' interests and as a brake on excesses of management that, in many cases, used to lead to unacceptable and untenable quality of workforce treatment. The onus is therefore clearly on the organisation to produce and enforce the required standards, otherwise staff members will simply seek support and security in union membership (see Example Box 16.7).

Whichever strategic approach is adopted, boundaries must be established by organisations as follows:

- standards of performance required
- standards of ethics, behaviour and attitude
- parameters of industrial relations activity and where those parameters end
- procedures for the management of disputes, grievances, discipline and dismissal, including the conditions under which there is recourse to arbitration (see Example Box 16.8)
- consultative, participative and communication structures
- the precise forms of workforce representation, including the recognition of trade unions
- the desired aura of workplace staff relations.

The 'aura' is the backdrop or general impression created. It is reflected in the nature and numbers of accidents, disputes and absences at the place of work; it may also be indicated by rates of staff turnover or problems with particular staff categories.

Whatever standpoint is adopted, it is important that both managers and staff understand it so that they can identify their mutual expectations. Needless disputes are kept to a minimum, as long as everyone understands the position of everyone else.

It is also necessary to recognise the pressures placed on staff management, HRM and IR by the following.

- **The structure of the workforce:** operational aspects; dispersion; departmentalisation and groupings; particular ways of working.

EXAMPLE BOX 16.7 Conditions for Effective Single Table Agreements, Single-Union IR, and IR without Unions

If these approaches to IR are to be effective, the following elements are required.

- It must mirror the **philosophy, ethos, style** and **values** of the organisation concerned; there must be commitment to it, and a willingness on the part of the organisation to resource and underwrite it all.
- Managers and supervisors are trained in the **procedures** and **practices** of IR, the ability to manage staff on a basis free from inherent conflict, and the ability to solve rather than institutionalise problems when they occur.
- **Wage levels** tend to be at the upper end of the sectoral scale, and will also be good in relation to other variables such as regional considerations and the ability to compete for all categories of staff in both the sector of operations and the locality where work takes place. Wage rises are never backdated.
- There is **one set** of procedures, terms and conditions of employment only, operated by the organisation in conjunction with the recognised union. The procedures themselves, together with the rest of the IR policy, are devised and drawn up by the company and the union invited to participate on pre-set terms. The IR sphere is not a matter for joint negotiation or agreement.
- The union represents **all members of staff** at the workplace and there is no other IR format. Staff are encouraged to join the union but are not compelled.
- **Disciplinary and grievance practices** operate from the standpoint of resolution and prevention of the matters in hand, rather than institutionalisation. They are aimed above all at getting any recalcitrant employee back into productive work in harmony with the rest of the company as quickly as possible. Where recourse to procedures is necessary, these also are designed for maximum and optimum speed of operation. The purpose here is to prevent any issue that may arise from festering and getting out of control.
- The **disputes procedure** is normally that of binding pendulum arbitration and represents the final solution to the matter in hand. It is only invoked at the point where an official dispute would otherwise take place; there are cultural as well as operational pressures that ensure that this is used as rarely as possible.

This style of IR is above all designed to be a business-like approach and arrangement, designed as part of the process of ensuring the success, continuity and profitability of the organisation. As such it is integral rather than an adjunct to it.

- **Staff management aspects:** of core and peripheral work groups; specialist subcontractors, consultants and advisors; those on fixed-term or fixed-project contracts.
- **Balancing** and **reconciling** a great mixture of conflicting and divergent elements in the basic interests of organising and maintaining effective working methods and ensuring fairness and equity to all.

EXAMPLE BOX 16.8 Recourse to Arbitration

This is open to managers at all times in their attempt to resolve disputes at the workplace. Arbitration is available whether these disputes are individual (between a manager and a member of staff) or institutional (between an organisation and a union or body of employees). Used effectively, it represents a means of resolution that is both considered and subject to internal scrutiny, and which may also have the benefit of acceptability on the part of all because a third party has arrived at the conclusion.

Arbitration is not in itself a universal means of problem solving. It can only be applied when all other approaches have failed, or when there is an issue of presentation concerning the means of delivery of a decision.

It is not an industrial relations policy. Regular recourse to arbitration encourages extreme positions on the part of those in conflict so that any middle position recommended by an arbitrator is as favourable as possible. Internal credibility is lost. Continued recourse to arbitration leads to the frustration of those who can, and would, resolve their own problems and this, in turn, leads to the loss of IR skills, expertise and aptitudes, and therefore of control.

Recourse to arbitration thus becomes an additional tool to be used by managers when the context and situation requires. Its use and value will be pre-evaluated in the light of these situations, the advantages and disadvantages being weighed up by managers when they decide on whether to go to arbitration on a particular matter or not.

Pendulum arbitration

This is the term given to the instrument most commonly used in this situation; it is invoked only at the point where a strike or other industrial action would otherwise take place.

An arbitrator is appointed by agreement of both sides to the dispute. The arbitrator hears all the arguments, and then decides wholly in favour of one party or the other. Someone therefore always wins (and is seen to win); and someone always loses (and is seen to lose). The concept of pendulum arbitration is based on this: faced with the prospect or possibility of losing a dispute, each party will wish to resort to the negotiating table once again to resolve the differences. In particular in Japanese companies, there are strong cultural pressures on managers not to get into disputes, and not to lose them if they do.

Pendulum arbitration normally represents the final solution to any dispute, and there is no appeal against it; this is clearly stated in handbooks and agreements in which this is the instrument for the resolution of disputes. Those entering in to it agree to be bound by the outcome before the arbitrator hears the case.

- Balancing **harmony** and **contentment** with commitment, drive and organisation purpose.
- The establishment and provision of **standards** and **sanctions** for the enforcement of rules.
- **The capability of managers:** one of the greatest advances in the field has been the recognition of the qualities, aptitudes and attitudes necessary for the promotion and maintenance of effective and harmonious IR; and the training of managers and supervisors in this field.
- Balancing **formality** and **informality:** the extent to which managers are given leeway to deal with their own problems, or the extent to which everything must be institutionalised; whichever is adopted, a fundamental basis of equality of application and treatment must be ensured.

The framework of HRM and IR

The framework of HRM and IR is dominated by: the government and the EU; employees, their representatives and trade unions; and employers, their representatives and associations. Each has distinctive roles.

Government and EU

Governments and the EU are the single major universal influences on IR in Europe. In the UK, the government is the single largest employer, responsible for the pay, terms and conditions of employment of the civil service, the armed services, the police, the emergency services, local government and services, nationalised industries and utilities, health and social services. As dominant employer, it sets standards of employment and IR practice that others will be expected to follow, and there is great scope for setting 'model' terms and conditions. Major public activities (especially large hospitals, government functions, nationalised industry premises) are often the dominant employer of a locality, directly affecting what others have to pay to attract staff to work for them.

Both the government and the EU make laws for employment and industrial relations as for everything else, and set the standards and boundaries of practice. They also establish codes of conduct, codes of practice and employment protection and encouragement policies. They may set contract compliance rules, requiring anyone wishing to tender for government contracts to adhere to particular standards of practice. Governments may also use the military, police and emergency services in times of industrial strife to keep essential services open and maintain the general national quality of working life.

Governments and the EU codify all aspects of workplace relationships: the rights and limits of trade union activities; the rights of individuals at the workplace; the rights of organisations and their managers; equality of opportunity; the right to strike; and the right to work.

Employees, their representatives and trade unions

The interests of employees at places of work are looked after by trade unions, staff associations, some professional bodies, and the individuals themselves. Over the years the greatest single influence has been trade unions (see Example Box 16.9).

In recent years, trade unions in many parts of the world have lost influence and reputation as the bases of much of their power and membership, the manufacturing and primary sectors, have declined. New jobs created have been in the assembly, service and retail sectors, where no traditions of unionism exist. Legislation has been enacted to ensure that proper procedures are followed before strike action or other disputes take place. Governments have reduced the national influence and reputation of the unions by setting their own IR agenda, and by covering the widest possible range of employees' interests. Finally, automation and technological advance have eliminated most of the demarcation distinctions between occupations, and the move is now towards multi-skilling and the flexible workforce.

Unions have therefore had to seek new or redefined roles. They have retreated from national lobbying and returned to effective action at individual workplaces on behalf of individuals and groups of members. They have engaged in cooperative agreements with organisations, including productivity, training and no-strike arrangements. They offer members benefits such as advantageous rates for personal and possessions insurance, and for health care. They have engaged in mergers and membership drives in order to maintain and improve on the levels of influence that they have.

EXAMPLE BOX 16.9   The Donovan Commission

Part of the review of the Royal Commission on Trades Unions and Employers' Associations (the Donovan Commission of 1965–7) was to define for the first time what the real roles of unions were. In summary, the findings were that unions:

- bargain for the best possible wages, terms and conditions for members
- lobby for an improved share in national wealth for members
- influence government policy and the legal framework on behalf of members
- lobby for social security for all
- lobby for full employment, job security, better wage levels, and cheap housing for the poor
- bargain nationally, regionally, locally, industrially, for organisations and individuals
- represent members at disputes and grievances and for any other reason according to need.

In the UK at present, there is overwhelming emphasis on this last point. Many individuals continue to maintain trade union membership as a form of 'employment protection insurance' so that if they do get into difficulties at the place of work, they have access to expert advice. This is not confined to those in traditional areas; many senior managers in industry, commerce and public services continue to maintain their union membership for exactly these reasons.

Source: D. Donovan, *Report of the Royal Commission on Trades Unions and Employers' Asociations*, HMSO, 1967.

Employers, their representatives and associations

The third party to the framework is the employer, represented by employer and trade federations and associations, individual companies and organisations. The influence of employers is currently at its highest level, and rising, in the conduct of workplace industrial relations, though as with the unions, the employers' lobby has declined at national level.

The function of the employer in IR is to set standards of staff management, attitudes, behaviour and performance for the organisation or company; to set terms and conditions of employment, and pay levels and methods; to act in a fair and reasonable way towards all employees at the workplace. They may take part in national arrangements to set minimum standards for the sector concerned. They may choose to recognise trade unions or not. They will make representations to government on their own behalf, through their associations and federations.

In recent years, the area of IR has become recognised for the first time as an area of profitable and effective activity. Managers are now being trained in the skills of staff relations and problem solving. Great emphasis is increasingly emerging in the devising of human resource policies, the tone and style of staff handbooks, the attitudes and approaches to staff and workforces. Companies are looking at fresh and creative approaches to HRM issues, and staff and IR management problems.

Conclusions

The general level of understanding and appreciation required of the managers if they are to be truly effective in this field is clearly deep and complex. They must create the basis of a harmonious, productive, working environment so that effective work can be carried out. Employee motivation must be maintained. The managers must establish formal, semi-formal and informal chains of communication with workforce representatives (if there are any) and with employees at large.

Managers have to develop a range of skills to use in the day-to-day handling of staff matters. Negotiations, dealing with disciplinary and grievance matters, handling disputes, and other problem-solving activities may have to be undertaken. They may have to balance conflicting demands and may only be able to resolve one issue at the expense of another.

Managers may be fortunate enough to be able to conduct HRM in an atmosphere of positivism and industrial harmony. Conversely they may constantly be working in an atmosphere where mistrust is endemic and outright conflict is just below the surface. In such circumstances, the best strategy may simply be to move from problem to problem if, by doing so, the manager can at least ensure a modicum of output. The ability to make any progress and shape a more positive and effective future in such circumstances will stem from an understanding of the status quo in the first place. Beyond that, a full appreciation of the principles outlined here and a commitment to change from the organisation in question, together with a clear vision of what that change should be, are essential for such progress to be successful.

Moves towards full workforce flexibility have also been made and the concept is now familiar and understood. However, it is not yet fully implemented in public services or the multinational sector. The full human resource and wider managerial implications have also yet to be thought through fully. Many organisations are still

---

EXAMPLE BOX 16.10 Comparative Industrial Relations

It is relevant to draw attention here to the uniqueness of the UK IR system and its divergence from others. This is especially true of the trade union movement. Until 1993, all UK trade unions took at least a collective standpoint and most were overtly socialist, at least in their leadership. The Labour Party was originally founded to represent the interests of the unions in Parliament, the major stakeholders in the party remained the trade unions. Only now is this relationship being seriously examined for the first time.

The other quirk specific to UK trade unions is their sectoralisation and specialisation. The titles – National Union of Teachers, Rail and Maritime Trade Union – define spheres of influence and interests. They are drawn from a tradition of demarcation and specialisation and, again, this was only being examined for the first time in the last decade of the twentieth century, when there started to be moves afoot among certain sectors to refocus their outlook.

This may be contrasted with unions elsewhere. In the USA they are professional lobbies. They work in the same way as any other such lobby to promote and defend their interests through the media, political representatives, and industrial and commercial councils and committees. They are neither as universal nor as institutionalised as in Europe and the UK, nor do they carry the same influence (indeed they have lost credibility and influence in the wake of corruption scandals in recent years).

In the countries of Europe, unions adopt a much wider brief than their UK counterparts, representing 'public services' or 'the car industry', for example, rather than a particular occupation or sub-section of it. They also adopt a much wider variety of stances and affiliations, ranging from communism and socialism to conservatism, Christian democracy and Roman Catholicism.

Finally, a much wider view of IR is taken in Europe. This ranges from conflict (e.g. France, Italy) to concentration on welfare benefits as much as wages (e.g. Holland); others adopt the stance that a productive, harmonious and profitable undertaking is good for everyone including their members (e.g. Sweden, Germany).

---

enmeshed in a great array of differing terms and conditions of employment, complicated working arrangements and restrictive practices, and these are maintained at the expense of operational effectiveness.

There must be a universal commitment to the development of all employees. As the value of this becomes more widely recognised and the benefits can be seen to translate into increased profits, service quality and organisation stability, flexibility and continuity, so the profile and priority of development activities will rise. Alongside this must come a greater awareness of the purpose and benefits of effective performance appraisal, and of the wider relationship between the efforts of staff and the prosperity of the organisation.

A general appreciation of the traditions, history and background of IR is also essential if managers are to understand both the current general state of IR thinking and that of their own organisation in particular. These traditions are underpinned by mythology, legends and folklore that still engender great pride in certain sectors of the population. This mythology has its roots in real grievances, deprivation and a style of entrepreneurship and management that was very often entirely unacceptable by any standard against which such practices should be measured in the world of today.

As a field of study and of managerial practice, human resource management is developing all the time. There exists now a much more universal understanding of the principles of human resource management, how these should be applied and what they are supposed to achieve. More widely, it is recognised as a business activity, a key function that contributes to both the effectiveness and the profitability of the organisation. In line with this, organisations are now setting their own HRM agenda rather than relying on traditional ways of doing things.

CHAPTER SUMMARY

Whatever the approach to human resource management and industrial relations at particular places of work, it is essential to understand the relationship between this and long-term organisational performance, effectiveness and viability. A survey carried out in the City of London in October 1998 established that there was some evidence to show that directors and chief executives were beginning to understand the relationship between workforce attitudes to the workplace, and profitable business and effective public services. Attention was required to all aspects of the working relationship; above all, problems could not be resolved simply by throwing more money at them, especially where wage levels were already high. Directors and senior managers were at last becoming aware of the fact that loyalty had to be earned, and could not be bought. This view especially prevailed among senior human resource directors; three-quarters of those surveyed saw a direct relationship between happy, highly motivated staff, and increases in company profits. However, the survey also found that only 18 per cent of HR directors felt that their companies were actively encouraging such an environment (Office Angels, 'Staff Satisfaction in the City of London', October 1998).

It is also important to ensure that staff management, human resource management, and industrial relations policies work in harmony with the interests of the organisation, rather than those of HRM and IR specialist functions. Especially where the quality of the work of such specialists is measured in terms of their capability to solve problems, they will inevitably find problems to solve. In these case, staff management, HR and IR problems can get very much worse before they get better, and this is because they will be used by the experts to make a name for themselves rather than to resolve the particular matter in hand. Many organisations are coming increasingly to the view that HRM is a strategic rather than operational issue; and that this, in turn, means that day-to-day HRM issues should be tackled and resolved by the particular line managers and supervisors involved, rather than referring them to specialist functions.

There is clearly an ideal pressure for this strategic approach to be developed and enhanced. With the increased complexity of organisational structure, uncertainties of markets and the continuing need for the development of expertise, a strategic approach to HRM is much more likely to make a long-term and enduring contribution to organisational effectiveness through following this agenda than through concentrating on specific issues and minutiae in functional departments and divisions. The strategic HR role also requires specific attention to establishing, maintaining and developing the required organisational management style and culture, and to engaging management development programmes in support of this. Staff development, expertise and technological training are also much better managed from a strategic point of view. Finally, the procedures that underwrite the required and desired human resource management style and strategy are much more likely to be effective if they are written from a strategic, rather than operational, point of view.

DISCUSSION QUESTIONS

1. What are the problems with long-term staff planning activities, and how might these be overcome?

2. Draw up a person specification for an occupation with which you are familiar. State why you have included these elements, and how you are going to test or infer them at the interview and selection stage.

3. Discuss the view that those on very high wages and salaries (e.g. sports and entertainment stars, top managers and directors of companies) work for job satisfaction, while those on very low wages (e.g. bar and waiting staff, food fryers and cleaners) work purely for the money.

4. If an organisation consciously adopts an adversarial approach and attitude to its staff, what costs and charges (both overt and hidden) are incurred as a direct consequence?

CHAPTER CASE STUDY

Sanyo Industries (UK) Ltd: Staff Handbook

1. Sanyo (UK) and the Amalgamated Engineering and Electrical Union hereby agree the following.

2. This is a business agreement.
    1) All aspects of the Establishment and its operations will be so organised as to achieve the highest possible level of efficiency performance and job satisfaction so that the Company shall:–
    (i) be competitive and thus remain in business
    (ii) provide continuity and security of employment for an effective work force
    (iii) establish and maintain good working conditions
    (iv) establish and maintain good employee relations and communications by supporting the agreed consultative negotiating grievance and disciplinary procedures set out in this Agreement
    2) Both parties accept an obligation to ensure that the Establishment will operate with effective working methods with the best utilisation of manpower and without the introduction of wasteful and restrictive working practices and this objective will be achieved by:-

(i) the selection, training, retraining and supplementary training of employees, wherever necessary, to enable such employees to carry out any job

(ii) the maximum co-operation with and support from all employees for measures and techniques used in any area to improve organisation and individual efficiency and to provide objective information with which to control and appraise the performance of individual employees and the Establishment

(iii) the maximum co-operation and support from all employees in achieving a completely flexible well motivated work force capable of transferring on a temporary or permanent basis into work of any nature that is within the capability of such employee having due regard to the provision of adequate training and safety arrangements

3) Both parties recognise that the well-being of the employees is dependent upon the Company's success and that the high standards of product quality and reliability are essential if the products produced at the Establishment are to become and remain competitive and that therefore the maximum co-operation and support must be given to measures designed to achieve maintain and improve quality and reliability standards.

3. The following matters have been agreed in connection with the Union:-

1) Employees will not be required to become union members but the Company will encourage all employees covered by this Agreement to become a member of the Union and participate in Union affairs and in this connection the Company will provide a check off arrangement for the deduction of union subscriptions

2) Union representation will be established in the following manner:-

(i) The number of representatives of the Union together with the constituencies which they will represent will be agreed between the Union and the Company

ii) The representatives will be elected in accordance with the Union Rules by union members in each constituency

(iii) Each such representative ('the Constituency Representative') will be accredited by the Union and the Union will then send details of the credentials of such representative for approval to the Head of Personnel who will confirm such approval with the Union and thereafter inform the appropriate line management concerned of the appointment

3) The elected representatives will elect from amongst themselves a senior representative ('the Senior Representative') in accordance with the Union Rules

4) The Senior Representative will be responsible for controlling and coordinating the activities of the Union in accordance with the terms and conditions of this Agreement and within the Union Rules and Regulations and will ensure that each elected representative shall have a working knowledge of the Union Rules and Regulations and in this connection in conjunction with the Personnel Department of the Company the Senior Representative shall ensure that the representatives shall have a comprehensive understanding of the industrial relations procedures and practices of

the Establishment and of general industrial relations procedures and practices and it is agreed that all communication between the representatives and the full-time official(s) of the Union will be made through the Senior Representative

5) Each elected representative must be employed in the constituency which he represents

6) The Company will provide adequate facilities to ensure that all Union elections and ballots of members shall be carried out in secret and by the use of voting papers and not by way of a show of hands

4. It is agreed by the Company and the Union that all matters of difference should wherever possible be resolved at the source of such difference as speedily as practicable and it is the intention of the parties that all such matters will be dealt with in accordance with the agreed procedure and in this connection:–

1) Where a matter relates to an individual employee covered by this Agreement such employee must in the first instance raise the same with the supervisor who will then be given the appropriate time necessary to resolve the situation PROVIDED ALWAYS that:-

(i) if the employee is not satisfied with the solution proposed by the supervisor then the employee may request the services of the constituency representative to reach a solution with the supervisor

(ii) if the constituency representative and the supervisor shall fail to reach agreement then the constituency representative will discuss the matter with the Department Manager or his representative

(iii) if after careful deliberation a satisfactory solution cannot be found then the constituency representative shall be entitled to raise the issue with the Senior Representative who will then decide if the grievance should be discussed at a higher level of management within the Company and the services of the Personnel Officer may then be called upon if it is considered that this will help to resolve the matter

(iv) failing such resolution discussions will then take place between the Senior Representatives of the Company normally including the Head of Personnel together with the Senior Union Representative and the constituency representatives on the Joint Negotiation Council ('JNC') referred to in Clause (5) below

(v) in exceptional circumstances the services of the National Officer of the Union may be requested to assist in the matter either by the Union or by the Company and in such circumstances the Company will arrange an appropriate meeting to be attended by senior representatives of the Company and the Union as well as the National Officer or the Full-time Official

2) Insofar as differences shall arise in connection with issues of a Departmental nature then the procedure shall commence with a meeting between the constituency representative and the Department Manager or his representative

3) In the case of an issue concerning the Establishment or the Company as a whole the matter will commence on the same basis as is set out in Sub-Clause (iii) above

5. The Company and the Union will establish a Joint Negotiation Council ('JNC') for the purpose of providing a forum through which discussions regarding improvements to employment conditions and other major matters can be discussed and in this connection:-

    1) The JNC will consist of representatives from the Company including the Head of Personnel and Senior Company Representatives and on behalf of the Union the Senior Representative from Production/Warehousing and one constituency representative from Administration.

    2) Discussions regarding substantive improvements to employment conditions will normally be held on an annual basis during December in each year and such discussions will not include changes arising as a result of promotions transfers or changes to job content which can be implemented at any time as agreed

    3) Matters agreed by the JNC will constitute one of the terms and conditions of employment for each employee covered by this Agreement

    4) The Senior Representative will be given appropriate facilities to consult with Union Members Constituency Representatives and the Full-time Official or National Officer of the Union to enable the Senior Representative to conduct a meaningful collective bargaining exercise

    5) All claims on behalf of Union Members must be made in writing by the Senior Representative to the Head of Personnel who will convene the appropriate meeting of the JNC

    6) It is recognised by both parties that whilst discussions are taking place all business and negotiations discussed at the JNC will remain confidential to its members and the Company recognises its responsibility to ensure clear communication to employees of the results of such discussions and negotiations and in this connection the Head of Personnel will be responsible in consultation with the members of the JNC for announcing the details of any offer to be made to employees following such discussions and negotiations as aforesaid

    7) In exceptional circumstances the services of the National Officer or the Full-time Official of the Union may be requested by the JNC and in such circumstances the Company will arrange an appropriate meeting to be attended by representatives of the Company and the Union and the National Officer

6. In addition to the JNC the Company will establish a Joint Consultative Council ('JCC') and the following provisions shall apply thereto:-

    1) The membership of the JCC shall consist of the Head of Personnel (as Chairman) and appropriate members of the Company's Senior Executives and the Senior Representative together with one constituency representative from each of Production, Engineering and Administration and a further constituency representative on a rotating basis as a co-opted member and in addition the Managing Director of the Company shall act as President of the JCC and shall attend meetings from time to time

    2) The JCC shall meet on a monthly basis for the purposes of discussing issues of a mutual nature and one week prior to each JCC meeting the Personnel Officer will publish an Agenda agreed with the Senior Representative who

will be responsible for submitting items for discussion on behalf of the Union in time for such items to be included on the Agenda

3) Items to be included for discussion at JCC meetings will include:-

(i) manufacturing performance

(ii) operating efficiency

(iii) manufacturing planning

(iv) employment levels

(v) market information

(vi) establishment environment

(vii) employment legislation

(viii) union policies and procedure

(ix) level of union membership

4) Following each meeting of the JCC the Head of Personnel will be responsible for communicating to all employees the nature and content of the discussions and in this connection the Company and the Union recognise the need to conduct meetings of the JCC in constructive manner for the benefit of the Company and all its employees

7. In the event that the Company and the Union shall be unable ultimately to resolve between themselves any discussions or disputes they may jointly agree to appoint an arbitrator and in this connection:-

1) The Arbitrator will consider evidence presented to him by the Company and the Union and any factors that he believes to be appropriate

2) The Arbitrator will decide in favour of one party

3) The decision of the Arbitrator will be final and binding and will represent the final solution to the issue

8. DISCIPLINARY MEASURES

It is in the interest of the Company and its employees to maintain fair and consistent standards of conduct and performance. This procedure is designed to clarify the rights and responsibilities of the Company, the Union and employees with regard to disciplinary measures

Principles

The following principles will be followed in applying this procedure:–

8.1 In the normal course of their duties, the Company will make employees aware of any shortcomings in performance or conduct. This counselling stage is separate from the disciplinary procedure as such

8.2 When the disciplinary procedure is invoked, the intention is to make the employee aware that the Company is concerned with their conduct or performance and to assist the person to improve to a satisfactory level

8.3 When any disciplinary case is being considered, the Company will be responsible for fully investigating the facts and circumstances of the case

8.4 The procedure will operate as quickly as possible, consistent with the thorough investigation of the case

8.5 The employee will always be informed of any disciplinary action to be taken and the reasons for it, indicating the specific areas for improvement

8.6 Normally the formal procedure will commence with the issuing of the first formal warning, however, the disciplinary procedure may be invoked at any stage depending on the seriousness of the case

8.7 Each formal warning will apply for 12 months. Should the employee improve their conduct or performance to an acceptable level and maintain the improvement for the duration of the warning, this will result in the deletion of the warning from their record

9. DISCIPLINARY PROCEDURE

The stages of the disciplinary procedure are as follows:-

9.1 *First Formal Warning*

A formal warning at this stage represents the outcome of investigation and discussion into an employee's conduct or performance. If a first formal warning is issued, the individual concerned will be advised to this effect both verbally and in writing by the Company representative conducting the hearing, indicating the duration of the warning (which will be 12 months), the reasons for the warning and the specific areas for improvement

9.2 *Final Warning*

If there is no significant and sustained improvement in the employee's conduct or performance, then the next stage of the procedure is the final warning. If a final warning is issued, the individual concerned will be advised to this effect by the Company representative conducting the hearing, both verbally and in writing, indicating the duration of the warning (which will be 12 months), the grounds for the warning and the specific areas for improvement

9.3 *Dismissal*

If there is no significant and sustained improvement in the employee's conduct or performance during the period of the final warning, then following thorough investigation by the Company, the next stage of the procedure will be the dismissal stage. This stage will also be invoked in cases of gross misconduct (see Establishment Regulations). If an employee is dismissed he will be advised in writing of the principal reasons for the dismissal, and the notice periods which will apply to him

9.4 *Union Representation*

At all stages of this procedure and consistent with the circumstances of the issue the Company will ensure the involvement of the appropriate constituency representative. When, following careful investigation, disciplinary action is contemplated by the Company, the union members concerned will be afforded the services of the Union constituency representative

10. APPEALS

Appeals against disciplinary action will follow the procedure as outlined below.

10.1 All appeals will be in writing by the Senior Representative within two working days after the disciplinary action shall have been taken by the Company

10.2 The appeal will be made to the Personnel Officer who will arrange the formal appeal hearing within two working days of the appeal

10.3 The appeal will be heard by a Senior Personnel representative and a Senior Manager of the Department concerned who has not been involved in the case

10.4 The appeal will be conducted on the employee's behalf by the Senior Representative accompanied by the Department representative

10.5 The employee appealing, his Supervisor and other appropriate employees may be called to give evidence if is thought their involvement is essential to the outcome of the hearing

10.6 The decision of the hearing is final. It is recognised that the Union may wish to discuss the matter as a collective issue

11. INDUSTRIAL ACTION

The Company and the Union undertake to follow the procedures agreed to and recognise that this Agreement provides adequate and speedy procedures for the discussion of Company related affairs and the resolution of problems and as such precludes the necessity for recourse to any form of industrial action by either the Company the Union or the Employees.

Source: Sanyo (UK) Ltd, 1982. Used with permission of Sanyo Industries (UK) Limited, Oulton Works, School Road, Lowestoft, Suffolk NR33 9NA

QUESTIONS

1. What responsibilities and obligations are placed on the staff, the union and the management as the result of adopting this approach to HRM and IR?
2. What are the key features adopted? Compare and contrast these with the traditional approach. What are the benefits and drawbacks?
3. Draw up a training and development plan for all staff and management involved, that has the purpose of making this approach work well. Specify aims, objectives and deadlines, and how, when and where you are to measure this for success/failure.
4. Outline the main objections to the 'no strike' deal. What other conditions must exist in order to ensure that this operates as stated?

Part IV
Management in action

17 Management Influence, Power and Authority

'With power comes responsibility.' Charles de Gaulle, French President, 1945.

'Authority flows from those who know.' Anon.

'In times of turbulence and change, it is more true than ever that knowledge is power.' J.F. Kennedy, US President, Inaugural Address, 1961.

CHAPTER OUTLINE

The relationship between influence, power and authority

Managerial prerogative and responsibility in wielding influence, power and authority

Sources of power and influence in workplaces; responsibilities in the management of these

Legitimate and non-legitimate uses of power, influence and authority.

CHAPTER OBJECTIVES

After studying this chapter, you should be able to:

understand the sources of power that exist within organisations, and the responsibilities and consequences imposed on managers as the result

recognise and take steps to ensure that unacceptable uses of power and authority are nipped in the bud whenever they first become apparent

recognise the necessity for effective managerial authority, and understand sources of this, and how it is built up

recognise the potential for power bases within organisations, and take steps to ensure that these are managed in the interests of all concerned, and of the organisation overall.

Introduction

Influence, power and authority are present in all organisations and these stem from a variety of sources. It is first necessary to distinguish between them.

- **Influence** is where a person, group or organisation changes the attitudes, values, behaviour, priorities and activities of others.
- **Power** is the capability to exercise influence in these ways.
- **Authority** is the legitimisation of the capability to exercise influence and the relationship by which this is exercised.

Power and influence are therefore resources. Authority is a relationship based on recognition and acceptance of the right and ability to restrict the freedom to act, to set boundaries and to encourage or order sets of activities for given reasons. Responsibility and accountability normally come with authority, especially in relation to the results achieved by the given activities and the ways in which these are ordered and conducted. Authority also refers to the establishment and enforcement of rules, regulations and norms.

Similarly, someone who is an authority – a source of knowledge and expertise, and therefore power – on a given area, is able to influence the acts of those who come to them for advice and guidance. The quality of this may lead also to the building of a wider and deeper relationship and reputation, and the authority figure thus gains further influence.

Power and influence are to be seen as positive and negative. The positive occurs where power and influence are used to energise, enhance and develop productive and profitable activities. The negative is where they are used to block or diminish activities, to limit the ability of others to succeed through the capability to restrict resources, money or information for example; or to bully, victimise and harass.

Influence, power and authority are all themselves limited by organisational structures and methods of behaviour. Authority is normally given over a limited range of activities or people only, and the extent of influence and the ability to wield power are therefore also limited. Authority also normally impersonalises: that is, when people act with authority they do so in the name of the organisation and not in a personal capacity. The need to exercise authority will be founded on both personal and professional judgement; the actions carried out are in ways prescribed by the organisation.

Sources of power

There is a range of sources of power and influence that, in turn, affect the authority relationship. These are:

- **Physical power:** the power exerted by an individual by reasons of his/her bodily shape, size and strength in relation to others. Large multinational and multi-location organisations exert their own equivalent of physical power in the pursuit of market or sector domination, in the ability to select their own preferred range of prices to determine the ways in which markets will operate, and in the ability to command staff expertise and resources. Physical power is also used to intimidate, bully and victimise.
- **Traditional power:** whereby the ability to command influence derives from accepted customs and norms. For example, traditional power is present in the hereditary principle whereby the office or position is handed down from parent to child. This happens with kings and queens and the aristocracy. The same thing happens in family businesses, and those who work in them are likely to find themselves receiving direction from the next of kin at particular points in time. Other social offices and positions carry varying degrees of power and influence based on tradition; examples are priests and town mayors.
- **'Divine right' and 'the natural order':** both have been used in the past to reinforce the position and influence of those in power. Divine right was ascribed to European monarchs over the Middle Ages and beyond; it attributed their position

to the will of God so that anybody who was in rebellion against them was also attacking God. The natural order was – and is – a more general view in support of the status quo. It is usually propounded by those who are currently benefiting from this and in their own support.

- **Expert power:** based on the expertise of an individual or group and the demand for this from other parts of society. The power and influence that stem from highly prized expertise are dependent upon the volume and nature of demand, the location of the experts and their willingness to use their skill. Expertise comes as professional and technical skills, knowledge, aptitudes, attributes and behaviour. It also includes situational and social knowledge.

  This normally carries an economic value, depending upon the nature of the expertise, the value placed on it by those requiring it, and overall levels of demand.

  All expertise may be offered for sale, rent or hire.

- **Referent power:** based on the degree of attractiveness of the person in the position of power. For example, people with a high level of desired expertise may not be hired because of other undesired characteristics (for example, they may be scruffy, bad time keepers or hold extreme political views) while, on the other hand, people with a lower level of expertise may be hired because their wider characteristics or points of reference are considered more suitable. Referent power is also based on the personal relationships and friendships that are found in working situations.

- **Charismatic power:** charisma is the effect of one personality on others, the ability to exert influence based on force of personality. It is also the ability to inspire high levels of confidence and identity among other people. It is to be found in all parts of society. On a global scale Hitler, Napoleon and John F. Kennedy are all known to have had this. In the world of business, it is found for example, in Richard Branson and Anita Roddick. It is also present in people in all groups, clubs, organisations and teams (see Example Box 17.1).

- **Resource power:** the ability to influence others based on the command of resources. This may be beneficial and positive: the giving and allocating of resources to enable someone else to succeed, the result of which is a feeling of well-being towards the resource giver. It may be negative, threatening or coercive, based on the ability to limit or cut off particular resources if the receiver does not behave in certain ways.

- **Reward power:** the ability to influence behaviour and activities by holding out and offering rewards for compliance and acceptance. The extent of influence exerted in this way is dependent upon the nature and volume of rewards and the extent to which these meet the needs of those over whom influence is sought.

- **Power to punish:** the reverse of reward power. Again, the extent of the influence exerted depends upon the nature of the punishment being threatened and whether this is felt to be important by those affected (see Example Box 17.2).

- **Reputation and confidence:** organisations and individuals are able in some circumstances to exert influence based on their achievements to date and the respect and esteem in which these are held. Past reputation and influence, past triumphs and successes are used as the basis for securing future work for example.

- **Coercive power:** the ability to bribe, bully or threaten someone into doing something that they would not otherwise do. This is usually based on physical or

> ### EXAMPLE BOX 17.1 Charismatic Power and Influence
>
> Many of the recent wave of leaders, managers and creators of companies have also become known as having charisma or a great force of personality. For example:
>
> - Stelios Hadjoannou, founder of the low-price airline EasyJet, has created a very strong and positive public image for himself (as well as bringing benefits to his company) through never refusing to appear on radio or television when requested.
> - Brent Hoberman and Martha Lane-Fox gave great impetus to the dot.com revolution because of their youth, vibrancy, personality and glamour at the time of the foundation of their company, LastMinute.com (this force of personality has undoubtedly helped to sustain the company through operating difficulties, and to gain a joint venture with Thomas Cook).
> - Michael O'Leary, founder of Ryan Air, also a low-price airline, managed to buck the trend in the airline industry by continuing to expand both the route network and also the aircraft fleet; this continued to apply even after the global airline recession brought on by the terrorist attack on the World Trade Centre in New York on 11 September 2001.
> - Alex Ferguson, manager of Manchester United Football Club, through a combination of personality and expertise, was able to transform an under-performing (if glamorous) entity into the largest company in this particular global industry.
> - Tony Adams, captain of Arsenal Football Club for nine years, gained the respect of the whole of his industry when it became known that his strength of character had enabled him to overcome battles with alcohol and depression.

economic strength, and reinforced by negative and threatening attitudes and behaviour.

- **Conformity:** this is where organisations and leaders set distinctive norms, attitudes, values and behaviour standards which those who wish to be a part of the situation are required to accept. This may be imposed formally by the organisation in the setting of rules and standards of behaviour and activity, or informally by groups exerting their own autonomous and informal pressures and norms. Pressure to conform may again be positive – holding out rewards and success for those who choose (and are chosen) to follow the given path – or negative, coercive and threatening.
- **Position power:** this is where someone is given power and influence according to the position or role held. Military and organisational ranks carry different forms and extents of this depending upon their position in relation to others. The nature of power also varies according to the positions involved. For example, a production supervisor has a direct influence on the daily activities of their work group; the production controller is likely to be responsible for the overall activities of the supervisor's group and directly for the activities of the supervisor; however, he/she

---

EXAMPLE BOX 17.2 Authority and Impersonalisation: Nazi Concentration Camps 1935–45

The Nazi regime in Germany (1933–45) established these camps from 1935 onwards as an integral feature of the management of the German Empire – the Thousand Year Reich. Their purpose was:

- to house and re-educate dissidents and those who held views contrary to those of the establishment
- to house and hold hostage the families and friends of dissidents
- to remove 'undesirables' (for example, homosexuals and the disabled) from society at large)
- to exterminate 'inferior' races and populations (Poles, Slavs, Gypsies and above all, Jews).

People were sent to camps for fixed periods or for life. A total of 300 camps were constructed and operated over the period. Most of the camp commandants and administrators were bureaucrats, civil servants working for ministries in certain locations and following career paths. The guards were either soldiers or members of the prison service. All involved had power and influence over the lives of the inmates. Above all, they all had authority to act in the name of the State, in the terms of the Nazi Empire.

   This, in essence, is why the horrors lasted for so long and affected so many. It was because the camps were run by instruments of the State and acted with its authority.

---

is likely to exert little direct influence on the daily activities, in spite of holding a superior position.

- **Legal/rational power:** this is the limitation, ordering and direction of power and influence in the name of organisations. It is based on the setting of rules, procedures, regulations and norms for each job, role, department, division and sector, and for the individuals who carry out the work. It is based on certain principles:
  - the right and duty of organisations to establish what they consider to be the best ways of working
  - the managerial prerogative: the establishment of persons in positions of command, responsibility and accountability to ensure that these are put into practice
  - the willingness of subordinates to accept direction and the right of superiors to expect this
  - duties of care placed on organisations by legal, social and ethical pressures so that that they will seek to operate in efficient, effective and profitable ways without being punitive or coercive (see Example Box 17.3).
- **Commercial power and influence:** based on the ability to command and dominate market sectors, the habits and consumption patterns of customers and other factors related to commercial life: the ability to attract financial resources,

---

EXAMPLE BOX 17.3 Rational/Legal Power and Authority

In the UK there are three tests of this as follows.

- The master–servant relationship, in which it is held that all working relations are based upon the ability of one – the master – to direct and order the work of others – the servants – as they see fit. This is often currently called the managerial prerogative. Masters are required to take good care of their servants. Work and workplaces must be safe and not detrimental to personal health. The work may be hard but not punishing. Servants are expected to work hard and to the best of their capabilities. They may not be worked to death, disease or illness. Masters may exert discipline and servants are required to accept it, provided that this is positive and not punitive.

- The wage–work bargain. Once people are hired by an organisation they must be paid (whether or not they actually carry out any work) according to the terms offered. The work carried out must also reflect expectations. For example, a secretary who has been told that he/she is to receive a salary of £12 000 per annum, payable in instalments of £1000 per month, must receive this and may expect in return to be asked to carry out secretarial duties (as distinct from carpentry for example). Both salary and duties may be varied by mutual agreement. Training may be necessary or desirable if this is the case, and may be requested by either or both parties. If no agreement is forthcoming then the relationship may be changed and alternative work offered or sought within the organisation. If the original work has ceased or diminished and no alternative is available, the organisation and the employee may sever the relationship in accordance with the law and the organisation's own procedures.

- Fairness and reasonableness. Organisations and their employees are required to act fairly and reasonably at all times. This especially is the test that is placed by courts and tribunals when adjudicating on employment law cases brought before them. This is because required standards of behaviour and demeanour vary between organisations. For example, attitudes and relationships among staff are different on a building site from those at a high fashion and exclusive clothes shop; the forms of dress required to work in the fields in winter are different from those in a public relations company. The question of fairness and reasonableness is always considered from this point of view.

These factors constitute the absolute boundaries of legal/rational power and authority in UK organisations.

---

technology and expertise; the ability to gain access to sources of components and raw materials, market outlets and means of distribution. This influence is based on a combination of reputation, esteem and confidence, together with economic size and strength. In many cases there are dominance–dependency issues to be considered (see below). Commercial power also sometimes leads to the ability to command or dominate the use of particular technology and expertise in ways that restrict its usage and availability to others and which force other organisations in similar activities to seek alternative means of operating.

Much power and influence therefore stems from the ability to recognise, combine and use these resources effectively. For example, a highly charismatic individual may also have his or her position reinforced by a formalised position that enables conformity to be imposed on a given group. Power is used in the energising of work, in the operation and enforcement of rules and procedures, in the creation, maintenance and development of working relationships and in the organisation, direction and management of people. Understanding of the nature, extent and sources of power is also essential when changes are being considered (see Figure 17.1).

Each of the factors indicated in Figure 17.1 constitutes a building block in the

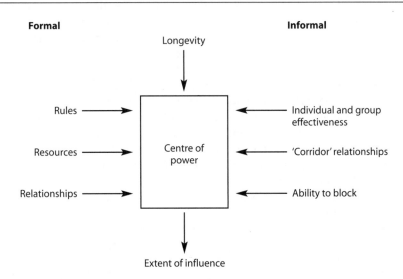

Longevity: people, groups and institutions become behaviourally both strong and influential when they have been in place for a long while. This has implications for need and demands for change, reorganisation and restructuring.

Blocking: this is the power to prevent things from being done. It exists in most situations and is a combination of resource and reward restriction and work prioritisation. It is also the ability to call upon other resources and influences to ensure that the blocking process is effective.

Corridor diplomacy: this occurs as a route to be considered around problems when the formal procedures of the organisation have been exhausted. Power and influence are used between the parties concerned on an informal basis to try to explore other means of resolving the issue.

Success and failure: a run of successes may lead to individuals or groups becoming acknowledged as experts enabling their influence to grow. Conversely, a series of failure is likely to lead to loss of influence, whatever the absolute standard of the expertise present.

Group energy: this is the ability of the group as a whole to influence things, both positive and negative. Especially negative, groups can become very effective in dissipating the energies of those who come to them. For example, those dealing with bureaucracies and who are constantly handed on from one person to the next expend a great deal of energy in this and may well give up altogether if the goal is not important or if some other way of achieving it can be found.

Factors relating to the centres of power   *FIGURE 17.1*

power base of the particular individual or group. The nature, prevalence and mixture of these varies both between and within organisations.

Centres of power in organisations

Each department, division, function and group always has its own power base to a greater or lesser extent as follows.

- The nature of their own function in relation to all the others present, and the nature and extent of the influence that they are able to exert.
- The nature and volume of resources that they command and use, the ways in which resources are allocated, and the wider question of availability of resources.
- The nature of inter-group and inter-departmental relations, the extent to which these are positive and cooperative or negative, dysfunctional and divisive.
- The physical size of certain groups and departments, the numbers of people involved and the scale and nature of resources and technology commanded.
- Relations between operating departments and functions, and the organisation's top management (invariably the supreme centre of power).
- Elements of group hierarchies. These are often found in sophisticated and diverse decentralised organisations for example, where the head office and its functions have greater proximity to senior managers and directors, and therefore the physical capability and location to bid for resources, establish priorities, establish personal relationships and get ahead of the more distant activities.
- The extent and nature of the authority vested in given officials, ranks, departments, divisions, groups and individuals; and the extent of autonomy and devolution that goes with this.
- The capabilities of managers and group leaders, both in absolute terms – the extent of their managerial expertise – and in relation to each other.
- Critical factors such as the ability to command, limit, edit and filter information; the command of critical technology or expertise; and the influence of this upon the ways of working of other functions and groups, and of the organisation as a whole.
- The structure of the organisation and the extent to which certain functions are accorded higher status, importance, influence and authority than others in the formal structuring.
- The priorities of the organisation in its dealings with its customers, clients and markets, and also internally in terms of its operational ways of working.
- The culture of the organisation as a whole, and of its different functions and groups (if a distinction can be drawn between the two). This includes reference to prevailing shared values, attitudes and beliefs, and to general levels of motivation, morale, mutual trust and respect; ethical considerations; and any absolute standards of integrity and activity.

Other centres of power in organisations are also present. These influence their capabilities to act and the ways in which both operations and management are carried out.

- **Vested interests, pressure groups and lobbies:** whether internal and external, these bring their own point of view to bear on particular proposals and activities. For example, internally a lobby may work for improved facilities for itself, on the grounds that many people have already left the group, and that they are difficult to replace. Pressure is then exerted on the organisation to consider the request and if necessary reallocate and reprioritise resources in order to comply. Externally, organisations are subject to public pressure groups wherever they contemplate engaging in activities that are, or are perceived to be, detrimental to the environment (for example construction, infrastructure projects and waste disposal always have to cope with this).

Pressure groups may also arise among shareholders and other stakeholders as the result of, or in response to, proposed sets of activities; or conversely, they may propose or attempt to influence these sets of activities themselves. They may also consist of cluster groups of managers, supervisors, technical and professional experts; specialist groups; trade unions and employee representatives.

- **Over-mighty subjects and over-mighty departments:** these wield great levels of influence and autonomy in certain conditions, particularly in locations physically removed from head office and the main directorate and where a large measure of independence of operation is granted. Over-mighty departments occur where, for operational reasons, they are required to act autonomously. Over-mighty subjects arise where, again for operational reasons, they are required to act in the name of the organisation in all aspects of work. The issue is compounded when the over-mighty subject or division is stationed overseas from the organisational head office and in particular situations where the nature and delivery of the service is given broad or general supervision only by the managing officials. This may again be influenced by organisation tradition: where for example, a long-serving individual is always allowed to air his/her views and have these taken into account by the organisation. Such individuals then become the target of lobbyists (see Example Box 17.4).
- **Mutual interest groups and alliances:** these occur among individuals, groups and functions to try and exert wider pressures on their organisations. This happens for example where one of these has failed and where there is nevertheless a widely perceived need for particular changes or activities to be undertaken.
- **The extent and prevalence of other means of interaction, participation and involvement:** this includes departmental and group staff meetings, work improvement groups, quality circles and project groups. It may also include pioneering activities, research and development functions where those involved are drawn from across the organisation.
- **External consultancies, agencies and statutory bodies:** such groups may be cited or called in to support particular points of view. For example, consultants carry great influence when engaging in restructuring operations; changes in working practices may lead to health and safety experts being called in; in some cases, trade unions exert influence when the restructuring of work and changes to working practice are being considered.

Power and influence relationships (realpolitik)

These exist within and between all groups, divisions, departments and functions; and also between the individuals involved. The main features are explained below.

> **EXAMPLE BOX 17.4 Informal Power and Influence: Over-mighty Subjects**
>
> In sixteenth-century England the Tudor kings and queens were burdened with what came to be known as their over-mighty subjects. These were the land-owning nobility whose support the monarch required to keep the peace in outlying parts of the country and who, if support was not forthcoming, constituted a real threat to the monarch's position. Their support was therefore generated by hiving off parcels of land, local ruling rights and general autonomy to these nobles, in return for their continuing support to the Tudor dynasty. The kings and queens went on regular progressions throughout the country to try to ensure that the bargains that had been struck were adhered to. In practice however, great areas of the country were effectively the personal fiefdoms of these nobles.
>
> The same situation exists in many organisations today. Effective control of large parts has often to be left in the hands of particular individuals. The relationship is normally based upon the organisation conceding large measures of autonomy and freedom to act to the individual in return for addressing and pursuing the organisation's interests in the particular area. Organisations often also become dependent upon these individuals in key critical and functional divisions and areas.

Orders of priority

The position of each individual group or department in relation to all the others involved is often called 'the pecking order'. It is established as a result of a combination of factors: the respect and regard held for the group or individuals by the organisation's top management; demands for resources and the ability to command these; the extent of a department's influence on organisation output; the extent of its influence on internal ways of working; the size of the group and the nature of the expertise that it wields; its physical location; and the nature and quality of its leadership, output and results, both in absolute terms and in those required and valued by the organisation.

Dominance–dependency

This is the extent to which some groups are able to influence, direct and dominate the courses of action of others, and the benefits and consequences that arise as a result.

All those who work in organisations are dependent upon them for rewards and continuity of employment. This requires at least acquiescence, acceptance and compliance with given ways of working; and indicates the general level of managerial and supervisory responsibility required.

Long-term effective working based on the retention, motivation and commitment of staff requires acceptance of the specific responsibilities that consequently arise. Organisations depend on staff to maintain required levels of output and so must create the conditions in which this is possible. The following should also be understood.

- Captive markets are dominated by their suppliers and providers and this brings responsibility in terms of level, volume, quality and frequency of supplies and service, and the prices that can be charged – and the prices that *should* be charged.
- Staff and workforces are dominated by their employers; the potential for this increases at times of increasing unemployment, causing some organisations to take a more expedient view of the working relationships.
- Locations may be dominated by a single employer or industrial, commercial or public service group; this brings with it responsibilities in terms of corporate citizenship, as well as the local dependency for employment.
- Individuals may dominate an organisation or work group through their expertise, as well as force and strength of personality and charisma.
- Experts may dominate in particular situations, especially when their expertise is urgently required, or highly prized. This leads to the ability to charge at very high levels (economic rent); and experts may also choose to limit or filter their expertise, or else to prioritise those with whom they have dealings.
- Owners and controllers of rare supplies, raw materials and specialist information may, from time to time, exert undue influence at specific points during the relationship (see Figure 17.2).
- Resource, especially finance, command and control is, in many cases, a dominant-dependency issue. This especially occurs where organisations require their staff, managers, departments, divisions and functions to bid against each other as part of the allocation process. This is always morally questionable and operationally inefficient. Those involved nevertheless have to engage in bidding activities in the particular environment and context. For some groups, this requires the need for alliances and other forms of support.

Dominance–dependency also exists as a consequence of physical and psychological distance. Those in remote locations find themselves powerless to influence the course of events; and this is compounded when organisations have preconceptions about particular locations based on prejudice rather than strategic and operational assessment (see Example Box 17.5).

Dominance–dependency may therefore be seen as a process in which mutual responsibilities exist, and in which sources of power clearly lie. While groups are dependent

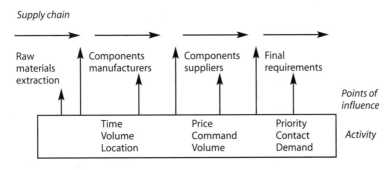

The supply chain and points of influence

FIGURE 17.2

EXAMPLE BOX 17.5   Birds Eye: Skelmersdale, Lancashire, UK

The Birds Eye Factory at Skelmersdale, Lancashire, was established in the 1950s and produced frozen meat and vegetables for the UK domestic and wholesale sectors. It was part of a large international manufacturing company that had four other factories in the UK. The factory employed 1500 people and was the largest single employer in an area where there was high unemployment following the demise of the of the nearby Liverpool dockyards. By the mid-1980s this was about 20 per cent. The factory, with its long local history, was an integral part of the community.

The workforce was represented by several trade unions. Management–union relations were reasonably good at the informal level; however, at the formal level there was a long history of conflict. The unions were described as militant in their approach to negotiations and general dealings with the company.

In terms of productivity, this was the least efficient factory out of the five in the UK. Top management of the parent company blamed various groups: some blamed poor local management over the years; other the outdated policies of the unions; others still, the negative attitudes endemic in the local community culture.

The community was dependent upon the factory for employment and the prosperity that this brought. This in turn directly affected the numbers of shops and leisure facilities in the area; if anything were to happen to the factory, then there would be a knock-on effect on these other activities.

The company that owned the factory eventually closed it down. The effect was to remove the largest single employer from the locality. This greatly increased levels of unemployment and also had the knock-on effects indicated above on the rest of the commercial activities of the area. The reasons quoted by the company for the closure were those indicated earlier; above all, the company head office in London had institutional negative attitudes and prejudices about the local community. The community perceived that the company head office saw the situation only in terms of its own dominance, its ability to act in this way 'because it could'. Frozen food manufacture had survived and grown during the recessions of the late twentieth century, and there was no operational reason why the factory should be closed. Consequently, those affected perceived that at no stage did the company ever acknowledge its dependency on the factory to achieve a certain level of production. Neither did it acknowledge its responsibility to those who had given large portions of their lives to the company over the period for which it had been open.

upon the continued confidence of top managers for continuity and allocation of resources, the top managers are dependent upon the groups to produce results. There is therefore, a clear mutuality of interest in understanding the nature of the relationship, and accepting responsibility to ensure that it works.

Hierarchy

Organisational hierarchies are normally based on a combination of rank and function and this is reflected in job titles (marketing director, quality manager, production supervisor, personnel assistant). This is normally well understood by those in particular organisations. The process is clouded by job titles such as secretary, officer, executive and controller, and again these have to be understood by those involved.

The hierarchy is a feature of organisation design and is composed of structure, job and work allocation, and rules and procedures. It indicates where power and influence lie and their extent and nature. It indicates spans of control, areas of responsibility and accountability, chains of command (the scalar chain) and reporting relationships (see Figures 17.3 and 17.4). As well as a functional and divisional map of the organisation, the hierarchy is a representation of the nature and limits of power and influence.

Status

Status influences the perceptions of power relationships in organisations and is also a reflection of general perceptions of influence. It is a reflection of the rank or position of someone (or something) in a particular group. Relative status is based on the interrelationship of each position. Status is based on the importance and value ascribed to the rank by the organisation and individuals concerned, and by the esteem and respect that accrue as the result of holding the given rank. It is also based on the ambition, self-esteem and self-worth of the rank holder: the ability to say with pride 'I hold job x' or 'I work for organisation y'.

Status is reinforced by the trappings that go with the rank held: personal office, expensive furniture, car, mobile phone, expense account; and by the volume and quality of such items.

It is also reinforced by the responsibilities of the rank held: size of budget, numbers of staff, performance requirements. It is often reinforced by the physical location of those concerned, for example, whether their office is in the 'corridors of power' (that is, the same as that of the top managers). In wider social circles it may also be reinforced by perceptions of glamour or excitement that are assumed to exist in certain occupations, such as show business, publishing or travel.

The components of status may be represented as in Figure 17.5.

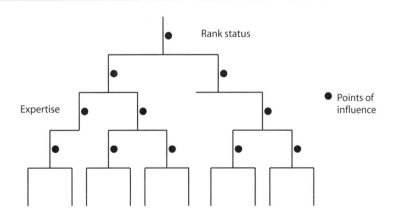

Hierarchies

FIGURE 17.3

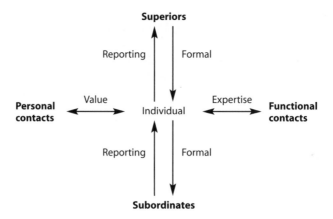

FIGURE 17.4 Influence relationships: the individual's position in the hierarchy

Friendships

Friendship influences power relationships in organisations where people who have positive feelings for each other also work together. A part of the way of working then becomes the desire to support friends and ensure that they derive some of the benefits that are to accrue from particular courses of action. The use of friendships, of personal contacts to resolve problems and address issues, is a general feature of the informal organisation. It represents the ability to use personal influence (referent power) to the organisation's advantage.

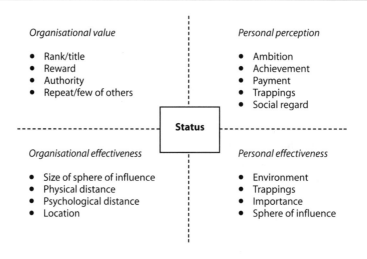

FIGURE 17.5 Status

Dislike

The converse is where antagonism exists between people. This is nearly always a barrier to effective organisational activities. It is used to block or hinder the progress of the other individual or group, and is compounded where operational reasons are given for the purpose of satisfying a personal grudge or grievance.

This is influenced by other personal emotions: envy, jealousy, hatred and resentment. It is also influenced by organisational and operational matters of expediency, especially where there is the need to find a scapegoat for a failure.

Delegation

Delegation is the allocation of work to subordinates accompanied by the handing down of:

- authority in the given area to carry out the work, make requests for equipment, materials and information, and act in the name of department, group or superior in the given area
- control over the process by which the work is to be carried out. This in turn normally involves relaxing a part of the process of work supervision. Activities taken in pursuit of the task are normally left entirely to the subordinate.

There is an effect on the wider issues of responsibility and accountability. Overall responsibility, especially to the wider organisation, normally remains with the superior. Any problems arising, especially questions of failure or ineffectiveness, therefore remain a matter between the superior and the rest of the organisation. However, this is invariably accompanied by discussions between the superior and subordinate. Where such problems do arise, to apportion blame to the subordinate when reporting back to the wider organisation leads to loss of morale and accusations of scapegoating.

Effectiveness

For effective delegation to take place, strong mutual trust, respect and confidence must exist. On the part of the superior, this is based on respect for the capabilities, motivation and commitment of the subordinates and the faith that they are interested in the work and wish to pursue it to a successful conclusion. On the part of the subordinates, it is based on an understanding that they will receive support and backing in their efforts to get the work done, help with any problems and a proper assessment of the end results. It is always enhanced where a strong and effective reporting relationship is already established and mutual trust and confidence are already in place. This is in turn influenced by the relationship between the task to be delegated and the staff available to carry it out. The greater the control the superior has over this, the more likely that confidence and trust are present and the greater the willingness of the superior to cede the required measure of control.

For both, work is likely to be successful only if expectations are clearly set out at the commencement of work. This is reinforced wherever possible with the establishment of proper, measurable, deadlined objectives. The subordinates can

EXAMPLE BOX 17.6 Empowerment

Empowerment, a current management buzzword, is a form of delegation that gives measures of control and responsibility to employees over their work, work processes and working lives. The concept of empowerment is based on the view that people seek as much personal satisfaction and fulfilment as possible from all situations, including work situations, and that responsibility and control lead to increased levels of satisfaction.

Such delegation is attractive to organisations, because by vesting these elements in front-line operative and other traditionally 'non-responsible' jobs, levels of supervision and management can be reduced. Expensive staff are no longer needed in current volumes. Complex and sophisticated supervisory practices, structures and controls can be simplified, thereby cutting down on overhead, non-productive processes and efforts, and the number of staff not actively engaged in primary output.

It is attractive to the staff (as long as the process is honest) because increased responsibilities are normally expected to lead to increased reward and benefit levels, and to increased prospects and opportunities. Potential may be identified that either the organisation or the individual may wish to develop. New levels and ranges of interest may become apparent.

Harvester

The following example illustrates the point.

Harvester, the UK restaurant chain, took steps to empower its restaurant and kitchen staff. The chefs decided what the menus for each week were to be and how often these were to be changed. They then became responsible for ordering the necessary levels and quality of stock, for ensuring that supplies were delivered, and then stored according to legal and best professional standards, and for chasing up any quality defects. They were responsible for setting ordering patterns, purchasing new kitchen equipment and ensuring that the place was clean. They dealt with the food and premises inspections and inspectors, and implemented any changes necessary as a result.

The restaurant staff (the waiters and waitresses) became responsible for all aspects of the eating area. They were required to clean and polish the tables, put out flowers and candles, and see that the restaurant was clean, tidy and welcoming to customers. They would greet customers, show them to their seats, take and process orders. At the end of the work period, they were to clean the restaurant area, check for security and close it down and lock up.

Both chefs and restaurant staff would handle any customer complaints directly, according to the nature of the complaint; rather than going through sophisticated managerial processes, these would be dealt with at the front line.

The company was therefore able to remove the differentiated, non-productive (or largely non-productive) jobs of head waiter, restaurant manager, work supervisor and general manager. Chefs and waiting staff were given large initial pay increases in return for accepting these ways of working.

> **Example Box 17.6 (continued)**
>
> The organisation adopted methods of supervision and control based on a roving and mobile area manager system (area managers would visit each of their sites at least once a week), a flexible but agreed budgeting system that enabled the staff to make a large range of decisions and an emergency/problem-solving 24-hour hot line to the area management.
>
> Empowerment is clearly very like delegation. It is useful to differentiate in this context however, in order to make the point that a great deal of organisational potential lies down the delegation path. This is in terms both of the operational capability of the organisation and the enhanced potential of and for the staff.

then be given enough autonomy over the process to see that the work is done (see Example Box 17.6).

Relationship structures and spheres of influence

These are built up as follows.

1. The conduct of the relationships. This is likely to be based on:
   - conflict, a power struggle, the need for ascendancy in a particular situation
   - cooperation: the establishment of areas of mutual interest; harmony – recognition of the need to resolve any issues for the greater good of all; openness – the extent to which each party involved is or feels able to declare its own position completely; expediency – the need to gain a result quickly for some reason
   - publicity: what others are to make of the outcome of the matter in hand once this is known (see Figure 17.6).
2. Structural factors such as divisionalisation, functionalisation and specialisation.

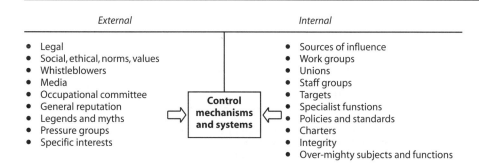

External	Internal
• Legal	• Sources of influence
• Social, ethical, norms, values	• Work groups
• Whistleblowers	• Unions
• Media	• Staff groups
• Occupational committee	• Targets
• General reputation	• Specialist funstions
• Legends and myths	• Policies and standards
• Pressure groups	• Charters
• Specific interests	• Integrity
	• Over-mighty subjects and functions

Control mechanisms and systems

Behavioural influences on organisation power and authority   *FIGURE 17.6*

The influences here are physical and psychological distance, and the relative positions of expertise and their importance in the particular relationships. Demarcation and restrictive practice – tight description and compartmentalisation of jobs and work – are an extreme form of structural influence in this context. Based on the principles of scientific management, these have at times given some groups so much influence (especially the ability to block work) that alternative work structures have not been sought.

3. Information, information chains and the means by which information is disseminated and distributed. Power and influence exist in each aspect. For example, organisations that put information out on a 'need to know' basis have first decided what it is that each group and individual 'needs to know'.

   Information is further distorted by the cascade process (see Figure 17.7) and the means by which the cascade is achieved. Briefing groups, notes, memoranda, newsletters and staff meetings may all carry the same substantive message and agenda. However this is varied by the media used, the person conducting the briefing or meeting and the interpretation that is put by each group that is being briefed on what is being transmitted.

4. Command of information technology is a source of power and this is exaggerated where others have neither the ability nor willingness to use it or understand it. This also applies to summaries of information, whereby a large volume is presented in a shortened and ostensibly useful format. In this case the influence lies entirely with the editor.

5. Technology and the expertise required to use it is also a source of power. This applies in all activities. The influence that this brings to individuals and groups is dependent upon the nature of the technology and the operations involved and, again, upon the willingness or otherwise of others to use it and understand it. However, this can be illustrated at its simplest: staff on the switchboard have a great influence on the initial impressions formed by those who telephone a particular organisation, through the greeting given, the way in which this is delivered, the tone of voice, the transfer-on. The technology itself also has influence both in the numbers of calls that it can take and how these are handled (for example, whether in a queuing system, engaged tone, pre-recorded voices, musical entertainment while the caller waits).

Professional	*Professional*
• Expertise	• Authority
• Direction	• Directional
• Usage	• Influential
• Audience	• Formal
• Content	• Accessibility
• Context	• Hardware and software
• Confidence	• Convenience
• Integrity	• Durability
Ethical	*Technological*

FIGURE 17.7 Influences on information flows and cascades

This also applies to production technology: the production controller's knowledge of the capacity of equipment and their ability to optimise its use; and the knowledge of the staff involved, the extent of their training and their understanding of their own ability to slow down and speed up the processes.

6. Access to key figures. This occurs where someone has influence in excess of their position in the hierarchy. Examples of such individuals include those currently in favour; trade union officials and staff representatives, and those who are known, believed or perceived to be supporters of particular 'fashionable causes'. For whatever reason, they are lobbied because of their proximity to sources of power and influence (see Example Box 17.7).

7. Cross functional groups and committees influence the views of those who take part in them. They may also be used as sounding boards for ideas and proposals for action. They may therefore exert influence and, again, this is likely to grow if their judgement is demonstrably sound. The same also applies to work improvement groups and quality circles.

8. Isolation. For whatever reason, isolation is a power relationship.
   - Physical isolation brought on because of the remoteness of a group from the rest of the organisation (for example, an overseas subsidiary) leads on the one hand to the feelings of loss of control and involvement on the part of the main organisation and, on the other, to feelings of autonomy and independence on the part of the subsidiary.
   - Psychological isolation is brought on by matters such as resource starvation, denigration and general lack of respect and regard for the work of the group or for its members. This leads to the adoption of a siege mentality on the part of the group affected as they defend themselves from the pressures of the rest of the organisation, and also on the part of the organisation as it seeks to make fresh inroads into the already beleaguered group (see Example Box 17.8).
   - Group think is also a form of isolation. For example, top managers and directors may create their own view of the organisation in its environment without reference to reality or on the basis of a historic perception and reputation.

EXAMPLE BOX 17.7 The Position of the Personal Assistant

In many organisations, senior managers have personal assistants, and these are courted by those wishing to gain influence for some reason. In particular, the personal assistant (PA) to chief executives normally exerts great informal influence. The PA is used as the manager's personal resource and as a sounding board and critic for possible and proposed courses of action. The PA therefore becomes an exerter of influence as the levels of mutual trust and confidence grow; and the relationship is reinforced if the judgement of the PA is shown to be sound.

PAs become the focus for lobbies and support from elsewhere in the organisation because they can (or are perceived to) provide a route to the sources of power. They have low status but high influence. They also become a source of quality information both to the manager for whom they work and potentially to the rest of the organisation.

EXAMPLE BOX 17.8 Strikes and Disputes

Strikes and disputes are used as any of the following:

- enhancement of charisma, authority and influence by the strike leaders
- rites and rituals in pay bargaining processes
- trials of strength between staff and managers
- trials of strength between organisations and strike leaders
- safety valves
- additional holidays
- catalysts for change, as well as for the resolution of grievances.

Where physical and psychological isolation occur, groups engage in strikes and disputes in order to draw attention to themselves, as part of a drive for gaining influence and being taken more seriously. Those involved also perceive that taking these forms of action may cause attitudinal changes on the part of those with whom they have the dispute. This can clearly be an extremely dangerous tactic; while it may increase their influence, there is always the possibility that senior managers will simply close operations down altogether.

Project groups and think tanks may also find themselves in this form of isolation if their relationship with the rest of the organisation is not carefully nurtured and managed.

Conclusions

The acquisition and use of power is a basic human as well as organisational need. The requirements and ability to control and influence the environment, and to make it comfortable and supportive, are factors in all behaviour. It is necessary to understand the ways in which people seek to do this in organisations, and the effects of this on aims and objectives, performance, behaviour and resource utilisation.

Power and authority come with responsibility and accountability. It is clearly necessary that managers are able to wield power and authority in the pursuit of achieving their priorities and outputs. In some cases, this self-evidently leads to misuse (see Example Box 17.9).

How power is used and what type of power is used affect all aspects of performance, as does the means of dividing and allocating responsibility and authority. From this point of view, a key part of the creation, design and structuring of organisations consists of creating patterns of control and influence. This is formalised in hierarchies, reporting relationships, functional and expert activities and results areas. Space is also created for the operation of communication and information systems, and group and inter-group relationships, both formal and informal.

It is also necessary to pay constant attention to the ways in which power, influence and authority are used and wielded within organisations, to ensure that this continues to be legitimate, and to ensure that conflict and organisational politics which might otherwise arise are kept under control.

EXAMPLE BOX 17.9 Misuses of Power and Influence

According to the Advisory Conciliation and Arbitration Service (ACAS) the extent to which power and influence is misused in the UK by people in organisations has never been greater. The main features are:

- **Favouritism:** the ability to influence an individual's career, prospects and advancement by virtue of a personal liking and at the expense of others.
- **Victimisation:** the converse of favouritism; the blocking or reduction of career prospects and advancement.
- **Lack of manners:** calling out rudely to people, abusing and humiliating subordinates in public.
- **Lack of respect:** treating subordinates with contempt, giving individuals public dressing downs, conducting discipline in public.
- **Bullying and harassment:** overwhelmingly by superiors of subordinates. This is usually found in the following forms: racial prejudice; sexual harassment (especially of female staff by males); bullying of the disabled by the able-bodied; religious manias and persecutions (for example, where a Catholic company bullies the elements of its workforce that are of other religions); expression of personal likes and dislikes – especially where the dislike is based on a perceived threat to the security of the senior's position.
- **Scapegoating:** the need to find someone to blame for the superior's errors.
- **Inequality of opportunity:** the setting of a priority order for the advancement of staff based on gender, race or disability elements.

ACAS report that some cases are so acute that people are being driven to despair, nervous breakdown or even suicide by the activities of managers. In 2001, 135 000 individual cases were referred to ACAS and the employment tribunal system of the UK; this figure has more than doubled over a four-year period (the number of cases referred to ACAS in 1997 was 65 000).

Curiously, managers and supervisors often do not see that they are bullying by the actions that they take. In many cases, they act this way because this is how they were treated and 'it made a man/woman out of me'. They confused being firm and assertive with bullying.

Some managers claimed that they only acted in this way because they perceived that it would help to get the job done. Others openly acted this way because they saw the opportunity to wield and use power – in some cases knowing the effects that this was having, in other cases not.

Source: *ACAS Annual Report* 2001, HMSO.

CHAPTER SUMMARY

In all organisations, everyone involved recognises to some extent the nature and prevalence of particular forms of power, authority and influence in organisations, and the ways in which these are wielded. They also recognise the presence or absence of integrity in organisational approaches to the management of the different power and influence bases that are present. Above all, they understand the extent of their influence in the given situations; they become especially disillusioned when they know that the management of influence is based on expediency rather than integrity.

The integrity of the organisation as a whole, and its managerial practices in particular, form the basis for the effective management of the different sources of power and influence. It is essential therefore that a full understanding of the true extent and nature of power and influence is established by those responsible for the strategy and direction of the particular organisation. This can then be translated into managerial authority so that this part of organisation management and activity is addressed effectively.

This is especially a problem when authority is devolved to those working in remote locations, or as a result of their distinctive expertise. It is for example very difficult for some health authority managers to confront expert surgeons and other medical practitioners, especially where such expertise is linked to an extremely powerful and dominant personality. It is very difficult for head office managers to exercise full authority over those who work in remote locations, or in the operational field, and this is often compounded by the lack of a full understanding of what the exact nature of this authority should be. The result, in each case, is that there is great potential for particular individuals to run their part of activities as their own monarchy, and for effective accountability and responsibility to be diluted or lost. Once problems such as these arise, they become extremely difficult to retrieve. Indeed, in some cases the situation may only be bought under control as the result of a scandal or disaster.

DISCUSSION QUESTIONS

1. Taking one group of which you are member (social or work), identify the ways in which you influence the others, and the ways in which they influence you. What conclusions and inferences can you draw from this?
2. What steps should organisations take to limit and control the potential for undue influence of: managers; experts; those working in remote locations?
3. What are the advantages and disadvantages of hierarchical management structures in terms of the ability to manage power and influence, and to determine where authority lies?
4. If a company commands 75 per cent of the total market in which it operates, what responsibility does the extent of this influence bring with it? To what extent do these responsibilities remain the same, and to what extent are they changed, for a company that commands 50 per cent of the market; 30 per cent of the market; 1 per cent of the market?

CHAPTER CASE STUDY

TROUBLE AT BOXWOOD PLC

Paul Hewson, Boxwood's chief executive, was reading the result of a strike ballot held at the company's main factory. The ballot paper had asked the staff whether they were willing to take all-out strike action against the company's final offer on pay conditions and restructuring. Staff had voted by 90 per cent to strike. With such a clear majority, there seemed little doubt that all production of car body parts would be halted, with effect from the end of the following week. With a full order book currently, this would mean delivery delays to customers, and this in turn would trigger penalty clauses for missing agreed deadlines. Moreover, as a major supplier to Ford, Nissan and Toyota, the last thing that the company needed was to get a bad reputation among such powerful customers.

Paul Hewson called together a crisis management committee. This consisted of Heather Platt, strategic planning director, Peter Davis, production director, and Dennis Gaffen, marketing and sales director.

The committee met and decided that there were three strategic options:

- engage in discussion with the staff and representatives, with a view to seeking compromise
- denounce the strike proposal, and make it clear that the company would not compromise
- denounce the strike proposal, and warn that if it went ahead the entire workforce would be dismissed and new staff recruited.

They debated each of the three options again. They came to no clear conclusions. As the meeting was breaking up, Heather Platt, the strategic planning director, said 'We could take advantage of the situation to de-recognise the trade unions, and reconstruct the workforce. I know this will lead to delays, but customers will understand, and the shareholders will be delighted.' As she developed her theme, it was clear that both Peter and Dennis were coming round to her point of view. The meeting broke up shortly afterwards.

Paul Hewson returned to his office, and discussed the matter over a cup of coffee with his secretary, Joan Campbell. Joan had worked for the company for 25 years, and understood it better than most. She listened to what had to say and then replied: 'You are assuming that we can get the staff with the necessary expertise and attitudes from anywhere. You should know that the workforce has skills developed over many years that are unique in this industry'. Paul shook his head and did not reply.

Meanwhile, staff representatives were meeting in the work's council office. They were all jubilant at the ballot outcome, for it seemed to them that after years of meek acceptance, their members were at last willing to take a stand against Boxwood's strident management approach. They speculated on the terms of any new offer that could be made by the management side.

For the rest of the day, both the chief executive and the work's council chairman fielded a series of questions from journalists. The Boxwood dispute was major national news because it might become the biggest private sector strike for many years. The factory employed 3500 people, and was the largest single employer in its location in the west country.

The next day, the morning papers were full of articles on the dispute. One newspaper condemned 'high and mighty union officials attempting to fight the class war all over again'. Another passed comment that 'the company's pay offer of 5 per cent seems reasonable, given the 2.5 per cent inflation currently. It is ambitious, however, to tie that in with moves towards fully flexible working, and changes in production processes, that would effectively mean that the staff could be requested to work whenever the company saw fit.' One of the tabloids said: 'This is madness. It should end. The workers should be grateful for any job – especially when it pays a basic minimum of £350 per week.'

After they had reviewed the press coverage, Paul and his colleagues met and agreed a further press statement as follows.

PRESS RELEASE

Boxwood plc

Boxwood plc regrets this campaign of misinformation by union officials has produced a ballot result that threatens the survival of the company. As only 30 per cent of employees actually belong to a union, fewer than half of all staff have voted for a strike. We therefore insist that the strike is called off. Should the strike take place, the company's senior management would take whatever action it deems necessary. Those who go on strike will be deemed to have broken their contracts of employment, and may be dismissed. The company will employ security agencies to ensure that those who do want to get to work can do so. Should the strike go ahead, the company also undertakes to de-recognise two trade unions: the AEEW and the TGWU.

The company's position is non-negotiable. Whatever action the staff take is therefore their responsibility and not that of the company.

Media commentators expressed surprise at the severity of the message. Particularly anxious were the local ITV station and regional evening newspaper. However, these both accepted assurances given by Paul Hewson that the strike would evaporate in the face of such a threat, together with the extremely generous pay offer.

Staff representatives received no direct communication from Paul Hewson and his colleagues. The first notice that they had of the company's intended line was when they read the evening paper. Staff throughout the factory abandoned their posts to look for union or management officials to clarify the situation. Coverage in the press only aggravated the situation, and the result was a total of 2500 staff hours were lost during that afternoon. By now there were plenty of journalists around, and plenty of people prepared to talk to them.

It began to become clear that the workforce felt that they had been exploited over the previous five years. They believed that the company's top management had deliberately used a period of uncertainty of employment as an excuse for under-mining the pay and conditions of manufacturing staff and their supervisors. One member of staff expressed this as follows.

First we were told about the value of de-layering the management. This was supposed to give us more responsibility, but all it did was to give us twice the work and hassle. Then came empowerment, which was intended to provide job enrichment, but all we got was more paperwork and longer working hours. At the same time, top management pay has moved ahead, and the ten senior managers of this company have managed to double their pay in the past three years.

For the rest of the week, little activity took place in the factory. The official strike was still nearly two weeks away, but there was little sense of urgency to complete work before then, either from the staff themselves or from supervisors. In fact, the threat of mass sackings had united factory managers, supervisors and staff; the common enemy was the crisis management team, headed by Paul Hewson.

The following day, in the local newspaper, the company's figures for the present year were published as follows.

Boxwood plc Company Accounts: Current Year

Profit and Loss Account	£m	*Balance Sheet*	£m
Revenue	120	**Fixed Assets**	32
Materials	(44)	Stocks	46
Labour	(40)	Debtors	26
Gross Profit	36	Creditors	(38)
Overhead	29	**Net Current Assets**	34
Interest	5	**Assets**	66
Operating profit	2	Loans	50
Tax	0.5	Share capital	10
Dividends	3.5	Reserves	6
Retained profit	2.0	**Capital**	66

QUESTIONS

1. Where do the sources of power and influence in this situation actually lie? Where should they lie?
2. What responsibility is being accepted and acknowledged by each of the participants in this situation for what is happening?
3. What are the advantages and disadvantages of wielding power and influence in these ways?
4. Produce a set of recommendations designed to:
   - resolve the situation as described
   - ensure that, as far as is reasonably practicable, the situation never arises again.

18 Leadership and Management

'I am the leader. Therefore I must serve.' Winston Churchill, 1940, on becoming Prime Minister.

'Leadership means crediting everyone for success; and accepting for yourself the blame and responsibility when things go wrong.' Gianluca Vialli, Chelsea Football Manager, 1999.

CHAPTER OUTLINE

The relationship between leadership and management

Leadership styles and traits

Leadership skills, knowledge, attitudes and behaviour

Leaders in their environment

The development of leadership qualities.

CHAPTER OBJECTIVES

After studying this chapter, you should be able to:

understand the range, scale, scope, expertise and responsibilities of being placed in a position of leadership

understand the importance of carrying out the leadership function in any management job or occupation

understand and be able to develop the particular traits and qualities required in order to be an effective leader

understand the consequences of bad, ineffective, or negligent leadership.

Introduction

Leadership is the core of all managerial and supervisory activities. This is more clearly observable in some areas than others: political leaders and chief executive officers are self-evidently 'in charge'. However, all those in managerial positions have a leadership function, and all those in leadership positions have managerial responsibilities. These are:

- to give vision and direction
- to energise
- to set and enforce absolute standards of behaviour, attitude, presentation and performance

- to see things through to completion
- where necessary, to surround themselves with expertise so that any gaps in their own capacities are filled.

Definitions and priorities

Definitions

Some useful definitions are as follows.

> A leader is someone who exercises influence over other people (Huczynski and Buchanan, 1993).

> Leadership is the lifting of peoples' vision to a higher sight, the raising of their performance to a higher standard, the building of their personality beyond its normal limitations (P.F. Drucker, 2001).

> A leader is: 'cheerleader, enthusiast, nurturer of champions, hero finder, wanderer, dramatist, coach, facilitator and builder' (Peters and Austin, 1986).

> The leader must have infective optimism. The final test of a leader is the feeling you have when you leave their presence after a conference. Have you a feeling of uplift and confidence? (Field Marshal Bernard Montgomery, 1956).

> Leadership is creating a vision to which others can aspire and energising them to work towards this vision (Anita Roddick, 1992).

> There is a need in all organisations for individual linking pins who will bind groups together and, as members of other groups, represent their groups elsewhere in organisations. Leadership concerns the leader themselves, the subordinates, and the task in hand (C.B. Handy, 1993).

> Leadership can be described as a dynamic process in a group whereby one individual influences others to contribute voluntarily to the achievement of group tasks in a given situation (G.A. Cole, 1994).

Priorities

Priorities may also be established:

- getting optimum performance from those carrying out the work in whatever terms that is defined
- ability to adopt an overview rather than to get bogged down in the detail of the situation
- ability to become engaged in the detail when necessary
- ensuring continuity, development and improvement in those carrying out the work; monitoring and evaluating both the work and those involved; taking remedial action where necessary

- relating the skills and capacities of those involved in the work to the work itself
- seeking continuous improvement in all aspects of the work environment; providing opportunities for continuous development and advancement for those in the organisation, department, division or function
- motivating and encouraging the staff, and promoting positive, harmonious and productive working relations
- leadership and management: either adopting managerial roles (as with supervisors and department managers), or ensuring that operational management activities are carried out (as with top managers and key figures).

Leadership and management

The key elements are as follows.

- **Results:** these are measured in terms of what leaders set out to achieve and what they actually achieved; how and why these were achieved; how they were viewed at the time and subsequently by posterity; and whether this represented a good, bad or indifferent return on the resources and energy expended in their pursuit.
- **Inspiration:** in order to achieve success, leaders must have their own clear understanding of what this is, at least in their own terms. To attract followers and resources to their cause, they normally translate this into a simple, direct and positive statement of where the leader is going, how and why this is to be achieved, and the benefits it is to bring to others as the result. Leaders must be capable of inspiring others; it is no use having a good idea if people do not recognise it as such.
- **Hard work:** to achieve their goals, leaders must have great stores of energy, enthusiasm, dedication, zeal and commitment. They have to inspire and energise people and resources in pursuit of the desired ends. They also set the standards for their followers; in normal circumstances, hard work cannot be expected of others if the leader does not set the example.
- **Respect and value:** which must be given, received and acknowledged among all of those working in the particular situation.
- **Honesty:** people follow leaders, either because they believe in them or because it is in their interest to do so (or a combination of the two). Leaders who fail to deliver are normally rejected or supplanted. Leaders who say one thing and mean another will not be trusted and people will only continue to work for them until they can find something else.
- **Responsibility:** leaders accept their own part in both triumphs and successes, and also disasters and failures. This extends to rewards and consequences (see Example Box 18.1).

Traits and characteristics

There have been a great many studies of leaders, directors and managers from all walks of life and all parts of history. By studying a range of leaders and managers from a variety of situations and background – sport, politics, the military, exploration, religion and business – it is possible to infer the basis for their success or otherwise, and the reasons and causes of this. The leaders' own contributions can be assessed and analysed in relation to the other elements and factors present.

EXAMPLE BOX 18.1 Leadership

Peters and Austin (1986) identified a long and comprehensive list of factors present in a 'leader'; and they contrasted this with the mirror attributes of the 'non-leader'.

Leader	Non-leader
• carries water for people	• presides over the mess
• open door problem-solver, advice giver, cheerleader	• invisible, gives orders to staff, expects them to be carried out
• comfortable with people in their workplaces	• uncomfortable with people
• no reserved parking place, dining room or lift	• reserved parking place and dining table
• manages by walking about	• invisible
• arrives early, stays late	• in late, usually leaves on time
• common touch	• strained with 'inferior' groups of staff
• good listener	• good talker
• available	• hard to reach
• fair	• unfair
• decisive	• uses committees
• humble	• arrogant
• tough, confronts nasty problems	• elusive, the 'artful dodger'
• persistent	• vacillates
• simplifies	• complicates
• tolerant	• intolerant
• knows people's names	• doesn't know people's names
• has strong convictions	• sways with the wind
• trusts people	• trusts only words and numbers on paper
• delegates whole important jobs	• keeps all final decisions for him/herself
• spends as little time as possible with outside directors	• spends a lot of time massaging outside directors
• wants anonymity for him/herself, publicity for the company	• wants publicity for him/herself
• often takes the blame	• looks for scapegoats
• gives credit to others	• takes credit
• gives honest, frequent feedback	• amasses information
• knows when and how to discipline people	• ducks unpleasant tasks
• has respect for all people	• has contempt for all people
• knows the business and the kind of people who make it tick	• knows the business only in terms of what it can do for him/her
• looks for controls to abolish	• looks for new controls and procedures
• prefers discussion rather than written reports	• prefers long reports

Example Box 18.1 (continued)

Leader	Non-leader
• honest under pressure	• equivocative
• straightforward	• tricky, manipulative
• open	• secrective
• as little paperwork as possible	• as much paperwork as possible
• promotes from within	• looks outside the organisation
• keeps promises	• doesn't keep promises
• plain office and facilities	• lavish office, expensive facilities
• organisation is top of the agenda	• self is top of the agenda
• sees mistakes as learning opportunities and the opportunity to develop.	• sees mistakes as punishable offences and the means of scapegoating

Peters and Austin add the following two riders to their version of these columns:

> You now know more about leaders and leadership than all the combined graduate business schools in America.
>
> You also know whether you have a leader or a non-leader in your manager's office.

Source: from T. Peters and N. Austin, *A Passion for Excellence: The Leadership Difference*, Harper and Row, 1986.

Attempts to identify the traits and characteristics present in successful leaders are largely inconclusive, in that none display all the attributes necessary to lead, direct or manage in all situations. However, the following are more or less universal.

- **Communication:** the ability to communicate regularly, continuously and in ways and language which those on the receiving end will be able to both understand and respond to.
- **Decision making:** the ability to take the right decisions in given situations, to take responsibility for them, and to understand the consequences of particular courses of action. Part of this involves being able to take an overall or strategic view of particular situations, to see the longer term and to take a wider general perspective. This is sometimes called 'the helicopter view'.
- **Commitment:** to both matters in hand and also the wider aspects of the organisation as a whole. This includes an inherent willingness to draw on personal, as well as professional, energies and to bring qualities of enthusiasm, drive and ambition to the particular situation.
- **Concern for staff:** respecting, trusting and committing oneself to them; developing them, understanding them and their aspirations and reconciling these with the matters in hand. Staff should be treated on a basis of equality and confidence.
- **Quality:** a commitment to the quality of product or service so that, whatever the

matter in hand, customers receive high value and high satisfaction, and the staff involved receive recognition for their effort.

- **A given set of values:** one with which others will identify, and to which they will commit themselves. There are few examples of leaders, directors or managers who succeed by being all things to all people in all situations.
- **Personal integrity:** this includes vision, enthusiasm, strength of character, commitment, energy and interest; it also includes the setting and establishment of high absolute standards of moral and ethical probity.
- **Positive attitudes:** held by the leader and transmitted to staff and customers.
- **Mutuality and dependency:** of leaders with their staffs; successful leaders know their own weaknesses, the importance and value of the people that go with them; above all, they know what they cannot do and where and when to go for help and support in these areas (see Example Box 18.2).

Leadership types

The following different types of leader may be distinguished.

- **Traditional leaders:** whose position is assured by birth and heredity. Examples of this are the kings and queens of England (and of other places in the world). They may also be found in family businesses, where child succeeds father as the chief executive or chair when the latter retires.
- **Known leaders:** whose position is secured by the fact that everybody understands their pre-eminence, at least in general. Kings and queens are examples again. Priests are known to be leaders of their congregations. Aristocrats are known to be masters or mistresses of their own domains. It is known also that they will be succeeded by one from their own estate when they die or move on.
- **Appointed leaders:** whose position is legitimised by virtue of the fact that they have gone through a selection, assessment and appointment process in accordance with the wishes and demands of the organisation and the expectations of those who will now be working for them. This invariably carries a defined and formalised managerial role in organisations.
- **Bureaucratic leaders:** whose position is legitimised by the rank that they hold. This is especially true of military structures and is reinforced by the job titles used and their known position in the hierarchy: corporal, captain, major, general. It is also to be found in complex commercial and public organisation structures. This also normally implies managerial responsibilities.
- **Functional or expert leaders:** whose position is achieved by virtue of their expertise. This form of leadership is likely to be related to particular issues; for example, the industrial relations officer may be a junior functionary who nevertheless becomes the acknowledged leader, director and problem-solver wherever industrial relations problems arise, whatever the rank or status of other people involved.
- **Charismatic leaders:** whose position is based on the sheer force of their personality. Many great world leaders (good or evil) have displayed this: Napoleon, Adolf Hitler, Winston Churchill, Margaret Thatcher, John F. Kennedy. In the business world, charismatic leaders include Richard Branson (Virgin), Anita Roddick (Body Shop) and Michael O'Leary (Ryan Air) (see Example Box 18.3).
- **Informal leaders:** whose position is maintained by virtue of their personality,

EXAMPLE BOX 18.2   The Leadership Functions Model

The leadership functions model recognises that certain traits, qualities, capabilities and aptitudes must be present in leaders; that these must be translated into action. It then reconciles this with emphasis on the work and the group that are the main features of the style approach to leadership. The qualities and capabilities required are:

judgement	integrity	human relation skill	dependability
fairness	dedication	cooperation	initiative
foresight	drive	decisiveness	emotional stability
ambition	objectivity		

The leader addresses the key tasks of achieving the task, building the team and paying attention to the individual members. Again, balance of the three is required. The leader who concentrates only on the task by going all out for production schedules, while neglecting the training, encouragement and motivation of the group, will always have problems of dissonance and dysfunction.

The leader who concentrates only on creating team spirit, while neglecting the job or individuals will not get maximum involvement and commitment, which only comes from an environment that is both harmonious and genuinely productive. Staff members would therefore lack any true feelings of achievement or success.

The key leadership functions required are:

direction	planning	communication	appraisal
decision making	coordination	control	creativity
assessment	development	resourcefulness	

Training courses were developed based around the concept of leadership functions. This was called 'action-centred' leadership. The courses were structured around a series of practical tasks: for example, the organisation of given sets of materials by leaders and groups into productive activities (such as getting across an open space without touching the floor; the organisation of carrying loads from one place to another).

Classroom exercises were centred around the study of war films such as *A Bridge too Far, Twelve O'clock High, Attack Alarm* and *The Longest Day*. Students on these courses assessed the general performance of the leader. They assessed in particular the attention paid by the leaders in the films to achievement of task, motivation and development of the group, and attention to individuals. From these activities, a body of first-hand experience would be generated by participants on which an evaluation of the effectiveness of particular approaches could be undertaken. This could then be related to group performance, individual performance, the extent to which the task was achieved and the reasons for this, and the contribution that the leader made towards it. It also enabled the relationship between the total purpose and sub-objectives to be assessed; for example, in some cases individuals made very strong and effective contributions to groups that nevertheless ultimately

Example Box 18.2 (continued)

failed. The study of the film *A Bridge too Far* and *Twelve O'clock High* in particular illustrates the need for coordination of effort between groups as well as within them.

Source: John Adair, *Action Centred Leadership*, Cambridge University Press, 1975.

EXAMPLE BOX 18.3   Charisma: Identity – and Rejection

It is very easy for people to identify with someone who holds a position of influence and who has a strong, dominant or forceful personality.

- Arthur Scargill generated overwhelming support for himself both when elected as President of the National Union of Mine Workers in 1979, and again in pursuit of the National Mine Workers strike of 1984/85.
- J.F. Kennedy conducted both his election campaign and the years of his Presidency on the basis of his personality – his charm, his freshness, his vitality, his appearance and looks – rather than his expertise and potential for running the country.
- Adolf Hitler had great personal presence with which he generated both pride and identity among the German nation of the 1920s and 1930s at a time of national bankruptcy.
- Margaret Thatcher fought the 1979 General Election in the UK, not on the basis of detailed and well-analysed policies, but rather on the slogan 'I will make Britain great again'.

Identity can quickly turn to rejection.

- Arthur Scargill is still held in high regard by a majority of his union members. When he became President of the National Union of Mine Workers in 1979 there were over 300 000 members. The Union now has 8000 members. For most of those lost along the way, extreme disillusion has set in.
- The USA has had great cultural and national problems reconciling the glamour and the martyrdom of J.F. Kennedy with subsequent revelations about his private life, the activities of the rest of the Kennedy family, and rumoured Mafia connections.
- The entire civilised world has turned against Hitler and everything that he built following the brutality of the way in which his armies fought the Second World War and also the great evil perpetrated in the concentration camps.
- The validity and extent of Margaret Thatcher's political legacy to the UK is coming under increasingly heavy scrutiny. At the start of the twenty-first century, she still remains the most influential figure within her party.

charisma, expertise or command of resources, but whose position is not formally legitimised by rank, appointment or tradition. This position may also be arrived at by virtue of some other activity for which they are particularly responsible, for example local trade union representative.

Leadership styles

The rationale for studying management styles is that employees will work better for managers who use particular styles of leadership (see Table 18.1 and Figure 18.2).

There are caveats however. Any management style must be supported by mutual trust, respect and confidence between manager and subordinates. If these qualities are not present then no style is effective. There must be a clarity of purpose and direction in the first place, and this must come from the organisation. Participation can only genuinely exist if this clarity exists also; it cannot exist in a void. Leadership and management styles must also be suitable and effective in terms of cultural and environmental pressures, as well as personal, professional and occupational acceptability.

The factors are interrelated. Account must also be taken of the fact that where leadership style is to be truly democratic, the decisions and wishes of the group must be accommodated, whatever is decided and whether this is 'right' or 'wrong' in terms of the demands of the work and the pressures of the wider environment.

The relationship between the leader, the work, the group and the environment may also be represented as in Figure 18.3. It must be understood both that there are demands exclusive to each element, and that it is necessary to integrate them all.

The participative/consultative style is supported by the work of Likert (see Chapter 20). The benefits that are held to accrue from this include the following.

FIGURE 18.1 Leadership functions model

Leadership and management styles   *TABLE 18.1*

Autocratic (benevolent or tyrannical)	Consultative/participative	Democratic/participative
1. Leaders makes all final decisions for the group.	1. Leader makes decisions after consultation with the group.	1. Decisions made by the group, by consultation or vote. Voting based on the principles of one person, one vote; majority rules.
2. Close supervision.	2. Total communication between leader and members.	2. All members bound by the group decision and support it.
3. Individual member's interests subordinate to those of the organisation.	3. Leader is supportive and developmental.	3. All members may contribute to discussion.
4. Subordinates treated without regard for their views.	4. Leader is accessible and discursive.	4. Development of coalitions and cliques.
5. Great demands placed on staff.	5. Questioning approach encouraged.	5. Leadership role is assumed by chair.
6. Questioning discouraged.	6. Ways of working largely unspecified.	
7. Conformist/coercive environment.	7. Leader retains responsibility and accountability for results.	

- **Communication:** two-way communication is a key feature which provides a general basis of mutual understanding. This leads to problems being identified early, enabling steps to be taken before they become dramas and crises. It also enables understanding and support to be generated for particular activities and a mutuality of interest to be established.
- **Satisfaction:** where people can take some part in structuring and ordering their work, and have a measurable autonomy and responsibility for its outcome, they can develop their jobs to greater limits and identify potential for preferred directions and choices for the future.
- **Supervision:** this is always present. In participative situations this is not close or coercive or domineering. It is based on mutual interest and accessibility: the ability of the supervisor to identify and take remedial or developmental action where necessary; and the ability of the subordinate to approach the supervisor with confidence when problems and issues do arise.
- **Understanding:** the more participative and open the style adopted, the greater the development of full understanding by all involved of their colleagues' points of view, hopes, aims and aspirations. Again, this contributes to the early identification of problems. It also leads to the development of mutual respect and trust, the ability to ask questions openly of each other and the development of a general mutuality of interest that is both positive and productive.

(a) Leadership continuum

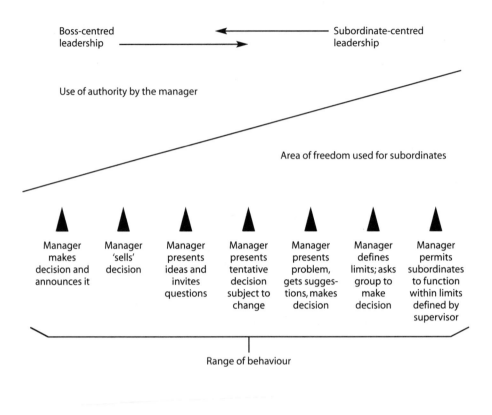

Boss-centred leadership → ← Subordinate-centred leadership

Use of authority by the manager

Area of freedom used for subordinates

| Manager makes decision and announces it | Manager 'sells' decision | Manager presents ideas and invites questions | Manager presents tentative decision subject to change | Manager presents problem, gets suggestions, makes decision | Manager defines limits; asks group to make decision | Manager permits subordinates to function within limits defined by supervisor |

Range of behaviour

Summary

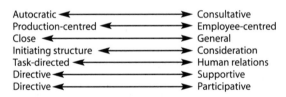

Autocratic	←→	Consultative
Production-centred	←→	Employee-centred
Close	←→	General
Initiating structure	←→	Consideration
Task-directed	←→	Human relations
Directive	←→	Supportive
Directive	←→	Participative

FIGURE 18.2 Leadership spectrum

- **Barriers:** these tend to be broken down when there is a participative style. This is because of the generation of mutuality of interest and direction. It is related to the volume and quality of communications. It also constitutes much of the groundwork that enables a general fairness and quality of interest for all involved to be generated.
- **Objectives:** organisational, group and individual objectives are invariably different and potentially conflicting. Participative styles are more likely to bring these out into the open enabling the mutuality of interest to be emphasised.
- **Preferred style of the leader:** preferred position on the autocratic–consultative–

(b) The leader in the environment

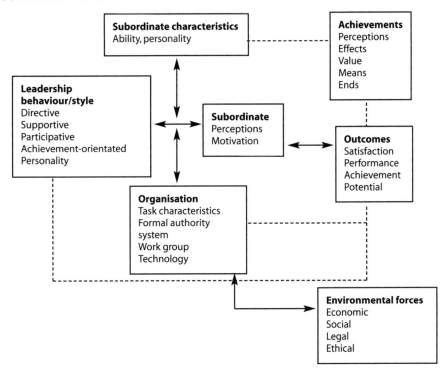

Leadership spectrum (continued)

FIGURE 18.2

participative–democratic continuum. This is partly related to the personal comfort of the leader, partly to the nature of the task and partly to the desired relationship with the group. There may also be environmental pressures: for example, the organisation may have a generally preferred leadership style that leads to pressures to conform on those responsible for particular groups. Groups may also seek to influence the nature of the style.

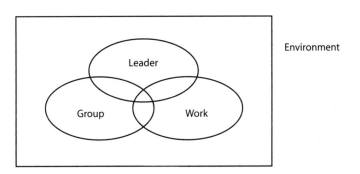

The leader, work, group and environment mix

FIGURE 18.3

- **Confidence:** personal, professional and operational confidence related to the need to gain results from the group involved. A highly experienced group may be left largely to its own devices once the broad nature of the work is understood. A new and inexperienced group may need strong and regular direction, work structuring and individual, as well as overall, schedules and targets.
- **Environmental pressures:** which include:
  - the structures and systems of the organisation, its overall, culture, values and attitudes, reporting relationships, realpolitik and overall leadership style. The style adopted by managers in relation to particular groups and activities has to be in harmony with the rest of the organisation
  - wider legal, social and ethical pressures, the values of the community and environment in which activities are conducted
  - pressure for results in terms of volume, quality and time. These have to be reconciled in turn with budget and resource constraints and the agenda of other individuals and groups.

Ineffective leadership style

Ineffective leadership is based on:

- ruling with an iron hand
- punitive approaches to problems, apportioning individual blame
- criticising others in public
- seeking scapegoats from among the group
- insisting that everything is done the leader's way, refusal to explain actions, refusal to consider other points of view
- lack of general consideration and empathy.

Ineffective work is based on:

- lack of clear purpose, aims and objectives
- lack of clear planning and scheduling, letting the work drift
- lack of appropriate technology, equipment and expertise
- letting people do work in ways that they think best without monitoring and evaluating performance
- the allowance of interruptions and diversions.

The clear requirement for a complete and effective style of management is attention to both group and task.

Over-emphasis on the group – employee-centred leadership – is likely to lead to general feelings of comfort but a lack of attention to the work. It may also lead to group-think and lack of consideration of its relationship with the wider environment.

Over-emphasis on the task – job centred leadership – invariably leads to feelings of dissatisfaction among the staff. This is brought on by general perceptions that they are unvalued and that they are merely instruments in the pursuit of output. Expertise and attention is therefore required in both aspects, and this has then to be integrated with the nature of the style adopted (see Example Box 18.4).

EXAMPLE BOX 18.4 Leadership Style: A Military Example

'You cannot expect a soldier to be a proud soldier if you humiliate him. You cannot expect him to be brave if you abuse him. You cannot expect him to be strong if you break him. You cannot ask for respect and obedience and willingness to assault hot landing zones, hump back-breaking ridges, destroy dug-in emplacements if your soldier has not been treated with respect and dignity which fosters unit and personal pride. The line between firmness and harshness, between strong leadership and bullying is a fine line. It is difficult to define, but those in authority who have accepted a career as a leader of men must find that line. It is because judgement and concern for people and human relations are involved in leadership, that only people can lead and not machines. I entreat you to be ever-alert to the pitfalls of too much authority. Beware that you do not fall into the category of a little man, with a little job, with a big head. In essence, be considerate, treat your subordinates right and they will literally die for you.'

Source: General Melvin Zais, quoted in T. Peters and N. Austin, *A Passion for Excellence: The Leadership Difference*, Harper and Row, 1986.

Blake and Mouton (1986): the managerial grid

The managerial grid is a configuration of management styles based on the matching of two dimensions of managerial concern: those of 'concern for people' and 'concern for production/output'. Each of these dimensions is plotted on a 9-point scale and an assessment made of managerial styles according to where they come out on each axis (see Figure 18.4). Thus, a low score (1–1) on each axis reflects poverty in managerial style; a high score (9–9) on each reflects a high degree of balance, concern and commitment in each area. The implication from this is that an adequate, effective and successful managerial style is in place.

The 9–9 score is indicated as the best by Blake and Mouton. This illustrates the targets to be striven for and the organisation's current position in relation to each axis. It also implies that the best fit is along the diagonal line: concern for the task and concern for the people should be grown alongside each other rather than one being emphasised at the expense of the other.

The information on which the position on the grid is based is drawn from structured questionnaires that are issued to all managers and supervisors in the organisation, section, unit or department to be assessed, and also to all their staff.

There are specific situations where a greater measure of direction is required. These include: emergencies, extreme conditions of hardship, and activities where there are prescribed right and wrong ways of doing things. There is no scope for debate in these areas and the benefits to be accrued from participation have to be sought in other ways.

Some organisation and social cultures cause people to *want* direction and prescription so that they have a clear point from which to take a lead. Those organisations and individuals that are not used to participation have to be trained and developed in

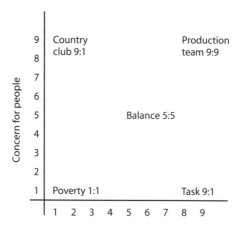

Other styles identified are:

- **9-1**: the country club: production is incidental; concern for the staff and people is everything; the group exists largely to support itself
- **1-9**: task orientation: production is everything; concern for the staff is subordinated to production and effectiveness. Staff management mainly takes the form of planning and control activities in support of production and output. Organisational activity and priority is concerned only with output.
- **5-5**: balance: a medium degree of expertise, commitment and concern in both areas; this is likely to produce adequate or satisfactory performance from groups that are reasonably well satisfied with working relations.

FIGURE 18.4 The managerial grid

such activities if they are to become fully effective. Conversely, others expect participation and involvement as a matter of course, and have equal difficulty where this is absent or removed.

It should also be noted that many of the organisations that are currently most successful have adopted the consultative (rather than participative) approach. Again the benefits indicated in the participative or supportive style are to be drawn from elsewhere, and there is evidence (as we have seen) that they are. The management style of McDonald's, Body Shop and Virgin Atlantic is prescriptive and directive. So also is that of Sanyo, Sony and Nissan. Many older and more traditional organisations, in both the public and private sectors, are seeking to learn lessons from these model organisations and transform their management styles in pursuit of comparable results.

Contingency approaches

Contingency theories of leadership take account of the interaction and interrelation between the organisation and its environment. This includes the recognition and accommodation of those elements that cannot be controlled. It also includes recognising that those elements that can be controlled and influenced must be addressed in ways that vary in different situations; that the correct approach in one case is not a prescription to be applied to others. There is a constant interaction between the leader's job and the work to be done; and between this and the general operations of the organisation in question. There is also the requirement to vary the leadership style according to the changing nature of the situation.

The concept of contingency approaches to leadership was first developed by F.E. Fiedler in the 1960s. Above all, the work identified situations where directive styles of management worked effectively as follows.

- Very favourable to the leader, where favourable was defined as a combination of circumstances: the leader was liked and trusted by the group; the task was clearly understood, easy to follow and well defined; the leader enjoyed a high degree of respect within the group; the leader had a considerable influence over the group members in terms of reward and punishment; the leader enjoyed unqualified backing from the organisation.
- Very unfavourable to the leader, where unfavourable was defined as the converse of this; and also where the task was not clearly defined; and where the work was to be carried out in an extreme environment (discomfort, working away from home).

Leadership styles may be effective or ineffective, depending upon their application and appropriateness to given situations. This is developed into a three-dimensional (3D) model by W. Reddin (see Figure 18.5).

Appropriate, effective leadership

- **Bureaucrat:** low concern for both task and relationships; appropriate in situations where rules and procedures are important.
- **Benevolent autocrat:** high concern for task, low concern for relationships; appropriate in task cultures.
- **Developer:** high concern for relationships and low concern for tasks; appropriate where the acquiescence, cooperation and commitment of the people is paramount.
- **Executive:** high concern for task, high concern for relationships; appropriate where the achievement of high standards is dependent on high levels of motivation and commitment.

Inappropriate, ineffective leadership

- **Deserter:** low concern for both task and relationships; the manager lacks involvement and is either passive or negative.
- **Autocrat:** high concern for task, low concern for relationships; the manager is coercive, confrontational, adversarial, lacking confidence in others.
- **Missionary:** high concern for relationships, low concern for task; the manager's position is dependent on preserving harmony and there is often a high potential for conflict.
- **Compromiser:** high concern for both tasks and relationships; manager is a poor decision maker, expedient and concerned only with the short-term.

Best fit

Best fit adopts the view that all leadership theories have a contribution, and that none by itself is the right or complete answer.

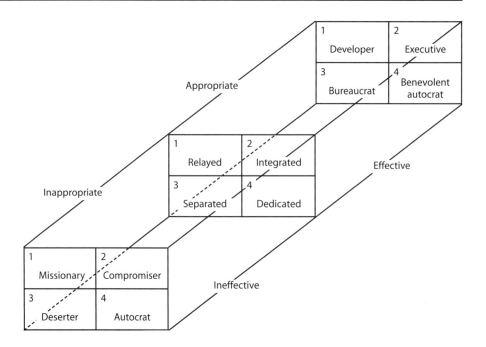

Purpose: The middle set of boxes identifies the four archeype leaders of Reddin's theory. These archetypes may then be translated into *appropriate effective* or *inappropriate ineffective* personal types.

FIGURE 18.5 W. Reddin: leadership and management behaviour

Best fit relates the leader, the subordinates, the task in hand and the environment. These elements are both interactive and mobile.

This must be developed further. For example, if the group is ineffective it becomes easy to state 'best fit was not achieved' without necessarily carrying out any further investigation; this is very superficial.

Handy (1990) describes best fit as consisting of:

- support: behaviour that enhances group members' feelings of personal worth
- interaction facilitation: encouraging members to develop mutually satisfying and supportive relationships
- goal emphasis: behaviour that stimulates desire and drives for excellent operational performance
- work facilitation: classical management activities of scheduling, coordination and planning.

Peters (1986) states that to this may be added the need to nurture qualities of flexibility, commitment, responsiveness and drive. This is achieved by a combination of direction and support on the part of the leader, and is a responsibility of anybody who conducts any form of leadership or supervision.

Furthermore, in many parts of the Western world there has emerged a consensus culture. In its widest terms this means that people need, want and are entitled to know where they stand, so that they may consent to work and that they may understand the basis on which this consent is requested or demanded.

The complexities of leadership

Understanding the complexities of leadership requires consideration of:

- assumptions
- functions
- roles.

Assumptions

Leaders act in the name of their particular organisation, department or function. They therefore have a degree of power, influence, authority, responsibility and accountability. This is to be used in the pursuit of effective leadership performance. These prerogatives may be enhanced, diminished or withdrawn by the organisation at any time (in Western organisations, this is usually but not always as the result of some form of consultation or appraisal of performance).

The leader must be acceptable to all those with whom he/she comes into contact. This applies both inside and outside the organisation. The range and complexity of relationships that leaders must develop are dependent on this.

The leader has certain clearly defined tasks, activities and directions. The leader also has a sphere in which personal judgement and initiative are to be exercised. This includes the qualities of flexibility, dynamism and responsiveness. It also includes characteristics of honesty, trustworthiness and integrity.

Leaders must have a working knowledge and understanding of the tasks being carried out by those in their sphere of influence. This does not mean being a technical expert. For example, managers who have secretaries cannot always type, but they must understand what typing is, how long typing takes, what is an acceptable level of performance and presentation, what is the most suitable machinery and so on; this extends to all spheres of activity. Where there is no such understanding dysfunction always occurs.

Functions of leaders in organisations

This is a general list of these functions, which may be found in all directorial, managerial and supervisory roles to a greater or lesser extent:

- setting, agreeing and communicating objectives
- providing suitable equipment, resources and environment to enable people to meet their objectives
- monitoring, evaluating and reviewing performance; appraisal of groups and individuals
- giving feedback
- setting standards of attitude, behaviour and performance
- solving problems, both operational and human; administering rewards and punishments wherever necessary; dealing with grievances and discipline
- organising and harmonising resources

- ensuring inward flows of materials
- ensuring that deadlines for outputs are met
- taking effective decisions
- developing the capabilities and performance of the group and its members
- developing the efficiency and effectiveness of the group and its output
- acting as figurehead and representative inside and outside the department
- parenting.

Leadership roles

The main leadership roles are as follows.

- **Figurehead:** in which the leader acts as the human face of the department, division or organisation to the rest of the world. For senior managers, politicians, public figures and other charismatic leaders, this is straightforward, and the effect is often enhanced by stage management and presentation techniques (see Example Box 18.5).

  At departmental, divisional and functional level, managers and supervisors act as figureheads in dealings with others. This requires attention to both the merits of particular cases or arguments, and the effectiveness of presentation and delivery. The key to being an effective departmental or divisional figurehead is extensive preparation, and the development of high-quality communication skills.
- **Ambassador:** in which leaders act as advocates, cheerleaders and problem-solvers on behalf of their department, division, organisation and staff. Again, for high profile public leaders this is straightforward (see Example Box 18.6).

  Every high profile public figure playing this role requires expert briefing and preparation, as well as sound knowledge and understanding of the particular situation into which they are going. This must also apply to organisation, departmental and divisional supervisors and managers when they have to carry out these functions.
- **Servant:** this view of leadership and management is based on the premise that the manager is the ultimate supporter or servant of staff, product and service output and quality, and markets, customers and clients (see Figure 18.6).
- **Maintenance:** this role requires:
  - daily maintenance: attending to problems and issues as they arise
  - preventative maintenance: continuous improvement of the work, working environment, and procedures and practices; attention to staff development
  - breakdown maintenance: handling crises, blow-ups and storms in a quick and effective manner.
- **Role model:** leaders, managers and supervisors set the style, standards, attitudes and behaviour for those who work for them. If leaders show qualities of commitment, enthusiasm, energy and honesty, these may be expected to arise in subordinates (see Example Box 18.7).
- **Ringmaster:** in their own particular spheres, all managers and supervisors are ringmasters. This is quite apart from any particular knowledge or aptitude for the task in hand.

The role elements indicated here are essential to effective leadership and direction at

EXAMPLE BOX 18.5 Lessons from the Nazi Era

Nobody would ever have heard of Adolf Hitler if he had not managed to secure the backing of the German military, who were happy to lend their support to anyone who would give them back their status, pride, prestige and influence. This backing, in turn, was used to secure the support and expertise of Leni Riefenstal and Josef Goebbels so that the Nazi message could be preached and filmed in ways that would be received favourably by the mass population.

When war broke out in 1939, the UK Prime Minister was Neville Chamberlain. He resigned in 1940 to be replaced by Winston Churchill. Churchill quickly realised that his own vision and utter dedication would not be enough. He accordingly spent extensive periods of time learning voice projection and the art of being filmed in particular situations. A Pathe news crew was with him at all times. Newsreel films were relayed at all cinemas throughout the country. Churchill's radio broadcasts were put out at times when it was known that there would be mass audiences available, and when they were unlikely to be disrupted by bombing.

EXAMPLE BOX 18.6 Lessons from Leaders in the Twenty-first Century

- **Stelios Hadjoannou (EasyJet):** Stelios Hadjoannou normally appears in public upon request, whether to address specific problems or complaints about the EasyJet airline, or to offer opinions about other things; he takes the view that this enhances the profile and reputation of his company. In 1999, his company featured in a 'fly on the wall' television documentary series 'Airline'. This was so successful with viewers that it continues to run commercially.
- **Richard Branson (Virgin):** Richard Branson has had to counter adverse criticisms of the quality of some of his activities, especially railways and financial services. On each of these occasions, he has used the media to acknowledge the problems, to gain general positive publicity for the Virgin Group, and to act as the company's general cheerleader.
- **Anita Roddick (The Body Shop):** Anita Roddick was forced to take an active part in stock market education when both brokers and media analysts failed to understand the basic business premise of The Body Shop: long-term security and viability (and therefore owner value), rather than short-term share price advantage.

Each of these examples illustrates the point of view from which the ambassadorial role may be seen. In each of these cases, the contribution is positive, addressing the specific issues, as well as enhancing general profile and value.

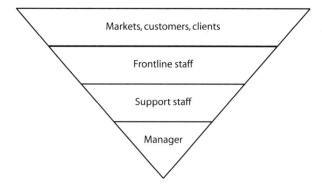

The manager or supervisor is placed at the bottom point, prima facie supporting and serving the workforce rather than sitting on top of it.

FIGURE 18.6 The inverse pyramid

whatever level. To be an effective leader the individual must accept an overwhelming responsibility to adopt these roles and the responsibilities inherent within them. It is also incumbent upon the person concerned to develop any of the qualities required in which he or she is not proficient.

Measures of success and failure

When the performance of leaders is being assessed it is again necessary to look at both the simple and the complex. In simple terms the criterion (as with anything else) is to measure performance against preset objectives and the extent to which these were achieved.

In practice, measurement of the leadership task and function is more complex. There are hard and soft elements. The hard elements will normally indicate quantifiable targets (to produce a return of x per cent, to generate y in income, to reduce costs to z, and so on). The soft include measures of confidence, respect, loyalty and identity.

Confidence

Thus, the chair of a publicly quoted company must maintain the confidence of the world's stock markets. Without this the share price falls. If this continues and shares continue to fall despite the activities and directions proposed by the executives in question, they will normally leave. This may also occur as the result of a bad set of company figures, either for a period or on a more continuous and long-term basis.

Confidence may also be lost among other backers and stakeholders. The leader in question may lose the respect and regard of the staff, as the result of some dishonest, expedient or unjustifiably punitive action for example.

Executives may lose the confidence of the markets in which business is conducted. This occurs for example, if a product is launched during their tenure that subsequently fails commercially, has a bad image or which it becomes apparent is unsafe or dangerous.

EXAMPLE BOX 18.7 Disasters and the Model of Leadership

In 1987 the *Herald of Free Enterprise*, a car and passenger ferry operating between the ports of Dover, Calais and Zeebrugge, sank outside Zeebrugge Harbour with the loss of 200 lives. The cause of the disaster was water rushing in through the bow doors, which had been jammed open. The ship had put to sea before the doors had been closed. The inquiry into the tragedy described the ship's owners, Townsend Thoresen, as a company 'riddled with the disease of sloppiness'. Nobody had thought it important enough to check or ensure that the doors were closed before the ship set sail. A key finding of the inquiry report was that the staff had behaved in ways that they perceived that they were required and expected by the organisation's top managers.

In 1988 there was a serious fire at the underground station at King's Cross, London. Thirty-one people died. During the inquiry it came out that the conditions and circumstances which caused the fire had been known to exist for a long while. They had constantly been reported by safety representatives and committees over a period of years. Particular attention had been drawn to the wooden escalators, the build-up of oil and rubbish underneath these, and the fact that travellers were allowed to smoke on the underground system. Nothing was done about this. In the end a cigarette dropped on to the floor set fire to the rubbish that had accumulated and this, in turn, set fire to the escalator. The fire then spread to the rest of the station.

In each case, the way in which those directly concerned reacted reflected the model behaviour that had been established by those at the top of the organisation and responsible for its direction and activities, and the standards by which these were to be conducted.

The converse of this is 'leaving a void'. This is where the confidence and identity of the organisation with the leader are fully integrated. Any question of the leader departing is therefore viewed with great alarm. For example commentaries on the Virgin Group always include questions of 'What happens to the organisation if anything happens to Richard Branson?'

Confidence is only maintained through honesty and integrity. Where the leader (of anything) is caught lying, the instant and unambiguous message given out is that 'he/she is a liar'. Any subsequent dealing or transaction with this particular individual is therefore invariably prefixed by questions of how far the person may be trusted. It is in turn exacerbated during briefings for those who are to be involved with them along the lines of 'don't believe a word they say' and 'get something in writing and get their signature'.

The complex view

Measures of success and failure will also address the question of what else was achieved during the particular period of office. The direction taken may have opened up a great range of subsequent opportunities and a part of this measurement will relate to the extent to which these were exploited.

This is also to be seen in the complexity indicated. The hard targets may be achieved for example, but only at the expense of the soft: the destruction of staff relations, motivation and morale. Conversely a superbly integrated and supportive group may be built that never actually produces anything of substance. The targets that were set may turn out to have been immeasurable, hopelessly optimistic or far too easy. In the latter case in particular it is both easy and dangerous to indulge in an entirely false sense of success.

The legitimacy of the objectives and performance targets must also be generally and constantly questioned. To return to the hard examples quoted above: increases in output, profit and cost effectiveness of x per cent should always be treated with scepticism. They assume that the basis on which the percentage is calculated is legitimate and valid, and that the increase constitutes the best use of organisation resources. They also assume (this especially applies to public services) that adequate and effective activity levels can be maintained.

It should be clear from this that the setting of organisation performance targets is a process capable of rationalisation and must be founded on the understanding of general organisation requirements. In the particular context of leadership, it should be clear also that ultimate responsibility for success or failure in achieving these targets rests with the leader.

Conclusions

When studied in this way it becomes clear that, for all its dependence upon quality, styles, roles and assumptions there is much in the concept and content of leadership that can be pinned down fairly precisely. We have said little about appearance, manner or bearing: that is, the extent to which individuals look the part, sound the part, act the part (anything in fact rather than being the part). Rather, it is clear that there is a substantial body of knowledge and expertise upon which to draw both in the assessment of what leadership is and also in the identification of who will make a good leader (and who will not). There are lessons here for those in charge of organisations, and for personnel and human resource professionals. It is possible to take positive, informed and enlightened steps towards the successful identification, development and appointment of the right people for leadership positions.

It is also clear that leaders are made and not born. People can be trained in each of the qualities and elements indicated so that (as with anything else) they may first understand, then apply, then reinforce and finally become expert in the activities indicated. This is understood to be on the same basis as aptitude for anything else however. Not everyone has the qualities or potential necessary in the first place. There is nothing contentious in this – not everyone has the qualities or potential to be a great chef, racing driver, nurse or labourer and in this respect leadership is no different.

CHAPTER SUMMARY

In business, commercial and public-sector organisations, leadership is that part of management that provides the vision, direction and energy that give life to policy, strategy and operations. It provides everyone involved – above all, the staff, but also suppliers, customers and community groups – with a point of identity and focus, a personification of the organisation with which they themselves are involved, and with which they are dealing. Problems always occur when the leader, for whatever reason, is either unwilling or unable to accept the full responsibilities of the position. These problems are compounded when it becomes known or perceived that the leader is acting without integrity, and is seeking to blame either circumstances or other people for organisational, strategic and operational shortcomings. In these cases, staff only remain in employment so long as they believe it in their interests to do so, and this invariably leads to the early loss of high-quality staff. Problems also arise when leaders accept their responsibilities to one group of stakeholders, in preference to others; this is a serious problem in large public and multinational corporations when senior managers discharge their responsibilities to shareholders, political interests and the drives of boards of directors and governors, at the expense of staff, suppliers, customers and clients.

Those who aspire to leadership positions must therefore be prepared to accept that there are certain qualities that go with the job – above all, enthusiasm, ambition, clarity of purpose, energy and direction – and must be prepared to develop these as the condition of employment in these positions. It is also important to recognise that this part of management development cannot be achieved except through a period of long-term, prioritised, intensive and demanding training, supported with periods of further education either at a university or conducted through the private sector. It is impossible to develop leaders purely on the basis of single or isolated short periods of training, unsupported by activities at the workplace. Moreover, it must be stressed again that the best practitioners of a particular trade, profession or occupation do not necessarily make the best leaders and managers of groups of these staff; assessment for leadership and management potential must be carried out on the basis of the ability to observe the fledgling qualities required rather than existing professional and technical expertise.

It is clear that this part of management development is going to become very much more important in the future. Organisations are certain to value much more highly the all-round capabilities and willingness to accept responsibility of those whom they place in top positions. In the medium to long term, the ability to satisfy dominant shareholder or political interests is certain not to be enough.

DISCUSSION QUESTIONS

1. What are the key attributes of a good leader? Give examples that illustrate these. To what extent can effective leaders lead in any organisation or situation; and to what extent is their effectiveness limited by the constraints in which they find themselves?
2. To what extent may the last three UK Prime Ministers be considered successful? Identify the criteria and means by which they are judged and state whether or not you think these are valid and reliable.
3. What is the role of organisational leadership in a crisis or disaster?
4. Devise a leadership training programme for junior managers and supervisors with aspirations to become more senior. This should be of six to twelve months duration. The programme should indicate aims and objectives, content, learning methods and the means by which success or failure would be judged and evaluated.

SUNFLOWER SEEDS LTD

Stephen Nash inherited Sunflower Seeds Ltd, a single-site nursery and garden centre, from his uncle. The business, set on the edge of a market town in south-eastern England, enjoys a good local reputation. At the weekends especially, large numbers of customers come from both the town and the outlying villages, and business is brisk.

However, it becomes clear to Stephen that everything is not quite as it should be. Sales and purchases are not properly recorded, and the only paperwork that is always retained are Visa card receipts and delivery notes.

The nursery employs 30 staff. Six of these are gardeners, who work tending the plants in allotments at the side of the centre before they are ready to be sold. A further ten are concerned with customer service and sales. Four work on the purchasing side: travelling to and from wholesalers, and making purchases as they see fit. There is an office staff of three who handle wages and other personnel matters, and also deal with the sales and purchasing reconciliation. The remaining seven are school and college students who work part-time on Saturdays and Sundays.

It seems to Stephen that some of the employees are a bit slapdash. One of the gardeners, an old gentlemen who has worked for the company for forty years, clearly regards himself as the senior manager. Two of the others only came into nursery work after losing jobs in local factories. The part-time staff tend to turn up and leave when they feel like it on Saturdays and Sundays, and sometimes do not come in at all.

In the shop, things are not very much better. The appearance of the shop is treading a very fine line between being fully, if rustically, stocked, and being a mess. When Stephen has enquired politely about this, he has been told 'This is what the customers expect to see. This is the way that it always has been.'

Stephen has also looked at the books. The company's accountant has produced figures at the bottom of which he has stated: 'These are accurate on the basis of the information that I have received.' It is clear that while income turnover is rising, expenditure is going up much more sharply and the figures for this and the previous two years are as shown opposite.

There is a full canteen in which the staff eat their lunch and take their breaks. On the wall of this, there is a tatty old sheet, written by another of the uncle's old retainers. This person, a man in his fifties, seems to have assumed the general responsibility for everything, and oversees all of the financial transactions. He is very

	This year £m	Last year £m	Previous year £m
Turnover	8.2	7.6	6.9
Goods inward	4.8	2.1	0.5
Labour costs	1.0	0.8	0.6
Overhead	0.5	0.5	0.4
Operating profit	1.9	4.2	5.6
Tax	1.2	0.5	0.3
Interest	1.1	1.0	0.3
Net profit	(0.4)	2.7	5.0

fierce about everyone starting work on time and not finishing until six in the evening. The trouble is that he himself is never there until 10.30 in the morning, and once he arrives he spends all his time either on the phone to his favourite contacts within the business, or else wandering round prying into everybody else's business. This has rubbed off on the rest of the staff, and everyone seems to be a little careless. Garden tools are often put away dirty at the end of the day, and the whole nursery has a muddy, unkempt look about it. Overall, therefore, behind the scenes, the prevailing attitude is one of 'couldn't care less'.

The firm continues to have an excellent name in the neighbourhood, but it has become apparent to Stephen that the overriding reason for this is that there is no local competition.

QUESTIONS

1. What leadership style should Stephen adopt and why? What actions is he going to have to take in order to make this acceptable to everyone involved?
2. What responsibilities does Stephen have in tackling each of the problems indicated above?
3. What problems might be foreseen in the future, and what actions should Stephen be taking now in order to minimise their effects?

19 Teams and Groups

'I am proud to be the Group's Chief Executive, and I am convinced that it is perfectly consistent for us to focus on our customers and profitability, while also ensuring that we live family-friendly values.' Barry Gibson, Group Chief Executive, Littlewoods, *Management Today*, October 1999.

'The first thing that I needed to do was to get this collection of excellent players working as a team.' Vicente Del Bosque, Coach, Real Madrid, on taking up the job in September 1999.

'We should celebrate our individuality and our differences. That is what gives strength to the whole Department.' Andrew Scott, Director, Management Studies Centre, University College London, January 2001.

CHAPTER OUTLINE

Group composition and priority

Key features of group management

Key features of group behaviour

Problem areas in the constitution and management of groups

Group development and progress.

CHAPTER OBJECTIVES

After studying this chapter, you should be able to:

understand the behavioural and operational features and constraints of group work

understand the management priorities in the ordering and direction of groups

understand the universal problem areas that arise in the management of groups

understand the key processes that have to be used if effective groups are to be constituted.

Introduction

Teams and groups are gatherings of two or more people that either exist or are drawn together and constituted for a purpose. This purpose is understood and accepted by all those involved. This purpose may be:

* largely social: sports and leisure clubs

- work or task oriented: workplace groups, committees, task and project groups, other ad hoc but organised gatherings
- based on the norms and expectations of society: above all the family (nuclear and extended)
- based on the beliefs and values of the members: churches and religious groups
- based on the expertise of members: the professional bodies, legalised associations
- mutual interest: trade unions; also hobbies and interests.

Joining organisations and their departments, divisions, functions, locations and activities also constitutes team and group membership.

In society, people become members of groups and teams from an early age and move into and out of them throughout their lives. Very young children often go to play groups. A child may first join the Cubs or Brownies and later move on to the Scouts or Guides because there is an age barrier to membership of each. More generally, belonging to a class or sports team at school constitutes group membership. The process of belonging to, and joining and changing, groups is established at an early age and is part of the wider and general socialisation process. By the time of joining a workplace this is well understood.

Additionally, groups may usefully be defined as:

- **Formal:** constituted for a precise purpose. Formal groups normally have rules, regulations and norms that support the pursuit of that purpose. Formal groups also normally have means and methods of preserving and enhancing their expertise. There are also likely to be means and methods that enable people to move into, contribute and move out of a given group.
- **Informal:** where the purpose is less precise but still clearly understood and accepted by all involved. A card school falls into this category, as does a Friday night gathering of friends and colleagues at the bar.
- **Psychological:** viewed from the point of view that membership is dependent upon people interacting with each other, are aware of each other, and perceive themselves to belong.

Groups may be distinguished in these ways from general gatherings of people drawn together for a more general purpose: for example, queuing to pay at the supermarket or waiting for a bus or train. Even in these circumstances a group identity may start to form. If the queue takes a long while to clear or if the bus or train is late, people start to form an identity at least for the moment based around the particular set of circumstances. This may lead to the constitution of a more enduring group for the future: a travelling group on the train for example.

From this, an initial general set of group characteristics may begin to be identified. These are:

- Each member is able to communicate with every other member of the group.
- There is collective identity based on a combination of the circumstances and environment in which members find themselves.
- Groups have shared aims and objectives. In the examples indicated above, these are the ability to travel and arrive at the required destination; the expectation (hope) that eventually those present will be served by the cashier at the

supermarket; and the need to pass the time involved productively and comfortably in the activities indicated (i.e. waiting and travelling).

- There are roles and structure. In the examples indicated these may be: a joker; the finder of a compartment in which to sit; the provider of newspapers and magazines; and so on. The leadership structure may begin to be based around one who makes suggestions: 'Why don't we move to another queue/call the supervisor?'; 'Why don't we bring sandwiches/tea/ beer/cards?'; and so on.
- Groups have norms and rules. Personal behaviour starts to become modified as the result of membership of the group. Smokers may resist or curtail their habit when in the presence of group members; patterns of dress may start to emerge. This is the general basis on which organisational groups are structured and developed.

Purpose

Organisational groups are constituted for a purpose, to meet a set of aims and objectives. These purposes generally fall into one of the following categories:

- distribution of work, by department, division, function, location, skill, aptitude, expertise and quality
- controlling work, through the placing of managers and supervisors at the head of teams and groups of people constituted for the purpose of conducting work
- project work and problem-solving, often constituted on an ad hoc basis for the life and duration of the specific matter in hand (though there are certain circumstances where this leads to future activities)
- creative activities, brainstorming, information pooling and gathering, the generation of bursts of energy and enlightenment in response to given issues
- to conduct inquiries into past activities, both successful and those which fail
- to investigate and resolve conflicts, grievances, disputes and arguments between individuals and groups
- clusters: of persons of the same profession or occupation from different departments; of equivalent levels of expertise in different fields; of equivalent rank (for example managers and supervisors); for the purposes of exchanging and gathering general information and knowledge; and a wider understanding of the total organisational and professional picture
- to take responsibility for the direction and management of a particular organisation's activities and services
- to coordinate and harmonise sets of activities often from different sources, functions, departments, divisions and expertise
- to implement initiatives, directions, policies, strategies and decisions
- for other specific organisational matters, especially health and safety, staff relations and consultation.

Through membership of work groups individuals also seek the following:

- distinctive work roles within which they can be comfortable and happy; and which satisfy their feelings of self-esteem
- establishing a self-summary and self-concept which can be presented both to others in the work group and to the world at large

- contribution to productive, positive, profitable and effective activities. This in itself leads to satisfaction, feelings of personal success and raised levels of self-esteem
- the ability to fulfil personal aims and ambitions which normally have to be harmonised and entwined with those of a particular organisation.

These reasons for belonging overlap and conflict (see Figures 19.1 and 19.2). Group norms and processes may also create distinctive pressures on individuals to perform in given ways, at certain speeds and to adopt given patterns of behaviour (see Example Box 19.1).

The creation of effective groups

Tuckman (1965) identifies four elements as follows.

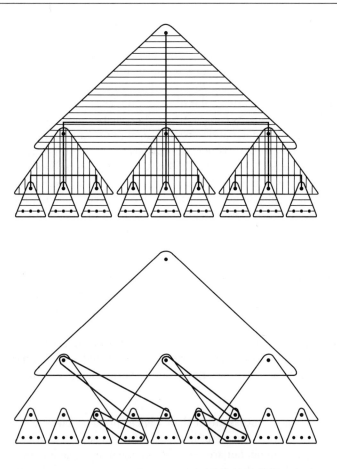

The linking pin model of Likert: the interrelationship   *FIGURE 19.1* of groups

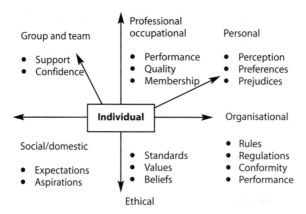

FIGURE 19.2 Divided loyalties

- **Forming:** (the coming together of the individuals concerned; beginning to learn about each other – personality, strengths, capabilities; assessment of the group purpose; introduction to the tasks, aims and objectives; initial thoughts about rules, norms, ways of working and achieving objectives; initial social and personal interaction; introduction to the group leader/leadership; acquiring and setting resources; constraints, drives and priorities.
- **Storming:** the first creative burst of the group; energising the activities; gaining initial markers about its capabilities and capacities and those of its members; creating the first output and results; mutual appraisal and assessment of expertise and process. Initial conflicts tend to become apparent at this stage, together with the need for means for their resolution. Opportunities and diversions may also become apparent. Conflicts between group and personal agenda start to emerge.
- **Norming:** the establishment of norms – the behavioural boundaries within which members are to act and operate; the establishment of rules and codes of conduct that underline and reinforce the standards set by the norms. By doing this the group provides itself with means of control and the basis of acceptable and unacceptable conduct, performance and activities.

  For rules and norms to be effective they must be clear, understood and accepted by all. They must be capable of doing what they set out to do. They must reinforce the mutuality, confidence and integrity necessary to effective group performance.
- **Performing:** the addressing of matters in hand; attacking the tasks to be carried out; getting results; assessing performance. This includes attention to group effectiveness and cohesion, as well as absolute performance measures; the two are invariably entwined.

This is to be seen as a process rather than a linear progression or series of steps and stages. For example, early successes in the life of the group may, strictly speaking, be categorised as 'performing' but are nevertheless essential to produce the mutual confidence, trust and reliance that are integral to effective 'forming'. Regarding this as a process also underlines the need for attention to the behavioural as well as operational aspects (see Example Box 19.2), especially group maintenance.

EXAMPLE BOX 19.1 Group Responsibility

Handy (1990) states that 'groups take riskier decisions than the individuals that comprise them would have done if they had been acting independently'. They behave more adventurously.

Fear of non-conformity contributes to this. When a newcomer joins a group he/she is normally willing and eager to accept its norms and rules. A range of research underlines this.

- The **Milgram** experiments of 1974 were based on the question: 'Would you torture someone else simply because you were told to do so by a person in authority?' The experiments involved volunteers acting as 'teachers' of those trying to learn word pairs. If the subject got the pairs wrong the 'teacher' administered an electric shock. The shocks increased in intensity, the greater number of mistakes made.

  In fact, no electric shocks were administered. However the volunteer 'teachers' nevertheless pressed the switch that supposedly gave the shocks when directed to do so by someone 'in authority'. Defiance only occurred when the subject was first encouraged to do so by 'rebellious elements' drawn from among the other group members. Little defiance was exhibited by volunteers working alone (Milgram, 1974).

- **Philip Zimbardo** (Zimbardo *et al.*, 1973) created a simulated prison to observe the impact that the adoption of roles had on individual and group behaviour. The group of volunteers were divided into two sub-groups, prisoners and warders. Within a very short space of time each adopted the expected, desired or inferred behaviour of their role. Thus the warders became aggressive, domineering, even bullying and violent. The prisoners at first became cowed and submissive. Later they sought ways of escaping. After 36 hours one prisoner left the experiment suffering from a nervous breakdown and three more followed during the next three days. Others promised to forfeit their fees for taking part in the experiment if only they would be released.

Issues facing work groups

These are as follows:

- atmosphere and relationships: the nature of relationships; closeness, friendliness, formality and informality
- participation: the nature and extent to which participation is to be allowed
- understanding and acceptance of aims and objectives and the commitment required for this
- availability, access and use of information
- means for handling disagreements and conflict
- means and methods of decision making
- evaluation and appraisal of member performance
- evaluation and appraisal of group performance

EXAMPLE BOX 19.2 Foundations of Corporate Norms

People seek to belong to peer groups wherever they congregate; this includes in organisational and corporate surroundings.

The tendency towards exclusivity exists in open-ended and corporate situations where people come and go. The formation of groups is influenced by the fact that fellow workers have been thrown together from the start in overtly unnatural mixes. At a large cocktail party, groups will drift together and apart without constraints but in a company people with different backgrounds and views are forced to work together and form groups. The bigger the company and the wider the range of social attributes among individuals, the better the chances are that there will be numerous groups with tight-knit and defensive norms.

Where both formal and informal norms coexist, as they do in companies, the informal norms transcend the formal. This leads to what has been called 'shadow organisation' in which the apparent management structure is actually superseded in importance by the mesh of group-norm dictates.

Individuals will go to extreme lengths to live up to (or down to) the expectations placed on them by others, even doing things that in other circumstances they recognise as going counter to their own best interests, their characteristics, their normal standards of ethics and behaviour. They can persevere in this behaviour however with the easy rationalisation that 'everybody else is doing it'.

Norm-imposed habits are lasting. Even when the original members of a group have disappeared and/or when the norms themselves have lost their original purpose, there will be strong norm remnants unthinkingly respected by new members.

Negative norms cannot be changed unless the norm follower is made aware of their existence, because most people respect and go along with the norms quite unconsciously; this is reinforced by pressures to conform.

- expression of feelings: how this should be done, the consequences of this, whether penalties (formal or informal) are to be issued and if so by whom
- leadership: relating both to the leadership of the total group and also to the individual tasks for which it has been constituted
- maintenance activities: including the development of group members and the bringing in of new and fresh talents and expertise as and when required.

Adjourning

It is usual to add a fifth element signifying the end of the group. This is where the group disbands, either because the task is completed and there is nothing else for it to do; or because it is told to do so; or because it is broken up on the orders of a higher authority (for example a site or operational closure).

In any case, for all but the smallest and shortest-lived groups, some people will leave and others join. Parts of the adjournment element are therefore a re-formation, integrating new members. A part of this is also concerned with celebrating the

Characteristics of effective and ineffective groups   *TABLE 19.1*

Effective groups	Ineffective groups
Informal relaxed atmosphere	Bored or tense atmosphere
Much discussion, high level of participation	Discussion dominated by one or two people
Tasks, aims and objectives clearly understood	Discussion often irrelevant, unstructured and away from the point
Commitment of members of the groups to each other	No common aims, objectives and purposes
Commitment of members of the groups to the tasks, aims and objectives	Members do not value each other's contribution nor do they listen to each other
Members respect each other's views and listen to each other	Conflict is allowed to develop into open warfare; it may also be suppressed
Conflict is brought out into the open and dealt with constructively when it arises	Majority voting is the norm; pressure is put on minorities to accept this
Decisions are reached by consensus; voting is only used as a matter of last resort	Consensus is neither sought nor achieved
Ideas are expressed freely and openly; rejection of ideas is not a stigma	Criticism is embarrassing and personal
Leadership is shared as appropriate, and is divided according to the nature of the tasks; ultimate responsibility, authority and accountability rests with the designated group leader	Leadership is by dictat and orders are issued by the group leader only
The group examines its own progress and behaviour	The group avoids any discussion about its behaviour

Source: from D. McGregor, *The Human Side of Enterprise*, Harper and Row, 1970.

achievements of those who leave, for example with group parties and eulogies. These activities punctuate the life and progress of the group as a whole.

The final curtain

Owen (1985) finds that it is better for the future of the individuals concerned if a celebration of the group's achievements is held when it finishes. This gives everyone a point of reference for the work that has been done and the personal and professional commitment that was made. This is the equivalent to a funeral or wake, both mourning and celebrating the group's passing. Those involved then go on into the future knowing that the past is complete and behind them and that a successful job was done with good people.

Group factors and characteristics

The main factors that affect the cohesion, behaviour and effectiveness of groups are as follows.

Size

This relates to the numbers of people involved and the nature of their involvement. Some authorities have tried to identify optimum size for work groups. This has to be seen in the context of the nature of the task to be carried out: if a particular process needs two or fifteen people then this is the optimum size in the circumstances (see Example Box 19.3 and Table 19.2).

Leadership

The particular responsibilities of leadership towards the organisation and direction of groups call for attention to a range of factors. In group situations, leadership is especially concerned with the following.

- **Management of the task:** setting work methods and timescales, gathering resources, problem-solving and maintenance functions.
- **Management of the process:** the use of interpersonal skills and the interaction with the environment to gain the maximum contribution from everyone involved.
- **Managing communications:** between different work groups and sub-groups and the disciplines and professions involved to harmonise potential conflicts and to ensure that inter-group relations are productive and not dysfunctionally competitive.
- **Managing the individual:** making constructive use of individual differences and

---

EXAMPLE BOX 19.3 Group Size

There is a range of factors to be taken into account here. There are some absolutes: the size of a tennis doubles team is two; of a rugby team fifteen. In work situations the technology used may determine that a group size is three, eight, thirty or whatever.

In general terms there is a balance involved between size, contribution and participation: the larger the group, the greater the range of expertise and quality is drawn in, but the lesser the chance of full participation by individual members.

Larger groups also have a greater risk of splitting into sub-groups (either formal, based on the work, or informal, based on workstation location, friendship, establishment of common bonds and interests). Total group identity may then become diluted. The interaction between the sub-groups becomes a barrier to the progress and achievement of the full group. The sub-groups create their own barriers themselves, especially if they have become constituted around the distinctive expertise of members. If this is in high demand by the rest of the main group, the sub-group establishes its own filter and priority systems based on its preferences and criteria.

On the other hand, smaller groups tend to avoid the sub-grouping effect; they may however develop a group identity so strong that it tends to lead to belief in its own infallibility and indispensability.

The size of any group therefore has clear implications, both for their management and leadership and also for participants, if these pitfalls are to be avoided.

The analysis of groups: the Handy model TABLE 19.2

The group	The task	The environment
Size	Nature	Norms
Member characteristics	Criteria for effectiveness	Expectations
Individual objectives	Salience of task	Leader position
Stage of development	Clarity of task	Inter-group relations
	Choice of leadership	External constraints
	Choice of leadership style	Pressures to perform
	Choice of processes and procedures	
	Motivation	
	Productivity	
	Member satisfaction	

ensuring that individual contributions are both valued and of value (see Example Box 19.4).

- **Management style:** the creation and adoption of a style that is appropriate and suitable to the situation.
- **Maintenance management:** ensuring that the effectiveness of both the work and the group itself are supported, appraised and developed.
- **Aims and objectives:** establishing common goals that are understood, valued and adopted by all group members.
- **Standards:** establishing shared values and absolute standards of honesty and integrity.
- **Group and team spirit:** creating an effective and positive atmosphere among the group.

EXAMPLE BOX 19.4 Individuals and Group Culture

Some archetype variations in individual behaviour include the mild, pleasant and kind individual who:

- is good to the family
- becomes an aggressive demon on the sports field on a Saturday afternoon
- in the work role of chief executive displays both vision and ruthlessness
- swears liberally in management meetings
- whose mother has heard but simply does not believe the swearing or aggression stories.

All of these variations are brought out by the individual's membership of the different groups indicated: the family, the sports club, the work place, committees and the extended family.

The determinants of group effectiveness

These include the following.

- **The group itself:** this is the extent to which membership satisfies the social and psychological needs of belonging, identity, pride and esteem anticipated. It also concerns the professional and operational reasons for belonging: the extent to which membership has furthered the individual's ambition, professional or technical development.

- **The work and tasks:** this is the successful output, production and productivity of the group. Effectiveness depends partly on the results achieved, partly on the members' perceptions of their own achievements, and partly on the wider organisation's view of these achievements. High levels of productivity and outputs are themselves a source of psychological satisfaction. Under this heading should also be included the resources, technology and accommodation necessary to carry out the task effectively. The group normally understands the effects on output where these are inadequate and that therefore the work cannot be completed to the desired standards anyway.

- **Procedures and processes:** this is the extent to which the group's ways of working enhance the work in hand and the behavioural strength of the group. Inappropriate processes and procedures are likely to get in the way of effective activities and diminish the regard that members have for each other because they hold up progress, divert and dilute resources, and reduce the time available for task completion and group maintenance.

- **Leadership, direction and management style:** this is based on absolute standards of honesty and integrity. It is developed in relation to the differing nature of group members, the mixture of expertise present, the work that is to be carried out and the maintenance activities required in support.

- **The synergy principle:** this is the extent to which the different qualities, elements and expertise present are moulded into a cohesive unit in order to produce results that could not be achieved by members working individually.

- **Morale and satisfaction:** this is monitored through the study of absenteeism, accidents, member turnover and the ability to attract, retain and develop new talent. It is established and developed through a basis of full understanding of the tasks and activities to be carried out, and by fulfilling the expectations of group members.

- **Group ideology:** this is normally based around concepts of participation, involvement and recognition of the value of the contribution that each member makes. It is underpinned by norms and rules. Individuals may also choose to belong to a group (or seek to join it) because of the strong and distinctive ideology. Trade unions and religious institutions are clear examples of this. Some organisations – for example, Body Shop, Nissan – also attract people because of their strong commitment to the environment or product and service quality.

- **Group spirit:** which must be positive and harmonious, and capable of acceptance and value by all; conflict and dysfunction occur where this is not present. This also recognises that, in all cases, individuals have their own reasons for belonging to the group, in addition to professional, occupational and intrinsic membership value; where group spirit is either negative or not present at all, individuals revert to professional and occupational (rather than group or organisational) identity.

- **Conformity:** a measure of conformity is normally expected of individuals by the groups to which they belong. This works best where the individual aims and objectives are capable of being harmonised and integrated with those of the group. Conformity is reinforced by:
  - physical identity, including the wearing of uniforms
  - social identity: the use of particular modes of address, manners, and approaches to each other by group members
  - the positive: in which the standards, attitudes and values to which individuals are required to conform are positive
  - regimentation: in which the standards, attitudes and values to which individuals are required to conform are imposed and unvalued.
- **Power and influence:** this is the position of the group in relation to others in the organisation. It is based on both behavioural and operational factors.

  The behavioural factors mainly concern the matters of relative respect and regard in which the group is held by others in the organisation. There are also questions of perception, related for example to the extent to which the given group is seen or believed to be high status, a stepping stone on the path to success, or a cul-de-sac from which no one ever emerges with credit.

  The operational concerns include the nature of the work carried out and the value that this adds to the organisation's activities. It also concerns the ability to command and wield resources and information.

  There are also elements of realpolitik involved: for example, the ability to block progress, to filter resources and information, to determine the speed, volume and quality of work.
- **Factors outside the group's control:** these are environmental pressures and changes; changes of organisation direction and priorities; organisational and operational realpolitik; and changed/imposed group leadership. Any of these may raise, as well as lower, the profile and status of the group and the importance and value of its work. The raising of the profile may not always be good; it may place hitherto unfelt (and unacceptable) pressures on members. The lowering of the profile may not always be bad; in the short term it may enable members to produce results without constant checks on progress being made from outside the group.

Group cohesion

Cohesive groups are most likely to be achieved where there is: proper attention to the division, allocation and structuring of work; the creation of a behaviourally suitable working environment; and the installation of a leader or manager who is aware of the pressures and potential problems, and is acceptable to the rest of the group.

- **Division of work:** this is to ensure that capabilities and expertise are used to greatest effect. It also includes enabling people wherever possible to follow their personal and professional preferences as long as this can be offered to everyone. Unpleasant, mundane and routine tasks are also to be shared out on a basis of equality.
- **The creation of a suitable environment:** as well as general suitability and the availability of required technology and equipment, this must include proximity

wherever possible. Difference of location is a physical barrier to group identity and therefore effectiveness. This difference may be a matter of yards, or thousands, or hundreds of miles. A suitable environment is created only if this is first recognised and then underpinned with adequate and effective methods and systems of communication (see Figure 19.3 and Example Box 19.5).

- **Eccentricity:** organisations are normally prepared and willing to accommodate eccentricity for their own purposes, for example where particular individuals have rare or special skills that are required. Forms of eccentric behaviour may be encouraged and nurtured by the organisation as part of its own creative processes. Research and development departments, for example, require creative and imaginative individuals, those who defy and question conventions.

    The main organisational behavioural problem is the extent to which such organisations are both prepared and willing to accommodate this behaviour. This is less trite than it may first appear. Eccentricity may be dysfunctional to the rest of the organisation. It may in itself create resentment among those in mainstream and steady-state departments and functions. It may create the perception (or indeed the reality) that eccentricity is tolerated, or even rewarded, in some parts of the organisation but not others.

Sources of potential group stresses and strains

The following must always be considered.

- The nature and mixture of the personalities involved and the nature of activities that are engaged in with the purpose of reconciling these.
- The nature and mixture of the expertise and talent that is brought to the group by its different members. This is especially important where some members of the group have expertise that is either rare or else of high price/high value.

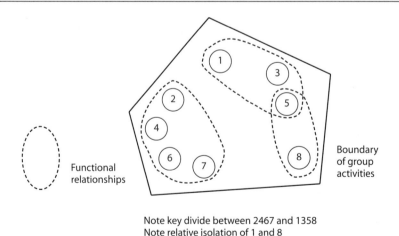

Note key divide between 2467 and 1358
Note relative isolation of 1 and 8

FIGURE 19.3 Group cohesion: sociogram of an eight-person group

EXAMPLE BOX 19.5 Canteen Cultures and Networking

These terms are used to describe the non-formal, unofficial (and often unwanted) ways in which groups think, behave and act. They derive from unofficial meetings and interactions between members (for example in the works or office canteen) where the real views, aspirations, attitudes – and prejudices – of those involved are nurtured and developed.

Variations on this theme also abound, for example the managers' dining room, the officers' mess, the workers' cafeteria – and also 'the old school tie', 'one of us/not one of us'. These clearly differentiate between different grades and classes of staff. This reinforces group identity among those so labelled. It also provides exclusions and barriers to those who do not carry the particular label.

The canteen culture is often a very powerful organisational force, especially negative. Ways of working and patterns of behaviour are derived and developed according to the wants of the groups involved rather than the needs of the work groups of which they are also (invariably) members.

This culture is also used as a form of networking by people who wish to gain access to particular work groups, departments, projects and activities. They use these informal channels rather than those devised by organisations if they appear to constitute the best and most certain routes of success and acceptance.

- Divergence of objectives between group members and between individual agenda and the objectives of the total group. This is inevitable; stress and strain comes about when these cannot be (or are not reconciled).
- The nature and mix of other and more general strengths and weaknesses that each of those involved brings with them to the group.
- Means and methods of communication, consultation and participation; the availability of good quality information. Stress and strain is created when these are inappropriate, inaccurate, dishonest or incomplete.
- The changes in group composition and membership; changes in influence of particular members as the task unfolds; the bringing in of new members; the phasing out of those whose part of the task is done.
- The clarity of purpose of the group.
- Levels of confidence, trust, respect and regard held by each member of the group in regard to the others and to their position in the group.
- The nature of the working environment including ergonomic factors, technology, location and design of workstations, and the physical distance/proximity that exists between group members. This also includes extremes of temperature, climate, discomfort, danger and location.
- The form of management style adopted, its suitability to the situation and task in question and to the understanding of this on the part of all concerned. This includes means of communication and a nature of decision-making processes.
- Levels of performance. Stress and strain are more likely to occur when the particular group is going through a bad patch or achieves no tangible result

for a long period of time. Stress also occurs during levels of very high performance when individuals start trying to take credit for the team's total achievement.

- Matters outside the group's control. To minimise the effect of these it is necessary to recognise what they are and the extent and frequency of their occurrence. Worrying about them is both unproductive and debilitating.
- Team and group malfunction. Causes of team and group malfunction are:
  - lack of clarity of purpose, direction, aims and objectives; conflicting directions, aims and objectives
  - lack of leadership and direction; inappropriate leadership style; extended and complex chains of command
  - lack of resources; inadequate and inappropriate resources, including finance, expertise, premises and technology
  - lack of mutual confidence, trust, respect and regard among group members
  - lack of responsibility and autonomy (within the broadest context); lack of control; lack of ability to shape and influence its own destiny
  - inappropriate, convoluted or complicated administration, reporting relationships and procedures
  - lack of balance of group maintenance and operational elements, usually causing the group to spend all its time on its own development to the detriment of the work in hand
  - lack of wider regard and respect (on the part of the organisation and other groups) for what the group is trying to achieve, for its achievements, needs and wants
  - lack of recognition of progress and achievement; lack of measurement and assessment of progress and achievement
  - lack of ability to act as its own advocate, lobby, self-promoter
  - lack of interest in the work; lack of perceived respect and value of the work on the part of the wider organisation
  - lack of equality of treatment, value, regard and respect of group members; lack of equality of treatment of the group itself in regard to the rest of the organisation
  - lack of consultation, participation and involvement in the communication, decision-making and directorial processes
  - failure to play to the strengths and talents of group members; giving tasks to people who have no aptitude for them.

These elements may arise through neglect and indifference on the part of the organisation concerned. They may occur simply because the work of the group in question is a little way down the order of priorities (even though it is actually valued).

Dysfunction can also be engendered. This occurs in the worst forms of inter-departmental strife. It also happens where the organisation makes a point of moving its malcontents or failures to one particular location.

Symptoms of group and team malfunction are as follows.

- Poor performance in which deadlines are missed, output is sub-standard and customer complaints increase.
- Decline: members decline or reject responsibility for their actions and those of the

group itself. They become involved in lobbying and seek to blame others for their shortcomings. The group breaks up into sub-groups and elites are created within it. Individuals claim rewards and bonuses for team efforts. Scapegoating and blame occur with destructive criticism and dismissive behaviour towards others both inside and outside the group.

- Becoming involved in grievances with other group members; increases in the numbers of these; personality and personal clashes; over-spill of professional and expert argument into personal relationships.
- Increases in general levels of grievances, absenteeism and accidents; moves to leave the group.
- Lack of interest in results, activities, plans and proposals of the group.
- General attitude and demeanour that exist among group members; the general attitude and demeanour of individuals within the group; lack of pride and joy in the group; moves to leave the group; difficulties in attracting new members to the group.
- The presence of an individual or sub-group that is known, believed or perceived by the rest of the members to be holding them back from greater achievements and successes. It is a very short step from this attitude to the presence of bullying, victimisation and harassment.

Some of these are clearly specific to particular group activities and functions. Others are more general symptoms that should be considered in the group context as part of the continuing monitoring of its effectiveness. Each gives an inlet for the person concerned with identifying and assessing trouble and potential problems with a view to tackling them (see Example Box 19.6).

Group development

The creation and formation of effective teams and groups is not an end in itself. To remain effective, cohesion, capabilities and potential must be maintained and developed. This takes the following forms.

- Infusions of talent from outside, bringing in people with distinctive qualities and expertise to give emphases and energy to particular priorities and directions.
- Infusions of new skills, knowledge and qualities from within through the identification of potential from among existing members and having them receive training and development, and targeted work that has the purpose of bringing out the retired expertise.
- Attention to group processes when it is apparent that these are getting in the way of effective task performance; and attention to task performance when it is apparent that this is ineffective.
- Attention to the relationship between team and task. This may involve using a good team to carry out a difficult or demanding task; or using the difficult and demanding task to build a good and effective team. From either standpoint, the results will only be fully effective if the task is within the capabilities of the group. As long as this is so, the rewards of success are likely to contribute greatly to overall group performance, well-being and confidence among members.

EXAMPLE BOX 19.6   The 0.5 Per Cent Rule

This is the rule that says that 99.5 per cent of people are penalised for the misde-meanours of the 0.5 per cent. Rules and procedures are created with the stated purpose of standardisation of behaviour without reference to the fact that most people behave as they are required all of the time.

Thus, for example, when someone steals something everyone on the premises is subject to searches and security checks. When someone is seen to be late arriving for work, sophisticated clocking in and signing in procedures are devised.

The certain result of this is the alienation of all of those who do not steal and who do turn up on time. If there is a problem with an individual, it is a problem that must be addressed as an individual issue.

There are knock-on effects both ways. The more sophisticated the set of rules, the greater the length of time spent on them in consultative, joint negotiating and other group management and industrial relations activities – and the greater the consequent waste of organisational resources. Conversely, if individual problems are dealt with on an individual basis by managers as and when they arise, all the time, energy and resources otherwise wasted are freed up for other things. If the manager in question is doing his/her job properly, misdemeanours happen only rarely and are dealt with quickly when they do occur.

Either approach underlines the level of respect and regard in which the staff are held. The greater the level of this type of regulation and procedure, the lower the level of respect and regard. Above all, the converse is true: the fewer such rules and regulations, the greater the level of respect and regard in which the staff are held. In the latter case the staff are treated as adults and are much more likely to respond as such when required. The approach also requires that the general malcontent or criminal is dealt with on an individual basis. Rules are no substitute for judgement in any circumstances.

- Attention to team roles, both to build on strengths and to eliminate weak-nesses. This is likely to involve reassessing requirements and priorities, and reassessing the strengths and weaknesses of each individual. It may lead to reallocation or rotation of roles and infusions of new talent, either from within or without.

- Attention to team roles and expertise, bearing in mind that different qualities, expertise and capabilities are likely to be more or less important at different phases of activity. This may lead to infusions again, or to the buying in of expertise (for example, using consultants) on an 'as-required' basis. It may also involve the recognition that members of the group may become redundant once they have made their particular contribution.

- Recognising the concept of group life cycle. Akin to that of the product life cycle, it recognises points at which infusions and divestments may need to be made. It also recognises the more general requirements for re-energising, revitalising, rejuvenating – or even ending – again, along similar lines to products (see Example Box 19.7).

EXAMPLE BOX 19.7 The Trouble with Teams: Togetherness Has Its Perils

Peter Cook, the British satirist who died on 9 January 1995, loved to poke fun at British private schools and their cult of team spirit. But if you listen to management theorists you would think that these schools had unwittingly stumbled upon the magic secret of business success. With teams all the rage, management theorists are earning fat fees by proffering advice on how to build teams and how to inculcate team spirit.

At first sight, the virtues of teamwork look obvious. Teams make workers happier by giving them the feeling that they are shaping their own jobs. They increase efficiency by eliminating layers of managers, whose job was once to pass orders downwards. They also enable companies to draw on the skills and imagination of the whole workforce instead of relying on specialists to watch out for mistakes and suggest improvements.

Having started with corporate giants such as Toyota, Motorola and General Electric, the fashion for teams has spread rapidly. A recent survey suggested that cell manufacturing, in which small groups of workers make entire products, is being experimented with at more than half of America's manufacturing plants; and teams are growing more powerful as well as more numerous. Their task was at first to execute decisions under the supervision of managers, not to make decisions. The current fashion however, is for self-management.

Companies as different as Xerox (office equipment), Monsanto (chemicals) and Johnson & Johnsville Sausage (foodstuffs) are allowing teams to decide on everything from hiring and firing to organising the flow of work. At New United Motor Manufacturing, a joint venture run in Fremont, California, by General Motors and Toyota, teams of workers elect their own leaders and invent ways of improving quality and efficiency.

Hewlett-Packard, a computer maker, has gone even further in mixing the specialisms represented in single teams. Its teams bring together engineers, technical writers, marketing managers, lawyers, purchasing professionals and shop floor workers. At Corning's, a ceramics plant in Erwin, New York, teams are fed business information so that they can understand how their plant is faring in the market. Informed workers, it is assumed, are less likely to make unreasonable wage demands. Still it would not surprise every inmate of a British private school to learn that teams are not always lawless ways to motivate and inspire people. Like many management fads, the one for teams is beginning to produce its trickle of disappointments. A.T. Kearney, a consultancy that continues to favour teams, found in a survey that nearly seven out of ten teams failed to produce the desired results.

A common error, says A.T. Kearney, is to create teams instead of taking more radical decisions. In many businesses it is still more effective to automate work than to reorganise the workforce. Years ago, Sweden's Volvo was praised for introducing self-governing teams in its car factories at Kalmar and Uddevalla in order to make the work more interesting. More interesting it duly became, but also so expensive that the company was forced to close the experimental

Example Box 19.7 (continued)

plants and concentrate production at Gothenburg on a traditional assembly line.

Even when creating teams really is the appropriate solution to a firm's problem, managers often make a hash of running them. A typical mistake is the failure to set clear objectives. Another is to introduce teams without changing the firm's patterns of appraisal and reward from an individual to a collective system. That can send the workforce fatally mixed signals: employees are expected on the one hand to pull together, on the other to compete for individual rewards.

Teamwork, moreover, costs money, the biggest additional expense being training. Not unreasonably, members of supposedly self-managing teams start wondering how to manage. This gives birth to an epidemic of woolly courses on conflict management and stress resolution. Meetings swallow time as empowered workers break off from the tedium of making things and chat endlessly instead about process improvement or production imperfections.

Although many such courses are superfluous, advocates of team-based production can see that the best teams are made up of people with broad enough skills to step easily into each other's shoes. Providing such cross training, as the theorists call it, is arduous. In some of the more complicated team structures such as those in chemical plants it can take team members between six and ten years to learn all the jobs they might be called upon to do.

However, the chief problem with teams is political. Almost invariably their creation undermines some existing distribution of power in a firm. Middle managers often see shop-floor teams as a threat to their authority and perhaps to their livelihoods. Many workers see teams as a source of division and a goad to overwork. On at least two occasions, American unions have used the National Labour Relations Act of 1935 which makes it unlawful for an employer to dominate or interfere with the formation or administration of a labour organisation to foil attempts to introduce teamwork.

Besides, although the cheery vocabulary of teamwork makes excitable use of words such as empowerment, teams usually replace top-down managerial control with peer pressure, a force that is sometimes no less coercive. 'People try to meet the team's expectations', says one worker at New United Motors in Fremont, 'and under peer pressure they end up pushing themselves too hard'.

Some workers may prefer being told what to do, to shouldering the burden of decisions themselves. Those who welcome responsibility sometimes find it hard to discipline their wayward colleagues. And there is always the danger that teams will impose a deadly uniformity and stifle the special qualities of individuals. As many a graduate of Britain's private schools will tell you, such places have made little use of the brainy wimp who hated rugby and spent a childhood shivering on the sidelines. That, in a way, was Peter Cook's point, and one that management theorists have been slow to notice.

Source: *The Economist*, 14 January 1995.

High performing teams and groups

The characteristics of high performing teams and groups may be summarised as follows.

- High levels of autonomy, the ability to self-manage and self-organise. This also includes team responsibility for self-regulation and self-discipline. It encourages the fast and effective resolution of problems and a commitment to dealing with issues before they become problems.
- Clear and unambiguous performance targets, capable of achievement and related to overall organisation purpose; these must be understood, accepted and committed to by all concerned.
- Full responsibility for all aspects of production and output process, quality assurance, customer relations and complaints. Issues and problems are identified and addressed to the particular team so that improvements can be made directly without going through sub-processes and procedures.
- Job titles do not include references to status, differentials or trappings, or other elements of psychological distance.
- Team-based reward systems available and payable to everyone who contributed, based on percentages of salary rather than occupational differentials.
- The open approach: to environment layout (no individual offices, trappings, barriers or other factors of physical and psychological distance); self-commitment for the whole team; open communication systems and high-quality communications; open approaches to problems and issues; open airing of grievances and concerns – these are usually very few in such circumstances, so that when they do arise full attention is paid.
- Federal relationship with the core organisation with reporting relationships based on monitoring, review and evaluation of production targets and other task-based indicators. General management style must be supportive rather than directive, bureaucratic or administrative.
- Fast and easy access to maintenance and support staff to ensure that equipment breakdowns are repaired as soon as possible and that production levels can be kept as high as possible for as long as possible.
- Full flexibility of work, multi-skilling and interchangeability between task roles. Group roles are assigned to people's behavioural strengths.
- Continuous development of skills, knowledge, qualities, capabilities and expertise; continuous attention to performance quality and output; continuous attention to production, quality, volume and time; continuous attention to high levels of service and satisfaction.
- High levels of involvement, confidence, respect and enthusiasm among group members, both towards each other and the work.
- Attention to equipment and technology to ensure that these are suitable and capable of producing that which is required to the stated and expected standards of volume, quality and time.
- Simple, clear and supportive policies and procedures covering organisational rules and regulations, human resource management and discipline, grievance and disputes.
- Continuous monitoring and review to ensure that the intended direction is

---

EXAMPLE BOX 19.8 Managing High Performance and Expert Groups

All organisations seek to develop work groups to their maximum potential and capability. This however, is not an end in itself. Problems arise in managing the following:

- highly expert and dedicated groups
- groups that enjoy high levels of autonomy
- groups with strong, dominant, arrogant and aggressive personalities
- groups that are known, believed and perceived to be very successful (difficulties also arise with groups that have a long history of failure, demotivation and lack of output)
- groups that enjoy high levels of favour, prestige and status.

The potential for problems lies in the perceived inability of managers to deal with group members on the basis of equal status and prestige, whatever the rank of the manager. Problems are compounded when the group's managers are not present all of the time, and are located away from the group's place of work. Psychological distance may also be reinforced by group professional and occupational attitudes of contempt towards managers; this is a form of bunker mentality and group think, and needs to be addressed.

  In these situations, all managers must establish and develop visibility and a physical presence. This is instituted by 'managing by walking around' the location of the group. It is reinforced by establishing a series of regular staff meetings that all group members must attend. Barriers have to be broken down so that the group learns that its expertise, prestige and value have still to be delivered in the total context in which it was created in the first place. The physical presence also institutes, develops and reinforces the ties between the group and the rest of the organisation.

---

pursued and that group activities are in accordance with this (see Example Box 19.8).

Conclusions

The characteristics and effectiveness of groups have been extensively researched and there is a measure of agreement around the critical elements and factors: clarity, conformity, harmony, achievement, spirit and maintenance.

  The effective use of groups is a concern for all organisations because of the nature of work and the different skills, qualities, aptitudes and expertise that have to be harmonised. Some organisations have made this their central feature. The Body Shop is created around a tribal culture according to its founder Anita Roddick. The effectiveness of the company is dependent upon the adoption of this by all those who come to work for it. Those who do not share this vision do not stay. A part is a requirement

Archetype team members   *TABLE 19.3*

Type	Symbol	Typical features	Positive qualities
Company worker	CW	Conservative, dutiful, practicable	Organising ability, practical common-sense, hard-working
Chairman	CH	Calm, self-confident, controlled	A capacity for treating and welcoming all potential contributors on their merits and without prejudice. A strong sense of objectives
Shaper	SH	Highly strung, outgoing, dynamic	Drive and readiness to challenge inertia, ineffectiveness, complacency or self-deception
Plant	PL	Individualistic, serious-minded, unorthodox	Genius, imagination, intellect, knowledge
Resource investigator	RI	Extroverted, enthusiastic, curious, communicative	A capcity for contacting people and exploring anything new An ability to respond to challenge
Monitor-evaluator	ME	Sober, unemotional, prudent	Judgement, discretion, hard-headedness
Team worker	TW	Social orientated, rather mild, sensitive	An ability to respond to people and situations, and to promote team spirit
Completer-finisher	CF	Painstaking, orderly, conscientious, anxious	A capcity to follow through to perfection

Source: R. M. Belbin, *Superteams*, Prentice-Hall International, 1999.

for all members to take part in environmental and social projects on one day per month.

Japanese employees introduce themselves by giving the name of their company first: 'I work for Honda', 'I work for Nissan'. The strength of team and group identity is with the company. This is distinct from the identities found, for example, among the English, whose first identity is with their generic group or profession – 'I am a nurse', 'I am a bus driver' – rather than the company. This is sometimes perceived to lead to divided loyalties (see Figure 19.2) especially where there is no clear set of priorities. By contrast, the employees of both The Body Shop and Japanese companies place their organisations at the top of this list.

Japanese organisations reinforce this through the attention that they pay to the creation of work groups, the training of these once they are constituted, the provision the best technology and equipment, and the selection of the right leader. Again, a contrast may be drawn: the leader of a Japanese work group must be acceptable to the group members, while leaders of Western groups are likely to be externally appointed on the basis of their technological or professional expertise.

The creation of effective work groups increases the burdens placed on organisations and their managers in terms of attention to behavioural as well as operational factors. Successful groups come about as the result of a combination of the effectiveness of both these elements. Group members and group managers alike require the ability to think things through, develop and present arguments, make judgements and persuade others to their point of view. The rewards to be gained by organisations are found in consistent and high levels of output delivered by committed people with a real concern for satisfaction and success. This is the rationale for constituting effective work teams.

CHAPTER SUMMARY

Everybody belongs to groups. To be effective in working situations, it is essential that there is as great a measure of mutual trust, respect, identity, cohesion and clarity of purpose, understood and accepted by all, as is possible in the circumstances. It is also essential that attention is paid to the human values – the shared values – necessary for effective functioning as a working group.

learn

The critical nature of the relationship between the leader and the group should therefore be apparent. It is essential that the leader establishes both clear patterns of work, and the environment in which mutuality of interest and respect can be assured. This is the cornerstone on which cohesion and effectiveness are founded. Without this, there can be no secure basis for group development, or for the progress and enhancement of the expertise of individual members. Indeed, lack of cohesion means that individual members only use the group situation so long as it remains in their interests, that their performance will decline, and they will move on as soon as it becomes apparent that they have no respect or value for what the group is trying to achieve.

Effective groups therefore require a combination of early and continued operational successes, together with a mutually enhancing and developing personal and professional respect among the members. All group activities that are proposed must be considered from each of these points of view. If something is contemplated which is perceived as having a damaging or divisive effect on the group then, where possible, that initiative should be abandoned or repositioned in order to ensure that everybody receives some form of benefit. Where it is not possible to abandon the initiative or proposal, then recognition of the likely effects on group cohesion must be acknowledged and understood. Steps can then be taken to remedy the situation as early as possible, and from the point of view of understanding and pre-planning rather than surprise.

It is also particularly important that attention is paid to the rewards (both financial and non-financial) that are available to group members. Merit, performance and profit-related financial rewards should ideally be paid on the basis of fairness and evenness, and the current prevailing wisdom is that all members should receive an equal percentage of their salary in these cases. Where for some reason it becomes necessary or right and proper to pay an individual above and beyond the rewards available to the rest of the group, the reasons for this should be made plain to everybody. If these are honest and straightforward, then they will be understood. If they are not, then the leadership and direction of the group is always called into question.

Finally, it is necessary to understand that all groups come to an end. They either outlive their useful life, or else the leadership changes, or else the nature of the task and work activities changes to such an extent that the requirement for the group as presently constituted no longer exists. It is essential to manage this end phase so as to avoid feelings of loss and deprivation on the part of members. As stated above, many organisations provide wakes and other celebrations at the end of particular group functions, projects, or periods of activity. Even if this is not carried out, acknowledgement of the group's contribution must be made formally. This enables everyone involved to recognise for themselves that a particular period of work has come to en end, and to have this publicly acknowledged. They are then able to move on within themselves to the next part of their working life.

DISCUSSION QUESTIONS

1. What are the major disadvantages of committee work and how can these best be overcome?
2. What are the major symptoms of group-think or 'the bunker mentality'? What steps should organisations take to ensure that these do not arise in the first place? How should organisations address them when they do arise?
3. Identify the main reasons why canteen cultures arise and the steps that organisations should take for dealing with them.
4. Identify the main roles and functions of group leaders. What are the best ways of identifying these? How can individuals best be trained to be effective group leaders?

CHAPTER CASE STUDY

Magellan Ltd

Deborah Shiel has just been appointed manager of the information services department of Magellan Ltd, an advertising and public relations agency in Bradford. Last week, she was offered the job, accepted it, and was taken to meet her new staff. She has seven staff, and they all greeted her politely but, she thought, a little bit formally. She was slightly nonplussed, and this soon turned to anxiety when she started talking the job through with Helen Worth, her new manager. Helen told her that the job had been vacant for six months since the previous post-holder, Paul Jarvis, took early retirement. Since then, the department had been in a state of limbo. Helen had kept an eye on things as far as she has been able, but she had been very busy. As the result, Thomas Lynas, the longest-serving member of staff, had assumed power, and the rest of the group appear to fear and hate him. There have been rumours that he hit David Johnson, the newest member of staff. The other male member of staff, Abdul Qadir, has spent entire working days on the telephone to employment agencies, trying desperately to get another job.

The rest of the staff are women. There is friction between two of them, Frances

Collins and Irene Ward, and this dates back to the last Christmas party. They now have regular shouting matches, and the agency once lost a contract because the client's representatives saw them having a very heated argument. Frances and David do not speak to each other at all.

Of the others, Sally Rivera will only do work for the firm's copy-writing department. She spends most of her time away her desk and with the copy-writers. The last member of the department is Kirsty Ali, and she is also looking for another job. She however is the only member of staff that Thomas listens to or talks to.

The following Monday, Deborah Shiel arrives to start her new job. Helen has promised to meet her and take her into the department, but is nowhere to be seen. Eventually the receptionist tells Deborah, 'I'm very sorry but Helen has been called away. She says to go up to the department, meet the team, and start work. She will come and find you later.'

Anxiously, Deborah makes her way to the department. The first person that she meets is Thomas. She takes a deep breath, and puts on her brightest smile. 'Good morning Thomas,' she says cheerfully.

'It's Mr Lynas to you. Morning it may be. Good it most certainly is not.' He turns on his heel and walks away.

QUESTIONS

1. What should Deborah do immediately about Thomas?
2. Produce an outline strategy for Deborah that has the purpose of getting this group of disparate and conflicting individuals into a cohesive working team. What factors have got to be considered, and how should this be measured this for success or failure? How long should the exercise be given to work?

20 Management and Motivation

'The wishbone will never replace the backbone.' Ron Saunders, Manager, Manchester City Football Club, 1973.

'I have a dream.' Martin Luther King, Birmingham, Alabama, 1962.

'To turn the dream of First Tuesday into reality, I worked 100 hours a week non-stop for three years. I had no other life – it was all First Tuesday. That's what it took to turn the dream into reality.' Julie Meyer, interview for *Management Today*, May 2000.

CHAPTER OUTLINE

The main theories of motivation; their relationship with organisational and managerial practice

Motivation and demotivation: causes, effects, and remedies

The relationship between capability and willingness

Motivating people in workplaces.

CHAPTER OBJECTIVES

After studying this chapter, you should be able to:

understand the major theories of motivation, and their relationship to human behaviour and work performance

understand the conditions that have to be in place if long-term commitment to work is to be sustainable

understand the steps that need to be taken when low levels of motivation and morale are present

understand and be able to apply specific lessons, with the objective of raising levels of commitment and morale.

Introduction

Motivation is a reflection of the reasons why people do things. All behaviour has a purpose (often several). All behaviour is therefore based on choice: people choose to do things that they do. Sometimes this choice is very restricted (sink or swim for example). Sometimes it is constrained by the law (for example, stopping the car when the traffic lights are red). And again, it is constrained by the norms and processes of society: for example, people tend to wear smart clothes to a party where they know that everybody else will be well dressed. In each case however, there is a choice, though the propensity and encouragement to choose one course of action rather than the other in the examples given is strong, if not overwhelming.

Definitions

Huczynski and Buchanan (1993): a combination of goals towards which human behaviour is directed; the process through which those goals are pursued and achieved; and the social factors involved.

Luthans (1992): motivation is a combination of needs, drives and incentives. Motivation is defined as 'a process that starts with a physiological or psychological deficiency or need that activates behaviour or a drive that it is aimed at a goal or incentive'.

Mullins (1999): the underlying concept of motivation is some driving force within individuals by which they attempt to achieve some goal in order to fulfil some need or expectation. Mullins also distinguishes between extrinsic motivation related to tangible rewards such as money; and intrinsic motivation related to psychological rewards such as the sense of challenge and achievement.

Some key factors begin to become apparent.

Key factors

These include the following.

- **Goals and ambitions:** these must be both realistic and achievable if satisfaction is eventually to occur. Problems arise when the goals set are too low (leading to feelings of frustration), or too high (leading to the constant lack of achievement). They must also be acceptable to the individual concerned – in terms of self-image, self-worth, and self-value – so they are likely to be positive and based on the drive for improved levels of comfort, capability and well-being. They must also be acceptable (or at least not unacceptable) to the society and environment in which the individual lives and works, and capable of being harmonised and integrated with them.
- **Recognition:** a critical part of the process of developing self-esteem and self-worth lies in the nature and levels of recognition accorded to the achievement of particular goals. The need for recognition itself therefore becomes a drive. Individuals thus tend to pursue goals that will be recognised and valued by those whose opinion and judgement is important to them: family, friends, peers and social groups, as well as work organisations. Dissatisfaction occurs when this recognition is not forthcoming.
- **Achievement:** the components of achievement are the anticipated and actual rewards that the fulfilment of a particular goal brings. High levels of achievement occur where these overlap completely. High levels also normally occur where real rewards exceed those that are anticipated. Low levels occur where the anticipated rewards are not forthcoming; this devalues the achievement. High or complete

achievement is normally seen and perceived as successful. Low achievement or failure to achieve is seen and perceived as a failure (see Example Box 20.1).

From this, in turn, other aspects of motivation become apparent.

- **The need for success:** people tend to set their sights at what they know or think they can do, or think that they may be able to do, so that success is forthcoming.

EXAMPLE 20.1 Achievement Motivation Theory: D.C. McClelland

McClelland identifies relationships between personal characteristics, social and general background, and work achievement.

Persons with high needs for achievement exhibit the following characteristics:

- task rather than relationship orientation
- a preference for tasks over which they have sole or overriding control and responsibility
- the need to identify closely, and be identified closely, with the successful outcomes of their action
- task balance: this has to be difficult enough on the one hand to be challenging and rewarding, to be capable of demonstrating expertise and good results, and gaining status and recognition from others; on the other hand it needs to be moderate enough to be capable of successful achievement
- risk balance: in which the individual seeks to avoid as far as possible the likelihood and consequences of failure
- the need for feedback on the results achieved to reinforce the knowledge of success and to ensure that successes are validated and publicised
- the need for progress, variety and opportunity.

Need for achievement is based on a combination of:

- intrinsic motivation: the drives from within the individual
- extrinsic motivation: the drives, pressures and expectations exerted by the organisation, peers and society.

It is also influenced by education, awareness, social and cultural background, and values.

McClelland identified a potential problem in relation to the appointment of high achievers to highly responsible managerial and supervisory positions. Because the higher achievers tended to be task rather than relationship driven, many did not possess (or regard as important) the human relations characteristics necessary to get things done through people, nor did they understand that they would need to develop these if they were to be successful in the future.

Source: D.C. McClelland, *Human Aspects of Management*, John Wiley, 1971.

Genuine successes, victories and triumphs enhance feelings of self-esteem and self-value; failures diminish these.

- **The need for rewards:** both extrinsic and intrinsic; rewards must be valued both by the individual receiving them and by the wider society, organisation, occupation and profession.
- **The need for acceptance, recognition and being valued by others:** this is a combination of pursuing things that individuals know or perceive will be valued by those around them (as stated above) and also of seeking out those who will value the achievements for themselves.
- **The need to develop and improve:** this is a positive statement of need. If satisfaction is not forthcoming in one field, individuals are likely to lose interest and find something else to pursue. As well as matters of comfort and well-being, it also includes broadening and deepening experience and variety of life (including working life), as well as developing new skills, capabilities and interests with the view to enhancing personal potential as far as possible.

These are social and behavioural needs, wants and desires; they are influenced, developed and conditioned by societies and organisations, and groups within them. They are based on more fundamental human needs.

- **The need and instinct for survival:** when individuals are hungry or thirsty, their prime motivation is for food or drink. When they are cold, their instinct is to find warmth and shelter. When the life of an individual is under threat (for example, from war or disaster), the instinct is to take actions that preserve life.
- **The need and instinct for society and belonging:** this is a reflection of the need for esteem, warmth and respect. More fundamentally, it is the need to belong, to interact and to have personal contact with those whom the individual identifies with, respects, likes or loves. It also involves being drawn to those who have similar hopes, aspirations, interests and ambitions.
- **The need to be in control:** this is the ability to influence the actions and feelings of others, and the ability to influence the environment, to make it comfortable and productive in response to the particular needs, wants and drives. Control is a function of purpose: the organisation and arrangement of particular resources (including other people) for given reasons.
- **The need to progress:** this is a reflection of the capacity to develop, to enhance knowledge, skills and capability. It includes:
  - economic drives for better standards of living, quality of life and enhanced capacity to make choices
  - social drives to gain status, respect, influence and esteem as the result of enhanced capability and economic advantage
  - personal drives reflecting ambition and the need to maximise/optimise the potential to achieve
  - opportunistic drives, the identification and pursuit of opportunities that may become apparent and attractive to the individual
  - invention and creativity, the ability to see things from various points of view and create the means by which quality of life can be enhanced.

Development, adaptation and creativity are also features of the needs for survival, society and control. They are a reflection of the extent to which individuals can influence their ability to survive, belong and control their environment.

Except at the point of life and death, when the instinct for survival is everything, these needs constitute parts of the wider process of adaptation and interaction. At given moments therefore, some needs will be stronger than others; there is no linear progression from one to the next.

Major theories of motivation

Rensis Likert: System 4

Likert's contribution to the theories of workplace motivation arose from his work with high-performing managers: managers and supervisors who achieved high levels of productivity, low levels of cost and high levels of employee motivation, participation and involvement at their places of work. The study demonstrated a correlation between this success and the style and structure of the work groups that the managers created. The groups achieved not only high levels of economic output, and therefore wage and salary targets, but were also heavily involved in both group maintenance activities and the design and definition of work patterns. This was underpinned by a supportive style of supervision and the generation of a sense of personal worth, importance and esteem in belonging to the group itself.

The System 4 model arose from this work. He identified four styles or systems of management.

- **System 1: exploitative authoritative,** where power and direction come from the top downwards and where there is no participation, consultation or involvement on the part of the workforce. Workforce compliance is thus based on fear. Unfavourable attitudes are generated, there is little confidence and trust, and low levels of motivation to cooperate or generate output above the absolute minimum.
- **System 2: benevolent authoritative,** which is similar to System 1 but which allows some upward opportunity for consultation and participation in some areas. Again attitudes tend to be generally unfavourable; confidence, trust and communication are also at low levels.

In both Systems 1 and 2, productivity may be high over the short run when targets can be achieved by a combination of coercion and bonus and overtime payments. However, both productivity and earnings are demonstrably low over the long run; there are also high levels of absenteeism and labour turnover.

- **System 3: consultative,** where aims and objectives are set after discussion and consultation with subordinates; where communication is two-way and where teamwork is encouraged at least in some areas. Attitudes towards both superiors and the organisation tend to be favourable, especially when the organisation is working steadily. Productivity tends to be higher, absenteeism and turnover lower. There are also demonstrable reductions in wastage, improvements in product quality, reductions in overall operational costs and higher levels of earning on the part of the workforce.
- **System 4: participative,** where three basic concepts have a very important

effect on performance. These are: the use by the manager of the principle of supportive relationships throughout the work group referred to above; the use of group decision making and group methods of supervision; and the setting of very ambitious high-performance goals for the department and also for the organisation overall.

Abraham Maslow: a hierarchy of needs

Maslow (1960) was a behavioural scientist whose researches led him to depict a hierarchy of needs which explained different types and levels of motivation that were important to people at different times. The hierarchy of needs works from the bottom of the pyramid upwards, showing the most basic needs and motivations at the lowest levels and those created or fostered by civilisation and society towards the top (see Figure 20.2).

The needs are as follows.

- **Physiological:** the need for food, drink, air, warmth, sleep and shelter; these are basic survival needs related to the instinct for self-preservation.
- **Safety and security:** protection from danger, threats or deprivation and the need for stability (or relative stability) of environment.
- **Social:** a sense of belonging to a society and the groups within it, such as the family, the organisation, the work group. Also included in this level are matters to do with the giving and receiving of friendship, basic status needs within these groups, and the need to participate in social activities.
- **Esteem needs:** the needs for self-respect, self-esteem, appreciation, recognition and status on the part of both the individuals concerned and the society, circle or group in which they interrelate; part of the esteem need is therefore the drive to gain the respect, esteem and appreciation accorded by others.
- **Self-actualisation:** the need for self-fulfilment, self-realisation, personal development, accomplishment, mental, material and social growth and the development and fulfilment of the creative faculties (see Example Box 20.2).

Maslow's work was based on general studies of human motivation and as such was not directly related to matters endemic at the workplace. However, matters concerning the last two items on the pyramid, those of self-esteem and self-actualisation, have clear implications for the motivation (and self-motivation) of professional, technical and managerial staff in organisations, as well as underpinning wider standards of attitudes and behaviour required.

Frederick Herzberg: two-factor theory

The research of Herzberg was directed at people in places of work. It was based on questioning people in organisations in different jobs, at different levels, to establish:

- those factors that led to extreme dissatisfaction with the job, the environment and the workplace, and
- those factors that led to extreme satisfaction with the job, the environment and the workplace.

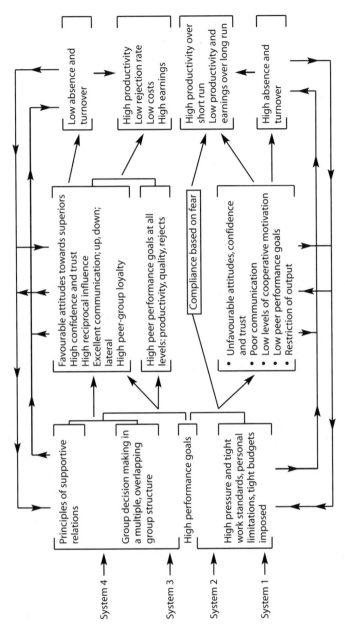

System 4

FIGURE 20.1

Source: R. Likert, *The Human Organisation*, McGraw-Hill, 1967.

The factors giving rise to satisfaction he called motivators. Those giving rise to dissatisfaction he called hygiene factors (see Figure 20.3).

The motivators that emerged were: achievement, recognition, the nature of the work itself, levels of responsibility, advancement, and opportunities for personal

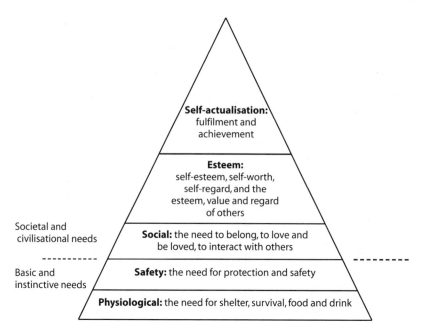

FIGURE 20.2 A hierarchy of needs

Source: A. Maslow, *Motivation and Personality*, Harper and Row, 1960.

growth and development. These factors are all related to the actual content of the work and job responsibilities. When they were present in a working situation they led to high levels of satisfaction on the part of the workforce (see Example Box 20.3).

The hygiene factors or dissatisfiers that he identified were as follows: company policy and administration; supervision and management style; levels of pay and salary; relationships with peers; relationships with subordinates; status; and security. These are factors that where they are good or adequate will not in themselves make people satisfied; ensuring that they are indeed adequate may remove dissatisfaction but does not in itself generate satisfaction. On the other hand, where these aspects were bad, extreme dissatisfaction was experienced by all respondents.

Organisations that fail to provide adequate hygiene factors tend to have high levels of conflict, absenteeism and labour turnover and low general morale (see Example Box 20.4).

The work of Herzberg has tended to encourage attention on such factors as:

- good and adequate supervision that encourages and extends the workforce rather than restricting it
- job satisfaction, which can often be increased through work restructuring, job enrichment and job enlargement programmes
- the setting and achieving of targets and objectives based on a full understanding of what they are and why they have been set.

Some organisations have also concentrated on removing the dissatisfiers or hygiene

EXAMPLE 20.2 Self-actualisation

Self-actualisation refers to the ability and drive of individuals to realise their full potential, to progress as far as possible and to be fulfilled. This includes recognition and value by others. Self-actualisation also addresses the need for challenge, responsibility and pride in work and achievement, as well as technological or professional expertise.

Two views of self-actualisation are taken. The first is that self-actualisation is available only to the very few. It is limited by the inability to develop sufficient qualities and capabilities for this to take place. This is due to the limitations of the social background of many people and, above all, of education, training and other means by which skills, knowledge and expertise are developed.

The second view is that self-actualisation is achievable by almost everyone in their own particular circumstances. Whatever the limitations placed by society and education, individuals nevertheless exhibit a range of capabilities and qualities which can be harnessed and developed in the pursuit of highly rewarding lives in their own terms. Self-actualisation is therefore an individual and not an absolute process.

The latter view currently holds sway. It is of particular value in understanding that all individuals have needs for respect and esteem; whatever the nature, level or content of work carried out, they will tend to seek variety and enhancement if this is at all possible. If this is not possible at the place of work, they will seek it elsewhere. This view tends to militate against traditional and classical organisation features of task specialisation and administrative hierarchies, which expect individuals to restrict their capabilities, work as directed and operate machinery and systems, rather than develop and use their capabilities and talents to the full.

factors to ensure that causes of intrinsic dissatisfaction with the workplace and its environment are minimised.

Herzberg's work carries a number of clear implications.

- Management style, attitude and approach to staff must be based on integrity, honesty and trust, whatever the nature, limitations or technology concerned in the work itself.
- The working environment is to be comfortable, functional and suitable in human terms, again whatever the operational constraints and limitations may be.
- General factors of status and importance should ensure that every member of staff is respected, believed in, treated equally and given opportunity for change, development and advancement within the organisation.
- Effective and professional operational relationships between members of staff should in turn promote profitable and successful activities across the entire organisation. This includes recognising the existence of barriers and potential conflicts between departments, divisions and functions and taking steps to provide effective counters to these.
- Pay and reward levels must meet expectations, as well as providing adequate

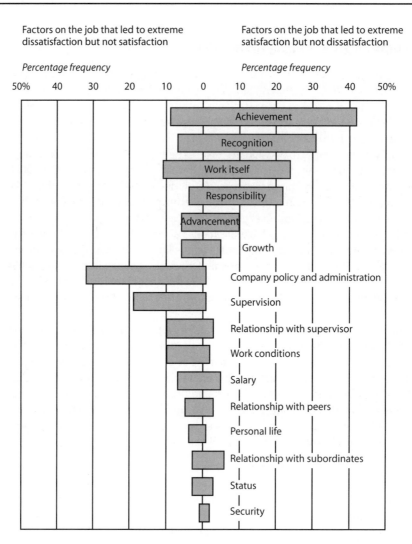

Factors on the job that led to extreme dissatisfaction but not satisfaction

Factors on the job that led to extreme satisfaction but not dissatisfaction

Percentage frequency

Percentage frequency

FIGURE 20.3 Two-factor theory

Source: F. Herzberg, *Work and the Nature of Man*, Free Press, 1967.

levels of income so that individuals feel secure in both life and work. There are collective, cultural and social requirements to increase pay and reward levels; it is also becoming increasingly accepted that there is a moral responsibility placed on organisations to share the fruits of their success (for example through profit and performance-related pay). However, it is also necessary to recognise that high levels of pay do not make work more interesting or worthwhile – though they do certainly make it more bearable, especially in the short term.

- Administrative support and control processes and mechanisms are to be designed both to make life easy for those working at the front line, and at the same time provide the necessary management information. This particularly refers to the nature and effectiveness of the roles and functions of corporate

EXAMPLE BOX 20.3 Theory X and Y

McGregor (1970) identified two distinctive sets of assumptions made by managers about employees; and identified these as follows.

- **Theory X:** in which people dislike work and will avoid it if they can; they would rather be directed than accept responsibility; they must be forced or bribed to put in the right effort; they are motivated mainly by money, which remains the overriding reason why they go to work; their main anxiety concerns personal security and is alleviated by earning money; people are inherently lazy and require high degrees of supervision, coercion and control in order to produce adequate output.
- **Theory Y:** in which people wish to be interested in work and, under the right conditions, will enjoy it; they gain intrinsic fulfilment from work; they are motivated by the desire to achieve and to realise potential, and to work to the best of their capabilities; they will accept the discipline of the organisation and also impose self-discipline.

Effective work motivation is therefore a managerial responsibility. The core of this responsibility lies in understanding the collective attitudes of the organisation and designing motivation and incentives around this. Organisations that adopt a largely Theory X approach cannot expect long-term enduring high levels of production and output; organisations that adopt the Theory Y approach require much greater levels of investment in the behavioural, as well as operational, side of enterprises.

---

headquarters and the relationships between these and the front line operations indicated.

- Attention must be paid to the work itself, and how it is divided up. There is particular reference here to those parts of the work that are looked upon with disfavour but which nevertheless must be carried out adequately and effectively.
- Security of tenure ensures that people are employed on a continuous basis as far as that is possible. At the same time steps have to be taken to ensure that there is a

---

EXAMPLE BOX 20.4 Absenteeism

Absenteeism is a feature of the general level of satisfaction or otherwise at the place of work. The higher the level of absenteeism, the greater the level of dissatisfaction.

This translates as follows: for every hundred members of staff, every percentage point of absenteeism requires an additional person employed. Thus 5 per cent absenteeism requires 105 members of staff to do the work of 100; or conversely it takes 105 days to do 100 days' work.

steady and open flow of information, so that when changes do become necessary the staff concerned are both forewarned and positively responsive.

V. Vroom: expectancy theories

The expectancy approach to motivation draws a relationship between the efforts put into particular activities by individuals and the ways they expect to be rewarded for these efforts (see Figure 20.4).

This is compounded however by other factors: the actual capacities and aptitudes of the individual concerned on the one hand, and the nature of the work environment

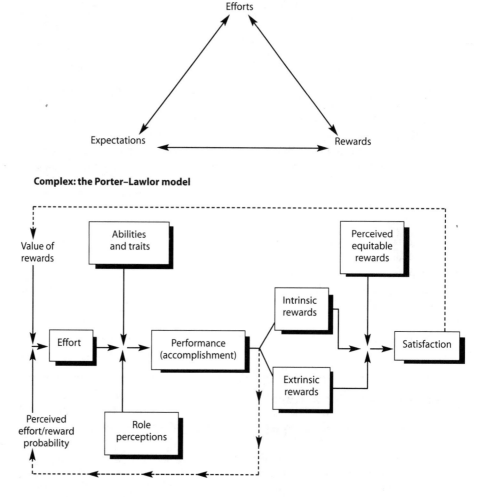

FIGURE 20.4 Expectancy theory

Source: F. Luthans, *Organisational Behaviour*, McGraw-Hill, 1992.

on the other. It is also limited by the perceptions and expectations that the commissioner of the work has towards the person who is actually carrying it out. There is a distinction to be drawn between the effort put into performance and the effectiveness of that effort: hard work, conscientiously carried out, does not always produce effective activity; the effort has to be directed and targeted. There has also to be a match between the rewards expected and those that are offered; a reward is merely a value judgement placed on something offered in return for effort and if this is not valued by the receiver it has no effect on their motivation.

The components of the expectation–effort–reward mixture are as follows.

- **Personal ambition:** the inner drive to make progress and the rewards that this progress brings with it. These are in terms of increased prosperity and disposable income (and, by extension, the uses to which that disposable income is put: the larger car, larger house, prestigious address, foreign holidays, higher-quality food and clothing, private education, better health care). They are to be seen also in terms of the status and esteem afforded by this: the feeling of well-being that accrues from for example the prestigious address or the children in private education.
- **Professional and occupational ambition:** the drive and desire to make it to the top of the chosen occupation, to become an expert (and to be regarded as such by both peers and the public at large). This includes the drive for constant self-improvement and self-development, pushing at the boundaries of the chosen field.
- **Situation:** the extent to which the situation can provide the anticipated rewards. This is constantly unfolding and changing. A situation that may have once been attractive can change quickly, particularly as the result of reorganisation. The situation may or may not bring the expected rewards. It may open up other opportunities that are either perceived or not perceived as opportunities. The individual may have gone into the situation with a variety of objectives, and the situation perhaps satisfies one or several of these but not all.
- **Performance:** this is the nature of the work in question, both present and future. Individuals are inevitably required to carry out a variety of tasks. They tend to gravitate towards those that are seen to produce the greater level of desired rewards. This may be at the expense of tasks which are just as essential but which do not carry the same motivational factors for the people in question.
- **Perception:** it follows from all of this that most of the drive comes from within the individual rather than being imposed or directed. The genesis is therefore what the individual feels or perceives to be important and worthwhile. Satisfaction derives from within, from the successful completion of activities that lead to it, rather than from the achievement of organisational targets per se. If one accepts the expectation model therefore, it follows that organisational targets and work methods must be dovetailed with individual expectations and aspirations for the best results. Indeed, to pursue this to its extremes, the source of organisational targets must be the satisfaction of those people working within it (see Example Box 20.5).

It is the responsibility of all organisations to find means of giving recognition, and provide opportunities for growth and advancement and measuring achievement. This

EXAMPLE BOX 20.5   Motivation, Achievement and Rewards

An alternative view of the expectation–effort–reward mixture consists of restating this as motivation, achievement, rewards. Drives for particular goals are enhanced by the capability to achieve them and the rewards that are to accrue as the result. These rewards are a combination of the following.

- **Economic:** monetary pay for carrying out the job, for special achievement for responsibility and accountability; this is expected to continue and improve in line with the relationship between organisation and individual, in terms of both current and future occupations and also loyalty and commitment. Economic rewards meet the needs and expectations of individuals, and also reflect the value in which they are held by the organisation.
- **Job satisfaction:** intrinsic rewards attained by individuals in terms of the quality of their work, the range and depth of expertise used, and the results achieved.
- **Work content:** the relative contribution to the output of the organisation as a whole and the feelings of success and achievement that arise from this. As stated elsewhere, operating a small part of the production process or administrative system tends to be limited in its capability to satisfy this part of the requirement for achievement.
- **Job title:** certain job titles give images of prestige as well as a description and summary of what the work is, and the respect and esteem in which it is held by individuals and their peers and social circles.
- **Personal development:** the extent to which individuals' capabilities are being used (or limited in their use); and the extent to which alternative means of achievement and reward may become apparent through the development of both current and new expertise.
- **Attendance and absence:** including the actual reasons why people come to work in the particular organisation, and why they make themselves absent from time to time; this is reinforced where there are 'long hours' cultures in managerial and professional circles.
- **Status:** the relative mark of value placed on the individual's rank, role, expertise and job by those whose views and opinions are valued. This invariably includes those of the particular organisation, because of the nature of the continuing relationship between the two. It is also likely to include, again, the views of social and professional circles.
- **Trappings:** these are the outward marks of achievement and success, material and visible benefits by which others can recognise its extent. They include:
  - Benefits: such as cars (both the fact that a car as been issued and also the value of the car itself); other business technology; business trips; sabbaticals; course and seminar attendance; health care. They are marks of achievement when presented in professional and social circles.
  - Autonomy: the ability of individuals to set their own patterns of work; to come and go as they see fit, to work from home; to attend the place of work

> ### Example Box 20.5 (continued)
>
> at weekends or other quiet periods in order to be able to work without interruptions (as distinct from having to attend at the same time as everyone else); to make work arrangements based on sole individual judgement without reference to higher authorities; to exhibit absolute, professional or technical expertise and judgement.
>
> - Secretaries, personal assistants and personal departments: normally integral to the nature of the work, they also constitute a trapping insofar as they are an outward representation to the rest of the organisation of the value and importance of the individual's work.
> - Accessibility: in many organisations, the inability to get to see someone, either because of their rank or because of their work loads, constitutes a mark of achievement (often perverse).
>
> The problems associated with these do not lie in their validity. This is not an issue since they are based on perceptions, expectations, the wider situation and the individual drives that accumulate from the achievement and possession of these. They rather indicate the organisation's capability of recognising the extent to which its employees need and want them, and its ability to satisfy them in these ways.

extends to front-line production and service activities as well as professional occupations. It involves taking a broad and enlightened view of what the whole purpose of the work is. Advocates of efficient but alienative traditional production and service methods point to the reductions in unit costs that are achieved by these, but usually take no account of the consequences of that alienation: absence, turnover, disputes and grievances and the additional levels of supervision that go with these. Above all, such approaches take no account of the resource base that is required is support these negative activities (see Example Box 20.6).

Edgar Schein: a classification of humankind

Schein classified people as follows.

- **Rational economic:** these people are primarily motivated by economic needs. They pursue their own self-interest in the expectation of high economic returns. If they work in an organisation they need both motivation and control. As they intensify the pursuit of money they become untrustworthy and calculating. Within this group, however, there are those who are self-motivated and have a high degree of self-control. This is the group that must take responsibility for the management of others. They also set the moral and ethical standards required.
- **Social:** these are social and gregarious people, gaining their basic sense of identity from relationships with others. They will seek social relationships at the place of work and see part of the function of the work group as the fulfilment of this necessity. The role of management in this case is therefore greatly concerned with

EXAMPLE BOX 20.6 Passivity and Activity

The transformation of individuals from states of passivity to those of activity occurs as a part of growing up and education. By the time individuals are ready for work, they require active rather than passive engagement. The key elements of this are as follows.

- An individual moves from a passive state as an infant to an active state as an adult.
- An individual moves from a state of dependency as an infant to a state of relative independence as an adult.
- An individual has limited behaviour as an infant but complex and sophisticated behaviour as an adult.
- An individual has short, casual and shallow interests as an infant but deeper and stronger interests as an adult.
- An infant's time span and perspective are very short; the infant concentration span is very short; it involves only the present; with maturity this widens into conception of the past and the future.
- An infant is subordinate to others and becomes a peer, equal or superior as an adult.
- Infants lack self-awareness and self-control; adults are self-aware and capable of self-control.

This is a theory of personality development, presenting the view that highly structured and formalised organisations are therefore unsuitable places in which to work. There is a fundamental lack of harmony – or congruence – between the needs of the individuals and the drives of the organisation. This tends to get worse as the organisation becomes more sophisticated and as its rules, procedures and hierarchies grow, and as the individuals concerned seek to progress themselves. This leads first to restriction, then frustration and finally, to conflict. Frustration and the potential for conflict are greatest at the lower levels of the organisation, where the ability to work independently is most restricted. It is also apparent where people at any level of the organisation and of any level of professional or technical expertise (or lack of it) believe themselves to be restricted in their potential to achieve by unnecessary and unproductive rules, procedures and systems.

From whatever point of view the matter is considered, the relationship between organisation and people is fundamentally unsound. The conclusion is that organisations create the conditions for disharmony and unproductiveness themselves by placing so many limitations on the potential and drives of their people. Staff apathy and lack of effort is the inevitable result of this approach to structuring and organising work. Effectively therefore, people are expected to behave in these negative ways.

Source: C. Argyris, *Personality and Organisations*, Harper and Row, 1957.

mobilising the social relationships in the pursuit of operational effectiveness and drawing a correlation between productivity and morale; and taking an active interest in the development of the work group.

- **Self-actualisation:** here, people are primarily self-motivated. They seek challenge, responsibility and pride from their job and aim to maximise the opportunities that these bring. They are likely to be affected negatively by organisational and management style, external controls, scarcity of resources and other pressures. They will develop their own ways of working and objectives, and integrate these with those established by the organisation. The inference is that this is strongest among professional, technical, skilled managerial staff. However, all work groups have tended towards higher levels of motivation and morale when given a greater degree of autonomy at work.

- **Complexity:** people are complex and sophisticated. They have 'varieties' of emotions, needs, wants and drives driven by personal circumstances, interactions and adaptation. They have many differing, diverse and contradictory motives that vary according to the matter in hand and the different work and social groups in which they find themselves. They will not fulfil every need in any one situation, but rather require a variety of activities in order to do this. They respond to a variety of stimuli according to needs and wants at a given moment. Schein's view of 'complex man' in organisations is that of a psychological contract, based on mutual expectations and commonality of aspirations. It is therefore a psychological partnership.

The psychological partnership

The psychological partnership is based on the motivation to:

- seek out particular types of work, follow a particular career, work in particular sectors, occupations, trades, professions and crafts
- apply for specific jobs, with specific employers, complete the application process and subject oneself to the recruitment and selection processes
- accept job offers, accept the salary/occupation/prospects mixes of particular organisations
- turn up for work on the first day
- turn up for work on the second day, and continue turning up on a daily basis; and to start and continue to produce effective and successful work on behalf of the organisation
- earn a living, and both ensure and increase the standard of living
- progress, develop and advance
- seek physical and occupational variety; and to apply skills and expertise in a range of situations, and problems and issues (see Figure 20.5).

Some job titles are, in themselves, demeaning and dissatisfying. Titles such as typist, dustman, operative (and their politically correct alternatives of clerical assistant, refuse executive, crew person) are given by organisations as proof of status as much as occupational indicators.

Job enrichment, job rotation, job enlargement and empowerment activities have to address all aspects if they are to be effective. If they are carried out successfully,

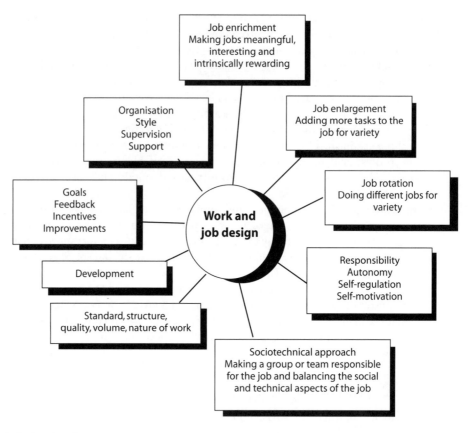

FIGURE 20.5 Job design

motivation and commitment can be generated in any staff or occupational group, whatever the working situation, provided that the behavioural satisfaction aspect is also addressed.

It is also to be noted that the converse is true: that where jobs and occupations are not effective, productive and satisfying, demotivation and demoralisation occur whatever the interests inherent in the particular profession may be.

Motivation and rewards

Monetary rewards

Money – in the form of wage and salary – is the reward for performance, especially and ideally, effective and successful performance. Wages and salaries are paid by organisations to individuals to reward them for bringing their expertise into the situation and for their efforts. The payment made must therefore reflect:

- the level of expertise brought by individuals and the ways in which they are required to apply it
- the quality and intensity of effort

- the effectiveness of individual performance, and the effectiveness of overall performance
- the value that the organisation places on the presence of the particular expertise
- the value placed by the individual on the expertise
- the expectations of the individual for particular levels of reward
- the anticipation of continuity of improvement in reward levels.

Perceptions and value

There is a strongly perceived relationship between pay and job importance. A chief executive who declares an annual salary of £20 000 will be widely considered not to have a great deal of responsibility or authority. A marketing officer on £80 000 a year will be generally perceived to have a responsible and high powered job. This now extends to the individual: if someone perceives themselves to be on 'only £x', it affects their self-esteem and self-worth because it is a statement of limited value. The converse is also true: where people can state that they are on 'good money' this underlines feelings of high value.

In times of turbulence and uncertainty the drive is for higher immediate rewards, part of which is a hedge against the vagaries of the long-term future.

Levels of pay and value quite legitimately indicate expectation levels. The higher the level of pay, the greater the levels of expectation placed on the employee; and the more disposed the employee is to accept these raised levels of expectation (see Figure 20.6).

Comparisons

Ultimately pay comparisons between different jobs in different organisations are spurious. However, they have a very strong psychological drive. If one person is

Motivation, perceptions and value in advertising   *FIGURE 20.6*

receiving a particular salary for carrying out a given job, and then finds out that 'the same job' in the neighbouring firm carries a salary of double what they receive, he or she becomes dissatisfied and frustrated. If a vacancy occurs at the neighbouring firm, the person may then put in for it and even get the job, only to find out that the nature, volume, content and commitment in the new job are nothing like the old.

The going rate

This occurs where the problem of comparison is overcome by setting local, regional and national rates for the same (or very similar) generic occupations. It applies especially to public professions, such as teaching, nursing and social work; while the job content and application of expertise may vary widely between establishments, the job output and expertise required are very much the same.

This also applies to pay rises. If one sector or occupation gets a rise of 5 per cent for example, then those in others that get only 4 per cent will tend to feel slighted, while those who get 6 per cent will tend to feel that they have done rather well.

Percentage rises in general also underline the value – or lack of value – placed on categories of staff. A low percentage therefore tends to give feelings of being under-valued or unvalued, even where the percentage may be known to reflect a low rise in the cost of living and seek only to compensate for this (see Figure 20.7 and Example Boxes 20.7 and 20.8).

Conclusions

The standpoint taken is that people work better when highly motivated, that there is a direct relationship between quality of performance and levels of motivation, and that volume and quality of work decline when motivation falls or when demotivation is present. The need to motivate and be motivated is continuous and constant. Some specific conclusions may be drawn.

- Motivation comes partly from within the individual and partly from the particular situation. It is therefore both constant and subject to continuous adaptation.
- Value, esteem and respect are basic human requirements extending to all places of work and all occupations (and indeed, to every walk of life). The key features of this are the integrity of relationships, levels of knowledge and understanding, general prevailing attitudes (whether positive or negative) and the nature of rewards, including pay.
- All people have expectations based on their understanding of particular situations, and they will be drawn to, or driven from these in anticipation of rewards and outcomes.

FIGURE 20.7 (opposite) The relationship between pay and performance

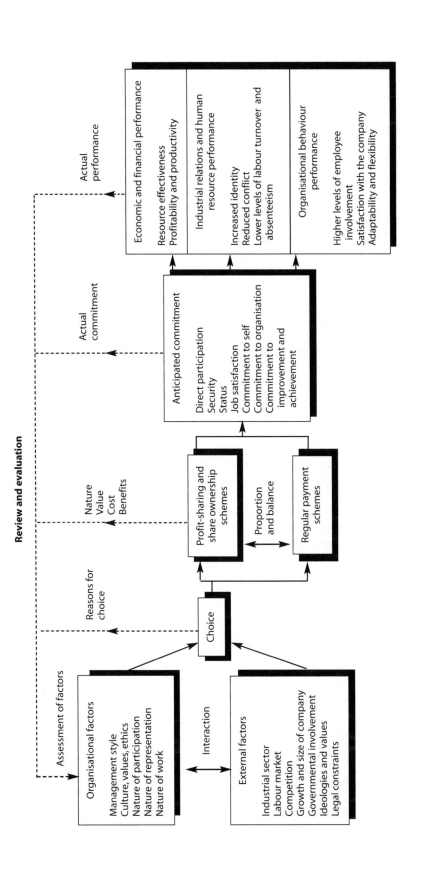

EXAMPLE BOX 20.7 Frustration

Frustration occurs when the relationship between expectation, effort and reward is skewed for reasons outside the individual's control. It is caused by a range of factors.

- The removal of anticipated rewards during the effort phase. For example, an individual may pursue qualifications in the expectation – even near certainty – that he or she will receive job promotion, enhancement and opportunities when he/she has finished the course. Towards the end of the course, if the organisation is taken over, or moves into new fields, or if the individual's superior changes jobs, the reward disappears.
- The cancellation of anticipated rewards through arbitrary (or even rational) action by the organisation. To take a similar example, the achievement of qualifications may have led in the past to pay rises – and then there is a change of policy during the course of the individual's studies and the rewards are now no longer available.
- When promised or indicated opportunities for training and development do not materialise for whatever reason.
- When the intrinsic satisfactions afforded by the job do not meet the wider needs (especially esteem and economic) of the individual. This has occurred in recent years in the UK with public services in occupations such as teaching, nursing and social work.
- When the nature of opportunities afforded and those anticipated do not match up, owing to misperceptions on either part.
- When individuals know or strongly believe that they are not being offered the opportunities that their talents and qualities merit; this occurs especially when they feels that this is as the result of the perceptions of their superiors.
- Where opportunities are simply not available, causing individuals to have to look elsewhere for their future prospects.
- Restriction of the capability to act by rules, regulations and procedures.

- People respond positively to equality and fairness of treatment, and negatively when these are not present.
- People respond positively to variety, development and opportunities when they know or perceive it to be in their interests to do so. They are less likely to respond to genuine opportunities if they do not understand or perceive them as such.
- People respond positively when they know the attitudes, behaviour, values and ways of work required; and negatively or less favourably when these are not apparent or not strong.
- People need constant attention to their individual wants and needs and will seek this from many sources, including work. If the work is demotivating, they will seek it elsewhere.
- The key to positive motivation is the establishment of a high level of mutual trust,

---

EXAMPLE 20.8 Failed Attempts at Motivation

Each of the following cases demonstrates the need to understand fully the nature and process of human and workplace motivation, and above all the futility of either throwing money at problems, or failing to recognise the broader aspects that have to be understood.

- The Allied Irish Bank gave an additional week's holiday to every member of staff who took no time off for sickness during the previous year. Once people had had a day's sickness, they would therefore tend to take at least another five working days to ensure that they did not miss out anyway.
- The Batchelor's Food Company imposed a policy which stated that anyone who was more than 10 minutes late for work would lose half a day's pay. The result was that anyone who was more than 10 minutes late – whether at the start of the day or returning after lunch – would simply take the rest of the period off.
- Early in the twenty-first century, public professions in the UK – especially teaching, medical and social care – are having great difficulties gaining new staff because the wider conditions of service are known, believed or perceived to be so poor that they place a lack of value on those who work in them.

---

commitment and responsibility. The main obligation here lies with the organisation. Individuals may be expected to respond positively when these qualities are present. Such values cannot be expected from individuals when the organisation is itself uncommitted to them, or where it takes an expedient, confrontational and adversarial view of its staff.

- People need constant feedback on the quality of their performance. The key contribution of general managerial and supervisory visibility is the ability to reinforce and develop positive attitudes and commitment; and the early identification of problems. People expect to be told constantly how well they are doing, even if they are doing well all of the time.

CHAPTER SUMMARY

Highly motivated and committed staff produce high-quality work over long periods of time. The highest levels of motivation occur in organisations which:

- respect and value their staff as people; treat them equally; offer opportunities on an even and equal basis; concentrate on performance not personality; pay and reward their people well
- generate a positive and harmonious culture; take early action to remove negative attitudes when they start to emerge; reward contributions to organisational performance
- recognise that everyone has personal, professional and occupational drives,

TABLE 20.1   Motivators and demotivators

Demotivators	Motivators
Management/supervisory style	Value
Administrative overload	Respect
Length of chains of command	Esteem
Attention to procedures rather than output	Responsibility
Bad communications	Progress
Lack of respect/value/esteem	Achievement
Status/importance based on rank rather than achievement	Communications

aims and objectives that require satisfaction; and take steps to harmonise and integrate these with organisational purposes

- balance the key behavioural features of expectation, effort and reward
- recognise and reward achievement, development and progress
- balance the attention given to the work in hand, the activities of work groups, and individual performance
- recognise the prevalence and influence of those elements that, if right, tend to motivate; and those that, if wrong, tend to demotivate.

The fundamental concern is to have capable people on the staff who want to work. The best and most rewarding jobs in the world can be – and are – destroyed by negative styles and attitudes of management. The most overtly mundane jobs in the world can be – and are – transformed and made excellent by positive and supportive styles of management and by offering respect, value and recognition where it is possible.

High levels of motivation

High levels of motivation are indicated by:

- low levels of absenteeism
- low levels of turnover
- low levels of accidents, sickness and injury
- few disputes, personality clashes, inter-departmental wrangles
- an open approach to problems; early recognition of and attention to potential problems
- active participation in consultation, organisational initiatives, suggestion schemes.

In each case, these are reinforced by open and participative styles of management, ready access to organisational, functional and personal information, and clear and simple systems and procedures.

Low levels of motivation

These are indicated by:

- high/increasing levels of disputes and grievances; high/increasing levels of disciplinary cases and the use of disciplinary procedures
- high/increasing levels of accidents, sickness and injury
- high/increasing levels of absenteeism and turnover
- a steady decline in quality and quantity of performance over the medium to long term. This is reinforced by the concentration on procedures and systems rather than output; and by the proliferation of new systems, procedures and monitoring and support functions.

These are the initial indicators of high and low levels of motivation. The key areas to address when assessing levels of staff motivation and morale are:

- the level and nature of identity that the staff have with the organisation; the extent to which status, esteem and rewards are issued for productive output as distinct from adherence to procedures
- the ability to offer fulfilment, and recognition of accomplishment to all levels and grades of staff.

Everyone has basic needs for a sense of belonging, self-respect and self-worth, for the respect and value of others, and for growth, development and progress. Initial enquiries in this area are, therefore, to be made along these lines; and these are the key features to address where problems are found to exist.

DISCUSSION QUESTIONS

1. Why do some top sports stars, on huge salaries, become demotivated and unwilling to perform to the best of their capability? What lessons are there in this for managers in other situations?
2. Identify the motivating and demotivating effects that different performance-related pay schemes can have on people in organisations.
3. In what circumstances does the 'Theory X' view of the world apply? In these circumstances, what actions can be taken by managers and individuals to improve the quality of working life?
4. Outline the motivating and demotivating effects present in job sharing and enrichment programmes, twilight shift working and nightshift working. What other factors do organisations have to be aware of when employing people under these conditions?
5. Identify the reward package that you would put together for: hospital nurses, double-glazing salespeople, call centre operatives and factory production workers. What motivators have you addressed, and what demotivators have you addressed, and why?

BORTON BOROUGH COUNCIL

Drumcree Ltd is a top-quality outward bound centre situated on the shores of Loch Lomond in Scotland. It runs courses for people from all walks of life, including parties from schools and colleges. Its top-brand, flagship course, however, is for management development. This is very expensive. Drumcree takes groups of no more than ten, and puts managers through a series of physically demanding, and mentally gruelling, exercises. The purpose of this is to identify the character and determination necessary to be a top manager in a large and sophisticated or complex organisation. Everyone who goes on these courses is assigned a personal tutor. The activities are recorded on video, and the Drumcree staff write extensive and detailed reports for the delegate's employers at the end of the courses. For this, Drumcree charge £3000 per delegate for a week's course.

Borton Borough Council sent seven of its staff on this flagship course. All had been identified as high fliers, potential senior management material. All were in middle-ranking executive posts, and ready to take the next step up the career ladder. They were:

- Anna Johnson, 32, from the Education Department
- Bob Friend, 37, from Corporate Personnel
- Caroline Hicks, 38, from the Highways Department
- Dev Desai, 35, from the Planning Department
- Eric Ameoli, 33, from the Social Services Department
- Faisal Ahmed, 39, from the Careers Department.

This was an important course for Borton Borough Council, and also for those attending. For as well as developing their leadership skills, the course would help in identifying who had the character and determination necessary for a senior corporate policy job in the Education Department for which they had all been shortlisted. Their assessment on this course would be a key feature of the decision to appoint. Accordingly, the staff at Drumcree were asked to prepare a special programme, which would require the equal commitment of all seven if it were to be completed satisfactorily.

All of the delegates knew each other by sight, having met at management meetings. They were all physically fit enough to undertake the activities. Indeed, the physical demands Drumcree made on its participants were never particularly arduous. It did, however, set great store on placing them in unfamiliar and stressful situations.

The seven travelled from Borton to Drumcree on the Sunday. That evening, they received a full briefing from the Drumcree staff. They met their personal tutors, all of whom had either been members of the military, police or emergency services. The course had been prepared especially for Borton Borough Council by Austin Layard, the Centre's founder and chief executive. He had spent twenty years designing and delivering courses for this kind of client. The brief was understood, the objectives agreed. On the Sunday evening, the group had its first short exercise, moving a heavy log up a muddy slope. During the exercise, Bob slipped and fell down the slope, and lay writhing in agony. The exercise was abandoned, and they all trooped back to the centre disappointed. A doctor was called to see Bob, and his ankle was heavily strapped.

Layard and the remaining six met later. Layard said to them: 'This is a bit of a nuisance. The course was specifically designed for seven of you. Now that we have only six, I do not know what we should do.'

The other six went into a brief huddle, then emerged and replied to Layard: 'We will carry out the course. Your staff will be present at all times, so if there is anything that we genuinely cannot do, we can simply abort the particular exercise.'

After a short discussion, it was agreed that the course would proceed as planned, but without Bob.

The remaining six completed all the exercises designed for them. Many of the activities placed considerable stress and strain on individuals, because they were one person short. However, as the week wore on, they got used to the idea that they were short-handed, and completed everything without any help from the course tutors. At the end of the course, they returned to the centre for the debrief. Layard spoke to them.

'You are, without doubt, the best group that we have ever had on one of these courses. We did not think that the seven of you would be able to complete it; indeed, we were told by your employers to make sure that you could not. The fact that the six of you have managed so well is a tribute to the character, determination and willingness shown in the face of adversity by every one of you. I am very proud to have had you along. The reports that we will be sending back to Borton will be the best that we have ever written.'

There was a short silence. Then Anna spoke. 'Where is Bob?'

Layard replied, 'Oh, he's gone. Fortunately there was nothing too much wrong with his ankle. The doctor had a look at it on the Monday morning. He pronounced it nothing more than a sprain. Bob caught the next train home, saying that he was going to have the week off.'

The others were briefly disappointed. However, such had been the development of their team spirit and group cohesion, that they thought little of it, and went off to celebrate a successful week.

The following Monday they returned to Borton Borough Council. A week later, they were summoned by David Griffiths, the Personnel Director of the Council, for the announcement of the Corporate Senior Officer post in education. Griffiths looked round at them all and then said: 'I am delighted to be able to tell you that we have appointed Bob Friend to this senior post. I am sure you will all want to congratulate him on this marvellous achievement.'

QUESTIONS

1. On the basis that successful completion of the outward-bound course was supposed to be a key determinant of the Senior Officer appointment, produce a logical, rational and honest explanation for the decision.
2. What are the likely effects on the motivation, morale and commitment of the other six?
3. Discuss the reasoning and validity of using this form of activity as an assessment of motivation and commitment.

21 The Management of Conflict

'I have the greatest confidence in the Chancellor of the Exchequer.' Margaret Thatcher, Prime Minister, one week before she dismissed Nigel Lawson from this post, 1986.

'The USSR is an evil empire.' Ronald Reagan, US President, on the Soviet Union, 1983.

'The strikes of the winter of discontent could have been settled easily, if only the trade union leaders had acknowledged that they were wrong and I was right.' James Callaghan, outgoing UK Prime Minister, 1979.

CHAPTER OUTLINE

Argument; competition; warfare – including open warfare, sniping and guerrilla tactics

The extent and prevalence of conflict in all human situations in general, and organisations in particular

Symptoms, sources and causes of conflict

The strategies for the management of conflict

Establishing and maintaining an environment in which conflict is managed positively.

CHAPTER OBJECTIVES

After studying this chapter, you should be able to:

understand the potential for conflict in all human situations, and how to recognise this

understand different strategic approaches to the management of conflict, once it becomes apparent that this exists

understand the organisational and managerial steps that need to be taken in order to ensure that a productive working environment is not disrupted

understand the expense of allowing conflict to develop

understand and apply particular remedies to specific situations.

Introduction

Conflict exists in all situations where individuals and groups are in disagreement with each other for whatever reason. This potential therefore exists everywhere, where two or more people are gathered together; a world without differences and disagreements is inconceivable! Much of the conflict of the world stems from the basic lack of recognition of this, and the inability to address it in ways designed to alleviate its effects or, better still, identify the positive and beneficial potential that is inherent in most situations.

Prima facie therefore, the potential for conflict exists in all forms of organisation. It is essential that all those concerned with the conception, direction and ordering of organisations understand its sources and causes, and are able to address these positively (see Figure 21.1).

Levels of conflict

The following levels of conflict may be distinguished: argument, competition and warfare. Argument and competition may be either positive, healthy and creative or negative, unhealthy and destructive. Warfare is always destructive.

The nature, symptoms and causes must be understood and these then become a focus for management action in striving for productive and harmonious places of work. It is useful therefore at the outset to establish the presence of conflict in organisations (as in all human situations). Conflict may be seen as positive and beneficial, a force capable of being harnessed for the greater good and contributing to organisation effectiveness. It is also clearly negative in many forms. Three distinctive variations on the theme are also apparent.

Argument, discussion and debate

This takes place between groups of two or more people and brings about (whether by accident or design) a better quality, more informed and better balanced view of the matter in hand. Provided that it is positive, the process of argument and debate leads to greater understanding also of the hopes, fears and aspirations of other group members. In addition it can identify gaps in knowledge and expertise, which can then be remedied, either through training or the inclusion in the debate of persons with the required expertise. It helps in the process of building mutual confidence and respect. It also

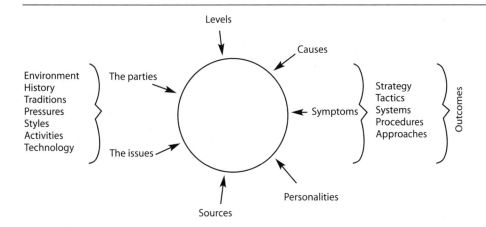

The nature of organisation conflict   *FIGURE 21.1*

encourages individuals to dig into their own resources, expertise and experience and to use these for the benefit of all concerned. It helps to build group identity. It leads to a better quality of decision making, and to understanding and acceptance of the reasons why particular directions are chosen.

Argument, discussion and debate become unproductive if they are not structured. People must be clear what they are debating. Otherwise they will inevitably argue about different things. At the very least this leads to group dysfunction and disharmony in the particular situation. The key is therefore to be able to set out the desired aims and objectives of the discussion and to have available as far as possible all necessary information.

The form of argument must be one that allows people to express strongly held views without sowing the seeds of potentially deeper and divisive differences. Attention should therefore be paid to the behavioural as well as structural side. An atmosphere of trust and confidence must be created if this is to be successful. People have to be supported in their views even if the group eventually decides to go in different directions.

Attention is required therefore to the outcome of the debate and the management of whatever is decided (always assuming that something is decided). Discussions and debates in committees for example, very often do not resolve anything, or determine courses of action, but rather agree to review the situation at a later date or else talk some more about the matter in hand. If this goes on for too long, the committee itself becomes the focus of resentment because it never achieves or decides anything. Assuming, however, that decisions are taken, the implications and consequences of these are to be fully understood and accepted by all.

Failure of argument, debate and discussion processes does not necessarily lead to more serious strife, though this may (and does) happen from time to time. The relationship is neither linear nor one-way. For example, a serious conflict that has recently emerged into the open may be managed and made positive through a continuous airing of the matter in debate and discussion. Where voices are raised and feelings run high in debate, this is not a problem as long as the group situation can accommodate this effectively and relationships return to normal after the event (see Example Box 21.1).

Competition

Competition exists between individuals and groups and within organisations. It also exists between organisations. It may be either positive or negative, healthy or unhealthy. At its best, competition sets standards for all to follow, whether within the organisation or within the entire sphere within which it operates. On a global scale, the standards of production, quality and managerial practice of certain organisations are held up as models to which the rest of the world should aspire. Some sectors arrange their organisations into league tables, thus shining a competitive light on some aspects of the activities carried out.

The nature of competition

This may be:

- **Closed or distributive:** one party wins at the expense of others.

EXAMPLE BOX 21.1 Rules for Productive Argument, Discussion and Debate

These are:

- Mutual interest of all concerned in the resolution of the matter in hand.
- Commitment to the debate itself and to the matters on the agenda.
- Honesty and openness so that differing views may become public and be heard without prejudice or penalty to the holders.
- A structure for the debate that addresses issues, facts, feelings and values, and which has a clearly understood purpose. This is true of all good discussions. Creative acts such as brainstorming have the clear intent of producing a wide range of ideas in as short a time as possible. The best committees work to an agenda, remit and terms of reference.
- Mutual trust and confidence in the personalities and expertise of those involved.

There are negative as well as positive aspects of the argument, debate and discussion process. It is likely to indicate where more serious differences may lie, especially if these indicate persistent clashes between particular individuals who adopt contrary positions merely to counter each other's views. Conversely, alliances may start to form in the debating chamber and carry on after the debate has finished, and these may divide the group itself into factions.

In these cases, argument itself is not going to resolve the problems and it is necessary to look more closely into the situation. Invariably, there will be deeper and underlying conflicts that need to be addressed if the group is to be made effective again.

- **Open or integrative:** there is scope for everyone to succeed.
- **Collaborative:** the boundaries of operations of each party can be set to ensure that everyone has a fair share of 'the cake': whatever is being competed for. The competitive environment may be dominated by one party or a few large parties who each take what they want from the situation while whatever is left over is to be disputed among the remaining players.
- **Based on positive or negative attitudes:** competition is only genuinely fruitful in the long-term if it is based on positive attitudes.

Competition is more likely to be successful and effective if it is open, if the rewards for competing effectively are available to all. Competition is likely to degenerate into conflicts where for example, competition for resources or accommodation is closed and one party is to succeed at the expense of the others.

The purpose of competition

This needs to be carefully managed. Competition between groups is much more likely to degenerate into conflict or warfare if this form of relationship is simply encouraged without adequate structure and without due consideration of its purpose and the goals of those involved. Competition between individuals within groups is also likely to become disruptive if this is the case.

For competition to be positive and productive a number of conditions must exist. The rules of the competition must be fair (and be seen to be so) to all concerned. They must be understood and accepted by everyone. The rewards of competing must be available to all involved and given to those who succeed. The competitors' destinies must be in their own hands: they are to succeed or fail by their own efforts and not by the arbitrary decision of persons elsewhere.

The rules must be adhered to and groups who cheat should be punished not rewarded for finding alternative means to the given end. Those in charge of the situation have considered all alternatives and have arrived at the conclusion that this form of approach is the best way of achieving the stated goal.

Competitive relationships exist best within organisations where attention is positively given to standards, creativity, the nature of the groups and the purpose of creating the situation. The aim is to bring out the best in everyone concerned, to improve performance and efficiency, to set absolute standards for activities and from this to form a base from which improvements can still be made. If these elements and rationale are not present, then organisations should consider alternative means of achieving their purpose. A negative competitive approach is likely to lead to interdepartmental strife, especially where the form of competition is closed.

Conflict as 'warfare'

Warfare exists where inter-group relations have been allowed to get out of hand, where the main aims and objectives of activities have been lost, and where great energies and resources are taken up with fighting the corner, reserving the position and denigrating other departments and functions.

Causes

Resources

Internal organisation warfare is often centred around resource questions and issues. It emerges when departments and individuals perceive that those who have control over resources are susceptible to non-operational approaches. They are also perceived to have their own reasons for issuing resources to particular departments: for example the availability or potential for triumphs; gaining favour and acceptance as the result.

Influence

Competition for power and influence is also apparent. A multiple agenda is normally pursued. Particular groups and individuals present their achievements in the best possible light. This takes various forms and is to ensure:

- recognition of real achievements
- presentation of achievements in ways acceptable to the sources of power and influ-

ence (for example, chief executive officer, top managers, particular shareholders and stakeholders, the community at large)

- that the group is receptive to patronage and that there are rewards to be gained by both patrons and those who come within their ambit
- presentation of results as major achievements, the best possible return on resources and expertise put in
- presentation of departments or individuals as having high value and expertise themselves, available for higher favours, good jobs; and acknowledgement that they can be relied upon to produce 'the right results'
- attaching the results (where possible or desirable) to questions of organisation success.

Competition also takes the form of:

- showing other departments and individuals in an unfavourable light
- denigrating the skills, expertise, qualities and achievements of others
- stealing the achievements of others or attaching oneself to their coat tails
- identifying any slight disagreement as a major barrier to progress
- apportioning blame for failure to others.

Divide and rule

Warfare is the normal outcome of management styles based on divide and rule. It is superficially attractive because it breaks a whole entity down into component parts – along the lines that, for example a tonne of bricks cannot be lifted by one person, but each individual brick may be and so the tonne is eventually shifted.

The analogy is false and so is the premise on which it is based. Dividing the whole into small chunks in this way causes energy to be expended by the individuals and groups on fighting their own corner rather than bonding to the common cause. To complete the analogy, the individual brick becomes the centre of attention rather than the use to which they can all be put.

Organisations and their managers that practise divide and rule therefore create battlefields on which the wars for resources and prestige are to be fought. The rules of combat are normally simple: winning is everything; and the losers may expect to lose influence, prestige, resources and possibly also their jobs. The process is normally additionally complicated by the 'dividers and rulers'; victories and triumphs are handed out in non-rational (more non-rational) ways, but rather designed to ensure that everyone is 'kept on their toes' and 'takes nothing for granted'.

This is compounded again by clandestine meetings, denigrations and denunciations involving individuals and groups in relation to each other and the organisation's top managers in its dealings with some groups.

Struggles for supremacy

Individuals and groups follow paths very similar to those of nations at war as they strive to succeed in warfare situations (see Example Box 21.2). Alliances are formed between different parties and so factions grow up. These may be overt or clandestine. Groups seek a fifth column: sources of influence in the departments that hold power,

---

EXAMPLE BOX 21.2 Reigns of Terror

Reigns of terror have been used by rulers, emperors, kings and queens throughout the ages as a means of keeping their subjects in check. The idea is that if subjects live in a constant state of fear, this will prevent them from taking up arms against those with power and authority. Indeed, they will be too frightened to do anything lest it be construed as rebellion.

A direct parallel may be drawn with organisational behaviour and associated managerial practices. Reigns of terror are a form of 'divide and rule' in which dissidents and non-conformists are marginalised (and sometimes sacked). Once these have been removed however, the leadership looks for other marginal groups and if there are none apparent they will be created anyway. Everyone therefore becomes at risk.

Again, the idea is superficially attractive along the 'keeping everyone on their toes' lines. The result, however, is normally that indicated above: everyone is too scared to do anything and therefore production, output and morale all collapse.

Moreover, all reigns of terror ultimately fail. Caligula, Nero, Robespierre and Danton were all themselves assassinated during their own reigns of terror. Persecution of early Christians by the Romans went a long way towards ensuring the survival of the Catholic Church. In turn, the persecution by the Catholic Church of its own dissidents in the fifteenth, sixteenth and seventeenth Centuries helped to ensure the survival and success of the Protestant reformation. The Nazi Empire – the Thousand Year Reich – lasted only 12 years (1933–45) though it used every organ of state in its reign of terror.

There are therefore clearly lessons to be learnt by managers who are tempted by the divide-and-rule approach, and by organisations that encourage it.

---

sources of information in the departments with which they are working. Rewards are promised in the form of promotion, increased pay, prestige work or a prestige location for the next job to be delivered when victory is achieved.

Resources and expertise are gathered together. This especially includes information of a nature and quality that can be used to enhance the one cause and damage the others. Public relations, presentational and lobbying skills are also required to ensure that what is done and achieved is seen in the best possible light by those with influence.

The effects of these forms of internal strife are entirely negative. They direct people from their main reasons for being in the organisation. They are extremely wasteful of resources time and energy. Success is only possible in individual terms and in the very short term where, for example, the individual uses a warfare triumph as the means for getting his/her next job; if this is outside the organisation then it will need to be addressed in terms that are meaningful to the prospective employer.

From a wider perspective, the base from which organisation welfare and strife grows is founded on certain tenets that have an initial attractiveness to the unwary. This is to be clearly and fully understood. The outcome is wholly disruptive and destructive. It destroys morale, careers, people, output, quality and value – and will destroy the entire organisation if either encouraged or allowed to go unchecked.

Sources of conflict in organisations

Most organisation conflict can be traced back to one or more of the following:

- competition for resources and the basis on which this is conducted
- lack of absolute standards of openness, honesty, trustworthiness and integrity in general organisational behaviour and in dealings between staff, departments, divisions and functions between different grades of staff and between seniors and subordinates; lack of mutual respect
- lack of shared values, commitment, enthusiasm; poor motivation and low morale
- unfairness, unevenness and inequality of personal and professional treatment, often linked to perceptions (and realities) of favouritism and scapegoating
- physical and psychological barriers, especially those between seniors and subordinates, and also those between departments, divisions and functions
- inability to meet expectations and fulfil promises; this is always compounded by the use of bureaucratic (mealy-mouthed) words and phrases
- expediency and short-termism that interferes with or dilutes the results that would otherwise be achieved
- the nature of work and its professional, expert and technical context
- the structure of work, the division and allocation of tasks and jobs
- people involved, their hopes and fears, aspirations, ambitions, beliefs, attitudes and values (see Example Box 21.3).

A conflict in expectations can therefore again be seen. The individuals who desire to act professionally and seek scope to practise their expertise to the full experience frustration when required to spend what they consider to be inordinate amounts of time on non-professional, non-expert activities.

Conflict is also caused where the attitudes, values and beliefs of the organisation in general are not the same as those of the individuals who carry out the work. People may, from time to time, be asked to do something that is counter to their own personal beliefs. For example, they may be asked to lie on the part of the organisation (give a false excuse for the failure of a delivery for example), and then to sustain this in public at least. They may be asked to dismiss or discipline someone else in ways with which they have no sympathy. The outcome of each may be essential to the organisation's continuing integrity: it is a question of reconciling the ends with the means (see Example Box 21.4).

Symptoms of conflict

Conflict may manifest itself in many ways.

- There are poor communications between groups, individuals and the organisation and its components.
- Inter-group relationships are based on envy, jealousy and anger at the position of others, rather than mutual cooperation and respect. People turn inward to the members of their own group and away from others.

EXAMPLE BOX 21.3 Right and Wrong

Differences in attitudes, values and belief cause conflict. This occurs most often when the demands of the organisation and the standards, expertise and ethics of its staff are at variance.

For example, hospitals are required to work within management and administrative budgets, and this often means that the medical work has to be prioritised and ordered to keep within financial targets. On the other hand, doctors and nurses have an absolute professional commitment to treat all those who come to them to the best of their ability.

There is also the relative commitment to the profession and the organisation. Conflict occurs when the demands of the profession and those of the organisation cannot be reconciled and the individual is required to choose between them. Operational factors also have to be considered: the balance of professional with managerial and administrative work for example, and the willingness of the individual to accept this.

This is, in turn, compounded by the attitudes inherent in the wider working relationship between organisation and individual. If this is largely positive and supportive, there is likely to be a greater willingness to take on peripheral and extraneous duties. If it is negative, the individual is more likely to retreat from the organisation into the profession and find comfort among other members.

- Personal and professional relationships deteriorate and personality clashes increase.
- There are increases in absenteeism, sickness, labour turnover, time-keeping problems and accidents.
- There is a proliferation of non-productive, ineffective and untargeted papers and reports, the purpose of which is publicity and promotion of the individuals and the departments that issue them.
- Rules and regulations covering especially the most minor of areas of activities also proliferate; the problem is compounded where rules and regulations are known or perceived to require conflicting and uneven standards.
- There is a proliferation of changes in job title especially 'upwards'. Thus for example, a supervisor may become a 'section controller'; a financial manger the 'director of corporate resources'.
- Disputes and grievances arising out of frustration and anger (rather than antagonism at the outset) escalate, leading to personality clashes and antagonism as well as operational decline.
- Control functions proliferate at the expense of front line functions.
- People take sides and gang up when problems are identified, joining or supporting one side or the other. This happens with long running disputes and grievances; in these cases the original cause has normally long since been forgotten.
- Informal corridor and washroom gatherings persistently discuss wrongs, situational and organisational decline.

EXAMPLE BOX 21.4 The Auditor

Robert Shore worked as an auditor for a county council in the south-east of England. He was invited to the wedding of a colleague. He happily attended the church service and reception and wished the couple all the best for the future.

When he returned to work he was studying some papers that related to the colleague who had just got married. One of these concerned an invoice addressed to 'The Old Rectory' in the village where the wedding had taken place. Studying the papers closely, he found that the colleague had hired the person who lived at The Old Rectory to do some work for him shortly before he got married.

Robert brought this to the attention of the county council chief executive. A full inquiry and investigation was launched. The implication was that his colleague had presented the clergyman concerned with some work in return for conducting his marriage for free.

The investigation lasted for a month. The following transpired:

- The person who lived at The Old Rectory was not the clergyman but a management consultant who had been hired legitimately to carry out the work. He had been paid a fee of £400 for doing this.
- The clergyman's fee for conducting the marriage was £90.
- The County Council spent £1500 on the investigation itself.

Robert wondered whether he should feel ashamed of himself as the result of instigating this investigation and the way in which it had arisen.

- Myths and legends flourish on the grapevine; minor events become major events, small problems become crises, a slight disagreement becomes a major row.
- Use of arbitration increases, handing organisational disagreements to higher (and sometimes external) authorities for resolution. The main cause of this is the need not to be seen to lose, especially as the result of personal efforts. At the point of decision therefore, the matter is handed on to a different authority to remove the responsibility for the outcome from the parties in dispute.
- Organisational, departmental, group and individual performance all decline. This is often mirrored by increases in customer complaints, relating either to particular individuals and departments or more seriously, to the organisation as a whole.
- People have disregard and disrespect for those in other parts of the organisation. This is mostly directed at management, supervision and upper levels by those lower down. It is also to be found among those at higher levels when they speak of employees in disparaging tones: 'the workers' and 'these people' for example (see Example Box 21.5).
- Too much attention is paid to the activities of other departments, divisions and functions, together with spurious and pseudo-analysis of the particular situation.
- There is a rise in non-productive meetings between persons from different departments, divisions and functions because individuals feel they need to defend their own corners and protect what they have.

EXAMPLE BOX 21.5 The Need for Victims

Many organisations, and their managers, find themselves in the position of 'needing victims'. This is an unacceptable aspect of organisation and managerial practice. In practice however, it is an extensive feature of large and complex multinational industrial, commercial and public service concerns.

In these cases, the organisation and/or managers seek 'victims': those on whom all the misfortunes of the organisation or department can be blamed. The individuals become stressed and traumatised through the bullying, harassment and discrimination that occurs as a result; they either leave or are forced out.

It is true that, in some cases, victims do receive compensation. Invariably however, the problem continues to exist within the organisation once the victim has departed, for the organisation and/or its managers simply find other victims.

Causes of conflict

The main causes of conflict in organisations are as follows.

- There are differences between corporate, group and individual aims and objectives, and the the organisation is unable to devise systems, practices and environments in which these can be reconciled and harmonised.
- Interdepartmental and inter-group wrangles overwhelmingly concerned either with:
  - territory: where one group feels that another is treading in an area that is legitimately theirs
  - prestige: where one group feels that another is gaining recognition for efforts and successes that are legitimately theirs
  - agenda: where one group feels that it is being marginalised by the activities of the other
  - poaching and theft: where one group attracts away the staff of the other and perhaps also their technology, equipment, information and prestige.
- Unequal status is awarded by the organisation to its different departments, divisions, functions, group and individuals. This is to be seen as:
  - formal relations, based on organisational structure and job definition
  - informal relations, based on corridor influence and possibly also personal relationships
  - favoured and unfavoured status, the means by which this is established and what it means to those concerned
  - the organisational pecking order and any other means by which prestige and influence are determined.
- Conflict also arises both from the status quo, where people seek to alter their own position, and from changes that the organisation seeks to make. For example, when an individual or group suddenly loses power, then a void is left which all the others rush to fill.

- Conversely, an individual or group may suddenly find itself in favour (for many reasons, operational necessity, expediency, the possibility of a triumph for the favour-giver) and the others rush to do it down.
- Individual clashes – both professional and personal – lead to conflict if the basis of the relationship is not established and ordered. For example, one individual sees a point of debate as a personal attack or questioning of his or her professional judgement; 'a lively discussion' may be regarded by one protagonist as the straightforward airing of a point of view, by others as questioning their expertise and integrity. This is also often the cause of feelings of favouritism, leading to clashes between the recipients (perceived or actual) of preferential treatment and the others around them. Bullying and scapegoating are also forms of individual clash, causing conflict between bully and bullied. This again may lead to conflict based either on support for the victim by others, or by others following the leader and setting upon the victim themselves.
- Groups may be drawn into conflict as the result of a clash between their leaders or between particular individuals.
- Role relationships have the potential to cause conflict. This is based on the nature of the given roles. For example, trade union officials are certain to come into conflict with organisations in the course of their duties; they are often representing the interest of members who have some kind of trouble or dispute. Other role relationships that should be considered are:
  - senior subordinates: conflicts of judgement, conflicts based on work output, attitudes style
  - appraiser–appraisee: where there are differences (often fundamental) over the nature and quality of the appraisee's performance and the action that this may cause to be taken
  - functional roles: conflicts between production and sales over quality, volume and availability of output; between purchaser (concerned with cost and quality) and producer (concerned with output); between personnel (concerned with absolute legal and ethical standards) and the departments which call on their services (concerned with solving problems, speed, expediency); between finance (efficiency) and other functions (effectiveness)
  - internal–external: the priorities and requirements of external roles (shareholder, stakeholder, bank manager, lobbyist, public interest group, community), and reconciling these with the organisation's aims and objectives and those of their staff and activities
  - parallel roles: clashes occur, for example, where two or more people are competing for one promotion; or where two or more people ostensibly carrying out the same job have (or are perceived to have) work of varying degrees of interest, quality, status and prestige.
- Internal customer/client or channel breakdown: clashes occur between people in any position or function when channels of communication, reporting relationships and hierarchical structures malfunction. If information or other output required elsewhere in the organisation is not forthcoming, attention focuses on the department or individual responsible in the search for an explanation.
- Conflict with the job held also occurs. This comes in the following forms.
  - Conflicts between job and job holder: this is largely related in the cases of expert and professional staff to frustration in terms of: the ability to use

expertise to the full; scope for professional development and advancement; ability to progress. In the case of the less expert, semi-skilled and unskilled staff it is normally related to routine patterns of work and the alienation and loss of self-worth that occurs as the result.

- Conflict between job and organisation: this concerns the relationship that exists between the two; the availability of opportunities; the extent to which these are offered; and the expectations that were placed at the outset on and by each, and the extent to which these have been fulfilled (see Example Box 21.6).
- Conflict between job holder and organisation: this is the extent to which pay, supervision, management style and the work environment are suitable and effective. Low pay leads to low feelings of self-worth, especially if there is little prospect of real increases in the future. Inappropriate supervision and management styles cause diversions away from effective work leading to feelings of frustration; this is compounded if the style is confrontational or abrasive. Frustration also occurs if, for example, the right equipment is not (or not always) available. It also occurs if the general ambience of the environment is tatty or

---

EXAMPLE BOX 21.6 Karen Wells

Karen Wells joined a large hospital in the south-east of England as a personnel assistant straight from college. She was impressed by the welcome that she received. She went through an expensive induction course and looked forward to starting work in earnest.

After a few weeks however, frustration began to set in. The job advertisement to which she had responded had offered 'a lively working environment, hands-on personnel experience, the opportunity to become involved in all aspects of human resource management work'. It also promised that professional training and development were to be available to the right person.

As the weeks and months went by, she found her frustration greatly increasing. She was employed on clerical and filing duties. Because she could type, her role quickly became a secretarial one. She regularly provided tea and coffee for meetings. She sometimes sat in on these and occasionally took minutes but was not allowed to participate.

After six months, she confronted her supervisor with her concerns. She was told: 'After the induction course we did not know what to do with you. All the personnel work is covered and so there is no opportunity for you there. We are pleased that we have found you a clerical job.' On the specific point about training and development she was told bluntly: 'You are not the right person and so training and development is not available to you.'

After this meeting, she reviewed her situation; she looked again at the job advertisement, which had said also 'starting salary up to £14 000'. She had started on £9 500. When she had mildly questioned this at the time, she had been told that it was normal practice and not to worry.

Karen Wells left the hospital after ten miserable months and now works for a major clearing bank.

unkempt, and this again leads also to feelings of reduced self-worth. It is seen as a reflection of the value placed on those who work by the organisation.

- Conflict also occurs where somebody works for two or more superiors. Again, the most common form is where each superior wants the same work done but the results produced in different forms or to different deadlines. In this situation, conflict also occurs where there is no agreement between the two superiors involved as to the nature of the subordinate relationship, especially in terms of commitment, time, energy and location. It is compounded where each party is determined not to make their position clear or to use precise, direct and assertive language (see Example Box 21.7).

- Giving credence, status and importance to the views of invested interests causes conflict. It especially causes resentment among those who do not lobby for their points of view and therefore lose out (or perceive themselves to do so) as a result. Conflicts normally come out into the open and may escalate into warfare as everyone forms themselves into vested interest groups or attach themselves to particular lobbies (see Example Box 21.8).

- The issuing of differentials causes conflict. Contentious items here include company cars, company parking spaces, personal computers and fax, mobile phones and other technology (executive technology), the flexibility to work from home, personal secretaries and assistants, differentiated office furniture. Conflict is caused when the allocation of these elements takes place (or seems to do so) from a point of view of patronage, prestige and status rather than operational necessity. This also enhances conflict and resentment where:
  - people receive differentials who do not (overtly) need them, while those who do need them do not receive them

---

EXAMPLE BOX 21.7 Causes of Conflict: Forms of Language

A symptom of some causes of conflict is to be found in language forms. These proliferate as the levels of conflict inherent arise. Some examples are given below.

- 'A plan exists': means that something has once or twice been discussed; it is perhaps required; no decision has been taken; and one should not be surprised if nothing happens.
- 'With the greatest respect' or 'I respect your views': normally means that the other person is thought to be talking or producing rubbish.
- 'I work too hard', 'I cannot leave things', 'I find it impossible to go home at night': become the normal statement of weaknesses at appraisal interviews if individuals perceive that they will otherwise be penalised.
- 'You move in exulted circles': normally means that the person being addressed has influence and prestige far beyond that which their level of perceived competence deserves.
- 'We did all we could': usually indicates that one individual or group is going to make it absolutely clear that they were let down by others in a situation where some form of failure has occurred.

> ## EXAMPLE BOX 21.8 Vested Interests and Hidden Agenda
>
> Hidden secondary and parallel agenda cause conflict. These proliferate where overall aims are not well or tightly drawn, where the aims do not accommodate those of the individuals involved, and where people feel that they are not likely to receive due recognition even if they do the work well. The parallel agenda therefore address these points: the need for individuals to progress; the need for recognition and the status and kudos that accrue as the result. At the very least, the organisation's purpose is diluted.
>
> In pursuit of this, other activities start to emerge. The department or group concerned is likely to start to engage in other means of achieving its objectives: use of any negative or blocking power that it has available, restricting and prioritising its own output, choosing deadlines to its own advantage.
>
> Those involved may also come to see or feel that the real issue is to fight for resources and/or prestige and reposition their activities accordingly. This is especially true where lobbies are seen or perceived to succeed at the expense of others.

- some people on a given grade receive them, while others on the same grade do not
- people on a given grade in one department or division receive them, while others on higher grades in other departments and divisions do not
- some people receive them (or some of them) because of operational necessity, while others on higher grades do not receive them either for operational necessity or for reasons of prestige.

Some common factors begin to emerge whatever the cause of conflict in a given set of circumstances.

- **Honesty:** the greater the integrity of the situation in terms of the relations between groups and individuals and the relationship between the organisation and its staff, the greater the likelihood of the effective management of conflict. This includes hierarchical and reporting relations.
- **Expectations:** conflict emerges when expectations are not understood and where they are not met.
- **Understanding:** much of this concerns empathy, a recognition of how people may be expected to behave in given situations and sets of circumstances.

    Destructive emotions, especially those of envy, jealousy, anger and greed, are brought into being when people are confronted with a situation in which they perceive themselves to be losing out. Fear and resentment flourish if the nature of the situation is such that those involved feel threatened by the success and prestige of others relative to their own position.

    Groups and individuals all seek to improve their position in all circumstances. They seek the capability to do this through any means, channels and resources available. Organisations either leave these open, remove them or close them down. If one group or individual pursues a channel successfully, others will follow. If this is not successful they will try other methods. Groups and individuals are attracted to the rewards that come from the improved position.

As well as a summary of the factors present in the causes, this indicates the main behavioural components of the conflict itself. Recognition of these therefore greatly contributes to an understanding of conflict itself and of some of the issues that have to be addressed if it is to be contained and if relations between groups and individuals are to be made positive and productive.

A complex picture of the potential for conflict, its emergence and strength begins to take shape. This involves:

- the level of conflict, and whether it is positive or negative
- the nature of conflict, whether positive or negative
- the source (or sources) of conflict
- the causes of conflict
- its symptoms.

To this may be added the following factors.

- The parties to the conflict. The simplest form of conflict involves two parties only. Much organisation conflict is more complex however.
- The issues in dispute; the strength of feeling that the parties involved have concerning them; the interests and agenda of those involved; the extent to which there is a hierarchy of contentious issues.
- The dynamics of the conflict: its causes; its sources of energy (see Table 21.1), the extent to which it is formalised; the extent to which it is personalised; the length of time it has been going on and is allowed to run on; the extent to which the eventual outcome is predictable; the range of possible outcomes.

At this point therefore, a basic conceptual framework exists for the understanding of conflict. It is important to know also that conflict, once it has been generated, is likely to feed off itself, gathering a life of its own if it is allowed to proceed unchecked (see Example Box 21.9).

It may deepen also if allowed to continue: professional disagreements and disputes may become personalised or generate into interdepartmental warfare (see Example Box 21.10).

Sources of energy in conflict   *TABLE 21.1*

The personalities involved	Expediency
The departments and functions involved	Need for triumphs, scapegoats and favours
The agenda of those involved	Relative necessity and compulsion to win
The organisational point of view	Wider perceptions of the dispute
The interests of those involved	Wider perceptions of the outcome
The presence and influence of third parties (for example, the CE, trade unions)	Alliances: the ability to call on outside support
Any absolute organisation standards, rules, regulations and practices involved	

EXAMPLE BOX 21.9 The Start of the First World War

At first glance, there is no apparent relationship between the assassination of a middle-aged nobleman in Sarajevo, Bosnia, and the death in northern and eastern Europe of 15 million soldiers from France, Germany, Russia, Britain and so many other countries. However the two are indeed cause and effect.

The Archduke Franz Ferdinand of Austria was assassinated by a Serb in Sarajevo on 1 August 1914. Austria immediately took this as an act of war and mobilised to invade Serbia.

At this point the domino effect of alliances became energised. Russia declared that any attack on its ally Serbia would constitute an act of war against itself. Because of a Franco-Russian treaty, France was drawn in as well. Austria sought help from its ally Germany, which sent a huge army across the Rhine and invaded northern France and Belgium. Britain, which had guaranteed the integrity of Belgium and had a long-standing 'entente' with France, declared war. Also quickly involved were the countries of the British Empire who rushed to the defence and support of the motherland. Battle lines were drawn across northern Europe for most of the next four years.

The war took less than a fortnight to start. The cause was quickly forgotten. What mattered was – winning.

Strategies for the management of conflict

Thus far it is established that the potential for conflict is present in every human situation, and organisations are no exception. Indeed, much of what has so far been discussed clearly applies to a variety of areas (for example, families, social groups, Guides, Scouts). Many issues present throughout society are emphasised and concentrated by the fact of their being in work organisations, and compounded by the ways, structures, rules and regulations in which these are constituted.

The first lesson, therefore, lies in the understanding of this. The second is to recognise that, if attention is paid only to the symptoms, overload is placed on the existing systems of the organisation as indicated above.

From this, in turn, derives the need to adopt strategic approaches (rather than operational) to the management and resolution of conflict. This is based on a framework designed at the outset that should:

- recognise the symptoms of the conflict
- recognise the nature and level (or levels) of conflict
- recognise and understand the sources of conflict
- investigate the root causes of the conflict
- establish the range of outcomes possible
- establish the desired outcome (see Example Box 21.11).

On to this framework can then be built strategies designed to ensure that the desired outcome is to be achieved.

It is clear from this that the symptoms are nothing more than the outward mani-

---

EXAMPLE BOX 21.10 The Outcomes of Conflict

- **Win–Win**: the integrative relationship in which everyone is content
- **Win–Lose**: the distributive relationship in which one side wins at the expense of the other (or others)
- **Lose–Win:** as Win–Lose
- **Lose–Lose:** leading to serious corporate strife.

The ultimate outcome of the distributive process occurs when the dispute escalates. In industrial relations terms this normally means recourse to strike or lock-outs (unless arbitration can be arranged) as a result of both sides becoming entrenched. In these cases a rational solution between the two parties is unlikely.

A result may eventually be gained internally if a dominant--dependency relationship can be called into play. From a workforce point of view this occurs mostly where the staff have control of output (for example, as used to happen with newspapers). In such cases the organisation will normally respond to economic necessity: the staff members have to be paid.

Arbitration may also be called upon to resolve disputes between individuals, especially those involving the superior–subordinate relationship. Many such cases lead to job loss, accusations of victimisation and prejudice, and are resolved only through the courts and industrial tribunals.

Note:

In all but integrative cases, the behavioural outcome is as important as the substantive. People do not like to be defeated. Neither do they like to be seen by others to have been defeated. A large part of the distributive process therefore covers the need to find suitable forms of words to address questions of wounded pride and loss of face that would otherwise occur. The great benefit of going to arbitration in these cases is the ability to present the outcome as an independent or outsider's view and therefore acceptable (see also the section on collective bargaining in strategies for the management of conflict).

---

festation that something is wrong; it is what has brought these to the surface that needs to be addressed. For example, it is no use sending sales and reception staff on customer care courses because of an increase in complaints if the causes of the problems lie within production functions. It is equally useless to train managers and supervisors in the use of disciplinary and grievance procedures without also giving an understanding of what discipline and grievance handling means in terms of a particular organisation.

The desired outcome therefore removes the symptoms of the conflict by addressing the causes rather than vice versa.

This is the starting point for effective conflict management.

Effective strategies for the management of conflict clearly vary in content between organisations and situations. In this context the main lines of approach are as follows.

- Attention to standards of honesty and integrity to ensure that people have a sound understanding of the basis on which the relationship between

TABLE 21.2 Operational and behavioural outputs of conflict

Operational	Behavioural
Dysfunction	Loss of face
Inefficiency	Wounded pride
Squandering of resources	Triumphalism
Loss of productive effort	Scapegoating
Customer complaints	Humiliation
Customer loss	Loss of faith
Loss of confidence	Loss of integrity
Loss of trust	Loss of morale
Loss of morale	Loss of confidence
Loss of performance	Loss of trust

Several of these items occur in each column. The purpose is to draw the relationship in terms of business performance as well as organisation behaviour.

themselves, their department, division or group and the organisation as a whole is established. This is brought about by absolute commitment by the organisation and those responsible for its direction, and transmitted to the required management staff by those responsible for the direction and supervision of the rest of the staff.

- Attention to communications to ensure that these meet the needs of receivers and that what is said or written is simple and direct, capable of being understood, honest and straightforward.
- Attention to the hopes, fears, aspirations and expectations of all those who work in the organisation. Much of this is based on empathy and mutual identity and commitment; it is dissipated by compartmentalising and differentiating between staff groups.
- Attention to the systems, procedures and practices of the organisation, to the ways in which these are structured and drawn up, and the ways in which they are operated. This especially means attention to equality and fairness of treatment and opportunity; the language and tone of the procedures themselves; and the training and briefing of managers and supervisors in their purposes, emphases and operation. It also normally entails the presence of sanctions for those who do not operate these systems with integrity.
- The establishment of organisational purposes common to all those present in the organisation, with which they can all identify and which transcend the inherent conflicts of objectives. This is the approach most favoured by Japanese companies in their operations in Western Europe and North America.
- The establishment of a universal identity and commitment to purpose. In organisation behaviour terms, this involves attention to the outputs of the stated purpose and the benefits and advantages that are to accrue as the result of their achievement. This is the starting point for the establishment of:
  - performance-related and profit-related pay schemes, and the generation of the identity, commitment and interest that are the key elements of the best of these

---

EXAMPLE BOX 21.11 Key Questions in Conflict Management

These are as follows.

- What is the likelihood of a dispute occurring? If it does, how long might it last? What are the wider consequences to ourselves, and to our staff?
- If it does occur, can we win it? What are the consequences of winning it? What are the consequences of losing?
- If it does occur, what costs are we going to incur? As well as financial cost, what of the questions of PR, media coverage and local feelings in our community? Is this a price worth paying?
- What happens when it all settles down? How will we interact and work with the staff afterwards? How long will any bad feeling last? What are the wider implications of this?
- What other ways are there around the matter or dispute in hand? Are we able to use these? What are the pros and cons of going down these alternatives, *vis-à-vis* a dispute?
- What are the behavioural and psychological aspects that surround this issue? If we win, what will be the effects on the workforce? And on managers? Are there questions of morale to be considered? If we lose, would loss of face be important? How could we save face, if that were necessary? What would be the response of the workforce and its representatives?

From consideration of the matter in hand this way, and by establishing the answer to these issues, the answer to the critical question emerges.

- Why are we seeking, entering, or preparing to enter this dispute?

This approach will form the basis of any strategic consideration of any conflict, or potential conflict, whether global, organisational, departmental, or divisional; or at team, group or individual level.

- briefing groups, work improvement groups and quality circles that reinforce the mutual confidence, commitment and respect of those involved.
- The removal of the barriers that exist between departments and divisions. This involves attention to matters of confidence and respect and to the level, quality and style of communications that impact on operational relationships.
- The establishment of organisation conformism based on the creation of desired means and methods of participation and consultation, and fused with absolute standards of honesty and integrity. Attention is required here to:
  - the representation of employees and the means by which this is to be achieved
  - their scope and structure
  - the agenda to be followed
  - the rules of engagement: the means by which these are to be operated.

These are the main organisational behaviour approaches required to address and tackle the sources and causes of conflict. They are based on the recognition of its universal potential to exist; the approach in particular organisations clearly varies. They arise from an understanding of the nature of conflict and of the need to recognise its causes rather than attack the symptoms. Energy devoted to dealing with conflict represents energy not spent on more productive activities; time and resources used in understanding and assessing the causes and dealing with these therefore bring their own pay-back in terms of reducing the time loss, stresses and strains caused by the reality of problems and disputes (see Example Box 21.12).

Conclusions

Understanding the sources and causes of conflict draws away from the hitherto accepted view that organisational strife is caused by troublemakers, trade unions,

---

EXAMPLE BOX 21.12 Operational Approaches to the Management of Conflict

The operational approaches used by organisations normally take the following forms.

- Developing rules, procedures and precedents to minimise the emergence of conflict and then, when it does occur, to minimise its undesirable effects.
- Ensuring that communications are effective in minimising conflict; bad communications may cause conflict or magnify minor disputes to dangerous proportions.
- Separation of sources of potential conflict which may be done geographically, structurally or psychologically (for example, through the creation of psychological distance between functions and ranks).
- Arbitration machinery may be made available as a strategy of last resort.
- Confrontation may be used to try and bring all participants together in an attempt to face them with the consequences of their action.
- Benign neglect: this is the application of the dictum that 'a problem deferred is a problem half solved'. This can normally only be used as a temporary measure while more information is being gathered or a more structured approach is being formulated.
- Industrial relations operations may be used for the containment and management of conflict; these include consultation, participation, collective bargaining and negotiating structures.

Whichever is used, each requires careful assessment as to its suitability for the situation. Each approach is then to be designed and implemented with the particular demands of the situation in mind. The choice of a single approach used piecemeal is never effective. More generally, each of these approaches is fraught with problems, if not adequately designed and implemented, and if the process is not managed.

Individual and organisational objectives

TABLE 21.3

Individual objectives	Organisational objectives
Money	Success
Prospects	Profits
Advancement	Effectiveness
Progress	Reputation
Perks	Confidence
Status	Development
Esteem	Progress
Respect	
Regard	
Development	

whistle blowers and other prima donnas, or over-mighty subjects or groups. Strategies and systems for the handling and management of conflict that are based on such a view clearly institutionalise rather than resolve conflict. They also tend to reinforce (rather than dissolve) more deeply held negative attitudes of mistrust, dishonesty and duplicity.

The current view therefore is that conflict is inevitable and that it is potential in all human relations and activities; and this includes work. In organisations it is determined by physical layout, physical and psychological distance, inter-group relationships, hierarchies, technology, expertise, and by the interaction of individual group and organisational aims and objectives. It is essential to realise the degree of mutual interest that exists between organisations and their staff. Understanding the extent and prevalence of the areas in which mutual interest exists is a key to effective conflict management. These can be seen in Table 21.3.

Differences in these objectives can easily be recognised; however, it is equally apparent that the establishment of where mutuality of interest lies is a major mark of progress in the management of organisational conflict.

Rather than the use of channels, procedures, institutions and forms, the desired approach is to give everyone a common set of values, goals and purposes for being in the organisation that both recognise and transcend the presence of conflict and reconcile the differing aims and objectives. Destructive conflict is minimised and resources otherwise used in the operation of staff management and industrial relations systems, are released for more positive and productive effect.

CHAPTER SUMMARY

The key to the effective management of conflict lies in recognising that it exists, at the three levels of argument, competition and warfare. From there, it is essential that the conditions are created that allow for constructive, open, honest and often heated debate, without this escalating into competition (proving oneself right and someone else wrong) or warfare (going to extreme lengths to demonstrate or prove a point). It is equally essential that all people are given the opportunity to voice their considered professional, occupational and personal informed opinion when required to do so, without fear of reprisal. It is extremely damaging, both to morale and effectiveness, if the honest expression of opinion leads to an individual being thought of as awkward or 'not a team player'.

Conflict based on prejudice, preconception and misperception is not to be tolerated either. Everyone has prejudices: for example, supporting a football club, or preferring one brand of baked beans over another. However, prejudices based on race, gender, occupation, ethnic origin, place of origin, religious background, sexuality and age are not to be tolerated. If proven, in every case, the perpetrators must be dismissed. If this does not happen, it sends a clear signal to the rest of the organisation that this form of behaviour is tolerated, and this becomes the defining point of the total lack of organisational integrity. Where preconceptions and misperceptions have been allowed to occur, it is essential that these are changed. It is the continuing responsibility of top management as well as divisional, departmental and section heads to ensure that they know as much as possible about the human, occupational and professional interactions, and create the conditions that ensure that any conflict is nipped in the bud when it becomes apparent that professional and occupational argument and debate is beginning to get out of hand.

It is also essential to recognise the extent and prevalence of conflict based on the abuse of rank, or professional or occupational status, when these forms of power, influence and authority are used to get something done that is illegitimate. It is a very short step from this to bullying, victimisation and harassment. This is personally, socially, occupationally and professionally damaging, as well as being morally repugnant and unacceptable. And it is endemic throughout organisations. A survey carried out by the University of Manchester Institute of Science and Technology (UMIST), the Institute of Management, and the Trade Union Congress (TUC) in the year 2000 published its results in March 2001. Among other findings were the following.

- One person in two suffered some form of stress or dysfunction as the result of workplace conflict.
- One person in four had suffered direct or indirect bullying over the past five years
- At the greatest risk were professionally or occupationally qualified staff, especially nurses, teachers, social workers, financial advisers, bank cashiers, computer operators and secretaries. For example, one teacher in every six complained of stress caused by conflict, bullying, victimisation or harassment in the past five years, and this applied to one nurse in every four.

Almost without exception, organisations and their senior managers did nothing about it. Health and education authorities were particularly crude in their attitude, and their response was summed as 'professionally qualified staff have to get used to a range of pressures, and conflict is always present. Robust organisational and managerial attitudes are therefore certain to prevail'. The same attitudes were found in the banking and oil industries, as well as the police service.

Conflict causes stress: organisational, occupational, group and personal. This, in turn, has a knock-on effect on organisational performance and output. Productivity falls, customers and clients are not served properly, and long-term profitability and effectiveness are damaged. There is also a professional and occupational marketing factor to be taken into account: those professions or occupations that come to be known, believed or perceived to suffer from stress and conflict have the greatest difficult in recruiting the next generation of staff. Moreover, it is increasingly expensive for organisations to accept the presence of stress and conflict without doing anything about it, because compensation levels for those who are able to demonstrate negative effects on their mental or physical well-being have risen sharply in the past few years. Many cases also attract extensive media attention, and this too has an adverse effect on the presentation and confidence of the particular organisation in the public eye.

In managing conflict, it is essential that there are clear grievance and disciplinary procedures, and that these are supported by full staff and management training. All procedures should be in writing, stating to whom they apply, and how, when and where they are to be used. Standards of required attitudes, behaviour and performance must be clearly stated. Especially when serious conflict exists, staff must have instant recourse to a named, senior and influential official to whom they can talk without fear of reprisals. If this is managed effectively, then it goes a long way to ensuring that organisational conflict is kept to an absolute minimum; indeed, that it only arises as the result of genuine misunderstanding

DISCUSSION QUESTIONS

1. What are the advantages and disadvantages of the collective bargaining approach to the management and resolution of conflict? How, in your view, might these be improved?
2. Outline and discuss the benefits and drawbacks of referring every single dispute or argument to arbitration.
3. Choosing an organisation with which you are familiar, outline the extent and prevalence of conflict present, and the causes and symptoms. What approaches should those responsible be taking in order to reduce their effect (where the organisation you have chosen has little conflict, identify and evaluate the actions and management style already present)?
4. Identify, as fully as possible, the potential for conflict in:
   - a joint venture arrangement between large companies and subcontractors for a major engineering project
   - a transition from individual offices to an open-plan arrangement
   - a transition from demarcated jobs to fully flexible working.
   Outline a strategy for the management of each of these situations.
5. Comment on the language used in the quotes at the start of the chapter. What attitudes can you infer from each?

RED SPIDER

Kitchens hold great meaning for the workforce of Red Spider, a marketing strategy consultancy.

One a year, all of its 20 strong complement meet at a country house with self-catering arrangements, and it is now part of an annual ritual that they cook for each other. So perhaps it wasn't surprising that when a group of them on a recent trip to Spain, separated into two touring parties, spent the journey designing their ideal head office, both groups came up with the same plan.

'It was uncanny', says Charlie Robertson, Red Spider's Chairman and Managing Director.'Everyone came up with a well-lit space with a big table in the middle and said it should be like a kitchen. This was two separate groups, in two cars, driving to Madrid.'

The consultancy's people need this social cohesion, because the bulk of their working lives is spent apart. The ideal office was a mere fantasy, an exercise in creativity. In reality, Red Spider is a virtual company, every employee operating from home offices dotted around Europe and the US. They refer to each other as 'spiders' and communicate by e-mail, telephone and fax. Every six weeks or so, a handful of them meet as a project group. But the rest of the time, according to Robertson, 'you can take your laptop to the beach if you want. It doesn't matter where you work.'. It is an extreme example of fragmented culture.

However, the firm (set up four years ago) is now adopting some standard personnel procedures to bring more structure to its management. It has taken advice from HR consultant Mandy Partridge.

One result has been a statement of values and information about the company, the 'handifesto', which is sent out to potential recruits. Robertson explains: 'Recruitment is almost through osmosis. People we take on need to be like-minded. We describe the right people as "spidery". If you are working remotely, there has to be trust, and we have a huge amount of emotional commitment to each other. But we needed a better way of getting our culture across.'

The firm is setting up an appraisal system by which staff appraise their managers as well as vice versa (360 degree appraisal). It is thinking of introducing profit-related pay. It has also taken on a finance director (although he too had to be 'spidery').

In short, anarchy does not work in a fragmented culture any more than it does elsewhere.

Source: Jane Pickard, *People Management*, 29 October 1998.

QUESTIONS

1. Identify the potential for conflict that exists from as broad a perspective as possible. You should pay particular attention to:
   - potential conflicts of interest
   - potential conflicts between individuals
   - the potential for conflicts brought about as the result of the changes indicated in the last three paragraphs.

2. In the case study, the ideal employee is described as being 'spidery'. On the basis of what you are told, how would you assess potential recruits for these qualities and attitudes?
3. What is the potential for conflict caused by 'recruitment by osmosis'? Identify the full range of consequences.
4. Identify the potential for culture and personality clashes as the result of having such a diverse organisation, working in these ways.

22 Managerial Performance

'Beware of rashness. With energy and sleepless vigilance, go forward and give us victories.' Abraham Lincoln, 1865.

'No epilogue I pray you, your play needs no excuse. Never excuse.' William Shakespeare, *A Midsummer Night's Dream*.

'People like to work for a good guy, but they will only take it for so long, especially if they do not get their bonuses.' Ricardo Semler, *The Maverick Solution*, BBC, 1997.

CHAPTER OUTLINE

The context of managerial performance

The components of managerial performance

The complexity of managerial performance

The development of managerial performance

The introduction of specific skills and capabilities: wait a minute; on-the-spot negotiating; style and visibility; time; and survival.

CHAPTER OBJECTIVES

After studying this chapter, you should be able to:

understand the complexity of managerial performance

understand the need for constant development of managerial skills and qualities

understand and be able to apply specific skills and points of enquiry to generate problems

understand the opportunities, problems and consequences of undertaking particular courses of action, or particular approaches to issues and problems

understand the need for review and evaluation of every activity.

Introduction

The purpose of this chapter is to bridge the gap between the acquisition of the skills, knowledge and aptitudes required of the manager and an understanding of the complexities and application problems in functional terms, so as to combine them together to generate effective and successful managerial performance.

The department manager's role

The department manager requires both an understanding of the principles and practice outlined thus far and the qualities necessary to put them into effect in ways suitable to the function, operation and nature of the situation in which the manager has to work.

The manager is the department's figurehead, symbol and representation, generating an image and identity for the department in the whole organisation and among the others with whom they come into contact. Managers represent their departments at meetings; they carry the hopes and aspirations of the staff at all times in all dealings with the rest of the organisation. It is the departmental manager's role and duty to fight the department's corner and to ensure that the interests of both department and staff are put forward and represented. According to the nature of the department in which they are working, this function will involve belonging to a wide range of professional associations, cluster groups and functional lobbies and being an effective operator in all of these.

The manager must have a decision-making capability that is suitable to the purposes of the department. Again, this involves drawing on capacities and capabilities and using them in ways suitable to his or her own particular situation. In particular, part of this decision-making faculty must include an effective problem-solving method (see Figure 22.1). Again, the precise configuration of this will vary from situation to situation but essentially must address the basic process of identifying and defining the problem, assessing its causes, considering the variety of approaches that are possible and feasible in the situation, and deciding on appropriate courses of action.

Effectiveness in any managerial position requires both understanding and capability in these areas. If these are present there are additional benefits in terms of the creation of identity and pride among departmental staff. Finally, decision making constitutes a critical part of the backcloth that is in any case necessary to managing effectively in any work situation.

Attitudes and values

Forming and nurturing the 'right' attitudes is an essential part of the managerial task, and any manager or supervisor must have a full grasp of this and be able to do it. If enthusiasm is infectious, so is negativity; a workforce can easily become demoralised very quickly if certain matters are not picked up. In both multinational and public and health services this is manifest in the 'canteen culture', and has been partly responsible for engendering and perpetuating negative and undesirable attitudes. The overall purpose must be that everyone is happy, harmonious and productive on the organisation's terms and those of the manager and department in question. A clear and positive lead must therefore be given, and clear and positive attitudes engendered and formed.

Negativity, therefore, is to be avoided. Prevention of such attitudes is achieved through adequate and well-designed induction and orientation programmes so that every employee is given a positive set of corporate and departmental values, a clear identity with the organisation and its purposes, and confidence in the rest of the staff. Ultimately, people wish to feel good about the organisation and department for which they work.

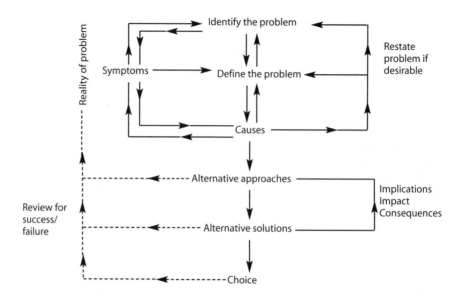

Purpose: to ensure that a rigorous and disciplined approach is recognised and understood as being necessary in all situations, or that it is adopted.
Points for consideration throughout the process must also include: the context and nature of it; when it is occurring; where it is occurring; why; its impact on the rest of the organisation, department or division; the extent to which it can be avoided; the extent to which it can be controlled; the consequences and opportunities of not tackling it (which is always a choice).

FIGURE 22.1 A problem-solving model

Cure of bad attitudes is harder. In isolated or extreme cases, people who do not wish to work for the particular organisation will be dismissed. In large or complex organisations they may be moved somewhere with the view of reforming their attitudes and getting a positive response from them. Marks of envy must also be dealt with; office executives who wish for the sales persons' cars should be informed that, without the efforts of the sales force, there would be no office job. Similarly, professional and technical experts may feel a much stronger loyalty and commitment to their expertise than to the organisation which actually employs them to use it. In general departmental managers will address such matters either at the point at which they first assume their post, or when new members of staff come into the department. They thus set standards of attitude and conformity to which all are to aspire in the pursuit of the goals of the department. One manager's view of such 'ground rules' is given in Example Box 22.1.

Setting goals

It is essential that all departments have clear aims and objectives and that all of those who work in them understand what they are and why it is the purpose of the particular part of the organisation to achieve them. It is invariably a feature of departments that malfunction, and of staff who are demoralised or demotivated, that they are not clear about this purpose or the requirements and directions of the part of the organisation for which they work.

EXAMPLE BOX 22.1 The Hard Line

'I believe in as hard a line as possible being taken by the management on the staff, a harder line being taken by the owners on the management and the hardest line being taken by the owners on themselves. Creating this environment is very difficult and so a strong approach must be taken in every area. The working atmosphere must be tightly controlled and be all-pervasive or it will not work. This seems contradictory to the "kind" approach of Maslow or Rogers. I think it is necessary however if their dreams of what people are capable of are to be achieved.

The vital ground rules must be ascertained (no more, no less) and then they must be stuck to absolutely rigidly. The Japanese conformity approach should be made to look weak, when it comes to the ground rules. On the other hand, once these rules are adhered to, as much flexibility as possible should be allowed. In this way individuality is achieved through conformity. As long as the important things are taken care of, people can do what they want and express themselves freely through their jobs. I don't care how they do something as long as the end product is good. Mavericks who can work within the guidelines are welcome and a great source of creativity and inspiration.

It may be possible to summarise the ground rules into simply one thing. You must keep to your agreements. This encourages the development of the person's integrity, their ability to make choices and their sense of responsibility. It then gives us the opportunity to ask them to agree to what we really want, i.e., be at work at 8.00 am. If they agree to this, we will hold them to it, precisely 2 minutes past 8.00 is not 8.00, and providing we can maintain enough front (and maintain this level of integrity ourselves) then we will pull them up on it.

Reasons are not relevant (e.g. the bus was late). It then becomes a matter of Personal Power, which we want to foster in the staff. It is possible to act as if you are responsible for everything that happens in your life whether it is true or not. Doing this eventually means it will end up as being true, in your reality. It is possible to look ahead and manipulate the environment. If you expect traffic then you can leave earlier. If they were paid £100 000 just for turning up on time, they would be there. This principle can be applied to everything we want, and although it may seem strange, in the long term it will benefit the individual as much as us.'

Source: David Scott, Artisan Group Ltd, *Business Plan*, 1993.

Such aims and objectives should be written down to give high levels of credibility and to serve as visual reminders to all concerned. They should also be positive, and reflect both aspirations and achievement. They should be 'personal' and be drawn up in ways with which everyone in the department can identify. They must be challenging and motivating and reflect the theme of constant improvements and achievements wherever possible. They must be prioritised; they will not all be instantly achievable but will set a progression and configuration of the value of the work of the department. They must also be realistic without introducing measures of complacency or inefficiency.

Objectives must be measurable; and this includes those established for managers and supervisors. This involves reducing any qualitative objectives wherever possible to a series of quantifiable measures. Where this cannot be expressed it is often nevertheless possible to break an objective down into useful, specific and more controllable sub-objectives. For example, where phrases such as 'a matter of urgency' or 'as soon as possible' are used, these should be replaced with particular timescales or deadlines; the phrases quoted bind nobody to anything in reality and will be read as such by those involved. Above all, goals, aims and objectives that are established must be clearly understood and valued by everybody. They must seek to combine the capacities and talents of everyone concerned in productive and effective effort and to reconcile the divergent and often disparate reasons that individuals within a department have for being there. Example Boxes 22.1 and 22.2 give model goal and objective formulations.

Managing by walking about

Managing by walking about (MBWA) enhances visibility, and also creates opportunities for productive harmony, early problem and issue resolution, and improvements in communications.

In behavioural and perceptual terms, the manager who is 'visible' is seen as approachable and acceptable. This will be reinforced by the manager who, while walking about, takes active steps to approach the staff members, get to know them,

---

EXAMPLE BOX 22.2 Objectives: An Example

A social service or welfare objective may be (and often is) written as follows.

> To promote the social well-being of groups with physical, mental and environmental handicaps; to enable them to function, as far as possible, as a community and within the community of their choice.

This is wrong. It is imprecise and unintelligible, and alienates people rather than drawing them in. It is written in 'politician- and bureaucrat-speak', and is thus full of opportunities for interpretation, and will be read as such.

The approach is wrong, therefore, unless what is actually desired is a clouding, rather than clarification of the issues raised. Assuming that clarity is what is wanted, the matter should be treated thus.

> In regard to each group of clients, the establishment of the following facilities and services .... by .... (a stated deadline).

Everyone is clear where they stand. Those working in the service have targets; the client group has expectations. There are included: performance achievement targets; measures of success or failure; and the basis of an operational review in relation to 'service' objectives.

understand their jobs, their problems and their concerns. More specifically, MBWA underlines the essential qualities of trust, openness, honesty and integrity, as well as visibility. It fosters a communication forum and informal meeting point between manager and staff that demonstrates the manager's care and concern and enables small issues to be brought up and dealt with on the spot before they become major problems. Such behaviour is an essential cog in the process of continually appraising the performance of staff. It enables any misunderstandings on the part of anyone concerned to be raised and rectified quickly.

Such behaviour also fosters the quality of empathy in the manager or supervisor, and gives a full general knowledge and background to the hopes, fears and aspirations of those who work in the department. This is an essential prerequisite to the process of motivating the staff successfully.

Such behaviour reduces both the physical and behavioural barriers between the manager and staff. The closed door, large desk and executive trappings are not only physically imposing; they also present a perceptual barrier that the subordinate has first to overcome because they reinforce the differences in rank and status between the two: MBWA dilutes these.

Related to MBWA is the need to lead by example, to set absolute standards. Good managers are always present whenever there is a crisis or emergency. Managers gain and improve their respect among their staff through their willingness to lead by example. Mark McCormack of IMG goes out with sales executives and consultants to demonstrate his own ability and preferred style in closing deals. Richard Branson of the Virgin Group regularly serves drinks and meals on his scheduled airline flights. Both also make a point of regularly telephoning those staff whom they have not seen during the week. Not only are they demonstrating their own willingness and capacity, they are also setting an example to, and for, their staff, and keeping an active eye on the day-to-day operations of their organisation. It is also excellent general marketing among both staff and customers.

MBWA is an essential tool for the manager and one that must be in constant use. If it is not, the staff will develop their own patterns and ways of working, their own means of problem and issue resolution, and control will pass out of the hands and office of the manager. In more sophisticated or complex organisations where there is a global, off-site, or other 'arm's length' supervision or direction mode, there should be an individual designated to act in the manager's stead, maintaining the visible face of the organisation and its management, taking the day-to-day decisions and resolving minor and operational issues before they become major crises.

Wait a minute

All managers should have a mechanism in some shape or form that constitutes a 'wait a minute' facility. This will be present in the formulation of policy or direction, the taking of decisions, and the implementation of strategy. At departmental and other junior levels the purpose is to ensure that no inconvenient operational precedent is being set by taking a particular line to resolve what may seem a simple and one-off problem. 'Wait a minute' is not an abdication of decision-making ability or of decision making itself. It need not take a 'minute'. It simply means ensuring that what is to be done has been questioned from every conceivable angle. It is more generally part of the monitoring, review, early and late warning systems that should be integral to all

---

EXAMPLE BOX 22.3 Wait a Minute

- Nike, the sportswear corporation, tried to devise a global travel policy for its staff. In particular the focus was on who should travel first class, business class or economy class on the world's airlines. Should this be based on the distance travelled, the part of the world to which the executive was travelling, the length of the journey, or the volume or value of business to be conducted?

- The Ceramics Industry Training Board summoned a meeting of junior field executives to its head office in Harrow, north-west London. The junior executives were from all over the UK, and overnight hotel accommodation was arranged for them. The meeting was unproductive and wasteful because two executives were unable to attend. These two lived in London and so no accommodation was arranged for them. On the day in question they were unable to travel because of a terrorist bomb. They also felt discriminated against, and slighted, by the accident of their location in London.

- John Stevens, an official at the London office of an international bank, asked to take two years' annual leave back-to-back (a total of two months) to visit friends and relatives in Australia. His request was granted. Mary Phelps, an official in an equivalent position and with longer service at the same bank, put in the same request for back-to-back leave to visit friends and relatives at Ullapool in Scotland. She underlined the request by stating that it would take longer for her to get to her destination than for Stevens to get to his.

---

aspects of the manager's task. The presence of a 'wait a minute' facility does not of itself ensure that the right decision is taken, but it does at least afford a moment's further consideration. If this is all that is necessary to confirm that what is being done is truly for the good of the organisation and the fair and equitable treatment of the staff concerned, it is a moment well spent. Example 22.3 considers three situations where 'Wait a minute' could usefully be used.

Control

All managers must have control mechanisms suitable to the department or unit concerned, relating to the staff and resources and to the operations that are carried out within it. This must apply even where the work in hand is of a professional, administrative, technical or qualitative nature. The overall function of control involves setting desired standards and measuring actual performance against them; from this, analyses of differences between the two will be made and remedial action will be taken where necessary. It follows from this that objectives must be fully understood by all concerned, so that involvement in the control of the work necessary and any remedial action that becomes apparent is adopted and understood by all concerned.

The methods and mechanisms to be used will therefore be department or task specific; and linked to and in harmony with the overall methods adopted by the organisation. They must reconcile the necessity to produce clear results with the need to be flexible and objective in operation, and must also be economical and simple. Presentation of control information in ways that everyone can understand and have regard to is essential. It is necessary not only to indicate deviations from required performance but also to provide the means of establishing the causes of these: where the failures are occurring, why this is so and what to do about them. Within this context managers will draw up and use their own control methods. These will include:

- **Forecasts:** based on the resources – staff, financial and technological – available, and related to the outputs that the organisation requires.
- **Budgets:** for all the activities within the manager's sphere, covering such matters as staff, production, outputs, operational costs, administration, other overheads, cash and daily expenditure, and possibly also an overall department reconciliation of these matters.
- **Management information systems:** including the gathering and promulgation of information within the department and the reconciliation of this with desired levels of performance; these also provide a vehicle for the manager's contribution to the information systems and requirements of the organisation.
- **Reporting systems and relationships:** designed to highlight any deviations and problems immediately, and to identify means by which such situations may be remedied; in any case, they should be able to provide information that can be used on an organisational basis for future planning and direction setting.
- **Job and work design:** to allocate work so as to ensure effective long-term organisational, departmental and individual performance, and an even distribution of the bad or unattractive parts of the work. This is likely to require attention to the ability to attract and retain staff, and to the design of effective (and often flexible) working patterns.
- **Feedback:** part of the control process is the communication process that constitutes keeping the departments informed of progress on a continuous basis. There is a control function inherent in the nature and content of feedback that is given; part of this may also be achieved through any performance appraisal scheme that is in place.
- **Conflict resolution:** part of the purpose of having control methods and procedures in place must be to ensure that conflicts or disputes between members of staff are resolved as quickly and effectively as possible.
- **Control methods and means:** these should be integrated into the general review, monitoring and process assessment that should be in place in all departments. To be fully effective, they require full understanding on the part of all concerned: the manager, the staff and those other departments and units with whom they interact. They should also mirror the aims and objectives of the departments if they are to be fully effective. Example Box 22.4 lists the number of problems a manager may have to field even when events are outside his or her control.

Time

Time at the workplace may be divided into productive time, non-productive or stoppage or downtime, maintenance time, and wasted time. From this, priority, crisis, wastage, overload and underload can be identified; and a time–resource–energy dimension put on each. The purpose is to ensure that what happens in reality accords with what managers think happens. Other dimensions and variables will also be

---

EXAMPLE BOX 22.4 An Airline Manager Working in the Middle East

This manager regularly fields questions from powerful and influential people in his region. Problems handled have included the following.

- Why the daughter of a diplomat had to wait 20 minutes for an orange juice on her flight back to London.
- Why packages and parcels carried by a worldwide courier organisation had to go through security screening and not straight on to the aeroplane.
- Why it took two hours for a particular cargo to be cleared from the airport by customs.
- Why Europeans have to go through the full immigration procedure upon arrival in countries of the Middle East.

The point that each of these items has in common is that they are all outside the manager's control. They are nevertheless raised by the firm's customers and clients and he/she must therefore either deal with them or find someone else to provide a suitable and adequate answer.

---

included. These include the complexity and difficulty of the task in hand, its importance, its urgency, and its frequency. The value of what is done, whether derived or implicit, will also have a time configuration to it. What is therefore required is an attitude of continued questioning of time usage based on the premise that anything and everything can always be improved and made more efficient and effective (see Example Box 22.5).

In order to maximise or optimise time usage, certain steps can be taken. The first is for the manager to be aware of the time issue. Part of the process that arises from this is:

- to set priorities for the department
- to set a pattern of delegation of tasks and activities
- to produce suitable and effective work schedules
- continuously to assess the work in hand against time constraints, as well as against constraints placed by other resource implications.

Next the manager should identify those things that waste time. These may consist of:

- long, unnecessary or habitual meetings, or those which are procedural rather than executive in content
- interruptions and the nature of these in his or her work
- idle conversations; unnecessary bureaucracy, reporting systems and record keeping
- the balance of travelling time against effective business conducted
- task allocations: especially the allocation of the easy tasks which should be

> **EXAMPLE BOX 22.5 Waste of Managerial Time**
>
> A report published jointly by the UK Industrial Society and the BBC at the end of the twentieth century drew, as its main conclusions, the following.
>
> Managers spend up to 20 per cent of their time or the equivalent of one whole day per five-day working week in meetings. Furthermore, they spend up to a third of their working time on paperwork, routine and administration. The main time-wasters identified were interruptions from colleagues, handling telephone calls that a junior or subordinate should have fielded, and dealing with untargeted bureaucracy and memoranda. The main operational causes of hold-ups were found to be computer problems and system failures.
>
> The stark conclusion to be drawn from this is that managers represent an over-paid niche of the workforce in relation to the quality of their output. Operations, contributions and key results require better targeting, and better definition; and an understanding on the part of the organisations and their top executives of the outputs required of their subordinates and the way these are to be achieved.
>
> This was reinforced by studies carried out and published in early 2001, also by the Industrial Society. These stated that the knowledge and understanding that so much time was wasted in these activities was having a seriously adverse effect on the morale of many junior and middle management staff. At the same time, the Institute of Management, following a survey of its members late in the year 2000, concluded that at no previous time had managers felt under so much 'pressure to perform', and that this was in many cases compounded by a lack of knowledge or understanding of what 'perform' actually meant. The Institute found that the overwhelming pressure was to attend for long hours, whether or not any productive work was carried out.

conducted on a basis that leaves those of high capacity and quality to carry out key, critical or other activities that match their capabilities, not filling up their work schedules with items that are well within them.

The manager should also be aware of creative approaches to time management in terms of machine, equipment and plant usage; working patterns and shift arrangements; personal planning; the setting and maintenance of deadlines; and giving clarity of purpose to meetings. There are opportunity costs of time usage and especially time wastage that can never be made up. All managers and their departments should have a system of time measurement that is suitable to its purpose, and that encourages efficiency and effectiveness of performance in regard to this resource.

Interpersonal skills and assertiveness

Everyone has interpersonal skills. For managers, these additionally constitute a tool that is essential to them in the pursuit of their daily occupation. They are instrumental in creating and reinforcing the management style adopted. They are part of the process of MBWA and the visibility that goes with this. They reinforce messages of honesty, openness and trust. They have implications for general levels and states of communication within the department, and for particular issues concerned with the handling of meetings and briefings within it (see Example Box 22.6), the wider handling of public presentations, and the ways in which these in turn reflect on the department.

The first and most important thing that a manager's use and application of his interpersonal skills will represent is the degree of trust and confidence in the staff and the basis on which they are to be treated. Overall it sets the tone and tenor for the whole department and its way of working. Managers will therefore apply their interpersonal skills in the following ways. They will never criticise members of staff either in public or on a personal basis when the problem is related to work. If there is a personal issue that requires managerial activity and concern this will be conducted in private and remain a matter between the manager and the individual. If it is necessary to criticise somebody's work performance, then it must be done in a clear and straight-

---

EXAMPLE BOX 22.6 The Chair: Leading Meetings, Discussions and Briefings

- **Before the meeting:** the chair establishes that a meeting is the best and most effective format for covering the matters in hand, and sets a suitable and effective agenda; arranges the room, facilities and environment in a way suitable for this matter; pre-briefs all those attending so that they know: what the nature of the meeting is, what their function in it is, what they are supposed to get from it, and the extent of their potential effect on the outcome of any resulting discussions. Finally, the chair will establish an effective order of business to be conducted and an application of general communication processes in ways suitable to the matter in hand.

- **During the meeting:** the chair has to strike a balance between allowing people's contributions and moving through the agenda in a suitable and effective way. If there are time constraints these should be made clear at the outset. Under such constraints contributions should also be limited so that all concerned get the opportunity to put their point of view. The correct atmosphere must be generated and maintained. The chair must also balance making sure that the matter in hand is kept to with allowing genuine opportunities for discussion and also the exploration of possibilities not previously thought of. The chair must know when to allow the discussion to continue and when to curtail it. Overall this aim must be to keep to the purpose and to move matters forward. A decision-making process should be published beforehand so that if there are decisions to be taken persons in attendance know what these are and how this is to be achieved (for example, through vote, through consensus, through the chair). Finally, nobody should be in any doubt as to the outcome of the meeting.

- **After the meeting:** it is invariably necessary for some form of follow-up to be effected. This normally takes the form of circulating a note, minutes or summary of what went on together with the main conclusions arrived at and decisions taken, and an indication of what is to happen next.

forward way with the emphasis upon remedy rather than apportioning blame. Effective criticism is always constructive; the end result must be to reinforce the importance of the individual as a member of the department. If it is possible, such criticism should be reinforced by finding areas of work to be praised at the same time. In this way also, the work remains at the centre of the concern.

It follows from this that praise should be extended where it is due. It is a powerful form of recognition and a universal motivator. Every manager should avoid only dealing with staff when there are negative concerns. Praise makes the individual concerned feel identity with the organisation, respected and important. It should be handed out whenever and wherever due, and it should be conducted in public.

Managers also use interpersonal skills to instil pride and enthusiasm for the job, the work and the department. The best managers inspire and generate pride and enthusiasm by the ways in which they behave in relation to the department's work and the people carrying it out. It is the manager's job to instil this feeling, and to promote this attitude among the staff, and the interpersonal relationship with the staff is instrumental in this.

Above all, work should be a matter of enthusiasm; and a matter of enjoyment as well as fulfilment. Again, the interpersonal skills of the manager are instrumental in creating this background.

Other qualities of leadership that become apparent through the use of interpersonal skills are: the courage of the manager concerned; job knowledge; self-control and self-discipline; a sense of fairness and equity; standards of personal conduct and behaviour that reflect the standards required in the department; and a sense of humour. It is also a reflection of the interpersonal qualities of the manager that ensures that the correct and appropriate standards of dress, language and manners are established. This is particularly important in departments and units where dealings with the public are an everyday feature.

The purpose overall must be to establish an adult and assertive means of interaction within the department (see Example Box 22.7). The prime purpose of the manager's interpersonal skills and approach in the situation is the promotion of effective work. These factors are an essential and integral part of this promotion; and without it actual standards will always fall short of the ideal.

This extends to giving negative messages; the fact that a message is negative does not mean it must have any lasting effect upon the motivation and morale either of the staff member who is to receive it or of the department at large. If it is necessary to deny someone a request, this should always be done quickly; the reason for the negative response should be made clear and should be the truth. The manager should never hide behind phrases like 'it's not company policy'. The reason given for the negative response should always be operational, and it should be clearly and unequivocally communicated.

The end result of all this is that the staff and manager know where they stand in relation to each other, and that the interpersonal skills applied and relationship generated support this. It provides the basis for effective work transactions and ensures that disputes and misunderstandings are kept to a minimum.

It also ensures that when these do occur they can be quickly and effectively remedied without lasting effect and, above all, negative consequences for the department as a whole. The particular issues are:

EXAMPLE BOX 22.7 Assertiveness in Action

The following is a summary of how to apply the principles of assertive behaviour and communication

- **Language:** assertive language is clear and simple. It is easy to understand on the part of the hearer or receiver. The words used are unambiguous and straightforward. Requests and demands are made in a clear and precise manner, and with sound reasons. Weasel words, political phraseology, ambiguity, and 'get-outs' are never used.
- **Delivery:** assertive delivery is given in a clear and steady tone of voice. The emphasis is on important words and phrases. The voice projection that is used is always even, and neither too loud nor too soft. Assertive delivery does not involve shouting, threatening, or abuse, at any time or under any circumstances; nor does it resort to simpering or whining.
- **Face and eyes:** the head is held up. There is plenty of eye contact, and a steadiness of gaze. The delivery is reinforced with positive movements that relate to what is being said (e.g. smiles, laughter, nodding; or a straight face where something has gone wrong).
- **Other non-verbal aspects:** the body is upright (whether standing or sitting). Arms and hands are 'open' (in order to encourage a positive response or transaction). There is no fidgeting or shuffling, nor are there threatening gestures or table thumping; or other outward displays of temper.
- **Situational factors:** assertive delivery is based on an inherent confidence, belief and knowledge of the situation, and the work that is done. Openness, clarity, credibility, and personal and professional confidence, all spring from this.

Any clarity of purpose or delivery will inevitably be spoilt through having to operate from a weak position or one which is not fully known or understood. In such cases, important issues are either clouded or avoided altogether. In extreme cases the people involved often interact aggressively or angrily in order to try to compensate for this basic lack of soundness, clarity or understanding.

Assertive behaviour is also the best foundation for effective negotiations and problem-solving activities. The approach taken is the determination to get to the bottom of the particular matter in hand and to resolve it to the satisfaction of everyone. Where in practice it becomes necessary to resort to more expedient means, there is invariably resentment somewhere at the outcome.

- **Discipline:** establishing absolute standards of behaviour and performance based on both ordinary common decency and absolute organisational demands; and ensuring that when disciplinary procedures are invoked, matters are dealt with quickly, fairly and effectively.
- **Dismissal:** ensuring that offences such as vandalism, violence, theft, fraud,

bullying, victimisation, discrimination and harassment are dealt with fairly and effectively; and that when these are proven, the perpetrators are dismissed.

- **Grievances:** handling and resolving issues rather than institutionalising them; ensuring that the full facts of the case are covered; and ensuring that everyone understands what outcome has been reached and the reasons for this.
- **Health and safety:** creating and maintaining the conditions whereby a healthy and safe working environment exists; taking remedial action where unsafe practices and unhealthy aspects are found.
- **Occupational health:** above all paying attention to stress, repetitive strain injuries, and the causes of these; recognising the potential for their existence; addressing and remedying working practices when these are found.

In each of these cases, it is essential that managers understand that there are procedures to be followed, and that failure to do so normally constitutes a breach of employment law. Managers must therefore become fully knowledgeable in the procedures, and expert in their application (see Example Box 22.8).

Continuous performance assessment

It is implicit in much of the above that the manager must be able to assess and judge the levels and quality of performance in the department and to measure it against the required standards, taking remedial action where necessary. This will apply at several levels. If there is a shortfall at departmental level, he or she may need to conduct a range of activities to find out why this is so and to make judgements from this. Such activities may consist of, for example, a walk-through of the processes and procedures of the organisation or department; an observation or sampling of departmental activities, harmony and cooperation; or the assessment and identification and remedying of blockages, again either in processes, procedures or the operations themselves.

At team level it may be necessary to institute a process of examination of the workings of the team in question, to assess where performance is falling down, why this should be so and what is causing it. From this, the manager should be able to make a more accurate compartmentalisation and definition under one or more of the headings of attitude, conflict, processes, procedures, communication, decision making and interrelations. Furthermore, where such an approach is adopted, the problem area may become apparent and remedy applied to it in the interests of reforming and recreating a positive and productive team.

At individual level a two-fold approach is necessary. One is to ensure that those in the department receive organisational feedback on the nature of their work, praise for good performance and a quick and effective remedy for any shortfall. The organisation's formal appraisal methods may in any case require this and may use these methods as the means of allocating training, development, secondment, the next move and pay rises. In all these cases it will be important to the members of staff that such appraisal is carried out in accordance with expectations and is generally effective.

The other part of the approach to the individual here concerns the general monitoring of the work of the department by the manager concerned. Performance will actually be continuously assessed as part of the manager's 'leadership' role in the department. Effectively conducted, this enables the manager to know the state and the performance of the department on a current and continuing basis. Issues

EXAMPLE BOX 22.8 Office Staff Practices, 1852

1. Godliness, Cleanliness and Punctuality are the necessities of a good business.
2. This firm has reduced the hours of work, and the Clerical Staff will now only have to be present between the hours of 7 a.m. and 6 p.m. on weekdays.
3. Daily prayers will be held each morning in the Main Office. The Clerical Staff will be present.
4. Clothing must be of a sober nature. The Clerical Staff will not disport themselves in raiment of bright colours, not will they wear hose, unless in good repair.
5. Overshoes and top-coats may not be worn in the office, but neck scarves and headwear may be worn in inclement weather.
6. A stove is provided for the benefit of the Clerical Staff.
7. No member of the Clerical Staff may leave the room without permission from Mr Rogers. The calls of nature are permitted and Clerical Staff may use the garden below the second gate. The area must be kept in good order.
8. No talking is allowed during business hours.
9. The craving of tobacco, wines or spirits is a human weakness and, as such, is forbidden to all members of the Clerical Staff.
10. Now that the hours of business have been drastically reduced, the partaking of food is allowed between 11. 30 a.m. and noon, but work will not, on any account, cease.
11. Members of the Clerical Staff will provide their own pens. A new sharpener is available, on application to Mr Rogers.
12. Mr Rogers will nominate a Senior Clerk to be responsible for the cleanliness of the Main Office and the Private Office, and all Boys and Juniors will report to him 40 minutes before Prayers, and will remain after closing hours for similar work. Brushes, Brooms, Scrubbers and Soap are provided by the owners.
13. The New Increased Weekly Wages are hereunder detailed:

Junior Boys (to 11 years)	1/4d
Boys (to 14 years)	2/1d
Juniors	4/8d
Junior Clerks	8/7d
Clerks	10/9d
Senior Clerks (after 15 years with owners)	21/–d

The owners recognise the generosity of the new Labour Laws but will expect a great rise in output of work to compensate for these near Utopian conditions.

will be remedied before they become problems, and problems before they become crises.

The final part of this activity is a continuous measure of performance against targets and objectives, the criteria against which the success or otherwise of the department will be assessed. Part of this requirement, therefore, is to see the department in this way and to be able to measure and judge its performance along these lines also.

Realpolitik

This is the art of survival in the organisation in which the manager is working (see Example Box 22.9). It requires knowledge and understanding of the nature of the particular 'jungle' in question. From this managers will devise their own methods and means of becoming effective and successful operators therein. They must be able to survive long enough to do this. It follows that they must understand and be able to work within the formal and informal systems of the organisation and to establish their place in them. Especially in the informal system, they may require to find their own niches and from there go on and develop networks and support within the organisation. Large, complex and sophisticated organisations have series of 'cluster groups' determined by profession, location and status; people in such situations must discover those that are suitable and make sure that they are involved in them to their advantage. They will develop a keen 'environmental' sense. This comprises: first, the ability to spot straws in the wind, indicating possible changes, developments, innovations or crises; second, the recognition of the departments and individuals where actual power and influence truly lie; third, sources of information within the complexities of the organisation; and fourth, 'managerial antennae' which are finely tuned to perceive any shifts in the other aspects or across the environment in general.

Managers will assess their own positions in the pecking order, the competition for power and influence and the qualities that they bring to the organisation's internal political situation. They will assess their own strengths and weaknesses in it, and the capabilities and capacities that are required in order to be effective and professional operators in the given situation.

They will identify where the inter-group frictions (and sometimes hostility) lie and assess the reasons for them. From this standpoint they will similarly assess the position of their own departments in the whole, and look to be able to lobby for support and influence where they are most likely to get it in the pursuit of these interests.

They must adapt their managerial style to the situation. For example, a highly open and task-orientated approach is not likely to work in a bureaucratic set-up. By adopting it anyway, because of preference, the manager would simply throw away

---

EXAMPLE BOX 22.9 'After the Staff Meeting'

'...so I went to the leader, and I asked him to build me a wall for my back, so that when the knife came, I would be able to see it. And he agreed, and he built me my wall; but he left a hole in it, just in case...'

Source: R. Pettinger, unpublished Minisaga, 1988.

> ### EXAMPLE BOX 22.10 The Choice of Ministers
>
> Machiavelli wrote that 'the first opinion formed of a ruler's intelligence is based on the quality of the men he chooses to be around him. When they are competent and loyal he can be considered wise, when they are not the Prince is open to adverse criticism.'
>
> The prince has 'an infallible guide for assessing his minister: if the minister thinks more of himself than of the prince, seeking his own profit rather than the greater good he will never be a sound minister nor will he be trustworthy.'
>
> Source: Machiavelli, *The Prince*.

any advantages held and the political positioning necessary to operate in the environment. This would also impinge upon both the effectiveness of the department and its own regard in the organisation. (Consider Example Box 22.10).

Other factors that affect the political and operational environment in the organisation may be identified. There may be a question of role ambiguity, whether among departments or staff, where particular lines of activity, authority, job and task boundaries are not clearly delineated. There may also be more general problems in this area relating to lack of clarity of aims and objectives, where departments are unsure of their remit and consequently operate in a void. Furthermore, where aims are unclear departments may use this to push their own boundaries outward and build or extend their empires. Lack of clarity in the fields of performance and output standards also relates to this. It can lead to interdepartmental wrangles and conflicts based upon the consequent inevitable shortfall in performance and the necessity to draw attention away from that which relates to the department of the manager in question and towards other departments.

Throughout the operational environment there will also be various agenda that are to be followed. Departments and their managers have secondary and hidden agenda, especially to do with the advancement of a particular course of action but also, more generally, in the promotion of the department or its manager in the pecking order of the organisation. Departments may engage in unhealthy, negative competition that has nothing to do with the pursuit of effective operations but rather, negatively encourages success at the expense of other departmental failures. It becomes a drive for power and influence in itself, motivated by the need to gain the ear of the chief executive or other spheres of influence.

The situation may be exacerbated by bad and inadequate communications and communication systems so that people find things out via the grapevine or other vested interests; in such situations especially, trade union officials prosper and flourish. There is a consequent increase in the numbers of disputes, including those between departments, and an increase also in those disputes and grievances that get put on a formal basis and go either to arbitration or to the top of the organisation for resolution. Rules and regulations in such situations become the end and not the means to an end. Where such situations are allowed to persist over long periods of time, bureaucratic superstructures are devised and additional staff and procedures taken on and adopted, and such interdepartmental and organisational wranglings become institutionalised and part of the ways of working.

In such situations also information becomes a critical resource to be jealously guarded and to be fed out in the interests of the information holder rather than the organisation itself. Impurities are fed into information systems by vested interests and those seeking increased power and influence for themselves and their own unit or sector at the expense of others. In such situations, over-mighty subjects prosper, again at the expense of others (as do designated officials such as union representatives). A manager must therefore recognise these components and vagaries of the work environment; and must be able to work his way around them, accommodate them, and where necessary, tap into them and feed into them in the pursuit of his or her own effective performance.

Conclusions

In the conduct of variant and divergent activities, the manager is responsible for devising and implementing work methods, patterns and styles – and a managerial approach that reflects these – in the interests of getting productive, effective and profitable outputs from the department. This has to be seen from the widest of all angles. For example, taking time to induct a new member of staff may seem a profligate use of precious and expensive managerial time, but the payback on it will be seen:

- when a problem has arisen due to the ignorance of the new member of staff or his/her lack of expertise or cultural awareness
- in terms of the manager not having to waste time on resolving such an issue because of the time spent in induction.

Similarly, resources spent on the department's ambience and environment may seem profligate in certain circumstances but the returns are measured in terms of low absenteeism, a general positive wish on the part of the staff to attend the department, high levels of output, low levels of labour turnover and a productive and harmonious attitude to work activities.

CHAPTER SUMMARY

The issues raised and discussed in this chapter are those common to all situations: projects, operations, industrial, commercial and public services sectors. Each has to be addressed on a daily basis. It is essential, therefore, that all managers ensure that they have their own ways of establishing specific standards in each of these areas, and uphold them.

The managers' performance in the eyes of their subordinates is underpinned by their determination to know and understand the field of operations in which they are working, even if they have no professional or occupational expertise in it. Preaching perfection, all managers are duty bound to ensure that they know as much as possible about the field of activities as a whole, and also the pressures and constraints on every activity for which they have direct responsibility, and the professional and occupational boundaries for which they are ultimately responsible. Cohesion of managerial activities with professional and occupational operations is essential if long-term effective organisational performance is to be sustained. This does not always happen; indeed, in some organisations, the overwhelming impression is that management and activities run parallel to each other, with very little direct contact. The public services sector has an enduring reputation for this; indeed, many school head teachers and hospital ward managers can go for weeks without any direct contact from those to whom they are ultimately answerable. However, this is not confined to the public sector; many multinational and multi-site industrial and commercial organisations run in exactly the same way. For example, a large oil company decided that it was going to undertake a programme of strategic change. Consultants were hired, and an outline strategy agreed. The consultants found that a key perception of those working as oil engineers in the field was that they did all the work, while head office consumed the fruits of their labours. Accordingly, proposals were drawn up to make sure that nobody spent more than three years at head office without doing at least six months in the field somewhere in the world.

It is essential that all managers have visibility and integrity of style and personality. This applies whether the manager is autocratic, democratic or participative (there is no reason at all why autocrats should not also be honest). Participation and consultation should never be used as excuses for sitting on the fence. Many managers use their overtly participative style as an excuse to avoid taking decisions or confronting awkward problems and individuals. Once the staff know, believe or perceive that a manager's style is solely concerned with the abdication of responsibility, a 'hands-off' approach, the position becomes very difficult to retrieve.

It is stated elsewhere in the book that the key qualities underlining all effective managerial performance are enthusiasm, ambition, dynamism, flexibility, responsiveness, and the acceptance of responsibility and accountability. To these must be added a willingness to accept one may be wrong and to admit mistakes, a willingness to put things right, and characteristics of integrity and truthfulness. It is important to recognise, however, that such approaches are not always welcome in organisations. Political systems, the demands of top managers, and other corporate boundaries often make it extremely difficult to accept responsibility without being made a scapegoat for a particular failure. It is important to recognise that it may be necessary in the short term to adopt the rules and norms of the organisation's realpolitik. If this continues over the long term, however, integrity, professionalism, and working relationships are damaged and ultimately destroyed. It is a very short step from this to steep declines in organisational, departmental and managerial performance.

DISCUSSION QUESTIONS

1. You are a departmental manager. You have just returned from your lunch to find that one of your staff has had a very bad accident. Another member of

the group has taken them to hospital. What immediate actions are you going to take and why?

2. Why is it very difficult to maintain long-term integrity of organisational and superior–subordinate relationships?

3. There still exists a widely-held view that the performance of managers is largely down to 'common sense'. If this is the case, why are so many mistakes made at the day-to-day performance sharp end?

4. Two members of your staff come to see you, each requesting the following day off. Operational pressures mean that you can only let one of them have the time off. Outline the strategy for the negotiations that you are going to undertake. What alternatives are available to you? What are the advantages and consequences of each approach?

5. To be successful and effective at 'managing by walking about', what other factors have to be present?

CHAPTER CASE STUDY

Autumn Publishing Ltd

The Autumn Press Ltd is a printing establishment, employing a labour force of 400 people. Fifteen per cent are women and they are concentrated at the finishing end of the works: the binding department. There are also about 40 men in the department. Anthony Thompson is the binding department manager.

Anthony's deputy is Ted Adam. Ted has been with the company for 28 years and has worked his way up by experience rather than by any technical or scholastic achievement. He does not have any formal management or technical qualifications. Ted relies heavily on Jack Phillips, his deputy, for technical advice as he is not familiar with the most modern machines recently installed in the department.

Jack Phillips was employed five years ago on the personal recommendation of Ted after qualifying at the local technical college. He is a good member of staff and a very able administrator but he drinks a lot. On many occasions, he has come into the works heavily drunk and Ted has taken him home. At times, he has not come back to work for days immediately after pay days. And when he did return, he presented medical certificates to cover the days he had been absent. You have questioned Ted about this, but all that Ted has said is that 'Jack has a lot of domestic pressures', and you have not so far followed these up.

One morning, Angela, one of the women members of staff, approached Ted for permission to see a friend off to Rome from the local airport. Ted refused as the work she was doing would have to be delivered at noon that day. Angela was annoyed and said, 'You won't let me have two hours off, but if it were Jack, he would be taken away home in your car and would remain at home for days.' She picked up her handbag and went off to the airport. The result was that the work was not completed on time, and now you have the customer – a large national bookshop chain – on the telephone demanding compensation.

QUESTIONS

1. How are you going to resolve the immediate situation? Why are you going to take these actions?

2. How are you going to resolve the broader situation, bearing in mind that you have rather allowed it to slide for a long period of time?
3. What general lessons are there to be learned from this situation in developing effective managerial performance?

23 Managing for the Present and Future

'I like good generals. Of course I like them. But I like lucky generals best of all.' Napoleon.

'The harder I practise, the more I work, the luckier I seem to get.' Arnold Palmer, top professional golfer.

Introduction

It is stated in Chapter 1 that the primary concern of management is to make best use of scarce resources in a changing and uncertain environment, to cope with change and uncertainty. From that point of view, managing in the future is likely not to be all that different from managing at present and in the recent past.

It is certain, however, that a much greater understanding of what 'coping with change and uncertainty' actually means is required. Effective managers are going to be required to lead and direct change, to create structures and cultures that accommodate this, to do it profitably and effectively in the long term, and from the point of view of the organisation's enduring best interests, and those of all its stakeholders. This is certain to apply to all managers, whatever their level of responsibility, seniority or occupational position. Organisational long-term effectiveness, profitability and viability is only possible if this approach is adopted universally (see Example Box 23.1).

Clarity of purpose and direction

The aim of all organisations should be long-term effectiveness and profitable existence in a turbulent and competitive world. Lack of expertise in strategic management and organisational behaviour has meant that this has all too often been ignored in the pursuit of short-term gain, or satisfaction of the financial interest alone. In these cases this clarity has been replaced with:

- the hiring of high-branded consultancies, leading in many cases to a hype in the share price in the short term in spite of the fact that the consultant's remit and prescription had not yet been agreed
- the use of parallel communications, using management speak and professional babble to give an impression of direction and clarity (see Example Box 23.2).

Beyond this, full market, production, customer and client assessment is regularly not fully carried out. This in turn leads to:

- fashion-based drives; for example we must have a website, we must have every office/school/airliner equipped with computers and other portable technology as ends in themselves
- hiring strategy consultants and accepting their findings unquestioningly and blindly
- sending staff on unrelated professional, management, occupational and organisational development programmes without relating these to the needs of the organisation or the individuals concerned
- concentrating on peripheral rather than core issues (see Example Box 23.3).

Core and peripheral business activities

All organisations and their top managers must understand where the core activities lie. It is very tempting to draw attention, and therefore resources, away from these two fashionable alternatives, and to give the illusion of globalisation. This varies between organisations. In some organisations the core business may not even be clear to top managers. Core business has to be assessed from the point of view of one of the following: what attracts, what sells, what makes money and why this should be so. Attention is needed in each of these areas, not just to the narrow issue of 'what makes money'. From the point of view of attract/sell/make money, core business has also to be seen in terms of enduring customer and client reputation, and brand loyalty and identity (see Example Box 23.4).

Dominant stakeholder drives

In industry and commerce, these drives relate to the desired priorities of shareholders' representatives, other financial interests, backers, and powerful and

---

EXAMPLE BOX 23.1 'We Are Doing All We Can'

In the later years of his term, Ronald Reagan, President of the United States, used this phrase as a catch-all whenever he was asked awkward questions by the media about particular issues. The phrase was coined for him in a whispered aside by his wife, Nancy, when he was stuck for an answer on the Gulf Crisis of 1984. It was subsequently adopted as a public relations mantra, and survives to this day, particularly in political circles.

In many organisations, this is plainly not enough. A number of examples show this.

- Throughout the 1990s Tarmac, the civil engineering and quarrying company, was faced with a series of accidents and safety concerns. The company's response, quoted both in annual reports and in press releases was that 'we are doing all we can'. This did not prevent the company from having to change its name from Tarmac to Carillion in 1999.

- British Steel cut both production and staffing during the 1990s, and reduced expenditure on safety procedures in the face of 'declining world markets'. In 1999 it was taken over by Corus, the Dutch steel producer. In 2001 the company was faced with further problems of over-capacity. Clearly it has not done 'all it can' to generate new markets.

- Ford UK, at its Dagenham plant, had been known to have problems of inter-racial strife since the mid-1980s. The company produced procedures and sent managers on racial awareness training course over the period 1985 to 1999. This did not prevent problems from becoming very much worse. In 1994, 1996 and 1999 there were riots at the plant, generated by the continued perception that the company tolerated racial strife.

- During the last months of its life, boo.com faced declining interest and inadequate sales. Right up to the end, when the company went bankrupt in January 2000, the approach to the commercial problem began and ended with the fact that 'the company was a lovely place to work'.

In each of these cases, clearly the companies had not done 'all they could'. British Steel/Corus made no genuine attempt to develop new markets; Tarmac made no genuine attempt over the period to reduce its accident rate; Ford had excellent procedures, but poor implementation; and boo.com concentrated on internal harmony, rather than external commercialisation.

---

influential figures who drive their organisations into their own preferred core business. In public services the dominant stakeholder is the government, which sets performance priorities and targets according to political need; there is a divergence here from the majority stakeholder – the public – whose interests call for high quality, enduring, good value public services. In the not-for-profit sector, many large charities now take the view that in order to provide the best possible service for their client groups, it is necessary to engage in fully commercialised fundraising activities; in these cases the core business becomes the conducting of marketing campaigns.

EXAMPLE BOX 23.2 Management-speak and Professional Babble

Various phrases are used by senior managers or corporation representatives to avoid explaining in detail their actions to the media, staff interests, customers, lobbies and other legitimate vested interest and stakeholder groups. They are designed to give the overwhelming impression that the precise mysteries of the organisation and its activities are well in control, but that to explain these in detail is clearly unproductive as nobody would understand them.

- 'We must tighten our belts': that trading or operational conditions are bad. Invariably how exactly the belts are to be tightened is never fully explained – or justified.
- 'We must hit the ground running': meaning that the time has come for action. How this action is to be engaged or implemented is never made clear.
- 'We must keep our eye on the ball': usually a response to criticism, or an apparent imperfection.
- 'We must work smarter, not harder': normally an exhortation for front-line staff to indeed work harder so that non-productive corporate lifestyles may be maintained.
- 'We must think outside the box': an encouragement to creative thinking (which is wholly laudable), but normally issued by organisations that stifle creativity, especially in the wrong places.
- 'We will achieve synergies or economies of scale': a phrase extensively used by directors and top managers in their dealings with the media; somehow the media never fail to follow up and to ask where, how and why more is to be produced using the same or a reduced resource base.

Other factors that indicate the true dominant stakeholder drives are as follows:

- balance of primary and support functions in terms of resource consumption
- what the organisation values and rewards in terms of output and what it does not
- the effectiveness of administration and bureaucracy (in many cases the domination of administration and bureaucracy).

In extreme cases the 'core business' of organisations is dominated by support functions, and the core business is therefore effectively to provide career patterns for individuals.

Economic and social demands and pressures

Managing economic and social demands and pressures requires constant attention to the broader competitive environment. This is one reason why undertaking and using the Five Forces model (see Chapter 6) is so vital. This especially involves taking the broadest possible view of the threats that may arise.

EXAMPLE BOX 23.3 High Profile Peripheral Issues

- Supermarkets and department stores: as companies within these sectors become known for their high-profile UK reputation, market position, and familiarity, they seek to differentiate themselves by calling attention in annual reports and press releases to overseas expansion and globalisation. This is dangerous if it is overdone because it calls into question the organisation's commitment to its core market in the UK. In some cases the market bites back: for example Marks & Spencer in its annual report for the year 2000 drew attention to its global reputation and continued expansion on mainland Europe; this was abruptly turned around in March 2000 when it announced the closure of all its non-UK operations.
- National Health Service: the UK NHS has concentrated all its efforts on managing specific statistics – reducing waiting lists and according priority treatment to some diseases. The core of the problem is the lack of staff, facilities, equipment and investment; no substantial improvement will occur in the services that it provides until it increases pay and status for front-line medical staff, and enhances their terms and conditions of employment.

- Threats of entry, where new rivals or key players can conceivably emerge; for example: 'If we can set up there, there will come a time when others can set up here.'
- Threats of substitution, such as the sourcing of textile manufacture all over the world by western companies; while this may not always be wholesome or ethical

---

EXAMPLE BOX 23.4 Core Business at the Start of the Twenty-first Century

Many organisations have found themselves diverted away from this by media, public relations and stakeholder pressures. They have consequently found themselves over-committing to peripheral or unfashionable business in the pursuit of media coverage. Many organisations have created their own websites on the basis that they perceived that they had to have one regardless of any contribution that it would make to long-term effectiveness, profitability and viability.

In an attempt to redress the balance, Porter wrote:

At the end of the day there are no new business models or paradigms. There is no virtual industry. There are no easy rides, quick fixes or absolute certainties. Nothing can be fixed through public relations alone. There are no virtual markets. There is only competition – the pursuit of real customers for real businesses who are going to avail themselves of products and services at prices they are willing to pay.

Source: M E Porter, 'Competition in the Twenty-first Century', *Harvard Business Review*, 2000.

or enduring, it provides immediate cost pressures on those who would compete with the particular sector. The alternative approach to this form of sourcing is to determine to pay western prices for imports from the Third World as The Body Shop does with the crops it purchases to manufacture its cosmetics.

- Threats of entry from players that used to conduct activities in an area or sector, but have withdrawn for the time being. This especially applies to the re-entry of airlines into mothballed routes; re-entry of defence electronics companies into commercial and consumer products; re-entry of private hospitals into emergency and urgent surgery (this is going on at present by arrangement with the National Health Service in the UK, and may become a service that is purchased universally over the long term).
- Threats from suppliers when new players can command greater access to suppliers, thanks to initial investment levels and willingness to pay. This may lead to supply auctions, which some existing players may not be able to afford.
- Threats from customers and clients when product and service levels decline; where the existing is superseded by the same thing at better price, quality and value; where the existing is replaced by something altogether new.

The Five Forces model may therefore be re-presented in the form shown in Figure 23.1.

It is also essential that the macro environment is continuously analysed and evaluated. This is so that as broad a view as possible of likely and potential – and unlikely – change is always kept fully in mind. Organisations and managers that do this are much less likely to suffer from foreseeable if unlikely events such as:

- the energy crash in California 2000–01
- loss of confidence in global airline travel 2001–02
- the stock market uncertainties of March 2001

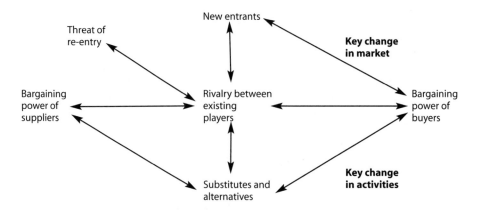

FIGURE 23.1 Five forces model (adapted)

Sources: M.E. Porter, *Competitive Strategy*, Free Press, 1980; R. Cartwright *Mastering the Competitive Environment*, Palgrave, 2000.

- the UK and European Union Foot and Mouth epidemic 2001
- the UK railway and transport crisis 2000–02
- The war in Afghanistan 2001–02.

The organisations and industries worst affected by such events are those that become so used to their environmental conditions that they come to regard these as certainties. Assumptions, forecasts and projections then take on a life of their own, based on historic stability, and the perceived 'certainty' of the durability of the sector.

Investment

The traditional – almost cultural – view of investment concerns the placing of finance and other resources into a situation or venture in the expectation of more or less predictable returns. This is founded on the widely-held behavioural aspect of placing money in individual deposit accounts, on which a rate of return is guaranteed or predicted. Even though this is less certain than in the past, and returns tend to be lower, the psychological drive to look at all investment from this point of view remains very strong, and this still applies to industry, commerce and public sector investments. For the future, however, a much more active managerial expertise and responsibility in this area is essential.

Investment in production, service and information technology must be undertaken on the basis that it may be necessary to discard it overnight in order to remain competitive and effective, because new equipment is now available to competitors. Appraising potential investment in technology therefore requires the best possible projection of whether competitive activities around price, quality, output and retention of market share would be sustainable should alternative technology suddenly become available. A key part of the management of investment in industrial, commercial and public service situations is therefore certain to require a continuous and active 'what if...' approach, focusing on questions such as:

- What if this technology becomes obsolete overnight?
- What if we have to replace a particular system at short notice?
- What if a competitor gains access to technology that can produce the particular product or service in a quarter of the time?

Greater expertise in forecasting a projection is required overall. This applies especially in those sectors that operate under mega-project conditions, where the true costs and returns on activities may not be realised for many years. Several current and recent high-profile examples of this in the UK must cause a radical rethink of how projections and forecasts are carried out (see Example Box 23.5).

This also applies to investment in production, service and public sector technology by individual organisations and departments. This requires a much greater projected understanding of density and frequency of usage, speed and convenience of product and service, and quality enhancement and insurance, as key elements of assessing returns on investment.

Much greater attention is required to the behavioural side of investment if the required or desired return is to be achieved. Conditions in which effective investments are carried out must be assessed from the point of view of stakeholder agreement and

---

EXAMPLE BOX 23.5 Projections for Costs and Reality

- The Channel Tunnel project was an early indicator that financial projection and forecasting from a managerial point of view were seriously flawed in such situations. This is reinforced by the experiences of the following:
- Millennium Dome: financial forecasts for this project were based on assumptions that it would be self-financing provided that 12 000 people per day would visit the Dome at full cost once it was completed. This meant that it would have to out-perform national tourist institutions such as Madame Tussauds by a factor of six, and the Tower of London by a factor of five. Yet the projections and forecasts were accepted without question. When the project closed in December 2000, it had attracted just over 6 million visitors (half of what had been projected), though it remained far and away the most visited single-ticket admission tourist site in the UK.
- Wembley Stadium redevelopment: the original projections for this quoted a project cost of £250 million. The perceived enduring appeal of top-class football as mass entertainment supposedly guaranteed that the project would be self-financing. Proposals to make the stadium more universally attractive by including athletics facilities were rejected. The original projection was produced in September 1999. When the project was returned to the drawing board in January 2001, the estimated cost had risen to £650 million.

---

liaison, and the stakeholders must be included in the process. It is very easy for any project to be launched and gain a life of its own because of the influences of one or two parties. It is then the others involved who have to make it work and/or suffer the long-term consequences. In each of the cases in Example Box 23.5, the return was late, and less than projected and therefore assumed, while costs were much higher. With the exception of the Channel Tunnel, each was driven by a dominant stakeholder interested primarily in short-term advantage; and in each case the returns projected in advance took on an overwhelming semblance of fact. This was overwhelmingly because the influence of those driving the venture was greater than their knowledge. (See Figure 23.2.)

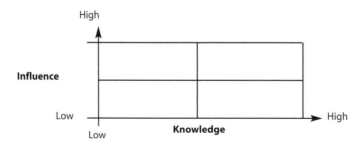

FIGURE 23.2 The knowledge influence spectrum

Both behavioural and financial issues therefore directly affect the outcome. This is also especially a strong drive in government ventures in partnering, private finance initiative, and public private partnership projects and ventures (see Example Box 23.6).

Mutuality of interest and confidence between the core stakeholders – financiers, backers, venturers, contractors, political interests, suppliers, sub-contractors, clients and end users – must be ensured as far as possible. Ideally this should also extend to peripheral stakeholders: lobbies, vested interests, social and pressure groups, and the media. If this is not possible among the core group, serious consideration ought to be given to the enduring viability of what is proposed, because it is unlikely that results can be achieved where there is not full confidence or mutuality of interest; this becomes all the more certain where there is a known, believed or perceived conflict of interest.

Investment in technology projects and expertise has therefore to be viewed as a sunk cost from a managerial point of view, one on which there may not be any direct or apparent returns. This flies in the face of the widespread current behavioural need to make simple the calculation of return on investment. It should be apparent that this is not possible in absolute managerial terms. Moreover, the return on investment is in

---

EXAMPLE BOX 23.6 Private Finance Initiatives

The private finance initiative, together with partnering arrangements and public–private partnerships, represent a political drive by the UK government to attract private funds and expertise into the creation and management of public facilities and services.

To date the Home Office (prisons), the Department of Transport, Environment and the Regions (roads, railways and bridges) and local government (care of the elderly and at-risk members of society) have all commissioned projects that are to be conducted under the private finance initiative. In essence they are to be designed, built, owned and operated by the private sector. Investing companies fund the costs of the project; when it is completed, the companies are either paid a lease or allowed to recoup their costs through charges to the end users.

The government's objectives were to attract short-term finance and expertise to accelerate and enhance the facilities available for the long-term provision of public facilities.

The objectives of the private companies involved were founded on the opportunity to attract short-term capital injections, to take up spare capacity in their organisations, and to ensure guaranteed rates of return.

Clearly some harmonisation of these aims and objectives is possible. However, the overwhelming political drive has ensured that most ventures have been inadequately constituted, and that returns have been measured in narrow political terms, with only secondary reference to the quality and durability of the projects, ventures and services. This has led, in almost every case documented, to a poorer quality of project and service delivery, greater costs to the public purse, and reduced total quality of project and service.

every case the subject of personal and professional evaluation, and these judgements may quite legitimately vary.

Investment in expertise is dependent at the outset on whether staff are valued as assets or liabilities, and the basis on which this is calculated. This also varies in each case; and is likely to vary within organisations according to:

- The nature of particular staff in different functions, and their relative and absolute expertise.
- The ease or otherwise with which they can be replaced or transformed through retraining and redeployment.
- Specific industrial, commercial and public service advantages (and liabilities) that they bring. This is particularly true of highly capable and well-known key figures in industry and commerce (such as Michael O'Leary at Ryan Air or Alex Ferguson at Manchester United). It also applies to public services (for example, Magdi Yacoub and Robert Winston in health services, or Peter Hall in town planning).

This is clearly a double-edged sword; individuals remain assets so long as they deliver their expertise in ways compatible with the priorities of their organisation, and there may be a loss of confidence on the part of key backers and stock markets should such a figure suddenly move on. On the other hand, no organisation should be dependent upon an individual, however great his or her expertise, for its future survival.

Investment in expertise is also required at the 'all staff' level. This involves underwriting whatever steps are necessary to ensure that effective, productive and positive conditions are created, maintained, enhanced and improved so that high-quality industrial, commercial or public service output may be maintained. It is also essential to ensure these conditions include the capability and willingness to transform when required.

Mergers and takeovers

All this is reinforced when considering the enduring managerial responsibilities in mergers and takeovers. Investment in mergers and takeovers requires managerial attention to the the findings of two surveys carried out in 1996 and 1998 by the Institute of Management and Industrial Society. These found that 87 per cent of such ventures do not work at all or fully in the long term. The reasons for this were found to be exactly those considered elsewhere:

- Lack of attention to behavioural and cultural aspects.
- An assumption that these would simply fall into place once the financial deal was completed (see Example Box 23.7).
- Lack of attention to the long-term staff management, management style, human resource and industrial relations issues to be faced, coupled with the lack of requirement for or understanding the necessity for, a long-term and sustainable staff management strategy as a precondition of the particular venture.
- Lack of precise definition of what synergies or economies of scale were projected or forecast and the nature of investment necessary to achieve them. This especially

---

EXAMPLE BOX 23.7 The SmithKline-Beecham and Glaxo-Wellcome Merger

The merger of SmithKline-Beecham and Glaxo-Wellcome was first mooted in 1998. If successful, it would have completed the largest ever merger between two companies anywhere in the world and would have created the world's fifth largest company. The first attempt foundered because the 12 most senior figures involved could not agree who was to do what job in the newly merged company.

The merger was finally completed in September 2000. To this day, there remain problems with the divisionalised and functional structure; these have yet to be resolved fully. Some senior executives have left; others have been required to take on jobs that they initially had no desire for. The company is able to operate in this way, ultimately, because it can afford to do so.

This may be contrasted with the proposed takeover of the Superdrug chain by the German company Risparti. Superficially attractive at first, the venture was called off by Risparti on the grounds of 'a lack of cultural fit'.

---

referred to technological incompatibility; and again it was found that a lack of cultural fit and the necessity for culture transformation and change programmes were not sufficiently well thought out or costed.

- Design of the merger or venture to satisfy short-term financial demands, shareholder interest and the reactions of the media and stock markets, rather than long-term enduring customer satisfaction in terms of their relations with the new merged organisation.

Those in senior positions with strategic responsibilities are therefore required to understand and acknowledge the full range of concerns, when seeking opportunities and enhancements in this form of investment. It is also incumbent upon those in departmental, divisional and functional positions to understand the pressures that mergers and takeovers bring with them, especially if it is known or perceived that overwhelming attention has been given to the narrow financial interest.

Customers and clients

Developments in the management of customers and clients have caused organisations to look much harder at every aspect of product and service delivery, marketing and presentation. This means addressing the following continuously:

- Competing with whom? Who are our strategic competitors? Who are our competitors in particular given locations? What causes customers to use them? What causes customers to use us and why? What causes customers to return to us? What causes customers to leave us?
- Competing for what? Which part of the customers' spending priorities are we targeting? What proportion of the customers' disposable income are we targeting? Are these real needs, perceived needs or wants?

- Assessing the speed, access and quality of input, raw materials and other sources, and the positive and negative contribution that each makes to the total quality of products and services. This assessment is conducted alongside the recognition that, even if what is done today is satisfactory and acceptable to customers and clients, other organisations may perceive better and higher value ways of doing things that could cause people to look elsewhere once their expectations had changed.
- Assessing the habits and behaviour of the customer and client bases. This means continued attention to perceived convenience and value, especially where there is heavy dependence upon convenience rather than loyalty.
- Assessing rather than assuming the benefits that customers and clients gain from products and services, and making sure that these continue to match demand. This includes the 'relationship benefits': the levels of satisfaction that are gained by customers and clients as a result of their identity with a particular organisation's products and services.
- Understanding the causes of increasing levels of satisfaction on the part of customers and clients, and from this taking action to ensure that this is maintained and enhanced.
- Understanding the causes of decreasing levels of satisfaction on the part of customers and clients, and taking action to remedy this. If no action, or the wrong action, is taken, then loss of customers will occur if there are adequate alternatives. This especially applies to:
  - Companies such as Marks & Spencer at the beginning of the twenty-first century. Marks & Spencer attracted adverse media coverage concerning its decline in financial performance when it appeared that customers' expectations were no longer being met.
  - Companies such as British Airways that have to tread a very fine line between overall convenience, market domination, premium prices and customer satisfaction. Again losses to low-priced, good-value airlines have occurred on certain routes.
  - Local shops, pubs, restaurants and other public and commercial facilities that depend on an actively loyal customer base.
  - Public services: part of the enduring problem with UK public services at the start of the twenty-first century is that the groups they serve now have such low expectations that they anticipate trouble, inconvenience and lack of quality, and so they look for and find signs that reinforce these perceptions.
  - Dot.com companies and those in the mainstream with commercial website activities: in these cases it is essential that the websites themselves are sufficiently consumer-friendly to attract and retain interest, are perceived as convenient, and supported with levels of customer service at least equivalent to mainstream activities. Where any of this is not satisfactory, customers will simply revert to the mainstream, not only for consumer-based activities but equally in business-to-business transactions.

In summary, all the above points centre around developing product, service and marketing strategies, opportunities, priorities and activities in the light of what is known – rather than merely believed or perceived – about customer, client and consumer demands, and fitting products and services to this. It is also essential to develop expertise in anticipating and developing new products and services to meet future demands based on the fullest possible understanding of what customers, clients, consumers and end users are likely to need and want.

Staff management

Effective staff management in the future is certain to be based on the development of management styles based on openness and access to information, and basic honesty and integrity. This is to apply whatever the leadership and management style chosen: autocratic, participative, democratic, hands-on, hands-off or consultative. For there is no reason why any organisation should have an emergent rather than a designed management style, whatever the sector or nature of activity. There is quite sufficient management literature, training and expertise (together with examples of good and bad practice) around, to ensure that all those responsible for the design and direction of an organisation establish this from their own particular point of view.

Once this is established then it is possible to address the key elements of the working relationship, paid work bargain, and quality of working life and environment to establish:

- what organisations and their managers require of their staff, why, when, where and how often
- what staff require of their managers and organisations, why, when, where and how often
- whether these requirements are practicable, feasible or possible in the particular set of circumstances (see Example Box 23.8).

It is increasingly apparent that there are some principles of staff management to understand.

Rewards

While everyone values intrinsic rewards – esteem, value, achievement, personal, professional and occupational satisfaction – these only satisfy in the long term where the extrinsic rewards are also at least adequate. For example:

- Voluntary Service Overseas and other voluntary activities (such as charity work or caring for dependent relatives) only work because the nature of the relationship is clearly understood and accepted to be voluntary or social at the outset. Caring for dependent relatives is in any case becoming more of a social problem because of the real and perceived economic as well as personal stress that is placed on the carers.
- Public service jobs in health care, teaching and social work continue to offer high intrinsic reward levels. However, in UK public services at the start of the twenty-first century these intrinsic rewards are more than offset by the low and declining quality of working environment, staff and resources shortages, and low pay – and a lack of political willingness to tackle these as core staff management issues.

High levels of pay and remuneration are required to compensate people as follows:

EXAMPLE BOX 23.8 Developing the Relationship Between Staff and Their Organisation

This is a lesson that many organisations never learn. It is also not always acceptable from either the staff or management point of view. For example:

A consultant was engaged in drawing up a marketing plan for a small manufacturing company. The company employed 22 staff and produced souvenirs for the seasonal seaside trade. She had been asked to look at the prospects of business development because, while the seaside trade itself was booming, sales of the particular products to outlets were declining.

She was working on her plan when she heard the company chief executive bawling out a member of staff. The chief executive, a man in his fifties, then came in to see her, rubbing his hands with glee. 'I always treat my staff like that', he said with evident relish, 'it keeps them on their toes. Most of them are on a final warning'.

The marketing consultant put down her pen. She said to him, 'No marketing plan for this company will be ever fully effective until you agree to treat your staff with a great deal more respect'.

The chief executive promptly dismissed the consultant and she did not get paid. At the end of the season, the company went into receivership.

A member of staff of a children's charity sought to enhance his income through constantly nagging for increases in allowances, evening shift and weekend work. He took out grievances aimed at pushing up these fringe areas of remuneration. Matters came to a head when the chair of the charity's governors asked him, almost as an aside, why he did not get another job, as plainly he was dissatisfied with everything that he was doing.

- economic rent (the reward for known, believed and perceived excellence or expertise, as in the case of sports stars or those in entertainment, the stock market or financial services)
- lack of wider social respect and regard (e.g. public service chief executive officers and top managers)
- lack of work variety (e.g. factory work and financial services; much of this work is still carried out in repetitive and tedious work patterns)
- extreme working environment, or extreme levels of responsibility (e.g. railway, public transport, airline pilots and crews)
- enduringly profit-effective and high-quality output of products and services.

Staffing problems occur where the relationship between rewards and work is not effective. These are compounded when the level of extrinsic reward is known, believed or perceived to be so low as to represent an overall lack of respect, value and esteem for the work itself; this is an especial problem in public service professional occupations. Problems are compounded when there is a great spread of rewards between the highest and lowest levels on offer within a particular organisation; staffing problems are reduced when the spread is narrow, and enhanced when the spread is very wide.

In staff and workforce structures where the managers continue to organise themselves on traditional or current lines, as in those where they adopt more flexible patterns of approach, effective operations are dependent upon:

- Integrity of working relations, including management and staff hierarchies, and above all paying attention not only to operational matters but also to human problems. These are particularly intense where people are working flexible hours, away from the organisation location for extended periods, or from home or on call, but the principle applies equally to those following regular patterns of attendance.

- Applying physical means of supervision such as clocking in or logging on universally or else not at all. This applies to factory and production staff as well as those in administrative and support functions. Those who work from home or in the field should never be made to log on or ring in if this does not also apply to their office- or location-based colleagues.

- Paying people for their flexibility and willingness, as well as their expertise. Where it is necessary for staff to work unsocial hours (as in financial services and other direct personal sales), or where they are expected to be fully responsive at short notice (e.g. supply teachers, agency nurses, social workers, ferry and airline crew replacements) this must be recognised and premium rates paid; many organisations also pay retainers for this.

- Managing by walking around, managing by ringing around, and any other means available for ensuring that continuity and visibility of relationship are maintained. Those who work in the field should be called into the office upon a regular basis, and part of the time spent on these occasions must include the opportunity for social interaction. This is both a consequence and responsibility of organising activities along these lines.

- Balance of primary and support activities: there is an ever increasing managerial need to look very hard at support functions in terms of overall cost, resource utilisation and consumption, and contribution to operational effectiveness. This does not mean that administration and support are no longer necessary. It does mean that organisation systems and bureaucratic operations must be as simple, flexible and responsive as possible, and designed in direct support of the primary activities. This in turn means attention to the effectiveness of overall organisation culture, and individual, professional and occupational career paths, especially those provided by head and regional offices.

Structures and cultures

The demand here is that top managers take a continuous, positive interest in the ways in which activities are carried out, in order to ensure that the organisation of staff continues to fit operational demands. Problems are caused when ranks and hierarchies work in favour of individuals and groups but cause blockages in operations and activities. It is therefore essential that questions of culture and structure change are addressed as part of any wider staff management strategy, and that these elements are related directly to organisational policy, priority, direction and performance.

A starting point for this is to look at structures and cultures from the point of view of the extent of fit. The initial enquiry is to establish whether:

- Structure, culture, strategy and staff management style clearly fit and match.
- Structure, culture, strategy and staff management style fit in some parts but not others.
- Structure, culture and staff management style do not match and fit with strategy direction at all.

One clear indicator of this is to assess what is rewarded and punished, and what is not.

This enquiry causes attention to be drawn to the whole relationship between behaviour, operations, activities and direction. It is often not considered or not addressed fully because:

- its importance is not fully understood by directors and shareholders' representatives
- there is a history of paying attention to 'the bottom line' rather than how the bottom line is achieved
- it is not fully understood conceptually by top managers; or it is assumed that once direction is established, everything else will automatically fall into place.

Management and organisation development

The present view of management and organisation development is that in order to professionalise and make expert practice of management, and develop the expertise of individual managers, it is necessary to learn about and put into action a body of skills, knowledge, attributes and qualities.

In essence this consists of each of the areas covered in this book, together with a commitment to take an active interest in keeping abreast of future developments. Beyond this management training and development is addressed from the point of view of:

- Further and higher education: syllabus-based management teaching and learning programmes, ranging from Higher National Diploma courses through undergraduate programmes; the main standard management education remains the MBA course.
- On and off the job balance: in which those in supervisory and junior managerial positions, or those coming into managerial positions for the first time from functional or practitioner posts, follow courses in supervisory studies, acquire certificates and diplomas in management, and take management modules and units as part of continuing technical and professional development. National Vocational Qualifications, especially at Levels 4 and 5, require the production of portfolios of practice and evidence demonstrating understanding and application of this expertise.
- Short course provisions in areas of skills, knowledge, expertise and current affairs development, including seminar programmes and the activities of professional bodies.

EXAMPLE BOX 23.9   New Fads

It is the sort of thing that gets handed on to consultants. This is all very well provided that a genuine brief is worked out with the consultants, based upon full assessment of the situation. Many consultancy firms have taken advantage of this gap in organisational managerial expertise to sell off-the-shelf solutions such as:

- Business process re-engineering: which is overwhelmingly taken to mean reductions in head count, de-layering, and increases in workload for the front line.
- Down-sizing, right-sizing, resizing: the outcome of which is normally a structured design suitable for the present rather than the future.
- Empowerment: normally resulting in pushing further responsibilities onto often overstretched front line staff.
- Synergies and economies of scale: concentrating again on a narrow economic rather than broader context of behavioural aspects.
- Facilitation: guiding companies through extended programmes of change.

In many cases, this leads to a long-term relationship between consultants and client organisations. One way of looking at this is to consider 'the circular flow of consultancy'. This works as follows:

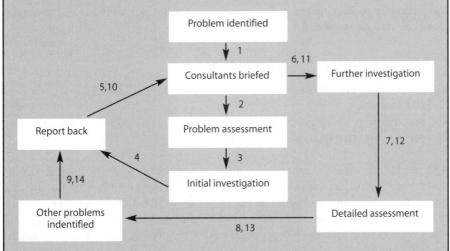

Fee levels charged by top brand consultancies make it behaviourally very difficult to turn down their recommendations. There is also a collective perception that if fee levels are very high, then the consultants must necessarily know what is best for the organisation. Many organisations and their top managers come, therefore, to depend on the consultants that they have hired.

Effectively, consultants are asked to come in. They provide an initial organisational assessment, leading to the conclusion that 'the organisation needs some work doing'. Consultants then produce further investigations and a report to the effect that 'you need some more work doing'.

- Project work, planned placements and secondments, supported by mentoring, coaching and counselling.

These approaches are generally well understood and represent, almost by common consent, the known ways in which the required body of knowledge, skill and expertise is imparted.

To this must be added the following.

- Common standards of integrity in all dealings. This is an active, collective responsibility as well as one placed on individual managers and supervisors. Moreover while this may stand to reason in theory, in practice, many managers do not approach all their dealings from the point of view of this absolute standard. It needs to be clearly understood that customers, clients, suppliers and staff all come to know very quickly when the person or organisation with whom they are dealing is trustworthy, and when they are not. When the person or organisation is proved to be untrustworthy, they will move elsewhere if they possibly can.
- The need to develop a distinctive, positive and collective management style. This reinforces culture, values, attitudes and behaviour, and is reinforced by the approaches and activities of individual managers. It matters much less whether this style is autocratic, participative or anything in between, than that it is common, open, honest and universally delivered.

It is necessary to develop the style, attitudes and behaviour of individual managers along the above lines. Key priorities have to be:

- visibility
- openness of communications
- the building of the person as well as occupational and professional aspects of relationships
- the ability to develop suitable long-term work group cohesion, expertise and performance (see Example Box 23.10).

Also needed is continuous professional development. Many professional and occupational bodies now demand this as a condition of continued membership. In any case part of the professional and personal responsibility of all managers is to keep abreast of developments in the whole field, to learn lessons as they become available, and to study and evaluate practice in other organisation sectors and locations. For example:

- One supermarket chain requires all its staff to go into competitors on a regular basis and to return with at least one example of what the competitor does better; to return and say 'there is nothing we can learn from them' is not acceptable.
- A dot.com travel agent, despairing at the lack of real customers, at last sent its staff into its high street competitors to study the real demand of customers; it consequently redesigned its approach and website to take account of these factors.
- A hospital reduced attacks on, and abuse of, its staff in its accident and emergency department by studying the management of long-stay customers and clients in airport lounges.

EXAMPLE BOX 23.10   Back to the Floor

In practice it is very easy for managers to loose sight of the day-to-day operational details that contribute so much to the enduring effectiveness of products and services. This reinforces the need for visibility, access at all times and the practice of managing by walking around.

It also ensures that overtly simply and straightforward details are not overlooked. The ideal is for managers to at least 'walk the job' as part of their own regular and enduring commitment to personal, professional and organisational development.

For several years, the BBC has produced a series of programmes entitled *Back to the Floor*. In these programmes, camera crews follow senior managers as they return to the front line of their operations and activities, and either shadow members of staff or adopt specific operational roles in order to better understand the particular jobs that they are asking others to do. Organisations featured have included:

- Sandals, the exclusive holiday resort, tour operator and wedding packing provider, in which the chief executive worked as a weddings co-ordinator
- Hamleys, the toy shop department store situated in the West End of London
- The London Borough of Southwark, in which the chief executive worked for a week as a housing assistant
- Galliford Property Services, in which the chief executive worked in a substandard building site and sales office.

This approach is a development of the action-learning scheme pioneered by Reg Revans in the 1970s. Revans' view was that the most effective management and organisational development was fostered by placing managers in unfamiliar operational situations, and meeting regularly in a support group to review progress. The action-learning sets or clinics were supported by expert facilitators, and full evaluation of the effectiveness and context of actions was undertaken. The 'Back to the Floor' approach is excellent at drawing attention to internal operational details and priorities, and again is only effective if it is reviewed and evaluated fully.

Source: *Back to the Floor*, BBC Television, 1997–2002.

- A single-location grocery store quadrupled its turnover in six months as the result of studying the range available at Tesco and Asda and increasing the perceived choice available to customers as well as convenience.

All of this is legitimate continuous professional development. It is as substantial as professional updates, technical studies and evaluation, and project work and secondment. Ideally continuous professional development should be planned and reinforced with the opportunity to put it into practice. Ultimately this is a matter of personal responsibility, whether or not it is actively encouraged by particular organisations.

Conclusions

The most important lesson for all managers to accept is that coping with change and uncertainty, and achieving things through people, come with a wide range of active responsibilities. Furthermore, the resources required for combining the various elements into productive, profitable and effective activities have to be gathered from a broader environment over which individual managers have very little control.

The purpose of this final chapter has been to illustrate the active steps that can be taken on a more or less universal basis to ensure capability and expertise in coping with change and uncertainty, organising and directing people, and combining resources.

Above all, genuinely expert managers – those who accept and understand the constraints under which they have to work and the expertise required as a result – are certain to become very much more highly prized in the future. As organisations come to query ever more precisely the actual added value of support functions and structures and hierarchies, the manager who can deliver enduring customer, client, supplier and end user satisfaction, is certain to become a most valuable commodity to organisations, and such expertise to be highly prized.

CHAPTER SUMMARY

For organisations at large, it is becoming increasingly apparent that the usual range of excuses for performance shortfalls, in industry and commerce at least, is simply no longer acceptable. Organisations that blame the following for their failings are certain to get left behind by those that do not.

- Fluctuations in interest rates, inflation, retail price indexes, currency values and other economic factors that 'simply could not be predicted or foreseen'.

- Currency collapses or surges that make activities either too expensive to complete, or too expensive to contemplate.

- Turbulence in the global economy, especially competitive surges from different parts of the world.

- Changes in consumer demand and confidence caused by unfair trading practices on the part of manufacturers and service producers in areas of perceived cheap activities. (It should always be remembered that the first countries to be accused of this were Japan in manufacturing, the Gulf States and Norway in oil production, and Switzerland in banking and finance industry practices.)

- Resorting to public relations campaigns, rather than managerial enquiry, to counter the commentaries by media on organisation and sectoral shortfalls.

- The practice of taking refuge in perceived sectoral league tables; this leads to the excuse that 'we are doing no worse than anyone else in our sector', or 'we are all beset by difficult trading conditions', as a substitute for active managerial responsibility.

In practice there is enough management literature, training, development, understanding and awareness, in every particular sector as well as overall, to ensure that each of these factors can be understood and accommodated. The most successful organisations in the long term are those that accept the constraints under which they have to operate, accept the potential for competitive and operational turbulence, and understand the factors outside their control within which they have to operate. In the future, the best managers are going to be those that take active responsibility for this, and continue to deliver high-quality, high-value, profitable and effective products and services, rather than those who take refuge in a ready-made list of excuses.

DISCUSSION QUESTIONS

1. Outline the ways in which you foresee the practice of management in public sector services changing over the next ten years.
2. A large children's charity has the opportunity to greatly enhance its profile through taking part in a television series about the exploitation of children in the Third World. What factors should it take into account before it agrees to do so?
3. How, when, where and by whom should investment in public service enhancement be measured? How, when, where and by whom is investment in public service investment currently measured? What conclusions can you draw from the differences to the answers to the first two parts of this question?
4. What steps should be taken by those responsible for customer management to ensure continuing high levels of satisfaction in: a website-based book shop; a village school; a premium price airline?
5. Outline a continuous professional development programme for a management trainee going to work in a hospital for the first time. What should be included in this, when, and how are you going to measure it for success or failure? Repeat the exercise for someone going to work as a trainee site manager at a civil engineering company. Compare and contrast the conclusions to which you have come.
6. On what basis should managers be rewarded for their expertise in the future and why?

CHAPTER CASE STUDY

SEMCO

'When I took over Semco from my father, it was a traditional company in every respect with a pyramid structure and a rule for every contingency. Today our factory workers sometimes set their own production quotas and even come in their own time to meet them without prodding from management or overtime pay. They help redesign the products, to make and formulate the marketing plans. Their bosses for their part can run our business units with extraordinary freedom, determining business strategy without interference from the top brass. They even set their own salaries with no strings. Then again everyone will know what they are, since all financial information at Semco is openly discussed. Our workers have a limited access to our books. To show we are serious about this, Semco with the labour unions that represent our workers developed a course to teach everyone, including messengers and cleaning people, to read balance sheets and cash flow statements.

We don't have receptionists. We don't think that they are necessary. We don't have secretaries either, or personal assistants. We don't believe in cluttering the payroll with un-gratifying dead-end jobs. Everyone at Semco, even top managers, fetches guests, stands over photocopiers, sends faxes, types letters and uses the phone. We have stripped away the unnecessary perks and privileges that feed the ego, but hurt the balance sheet and distract everyone from the crucial corporate tasks of making, selling, billing and collecting.

One sales manager sits in the reception area reading newspapers hour after hour, not even making a pretence of looking busy. Most modern managers would not tolerate it. But when a Semco pump on an oil tanker on the other side of the world fails and millions of gallons of oil are about to spill into the sea he springs into action. He knows everything there is to know about our pumps and how to fix them. That's when he earns his salary. No one cares if he doesn't look busy the rest of the time.

We are not the only company to experiment with participative management. It has become a fad. But so many efforts at workplace democracy are just so much hot air.

The rewards have already been substantial. We have taken a company that was moribund and made it thrive chiefly by refusing to squander our greatest resource, our people. Semco has grown six-fold despite withering recessions, staggering inflation and chaotic national economic policy. Productivity has increased nearly seven-fold. Profits have risen five-fold. And we have had periods of up to fourteen months in which not one worker has left us. We have a backlog of more than 2000 job applications, hundreds from people who state that they would take any job just to be at Semco. In a poll of recent college graduates conducted by a leading Brazilian magazine, 25 per cent of the men and 13 per cent of the women said Semco was the company at which they most wanted to work.

Not long ago the wife of one of our workers came to see a member of our human resources staff. She was puzzled about her husband's behaviour. He was not his usual grumpy autocratic self. The woman was worried. What, she wondered, were we doing to her husband?

We realised that as Semco had changed for the better, he had too'.

Source: Ricardo Semler *Maverick*, Free Press, 1993.

QUESTIONS

1. Why has this approach to the management of a manufacturing company been so successful?
2. What lessons are there to be learnt from Semco by those who work in more traditional multinational organisations and public sector services management?
3. What commitments must be undertaken by Semco management to ensure that this management style continues to be profitable and effective?

Bibliography

General bibliography

Adams, F., Hamil, S. and Carruthers, G. (1990) *Changing Corporate Values*, Sage.

Adams, S. (1999) *The Joy of Work*, Macmillan.

American Management Association (2001) 'The Value of Merger Activity', American Management Association.

Ash, M. K. (1985) On People Management, MacDonald.

BBC/Industrial Society (1993) 'Managerial Time and Performance', Industrial Society.

de Bono, E. (1984) Lateral Thinking for Managers, Pelican.

Brech, E. F. L. (ed.) (1984) *Organisations*, Longman.

Burns, T. and Stalker, G. M. (1968) *The Management of Innovation*, Tavistock.

Carnegie, D. (1936) *How to Win Friends and Influence People*, Simon and Schuster.

Cartwright, R. (2000) *Mastering Customer Relations*, Macmillan Palgrave.

—— (2001) *Mastering the Business Environment*, Palgrave Masters.

Cartwright, R. *et al.* (1994) *Management*, Blackwell.

Chattell, A. (1995) *Managing for the Future*, Macmillan.

Clark, E. (1988) *The Want Makers*, Corgi.

Cole, G. A. (1994) *Management Theory and Practice*, DPP.

Cornhauser, A. (1965) *Mental Health of the Industrial Worker*, John Wiley.

Donovan, D. (1967) *Report of the Royal Commission on Trades Unions and Employers' Associations*, HMSO.

Drucker, P. F. (1955) *Management by Objectives*, Prentice-Hall International.

—— (1986a) *Drucker on Management*, Prentice-Hall International.

—— (ed.) (1986b) *The Practice of Management*, Prentice-Hall International.

—— (ed.) (1988) *The Effective Executive*, Fontana.

—— (ed.) (1990) *Frontiers of Management*, Heinemann.

—— (1993a) *The Post Capitalist Society*, HarperCollins.

—— (1993b) *The Ecological Vision*, Transaction.

—— (2001) *Management Challenges for the Twenty-First Century*, Harper Business.

Fayol, H. and Urwick, L. F. (1946) *The Principles of Administration*, Allen and Unwin.

Fiedler, F. E. (1967) *A Theory of Leadership Effectiveness*, Harper and Row.

Gantt, H. (1919) *Organising for Work*, Harcourt Brace Jovanovich.

Gilbreth, F. and Gilbreth, L. (1916) *Fatigue Study*, Harper and Row.

Goldsmith, W. and Clutterbuck, D. (1990) *The Winning Streak*, Penguin.

Goldthorpe, J. H. *et al.* (1968) *The Affluent Worker*, vols. I, II and III, Cambridge University Press.

Hamel, G. (2001) *Leading the Revolution*, Harvard Business School Press.

Hamel, G. and Prahalad, C.K. (1999) *Managing for the Future*, Harvard Business School Press.

Handy, C. (1993) *The Empty Raincoat*, Penguin.

Hannagan, T. (1998) *Mastering Statistics*, Macmillan Palgrave.

Harvey-Jones, J. (1990) *Making it Happen*, Fontana.

Herzberg, F. (1967) *Work and the Nature of Man*, Free Press.

Huczynski, A. and Buchanan, D. (1993) *Organisational Behaviour*, Prentice Hall.

Industrial Society (2001) 'Management, Motivation and Morale', Industrial Society.

Institute of Management/Industrial Society (1996) 'Mergers and Acquisitions', Institute of Management/Industrial Society.

Institute of Management/Industrial Society (1998) 'The Lasting Effect of Merger and Acquisition Activity', Institute of Management/Industrial Society.

Institute of Management/UMIST/TUC (2000) 'Survey of Workplace Attitudes', Institute of Management.

Kanter, R. M. (1985) *When Giants Learn to Dance*, Free Press.

Kast, F. and Rosenzweig, J. (eds) (1985) *Organisation and Management,* McGraw-Hill.

London Chamber of Commerce and Industry (1998) 'Costs and Benefits of Merger Activity', London Chamber of Commerce and Industry.

Koontz, D. R. *et al.* (1984) *Organisations*, Longman.

Lawrence, P. A. (1984) *Management in Action*, Routledge and Kegan Paul.

Lawrence, P. A. and Elliott, K. (eds) (1988) *Introducing Management*, Penguin.

Lawrence, P. A. and Lee, R. (1984) *Insight into Management*, Oxford University Press.

Lessem, R. S. (1985) *The Roots of Excellence*, Fontana.

—— (1987a) *Intrapreneurship*, Wildwood.

—— (1987b) *The Global Business*, Prentice-Hall International.

—— (1990) *Transforming Management*, Prentice-Hall International.

Lewis, C. S. (1953) *The Silver Chair*, Puffin.

Lupton, T. (1984) *Management and the Social Sciences*, Penguin.

Machiavelli, N. (1986) *The Prince*, trans. G. Bull, Penguin Classics.

McCormack, M. H. (1983) *What They Don't Teach You at Harvard Business School,* Fontana.

—— (1989) *Success Secrets*, Fontana.

McGregor, D. (1970) *The Human Side of Enterprise*, Harper and Row.

Marcouse, I. (1990) *Business Case Studies*, Longman.

Milgram, S. (1974) *Obedience to Authority*, Tavistock Institute.

Mintzberg, H. (1979) *The Structure of Organizations,* Prentice Hall.

Montgomery, B. H. (1956) *Montgomery of Alamein*, W. H. Allen.

Morita, A. (1987) *The Sony Story*, Fontana.

Mullins, L. J. (1999) *Management and Organisational Behaviour*, FT Pitman.

Pascale, R. (1989) *Managing on the Edge*, Simon and Schuster.

Pascale, R. and Athos, A. (1983) *The Art of Japanese Management*, Fontana.

Payne, D. and Pugh, D. (1990) *Managing in a Corporate Environment*, Penguin.

Peter, L. J. (1970) *The Peter Principle*, Penguin.

Peters, T. (1986) *The World Turned Upside Down*, Channel 4 Television.

—— (1989) *Thriving on Chaos*, Macmillan.

—— (1992) *Liberation Management*, Macmillan.

—— (1996) *The Tom Peters Seminar*, Macmillan.

Peters, T. and Austin, N. (1986) *A Passion for Excellence: The Leadership Difference*, Harper and Row.

Peters, T. and Waterman, R. H. (1982) *In Search of Excellence*, Harper and Row.

Pugh, D. S. (1986) *Writers on Organisation*, Penguin.

Revans, R. (1967) *Action Learning in Practice*, Harper and Row.

Rice, J. (1995) *Doing Business in Japan*, Penguin.

Roddick, A. (1992) *Body and Soul: The Body Shop Story*, Ebury.

Rogers, C. (1947) 'Observations on the Organization of Personality', *American Psychologist*, vol. 2.

Scheen, B. (1988) *The Herald of Free Enterprise,* HMSO.

Schein, E. (1971) *Organisational Psychology*, Prentice Hall.

Semler, R. (1992) *Maverick*, Free Press.

Simon, H. A. (1967a) *The Simon Model of Organisations*, Free Press.

—— (1967b) *Organisations and Performance*, McGraw Hill.

Stewart, R. (1991) *Managing Today and Tomorrow*, Macmillan.

Tuckman, B. (1965) *Small Group Development*, Harper and Row.

Urwick, L. F. (1947) *Elements of Administration*, Pitman.

Winch, G. (1996) *Principles of Management*, University College London Press.

Woodward, J. (1961) *Industrial Organisation: Behaviour and Control*, Oxford University Press.

Zimbardo, P., Banks, W., Haney, C. and Jaffe, D. (1973) 'A Study of Prisoners and Guards in a Simulated Prison', *Naval Research Reviews*, Office of Naval Research, Navy Department, Washington D.C.

Strategy

Ansoff, H. I. (ed.) (1985) *Business Strategy*, Penguin.

Buchholz, R. (1982) *Business Environment and Public Policy*, Prentice-Hall International.

Christensen, C. R. *et al.* (1987) *Business Policy: Text and Cases,* Irwin.

Heller, R. (1998) *In Search of European Excellence*, HarperCollins.

Johnson, G. F. and Scholes, K. (1994) *Exploring Corporate Strategy*, Prentice-Hall International.

Pettinger, R. (1996) *Introduction to Corporate Strategy*, Macmillan.

Porter, M. E. (ed.) (1981) *Competitive Strategy*, Free Press.

—— (ed.) (1985) *Competitive Advantage*, Macmillan.

Thompson, J. L. (1990) *Strategic Management*, Chapman and Hall.

Behaviour of organisations

Adair, J. H. (1975) *Leadership*, Cambridge University Press.

Belbin, R. M. (1986) *Superteams*, Prentice-Hall International.

Berne, E. H. (1984) *Games People Play*, Penguin.

Biddle, D. and Evenden, R. (1989) *Human Aspects of Management*, IPM.

Buchanan, D. and Huczynski, A. (1985) *Organisational Behaviour*, Prentice-Hall International.

Cartwright, D. (ed.) (1959) *Studies in Social Power*, University of Michigan.

Drennan, D. (1992) *Transforming Company Culture*, McGraw-Hill.

Etzioni, A. (1964) *Power in Organisations*, Free Press.

French, J. and Raven, B. (1959) 'The Bases of Social Power', in D. Cartwright (ed.), *Studies in Social Power*, University of Michigan.

Groucutt, J. and Griseri, P. (1996) *In Search of Ethics*, Technical Communications.

Handy, C. B. (1984) *The Future of Work*, Penguin.

—— (ed.) (1990) *Understanding Organisations*, Penguin.

Harris, P. and Moran, R. (1991) *Managing Cultural Differences*, Gulf.

Henry, J. (ed.) (1992) *Creative Management*, Open University.

Hersey, P. and Blanchard, K. (1982) *Management of Organisational Behaviour*, Prentice-Hall International.

Hofstede, G. (1980) *Cultures Consequences*, Sage.

Kenney, J. and Reid, R. (eds) (1992) *Training Interventions*, IPM.

Lessem, R. S. (1989) *Managing Corporate Culture*, Gower.

Likert, R. (1967) *The Human Organisation*, McGraw-Hill.

Luthans, F. (1992) *Organisational Behaviour*, McGraw-Hill.
Maslow, A. (1960) *Motivation and Personality*, Harper and Row.
Mumford, A. (1989) *Management Development*, IPM.
Owen, H. (1985) *Myth Transformation and Change*, Collins.
Pedler, M., Burgoyne, J. and Boydell, T. (1991) *The Learning Company*, McGraw-Hill.
Pettinger, R. (1996) *Introduction to Organisational Behaviour*, Macmillan.
Reddy, M. (1991) *The Managers' Guide to Counselling*, Methuen.
Sternberg, E. (1995) *Just Business*, Warner.
Taylor, B. and Lippett, G. (1984) *Management Development and Training Handbook*, McGraw-Hill.
Vroom, V. (1964) *Work and Motivation*, John Wiley.
Vroom, V. and Deci, E. L. (1992) *Management and Motivation*, Penguin.
Warr, P. (ed.) (1987) *Psychology at Work*, Penguin.
Williams, A. and Dobson, P. (1991) *Changing Culture*, IPM.

Management of organisations

Back, K. and Back, K. (1982) *Assertiveness at Work*, McGraw-Hill.
Blake, R. and Mouton, J. (1986) *The New Managerial Grid*, Gulf.
Handy, C. B. (ed.) (1990) *The Gods of Management*, Penguin.
Handy, C. B. *et al.* (1981) *Making Managers*, Penguin.
Katz, D. and Kahn, R. L. (1978) *The Social Psychology of Organisations*, Wiley.
Pettinger, R. (1996) *Managing the Flexible Workforce*, Technical Communications.
Reddin, W. (1970) *Managerial Effectiveness*, McGraw-Hill.
Rees, W. D. (1990) *The Skills of Management*, Routledge.
Schumacher, E. F. (1986) *Small is Beautiful*, Oxford University Press.
Sereny, G. (1996) *Albert Speer: A Biography*, Macmillan.
Tannenbaum, R. and Schmidt, W. (1958) *How to Choose a Leadership Pattern*, Harvard Business Review.
Trevor, M. (1992) *Toshiba's New British Company*, Policy Studies Institute.

Marketing management

Baker, M. (1992a) *The Marketing Book*, Institute of Marketing.
—— (1992b) *Marketing*, Macmillan.
Buell, V. (1990) *Marketing Management*, McGraw-Hill.
Clark, E. (1988) *The Want Makers*, Hodder and Stoughton.
Cohen, W. (1986) *The Practice of Marketing Management*, Macmillan.
French, J. (1992) *Principles and Practices of Marketing*, Pitman.
Keegan, W. (1990) *Global Marketing Management*, Prentice-Hall International.
Packard, V. (1957) *The Waste Makers*, Pelican.
—— (1960) *The Hidden Persuaders*, Penguin.
Randall, G. (1992) *Marketing*, Routledge.

Human resource and industrial relations management

Cartwright, R. *et al.* (1994) *Personnel Management in Practice*, Blackwell.
Cheatle, K. (1996) *Code of Employment Practice*, NCVCCO.
Ferner, A. and Hyman, R. (eds) (1992) *Industrial Relations in the New Europe*, Blackwell.
Kessler, S. and Bayliss, F. (1992) *Contemporary British Industrial Relations*, Macmillan.
Livy, B. (1989) *Corporate Personnel Management*, Pitman.

Rodger, A. (1958) *The Seven Point Plan*, National Institute of Industrial Psychology.
Salamon, M. (1992) *Industrial Relations*, Prentice-Hall International.
Salomon, G. (1992) *Human Resource Strategies*, Open University.
Sisson, K. (1991) (ed.) *Personnel Management in Britain*, Blackwell.
Torrington, D. and Hall, L. (1992) *Personnel Management: A New Approach*, Prentice-Hall International.
Walton, D. and McKersie, A. (1965) *A Behavioural Theory of Labour Negotiations*, McGraw-Hill.

Operations management

Adam, E. and Ebert, R. (1990) *Production and Operations Management*, Prentice-Hall International.
Bresnen, M. (1990) *Organising Construction*, Routledge.
Clark, K. B. and Fujimoto, T. (1991) *Product Development and Performance*, Harvard University Press.
Cleland, D. and King, W. (1988) *Project Management*, Van Nostrand Reinhold.
Cuming, M. (1984) *Managers' Guide to Quantitative Methods*, ELM.
Davis, G. and Olsen, M. (1985) *Management Information Systems*, McGraw-Hill.
Gummesson, E. (1991) *Qualitative Methods in Management Research*, Sage.
Heizer, J. and Render, B. (1991) *Production and Operations Management*, Allyn.
Layard, R. (ed.) (1980) *Cost-Benefit Analysis*, Penguin.
Lockyer, K. (1992) *Quantitative Production Management*, Pitman.
Long, L. (1990) *Management Information Systems*, Prentice-Hall International.
O'Neil, J. J. (1989) *Management of Industrial and Construction Projects*, Heinemann.
Pettinger, R. and Frith, R. (1996) *Measuring Business and Managerial Performance*, STC.
Van Horne, J. (1990) *Financial Management and Policy*, Prentice-Hall International.
Welsh, G. *et al.* (1984) *Budgeting: Profit Planning and Control*, Prentice-Hall International.
Wright, M. E. (1980) *Financial Management*, McGraw-Hill.

Other books by Richard Pettinger

1997 *Construction Marketing: Strategies for Success*, Macmillan.
1999 *Mastering Organisational Behaviour*, Macmillan.
2000 *Mastering Management Skills*, Palgrave.
2001 *Investment Appraisal*, Palgrave.
2002 *Mastering Employee Development*, Palgrave.
2002 *Global Organisations*, Capstone.
2002 *Stress Management*, Capstone.
2002 *Learning Organisations*, Capstone.
2002 *Managing Flexible Workers*, Capstone.

Index